ARTHUR GRIFFITH

ARTHUR GRIFFITH

OWEN McGEE

MERRION
PRESS

First published in 2015 by Merrion Press
8 Chapel Lane
Sallins
Co. Kildare

© 2015 Owen McGee

British Library Cataloguing in Publication Data
An entry can be found on request

978-1-78537-009-0 (cloth)
978-1-78537-010-6 (PDF)
978-1-78537-012-0 (Epub)
978-1-78537-011-3 (Mobi)

Library of Congress Cataloging in Publication Data
An entry can be found on request

Contents

Acknowledgements

This book is dedicated to the memory of my late father Donard McGee, a musician and bank official who first stimulated my interest in history. Shortly before he died, he encouraged me to complete this book while he also left to me his histories of the banking and transport industries. This book was written over a three-year period. It was not possible for me to find academic support specifically for the idea of researching and writing a biography of Griffith but during 2008 a fellowship held at the National Library of Ireland gave me an opportunity to work with records that related directly to Griffith's later career and thus an interest in pursuing the idea, first entertained during 2006, was possible to sustain. I wish to thank Lisa Hyde of Merrion Press, who suggested the idea of a Griffith biography to me many years ago, as well as her publisher Conor Graham, for being willing to publish my book and for producing such a handsome volume. Thanks are also due to the Director of the National Archives of Ireland, UCD Archives and the UCD–OFM Partnership, the Parliamentary Archives (UK), Churchill Archives Centre, Westminster Diocesan Archives and the manuscripts department of the National Library of Ireland for permission to quote from manuscripts in their possession. Thanks are also due to the National Library for permission to reproduce several of the illustrations that feature in this book.

List of Plates

1. Griffith's birthplace at 61 Upper Dominick Street, photographed before its demolition by Dublin Corporation. (National Library of Ireland, O'Luing papers)

2. The earliest known portrait of Griffith (aged twenty-six).

3. Maud Sheehan (1876–1963) as a young woman. Griffith's future wife was a daughter of middle-class and Catholic parents whose two siblings entered religious orders and she may also have been so intended (note the crucifix belt). (National Library of Ireland, Griffith papers)

4. William Rooney (1872–1901), Griffith's assistant in the Young Ireland League. Like Arthur's sister Marcella (1866–1900), Rooney died as a result of a disease contracted in a Dublin slum tenement. He was the first literary editor of the *United Irishman* (1899–1901).

5. Griffith on a day-trip to Tara, Co. Meath, a few months before launching the Sinn Féin Policy to coincide with the creation of the Industrial Development Association (November 1905). The photo-shy man to the left of Fr. Forde is James Casey, the first secretary of the Gaelic League. On the far right is the Healyite Dublin city councillor Walter Cole, who arranged the release of Griffith's father Arthur C. Griffith (1838–1904) from the workhouse and became a long-term political ally. *The Leader* (1944)

6. Máire Butler (1874–1920), a wealthy Catholic writer and mutual friend of Griffith and Patrick Pearse. She gave the *United Irishman* and *Sinn Féin* a puritan tone through her work as their literary editor. A very frequent contributor to *An Claidheamh Solus*, she later died on a pilgrimage to Rome.

7. Jennie Wyse Power (1858–1941), a suffragette and treasurer to the Sinn Féin Party. The IRB's infamous republican proclamation of 24 April 1916 was written and signed in her home because of her husband's long-term association with Tom Clarke's political friends.

8. Arthur and Maud Griffith as newly weds sitting in the back garden of their home in Clontarf (1911). Note Griffith's orthopaedic boots. The couple had not been able to afford to marry during their previous six-year engagement. This house was a wedding gift to them from William O'Brien's political supporters within

the Gaelic League. By 1912, however, the home was already partly mortgaged due to financial pressures. (National Library of Ireland, Griffith papers)

9. Election card for Griffith during the East Cavan contest of June 1918. (National Library of Ireland, Griffith papers)

10. The 'Sinn Féin People's Bank Limited' at 6 Harcourt Street had a twelve-year history before its suppression in March 1921. Reflecting the unpopularity of Griffith's ideal of an Irish takeover of the country's financial institutions, no effort was ever made to revive it. *Irish Independent* (1921)

11. Griffith being celebrated after the end of nine-months imprisonment (November 1920–July 1921) he received for leading Dáil Eireann. The summer of 1921 marked the peak of Sinn Féin's popularity. *Daily Mirror* (1921)

12. In London with Mark Ryan, Eamon Duggan and Bishop Joseph MacRory while preparing to negotiate an unpopular and virtually preordained Anglo-Irish agreement (October 1921). *Daily Sketch* (1921)

13. Waiting in vain for the train to start: a frustrated Griffith on his way to Sligo (April 1922). Nationalisation of the railways was one of Griffith's plans to combat general poverty by promoting an infrastructure for business and employment in Ireland. *Irish Independent* (1922)

14. This contemporary political cartoon represented the common perception that the treaty agreement was an arrangement with an insufficient grounding, thus making it a potential death trap for Irish politicians. *UCC Multi-text*

15. Shots fired over Griffith's grave following his burial (August 1922). On the left looking pensively into the grave is Michael Collins, Griffith's former finance minister. The last leader of the IRB alongside Harry Boland, Collins seems to have been the only National Army officer at the graveside to keep his head uncovered as a mark of respect. In Boland's opinion, 'Griffith made us all'. (National Library of Ireland, Griffith papers)

16. Ida Griffith and Nevin Griffith (a future barrister) photographed around the time of their father's death. (National Library of Ireland, Griffith papers)

17. A *Dublin Opinion* cartoon representing the difficulties that Griffith faced during April 1922. W.T. Cosgrave would express the opinion that Griffith died primarily due to overwork and stress. *Dublin Opinion* (1922)

18. A portrait of Griffith by Leo Whelan R.H.A. that was unveiled in Leinster House on the occasion of the 25th anniversary of the formation of Dáil Eireann (21 January 1944) by Bishop Fogarty, the former Sinn Féin Party treasurer. This was one of three portraits of 'Founders of the Dáil' that was commissioned by a committee that consisted of W.T. Cosgrave, Joseph McGrath, Richard Mulcahy, James Montgomery, T.F. O'Sullivan and Senator Barniville. The other portraits were of Michael Collins and Kevin O'Higgins.

Introduction

I first became interested in the subject of Arthur Griffith when researching an undergraduate, social history dissertation on crime in Dublin during the mid-to-late Victorian period. Whether due to the phenomenon of unreported crime or inadequacies of contemporary statisticians, I found that records actually indicated that there was little or no crime in Dublin city during the 1870s (if that can be believed). Therefore, my initial immature vision of analysing Victorian Dublin life with a Charles Dickens' style social consciousness could not be pursued much further. What I did find, however, were cartons of Dublin police reports about nationalist protest demonstrations and the like. These records excited my historical imagination into addressing the subject of the Fenian movement, as they presented a very different and much more interesting picture of its world to what I had already acquired from the standard historical textbooks. In among these decaying police records, covering the period 1872–92, were reports of the movements of a teenage Arthur Griffith, while he was still in proverbial short pants or not long beyond that stage of personal development. He was engaged in debates relating to the Land League and a nascent British socialist movement. This was the world of Michael Davitt and William Morris, not that of Eamon DeValera or Winston Churchill, yet this was evidently Griffith's proverbial world at the outset of his political career.

The subject of the undergraduate dissertation was later expanded into a postgraduate thesis and this became a basis for a study entitled *The IRB: The Irish Republican Brotherhood From the Land League to Sinn Féin* (Dublin, 2005), which I wrote to get my PhD thesis out of my system, hopefully for good. However, it was then suggested to me that I should examine a later time period, from the beginnings of Sinn Féin up to the early years of the Irish state and, again, make the IRB the focus; in other words, start examining the world of Michael Collins and company. I was still hankering for the idea of pursuing more studies of the Victorian period, especially debates on church-state relations and how this impacted on the diverse political careers of men such as George Henry Moore, Thomas D'Arcy McGee (within the Irish diaspora) and the young John Dillon. It then occurred to me, however, that I had already found an interesting and little known link between these two time periods in history. That link was the life of Arthur Griffith. A specialist on the nineteenth century could also potentially tackle that subject in a manner that many historians of the twentieth-century

Irish state may have been a little less equipped to address. I was already familiar with the history of Dublin in 1871, into which Arthur Griffith was born, and thus I felt had a good grounding for analysing the subject. In addition, I had much experience studying debates within the nationalist community in Dublin up until the formation of Sinn Féin by this same Mr Griffith in 1905. A logical progression from my past research, therefore, would be to examine the evolution of that Victorian world in the light of Griffith's career up until 1922. This seemed like a worthwhile exercise, even if my conception of international relations in history was still rooted more in examining the worlds of Napoleon and Gladstone than that of the various statesmen of what twentieth-century historians not inaccurately refer to as 'the interwar years'.

It may be a cliché but it is also true to note that Europe was generally perceived to be a very different, as well as more 'democratic', place after the First World War than it had been before. If one abiding lesson was learnt from my past research on the Parnell era it was the reality that one cannot speak of concepts such as 'democracy', 'liberalism', 'nationalism', 'republicanism' or 'socialism' during the nineteenth century as having the same meaning, or currency, as they may be said to have had ever since the First World War. That is partly why the political history of the nineteenth century is so interesting. Aldous Huxley may have coined the catchphrase 'brave new world' in 1932 but people a century earlier—when the very concept of modernity was in the process of being born—felt themselves to be living in precisely such a world without the aid of hallucinatory drugs. This may explain why historians of the nineteenth or twentieth centuries frequently seem to be speaking a different language: the period of the First World War stands between them as a bridge that remains uncertain how to cross. When applied to Ireland, this historical conundrum can have peculiar results.

A common perception of Arthur Griffith has been voiced by the premier historian of the post-1917 Sinn Féin Party, when he suggested that 'among Irish nationalists who fought against British rule he was unusual, if not unique, in one respect: by the time of his death he had achieved most of his objectives.'[1] Griffith probably remains best known to the reading public for signing an Anglo-Irish agreement in December 1921. However, he did not live to see the actual implementation of that agreement, a year later, with the establishment in December 1922 of the Irish Free State; the precursor to the current Irish state known as Éire. Within many accounts of Irish nationalism during the twentieth century is the idea that Griffith 'achieved most of his objectives' precisely because a 'long revolution' began in Ireland during the First World War, but Griffith actually represented a compromise upon the ideals of that 'revolution' because he accepted the terms of the Anglo-Irish agreement of December 1921. Supposedly, this not only made Griffith an unusual man but also a 'counter-revolutionary' figure.[2] A revolution is inherently a dubious historical concept, however, because it implies the complete destruction of a past and the invention of a new future; in other words, a complete end to a sense of chronological time. When in human history can such a development be said to have truly come about?

The sense was certainly alive among Griffith's own contemporaries that his career fell between two stools—namely, those who are acknowledged leaders of society and those who do not merit that recognition—and so he was likely to be soon forgotten. Indeed, the colleague that paid the greatest possible tribute to Griffith's leadership skills also fully acknowledged that he 'did not possess the romantic personality which moves crowds', such as that of a 'spell-binding orator', and so he was both temperamentally inclined as well as encouraged by others 'to stay in the background'.[3] This book does not represent an effort to push the figure of Arthur Griffith into a historical foreground—a proverbial 'resurrection' of a forgotten man—but rather to readdress his life and times more fully according to the reality that his life began in 1871, *not* in 1917. I believe that there is much value to those interested in the history of twentieth-century Irish society to fully ground their perception in a deeper awareness of the realities of what is often termed 'the long nineteenth century' (1789–1914). As an introductory preface to the text that follows I would like to offer a few brief reflections on precisely this theme.

The history of nationalism in twentieth-century Europe is a deeply controversial subject. Two world wars have made a preoccupation with the concept of a nation-state anathema to many Europeans, not just to Vatican theoreticians of social justice, and quite understandably so. A deeper familiarity with the debates of the great age of nationalisms in Europe, during the proverbial long nineteenth century (1789–1914), can be illuminating in explaining the potential pitfalls for scholars who dare to explore that theme, however. Prior to the First World War and also, to some extent, during the inter war years, Europe experienced what many historians have typified as a cultural mania for building monuments to alleged national icons, including aristocrats and soldiers. To more contemporary eyes, these figures generally seem like 'romantic and often ridiculous national heroes', 'who seem to want to leap from their plinths into some titanic struggle':

> The obvious intensity of their desire to liberate, or resist, is in heroic though doomed contrast to the pigeons perched on the sabre they brandish or the foxing that spots their fading image. They are like the essence of the longings of another age, frozen in time.[4]

One need only pay a passing visit to the environs of Westminster to see numerous Victorian monuments that sought to encapsulate a nation's history in stone: from the conscious and symbolical juxtaposition of the Cromwell monument near the Royal Arch within the parliamentary grounds, to the larger-than-life monuments to various prime ministers of Britain's most imperial days in the facing square. Warlike or not, they fit within this Europe-wide tradition of creating national icons in stone.

Ireland experienced monument building phases of its own, while the most imposing such monument encompassed a debate in itself.[5] During 1875, the erection in Dublin of a monument to Daniel O'Connell consciously championed a conception of political liberation that was rooted *not* in the right granted to Catholics of political representation at the Westminster imperial parliament during 1829. Rather, it was rooted in O'Connell's election during 1840 as the mayor of a city that was then—in so far as one could still claim the existence of one—the financial capital of the island of Ireland. Simultaneous with O'Connell's election in Dublin, a foundation stone was laid in Armagh for the building of St Patrick's Cathedral for the Catholic Primate of All Ireland, while young Trinity College students, soon represented by the Young Ireland circle behind the *Nation*, began an enthusiastic and pioneering debate upon Irish nationalism. This was a world of great debate and enthusiasm that was very familiar to the young Arthur Griffith and it shaped his world and imagination.

Today, near the O'Connell monument stands two twentieth-century monuments to express a very different sense of Irish identity. In addition to a sense of identity, these monuments express a deep sense of conflict. Nevertheless, one of these figures appears equally as triumphant as O'Connell. This is a monument to the international labour activist James Larkin, who represented the ideal of promoting labour political activism without consideration of national political boundaries and a consequent complete detestation and rejection of the nationalist idea of Irish self-government espoused by Arthur Griffith. Nearby, the seemingly heroic and eternal figure of Larkin is a monument to a self-consciously Irish nationalist, yet very small, rebellion that was organised by friends of Griffith during 1916. This is a monument with very noticeably defeatist or fatalistic overtones. It takes the form of a pre-historic Fenian who is seemingly dying a slow and agonising death for all eternity. It stands barely visible through the window of a post office, like an embarrassment that should be forgotten, as the general public passes by with understandable indifference or even repulsion at such a grotesque sight: it seems to represent a life-denying death wish.

These two monuments, erected almost a century after the initial O'Connell monument, may perhaps be said to be an Irish reflection of a broader international trend. The schoolboy histories of nationalist battles and iconic soldiers that were sold to a century of European youths stand indicted today as a cultural phenomenon similar to that which once absurdly sent hundreds of thousands of young men charging into machine-gun fire during two world wars. Between the age of O'Connell and the two world wars, however, stands the lifetime of Arthur Griffith. If the European tradition of monument building reflects anything in terms of the culture of Irish society then it must surely be that Griffith's lifetime represents a culture that is now alien to the historical imagination to such an extent that the employment of sympathetic analyses— such as is first required to develop understanding of any historical subject matter—is one that is likely to be in relatively short supply whenever it is applied to Griffith or his contemporaries. This is an understandable but also relatively debilitating trend in historical studies.

The history of Europe during the long nineteenth century (1789–1914) was not a story of unrelenting warfare—although it certainly experienced its fair share of horrific wars—but of 'revolutions in science, technology, transport, communications and commerce', moving 'colossal quantities of people, raw materials, crafted and manufactured goods from one corner of the globe to another at unprecedented speeds'. This was the essence of modernisation. Meanwhile, in politics, 'dynamic new forces' stood together 'in uneasy balance': 'if liberalism was a characteristic response to these currents, so too was its cousin, revolutionary nationalism'.[6] All the conventional vocabulary of political journalists during the post-1918 age of universal suffrage—speaking of concepts such as 'democracy', 'liberalism', 'nationalism', 'socialism' and 'communism'— were a century earlier, or at least up until the 1848 rebellions in Europe (when the franchise was less than one per cent of adult males in most countries), almost exclusively the language of strange secret societies, or conspiracy brotherhoods, who were imagining brave new worlds.[7] By the time of Griffith's youth, with the formation of the Third Republic in France, these terminologies had slowly but surely begun to enter into the discourse of British university students as well as a new world of political journalism, with national circulations and aimed at a skilled working-class readership. This was the world of letters into which Griffith emerged. With this development also came the rise of a preoccupation with the hitherto revolutionary notion of establishing balanced state constitutions.

Historically, most European countries were based upon legal systems that employed precepts that were rooted not least in church traditions that emphasised the importance of placing the spirit of the law above the letter of the law. This was also a basis of the common law tradition. However, this consensus was challenged to its core in the wake of a Napoleonic Empire that introduced a strict civil code as a legal basis for national governments and administrations in the conquered territories. Would-be revolutionaries—generally typifying themselves as 'republicans' (then a catch-all phrase for 'nationalists', 'liberals', 'democrats' and 'socialists')—imagined during the post-Napoleonic era that the revival and maintenance of this tradition of civil codes was essentially to the process of modernisation and the creation of progressive constitutions; a concept then generally associated with that of the nation-state. In modern times, Ireland had always been a common law country. During the nineteenth century, as part of the United Kingdom, it remained one. The rise of nationalism did, however, stimulate debate in Ireland on the meaning of constitutions that mirrored developments throughout Europe in the wake of the French revolution. In this world of debate, in a manner comparable to the twentieth-century phenomenon of Marxism, the foreign offices of each of the European powers (perhaps most notably that of Britain) frequently sought to influence the tenor of debate within all potential rival countries for their own purposes. As a result, contemporaries throughout Europe were frequently divided on the question of whether all this revolutionary talk of republicanism truly represented a progressive development or else was simply a ruse of the foreign offices in an attempt to weaken whatever states could potentially prove to be an enemy on the international stage. In effect, with the rise of a debate on modernity came the birth of the fantasy world of the disingenuous ideologue in politics.

Youths who, like Griffith, spoke of republicanism echoed the example of the would-be constitutional revolts in Europe during 1848. However, the combination of the common law traditions of other English-speaking countries, such as the British colonies and the federal republic of the United States, reinforced the perception in Ireland and Britain that such radicalisms were best equated (at least outside of the American republic) with the potentially anarchical concept of democracy. For instance, in an act of defence against the European liberal or republican tradition of thought, the United Kingdom referred to itself as a 'liberal constitutional monarchy'. This was done to indicate that a common law country, with a monarchy, could be both 'constitutional' and 'liberal' without necessarily having to be 'a republic' with its own definitive written constitution or civil code. What did this 'liberal constitutional monarchy' idea mean in Ireland? Although some spoke in Ireland about republicanism, it was generally perceived that the common law tradition, to which the churches held very dearly, was too deeply rooted and popular in Ireland to ever become uprooted. For this very reason, Griffith's moderation of his republican views by espousing during 1904 the idea of an Anglo-Irish dual monarchy, akin to the situation in the Austro-Hungarian Empire, was understood by many to be both a practicable and a progressive idea. This legalistic issue of common law traditions versus republican civil codes has remained a constant feature of European political life ever since Napoleon, including the current-day relationship between the constitutions (written or unwritten) of various modern nation-states and the European Union.

In terms of national governance, alongside the issue of constitutions lay the question of finance. An issue that became of paramount concern to Irish contemporaries during Griffith's lifetime, even more so than during the lifetime of O'Connell, related to the financing of social services, particularly education and health. These issues greatly preoccupied the churches, especially a rapidly growing Catholic Church that was only in the process of re-establishing its authority in Ireland. The former question of education had certainly acquired greater connotations, however, as the traditional role of aristocrats in politics, business and government began to crumble upon the expansions of the civil service, local government and the electorate in the United Kingdom during the 1880s. The focus of education had now changed to facilitate a greater professionalisation of society.[8] Reflecting this, the prospect of an imperial civil service career now became as enticing to many in Ireland as in the rest of the United Kingdom. This development encouraged a greater Irish acceptance of British state centralisation ever since the 1820s in terms of the management of Irish finances and resistance to this development was actually limited. Nevertheless, Griffith would make this goal his abiding preoccupation in political debate. This is precisely what ultimately made him, as well as the issue of an Irish nationalism, a subject of great controversy.

What is now termed as 'globalisation' essentially refers to the development of a situation ever since the 1950s whereby many financial institutions and, in turn, major businesses have ceased to be based exclusively within specific nation-states. In virtually all countries, few banks or major businesses are not partly owned by banks or businesses in other countries. States now compete with each other by regulating competing taxation systems for business far more so than by the creation of international trade walls, while stock exchanges operate far more on the basis of the exchange rate for each international currency than specifically the exchange rate for a national currency. Matters were very different in Griffith's day. What might be termed as an economic nationalism was at the root of each state's self-interest, while each state also invariably had its own national bank. Griffith applied these concepts to Ireland and as a leader of Dáil Eireann between 1919 and 1922 he sought to win greater public acceptance of them in the wake of the introduction of American investment in Europe during 1918. This same trend of American investment in Europe may be said to have ultimately caused the 'globalisation' phenomenon born during the 1950s, although in Griffith's day it was a process that was only just beginning and it was not seen to have quite the same significant political connotations as it is supposed to have had in recent decades.[9]

Griffith and his colleagues were a people who protested that the small nations of Europe had the potential to make distinct contributions to European life and become viable political entities ('nation states') in their own right; principles that would ultimately become widely accepted internationally. This was done at a time when English debates on the proverbial British constitution (an unwritten and, therefore, not a republican constitution) essentially fell into the realm of a different field of analysis or debate. However, if Griffith was a great dissenter from accepted British norms even those in Ireland who favoured a continued connection with the United Kingdom held very dissenting opinions from the English majority and this, in turn, formed the context for a specifically Irish debate. Beyond that debate, Griffith's life cannot essentially be understood. The challenge for Griffith's biographer, therefore, is to address the fact that the precepts upon which the study of the political history of modern Ireland is based not only require a combination of a localised and a British imperial focus but also an analysis of the debates upon the concept of the nation-state that existed internationally throughout his lifetime.

If the birth of an Irish government during the twentieth century represented a new beginning it will be suggested in this book that it also reflected a deeper continuity in Irish life. Like many of his colleagues, or contemporaries, Griffith represented a particularly Irish response to the debates of the long nineteenth century. The answers they came up with provide a fascinating window into how the history of Ireland before and after the First World War not only met but also represented a greater continuity in modern history as a whole. Along with the remarkable social history connotations of Griffith's life—he was a quintessentially working-class figure who nevertheless died while virtually a head of government—this is what makes Griffith's life both a fascinating story in its own right and perhaps the greatest window available into the dynamics of what has, rightly or wrongly, been termed as an Irish revolution. The dynamics of Griffith's career also represented a longstanding debate within Ireland regarding the respective merits of state-centered or Christian-democratic solutions to the problems that modern political societies face within the context of common law traditions. In itself, this debate became the touchstone of both modern Irish nationalism and constitutional thought.

CHAPTER ONE

The Dubliner and Independent Nationalist (1871–96)

Arthur Griffith was a proud Dubliner all his life. He was born on 31 March 1871 into a working-class family in the city centre. In his youth, he rejoiced in learning intricate details of the city's history and its most colourful characters.[1] He also desired 'the cultivation of a Dublin literature'.[2] Ireland's deposed capital was once known as the second city of the British Empire. To Griffith's dismay, however, it lost its eighteenth-century grandeur under the Union. Deserted by its wealthiest inhabitants, by the 1870s Dublin city centre had become notorious for slums that were inhabited by a poor and unhealthy work force. The Griffiths were well aware of the peculiar reasons for this development and the decline of numerous city businesses and trades.[3] Nevertheless, they were one of very many Dublin families that remained locked into a downward economic spiral. During Griffith's childhood, his parents and grandparents lived in slum districts where disease and prostitution were rampant, while some close relatives spent much time in the dreaded workhouses.[4] Arthur was the third of five children in a family where the first had to emigrate in his mid teens and the second would die as a young adult from a poverty-induced disease.[5] Arthur, known as 'Dan' to his closest friends, was the next in line and had no greater prospects. With this socially insecure background, Griffith grew up as a very shy and private man. The reserved demeanour and caustic pen he would exhibit frequently in adulthood was undoubtedly shaped partly by the wounded pride and social frustration of his family.

Griffith's father, Arthur Griffith senior, was 'a well-read craftsman' and akin to 'a typical tradesman of the old Dublin school … in his craft reposed his first personal interest and pride'.[6] He was a trade unionist who was active in the local printers' union, but this did not prevent him from suffering many bouts of unemployment.[7] Traditionally, printers were a proud and envied guild among the working class because of their higher levels of literacy. In Dublin, however, they were a deeply frustrated group. Since the 1850s old firms were struggling and new firms were not being established. This was partly due to English competition but it was also because available work for printers was now confined mostly to acting as compositors for the newly burgeoning newspaper trade. Working as a compositor was a messy job that required over-night work and it was frequently paid less than an unskilled labourer's wage.[8] Whenever the printers' union attempted to strike in protest against these circumstances it backfired badly against its own members, leading to the dismissal of staff.[9]

One of Griffith's earliest memories was no doubt his father's involvement in the printers' union strike during the industrial recession of the late 1870s. A journal published by one of the union's members, *The Citizen and Irish Artisan* (Dublin), reflected the political outlook of the Griffith family as well as attitudes towards both labour disputes and municipal politics that Griffith would express frequently in adulthood. Adopting the slogan 'the wealth of a nation lies in the intelligence and handicraft of its sons', it maintained that 'socialism is the natural desire of men to improve their lot in life' and valued contemporary Irish nationalism, including its more radical varieties, only in so far as it was rooted in an understanding of socio-economic realities. It opposed any effort made by churches to introduce religious segregations into workers' unions or benevolent societies and, in doing so, professed to speak exclusively on behalf of the material interests of the 'working class'.[10] In keeping with the norms of contemporary labour politics, however, it did not include unskilled labourers within that definition.[11] Having no intrinsic sympathy with unskilled labourers, it was prepared to defend the lockout of striking labourers if the firms in question were deemed to be trustworthy and genuinely promoting the welfare of the city's inhabitants. Indeed, *The Citizen* perpetually distinguished between 'fair' and 'unfair' employers. The latter were compared occasionally to 'mercenary London Jews' who speculated on London Stock Exchange markets on the shares of all the (predominantly British) companies in Ireland and cared nothing for the economic welfare of the citizens of Dublin. Their principal sin was considered to be the importation of cheap labour, which was reducing the city's skilled artisans to pauperdom.[12] City landlords were denounced for charging exorbitant rents for unsanitary tenement flats, while municipal authorities were demonised for failing to address the problem that Dublin had double the mortality rate of any other British city.[13]

Griffith would repeat these arguments forcibly in early-twentieth-century Dublin. He inherited from both Victorian labour politics and his own family a purely materialistic nationalism. From this premise, Griffith considered that 'the poor have been left to rot in slum tenements because vested interests of both green and orange do benefit thereby'.[14] He was at odds with the manner by which the British imperial economy was defining both political allegiances and economic norms within Ireland.[15] As he was indifferent to Ireland's politico-religious divide, he refused to judge the validity of political arguments from that vantage point. He would draw extensively from the arguments of economists at Trinity College Dublin who, at various times, called for a radical overhaul of the existing financial basis of the Union. The fact that these arguments were made by men who held sympathies with an Anglican-biased Tory party did not matter to Griffith: if their points seemed to him reasonable and patriotic in their defence of Irish interests he would readily adapt them to his own perspective.[16]

Like his father, Griffith grew up to be a bookish young man. Though he liked to exercise, poor vision and a slightly deformed leg, which necessitated that he wear high-heeled orthopaedic boots throughout his life, militated against strenuous athletic pursuits.[17] By his mid-teens he was a voracious reader and accustomed to smoking tobacco and drinking spirits.[18] He had very little formal schooling. At the age of thirteen, after attending three different primary schools, his father arranged for him a seven-year apprenticeship with a mercantile printing firm that was run by a Protestant family who were enthusiastic about the history of Irish literature.[19] The printing trade, in common with the contemporary Irish revolutionary underground, had a very mixed religious composition in terms of its members' social background. This factor combined with the Griffiths' ancestry (a Catholic family offshoot from an established Ulster Presbyterian farming family) encouraged his anti-sectarian attitudes.[20] Through the patronage of his father's employer, Griffith was allowed the chance to prepare for an intermediate (secondary school) examination as an extramural student but he did not take this opportunity.[21] Instead, his apprenticeship prompted him to revel in a social world consisting of youths of similar backgrounds whose favoured medium for self-development was participating in literary and debating societies.

At the tender age of fourteen, Griffith was made the secretary of the 'junior branch' of the Young Ireland Society after winning an Irish history competition. Founded in Dublin in March 1881, this society was notable for encouraging serious political debate. Past members had included John Dillon (the future Irish Party leader), Thomas Brennan (chief organiser of the Land League), John Wyse Power (a future leading journalist) and Fred J. Allan (a future newspaper manager, secretary of City Hall and revolutionary activist). During the mid-1880s, its membership included C.H. Oldham and T.W. Rolleston, the founders of the *Dublin University Review*, as well as significant literary figures such as George Sigerson and W.B. Yeats.[22] At an event hosted by the Lord Mayor of Dublin, Griffith received as his prize from John O'Leary, an old Tory turned Fenian, books by John Mitchel, Charles Gavan Duffy and Thomas Davis; the editors of the original *Nation* newspaper of the 1840s.[23] In these books, the teenage Griffith believed that he had found a revelatory explanation for the world that he inhabited. These Trinity-educated authors styled themselves as all that was *left* of an Irish intelligentsia. They protested that ever since the economic reforms of the 1820s, British state centralisation was causing Irish leaders to abandon any sense of duty towards their own people.[24] The motive for Griffith's future Irish nationalism would be the belief that reversing this process of British state centralisation was essential to the survival of specifically Irish economic interests and, in turn, an Irish intelligentsia that was capable of sound political judgment. Reading these Young Ireland authors also convinced the young Griffith that being an adult was entirely a matter of 'having convictions'.[25]

Griffith's formative convictions were both individualist and antisocial. He believed that personal virtue was not something that could ever be learnt at school or from the example of political and religious leaders. Rather, it was something that could only be developed within. Distrust of all communal leaders and vigilant self-reliance was necessary to counter the reality that the exercise of powers of dominance in society was never based upon moral justice. To illustrate this point, Griffith drew up precepts such as 'do not scorn the beggar in the street ... he is nobler than your masters'; 'do not believe that a man who wears a tall hat and trousers is necessarily civilised'; and 'do not talk about "the dignity of labour" [a favoured subject of contemporary religious epistles]. Look up from the mud and behold the poorhouses [the fate of many rural migrants to the city].' As 'the only unforgivable sin is the sin of hypocrisy', Griffith believed that it would be better to be associated with 'honest scoundrels' than 'mix with dishonest swindlers'. Expressing negative emotions such as pity, anger and scorn should never be avoided if they were justified. Above all, it was essential 'to be frank'.[26] The political savvy adage that was favoured by John O'Leary—that the world is his who knows when to hold his tongue—was not part of Griffith's mindset. As a result, Griffith was often considered to be a cantankerous man who was incapable of doing anything to either to his own advantage or that of anyone else. According to the social norms of politics, such a man was quite simply best left alone.

Griffith did not view his youthful convictions to be a matter of inherently rooting for the underdog or the oppressed. Rather they reflected a belief that society was fundamentally dishonest and, therefore, the honest man would inevitably suffer and be punished by his peers.[27] Not surprisingly, he would grow up to recognise that he too had the capacity to offend 'honest as well as dishonest quarters'.[28] Nevertheless, his almost misanthropic belief that it was possible to counter dishonesty in society with the written word remained. This self-righteousness reflected not so much naivety as his basic temperament, which was that of a writer. Possessing the air of a man who was psychologically apart, his few friends never attempted to probe into his personal life out of an instinctive respect. It was simply clear that 'he is very sensitive' and was incapable of appealing to others for help.[29] Griffith's personal code of strict self-reliance was not only a quintessentially Victorian work ethic: it was also a psychological defence mechanism to maintain a determined resolve in the face of demoralising life circumstances. Respect, rather than personal intimacy, would be the touchstone of what he sought in his social relations. His private life and family was virtually a taboo subject. Even allowing for the norms of Victorian reticence, it was perhaps inevitable that Griffith's primary role in public life would be that of a maverick and frequently unpopular critic rather than a truly communal figure.

During the late 1880s, following a collapse of the Young Ireland Society arising from quarrels surrounding the management of the GAA, Griffith became a leader of the Leinster Debating Society. This was composed entirely of 'hardworking young men of humble circumstances' who in their determination to unmask social injustices typified themselves as 'strangers to cant and hypocrisy'.[30] Although it met at a venue that housed small republican and socialist clubs, its membership intentionally had a mixed political profile: as its leader Griffith would place advertisements for its meetings in opposing Tory and Parnellite newspapers.[31]

Griffith's attitudes towards Parnell and his party were not sympathetic. Although he chaired a meeting that denounced the British government for imprisoning William O'Brien MP (the most popular Irish Party politician and journalist of the day), Griffith wrote a scathing satire of Parnellite journalism. Meanwhile, the society's journal denounced Parnell and his followers as 'professional swindlers' who 'connive at blackmailing the Irish people' into supporting their party alone so they could become 'a well-fed, well-housed, "aristocratic" if you please, corps of professional agitators' while ordinary Irish people were left to face 'the poor house, the jail—a hand to mouth existence in this country or emigration'.[32] Such attitudes reflected a belief that Parnell and his Irish Party had betrayed the promises made by republican Land Leaguers earlier that decade to prioritise the welfare of the urban working class. Due to this failure, the society expressed sympathy with the Social Democratic Federation, a British socialist body then seeking to establish itself in Dublin. Griffith himself supported the argument that the remedy for strikes was the nationalisation of all means of production under a system of state socialism.[33] Strikes were actually quite common in Dublin at this time. Notwithstanding the formation of the first permanent Dublin Trades Council in 1886, the city's working class experienced a great economic depression with unemployment rising to high levels and slum tenements becoming more numerous than ever.[34] Such issues never surfaced in the columns of the Irish Party's press, however. It was therefore quite natural for Griffith to find himself at home within a republican or socialist culture of protest.

Griffith's interest in working-class protest politics was combined with a preoccupation with personal self-development. Reflecting his interest in journalism, Griffith gave papers about past political pamphleteers like Jonathan Swift as well as Richard Steele and Joseph Addison, two pioneering newspaper figures of early-eighteenth century England whose writings were still considered by Victorians as providing templates in style for any prospective journalist.[35] Reflecting his interest in literature, Griffith spoke on modern and early-modern Irish writers, English and American poets from Elizabethan times up until his own day and the classics.[36] His lack of formal education, however, was betrayed by his writing style at this time, which used vernacular language and no punctuation.[37] Most tellingly, he drew a contrast between the life that he felt he deserved and that which he had in reality. In poor verse Griffith depicted the privileged lifestyle of a university student, living a life of scholarship and dissipation without having to worry about any material concerns, before cutting abruptly to a description of the reality of his life, being almost penniless and performing solitary pub crawls in the early hours of the morning after 'every honest man was gone to sleep'.[38] In later life, Griffith championed the right of the working classes to receive state grants to enable them to attend university. This was an almost unheard of idea in contemporary Britain or Ireland but, reflecting a legacy of the Napoleonic Empire, it had many supporters in continental Europe.[39] Griffith generally impressed whatever company he was ever in as being extraordinarily well read. This was partly because he had a photographic memory.[40]

The power of Griffith's pen was suited best for satirical or insightful political analyses rather than literary or artistic creations. His almost religious preoccupation with notions of social justice perhaps made him a good candidate to become a persuasive journalist while he was certainly not a poet. In his youth, he expressed appreciation for the tradition of political street ballads. This viewpoint reflected his passing interest in writing such material. This was something he would do infrequently, however, confining himself to a few protest ballads at the time of Anglo-Boer War (1899–1902) as well as some bawdy doggerel to entertain fellow political prisoners during the post-1916 period.[41]

In 1890 Griffith renamed his club as the Leinster Literary Society and proposed that it should establish branches throughout the province, with a central executive in Dublin.[42] This plan for expansion failed because its members lacked means. The only successful literary society in Dublin at this time was the Pan-Celtic Literary Society. Formed by alumni of Blackrock College, it was associated with the Rathmines branch of the Irish Party's Irish National League and included several barristers and arts graduates.[43] The Pan-Celtic represented a suburban and comfortable Dublin Catholic middle class that was very distant from Griffith's social world.[44] Its members viewed the contemporary history of Irish writers and artists living in London, as well as the existence of Parnell's party at Westminster, as a national success story. By contrast, Griffith and his friends viewed Irish culture and politics through the prism of their socially disadvantaged experience. These two social worlds began to commingle, however, when Parnell's fall had the affect of shattering the unity of the Irish National League, the Irish Party's authoritarian support body. This led the minority pro-Parnell wing to appeal directly for working-class support; a development that was unprecedented and would also prove very short lived.[45] Nevertheless, this presented Griffith and his associates with a brief window of opportunity to play a part in formulating a political programme in conjunction with various middle-class activists. In turn, they were led to view Parnell, as distinct from the Irish Party's political machine (to which they remained intensely hostile), with a newfound sympathy.

Later, at a key turning point in the history of early-twentieth-century Ireland, Griffith would cite the former example of Parnell as a means of criticising the contemporary leadership of the Irish Party.[46] From this premise, future historians of twentieth-century Ireland mistakenly assumed that Griffith had idolised Parnell in his youth.[47] The reality, however, was quite different. Although, like most Dubliners (including Tories), he denounced those who were prepared to 'betray the country by voting against Mr. Parnell' at the request of the British Liberal Party, he insisted that his society's minute book would record that 'Mr. Griffith spoke as one who never was a supporter of Mr. Parnell but was an independent nationalist.'[48] This was also the stance taken by the Irish Republican Brotherhood (IRB) during this controversy.

Griffith was drawn into the controversy through the National Club Literary Society. This met in the same venue and under the same management as a new Parnell Leadership Committee; namely, John Clancy, a city councillor, the electoral registrar of Dublin and an old republican.[49] When Parnell announced his intention to pit his own candidate against that of the Irish Party at a Kilkenny by-election, virtually all contemporaries expected that the outcome would be decisive in settling the controversy. Parnell's candidate lacked any organisational support, however, except for that provided by P.N. Fitzgerald, the chief travelling organiser of the IRB and a personal friend of William O'Brien MP who was then wavering in his support of Parnell.[50] Griffith's society published an 'address to the men of north Kilkenny' in support of the Parnellite candidate (Vincent Scully) that was sent to various newspapers, politicians and a workingmen's club in Kilkenny City that was run by P.J. O'Keefe, the local IRB leader. James J. O'Kelly, a former IRB leader who became a founder of the Irish Party during 1880, was the only politician to take notice of Griffith's address, however. This was signed by Griffith using the pseudonym 'J.P. Ruhart'; 'Ruhart' being an anagram of Arthur, and J.P. standing for Justice of the Peace.[51]

Why Griffith, an unknown youth, chose to use this false name is unclear. He may have been aware that the police were watching his Leinster Literary Society's meeting place on Marlborough Street.[52] It is more likely, however, that he understood that his father's fortunate current status as the foreman-printer with the stridently anti-Parnell *Nation* meant that any public address in which 'Arthur Griffith of Dublin' denounced all opponents of Parnell could have led to the only bread-winner in the Griffith family losing his job. Griffith's willingness to support Parnell was partly motivated by the Catholic hierarchy's statement that no Catholic could support him any longer. Prior to the outbreak of the controversy, Griffith had given voice to anticlerical viewpoints and the clergy's critical role in overthrowing Parnell would encourage him to embrace an IRB-style anticlericalism, claiming that the continued presence of priests and bishops in politics would be 'fatal' to the development of Irish political society.[53] Many Irish Tory cultural nationalists, who naturally sided with Parnell against the Liberal Party, shared this perspective if only because they lamented the partial eclipse of the prestige of the disestablished Church of Ireland.

The Parnellite defeat at Kilkenny came as quite a shock to much of Dublin society. Griffith and his friends vented their spleen through a series of private debates in which various historical episodes were turned into platforms for giving voice to anticlerical viewpoints.[54] In Griffith's case, this was done primarily in the context of a debate on the French Revolution (1789–93). He described this event as a justifiable 'outburst of popular feeling against the corrupt and debauched nobility and clergy who governed the land' before he proceeded to defend the excesses of the French revolutionists in executing their perceived enemies.[55] Griffith's youthful tendency towards extremism, which certainly separated him from the Tory brand of contemporary nationalists, would also be reflected by a ballad he wrote on the Europe-wide 1848 revolutions. This depicted all established authorities as enemies of liberty that deserved to be 'stricken, in the anger of the people, to the dust'.[56]

By May 1891, Griffith was attending meetings that were organised by the IRB with the purpose of forming an executive for a new organisation that would create an alliance between all nationalist debating societies in the country. He represented the Leinster Literary Society at such a private convention, held at the National Club.[57] That summer, Griffith also worked with the National Club Literary Society in launching a tradition of holding annual Bodenstown demonstrations in honour of Wolfe Tone and began attending meetings of amnesty clubs. These clubs had been formed by James Boland, the Dublin IRB leader (and father of Harry Boland), to campaign for the release of John Daly and P.W. Nally, two IRB leaders who had received terms of life imprisonment several years before.[58]

Many years later, a newspaper contributor claimed that during 1891 Griffith addressed a rally of university students and 'old Fenians' outside of University College Dublin and made a direct personal appeal to T.C. Harrington, a lawyer and future mayor, to resign his Dublin parliamentary seat so that Parnell could contest it.[59] This seems unlikely, however, because Griffith never held a position in the new Parnellite Irish National League (the Irish Party's support body had renamed itself as the Irish National Federation). In July 1891 the National League rejected calls that representatives of debating and trade societies be admitted to its executive. By contrast, reflecting contemporary class dynamics, several wealthy Tories who represented business interests in Cork and Dublin cities were allowed admittance to its executive.[60] John R. Whelan, one of Griffith's maternal cousins, did read an address to Parnell at Kingsbridge (Heuston) Station on behalf of the Leinster Literary Society; an event at which Griffith was no doubt present.[61] This address was signed and quite possibly written by 'J.P. Ruhart' (Griffith). It began by expressing praise for Parnell's past use of obstructionist tactics in Westminster before emphasising that the true concerns of Irish nationalists had always far surpassed such considerations:

> To us, it matters not whether most or any of those representatives desert that policy and seek fusion with any English party. To us, it matters not whether ecclesiastical domination on the one side or Dublin Castle influence on the other prevail; our duty is imperative. The path of independence is before us. Independent of English politicians, and without Irish traitors and cowards, we will seek for freedom; or failing to obtain it, we will, like the Carthaginians of old, retire behind the embattlements of our rights and refuse to obey the dictates of any leader of an alien people. And we hereby emphasise that resolve by declaring in the words of John Mitchel: 'all Whig [Liberal] professions about conciliatory and impartial government in Ireland are as false as the father of Whiggery himself'.[62]

It is unlikely that Parnell was impressed with this somewhat self-righteous address. Shortly thereafter, Griffith was re-elected as president of the Leinster

Literary Society. In this capacity he attended Parnell's funeral and expressed condolences with the relatives of P.W. Nally, who died very suddenly in Mountjoy jail just prior to a date set for his early release.[63] Griffith also distributed circulars across the country with a view to creating a federation of nationalist debating societies.[64] This had led to the creation of the Young Ireland League (YIL) at the Dublin Rotunda that September under the presidency of John O'Leary.[65] The most prestigious club to become affiliated with the YIL was W.B. Yeats' new National Literary Society, which was popular with Tory cultural nationalists. Fearing the consequences of the bitter passions that Parnell's fall had aroused, Yeats' society forbade the discussion of party politics at its meetings.[66] This was an example that Griffith's lesser-known society chose not to follow, ultimately to its own detriment.

Griffith resigned as president of the Leinster Literary Society in December 1891 when he took up his first salaried job, which was as a compositor with the *Irish Daily Independent*. This was a recently established Parnellite newspaper that was partly funded by the Tories and managed by Fred Allan, a Dublin IRB leader who married into a Royal Navy family.[67] During 1892, the Leinster Literary Society expressed unanimous support for republican governments: Griffith even styled himself as the representative of 'the Republic of Ringsend and the Coombe'.[68] In the autumn of 1892, however, a Cork Irish Party supporter was admitted to its meetings and taunted its members by arguing that 'you are Parnellites here in Dublin but you would be anti-Parnellites if you were down in Mallow [the hometown of William O'Brien MP, whose decision to turn against Parnell had been pivotal in deciding the dispute]'. This incensed Griffith, who accused the Corkman of having made 'a charge of hypocrisy and an insult to the intelligence of the members'. Griffith's friend William Rooney, who had joined the Leinster Literary Society in February 1891 and was now its leader, did not agree with this assessment, however.[69] When the society voted to make the Corkman a member, Griffith immediately resigned from the society as a protest. The following week, when more 'Parnellite' sympathisers were deliberately taunted, most other members decided to resign as well. Rooney had now no choice but to dissolve the club that December.[70] Two months later, Rooney created a new society known as the Celtic Literary Society, which wisely resolved not to allow contemporary party politics to be discussed at its meetings. The disgruntled Griffith and his cousin Edward Whelan would not join Rooney's Celtic for some time, however. Instead, they took the opportunity to become members of the executive of the Young Ireland League (YIL), which was a far more influential body that campaigned for changes in the Irish education system.[71]

From the autumn of 1892 until late 1894 Griffith chaired many meetings of the YIL, the membership of which nominally included a few Parnellite MPs and many influential public intellectuals.[72] However, attendance at its meetings soon grew small and appeals by Griffith's circle to the society's more influential members to pay their subscriptions to the organisation and to attend meetings were invariably ignored. This occurred because the YIL insisted on championing the Irish Education Act (1892) despite the fact that the Irish Party, acting on the insistence of the Catholic hierarchy, refused to support the implementation of this measure; a fact that would ultimately cause this legislation to be dropped. Even prior to the introduction of the education bill, Griffith had expressed enthusiasm for the British government's proposal to abolish fees in all national schools and to make school attendance compulsory for children up until the age of fourteen.[73] Together with the rest of the YIL executive, Griffith was annoyed that Irish political and church leaders, with the exception of the Church of Ireland and (privately) some individuals within the Christian Brothers, refused to support the British government's proposal.[74] The refusal of local government bodies to use the authority vested in them to implement the measure without first securing the approval of a Catholic bishop (an approval which was not given), as well as the refusal of the recently-established Irish National Teachers Organisation to support the measure (again due to the Catholic bishops, who had founded the teachers' organisation), particularly outraged the YIL, which pondered whether or not it was intended to 'appoint the Bishop [Archbishop Walsh of Dublin] to carry out all the functions of the Corporation'. It also pointed out a great inconsistency in such public representatives claiming to represent a desire for an independent Ireland: 'The people sought the right of self-government, yet here was a body refusing to exercise the powers of self-government unless the Bishop so approved.'[75]

Griffith took local politics seriously, as was reflected by his perpetual anger at Dublin city council's failure to deal with housing and sanitation problems. He firmly believed that municipal authorities had the responsibility to act strictly in every tax payer's interest as much as any national government, without distinguishing between sectional interest groups, and that they should be made accountable to the public upon that financial basis alone. Griffith would argue that the town councils should not only have supported the education act in defiance of the Catholic Church but should also have appointed representatives of trade unions and women's groups to the proposed school attendance committees.[76] The Catholic Church justified its opposition to the act on the grounds that it supposedly constituted state encroachment upon families' freedom of choice. By contrast, Griffith's YIL maintained that the real problem was that the church was using the question of education as a political football, refusing to encourage support of any government measure until its political desire to have a state-funded Catholic university was first achieved; a purely selfish decision which was typified as an ongoing betrayal of the masses for the sake of the upper classes that had been going on in Catholic Ireland for the best part of fifty years.[77] In taking this stance, Griffith's circle claimed to be giving a voice to an underclass that had long understood that recognised leaders of Irish public opinion were failing to address vital needs of Irish society in matters of education.[78] In doing so, however, they discovered that ambitious individuals who were committed to political networking generally chose to remain silent rather than espouse any cause that might hurt their career prospects. In Catholic Ireland, this meant never questioning the right of the church alone to determine education policy.

The YIL Council, of which Griffith was an active member, drafted a bill calling for the establishment of elective county councils in Ireland such as existed in England since 1888 but that Parnell (with financial persuasion from Gladstone and Sir Cecil Rhodes of South Africa) had refused to demand for Ireland.[79] The YIL's one parliamentary supporter introduced this bill at Westminster but it never reached a second reading.[80] The MP in question was William Field, a pro-labour independent nationalist and patron of Irish technical schools. The son of a republican rebel of 1848, Field was currently GAA treasurer and a leader of the Irish cattle traders' association. The fact that he made his entry into politics as a supporter of the Amnesty Association meant that he was often associated in the public mind with the IRB. The real source of Field's influence, however, was the Tories who sided with him against Catholic businessman W.M. Murphy during the 1892 general election.[81] Over the next twenty-five years, Field and Murphy essentially represented two rival stances on matters relating to the economy of Ireland from their Dublin political support base. In addition to the YIL arguments regarding education, Field supported its demand that local government bodies collect new rates to establish public libraries in Ireland for the first time; another campaign that met a dead end.[82] In support of Field, Griffith himself petitioned the Lord Mayor of Dublin to call a public meeting on the compulsory education question. He also drew up a twelve-point resolution of the YIL in support of the act that was distributed to all members of Dublin City Hall, chaired a debate on the Chief Secretary's attitudes to the question and protested about the mayor's seeming subservience to church leaders in the matter.[83]

Griffith's embroilment in the politics of Irish education from the tender age of twenty-one highlighted a central dynamic of his career. Notwithstanding the fact that he had received some valued schooling from the Christian Brothers, Griffith would often find himself espousing a patriotism that was at odds with prevailing Catholic attitudes towards Irish nationalism. A key determinant of this situation was Parnell's decision in October 1884 to surrender control of the Irish Party's education policy to the Catholic hierarchy to enable his party's subsequent triumph at the election polls. This had led the idea of Irish nationalism to become wedded politically to the cause of Catholic education. To a very significant extent, this had the affect of divorcing the Irish Party from the broader economic realities that faced the general business community within Ireland. Furthermore, as the Irish Party would never reverse this stance, the business community generally remained sympathetic to the Tory party. This was reflected by the composition of the Dublin Chamber of Commerce, which had a good political relationship with William Field, and the composition of Trinity College's Statistical and Social Inquiry Society of Ireland, which was Ireland's top forum for economic debate.[84]

These trends led many educated contemporaries to the conclusion after 1886 that an Irish nationalism could only ever be a cultural construct and thus never become a meaningful political reality. Disputes in Dublin City Hall between Protestant Tory commercial elites and Catholic businessmen caused bigoted journalism (on both sides) to appear in those Tory and Irish Party weekly newspapers that were aimed directly at the lower classes. During 1886, this stimulated street violence in Dublin city centre on a much smaller scale, albeit according to the exact same dynamic, as had occurred in Belfast (the largest ever riots in the history of that city occurred during 1886), while Cork City Council was similarly divided.[85] Griffith's debating societies had reacted to this trend by forbidding any religious viewpoints to be raised at their meetings.[86] The fall of Parnell five years later simply amplified this same dynamic. A much more central dynamic at work than any religious factor, however, was the role of Gladstonian fiscal doctrine regarding the management of the British Empire in dictating government policy regarding Ireland.

In restructuring the British economy in the wake of the Anglo-French wars (1793–1815), London abandoned cherished promises that had been made to Irish politicians at the time of the Union of 1801 (enshrined in Article Six of that Act) by merging the Irish with the Imperial Exchequer. As a result, the Bank of England now banked all Irish customs and excise; the former national bank, the Bank of Ireland, began investing solely in British imperial defence stock in London; a parity was enforced between the Irish and English pound; and the formation of new Irish banks was encouraged, each of which tailored themselves not only to the new imperial economy (represented by the abolishment of all Irish customs houses) but also, in their search for customers, to the existence of strictly segregated religious communities within Ireland.[87] This was the political precursor to granting Catholics the right to parliamentary representation in 1829 and the ineffective Young Ireland protests, partly supported by an elderly Daniel O'Connell, against W.E. Gladstone, the president of the Imperial Board of Trade during the mid-to-late 1840s. Gladstone subsequently managed to 'permeate the thinking not only of treasury officials but of a generation of civil servants in virtually all departments of administration' by prioritising increasing England's economic control over all British territories while simultaneously appearing to address their desires for more autonomy in public. The much lauded mid-Victorian age of prosperity (1851–75) was actually a period defined by a largely unnoticed establishment of a complete English monopoly over all imperial markets, very often at the direct expense of the rest of the United Kingdom, while simultaneously cutting expenditure for all colonial governments or administrations.[88]

The relevance of this Gladstonian fiscal doctrine to Irish circumstances was highlighted during Gladstone's own tenures as Prime Minister. In the wake of the disestablishment of the Church of Ireland (a purely symbolical measure that nevertheless convinced some clericalist Catholic politicians that Gladstone favoured 'justice for Ireland'), Gladstone abolished the office of Vice-Treasurer of Ireland that had been established on the merging of the exchequers to guarantee there would be some regulatory measures in place to ensure financial fair play for Ireland. As a result, even those Irish businessmen who enthused over annual return figures for trade as an indication that they were operating within a prosperous economy admitted that they had no means of ever knowing either what these figures meant in practice for Ireland or what financial returns were ever being made to Ireland because of the arbitrary manner in which London was determining its figures and the fact that these figures only gave statistics for the United Kingdom as a whole.[89] In effect, Gladstone had succeeded in making all Irish politicians economically blind. This exacerbated a trend whereby Irish businessmen literally had to make London their headquarters if they were to be sufficiently well attuned to market trends to be able to survive in business at all.

Gladstone's masterstroke in forwarding this policy occurred during the 1880s. He abandoned his recent coercive policy in Ireland (imprisoning over 1,000 Land League officials without trial and establishing, for the first time in history, a permanent secret service in Ireland)[90] and suddenly announced his willingness to embrace the idea of 'home rule' for Ireland. Irish Tories, under Isaac Butt, had actually initiated an idea of home rule for Ireland during the early 1870s in protest against Gladstone's abolishment of the office of Vice Treasurer for Ireland. Now, however, Gladstone saw an embrace of the home rule slogan as a means of increasing existing levels of over-taxation in Ireland, which he had first established during the 1850s, while simultaneously cutting back on government expenditure in Ireland. In particular, by forcing Irish political representatives to sit in a completely powerless and subordinate assembly in Dublin with no fiscal autonomies, he intended to deny Irish political representatives any means of ever counteracting his policy.[91] Even though it was fully understood that 'Gladstone's proposed contribution from Ireland to England under the Home Rule Bill is more than Ireland could possibly continue to pay', Parnell's party went along with Gladstone's policy,[92] in the process tearing the Irish political community apart. Many former supporters of the Liberal party in Ireland, particularly within Ulster, now defected permanently to the Tories in opposition to Gladstone's initiative.

After 1886, Irish Tories protested that Ireland was legally supposed to be an equal part of the United Kingdom but it was now being governed in a purely exploitative manner in keeping with trends in Gladstonian foreign policy in third-world countries. This was why Parnell's willingness to depend on a Catholic Church that was completely indifferent to the economic well being of Ireland, except in so far as it affected its own private concerns, was equated with being willing to risk letting the country be economically ruined purely for the sake of a short-term electoral expediency. Irish Tory opponents of Parnell and Gladstone now described themselves as 'unionist', a political term they invented to denote their preoccupation with the terms of the original Union of 1801, but Gladstone's dismissal of their politics by noting that 'we are all unionists' was one to which Irish political commentators could offer no effective retort.[93] Indeed, after 1886 both Irish 'nationalist' and 'unionist' political organisations not only grew increasingly confessional but they were also frequently subject to ridicule because Irish politicians had neither the authority nor the means to ever establish a tribunal on the fiscal relations between Britain and Ireland. This meant they were inherently impotent in championing Irish economic interests.

The economic backdrop to the political operations of Griffith's YIL was that the fall of Parnell coincided with a shift in Tory economic policy in England. The exclusion of Britain from European free-trade markets around 1891 led English Tories to attack Gladstone's policy in that regard,[94] and this provided Irish Tories with an opportunity to step up their own criticisms of Gladstone. This was done by attempting to link the question of the financing of Irish education, which alone preoccupied the Catholic Church, with intellectual and cultural nationalist debate within Ireland in an attempt to highlight the existence of other political alternatives. However, the proverbial Irish nationalist response, as represented by the Irish Party, was simply to label the Tory-minded Parnellite press and the YIL that it publicised as an anti-Catholic faction. This reflected a central dynamic and deep paradox to the history of the Irish Party. From 1886 onwards it espoused a Liberal Party alliance for the sake of retaining support for the idea of home rule but in doing so it was actually defending a party that supported neither the economic interests of Ireland nor the principle of denominational education. Instead, the Liberal Party was simply prepared to allow for the greater promotion of Irish Catholic professionals within the British imperial civil service in order to further implement Gladstone's principles of fiscal administration.[95]

The Catholic Church welcomed this development purely because it assisted it in promoting its missionary work throughout the British Empire; a key issue as far as the Vatican was concerned. As far as Griffith was concerned, however, the only real defence that could be offered in favour of this policy was the opportunities it presented for individuals' professional development at the expense of Ireland itself. This was essentially true.[96]

Politically, Griffith's YIL occupied the position of being independent to such a degree that it fitted into no particular camp but instead found its audience primarily within the republic of letters. This was not necessarily a guarantee of obscurity during the 1890s. Many could identify with the protests of Griffith and his YIL friends that, judging from contemporary trends, the ideals of Irish nationalism had been completely forgotten in a race for civil service employments and that this was being masked and justified in public by disingenuous attempts by politicians to promote sectarian animosities purely in an attempt to hide their own personal, or careerist, ambitions.[97] Therefore, even if it was ineffective in a purely party-political sense, the fact that the YIL refused to obey MPs' request that it engage in electioneering and distributed copies of its resolutions to all parties, irrespective of whether or not they identified themselves as 'nationalist' or 'unionist' (according to the post 1886 party-political definitions) or whether or not they held government offices, was respected by all who disliked the tenor of Irish party politics ever since 1886.[98] In reviving debate on the ideals of the Young Irelanders of the 1840s, Griffith and his friends were also consciously echoing the green-white-and-orange symbolism of T.F. Meagher's republican tricolour of 1848.

Griffith's mentor in the YIL was Henry Dixon, a legal secretary at the Dublin Four Courts and former member of the Rathmines branch of the Irish National League. Now a professed admirer of both the Fabian Society in Britain and the Irish republican tradition, Dixon ran the avowedly republican National Club Literary Society with John MacBride (an IRB activist with links to the British naval port of Castlebar), launched the tradition of Bodenstown demonstrations and later became a business manager for one of Griffith's journals.[99] Indeed, Dixon was one of several YIL activists who later re-emerged as 'Sinn Féiners'.[100] These included Walter Cole (a future leader of Sinn Féin in Dublin City Hall), Peter White (the first secretary of Sinn Féin), Patrick Lavelle (Griffith's future solicitor) and Denis Devereux, a printer who tried to establish a journal for the YIL during 1894 and ultimately became the printer and manager of Griffith's first journal.[101] Reflecting the National Club's past attempt to mobilise support for Parnell specifically among town councillors nationwide, Dixon's circle combined a practical conception of the importance of promoting local government reform with a bookworm-style conception of Irish nationalism. Reflecting Dixon's friendship with leading Irish cultural nationalists like the republican-radical John Wyse Power and the great George Sigerson, the YIL also attempted to revive a partly successful, albeit short-lived, campaign from the early 1880s that appealed to church and school leaders to appoint more teachers of the Irish language.[102] This was a cause that the YIL first took up, partly on Griffith's suggestion, in May 1893.[103]

Griffith sent copies of a British government report on Wales, which became the basis of Westminster legislation that recognised that country's bilingual status, to members of all Irish education and local government boards with a request that they demand the same for Ireland.[104] As a member of the YIL's Irish Language Congress Committee, Griffith also issued flyers that claimed the present educational system in Ireland was 'indefensible' on the grounds that it did not make allowance for the existence of an Irish-speaking population.[105] Questionnaires to ascertain where and how much Irish was spoken and taught were sent not only to schools and colleges across the United Kingdom but also to a few in Europe and the United States.[106] Only the Catholic Irish College in Rome (which had an Irish language department) responded enthusiastically to this questionnaire, however.[107] In addition, the general results of the YIL survey were not encouraging: of approximately 8,500 national schools in Ireland, only forty-five taught Irish and this was only as an extra-curricular subject.[108] The YIL received negative replies from all Irish teacher-training colleges, the National Education Board at Dublin Castle as well as *ex-officio* members of that body, such as Chief Secretary Morley and William Walsh, the Catholic Archbishop of Dublin. Archbishop Walsh maintained that although he sympathised with the language movement, 'what you suggest is, at all events for the present, quite out of the question'.[109] At the YIL's Easter Week conference of March 1894, Griffith proposed that all local government bodies should be requested by the General Post Office in Dublin to 'have the names of some of the chief thoroughfares painted in Irish as well as in English'. Meanwhile, George Noble Plunkett (a Parnellite candidate for parliament who later became a papal count) and Michael Cusack of the GAA proposed that the electorate should vote only for those MPs who agreed to support the language movement.[110] Neither of these proposals had any effect, however.

Although it won the sympathy of a handful of significant individuals,[111] the YIL language campaign was essentially doomed because it had no organised body of support. With the British government's support, the churches had already established much control over Irish schools and the nominal existence of a 'national education board' for Ireland was meant to reflect this Irish divergence from the British and, indeed, European, as well as North American, trend of state-controlled education. This was great value of the Union to the Roman Catholic Church and the reason why the church encouraged the strengthening of that union after 1886. Full cooperation with the churches' educational policies was an essential prerequisite if any practical steps for educational reform were to be taken in Ireland. Douglas Hyde, who worked with the YIL through his membership of Yeats' National Literary Society, nominally founded the Gaelic League in July 1893 but he did not come to realise the necessity of working with the churches until late in 1896. Consequently, it was only from that time onwards that the Gaelic League began to emerge as a public body. By mid-1897, half of its executive consisted of senior Catholic clergymen and the remainder consisted of politicians and newspaper editors who first made it clear that they accepted the church's education programme.[112] By contrast, in championing the Irish language purely on its own merits the YIL had won no support whatsoever. In effect, it had refused to play the political game and so no bargain could be struck.

An additional reason for the YIL's failure was its attempt to emulate the original Young Irelanders of the 1840s by championing the non-denominational Queen's Colleges and calling for the conversion of Trinity College into a new, non-denominational, national university. Some Trinity graduates, although obviously not the Church of Ireland itself, favoured this idea. In opposition to this idea, Archbishop Walsh and the Catholic hierarchy never wavered in their conviction that non-denominational schools and universities were responsible for the growth of religious indifference (a reality that, at least when addressing the general Irish public, Walsh alleged to believe the British governing classes were incapable of appreciating) and that each Christian denomination in Ireland was therefore entitled to its own university.[113] By contrast, the YIL maintained that this policy would be very wasteful of the limited financial resources available for Irish education. It was openly critical of the idea of Irishmen seeking state funding for a Catholic university, claiming that if, instead, Trinity College was converted into a totally non-denominational and national university religious segregations would not continue to dominate Irish life.[114] This stance of the YIL encouraged Trinity-educated public intellectuals such as T.W. Rolleston and C.H. Oldham to offer their support to the Celtic Literary Society, which affiliated itself with the YIL during 1894, but it led Archbishop Walsh to request that the YIL cease to communicate with him under any circumstances, as 'I cannot undertake to answer questions put to me ... by unrepresentative and irresponsible bodies, such as that on behalf of which you have written.'[115]

Although this claim regarding the 'unrepresentative' and 'irresponsible' stance of the YIL was motivated by its political stance on education, to contemporaries it frequently had a cultural connotation as well.[116] This occurred because the YIL's citing of the legacy of the Young Irelanders of the 1840s could make debate upon Ireland historicist in tone. For instance, ever since the British-Catholic pact of 1886,[117] T.W. Rolleston (a Tory confrere of John O'Leary) and many others began repeating Thomas Davis' old example of celebrating the defunct eighteenth-century Irish parliament whilst denigrating Ireland's current representation in the imperial parliament.[118] Griffith was influenced strongly by this trend. Although this historic Irish parliament had been exclusively Protestant, the fact that control of the wealth of Ireland was still largely in the hands of its members' descendants convinced Griffith that many Irish Party supporters' simple equation of Irish nationalism with attempting to undo all existing manifestations of the historic Protestant ascendancy could only be politically self defeating. Reflecting this, Griffith's first-ever publication was a series of eight articles on notable eighteenth-century Irish personalities.[119] Although Griffith suggested that several of the figures examined presented 'somewhat of a paradox' ('whilst constantly asserting the right of Ireland to political freedom they were mostly at the same time inveterate and determined bigots'),[120] he suggested that the eighteenth century was a 'brilliant page in our history' that produced 'some of the ablest and a few of the greatest minds Ireland has produced'.[121] With regards to politics, Griffith believed that had Henry Grattan not 'played the generous fool, prating of Ireland's trust in English generosity', and instead listened to John Flood's economic nationalist arguments, the Act of Union would never have been passed and 'the misery of the last ninety years would have been impossible'.[122] He also believed that Ireland had become a prosperous country for the first time prior to the Union and that this act was motivated partly by a covert desire to undo this trend.[123]

Unlike Griffith, comparatively few contemporaries could blind themselves to the fact that the Young Ireland citation of the ideal of an Irish nationalism unaffected by religious divisions had only ever been a storybook ideal. It reflected neither the British government's fiscal management of Ireland since the 1820s (or indeed before) nor the Irish public's general acceptance of the equation of competing denominations with competing political interest groups on a fundamental, financial level.[124] This was a political actuality and to cite an ideal rather than dealing with existing realities was generally equated with poor political judgment. Reflecting this, if Griffith had entertained hopes of finding a political platform for himself after the fiasco of the YIL's education and Irish language campaigns, he did himself no favours during 1894 by appearing on various republican platforms (including one addressed by Jeremiah O'Donovan Rossa of New York) where all contemporary Irish politicians were denounced as royalist flunkeys.[125]

After delivering the annual IRB 'Robert Emmet lecture', Griffith began working closely with C.J. O'Farrell of Enniscorthy, an aging Francophile bookworm and Leinster IRB leader who was notoriously anticlerical.[126] Griffith's friends typified O'Farrell as 'a tall, dignified, grey-haired, handsome man, with a period moustache' who though 'normally retiring and gentlemanly only, periodically went on a spree and on these occasions he was volubly agnostic but always polite'.[127] As soon as the YIL began working with O'Farrell, however, a Wexford priest denounced them as young men with 'no more beards than brains' that were attempting 'to blacken and besmirch the character of the Irish priesthood'.[128] The Irish Party's press took up this accusation. At O'Farrell's Vinegar Hill demonstration, Griffith expressed strong approval for speakers' praise of the French Revolution. It was argued that the only hope for the nationalist cause in Ireland was if the youth were taught 'the true duties of citizenship ... to think for themselves regardless of the opinion of anyone else' and became prepared to demand 'the establishment in this country of a senate responsible to the people, and, if the country was so disposed, a government on republican lines'.[129] After a similar speech was made in New Ross, however, the Irish Party's press denounced the YIL as 'traitors'. This claim was rationalised because the YIL attempted to 'separate faith and fatherland' not only in their understanding of the history of Irish nationality but also in their attitudes towards Irish education: it was 'revolting', according to the Irish Party, that any body purporting to be Irish nationalists could think themselves entitled to criticise the Catholic hierarchy's stance on education.[130] Similarly, the following year, William Rooney was labelled by the Irish Party's press as a juvenile delinquent who had the 'cheek' to praise republicanism and the French Revolution and to 'read out a diatribe against the priests'.[131]

On a motion of William Field MP and George Coffey of the Royal Irish Academy, Griffith was re-elected as a member of the YIL Executive during 1895. However, Griffith declined the invitation to be the chief speaker at the 1895 Bodenstown demonstration (an event that attracted 5,000 people) and his attendance at meetings grew rare.[132] Indeed, with the exception of a few events (including a massive public funeral for James Boland that was organised by Field),[133] Griffith appears to have made very little public appearances for the best part of two years.[134] Why exactly this was the case is unclear. Although a pencil annotation in the YIL minute book read 'Griffith has been in France at Irish war and hurt himself',[135] this was evidently an addition made at a later date. The most probable explanation for Griffith's sudden reticence lay in problems in his personal life.

During the summer of 1891 Griffith's father was made unemployed again after T.D. Sullivan, a clericalist MP, characteristically folded the historic *Nation*, which was first founded by the Young Irelanders, and sold its franchise to the recently established *Irish Catholic*, which now became known as the *Irish Catholic and Nation*. Although he found some work with the Parnellite *Irish Daily Independent*, acute respiratory problems soon forced the father to take early retirement. This put real pressure on his son to compensate for the loss in family income. Griffith took on extra work as a copyreader and joined the Dublin printers' union in February 1894.

One acquaintance recalled that the Griffith family established a small shop at this time on Parliament Street, just opposite Dublin Castle.[136] This was possibly an investment made from a lump sum received by the father on his retirement. 'Griffith's For Bargains', a small market-stall selling discount household goods, existed in 'Parliament Street General Stores' during 1892,[137] while a reference exists to a 'Griffith Hardware and General Stores' at 16–17 Parliament Street as late as November 1895.[138] This shop was short lived, however, and its failure created a debt. Griffith's younger brother Frank, who was described by one family friend as a 'most attractive if somewhat feckless' character, also entered the workforce around this time, but his work as an usher in the Gaiety Theatre (a job that he stuck with for very many years) did little to supplement the family income.[139]

Griffith's withdrawal from public meetings in November 1894 coincided with the dismissal by the *Irish Daily Independent* of many of its staff. It is probable that he lost his job at this time and could not find another. Indeed, it seems that the Griffith family had to give up a rented home near Mountjoy Square, which had been acquired during the mid-to-late 1880s, during 1895 or 1896 and resettle in an unsanitary and crowded tenement flat such as they had lived in during the 1870s.[140]

Friends later recalled that Griffith fell into a serious depression at this time. George A. Lyons, a young Protestant evangelical clerk of republican sympathies who befriended Griffith in the Celtic Literary Society, recalled how the usually reticent Griffith admitted to him that he felt there was 'no prospects for him, either as an individual or as a nationalist'. Lyons also noted that 'some of his old friends suspected a disappointment in love' as an additional cause of his depression.[141]

Griffith had only one real girlfriend in his life, namely Maud Sheehan, the daughter of a Catholic middle-class and leisured family (one of her brothers was a keen amateur photographer)[142] that lived near Mountjoy Square. Griffith first met Maud during 1892 after he ruled that membership of the Leinster Literary Society should be open to women.[143] Later, she often played the piano to accompany singers at Celtic Literary Society social events and music became one of their common interests.[144] Like several YIL activists, Griffith was a supporter of women's suffrage and educational rights for women; the latter campaign being led in Ireland by Edith Oldham, a sister of C.H. Oldham. Maud had attended secondary school, was a devout attendant at Mass and suspected that Griffith suffered from acute ill health during 1895 and 1896 as, like everyone else, she saw very little of him at this time.[145] While they would fall in love (ultimately they married, fifteen years later), they rarely met during the mid-1890s as Griffith seemingly deliberately avoided her out of shame at his desperate material circumstances. While associates frequently attributed to Griffith 'an innate shyness',[146] poverty certainly limited his social self-confidence. In addition, it may well have been that the Sheehan family never approved of the Griffiths.

Lyons suspected that Griffith's withdrawal from public activities was also influenced by the fact that the IRB, 'to which in all probability he already belonged, was in a hopeless condition'.[147] Maud recalled that John MacBride was disgusted by the fact that the Dublin IRB organisation had become embroiled in dynamiting conspiracies involving *agent provocateurs* that were designed only to discredit Irish nationalism. She understood that this persuaded MacBride to leave the IRB and to follow Mark Ryan, a London doctor who set up a rival organisation that would concentrate exclusively on the cultural nationalist movement.[148] It is likely that Griffith felt similarly to MacBride. Ryan, the leader of the Parnellite National League in London, was notable for having friends in Irish Party circles as well as some secret contacts in various British colonies (Irish republican social networks often overlapped with those of British navy or army personnel). These networks included South Africa,[149] where two Irish Party members had recently gone to try gold prospecting. Utilising Ryan's contacts, MacBride left for South Africa where he found work as the foreman of a goldmine. In turn, word reached Griffith in Dublin that work was available and that a small Irish community existed in South Africa. In the autumn of 1896, Griffith as well as his cousin John R. Whelan made the decision to leave for the proverbial 'dark continent'.

Griffith's decision to emigrate coincided with the publication of a significant report by Hugh Childers, a former Chancellor of the Exchequer and cousin of Erskine Childers. Based on a Tory government commission of 1893–4, this report on the financial relations between Britain and Ireland showed Ireland to have been a victim of past economic mismanagement and to be deserving of 'a distinct position and separate consideration'.[150] After his return to Ireland, Griffith would use these findings to make a case in favour of an Irish economic nationalism. In time, this would prompt Andrew Kettle, a former Land League treasurer, to credit Griffith with being the only Irishman since Parnell's very brief flirtation with economic nationalist ideas during the early 1880s to have ever bothered making a rational effort to examine whether or not the idea of an independent Irish state could possibly make the slightest political sense.[151] This would do little, however, to reverse the firmly established trend of debate on Irish nationalism being confined largely to the non-political sphere—a supposedly purely cultural 'separatism'—as if it could inherently have no practical, economic connotation.

During the winter of 1896, Griffith took part in some Celtic Literary Society activities and an event occurred that must have been cheering.[152] On 29 December 1896, just before he was due to leave the country, a surprise party was held in his honour and a testimonial was presented to him.[153] No testimonial was collected for fellow immigrant John Whelan (until recently, the secretary of the Celtic Literary Society), which probably indicates that Griffith's poverty was better known than he wished.[154] Some public figures attended to wish Griffith well. These included John Clarke, the curator of the Linen Hall Library in Belfast and editor of the *Northern Patriot*, James Casey, the secretary of the Gaelic League, as well as sub editors with the *Daily* and *Weekly Independent* (J.W. O'Beirne and John Murphy) who had recently joined the IRB. Murphy, Patrick Lavelle B.L. and Edward Whelan spoke in Griffith's honour before Rooney concluded with a speech, noting 'how much the existence of many national organisations have owed to your support' and that 'associated with you as most of us have been for years in national work, we cannot but feel grieved that your counsel and your assistance, valuable and ever ready, are about to be withdrawn.' The Celtic Literary Society expressed a hope that they would be able to welcome Griffith home again one day.[155] Maud Sheehan was evidently impressed by this little event as she recalled, by way of comparison, that when MacBride left for South Africa nobody was there to say goodbye to him.[156]

Although still completely unknown to the Irish public at large, by the age of twenty-five Griffith had acquired a few notable contacts in the worlds of politics and journalism. He was also sufficiently well informed of intricate dynamics of political developments in recent times to be able to later draw upon this knowledge for various critiques.[157] He had not, however, acquired a livelihood or any degree of personal security. The combination of poverty and his individuality, as well as his refusal to abide by Archbishop Walsh's Christian-democratic shibboleths, may explain his failure to find a career, or a niche in politics, through existing patronage networks. This brought him closer to the revolutionary underground. Like many IRB men, Griffith was both a product of British imperialism, as would be demonstrated by his South African adventure, as well as a declared opponent of British imperialism, as would be demonstrated by his continued intellectual attraction towards nationalist ideologies. His self-definition at this time was that of a rebel but he was very much a rebel without a cause. The outbreak of the Anglo-Boer War would change this situation, however. It would allow Griffith to find patronage from both revolutionary and political circles that would, in time, enable him to embark on a definite career path as a journalist.

CHAPTER TWO

The Pro-Boer
Republican (1897–1902)

Erskine Childers, a leading theorist of Gladstonian fiscal doctrine for the British Empire, claimed that 'the whole history of South Africa bears a close resemblance to the history of Ireland'.[1] This idea was only justifiable according to the British Empire's plan after 1886 to turn Ireland into a similar colonial, financial entity. As Gladstone himself explained, the only motive of his Irish policy lay in imperial 'finance devices ... too subtle and refined' to be announced to the general public. For security reasons, however, it was 'of great consequence that in Ireland, with a view to holding in the people', these realities remained ones to which Irish public attention should never be drawn.[2] Some historians have claimed falsely that the provenance of Gladstone's Irish policy 'must be explained in terms of parliamentary combinations' arising from electoral results,[3] as if T.P. O'Connor's return for Liverpool in 1885 necessitated a dramatic alteration of government policy. However, the reality was quite different. 'Ireland's future had now become more unionist and imperial'[4] precisely because 'the position of the landlord in Ireland has been directly associated with [the formation of] State Policy all along' and it had now been simply arranged that the Irish Party would serve as a 'body of moderate men' suited 'to take their place' in forestalling any possibility of an opposition to British rule arising in Ireland. This was to be done not least by deliberately not acknowledging publicly in Ireland what the British government's policy for Ireland was in reality.[5] The perpetuation of a permanent secret service within Ireland was a reflection of this intent.

This trend in British governmental policy regarding Ireland was essentially why deep paradoxes arose in Irish party-political nomenclatures after 1886 and continued long thereafter. For instance, in Dublin, the independent nationalist MP William Field found his material support from Tory ('unionist') businessmen in demanding greater Irish fiscal autonomy and independence from Britain. By contrast, the chief 'home rule' parliamentary representative,William Martin Murphy, who was a 'nationalist' wholly committed, with the Jesuits' enthusiastic support, to overthrowing the historic legacy of the Protestant ascendancy, was one of three Irish Party figures who not only supported those British raids for South African gold that led to the Anglo-Boer War but also made and developed his fortune from the related British colonial ('gold coast') railway schemes in West Africa.[6] In this way, the general impact upon Irish society of the Anglo-Boer War might be typified as having been an illustration of the maxim that 'the bond of Empire was at all times stronger than that of [the] Union'. This was because 'the Empire ... offered career opportunities—male and female, clerical and lay, that were simply not available in Ireland', making the Empire seem like a more sensible guide to political and economic developments than the old (eighteenth-century) Irish nationalist adage of 'perish the empire and live the [Irish] constitution'.[7] Griffith would take a contrary view. In the short term, however, such considerations evidently mattered very little to him compared to the purely personal issue that he was receiving a working holiday. Indeed, as Griffith could never afford from his own wages to take a holiday longer than a few hours in the Dublin countryside,[8] his time in South Africa was undoubtedly one of the most colourful episodes of his life.

During his travels Griffith met people of various nationalities for the first time: native Africans, Indians, Dutch 'Boers', Portuguese, Germans, Egyptians, Japanese and even the English. Having travelled across England to Southampton, he boarded a steamship bound, via the Mediterranean and Suez Canal, for Portuguese East Africa (Mozambique). The ship stopped first at the tropical island of Zanzibar, a territory recently acquired by the British off the coast of German East Africa (Tanzania). Here he went on a British guided tour of the capital city, which brought to life for him 'a beloved storybook of our childhood':

> One cannot thoroughly appreciate or understand the *Arabian Nights* until he has visited an Arab city—until he has wandered through the narrow, tortuous streets with palaces towering to the sky ... Sometimes we went into the courtyards of the princely merchants ... and cooled ourselves under his palm-tree; sometimes we mingled with the whirling stream of Arabs, Swahilis, Singhalese, Egyptians, Japanese, Banyans and Parsees in the bazaar, and sometimes we explored the narrow dirty back streets, scarcely

three-feet wide, lit by occasional lanterns … [observing] the fish-market and the slave-market and a mosque or two.[9]

In Mozambique, Griffith spent most of the time 'lying all the morning round the deck, revelling in delicious laziness'. He learnt some phrases in a Hindu dialect and repeatedly defeated a German traveller in chess ('I comforted him with large beer and the assurance that I was the champion chess-player of the Celtic race').[10] At night, however, he invariably envied his fellow travellers for their female companionship. This prompted him to rely even more than usual on the traditional refuge of loveless young men: his pipe, which he christened as his companion 'Nicotina':

> On such a night—it is better to think Shakespeare than to quote him. Pray, what have I to do with lovers? I saw the Queen rising from the waves, and Helen and Maeve and Joan in her beautiful mob. Begone, O Aphrodite! Nicotina alone I serve—can your caresses drive her image from my heart? … My heart weeps …I cast aside my Nicotina. Shall I ever for one instant feel the divine joy of this one-time vilest of men, who loves and is beloved?[11]

Griffith shared in the British travellers' bemusement at the ostentatious aspects of Portuguese culture. A Portuguese port town appeared to him to be full of diminutive soldiers, 'black-moustached and yellow-faced', who were inappropriately 'carrying enormous sabres'. Life in the town appeared to Griffith as carnivalesque, bordering on the grotesque:

> Every third day is a great saint's day … The troops fire off their guns, the band plays at the kiosk, and the governor illuminates his residence. We go to the church and stare at the red-white-and-blue saints, dressed in tinsel-paper with cardboard crowns stuck on their heads …'These Portuguese', said a Saxon to me as we lay on deck that night, blowing our tobacco-clouds up in the face of divine Astarte, 'are useless in the world … If England or America had magnificent Delagoa the trade and commerce of South Africa would be doubled in five years; but these little pride-inflated, lazy nincompoops, with their big swords and ten thousand saints, are ruining the country.' [12]

Such manifestations of British cultural prejudice against less industrialised Mediterranean nations were not alien to the Dubliner Griffith. His strong sense of identification with his English companions would disappear, however, whenever they boasted of the political achievements of the British Empire. At Zanzibar, for instance, several English travellers asked Griffith for his opinion of Britain's performance in the recent Anglo-Zanzibar War. This had ended in just forty-five minutes after a British gunboat blew up the palace of the Sultan who had declared war. Griffith replied by expressing disapproval of the Empire, after which the English, who had hitherto been 'very pleasant fellows as travel-companions', turned on him with seething hatred, prompting Griffith to conclude that 'each had a tiger sleeping in his heart' that was born of a militant British nationalism.[13]

The nature of African town life led Griffith to the conclusion that Christian missionary work often went hand-in-hand with colonial exploitation. In one particular town, he found that the six richest men were Christian missionaries. Each man, it seemed to him, treated the natives simply as slaves:

> He came to enlighten the heathen and in the process of enlightenment acquired wealth sufficient to enable him to live comfortably … He had converted six heathens who hewed wood and drew water for him, while he smoked his pipe and said it was good. As money is the root of all evil he gave them none but he occasionally hired them out at so much per day to do work for other people.[14]

Griffith's sense of outrage at the colonists' treatment of the native Africans as children prompted him to typify the Negro as 'an old, old man':

> Once upon a time when your father and mine—my white brother— were lusty barbarians, the Ethiop was a mighty man, a warrior, a sailor, a poet, an artist, a cunning artificer, and a philosopher.[15]

Contemporary imperialist propaganda, issued by each of the European powers, invariably justified their financial exploits in Africa by portraying their adversaries as 'robbers and murderers with a penchant for harpooning pious Christians'. Griffith, however, typified this as a denial of 'the solemn truth the Japanese has grasped, that the Art of Destruction must be learned from the Christian nations'.[16] He even suggested that life in Africa had probably been 'comparatively godly' before the Europeans had built their Christian churches there, in the halcyon days when 'there were no crawling capitalist conspirators infesting the country'.[17] Griffith's cynicism regarding organised religion at this time included the Irish Jesuits, whom he accused of having substituted 'the Gospel of Khaki' (the British Army) for 'the Gospel of the Prince of Peace' (Christ) through their desire to benefit financially from British imperial colonialism.[18]

In Pretoria, Griffith discovered that the Dutch 'Boer' colony had become very militarised as a result of recent British raids into the territory. Here he met John James Lavery, a British businessman of Irish descent who had purchased a small newspaper in the town of Middelburg. Lavery was looking for some editorial assistance and Griffith seized this opportunity. Some local historians have dated the beginning of his editorial work to May 1897, although Griffith recollected that 'it was a pleasant autumn evening when I struck the town'.[19] The *Courant* was a badly printed country paper with a circulation of only 300 copies, some of which reached larger towns such as Johannesburg and Pretoria, and it was designed for the British citizens living within the Dutch colony.[20] The newspaper office was tiny and grubby and 'when I found the office I felt sorry I had come, but the die was cast … . We were sometimes short of type and often short of paper in the *Courant* offices, but our subscribers accepted this as inevitable.' Griffith typified his work for this paper as provocative, prompting readers to 'complain when I started writing in its columns':

> It had been the policy of the *Courant* to please all parties—the English for preference. I explained to its owner that if he wanted me to edit his paper, its policy must be one that would please myself. He agreed, and I pleased myself by arguing that the Boer and no one but the Boer owned the Transvaal, that the Queen's writ didn't run there and shouldn't run there, and the God Almighty had not made the earth for the sole use of the Anglo-Saxon race. This offended the Englishmen and they sent word they would drop round one evening, burn down the office and finish the editor off. But they didn't.[21]

In fact, Griffith's job consisted mostly of reporting on local business matters, although he also drew attention to the formation of Maud Gonne's *L'Irlande Libre* (Paris).[22] Life in the town itself was dull as it contained only 'two hotels, a Dutch church, an English church, and a jail':

> It was the centre of the coal-mining district … The young English managers of the mines played billiards all the month round in the town and 'let things rip', as they elegantly termed it. The shareholders in England paid for their fun.[23]

The most colourful episode to occur for Griffith in Middelburg was to meet Olive Schreiner, a daughter of Dutch and English Protestant missionaries who had the reputation in London, which she occasionally visited, of being the leading literary figure in South Africa. Prior to their meeting, Griffith had dismissed her literary reputation by arguing that 'she has not grasped, or mayhap "disdained", the fact that the literature of a people must be of and from the people'. He suggested that not unless someone 'arises who can understand and sympathise with the ideals and aspirations of the people of this portion of the world, black as well as white, there can be no African literature'. Such a writer, he noted, would need to have 'powers of expression and genius' but such qualities were 'as scarce in Africa as millionaires are plentiful'.[24] When he actually met Schreiner, however, Griffith found that she was 'a charming woman'. Later, he was delighted to find that she became a critic of British imperialism in South Africa,[25] as indeed many contemporaries did.[26]

Griffith's time with the *Courant* was cut short after he responded to the horsewhipping of an English townsman by a Dutch Boer landowner by writing that the former had received just what he deserved. The offended English party not only won a court case against the landowner but also pressed libel charges against the *Courant*, demanding five thousand pounds compensation from a paper that had a grand capital of thirty pounds. As a result, Lavery was arrested, receiving a sentence of either six months hard labour or a fine of one hundred pounds. Fortunately for Lavery, the population of Middelburg paid the fine but considerable ill feeling had developed and so the paper was disbanded.[27] Griffith left the town in October 1897 with neither regrets nor, it seems, any sense of shared responsibility for Lavery's misfortune. It was an example of which Griffith's hero, John Mitchel, probably would have been proud. Noting how 'I eventually managed to kill the paper', Griffith recalled that while 'there were some drawbacks to journalism in Middelburg … on the whole, it was exhilarating.'[28]

Returning to Pretoria, Griffith joined an Irish workers-benefit society named after John Daly, an imprisoned IRB leader who had recently been returned unopposed to parliament for Limerick city as a protest vote (his candidacy was immediately disqualified). Together with John MacBride, Griffith depended upon Solomon Gillingham, a successful baker of Irish descent and secret correspondent of Mark Ryan in London, to help him settle in the Dutch city. Through this channel, funds were forwarded to London for a fenian-amnesty agitation while an address was made to that wing of the American Clan na Gael that funded Ryan's London activities.[29] In this address, which was reprinted by W.M. Murphy's Dublin newspaper, Griffith expressed a desire that Irishmen worldwide would use the centenary of the 1798 rising as an opportunity to 'repudiate forever … the sham miscalled "constitutional action"',[30] which was the description that the Irish Party gave to their appeals to the British imperial parliament to better manage Irish affairs. Mark Ryan's American contacts, secretly known as the Irish National Brotherhood (INB), were not reliable. Their propaganda was valued, however: as early as 1894 Griffith had persuaded the Celtic Literary Society to become subscribers to the *Irish Republic* (New York).[31]

It has been rumoured that Griffith was involved in a secret conspiracy in South Africa that planned to rob a local goldmine in order to finance an Irish revolutionary organisation.[32] This seems unlikely, although the clear connection of his South African circle with a trans-Atlantic 'Fenian' communications network (this, as Griffith knew, had also existed during the first Anglo-Boer War)[33] does at least explain the existence of a rumour. Griffith *did* work for a time as an overseer in a gold mine near Johannesburg where he nearly had a fatal accident. He later told the orphaned Dublin Protestant writer James Stephens that 'I could have been a fairly wealthy man if I had the luck in those days to want to be dishonest' because many individuals doing the work he was doing 'were able to retire after a few years and buy theatres' due to their subtle larceny.[34]

In Johannesburg Griffith occasionally received letters from William Rooney,[35] which no doubt related to the activities of the 1798 centenary movement. Within weeks of Griffith's departure, a 1798 Centenary Committee, led by John O'Leary, Henry Dixon and Fred Allan, was established by the YIL. Shortly thereafter, at a YIL convention chaired by P.N. Fitzgerald, it was proposed that centenary clubs should be established nationwide with a view to creating a new nationalist organisation.[36] This 1798 centenary movement quickly grew large, but the Irish Party and the Catholic clergy launched a concerted campaign to wrestle control of the movement out of the IRB's hands.[37]

The first circular distributed by the Centenary Committee argued that if the celebrations were to have 'permanent beneficial results' they would need to encompass equally the viewpoints of 'the three great sects' in Ireland. It was also argued that the United Irishmen's greatest chance of attaining a fair constitution for Ireland had not been in the 1798 rebellion but rather in those political developments that had occurred prior to the government's suppression of the Irish Volunteers during 1794 and the driving of the reformist United Irish movement underground.[38] This argument was one that Griffith himself would repeat in later years.[39] It was based on the understanding that the rebellion had been provoked by Britain to do away with the Irish constitution and facilitate a political and economic union between Britain and Ireland in order to maximise the former's resources in fighting the Anglo-French War (1793–1815). Ireland, it would seem, could never quite escape from the demands of the British imperial economy. Griffith pointed out in 1911 that the existence of 'international' Irish republican conspiracies ever since that time was merely a cover to enable British consulates abroad to gather useful foreign policy information in their host countries.[40] This was an additional paradox in Irish political nomenclatures, which was perhaps best reflected by the fact that the author of the famous nineteenth-century Irish nationalist ballad 'who fears to speak of '98' was actually a leading unionist economist.[41] It was also the reason why most contemporaries judged that no greater revolution could possibly take place in Ireland than the development, for the first time in history, of a political community that was truly determined to revolve on its own axis.

Virtually all those who had been present at Griffith's farewell gathering at Dublin were prominent members of the 1798 Centenary Committee. A surprising exception was William Rooney, who was delegated instead to join Alice Milligan, the co-editor of the Belfast *Shan van Vocht* (which was partly funded, via Robert Johnston, by the New York *Irish Republic*), in doing insignificant propaganda work, such as organising small-scale historical lectures and exhibitions.[42] This may be explained by the fact that Rooney was now concentrating primarily upon the Irish language movement, having helped the Gaelic League to organise its first of many Feis Ceoil Irish music events.[43] Indeed, aside from contributing a ballad (as did Griffith) to Douglas Hyde's *Songs and Ballads of '98*, Rooney's only direct contribution to the 1798 centenary movement was to propose that all memorials erected in honour of the United Irishmen should bear Irish language inscriptions only.[44]

Griffith and other Irish immigrants were able to hold their own 1798 centenary demonstration in Johannesburg on 30 August 1898.[45] By that time, however, the centenary movement in Ireland had grown weak and two of Griffith's closest associates in the movement, Henry Dixon and G.A. Lyons, blamed John O'Leary and, to a lesser extent, Fred Allan, for this, owing to their eventual capitulation to the Irish Party's demand to have greater control over the movement.[46] Furthermore, as the YIL had been converted into the 1798 Centenary Committee (each of which, like the IRB, had been nominally under O'Leary's presidency), this meant that Griffith's friends in Dublin had lost their only available political forum.

It was sometime during the autumn of 1898 when Griffith made the decision to return to Dublin. By January 1899, he was working as a compositor in the City Hall office of *Thom's Dublin Gazette* and again attending meetings of the Celtic Literary Society.[47] Well-founded rumours existed in Dublin that the 'Parnellite' Independent Newspaper Company, which had promoted the YIL, was about to be liquidated. In addition, the *Shan van Vocht*, which had been established to eclipse the influence of John Clarke's *Northern Patriot* in the 1798 centenary movement (a task it accomplished), was ready to fold. This journal had been closely associated with the Celtic Literary Society and it was partly funded by Mark Ryan's London-Irish circle. Upon receiving word in late 1898 that it would cease publication, Ryan proposed that Rooney should become the editor of a new journal to replace it. As Rooney had no previous editorial experience, however, Griffith landed the job. An additional factor that worked in Griffith's favour here was that this enterprise was funded by capital previously forwarded to Ryan from South Africa.[48]

The *United Irishman* was founded in Dublin in March 1899 with Rooney and Griffith as its joint editors. It was expected by the IRB to be an organ for the surviving centenary clubs. Mark Ryan, by contrast, wanted it to promote a non-political cultural nationalism. In the face of these competing desires, Rooney and Griffith chose a similar stance as had Alice Milligan by adopting a middle course, declaring that 'here are opinions to suit all classes. You pay your penny and you take your choice.'[49] Up until a couple of months before his premature death in May 1901, William Rooney acted as the literary editor of the *United Irishman*, which was subtitled as a weekly review. Griffith took on the responsibility of tackling political subjects. These included the recent establishment of elective local government bodies and the role that the outbreak of the Anglo-Boer War had in influencing the whole question of where Irish political allegiances should lie in the wake of the 1798 centenary celebrations. Reflecting his antipathy to contemporary party politics, Griffith wrote regarding the creation of new county and urban district councils that he hoped voters would 'reject with equal contempt the slavish home ruler and the knavish unionist and vote for representatives, regardless of their party politics, who are honest men'.[50] Men of professed nationalist sympathies but not necessarily of any specific party allegiance won 75 per cent of all seats, including many individuals who had once been connected with the republican underground.[51]

The outcome of these elections highlighted significant undercurrents within Irish political society. New county and town councillors erected dozens of memorials to Irish rebellions in the wake of the 1798 centenary, while some old republican figures as well as many members of William O'Brien's new agrarian United Irish League (UIL) refused to follow requests from the Irish Party that they become justices of the peace because of the required oath of allegiance to the British crown.[52] In Limerick, the released convict John Daly was elected as mayor and acted nominally in republicans' interests by removing the royal coat of arms from City Hall and granting the freedom of the city to his fellow released convict Tom Clarke. Meanwhile, immediately upon the outbreak of the Anglo-Boer War in October 1899, resolutions of sympathy with the Boers were passed by six of the thirty-two county councils in Ireland (Limerick, Kilkenny, Mayo, Kings County, Sligo and Cork) as well as about two-dozen urban and district councils, town commissions and board of guardians (mostly in the counties Monaghan, Tipperary, Clare and Galway).[53]

This was a somewhat startling development. It reflected a motive of the secret compact behind the Anglo-Irish security negotiations of 1884–7 and the purpose of the recently established Resident Magistrate System, which was launched during 1881. During the mid-1880s the idea of creating elective local government bodies in Ireland was deemed 'unsound and dangerous' purely for security reasons.[54] The decision to withhold from the municipal authorities established in Ireland during 1899 the same financial autonomies as their British counterparts possessed since 1888 was a continuation of this legacy.

Griffith helped to found a small Pro-Boer movement in Dublin during June 1899 once it became clear that Britain was going to invade the Boer Republic. With the support of the Celtic Literary Society, local 1798 centenary clubs and Mark Ryan's recently established Irish National Club in London, Griffith formed the Irish-Transvaal Committee under John O'Leary's presidency. Three Irish Party members made a subscription to the Irish-Transvaal Committee, but the Boer War presented some problems for the Irish Party in promoting its nationalist reputation. This was because the Irish Party was expected in all British political circles, including South African ones, to celebrate the Empire.[55] Disingenuously or not, Griffith sought to capitalise upon this chink in the Irish Party's armour. The possibilities of doing so were limited, however, by republicans' lack of a viable political organisation of their own.

During 1899, IRB leaders in Dublin, Cork, Belfast, Limerick, Kerry and Mayo made efforts to keep the 1798 centenary clubs in existence. Their purpose in doing so was reflected in the political columns of Griffith's *United Irishman*, which called for the creation a new 'republican association' in the country that would be entirely public and based around the centenary clubs. Griffith's friend G.A. Lyons even made an exaggerated claim that 'if we had a '98 club in every town in Ireland, working as I know at least one to be working in Dublin, we would not fear for the future of an Irish republic'.[56] In Dublin, the IRB leader Fred Allan operated a body known as the Wolfe Tone Memorial Committee to which these centenary clubs were supposed to send subscriptions, just as they had previously done to the now defunct 1798 Centenary Committee. It was evidently intended that Griffith's *United Irishman* would act as the organ of this new movement. At the June 1899 Bodenstown demonstration chaired by P.N. Fitzgerald, Maurice Moynihan of Tralee, the new Munster IRB leader (and father of a future leader of the Irish civil service of the same name), called upon all nationalists to support 'that sturdy and patriotic little sheet, the *United Irishman*'. Moynihan advocated the establishment of 'an open organisation' because 'political opinion in Ireland at this time is in too unsettled, too chaotic, a state to start a real revolutionary movement'. Moynihan declared that the proposed new public organisation should have nothing to do with the Irish Party and its press but it need not 'decry any existing organisation, whether connected with land or labour', such as William O'Brien's United Irish League. Reflecting republicans' prejudice against land agitations, however, Moynihan felt certain that it was 'to the young men of the cities and towns we must look for the formation of a national organisation'.[57]

About 8,000 people, primarily from Dublin, were present at this Bodenstown demonstration. This may well have seemed as evidence to Griffith that his journal was about to become a significant seller. However, many centenary clubs disbanded soon after and whatever funds that were subscribed to the central Wolfe Tone Clubs of Dublin seem to have been financially mismanaged. Nominally, these funds were supposed to be used to erect a monument to Wolfe Tone (an idea that Dublin City Hall would reject in favour of the idea of a Parnell or a Gladstone monument) but instead they became funds of the IRB that were deliberately misappropriated by J.P. Dunne, the first secretary of the Wolfe Tone Clubs and a former admirer of John Redmond. Indeed, it is doubtful that the *United Irishman* received regular funding from this quarter. Although the *United Irishman* expanded to an eight-page journal after the 1899 Bodenstown demonstration, John Devoy, the IRB's American ally, recalled that Griffith considered the IRB as 'too stingy' in their support and so he looked elsewhere.[58] His alternative backers would prove to be no more reliable.

Historians have sometimes attributed to Griffith the political opinions voiced in 'Over the Border'. This was a front-page commentary on international affairs that appeared in the *United Irishman* during its first year of publication.[59] However, these articles were actually written by Frank Hugh O'Donnell, a London-Irish figure and associate of Mark Ryan upon whom the *United Irishman* became financially dependent. A graduate of Queens College Galway who had been expelled from the Irish Party in 1885 (Parnell had considered both O'Donnell and John O'Connor Power as too much of a personal rival),[60] O'Donnell had the reputation of being a controversial propagandist because of his tendency to overstate his arguments. By now, he had few admirers apart from Mark Ryan and some London-Irish Tories.

During the period of the Boer War, Irish Catholics' great hostility to the French Republic's state-controlled education programme (it would soon expel the Jesuits from France) encouraged the Irish Party's press to adopt a very pro-British treatment of current Anglo-French relations. These were strained due to Britain and France's rival colonial interests on the African continent. Acting partly on John O'Leary's advice,[61] the *United Irishman* chose to reflect an opposing viewpoint. To this end, O'Donnell, adopting the pseudonym 'the foreign secretary', wrote unquestioning defences of the French government from all international criticisms, including intensely anti-Semitic defences of the Parisian government's handling of the Dreyfus affair. Some historians have cited this as evidence of a strong anti-Semitic streak in Griffith, although this is an exaggerated claim.[62] O'Donnell was actually receiving funds from the French government to write this propaganda. He had used his connection with Mark Ryan's London-Irish circle as a cover for claiming to be an Irish revolutionary leader and had approached both French and Dutch embassies looking for financial support for an anti-British propaganda campaign. In this, he outmanoeuvred American agents of John Devoy's Clan na Gael (who attempted a similar objective, nominally on behalf of the IRB) and succeeded in acquiring funds to launch an Irish pro-Boer movement, his efforts in Paris having succeeded partly due to the assistance of Maud Gonne and her war-mongering French imperialist (ex-Boulangerist) associates on the Parisian city council. In this way, O'Donnell, Ryan and Gonne effectively financed the Irish Pro-Boer movement from London and Paris. It appears, however, that their circle was not above passing information to the British Foreign Office on French attitudes towards international affairs.[63]

In some Irish Party quarters (which were privy to what was taking place at Dublin Castle), it was rumoured not entirely without reason that the pro-Boer movement was also connected with more dangerous British secret service plots.[64] Whatever the case, Maud Gonne, who grew up in Dublin Castle social circles and took after her military father, clearly attempted to endear herself to Griffith at this time. She sent him a large signed photograph of herself and a copy of a novel *The Mountain Lovers*, both bearing an inscription pledging her friendship to him.[65] Reputedly, Griffith thereafter entertained serious romantic illusions about Gonne,[66] who had attained celebrity status as supposedly one of the most beautiful women of the day. If so, these hopes were no doubt short-lived: she was not known as Ireland's Joan of Arc for nothing. A political association remained, however, for at least the length of the Anglo-Boer War. Griffith even horsewhipped a newspaper editor for claiming to have proof that Gonne was a Parisian agent of the British Foreign Office.[67] This action led to Griffith's arrest and his violent action was very probably motivated by self-defence: it was well known that the *United Irishman* was financially dependent upon Gonne's circle. However, even if Griffith was in receipt of some monies that came from suspect sources—this being an almost inevitable feature of being associated with revolutionary organisations—this did not have a great bearing upon his own work.

Griffith's opposition to the Irish Party, which was more intense than that of any Irish Tory member of parliament, would become a defining feature of his political editorials. As had been the case since the late 1880s, it continued to be expressed primarily as a sense of outrage at the party's indifference to the urban working class. Griffith continued to believe in the idea of a state-sponsored socialism while opposing all notions of politically engineered class conflicts. He argued that the establishment of more state institutes of technical education for the working classes was the most pressing educational need facing the country and that state grants should be created to enable the working classes attend university, as was the case in France and Germany.[68] As a result of its decision to allow the Catholic hierarchy determine its policy on education, the Irish Party was understood by Griffith to have equated Irish educational needs with the question of denominational education alone.[69] He typified Irish Party politicians and journalists as royalist flunkeys for two reasons. First, they took part in loyalist social events. Second, there was an inevitably close working relationship between all the country's elected politicians and its police forces. This reality was presented by Griffith as a symbolic representation of parliamentarians' indifference to the urban working class.[70]

Griffith frequently gave voice to this quintessentially working-class perspective of police forces being inherently oppressive tools of social control for so long as he lived in poor circumstances himself. It underpinned his fascination with the history of the Fenian movement—regarding which he knew very intricate details [71]—as well as his fondness for attending republican commemorative events. For example, in expressing praise for P.N. Fitzgerald's 1901 Bodenstown speech against middle-class political opportunism Griffith drew the personal conclusion that police harassment of workers on their way home to Dublin from Bodenstown demonstrated what motives underpinned both middle-class political attitudes and all the activities of the police.[72] Catholic clergymen often attempted to dissuade working-class figures like Griffith from holding such attitudes. This was done by pointing out that secret revolutionary movements, in Ireland as much as in the rest of Europe, were invariably established by police forces as a tool to detect and manage sources of discontent among the poor. Old fenians like Fitzgerald sometimes attempted to counter this argument by telling their followers, in the same breath as they espoused the value of bearing firearms, that priests were, consciously or unconsciously, an ally of the police in oppressing the poor.[73]

Fr P.F. Kavanagh, a Franciscan monk and popular historian of the 1798 rising, gave valuable support to the pro-Boer movement by launching an anti-enlistment campaign. He challenged Griffith directly on the issue of secret societies in the pages of the *United Irishman*.[74] To refute Fr Kavanagh's arguments, Griffith argued that secret societies were very often a necessary evil in overthrowing tyrannical powers. His belief in this idea appears to have been rooted primarily in his appreciation for the fact that members of such organisations, by espousing a republican dichotomy between the concepts of citizenship and slavery, had often helped to sustain a sense of self-reliant patriotism in Irish political debate: 'we owe what national self-respect we still retain mainly to the secret society of the United Irishmen and the secret society of the Fenian Brotherhood ... They made men out of slaves.' Meanwhile, in an attempt to speak in defence of the existence of secret societies, Griffith also spoke of the underground nature of the early Christian church and argued that the modern church had lost its sense of perspective in these matters, thereby frequently becoming a bastion of aristocratic conservatism.[75] Griffith himself came to the realisation that there were many dubious features to the history of Irish revolutionary organisations, not least because he knew from his own youth in Dublin of horrific episodes that pointed to unsavoury conclusions regarding the true nature of all revolutionary undergrounds.[76] Overall, he evidently viewed the broad question of the relationship between agencies of social control and the activities of revolutionary organisations from a practical standpoint. He knew that secret machinations involving the police's political intelligence forces were an inherent feature of this environment. However, he also acknowledged that, in the pre-democratic age and semi-colonial political context in which he lived, such organisations often provided the only ladder available for men of his social background to gain an entry point into the power game that defined the world of politics.

If Griffith was willing to defend the history of Irish revolutionary organisations, his own activities at this time were less an underground conspiracy than a form of protest politics that was shaped by specific Dublin circumstances. The Irish Party was beginning to eclipse the Tories in Dublin parliamentary representation.[77] As Griffith would note, however, the city's politics was still governed by a unique partition that stemmed from the legacy of the imperial treasury's deliberate withholding, not long after the admission of Catholics to municipal office in 1840, of the city's quit and crown rents that were paid annually for the city's upkeep. Dublin was now the only city in the world where the suburbs, which were invariably the home of a city's labour force, housed its wealthiest inhabitants and contributed nothing to the upkeep of a city that was left to subsist if that were possible (generally it was not) only on the taxation of the city's labouring population.[78] It was not for nothing that Griffith typified Dublin city's completely unparalleled housing and sanitation problems as a totally avoidable 'Viceregal microbe'. The Dublin Chamber of Commerce had become a moribund body that, more often than not, maintained a deliberate and embarrassed silence, while contemporaries invariably associated wealthy Dublin society exclusively with royal court society, or the suburbs, and the poor with City Hall, i.e. the city's actual government, which was deprived of resources and then accused of incompetence.[79]

An additional factor that uniquely coloured Dublin life was peculiarities that existed on the level of political organisation and journalism. Although the Irish Party had progressively abandoned its association with Land League radicalism after 1881, continuities existed on the simplistic level of personnel. Reflecting this, ex-Land League officials from the provinces lacked influence equally with the Irish Party and the British government but nevertheless maintained a proud tradition of moving to Dublin in an attempt to act as behind-the-scenes party administrators or nationalist journalists. Although the age of the by-line had not yet arrived, men of this social background played a significant part in colouring political debate in Ireland, while unionist opinion generally took perpetual comfort from the British government's effective guarantee that 'Dublin does not lead Ireland as Paris leads France.'[80] Like many a nationalist journalist, Griffith wrote his columns as if this simply should not be the case. Unlike various ex-Land Leaguers, he had the additional vantage point, or motive, of being a native of Dublin; the home of many 'statesmen on the street corners'.[81] Although many fellow journalists typified Griffith's understandable attacks on the Irish Party as either counter productive or downright unfair, they nevertheless generally understood and respected his place in the world of Dublin letters.

Griffith's determination to act as a thorn in the Irish Party's side manifested itself several times during 1900. First, to coincide with the nominal reunification of the Irish Party under John Redmond's leadership, Griffith supported Mark Ryan in proposing that John MacBride be put forward for a south Mayo parliamentary by-election as a means of protesting against British rule. In doing so, they publicised the fact that MacBride had recently formed a small commando unit on the Boer side in the Anglo-Boer War. There was another context to this election, however, about which Griffith may well have been unaware. Under Dublin Castle's supervision, Ryan had recently met up with MacBride's Castlebar associates and spoke publicly of initiating arms importations along the Mayo coast. This action enabled Dublin Castle to achieve its longstanding ambition to persuade the British Admiralty to begin placing Royal Navy gunboats in Clew Bay.[82] This reflected a peculiar context of the social world of republican activists. This was always characterised by engagement with nationalist debating clubs, working-class political organisations (urban and, to a lesser extent, agrarian) and popular cultural nationalist organisations (most notably the GAA) within Ireland itself. This prompted most activists, including Griffith, to view themselves as engaged in a nationalist challenge to the authority of Dublin Castle. However, the latter's political intelligence work always had much broader ramifications than the local (friendly or unfriendly) DMP or RIC detectives who were standing on Irish street corners. In conjunction with various activities of the Foreign Office, War Office and the Admiralty, it was financed by the

Secretary of State's secret service fund to promote and protect British strategic or diplomatic interests worldwide, including the financing of both national and international security concerns.[83] Griffith claimed to have expected a negative result in MacBride's parliamentary campaign, but nevertheless attempted to use MacBride's defeat repeatedly thereafter as a means to criticise the Irish Party's supposed lack of patriotism.[84]

Griffith's next attack upon the Irish Party was equally indirect. Maud Gonne and Mark Ryan funded him to attempt to negate the political influence within Dublin of Fred Allan. As the former manager of the *Irish Daily Independent*, Allan was considered to be too personally sympathetic towards John Redmond, who was now chosen as a new leader for the Irish Party partly because it was considered that his political lineage (his family had been in politics since the 1850s) made him a good potential successor to Parnell as a man who could at least pose as an individual that was above 'mere' party politics and thus assume the standing of a prospective national leader. Allan had recently accepted the job as secretary to the lord mayor of Dublin to strengthen the hand of the Wolfe Tone memorial movement but was then embarrassed by the mayor's announcement that he intended organising a large welcoming celebration for Queen Victoria and so decided to offer his resignation to City Hall. However, John O'Leary dissuaded Allan from doing so (he deemed the Queen's visit to be politically insignificant). This prompted Gonne to fund Griffith to blacklist all corporation officials who took part in the royalist demonstration.[85] As a result, Allan lost his position as the leader of the Wolfe Tone Clubs in June 1900 in the same week as the United Irish League set up a central executive in Dublin and officially declared itself to be the supporting body of John Redmond and the Irish Party. Thereafter, Griffith also broke up a meeting in the Rotunda and gathered about 2,000 people to break up a relatively small rally in the Phoenix Park in an attempt to prevent the UIL from establishing branches in Dublin.[86]

These activities, funded by Gonne, reflected a peculiar and longstanding dynamic to the revolutionary underground in Ireland. In acting as a thorn in the side to moderate nationalist politicians, it frequently served unionists by diverting attention away from the manner in which they were being politically protected the most in the manner of oligarchs by the exercise of the golden rule in society. During the Queen's visit, Griffith published bitter *United Irishman* editorials against the Irish Party's willingness to pledge their allegiance to 'The Famine Queen', took part in Irish Socialist Republican Party street brawls with the police (Griffith was a skilled boxer)[87] and succeeded in getting himself arrested twice and his journal prosecuted.[88] Griffith's willingness to engage in street brawls was probably influenced by deep frustration in his personal life at this time. The previous winter, he was unable to save his father from the shame of being forced to enter the workhouse while his beloved older sister had just died from tuberculosis.[89]

T.D. Sullivan MP, a mayor of Dublin during the Land League days, knew the Griffith family slightly during the mid-1880s but he had recently announced his intention to retire from politics. He responded to the prosecution of the *United Irishman* by pointing out that it was an insignificant cultural nationalist organ of Maud Gonne's that did not represent a dangerous political movement. Therefore, it was absolutely ridiculous for Dublin Castle to have treated it, or, indeed, to have drawn great political attention to it, in the way that it did.[90] The political context of these developments was essentially the scheming of John Clancy, a key figure in Dublin republican circles for many years despite the fact that he was the electoral registrar and sub-sheriff of the city from 1885–99. He was now a representative of the new municipal ward of Clontarf.[91] Clancy supported Gonne and Griffith's failed efforts to get City Hall to confer the freedom of Dublin upon the president of the Boer Republic and to get released convict Tom Clarke appointed to a clerical position in the corporation (Clarke subsequently became the New York agent for the *United Irishman*). Acting on the advice of J.P. Nannetti, a printing-firm owner previously associated with the IRB but who now joined the Irish Party, that winter Clancy committed himself to the UIL and helped to establish it in Dublin by making it vocally supportive of a policy of removing all loyalists from the corporation.[92] This set the tone for subsequent developments.

Griffith had called previously in the *United Irishman* for the formation of a new movement that would commit itself primarily to removing all royalist flunkeys from Irish municipal politics.[93] These campaigns reflected a desire to undo a legacy of the 1892 general election, the first post-1886 general election to be held. This was a widespread tendency to abandon the old pledge of the Irish National League, set during 1882 and partly sustained by the Plan of Campaign of 1886–90, that nationalists should not take government offices.[94] The revival of the sectarian Ancient Order of Hibernians among the beleaguered Ulster Catholic population after 1904 would see this idea re-emerge as a factor in political debate.[95] It essentially remained a minority position, however, that, in the meantime, was championed mostly by Griffith's nascent political movement in Dublin. This was also the context for the launch of an anti-enlistment movement, for which Gonne financed the printing of 40,000 circulars and Fr Kavanagh declared the Boer War to be an unjust war according to the teachings of the Catholic Church.

Gonne also financed the creation of two new cultural nationalist organisations that were founded at the Celtic Literary Society meeting rooms in Dublin. The first was the Daughters of Erin, a small women's nationalist organisation, and the second was 'Cumann na nGaedhael (Confederation of the Gaels)', which expressed support for promoting the Irish language and held joint social functions with the Daughters of Erin. Only a few dozen people were present at its initial meeting, at which Griffith was appointed its provisional leader.[96] When its first convention was held, however, Griffith was not elected to any position. Instead, its executive consisted mostly of individuals who were elected *in absentia* due to their status as figureheads in the pro-Boer agitation, namely John O'Leary (president) and Fr Kavanagh, John MacBride, Robert Johnston and James Egan (vice-presidents).[97]

With Gonne's support, Fr Kavanagh also formed a branch of the Celtic Literary Society in Cork and subsequently wrote to the *United Irishman* stressing that the new movement must not be allowed to fall under the influence of men who held 'un-Catholic doctrines'.[98] In the light of his previous quarrel with Griffith, Fr Kavanagh may have used his influence to exclude him from its executive. This stance was motivated primarily, however, by a desire to marginalise all political activists of John Daly's generation who, through their association with surviving 1798 centenary clubs or trade and labour associations, were either sympathetic to the early radicalism of the United Irish League or the old school of fenian political anticlericalism. To marginalise all such men, Cumann na nGaedhael sought recruits exclusively among young members of the Gaelic League. Early adherents such as Terence MacSwiney and Liam de Róiste of Fr Kavanagh's Celtic Literary Society in Cork, as well as Bulmer Hobson and Denis McCullough in Belfast, made no secret of their distaste for political activities of the preceding generation. It was not a coincidence that this formation of Cumann na nGaedhael coincided with the establishment of D.P. Moran's *Leader*. This was a new Catholic newspaper that, although nominally an independent organ, existed to propagate a self-confident cultural nationalism that sought to undo, or screen over, all the divisions that had erupted in Irish Party circles after 1890.[99]

During the height of the pro-Boer campaign in the summer of 1900, Griffith had enjoyed the excitement of being brought by Robert Johnston, a wealthy Belfast republican, to Paris to meet Maud Gonne and her war-mongering French political associates.[100] A year later, however, Griffith was writing to John MacBride that there was 'not the ghost of a chance of my being able to go over' to Paris again and that he was 'all alone in Dublin now and half-dead'.[101] In March 1901, Rooney had fallen terminally ill due to a slum-contracted disease. He died three months later. Coming very shortly after the death of his own sister from the same cause and his father's incarceration in a workhouse, this hit Griffith particularly hard. Meanwhile, if Griffith's enthusiasm for the pro-Boer campaign had declined, this was only natural as the centre of the political controversy had shifted far away from Griffith's orbit, namely to Irish-America.

After expelling T.M. Healy and his clericalist followers from the party, the Irish Party discovered that the UIL, whose branches consisted of many parish priests, was not very willing to contribute to its funds. To counteract this trend, it was decided to send men to the United States to establish an American fund-raising wing of the UIL. Maud Gonne and John MacBride, who had fled from South Africa, went to America on Mark Ryan's orders. While Griffith believed they were opposing the Irish Party's mission, they actually worked for the American allies of Michael Davitt. Essentially acting as the Irish Party's fifth columnist, Davitt had resigned from parliament purely to supervise the development of the Pro-Boer movement. He went to the United States to attempt to shut down the old Clan na Gael organisation of John Devoy, which was currently promoting an American lecture tour for John Daly and no longer supporting John Redmond (the chief 'independent nationalist' after 1891) after he rejoined the Irish Party. Devoy complained to MacBride about this situation but the later justified this course of events by stating that Cumann na nGaedhael had been decided upon as the movement of the future, not the old republican networks. Reflecting Maud Gonne's strategy, he also wrote to the *United Irishman* that he believed that the public organisations identified with the new Irish-Ireland movement within Ireland itself, such as Cumann na nGaedhael, the Gaelic League and (increasingly) the GAA, were bringing 'a new soul into Erin' and he suggested that they adopt a new motto of 'Sinn Féin' to describe their objectives.[102] At the time, with Gonne's support, Mark Ryan was proposing to form a new international organisation, under MacBride's presidency, that would link Irish-American contacts with his own circle in London and Cumann na nGaedhael in Dublin.[103] It was intended that this would replace the old Clan na Gael-IRB networks and create a new movement that was more in line with mainstream Irish nationalism.

Not surprisingly, the political outcome of the Pro-Boer movement did not become evident until the Anglo-Boer War ceased in October 1902. That month, the Irish Party's fortunes were partly secured by the formal establishment of the United Irish League of America while the success of Davitt's mission meant that the Clan na Gael nearly disbanded altogether. The cessation of the Boer War also brought an end to the funding that had sustained the O'Donnell–Ryan–Gonne–MacBride network and, in turn, the *United Irishman*. Griffith was therefore left once again in the position of needing financial backers: due to its very limited advertising and sales revenue, the *United Irishman* had to rely on private donations from shareholders to keep afloat.

Mark Ryan still had sufficient funds to impose his will upon the old IRB organisation and attempt to create a new executive and strategy for that movement. Since the 1901 funeral of James Stephens, he had pressed for uniting his movement with the IRB on the condition that the latter would rebuild itself totally from scratch exclusively among young Cumann na nGaedhael or Gaelic League activists. As a result, P.T. Daly, an active Dublin trade unionist, was simultaneously appointed the first full-time travelling organiser for Cumann na nGaedhael, which soon developed branches in each major Irish and British city, and the secretary, or 'chief travelling organiser', of a new IRB organisation in October 1902.[104]

MacBride would soon call upon Devoy to fund both Griffith's journal and P.T. Daly's organisation through the medium of Mark Ryan in London.[105] However, Cumann na nGaedhael's status as a public organisation connected with the new Irish-Ireland movement meant that the necessary funding was more likely to be attained from entirely different quarters. This was a reality that was appreciated most by Maud Gonne. These trends would soon enable Griffith to take his first steps out of the police-supervised world of street protest politics and find a niche for himself in mainstream politics, thereby slowly but surely distancing himself from the revolutionary underground that had embroiled him in its dark secrets since 1894.

The clericalist wing of the Irish home rule movement led by T.M. Healy, W.M. Murphy, John Sweetman and their followers remained in favour of decentralising authority within the United Irish League. Unlike T.M. Healy and his followers, the Irish Party had failed during 1902 to support an English education act that was supported by the Catholic hierarchy because of the boost that it gave to denominational schools in England. This created a backlash against the Irish Party in Catholic circles in both Ireland and Britain. D.P. Moran's Irish-Ireland movement had already been established as a tool for putting pressure upon the Irish Party to obey the Catholic bishops, not the intellectual fashions of British public life or the Liberal Party, in the politics of education. Soon, Maud Gonne would take it upon herself to contact John Sweetman, a very wealthy former Healyite MP, looking for financial support for the *United Irishman*, noting that 'the editor Mr. Griffith is not aware that I am writing to you and to one or two more'.[106] Sweetman admitted to being a constant reader of Griffith's journal despite the fact that 'sometimes it annoyed me very much by some of its writers sneering at religion'. If this practice ceased entirely, however, he would agree to become its principal shareholder. Gonne let Griffith know the terms of Sweetman's offer and then informed the latter that 'I quite agree with you that all attacks on religion should be avoided … I am sure they will be.'[107] Soon afterwards, on Griffith's behalf, she persuaded Sweetman to increase his shareholding in the company further, as 'Mr. Griffith feels confident if things go on as they are going at present, in about 3 months the paper will be paying its way.'[108]

In addition to Sweetman, another valuable patron Griffith found at this time was Walter Cole. He was a successful Liverpool-born fruit merchant and Catholic community activist who served on Dublin city council as an alderman. A former Healyite within the YIL, Cole also admired Michael Davitt's politics. Upon joining Cumann na nGaedhael, Cole not only established a close friendship with Griffith but also offered him much needed personal financial assistance. This certainly did not go unappreciated. Henry Egan Kenny, Arthur's closest friend, once recalled that Griffith told him that 'Walter has been Mother, Father and ideal friend to me. I could not have lived through those days of stress without his unexampled care and princely hospitality.'[109] While Griffith's family had fallen completely apart due to poverty several years previously, after the cessation of the Boer War the support Griffith received from his new Catholic patrons allowed him to rescue his ailing father from the workhouse and the Griffith family were able to resettle in a small family home of their own, based in Summerhill, for the first time in almost a decade.[110]

At the relatively late age of thirty-two, Griffith's life began to undergo a significant change due to the fact that he had finally found a career. Thanks to Maud Gonne's initiative, he had found a means of leaving the very insecure life of poverty he had known behind him and to embark on a journalistic career with a degree of confidence because he had found stable financial backing from well-to-do individuals. After years of troubling ill health from living in slum conditions, he was certainly lucky to escape the same fatal fate of Rooney and his older sister Marcella, and to not have to follow the same path as had been taken by his brothers, most of his youthful friends (including former *United Irishman* contributors) and other former pro-Boer activists (including James Connolly), which was emigration to perform menial labouring jobs. Not surprisingly, he was not prepared to throw away his recent good fortune.

Arthur Griffith's days of working overnight for a minimum wage, dressed in the ink-stained overalls of a compositor or the sweat-soaked clothes of a South African miner, were now over. Instead, he would begin to revel in his newfound role as a respectable and well-dressed, if far from well off, editor of a 'national review'. If the stylish pince-nez that now adorned Griffith's face betrayed a degree of personal affectation, however, it was his already well-developed and incisive intelligence that would ultimately allow him to catch the public eye.

CHAPTER THREE

The Review Editor

Arthur Griffith's relationship with the journalistic profession might be typified as lifelong: his own father had a thirty-year association with the newspaper business. As a teenager, Griffith both satirised and celebrated the profession by writing fictional tales of a journalist 'smoking a cigar with the easy grace of a man about town'. He wins top jobs 'with the help of the muses and a glass of whiskey' due to his uncanny ability to convince newspaper editors that he was 'the grandest liar that the Lord ever breathed into' and so was unquestionably the right man for the job.[1] Many of Griffith's contemporaries pondered the significance of the trade. This was because the enfranchisement of sections of the working class during the mid-1880s coincided with the rise of the journalist to a position of political significance for the first time. Furthermore, as was demonstrated by T.P. O'Connor's burgeoning literary world in Britain, young writers such as George Bernard Shaw and other self-consciously 'modern' figures were not ashamed to have begun as 'lowly' journalists, even if it would take a couple of decades before O'Connor's journals were widely accepted.[2] In his teens, Griffith drew a contrast between revered past pamphleteers, such as Jonathan Swift, and contemporary writers for newspapers in order to defend the credibility of the latter. As an adult he would draw a different analogy; namely, between the journalistic profession and that of the barrister, claiming that this was the root of a prospective problem.

Griffith emphasised that 'most people in this country live under the impression that those who write the leading articles in the daily papers believe in what they write'. This, of course, was 'generally untrue'. It was the proprietor of a newspaper who sets and upholds 'a policy' for his own private business interests. Journalists were expected to be merely a pen for hire. Although, as Griffith noted, many journalists privately maintain that 'their position … is similar to that of the lawyer who indifferently accepts a brief', the fact remained that to most of his readers 'he is not ... speaking from a brief, but a tribune speaking from conviction' as if he were a passionate advocate upon their behalf. Unlike the impartial barrister, therefore, the journalist was potentially 'a man of superior knowledge or education who uses his superiority to mislead'.[3]

Griffith preferred to consider himself as a man who could never be guilty of playing such a dirty trick. He likened himself to his literary idol John Mitchel, a barrister turned journalist whose *United Irishman* publication was the model for Griffith's own. To Griffith, Mitchel's capacity to be an independent thinker came from his indifference to intellectual fashions: 'he was a sane Nietzsche in his view of man, but his sanity was a century out of date back and forward.' This was the reason why 'he never wrote a paragraph which there is not an intellectual pleasure in reading' and why, even in his 'fiercest polemics', he was capable of being a remarkably perceptive writer on the relationship between the narrow world of politics and the broader question of human nature. To Griffith, however, Mitchel was 'a man of superior knowledge or education' whom the Irish public failed to appreciate not because he had failed society but because society had failed him: 'Ireland failed Mitchel because it failed in manhood.'[4] This literary justification of extreme individualism, if a little perverse, was essentially a reflection of each man's shared temperamental incapacity of being a common party-political animal that subscribed to popular shibboleths. Republican in philosophy, they actually thought more like monarchs from behind their editorial chairs in defence of their conception of citizenship. This was why Griffith was better suited to being a review editor rather than an actual journalist. He insisted on being his own boss.

Griffith was fortunate that review editors still enjoyed an exalted reputation during his lifetime. This was because of a lingering prejudice within British and Irish society against the journalistic world of commercial newspapers, which was frequently typified as 'more a disease than a profession'.[5] Griffith sought to capitalise upon this cultural phenomenon in a disingenuous manner. He perpetually pointed an accusing finger at all contemporary Irish newspapers for operating equally out of London and Dublin commercial offices and accommodating themselves to business and political norms as if this was proof not only of their lowly and anti-intellectual opportunism but also their conscious betrayal of Irish interests. This stance essentially fooled nobody as Griffith could only operate his review publications under a protective immunity from the commercial pressures that governed regular newspapers. Indeed, it was no secret to most contemporaries that Griffith was using his status as a review editor as a cover for issuing what was often considered to be a suspect political journalism of his own. Be that as it may, although Griffith's journal was never printed in more than a thousand copies, had an even smaller readership and rarely broke even, the very fact that it was a weekly review rather than a newspaper meant that its capacity to influence bookish opinion in the country was significant.

The cessation of the Anglo-Boer War might have led to the permanent cessation of the *United Irishman* were it not for the ongoing political conflict over the financing of Irish education. In particular, the challenge that the Jesuits' university, University College Dublin (UCD), was posing to the state's universities, principally Trinity College Dublin (TCD), had become a very pivotal one because the Tory government had promised to establish a completely new 'national university of Ireland'. This stimulated a significant market for creating and perpetuating review publications, perhaps most notably UCD's *New Ireland Review*. Griffith would tackle the politics of the university question on a fairly regular basis but his readership was not generally an academic one.

The *United Irishman*'s popular front-page feature 'All Ireland' covered new publications and cultural events to make it a useful calendar for all who were interested in Irish literary life. This feature was compiled by William Rooney, up until he fell terminally ill in March 1901, and subsequently by Máire Butler, a Catholic fiction writer who was closely related to the propertied Galway family of Edward Martyn, the chief patron of Catholic sacred music in Ireland and a playwright.[6] This literary side to the review was enhanced by its weekly 'Ireland in London' feature, which was designed to keep writers in Ireland and London informed of each other's activities. Henry Egan Kenny ('Sean Ghall'), Griffith's closest friend, compiled this feature. Kenny now worked in London for the customs and excise office and also wrote (alongside Tomas Cuffe, a historian of Dublin) most of the Irish historical articles in the *United Irishman* (later, he was commissioned by historian Alice Stopford Green to do research for her publications).[7] The veteran journalist Michael Cusack, who turned Griffith into a particularly enthusiastic fan of 'the fine art' of GAA hurling, was the author of all of its sporting columns.[8]

Later, a myth developed that Griffith wrote virtually everything that appeared in his publications. This occurred because during a pivotal period of Irish political debate (the early 1910s) Griffith was forced to do so for a time and, all things considered, he shouldered this burden extraordinarily well. This was the exception rather than the norm, however. Particularly during the early years, aside from writing occasional book reviews under pseudonyms, Griffith's only personal contribution was to make political commentaries in brief editorials and to choose what Celtic Literary Society lectures to republish (the *United Irishman* was effectively the organ of this society). The latter practice ceased during 1902, as the Celtic began to crumble after Rooney, its founder, passed away. Ultimately, Griffith came to view his earliest days as a participant in debating societies as a youthful irrelevance; a viewpoint that reflected his sense that he had now moved on to more rewarding activities.

The formative stages of the *United Irishman* were commemorated by the publication of Rooney's historical ballads and essays as books. This initiative of Griffith's was supported by Seamus MacManus, a Donegal-born writer and frequent *United Irishman* contributor (he later became associated with Notre Dame University in Ohio), who also published in book format the poems of his recently deceased wife Anna Johnston ('Ethna Carbery' and daughter of Robert), the former co-editor of the Belfast *Shan Van Vocht*.[9] Griffith paid tribute to Rooney's memory by attributing to him an iconic image comparable to that which surrounded Thomas Davis, who had been Rooney's literary role model.[10] The *United Irishman*, however, had not been notable for containing original literature. Indeed, its declared intention to promote the ideals of long-deceased figures such as Davis and Wolfe Tone reflected a tendency to rely upon a simple historicism. Other writers, who were no less sincere than Griffith in their admiration of Rooney, lamented that he literally 'burnt himself out' through his futile attempt to repeat the example of Thomas Davis (a man who died equally young) as a historian who attempted to be an all-embracing essayist on Irish cultural matters.[11]

A focus upon Irish history had sometimes created religiously tinged disputes in the *United Irishman* columns. This was in keeping with contemporary trends. Catholic religious publications, being a lesser priority of the British firms who monopolised the market, were the chief product of Irish publishers.[12] In addition, clergymen often supervised Irish newspapers' literary supplements, which invariably included unremarkable melodramatic fiction with a religiously motivated punch line.[13] This trend, which became particularly noticeable during the 1880s,[14] was reflected in the *United Irishman* by Máire Butler's celebration of the didactic novels of Canon Sheehan, whose work she portrayed as the pinnacle of contemporary Irish literature due to the theologically-inspired intellectualism that underpinned all his work. While Butler viewed this as evidence of his realism, old republicans, by contrast, ridiculed his novels in the *United Irishman* as typically anti-republican and anti-individualist Catholic writings that were entirely unrealistic depictions of Irish society: 'a realist, by all the Gods! Let *any* Irish novelist try to do so and every Father Sheehan in Ireland will denounce him'.[15]

Religiosity certainly shaped many contemporaries' reaction to W.B. Yeats' launching of the Irish Literary Theatre, the forerunner of Edward Martyn's Abbey Theatre. This was perhaps inevitable because an Eastern-mysticism derived pantheism was the essential inspiration behind Yeats' art,[16] while his most talented playwright John Millington Synge, a depressed Darwinist, decided to focus on a perceived nature-worshipping tradition among peasants in the west of Ireland. Orthodox Christians, if not many artists and some intellectuals, equated Yeats and Synge's pantheism with retrogressive, or unhealthy, social tendencies. Griffith's reaction to this controversy reflected his own individual sensibilities. Unlike Rooney,[17] Griffith greatly admired Yeats' ability as a poet, crediting him with being 'the greatest of Irish poets' due to his facility in simultaneously 'interpreting the Celt to the world and to the Celt himself'. He reviewed a collected edition of Yeats' poems by suggesting that every Irishman should acquire a copy of the book even if he had to steal it.[18] Meanwhile, Yeats' greatest defender in these debates, the equally pantheistic painter and poet George Russell (AE), was described by Griffith as 'one of the few men whose good opinion I sincerely value'.[19] Nevertheless, Griffith was unconvinced of the value of the plays that Yeats patronised or produced. He ignored the religious criticisms of the plays. Declaring himself to be totally indifferent to 'the moral character of an artist', he noted that 'I should still love Byron's poetry were he ten times the libertine he has been painted' and he denied absolutely that religious figures had a right to censure artistic creations.[20] Instead, the *United Irishman* focused on the absence of a recent tradition of Irish theatre outside the staging of popular melodramas and described Yeats' attempts to draw inspiration from the classics ('the severe simplicity of Greek drama appeals to very scant audiences now')[21] as a novel but misjudged initiative.[22]

Griffith's prior criticisms of the South African writer Olive Schreiner had reflected his belief that modern literature needed to be grounded in realism, or experiences with which contemporaries could identify. In a survey of modern Irish novelists, he lamented the proliferation of writers with underdeveloped talents. He believed that this had occurred due to the persistence of the romantic, or introspective, tradition of the exploration of purely personal themes while ignoring the challenge of capturing the nature of Irish society itself.[23] As an urbane Dubliner hoping to witness the creation of a more realistic Irish literature, he had much reason to be disappointed with writers' choice of themes. Ireland was certainly not producing any Emile Zolas, while Griffith was not at all convinced that the obsession of Yeats' theatre circle with rural folklore was genuine, as their preoccupation was clearly with mythologies rather than the nature of contemporary rural Irish society. T.W. Rolleston's efforts to introduce Ivan Turgenev and Anton Chekov to an English-language readership had also failed to elicit an Irish response. Although Griffith felt that there was 'no … difference as to essentials' between his and Yeats' attitudes towards literature, he would infuriate Yeats by making a claim (which he defended in detail) that J.M. Synge's *In the Shadow of the Glen* was a story derived from classical Greek mythology and redressed as if it was an Irish creation. Griffith maintained that

Irish writers should 'not be allowed to go unchallenged' if they exhibited a desire to 'construct fifty "Irish" plays out of the Decameron':

> If changing the names of Greek characters and places into Irish ones can provide us with Irish plays, the converse should be true. Diarmuid and Grania, with an Hellenic baptism, should represent to the world Greek drama.[24]

Although its membership did not include a single novelist, the National Literary Society (the progenitor of the theatre movement) had spoken ambitiously since its inception of its desire to create a completely new Irish literature, but Yeats, the most notable writer in its ranks, was a poet, concerned with symbolisms, rather than an author of credible fiction (including theatre). Most of his compatriots, such as William Magee (a.k.a. 'John Eglinton'), were critics, not artists.

To Griffith, the National Literary Society's chief shortcoming lay in its members' social attitudes. Even the architecture of Dublin itself led many to view the city's Georgian past with far more sympathy than contemporary society, with which Griffith felt they were unable to connect due to their unwillingness to deal with themes of poverty (urban or rural). In turn, Griffith believed they were prone to a debilitating form of affectation that was born of social snobbery. This was a mentality that he repeatedly satirised with deliberately bad comic verses such as 'Oh Lucinda! My beaming, gleaming star, I would that I were good enough, to dwell in dear Rathgar [a strictly upper-class Dublin suburb].'[25] Even George Sigerson, the most convivial and intellectually gifted of the National Literary Society's leaders (he was a polymath, UCD science lecturer, prolific author and man of strong democratic–republican sensibilities), had, when dwelling on literature, nevertheless spoken of Irish society purely in terms of 'the lord and the peasant'.[26] W.P. Ryan's judgment at this time that 'literary Ireland, in fact, does not know itself' was another reflection of this disconnection between the world of Irish letters and Irish life.[27] Meanwhile, if contemporary Irish artists' attraction towards mysticism (which Griffith, as a self-professed realist, satirised as an obsession with 'spooks')[28] was spiritually enlightened—in so far as it was 'creationist'—it also reflected a deliberate disengagement from material realities. This essentially echoed past failures within Irish society rather than challenged them.

For the seven years that the *United Irishman* was in print, the touchstone of virtually all contemporaries' reaction to Irish cultural debate lay in their response to the rise of the Gaelic League and its propaganda. This had also been true of Griffith and Rooney. While they shared many attitudes on the national question, as their writing styles demonstrated, they were men of noticeably different temperaments. Rooney's prose always exhibited a desire to be impartial in the manner of a young student of essay writing: he enjoyed taking part in non-political cultural debates and was certainly open to persuasion. Griffith, by contrast, always believed in the importance of being persuasive at all times and, if necessary, to employ shorthand rhetorical techniques, such as witty satire or the declamatory tone of an ideologue, to undermine rivals in debate. Indeed, it was undoubtedly Griffith's acerbic prose that caused some readers (invariably religious individuals) to write to the *United Irishman* in protest against its offensive use of language,[29] just as many journalists would come to secretly admire Griffith's 'power of killing his adversaries with the point of his pen' without any seeming need for exegeses.[30] Michael MacDonagh, the greatest *Freeman* journalist of Griffith's lifetime who now led the much-respected Irish Literary Society of London, offered an alternative perspective. He credited Griffith's journal with being 'as clever and interesting a paper as Dublin has ever produced', but suggested that its 'lack of humour' was evidence that its young editors were still a little wet behind the ears.[31]

After he achieved a degree of fame, Griffith developed the reputation in some quarters of being a politically ambitious journalist. However, he never quite escaped his established role as a review editor. Even when his journals effectively became party-political newspapers (after 1917), they retained their reputation as reading matter exclusively for the bookish section of working-class opinion.[32] While most review publications contained several lengthy essays that were dressed in the academic garb of impartiality, the format of Griffith's publications was always singular. They invariably encompassed newspaper-column length digressions on political or cultural matters by various contributors that appeared alongside random commentaries by Griffith himself upon a potpourri of politicians, as well as other publications', activities. These commentaries were often delivered with a Mitchelite verbal punch and were presented as highly topical and political, but frequently they read as mere exercises in criticism.[33] This was because they originated in Griffith's own selection each week of whatever seemed to *him* as symbolic of how political events were developing.

This trait of Griffith's publications reflected the fact that he was more often than not a critic, including a comically satirical one,[34] rather than a preacher of original ideas. Even after he launched significant political initiatives of his own, their limited promise led him to write editorials that continued to focus primarily on other quarters, such as internal debates within the Ulster and Irish Parties. In doing so, Griffith invariably sided with William O'Brien's wing of the Irish Party as well as the dissenting 'Independent Orange Order' wing of the Ulster Party against their respective party leaderships. Often, this material was printed alongside articles of historical research that sometimes hinted at contemporary parallels. Griffith himself was probably much more familiar with intimate details of the history of both the Irish Party and the Orange Order than were many members of those organisations in his own day. Like Mitchel, he tended to subscribe to a cyclical conception of the course of history and, therefore, believed that quoting the past against the present could see similar fault lines emerge in society once again.

Often the logic of Griffith's prose was to assail all quarters in the expectation that this would prompt readers to follow his line of reasoning instead. However, as most of his readers were confined to subscribers to his publication rather than part of the fluctuating and larger demographic of newspaper consumers, he was effectively preaching to the converted, or whatever readers 'never tired as from week to week he reiterated his thesis in all the varied tones of appeal, denunciation, mockery and argument', utilising 'all the powers of a singularly clear, serene and forcible mind'. While Mitchel had acquired fame through adopting such tactics for about fifteen months, Griffith would do so 'when no other Irishman did it' for about fifteen years, and 'there hardly exists in the history of journalism another instance of such patient, passionate and consistent propaganda', as one of Griffith's more critical Ulster unionist readers noted:

> Very few men in such a task would not have made themselves tiresome and ridiculous and have brought upon their principles either hatred or contempt. What saved Arthur Griffith was his personality [as reflected in print] … It was not that he was always wise and right, for he was often wrong and unwise: it was not that he was always just and fair, he was often hard and sometimes curiously obstinate when most manifestly in the wrong; but he had the faculty of convincing his readers of his personal honesty and sincerity. His style was most marvellously adapted to his purpose: it was clear and sinewy and flexible, never rising to any great height of eloquence or passion but never slovenly or vague or weak. It was the direct expression of his character.[35]

Similarly, the mutual dislike between Griffith and George Moore did not prevent the latter from crediting Griffith with having 'the power of putting life into the worn-out English language'.[36] As many simply disliked Griffith, however, and equated him with an alien presence in the world of politics and literature because he did not always play the role that he was expected by his peers to play within what became known as 'the Irish Ireland movement'.

Rooney had been much more prepared than Griffith to overlook differences in politics among the membership of the Gaelic League, befriending, for example, J.J. O'Kelly (a.k.a. 'Sceilg'), a conservative and clericalist editor with the *Freeman's Journal*, the organ of the Irish Party and the favoured newspaper of the Catholic hierarchy. Although O'Kelly greatly admired Rooney's tolerant personality, he was never fond of Griffith who detested anyone connected with the *Freeman's Journal*,[37] which indeed was a semi-governmental organ that was closely connected with Dublin Castle. The manner by which the membership of the Celtic was absorbed into various Gaelic League subcommittees by October 1902 determined what role Griffith was expected by his peers to play as a review editor. As had been the case since 1892, the politics of Irish education continued to be the subject that polarised opinion.

The Celtic had lost the support of Trinity public intellectuals for opposing the Boer War. This prompted Catholic businessmen associated with the *Freeman* to step into this breach, assuming the status of the Celtic's patrons and discouraging it from continuing to champion non-denominational education. This occurred while a debate, dormant since the early 1880s, upon the possibility of Irish industrial development was revived in response to the establishment of new local government councils. Hitherto, socialists had joined Griffith and Rooney in arguing in favour of a state-controlled economy but disagreed with their ideal of Irish independence, which they deemed to be retrogressive.[38] Griffith was now persuaded to join a Gaelic League subcommittee set up to examine the Irish industrial question.[39] This became Griffith's connection with the Gaelic League, while his old anticlerical mentor Henry Dixon was persuaded to join a Gaelic League subcommittee on the question of public libraries, in the process disappearing from the public eye.

By 1902, the Gaelic League had the support of the leaders of Clonglowes College, Blackrock College, Rockwell College, Saint Patrick's Catholic teacher-training college in Drumcondra and Archbishop Walsh. It also had trans-Atlantic support from the recently revived Ancient Order of Hibernians (AOH) whose American wing succeeded in encouraging American Catholic universities to support the Gaelic League's mission in Ireland while priests as far as Argentina collected funds for the same purpose.[40] In Ireland itself, Catholic bishops began chairing most Gaelic League feiseanna while the AOH, a militant supporter of the Irish Party, was responsible for creating a demand to make Irish the nation's first 'official language'.[41] The politics of 'home rule' had taken on a definite new tinge, as if it was seeking to establish a separate cultural identity for that subordinate imperial parliament that had been envisioned by Gladstone. At the same time, however, Catholic support for the Gaelic League was undoubtedly motivated by a simple determination to use the absence of a linguistic nationalism in the state's education system as a means of bolstering the church's argument for a religiously-controlled education system and putting more pressure on the Irish

Party to stand by that Christian–democratic principle in the face of any potential British governmental opposition.[42]

Notwithstanding the Gaelic League's anti-Trinity bias, the Irish-Ireland movement's creation of an alliance between the cause of the language and religious education also made the Church of Ireland's national magazine sympathetic towards the Gaelic League, which could only be accused of being sectarian in so far as Archbishop Walsh and Douglas Hyde were being sectarian in maintaining that nationalist ideologues were mistaken in their Napoleonic equation of state control of education with the existence of the nation state.[43] Hitherto, Griffith had made no secret of his opposition to this anti-statist position. Just as he argued in favour of state grants to enable the working classes attend university and the establishment of more state institutes of technical education, he was particularly adamant that no education system, or university, could possibly be national if it was under denominational rather than purely state management:

> We do not believe with those who would keep the present Protestant University in College Green, establish one for Catholics at Saint Stephens Green or elsewhere, and one for Presbyterians somewhere in Belfast. If three such universities were in existence tomorrow, we would regard them merely as part of the system whose chief object is to keep the people of Ireland in two or three opposing camps—such a system, in whatever guise it comes, we will continue to oppose, however strong the influences that support it.[44]

In opposition to Archbishop Walsh, Griffith expressed support for the stance of the Presbyterian Church in Belfast, which declared that non-denominational schools and universities were not detrimental to religion and were also more conducive to the progress of the nation-state and the material wellbeing of its citizens.[45] This reflected the fact that the YIL's call for the conversion of Trinity College into a national university under non-denominational management had been more in keeping with egalitarian Protestant dissenter than Protestant Episcopalian or Catholic social attitudes. The possibility of continuing to promote such an idea had been undermined, however, by the fact that the Gaelic League's official organ, *An Claidheamh Solus* (edited by Eoin MacNeill, a militant supporter of the Catholic hierarchy's stance on education ever since the 1892 controversy), was using Trinity College's lack of support for the language movement as a basis for a political onslaught on that college, claiming that in the struggle for control of the future direction of Irish education 'the combatants are Trinity College and the Irish people'.[46] The sectarian divisions in Irish education were also an extension of the sectarian divisions that existed in the Irish business community, but it would be some time before Griffith came to understand the significance of this fact.

So long as Griffith defied the stance of Archbishop Walsh in the politics of education, both the *Leader* and *An Claidheamh Solus* were highly dismissive of the right of the *United Irishman* to have a voice in the debate on Irish education. Although Rooney had been co-opted as a member of the league's committee for organising Oireachtas meetings, he was always denied membership of its executive council.[47] Meanwhile, Griffith's relationship with the Gaelic League was often less than cordial. This is hardly surprising, as Griffith had initially made no secret of the fact that he wished 'a speedy extinction' upon all those who 'babbled of the Gael' while claiming that 'nationality is not a thing of rights, arms, freedom, franchises, brotherhood, duties'.[48] Griffith was a firm believer in the republican idea that a man was either a citizen or a slave, 'for there is no middle term',[49] and that patriotic citizenship was essential to the nation-state. By contrast, in keeping with papal encyclicals, Catholic educators throughout Europe and America defined both patriotism and the nation in purely cultural terms in order to minimise the power of state to control education. This was in keeping with a mainstream European trend whereby many writers and artists (including, perhaps most potently of all, musicians and composers; a trend admired by Griffith)[50] were simultaneously celebrating indigenous folk cultures while attempting to portray the progressive appeal of a cultural patriotism in an essentially modernist or didactic way. In central Europe, for instance, the Czechs succeeded particularly well in creating a new national theatre in their minority-spoken language, with Catholic clergymen's support, as part of a broader campaign in resistance to exclusive control of education by a central imperial parliament.[51] This was why, with the moral support of London Gaelic Leaguers, *An Claidheamh Solus* maintained that Irish writers would have to do the same and expressed a disappointment with contemporary Irish productions.[52] Griffith, whose own knowledge of the Irish language was limited,[53] disagreed, however. He cited the example of the United States and Switzerland as evidence of the fallacy of Schlegel's oft-quoted maxim 'no language, no nation' while, like many working-class figures, he also regarded the purely cultural definition of nationality embodied in the 'new patriotism' as a deliberate attempt to ignore political and economic realities.[54]

Griffith was not without prejudices of his own, of course, and it is clear that he was particularly annoyed that many Gaelic Leaguers questioned the capacity of fans of contemporary English literature to be Irish patriots. For example, he was not above typifying as 'ignoramuses' those pious Gaelic Leaguers who celebrated the fact that all surviving Irish language texts, dating mostly from early-modern times, were on religious rather than literary themes (a reality that motivated many priests' zealous support for the league):

> Years ago an ignoramus would have sneered at the language. Now the ignoramus yells out in bad English that all who do not speak it are mere Englishmen. This is a sure sign that the Gaelic League is going to achieve its object. A movement that at the same time is supported by the man of intellect and the profound jackass cannot fail ... [When the Gaelic League] tells us in its funny way that Emmet and Tone and Davis are not Irish, and that O'Grady and Yeats will never write a line that will touch the heart of a single Irish ignoramus, one feels compassion for the Gaelic League and trusts it may be saved from its illiterate friends ... The cause of the Irish language is a noble and national one, but it can be injured by allowing fools and hypocrites to pose as its champions.[55]

Thus spoke Griffith in 1901, but his ascribed role within the Gaelic League after 1902—to deal with the question of Irish industrial resources on a subcommittee that was headed by Fr Tom Finlay S.J.—potentially placed him in a subordinate role to that which was being played by the Jesuits.

The Jesuits viewed the Gaelic League as providing a forum whereby economic debate within Ireland could be made a vehicle for propagating Catholic ideas of social justice (creating a more caring and homogenous society without disturbing the Gladstonian fiscal consensus established during 1886) and whereby cultural debate within Ireland could be accommodated with what might be described as a Catholic variation of modernism. In particular, it was desired to counter critiques (popular with republicans and British nationalists) of Catholics' alleged failure to acknowledge progressive tendencies within the modern nation-state by arguing that Catholicism had inherent progressive tendencies that were compatible with any true programme of modernisation. As the intellectual cult of modernism, itself an anti-individualist philosophy, was frequently wedded to the cause of the nation-state, propagating a Catholic variation of modernism was seen as a necessary counter in the intellectual debates of the new (twentieth) century.[56] Meanwhile, to reflect the Jesuits' view that the British state was intrinsically Protestant *and* that a modern nation-state should not be defined without reference to religion,[57] D.P. Moran deliberately twisted republicans' traditional propaganda against any manifestations of royalist flunkeyism by maintaining that such flunkeyism was something that could only be expected from a Protestant.[58] His 'philosophy of Irish Ireland' also attempted to imbue the Gaelic League with a brash self-confidence that generally manifested itself as a refusal to listen to any claim that Catholics were capable of anything other than the most progressive or modernist of political tendencies.

While this was not essentially a popular Catholic position,[59] the success of the Jesuits in equating 'Irish ideas' with a Christian–democratic conception of church–state relations was made clear by the birth of a tradition whereby politicians who declared their support for the Irish language generally did so only as a means of indicating, or reaffirming, their support for the churches' educational interests without running the risk of openly saying so and thereby providing an avenue for ideologues (be they nationalists or socialists) to mount an effective political criticism of the Christian–democratic position. Meanwhile, in William Martin Murphy, a very successful business entrepreneur, dedicated financier of Catholic projects and political associate of T.M. Healy and John Sweetman (Griffith's new patron), the Jesuits found an ideal role model for presenting their vision of Irish economic development. Although never a popular man, Murphy was a highly professional figure whose success in establishing the *Irish Independent* as a non-party organ during 1904 and making it a far more popular newspaper in Catholic Ireland than the Irish Party's *Freeman's Journal* (whose sales perpetually dropped thereafter) marked a significant new departure;[60] one that actually provided an avenue for Griffith to find an audience of his own. Although Murphy's followers supported the existing British imperial economy, they had a more urban appeal than the Irish Party, whose members notoriously combined farmers' interests with a slavish identification with the culture of the British state. The role of Murphy's followers in encouraging a real element of social consciousness to Gaelic League propaganda could also make it appealing to young urban intellectuals. It was essentially the latter dynamic, however, that ultimately created a significant counter reaction from within the Gaelic League's own ranks.[61]

The first substantial critique of this trend in Irish politics came from Frank Hugh O'Donnell, the former *United Irishman* patron who later became a historical lecturer for the Gaelic League of London.[62] In *The Ruin of Education in Ireland*, O'Donnell argued that the Catholic education system was producing lay graduates who were ill equipped for entering various modern professions and civil services, being better suited to entering religious orders or else acting as teachers in schools where they had to surrender all personal and intellectual freedoms to the local bishop as much as any Catholic curate. Claiming to speak on behalf of dissatisfied Irish national-school teachers and unemployed Catholic university graduates everywhere, O'Donnell argued that the Jesuits who were directing the Irish educational movement were masking the fact that the church's ambition to control education was purely self-aggrandising, partly in their desire to create more priests, and that its ambition was also governed by avarice—charging school fees and opposing the nation-state policy of free education—rather than any altruistic wish for the good of Irish society. O'Donnell suggested that the European Catholic experience demonstrated that the reason why Catholic involvement in state universities had been discouraged for the past century, ever since the rise of Napoleon, was that it had always stifled productive critical analyses and creative thinking for laymen, if not for theologians, in the social science departments.[63] Owing to Archbishop Walsh's prominence on the National Education Board, these arguments were considered as too polemical for virtually any Irish political commentator to touch. Reflecting this, Griffith would not embrace such a polemical viewpoint, while O'Donnell, who was formerly close to T.P. O'Connor, was reputedly in the pay of London Tories.[64] The counter arguments being put forward by UCD students were not particularly persuasive either, however.

Tom Kettle was a celebrated figure among UCD academics and students because, as an essayist, he was perceived to have considerable literary skill in defending that idea to which each of them were necessarily wedded in a career sense; namely, that Catholic theories of social justice had an all-embracing applicability and the ethics of a Christian humanism was inherently more beneficial to society than a political rationalism.[65] This gave Kettle an appeal in contemporary Ireland comparable to that of the Englishman G.K. Chesterton, who considered the independent Irish clericalist politician T.M. Healy to be 'the most serious intellect in the present House of Commons'.[66] In his contributions to Griffith's and other journals, Kettle mirrored Chesterton's defence of Christian ethics in literature, albeit in a less inspired and humourless way.[67] On being appointed to a professorship of economics at Maynooth College by Archbishop Walsh, Kettle would reject the relevance of Griffith's analyses of the Irish Party's support of unionist taxation practices on the grounds that statistics were mere 'bloodless actualities' that meant nothing to the heart.[68] In an attempt to justify Catholic social theory as being more valuable to society than economic analyses, Kettle would also argue (to the delight of ambitious UCD students such as Kevin O'Higgins) that, ultimately, a government meant nothing more than the compassionate hearts of 'you and me and the man around the corner' and that 'the wise custom of scholasticism', inspired by St Bernard of Clairvaux and Thomas Aquinas' philosophies of education, was intellectually superior to statistical analyses.[69]

Accused by Griffith of being tongue-tied by his political loyalty to the Irish Party (for which he became the party's official finance spokesman),[70] Kettle's celebrated career in Irish Catholic academia was actually honour bound to Archbishop Walsh, whose patronage extended to allowing Kettle to become the sole layman to attend secret monthly Dublin diocesan convocations on how to increase the temporal power of the church in politics.[71] Kettle's literary role as a dilettante perhaps reflected the extent to which he was expected as a Catholic university academic to act more as a lay defender of the church's interests than as a purely independent professional. An essential context to his circle's grievances, however, was the belief that a long-term legacy of historic British discrimination against Catholics up until shortly before the British state effectively became secularist was that those Catholics who now wished to enter the professions were ill equipped to capitalise fully upon the rise of a modern professional society to a central place in British political and economic life in the wake of the UK educational reforms of 1880 and the resulting expansion of the civil service.[72] The Catholic University student who protested this point most eloquently during 1903 was Edward (later Eamon) DeValera,[73] who was destined to replace Kettle as the chief lay-confidant of Archbishop Walsh. Reflecting the logic of O'Donnell's critique, however, DeValera initially felt that he had no career options except to move to England to teach in a Benedictine school as a stepping-stone to becoming a priest. This ambition of DeValera's was partly shaped by his belief that priests 'are the natural leaders of the people and are looked up to as such',[74] as if the professional leaders of Catholic society were inherently the clergy themselves. Being denied this opportunity due to his illegitimacy, DeValera became but one of many well-educated Irish Catholic youths who combined part-time school teaching in Ireland with voluntary activism within the Gaelic League while acting under close priestly supervision. As the editor of a small review, Griffith himself was able to sidestep this need for church patronage to a significant degree and so hold tenaciously to his storybook Young Ireland ideal, while political developments that occurred during 1903 helped him to capitalise upon growing anti-royalist sentiment within the Gaelic League.

Griffith's republican protests against Queen Victoria's visit had failed to find an audience because the Irish Party, which favoured the visit, was focused on the challenge of reunifying their party. However, the British government's decision to send Edward VII to Ireland as a patron of the 1903 Irish land act coincided with a period of division in Irish Party circles that was represented by a rural–urban divide within the UIL. The UIL leader William O'Brien, who had inspired the land act through his negotiations with the Tory landed aristocracy, was driven out of the UIL and the Irish Party by John Dillon, the former Irish Party leader who always remained a far more significant figure than John Redmond, a former Parnellite with Tory connections, in shaping party discipline and policy (hence, many contemporaries' perception that Dillon was still the real party leader). In an attempt to capitalise upon this, Griffith defended O'Brien against Irish Party critiques and stormed a UIL meeting in Dublin in an attempt to force the Lord Mayor of Dublin to express opposition to the royal visit. Thereafter, with the support of Seamus MacManus and Maud Gonne, a new body ('The People's Protection Association') was formed that Griffith soon titled as the 'National Council'. This, he argued, existed to unite home rulers and nationalists upon the 'one purpose on which both can agree—the stamping out of flunkeyism and toadyism in this land'.[75]

Griffith's initiative won the support of Edward Martyn's new Abbey Theatre, various republicans as well as a couple of newspaper editors in rural Ireland, while John T. Keating (formerly of the Cork City IRB but now chairman of the American Clan na Gael) came to Ireland in support of their efforts.[76] A couple of days after Keating's return to the United States, Dublin City Council voted against issuing of a welcoming address to the King by a narrow margin (forty votes to thirty-seven). While Griffith claimed this as a victory for the National Council, it was J.P. Nannetti MP (who was elected as the new mayor the following year) who actually played the decisive role in defeating the motion by persuading many figures in the Dublin UIL to vote accordingly.[77]

Although this opposition to the royal visit did not spread elsewhere, these surprising events in Dublin led many to conclude that the Gaelic League and most young Irish nationalists were not supportive of the Irish Party. Meanwhile, with Clan na Gael support, a 'Keating Branch' of the Gaelic League was formed in Dublin and became a recruiting ground for the new IRB.[78] Catholic university students led by Tom Kettle responded by forming a new 'Young Ireland Branch' of the UIL in defence of the Irish Party. Meanwhile, sensing opportunities, Griffith noted gleefully that among the many dissenters from the Irish Party's politics there were 'many law bachelors who are Gaelic Leaguers ... these are the stuff of which politicians are made ... their influence could permeate every phase of Irish life.'[79] The deep reservations that Griffith had expressed hitherto about the cultural connotations of the Irish-Ireland movement now became far less important to him than his declared belief that it presented a far more potent means of overthrowing the established political order than a republican rebellion:

> The taking of the Bastille was an upheaval. A revolution is not an upheaval. A revolution is the silent, impalpable working of forces for the most part undiscerned in their action ... That nationalists feel the working of a new order of things in Ireland at the present day, no-one will be prepared to doubt.[80]

Seeking to capitalise upon this trend, Griffith would soon commit himself to drafting a comprehensive critique of the established political order in Ireland. As he was the editor of a review rather than a newspaper, however, it was fellow writers rather than politicians who generally took most notice of his efforts. Another reason for politicians to be dismissive of Griffith's critiques was the degree to which he merely echoed Irish Tory arguments. Griffith argued that it was O'Brien's willingness to work with the Irish Tories that had secured good terms for Irish tenant farmers, while he would also echo the Tories' response to Britain's difficulty in bringing closure to the Anglo-Boer War.[81] This was to claim that the Empire had become overstretched, necessitating the initiation of a nationalistic policy of economic protectionism by placing less emphasis upon the commercial value of the colonies.

The peak of Griffith's popularity among writers took place during the brief burst of literary fame he acquired upon the publication of *The Resurrection of Hungary: A Parallel for Ireland* (Dublin, 1904). This prompted various famous figures in the Irish literary world to act as contributors, making the period 1904–5 the peak of the *United Irishman*'s status as a notable review. The commercial success of this book also brought about another change in Griffith's lifestyle. Having escaped from real poverty two years previously, he now became the centre of a circle of professional and literary friends who met once or twice a week at private rooms in Bailey's, an expensive restaurant off Grafton Street. As he grew confident about the niche he had found for himself in the world of letters, Griffith would occasionally make fun of the loneliness of other writers, once claiming, for example, that he saw in George Moore's memoirs a determination 'to get people to laugh at him, for certainly none could have laughed with him ... I think there is not an unhappier or lonelier old man in the world.'[82] If Griffith no longer felt vulnerable in society, however, he remained an intensely private figure who did not win many friends. As his good friend James Starkey (the writer 'Seamus O'Sullivan') testified, 'in spite of the strong well-set jaw bone which gave Arthur Griffith a rather stern—even to those who knew him ... a rather militant, even a belligerent, expression', and in spite of his well-developed upper body which 'suggested immense strength' and strength of character, the impression Griffith always made on social occasions was 'an innate and unconquerable shyness'. Even if he could be 'a great companion', he was incapable of greeting friends by their first name and conversation could die quickly if he was not in the company of people who were also omnivorous readers and liked to talk about books.[83]

Close friends acquired at this time included Seamus O'Kelly and Darrel Figgis (notable Catholic writers and journalists), poet Padraic Colum, engineer James Montgomery, medical student Oliver St John Gogarty, future lawyer Constantine Curran (a mutual friend of Kettle) and painter Lily Williams, the latter being someone with whom Griffith could share his love of the countryside and, most of all, music; a trait he had inherited primarily from his mother Mary, whose family (the Whelans) were no less cultivated than the Griffiths.[84] George Russell (AE) began inviting Griffith to art exhibitions and even suggested that he work as an art editor but as Griffith did not feel qualified to be art critic he delegated Williams and especially Starkey to write on artistic matters in his journal.[85] Indeed, from 1905 onwards, Griffith generally confined his art commentaries to speculations on whether or not Dublin City Council overpaid for various paintings in municipal galleries; a purely materialistic perspective that few, if any, of his artistic or literary friends ever felt to be justifiable: 'poor Griffith; the devil is in him. Poor devil and poor him.'[86] St John Gogarty was initially responsible for introducing Griffith to various college students but, although he had dreamed of being a university student in his youth, Griffith initially found their company a little disconcerting. For example, when he was invited by Gogarty to attend a bizarre house-warming party at the Sandycove Tower that also served as a home for the young writer James Joyce, Griffith pleaded with Starkey to come with him to prevent him from feeling 'helpless and alone'.[87]

During 1907, James Joyce would take an interest in Griffith's writings due to Gogarty's sympathy for his journalism and willingness to write anti-enlistment articles for Griffith's journal.[88] Ultimately, Joyce's experimental novel *Ulysses* (Paris, 1922) would be set in Dublin on the same day (16 June 1904) as the last of Griffith's 'Resurrection of Hungary' articles appeared in the *United Irishman*. While it would use the political contest involving J.P. Nannetti and Griffith's National Council as a distant backdrop for its storytelling, Joyce would not depict this as a defining political moment but rather suggested, in a literary monument to inhumanity, that particularly exaggerated religious or political claims upon individuals' allegiance, such as frequently existed in Ireland, could perversely lead to the needs of a man and his wife to go unfulfilled.[89]

Griffith's own principal contribution to (non-political) Irish literature would be to publish the earliest works of James Stephens, a Protestant orphan who, like Griffith, had known great poverty in his youth living in inner-city Dublin tenements where 'no daring wind, light-hearted, from a garden blows, its sweetness here from any rose'.[90] In his earliest poems, which were published in Griffith's journal, and his first novel, *The Charwoman's Daughter*, a portrayal of an impoverished Dublin girl living in a tenement, Stephens might be said to have come closest to producing that Dublin literature which Griffith had desired to see come into being. During the 1910s, Stephens (a writer idolised by Joyce) arguably far surpassed Yeats, Lady Gregory or indeed any other living Irish writer in depicting a fantastical world inspired by mythology and he would also write the most immediate (and popular) account of attitudes in Dublin to the GPO rebellion of 1916, but his connection with his hometown lessened thereafter and it would be a long time before an Irish writer (with the notable exception of Sean O'Casey) would again embrace the world of the Dublin poor as his subject.[91]

Griffith's popularity with writers took a nosedive when his journal supported the Gaelic League boycott of Synge's *The Playboy of the Western World*, which was officially boycotted by both the league and UCD on moral grounds just as Yeats' *Countess Kathleen* had been boycotted a decade earlier. Characteristically, Yeats saw this as an ignoble betrayal of himself. Various factors were generally overlooked in this Gaelic League inspired controversy, however. First, Griffith's literary editor Máire Butler was not only a deeply religious Catholic (she died on a pilgrimage to Rome) but also close to Patrick Pearse, the editor of the Gaelic League's national organ *An Claidheamh Solus*, a publication to which she was also a chief contributor. Second, Griffith was at the time seeking the political support of John Sweetman, a strong advocate of literary censorship. In this way, Griffith had an editorial responsibility to reflect Gaelic League social mores at this time even if they did not quite match his own. As 'reparation', not long after the *Playboy* controversy ended, Griffith published a series of celebratory cartoons by Grace Gifford of contemporary Irish writers before concluding the series with a self-penned caricature of himself drawn in the image of Satan and 'depicted according to the idea and for the consolation of all who have been caricatured in *Sinn Féin*'.[92]

A common denominator to Griffith's attitude towards literature throughout his bachelorhood was his difficulty in accepting any production (including the *Playboy*) that did not match his own idealised vision of women. As a shy teen, he had written a fantasy about being loved by a beautiful blonde woman whose 'mind is as deep and pure as the deepest well'.[93] As an equally shy young adult, he had typified a failure to appreciate an idealised vision of romantic love from (what he imagined to be) a woman's point of view as 'thinking like a rascal Englishman'.[94] Meanwhile, his chaste relationship with Maud Sheehan, to whom he became engaged around the time of his father's death during 1904, was probably governed by a fear of losing her moral approval. She was not only a devout and reserved woman but also the sister of two Catholic monks in what was a close-knit and self-consciously middle-class family. Griffith, meanwhile, had not left his working-class social background behind. Both before and after his father's death in 1904, Arthur had to financially support his old mother (who lived for another fifteen years) and his younger (unskilled) sister Frances, with whom he lived in their Summerhill flat. He simply could not afford to marry Miss Sheehan. As his closest friend knew, 'to a man of such deep and tender domestic qualities, this was a severe cross'.[95]

Griffith's only real hope of acquiring a significant livelihood was through attaining a political success. This reality no doubt played upon his mind while he was writing his most substantial work, *The Resurrection of Hungary: A Parallel for Ireland*, which sought to readdress Anglo-Irish relations and, in the process, redefine Irish nationalist debate. Griffith would do so, however, while characteristically avoiding any direct engagement with what most *other* contemporaries judged to be the most pressing issues in current affairs.

CHAPTER FOUR

The Resurrection of Hungary and the Birth of Sinn Féin (1904–5)

Tom Kettle of University College Dublin considered *The Resurrection of Hungary* to be the publication that gave a policy to the Irish revolutionary underground for the first time.[1] This was because its unilateral definition of Anglo-Irish relations without reference to British requirements was informed by trends in Catholic diplomacy that also shaped the Irish Party's politics.

Hitherto, the clandestine activities of Ireland's self-styled republican conspirators had always reflected British foreign policy interests regarding the republics of the United States and France. This situation had changed by 1904 when an Anglo-French diplomatic alliance ended centuries of Anglo-French conflict: hence the sudden political retirement of Maud Gonne, amongst others. By 1904, the Austro-Hungarian Empire was effectively the last great Catholic power, or explicitly Catholic state, on the European continent. Since the days of the Congress of Berlin (1878) its significance in British foreign policy rested on its role as a key intermediary for Britain between Germany and Russia in all matters, as well as between Britain and Russia regarding the perpetual disputes over the Balkans. There was no actual link between Ireland and Britain's new principal enemy, Germany, aside from links between the Irish and German Catholic immigrant communities in the United States, both of whom now maintained that 'Europe, not England, is the mother country of Europe.'[2] This trend of opinion reflected the growth of a greater diplomatic role for the Catholic Church in the United States. This in turn made it a factor in Anglo-American relations.

There was nothing new about suggesting a parallel between the Anglo-Irish and Austro-Hungarian political relationship. It had occurred to several political leaders—British as well as Irish—during the mid-Victorian era and it still exercised an influence over political opinion during the mid-1880s.[3] Reviving this idea after 1904 could serve to remind politicians that the Catholic Church had been the key player in the Anglo-Irish agreement of 1885–86. Both the President of Maynooth College and the Catholic Archbishop of Westminster supported Griffith's publication. This development reminded the Irish Party that Catholic support was inherently conditional precisely because Griffith's book included a stinging criticism of the Irish Party in its conclusion. Reflecting this, John Redmond paid a personal visit to the Vatican shortly after Griffith's book became a top-selling publication to reassure the Pope that the Irish Party would again faithfully represent the Catholic interest in the British imperial parliament for both Ireland and Britain.[4] An essential context to Griffith's publication, therefore, was the church's ambiguous relationship with the Irish Party, which had connotations not only for Anglo-Irish relations but also the general tenor of Irish political debate.

Along with John MacBride, Griffith had essentially been the chief spokesman for the republican underground ever since his return from South Africa. They had maintained that 'there is no constitution in Ireland' because a constitution is something 'founded by the people and for the people' and that for any political community not to act upon this reality 'daily enfeebles the oppressed whilst it more than in the same proportion strengthens the usurper'.[5] In common with T.M. Healy's clericalist wing of the home rule movement and some Irish Tories, they also maintained that the obsessive emphasis of the Irish Party upon maintaining a monolithic political platform within Ireland had become deeply debilitating and unproductive, cultivating 'the habits of servitude', political idleness and lack of critical thinking among the Irish populace at large.[6]

The key general election of 1885 was preceded by preparatory actions by political elites in an attempt to manipulate the outcome within Ireland of the enfranchisement of half of adult British males. Parnell decided during the summer of 1884 to alter the financial management of Irish Party support bodies in both Ireland and America by placing them in Catholic clergymen's hands,[7] while Dublin Castle's security department simultaneously rounded up and imprisoned the IRB's leadership, leading to the implosion of the revolutionary underground on both sides of the Atlantic.[8] These developments formed the backdrop for several things: Parnell's decision to grant Catholic clergymen the right to be *ex-officio* members of all National League committees, the Irish Catholic hierarchy's decision to make a public statement in October 1884 that it was prepared to rely on Parnell's party to represent the Catholic interest in the

British imperial parliament and the launching of secret negotiations between Dublin Castle, the Irish Party and the Catholic hierarchy through the medium of Sir George Fottrell and the *Freeman's Journal*.[9] The results of these negotiations was that the Irish Party not only committed itself to trust in a slow, conservative evolution of the British political system but, at Dublin Castle's request, nationalist propaganda was also toned down in the press, men of seditious or nationalistic tendencies were removed from all the Irish Party's support bodies and the National League's more radical or democratic ideas were simply abandoned, hence the Special Commission of 1888.[10] This had been the price for allowing the question of home rule to be even raised in British politics. All accepted this consensus not least because the Irish Party, notwithstanding its being prised to win majority political representation with the church's support, represented neither the propertied interests nor the wealth of Ireland.

In the past, IRB and Land League revolutionaries had cited the Hungarian example of the 1860s in defence of the idea that Parnell's party should abstain from Westminster and unilaterally establish a parliament in Dublin in an attempt to dictate Irish nationalist terms to the British imperial parliament.[11] If the Irish Party had ever taken this option, however, it would have faced total opposition from the Irish banks, the Irish business community, the Irish legal profession and the country's principal property owners (who directed the militias of Ireland),[12] placing it in a completely powerless and self-defeating position. Twenty years later, nothing had essentially changed in this regard. Nevertheless, Griffith revived the idea. Michael Davitt's career partly explains why this was done.

The concordat established during the mid-1880s between the British government and the Catholic Church regarding the government of Ireland and the preservation of the Union later encouraged twentieth-century British government officials to look back fondly upon this time as marking the birth of 'the Ireland that we made'.[13] However, Michael Davitt's success, as an accredited lay representative of Archbishop Walsh, in convincing Pope Leo XIII to grant the leader of the Irish College in Rome official diplomatic status as the sole intermediary between the Irish Catholic hierarchy and the Vatican, independent of any British political arrangement or the status of the Catholic Church in the rest of the United Kingdom (a situation which lasted from 1886 up until 1929),[14] meant that the international organisation of the Catholic Church, especially the religious orders, had provided Irishmen with a diplomatic outlet outside the confines of the British Empire for the very first time in modern history. This was a significant development because irrespective of the church's great conservatism and the papacy's relative lack of clout in international affairs, Catholic diplomacy was naturally very well informed about the international political order as well as highly professional and securely independent in nature. It did not exist in a world of revolutionary make-believe or cloak-and-dagger conspiracies. Conterminous developments within Irish-America reflected this reality.

From the 1884 American presidential election onwards, Irish-American politicians (political friends of Davitt) emphasised the potentially great contribution to be made to the American Republic specifically by the Roman Catholic Church and Catholic schools. In turn, they abandoned their previous focus of acting as critical 'fenian' spokesmen on Anglo-American relations.[15] Reflecting the positive state of Anglo-American relations, over one hundred US congressmen of Irish descent expressed appreciation for Gladstone during 1886 for announcing his willingness to introduce a Government of Ireland bill in parliament.[16] Simultaneously, John Devoy lost his career as a newspaper editor and relative significance as an Irish-American public figure. By 1903, the American AOH, without formally expressing opposition to the Irish Party, was deliberately distinguishing itself from the United Irish League of America because the latter body had grown closer to the British business community in New York than to the American Catholic hierarchy (needless to say, all non-naturalised Irishmen in the United States were still British citizens). By targeting this Catholic AOH readership, Devoy was able to launch a very successful newspaper in September 1903, the *Gaelic American* (New York). Together with Davitt, Devoy expressed appreciation for Griffith's Hungarian Policy and, more or less, called for an end to the old Fenian tradition of political anti-Catholicism.[17] As Devoy was still its paymaster, the IRB in Ireland followed suit. In a sense, this brought the revolutionary underground on both sides of the Atlantic into line with the Catholic Church's diplomatic role in Anglo-American relations as it had developed since the mid-1880s.

Just prior to beginning his Hungarian series, Griffith had argued that nationalist revolutionaries should aim to 'capture the municipal administration of all Ireland' as a means of putting pressure upon the Irish Party to abstain from the imperial parliament and make a stand for Irish independence.[18] Griffith's idea of turning local government office into a platform for promoting this idea was one that failed to impress Michael Davitt, Mark Ryan and John O'Leary when he discussed it with them, however.[19] All bar the last few of Griffith's articles on the Hungarian theme dealt exclusively with recounting the Hungarian struggle for independence after 1848 involving parliamentarians and republican rebels. This was done primarily to influence the IRB and ex-Land League readership. Regarding this body of opinion, Griffith judged that 'it is the parallel rather than the logic which I think will most powerfully affect' them.[20] In particular, he hoped that this historical narrative would help to remind 'his compatriots' in the IRB that there was a practical 'alternative to armed resistance' that could bring about political freedom.[21] This was a fairly reasonable hope.

Since its inception, the IRB was nominally committed to creating a volunteer force for Irish nationalist purposes. However, it had never been a movement led by the landed gentry; the traditional creators of such volunteer corps. Instead, it was a movement of obscure lower-class political activists whose secret social networks frequently overlapped with British military figures, who owned much property in Ireland, as well as the country's police forces. Although the IRB had nominally been the most numerous Irish political organisation prior to the 1880s, like the British Chartist phenomenon which preceded it, its lack of control over public opinion, or impact on political elites, usually relegated it an insignificant position beyond having acted as 'a political school' for some notable individuals who went on to achieve more significant careers in other directions.[22] Those who left the organisation frequently justified their decision on the grounds of having grown 'weary to death of playing roles and striving to roll impossible balls up impossible hills'.[23] Some who remained spoke sadly of their frustrated determination 'to get in a blow at the power which has been banging me about the head—in common with my brethren—since I was born'.[24]

The political bankruptcy of the IRB's position hitherto lay in its response to British state centralisation. A brief debate in Chartist circles during the early 1840s as to whether or not 'physical force' was needed to back up the 'moral force' of their ignored petitions for reform had been elevated by British political leaders into an ideological standpoint to counter any verbal challenges to the constitution.[25] As a result, the IRB, in perpetually speaking of the moral justice of a rebellion, was essentially playing the same political game as those British elites that it professed to oppose. This made its existence a product of British security considerations as much as it was a genuine vehicle for sincere young Irish nationalists to attempt to come more fully to terms with the political society that they inhabited and, in particular, the ready-made debates that had been prepared for them. As both participants and auxiliaries to public Irish movements, members of the IRB frequently displayed considerable talent in initiating significant new departures, at least on the level of political debate. This was often done as a preliminary step to embarking on different careers. Griffith essentially stepped into this role during 1904 just as Davitt had done twenty-three years previously. There was good reason to expect that the IRB would follow Griffith's lead. The almost entirely new and slim-line IRB organisation established in the wake of the Anglo-Boer War was based entirely around the Gaelic League. Although some republicans disliked the Gaelic League's very conservative and avowedly non-political leadership, they nevertheless accepted it as their principal forum. The thought of engaging in conspiratorial work was neither entertained nor suggested. Over 50 per cent of the Gaelic League's membership were civil servants or national school teachers who worked for British state institutions, while its IRB membership was drawn mostly from that 25 per cent who worked as clerks or shop-assistants.[26]

At the time, Davitt was arguing that the vote of Catholic politicians of Irish descent in America had much more importance in the context of British international relations than Irish politicians' vote in Westminster. Griffith cited Davitt's argument to defend the idea that international Catholic diplomacy could aid the 'Hungarian Policy'.[27] This ignored the fact, however, that the potential of an Irish-American vote to influence the American government's attitude towards Anglo-American relations had no bearing whatsoever on the Anglo-Irish relationship itself, which was an entirely separate and purely British matter. Its very suggestion nevertheless reflected Griffith's growing political indebtedness to John Sweetman. The latter had long been a regular financial supporter of Catholic interests in the United States, the United Kingdom and Italy but had had no interest in Irish nationalism prior to its becoming wedded to Catholic interests during 1884. Sweetman was now a firm believer that the Irish Party's presence in Westminster was of no advantage to anybody.

Having taken part in the negotiations surrounding the 1893 Government of Ireland bill, Sweetman realised that the politics of home rule was a meaningless charade that was deliberately launched by Gladstone only to mislead the Irish public regarding how the country was really being governed. Disgusted by the fact that the Irish Party was now subsidised largely by the British Liberal Party, after failing to persuade the Irish Party to withdraw from Westminster, Sweetman resigned from parliament in 1895 and helped W.M. Murphy to establish his first newspaper, the *Daily Nation*. This championed the Healyite policy of decentralising authority within the Irish Party's support body and placing more power in its branches, which were governed mostly by priests.[28] During the Boer War controversy, Sweetman had formed the Irish Financial Reform League and the General Council of County Councils to protest against the over-taxation of Ireland and to encourage business activism in local government.[29] When Griffith was publishing his initial Hungarian articles in the *United Irishman*, Sweetman wrote to the *Freeman's Journal* calling upon all Irish Party supporters to pay very close attention to the series. Reflecting Sweetman's influence as one of the richest Irish Catholics (he was an estate and brewery owner as well as a major railway shareholder), Griffith was glad to note that the initial response to Sweetman's suggestion 'seems to indicate that the Parliamentary Party is not prepared to oppose the Hungarian policy very strongly. It does not commit them to any opposition.'[30]

Sweetman's London Catholic friends were the first group to support Griffith's Hungarian Policy. They had organised themselves into the Irish National Society of London. This was a small breakaway body from the United Irish League of Great Britain (the Irish Party's fund collection body in Britain, led by T.P. O'Connor) and it was also associated with the Gaelic League of London. The Irish National Society received a special blessing from Pope Leo XIII after it opposed the Irish Party on the grounds of the latter's failure (at the insistence of Liberal Party) to support a Tory bill at Westminster providing for state support for denominational education, including all Catholic schools.[31] Led by a wealthy architect Thomas Martin, the Irish National Society was closely associated with the Catholic Archbishop of Westminster who, for a time, ordered that the United Irish League of Great Britain be no longer permitted to use Catholic halls and schools as venues for its meetings.[32] Through this channel, various historic letters of Monsignor Persico of Rome to Cardinal Manning of Westminster were leaked to Griffith's *United Irishman*. The publication of these letters was meant to show that Irish Party figures were wrong to have criticised the church at the time of a papal rescript against an Irish agrarian agitation that demanded rent reductions during the late 1880s because this decision was (supposedly) not popular in Vatican circles. These letters were later republished in Catholic newspapers throughout the continent in order to present the Catholic Church as having democratic sympathies, thereby echoing the thrust of a notable papal encyclical of 1891. Griffith himself characterised them as proof that the Irish Party had always been a 'Castle Catholic' party whose pro-British leanings had caused them to become divorced from a true sense of social justice.[33]

During the summer of 1904, Martin's London society appealed to John Daly, the most well known republican politician in Ireland, and to T.M. Healy to help them organise an opposition movement to the Irish Party. This initiative won Healy's sympathy. Reflecting his ambiguous relationship with the Irish Party, however, Healy felt that he could not come out openly in support of a rival party as, rather like the bishops, 'my own share in politics must I fear be individual' or, at least, appear to the general Irish public to be so.[34] In August, Martin's friends travelled to Dublin to meet Griffith, Edward Martyn and aldermen Thomas Kelly and Walter Cole of Cumann na nGaedheal. Cole had recently worked with Sweetman and Charles Dawson, an ex-mayor of Dublin, in promoting the idea of holding an Irish national industrial exhibition as a riposte to Dublin Castle's international exhibition of British industry.[35] As the Dublin representative of the Irish National Society, Cole now convened a conference to discuss the idea of calling for the withdrawal of all Irish MPs from Westminster. In preparation for this, Griffith himself travelled to London to organise the visit of thirty local Gaelic Leaguers to this Dublin meeting. This was done with the cooperation of Art O'Brien and Michael MacWhite, two well-educated associates of Martin's in London who were also growing dissatisfied with the Irish Party.[36]

This circle evidently felt hopeful that if Griffith's articles were publicised more widely through being republished as a pamphlet, they could win the cooperation of known political allies of the Catholic hierarchy such as Michael Davitt, Eoin MacNeill and D.P. Moran.[37] To this end, John Sweetman purchased the vast majority of the *United Irishman* shares that winter and financed the publication of Griffith's articles as a pamphlet.[38] Due to Sweetman's close association with Daniel Mannix, the president of Maynooth College (who would encourage further publications of Griffith's writings),[39] much of Catholic Ireland, lay and clerical, were inclined to examine its contents and *The Resurrection of Hungary: A Parallel for Ireland* became a top-selling publication, selling tens-of-thousands of copies in a very short space of time.

Griffith was not blind to what political interests he now represented. While he had directly opposed the stance of Archbishop Walsh on education and criticised Maynooth College for promoting royalist attitudes in the not too distant past,[40] he would not do so again. He also understood, with delight, the political significance of Redmond's concern at Maynooth College's acceptance of the Hungarian Policy:

> Another fact, and one fraught with significance for the future of Ireland, is that the students of Maynooth, a few days ago, after a prolonged debate, decided in favour of the Hungarian Policy as the policy for Ireland. The future is with us and we face it with confidence.[41]

As early as December 1904, Griffith was writing to Sweetman that the Catholic clergy in Dublin and Leinster were 'all strongly advocating the policy in private'; that the *Irish News* (Belfast), associated with the new West Belfast MP Joseph Devlin (who was also president of the revived AOH), was becoming sympathetic; as was the Scottish section of the United Irish League. In addition, he felt that the expected victory by the National Council of 'the most compact and intelligent party' in Dublin City Hall combined with Sweetman's intention to promote Griffith's policy at the General Council of County Councils would give them a strong platform to build upon. This led Griffith to view the overall course of current affairs as 'foreshadowing the general adoption of the Hungarian policy'.[42] Banking on this expectation, Griffith finally mustered the courage to propose to Maud Sheehan (she accepted). It would be several more years, however, before Griffith could afford to marry, not least because his proposed programme would fail to find as many supporters as he had hoped. This was due to a fundamental paradox that it embodied.

Griffith's Hungarian Policy was attuned to Catholic disaffection with Westminster and the fact that Catholic Church diplomacy in the English-speaking, or Anglo-American, world was now of much more significance to Ireland's future than whatever preoccupation still existed amongst continental European powers regarding any potential strategic significance of Ireland.[43] However, its argument still had little or no relevance to the dynamics of Irish party politics. This was because of its retrospective focus and emphasis on an idea that nobody except the Tories, the self-styled 'unionists' of contemporary Irish party politics, was essentially prepared to support. This was that the Irish Party had led itself into a political 'cul-de-sac' in 1886 through committing itself to Gladstone's programme and that the 'vanity and selfishness' of its leaders was 'preventing them from admitting the truth and retracing their steps'.[44] It was all very well for Griffith to emphasise that the Irish public had spent over £600,000 to keep the Irish Party in Westminster ever since 1886 only to see a commensurate increase in the imperial over-taxation of Ireland.[45] This had indeed been Gladstone's intention. In itself, however, this did not offer a solution, only a critique. Likewise, Griffith's subsequent effort to justify the Hungarian Policy by using the Financial Relations Report of 1896 to show that 'in the memory of living man … no more excessive taxer of the Irish people has ever been known than William Ewart Gladstone'[46] was ineffective in a party-political sense precisely because Gladstone (who died in 1898) had already been retired for over a decade.

In the *Resurrection of Hungary*, Griffith suggested that the Irish Party revert to its independent political stance prior to 1884 and accept the 'one statesmanlike idea' that the elderly Daniel O'Connell had been tempted to follow, alongside the Young Irelanders, during the mid-1840s. This was to set up in Ireland a national council of three hundred representatives that would act unilaterally as an Irish parliament, establish their own arbitration courts (which Griffith believed could now be supported by the new local government bodies) and force the British government to abandon the unequal relationship that had come to define the Union by recognising Irishmen's right to political self-determination.[47] Looking back even further in time, Griffith suggested that those Gaelic Leaguers who declared themselves willing to promote Irish economic development should follow the example of the Irish Volunteers of 1779. This volunteer movement instigated a boycott of British goods in an attempt to force the British government to surrender its control of the Irish economy; the event that prefigured the establishment of Irish legislative independence in 1782–3.[48] Griffith cited this historic case study and the Irish Party's current toleration of the over-taxation of Ireland in order to drive home his argument that the Irish Party had completely surrendered all political direction to the imperial parliament, in the process ensuring that the Irish nation was becoming a defunct concept: 'a man who runs his business on such lines ends up in the bankruptcy court. A nation that runs its business on such lines must inevitably go smash.'[49]

As Sweetman had not been an MP since 1895 and Healy had refused to come out in favour of the Hungarian Policy, Griffith had no allies among Ireland's parliamentary representatives. Meanwhile, his sole claim to credibility as a spokesman on economic matters stemmed from his membership of the five-man executive of the Industrial Committee of the Gaelic League. However, together with Douglas Hyde, two of its members had been in favour of the British government's international industrial exhibition of 1903.[50] In addition, while Sweetman and the Catholic Church desired that Irish-America would henceforth fund the Gaelic League rather than the Irish Party,[51] in practice this ambition related primarily to the financing of Irish education, not the state of the nation. As an avowedly non-political body, the Gaelic League could not support Griffith's Hungarian Policy. Furthermore, while its Industrial Committee had declared its intention to draw on the advice of independent economic experts, its circulars requesting suitable nominations of personnel had received no names in return.[52] This reflected the fact that Gaelic League activities were primarily social, such as summer schools and dances that were run by travelling teachers and supervised by the clergy. Meanwhile, despite its nominally non-sectarian platform, its membership would soon become religiously segregated.[53] This was not a promising development.

Douglas Hyde's claim that the Gaelic League was non-political was disingenuous. It was closely connected to Dublin Castle, the Irish Party and the Catholic Church according to the consensus established during 1886. Dublin Castle's National Education Board accepted the league's exclusive identification with the principle of voluntary rather than state-run schools. The leader of its industrial committee Tom Finlay S.J., who unusually for a UCD Jesuit was the son of a Scottish Presbyterian, was also the vice-president of the recently established Irish Agricultural Organisation Society that worked with Dublin Castle's new Congested District Board and Department of Agriculture and Technical Instruction.[54] Some historians have typified the establishment of these bodies (inspired by Lord Dunsany's son, Sir Horace Plunkett, and led by Lord Monteagle) as marking a shift in British government policy regarding Ireland because they supposedly favoured interventionist activity in the economy.[55] However, their administrative lynchpin Sir George Fottrell, the secretary of the Irish Land Commission, was a Catholic administrator at Dublin Castle who, alongside E.G. Jenkinson, was knighted for his role in negotiating the secret Anglo-Irish security consensus of 1884–6.[56] This had involved a total Irish political acceptance of Gladstone's longstanding imperial fiscal plan for Ireland.

The Tories professed willingness to invest a higher percentage of Irish revenue in the Dublin Castle administration did not overrule or alter this consensus in the slightest. Reflecting this, Fr Finlay, with the moral support of George Russell and the enthusiastic support of D.P. Moran (who would continue to make no secret of his detestation for all Griffith's ideas),[57] accepted the judgment of the Congested Districts Board that the chief dynamic of both emigration and economic stagnation in Ireland was the absence of economically viable land holdings in the west of the country. The solution was deemed to be the creation of a rural economy that was more self-sufficient and that would not continue to be burdened by a surplus population.

At the inception of the United Irish League (1898), both William O'Brien and Michael Davitt had denounced this idea of labelling the west of Ireland as a 'congested district'. Laurence Ginnell, a passive sympathiser with Griffith's writings,[58] would soon attempt to revive a political agitation on behalf of the rural poor.[59] This agrarian tradition in Irish politics had always lacked power however.[60] Ever since the reunification of the Irish Party (1900), it was being labelled as reactionary in its response to supposedly progressive governmental reforms. In his capacity as a UCD professor of economics (formerly, he was a professor of moral philosophy), Finlay would shape the thinking of many future Irish political leaders. In doing so, he has been described as a conservative rather than a reactionary in his thinking.[61] However, Finlay was temperamentally inclined to judge all political matters far more from an ethical rather than a practical standpoint. Therefore, he was ill suited to conceiving of any potential initiatives and was content to let decision-making rest with Whitehall.[62]

Land law reform was a UK wide and in no sense specifically Irish phenomenon. Ever since the 1880s, the chief divergence between the British and Irish application of this reform was that the British reforms were designed to facilitate a prioritisation of the municipal authorities' capacity for promoting business over that of the traditional ruling landowning class. No such provisions were made for the development of an infrastructure for business within Ireland, however.[63] This made the Local Government (Ireland) Act of 1898 an insignificant reform. As an extension of this, current UIL branch leaders, which included many local government officials as well as parish priests, owned extensive grazing land themselves and had no interest in promoting Irish business. They conveniently forgot, or rather deliberately ignored, that the original ideal of the Irish National Land League (its 'Irish National' title had already been permanently erased from history books) was to conceive of the rural and urban Irish economies as one entity and to launch an Irish nationalist political agitation upon precisely that basis.[64] This had reflected the input of republican radicals into that agitation. Griffith's attitude towards both emigration and the general economy was rooted in this tradition. This made him reject the British government's policy that agriculture was inherently the basis of the economy of Ireland. Instead, Griffith focused on the indisputable fact that the union of the British and Irish exchequers was inherently the central dynamic of all economic developments on the island, both rural and urban. Therefore, this development combined with the imperial taxation regime launched by Gladstone was unquestionably 'at the root of the question of emigration and lack of employment in Ireland'.[65] Although entirely logical, this was a deeply unpopular stance. This was because it did not fit with the material interests of Catholic Ireland as they had developed. It also made Griffith the odd-man out on the Gaelic League's industrial committee (although, in time, Sweetman would succeed in getting himself nominated onto that body).[66]

During 1904–1905, the only member of the Gaelic League's Industrial Committee with similar attitudes to Griffith was Robert Lindsay Crawford of Lisburn, Co. Antrim. Together with Thomas Sloan, a Belfast Methodist street preacher, and Belfast trade unionist Alex Boyd, Crawford favoured a labour-led political uprising against the existing leaderships of both the Ulster Party and the Irish Party, each of which were deemed to be cowardly reactionaries and mindless clericalists in politics.[67] Crawford, however, was not a popular figure. The Ulster Party would soon work to have him removed as editor of the *Irish Protestant*. Crawford created an Independent Orange Order in opposition to the landed-gentry led Orange Order but his organisation never acquired a large membership. This reflected his powerlessness to overcome the legacy of the British government's handling of the Irish land question.[68] Dublin Castle officials typified the political consensus established during 1886 as serving the purpose of 'making Castle rule popular'. This was made possible because the Irish Party and its support bodies were henceforth allowed to 'know almost as soon as the Law Officers themselves everything which transpires in the secret councils of Dublin Castle'.[69] If this could be typified as a government by consensus, it had the result of making the Irish Party—not just the historic governing gentry class (who now concentrated on the new Ulster Party)—an instrument of clientelism. Priding itself on being a supposed government party with special insider political knowledge, the Irish Party now exacerbated a tradition in Ireland (common to all British imperial colonies)[70] of turning politics into a mere dispensary for private patronage networks, even within the civil service.[71] This was not an example of plutocracy at work so much as a deliberate curtailment of the potential relevance of party politics as an instrument of change. This made the establishment of effective platforms for demanding reforms of any kind almost impossible. This was particularly debilitating for those like Griffith who were attempting to establish such platforms.

Specifically in the Dublin area, in common with Griffith's two business allies Cole and Sweetman, William Field and James McCann had demanded fundamental fiscal and banking reforms in Ireland. They failed, however, to establish an effective platform for the Irish Financial Reform League (1897–1901); a movement that was also supported by Thomas Lough, the owner of the leading Ulster cooperative, and Ned (later Sir Edward) Carson of Dublin. This body was forced to disband soon after the reunification of the Irish Party and upon nominally joining that party, Field and McCann were requested to simply keep quiet.[72] A similar dynamic ensured that the chances of Griffith or Crawford using the Industrial Committee of the Gaelic League as a basis for establishing a platform for fiscal reform were negated.

J.P. Boland, owner of Boland's Mills in Dublin, and Tom O'Donnell, an Oxford-educated Kerry politician who, with encouragement from Maurice Moynihan (now electoral registrar for Tralee), toyed with the idea of promoting abstention from the imperial parliament,[73] professed sympathy for the Gaelic League's industrial committee. Their attempts to promote such ideals in the west of Ireland failed, however, due to the unwillingness of banks to fund their ideas. Indeed, the only recent companies whose formation was assisted by Dublin Castle's Congested Districts Board and its associated English banker J.H. Tuke (who also promoted all assisted emigration schemes in Ireland) was a handful of woollen mills that were run by the Catholic religious orders for their own private gain.[74] As a result, Field, McCann, Boland and O'Donnell were left in the position of standing still politically and grew increasingly isolated. A similar fate was to await Griffith's proposed Hungarian Policy.

Thanks to Sweetman, Griffith found a prestigious candidate to launch his Hungarian Policy in Dublin City Hall. Sir Thomas Henry Grattan Esmonde, MP for Wexford, was a former whip of the Irish Party who had also been the Jesuits' principal choice as an Irish Party MP in 1885.[75] Together with Sweetman, Esmonde had founded a body known as the General Council of the County Councils during 1899 in an attempt to compensate for the complete lack of directive powers that were granted to the new county councils by the imperial parliament. Esmonde, a descendant of Henry Grattan, convened a meeting of this body to adopt a historic resolution of the Irish Volunteers in Dungannon in 1782 as its own. This stated that 'no parliament is competent to make laws for Ireland except an Irish parliament sitting in Ireland' and that 'the claim of any other body of men to make laws for or to govern Ireland is illegal and unconstitutional'. It also argued that the Irish constitution of 1783, denying the right of the imperial parliament to overrule Irish legislation, should still have some jurisdictional relevance. However, no follow-up meeting could be held (representatives of four Ulster counties had also refused to attend this initial gathering). This was because the General Council of County Councils, which consisted mostly of UIL representation and legally had no jurisdictional powers, did not declare itself in favour of politicians withdrawing from the Imperial Parliament.[76]

Griffith attributed this development to the baneful influence of the UIL Directory, the executive of the Irish Party's political machine, and its associated newspaper the *Freeman's Journal*. He typified both as the political heirs to Leonard MacNally, a former *Freeman* editor who had worked covertly with Dublin Castle to bring about the Act of Union through underhand methods.[77] Although Griffith was also able to acknowledge the *Freeman's* history of quality newspaper reportage,[78] over the next decade, he would repeatedly equate the politics of the *Freeman's Journal* (whose former proprietor had been, with Fottrell, the central figure in the secret Anglo-Irish negotiations of 1884–6) with MacNally's historic legacy.[79] This was provocative and essentially foolhardy: Archbishop Walsh certainly had been and probably still was one of the *Freeman's* company directors.[80] To some extent it reflected Griffith's sincerity regarding his own political stance. According to two associates, Griffith turned down the offer of a very well paid position with the *Freeman*, as well as an offer to become a member of the Irish Party, because he viewed this as an attempt to bribe him into a political silence.[81] His willingness to attack the *Freeman* was also tactical. Sweetman and several Catholic bishops had already transferred their allegiance from the *Freeman* to W.M. Murphy's new *Irish Independent*. This led Griffith to typify the latter as a quality newspaper and even as a fellow traveller with his own journal in championing progressive political ideas:

> Every sound idea, every logical item, on the programme of the parliamentarians has been filched from the columns of the *United Irishman*. We don't grudge them these stolen ideas since they shall be ultimately of some service to Ireland—we merely invite them to come and steal ore.[82]

Such boastful claims to political relevance were always Griffith's favourite tactic in attempting to popularise his ideas. This may not have been an effective gambit, however. Fellow writers, who liked nothing better than a persuasive turn of phrase, generally admired Griffith's journalism, whether they agreed with him or not. Much of the contemporary middle class reacted to Griffith's affronts, however, by speaking about him with derisive contempt: why should a nonentity amongst Ireland's professional classes feel entitled to not only claim to understand the political situation much better than they did, but also claim a right to perpetually pass damning and blanket judgments upon them all?

The Irish Party hated Griffith for precisely this reason and so labelled him as 'a factionist in the pay of the unionists to smash home rule', which was their means of saying that they feared that if his ideas became popular this could undermine the basis of their own personal wealth as a newly-arrived middle class by destroying that political consensus upon which that wealth was based. On this level, Griffith was certainly a poor politician. He once typified the entire Irish reading public as 'human ostriches' because the political programme of his book was not being discussed, even though it had sold six times more than any publication of the previous five years.[83]

The Irish Party consciously attempted to confine debate on Griffith's programme to Tom Kettle's Young Ireland (i.e. UCD) Branch of the United Irish League. Kettle did point out some real flaws in Griffith's programme. Rather than appealing for the creation of a new Irish constitution, Griffith had referred back to the Irish constitution of 1782 and the Renunciation Act of 1783, which recognised the legislative independence of the historic (and exclusively Protestant) Irish parliament. Griffith maintained that if all Irish MPs united in declaring themselves in favour of this legal precedent and in demanding fiscal reform on the basis of the Financial Relations Report of 1896 then existing nationalist and unionist divisions would disappear and a united Irish nation would begin to emerge politically. By contrast, Kettle emphasised that a historic Irish constitution from over a century ago could have absolutely no material connotations or popular appeal in the present. In addition, the very existence of the Irish county councils, upon which Griffith placed so much emphasis, were subject to the law of the imperial parliament.[84] Griffith retorted that the non-requirement of taking an oath of allegiance upon entering local government office meant that Irish county councils could pledge their loyalty to the 1783 constitution without breaking the existing law.[85] He also claimed that

> No Irish movement can be constitutional unless it be based on the Irish Constitution, which the volunteers won for Ireland and which Ireland intends to retain, even though it may cause as much trouble in London as the retention of its constitution by Hungary caused in Vienna.[86]

Griffith's repeated justification of this policy by claiming that the Act of Union was actually illegal essentially explains why this was not done, however. The existence of a legal precedent of Irish legislative independence was an academic curiosity. In the present, however, it could not be the basis of a political policy that was anything other than seditious. Another reason for the deafening silence of Ireland's professional classes in response to Griffith's writings was a deep distrust of his association with the IRB. Reflecting this, Kettle suggested that 'this pamphlet [the *Resurrection of Hungary*] will have justified its existence if only it leads up to a working alliance between the two sections of nationalism, now standing deplorably apart'. As far as Kettle was concerned, 'there is nothing in the nature of things to prevent our separatists and "constitutionalists", our nationalists and nationists[87]—if I may invent a word—from cooperating' in support of the 'nationist' Irish Party in the British Imperial Parliament.[88]

A weakness in Kettle's critique was his deliberate decision to ignore Griffith's point about the Irish Party's support for both Gladstone's imperial fiscal policy and the over-taxation of Ireland. Instead, he focused purely upon Griffith's treatment of Hungarian history. Kettle emphasised that the Hungarians' decision to abstain from the Austrian parliament during the 1860s was the result of a process of constitutional experimentation (namely, the possibility of creating new representative assemblies) that had been taking place in central Europe ever since 1848, whereas 'the parliament we have to confront is not precisely a novice'. Kettle also repeated an argument against abstention that the Irish Party had made after Parnell's death. He argued that Bohemia was a closer parallel to Ireland's case than that of Hungary and yet the Czechs, after having tried the abstentionist policy for a number of years, decided that they were better off materially in the Imperial Parliament.[89] Griffith did not agree with this assessment, however. He typified Kettle's critique as being motivated by the simple fact that he 'writes from the parliamentarian side'. Although he agreed with Kettle that the policy required to be thought out 'clearly and exhaustively in terms of Irish politics' if it was to be of any benefit, he comforted himself with the idea that 'even if the people did fail it, there is consolation in the thought that it could not possibly leave the country worse off than it found it'.[90]

Griffith's intended trump card in defence of his programme was his claim that the contemporary home rule movement was slowly but surely disintegrating by becoming divorced from its political roots, having abandoned its initial nationalist radicalism, at Gladstone's request, during 1885–6.[91] Griffith could only really justify this claim, however, by emphasising the potency of IRB–Land League radicalism during 1879–1882. For example, John Morley's *Life of Gladstone* was quoted to show that Britain's temporary abandonment of the Transvaal to the Boers in 1881 had been justified on the grounds of a felt need to keep sufficient troops in Ireland to prevent the possibility of Britain losing control of the country to the Irish National Land League.[92] The reality of the time, however, was that this British political insecurity reflected little more than a fear of the potential political consequences of an eclipse of the power of landed gentry in Ireland, if not in Britain. A real security danger to the state can hardly be said to have existed during 1881. The IRB had been at its absolute all-time peak in terms of its financial, numerical and military strength at this time (curiously, the southern landed gentry, mostly Tory in politics, were simultaneously arming themselves), but neither a pitched republican battle with the aristocracy nor a nationalist rebellion had been contemplated, notwithstanding the imprisonment without trial of over one thousand Land League officials that winter.[93]

The most significant aspect of the political consensus established during the 1880s was that the Irish Party wholly agreed with the British cabinet that any changes in government personnel in Ireland should only ever be done very slowly, cautiously and gradually in order to prevent the risk of any possibility of disorder or sedition.[94] For this very reason, there was really no question of Irish local government bodies ever being used as a revolutionary platform in the manner that Griffith suggested. Furthermore, there was also the unavoidable professional reality that, from 1886 onwards, it was virtually a career necessity for members of all British and Irish political parties, as well as all lawyers and academics (including historians) within the universities (who were themselves civil servants), to accept the consensus established during 1886. Its provenance was no longer of any significance with the passage of time compared to its actual establishment and, in turn, its increasing hold over the public imagination. Essentially realising this, Griffith soon modified his Hungarian Policy. Instead, he launched on behalf of the National Council, a nominal organisation that was still Griffith's only platform, what he typified as 'the Sinn Féin Policy'. This was deliberately done to coincide with the launch of the Irish 'Industrial Development Association' (IDA) in November 1905. As a counter offensive, Dublin Castle and the Irish Party soon persuaded the National Board of Education to withdraw state funding from the Gaelic League.[95]

In launching the Sinn Féin Policy, Griffith explicitly sought to capitalise upon the existence of the Gaelic League. He argued that although 'the end of education is to make men patriots' such values did not exist in Ireland outside of a British state context and, therefore, it was essential to support the programme of 'a friend of mine in London' (Thomas Martin) to make voluntary schools in Ireland the basis for an Irish national education system. Such a goal, Griffith maintained, could be supported 'by the Irish people throughout the world',[96] or, in other words, those Catholics of Irish birth or descent within the English-speaking Catholic diaspora who gave their money to the church to promote Catholic schools. Upon this basis, Douglas Hyde would soon visit the United States to collect funds for the Gaelic League.

As he was an ideological nationalist at heart, Griffith was certainly not the most suitable Irish candidate to promote this ideal of education. His motive was reflected by a series of articles on various small nations in Europe that were written in an attempt to highlight 'what can little Ireland do'. In this series, Griffith presented most contemporary European nations as having more progressive attitude towards education than Britain due to their having a broader conception of the non-denominational basis of the Christian-democratic tradition. For instance, from this premise, Griffith suggested that 'Holland breeds Protestants and Catholics but she breeds no bigots' while, by inference, British secularism was a comparatively divisive and restrictive influence upon the development of political societies.[97] Following Sweetman's orders never to treat religion as a problematic political question, by 1905 Griffith was essentially giving implicit support to the idea that the churches could not possibly be at fault in politics. This led W.B. Yeats and George Moore to typify Griffith as having shifted his position under the new Sinn Féin banner to one analogous to that of the Christian Scientists, which was a contemporary Protestant reaction against secularist rationalism in Britain.[98] For Griffith, however, the essential question was simply to first acquire a political platform from his Catholic patrons on the question of education from which he could then begin to champion his vision of a political (i.e. economic) Irish nationalism. Without doing so, Griffith could have no patrons or platform whatsoever.

W.M. Murphy's *Irish Independent* once typified the establishment of the IDA as a direct outgrowth of the work of the Gaelic League's Industrial Committee. Reflecting this, Griffith's motive in launching the Sinn Féin Policy was evidently a desire to acquire a seniority of influence over that body. Noting that 'agriculture in Ireland is resolving itself into the cattle trade' alone, Griffith highlighted that the post-famine Irish economy had been so manipulated by the British government that the rural economy existed almost entirely to provide meat for the English market, while the urban Irish population was, in turn, being fed entirely by consumable English imports. At both levels, England alone was deriving full economic benefit from this,[99] but Griffith believed that 'there is no reason whatever' that this system should be made permanent. In particular, Griffith believed that it could be undone if Irish businessmen accepted the ideals of the American economist Henry Carey, the German economist Frederich List and several others on 'the national system of political economy'. These writers 'brushed aside the fallacies of Adam Smith and his tribe' by positing that the prerogatives of an imperial economy should not be allowed to dictate all government policies. As the economic history of Europe ever since 1860 had proved, this economic philosophy suited Britain but no other European nation.[100]

Griffith's essential concern here was that British economists were still maintaining 'that our destiny is to be the fruitful mother of flocks and herds—that it is not necessary for us to pay attention to our manufacturing arm, since our agricultural arm is all-sufficient' for the British Isles' needs. However, Griffith emphasised that 'a merely agricultural nation can never develop to any extent a home or a foreign commerce ... or make notable progress in its moral, intellectual, social and political development.' This was partly because

> A mere agricultural state ... is always economically and politically dependent on those foreign nations which take from it agriculture in exchange for manufactured goods. It cannot determine how much it will produce—it must wait and see how much others will buy from it.

From this standpoint, Griffith maintained that 'an agricultural nation is a man with one arm who makes use of an arm belonging to another person, but cannot, of course, be sure of having it always available. An agricultural-manufacturing nation is a man who has two arms of his own at his own disposal' at all times.[101]

Fr Finlay's espousal of the idea of creating a more self-sufficient agrarian economy in Ireland had reflected the economic ideal of protectionism that was championed by both the Tories (who had been in power since 1896) and Horace Plunkett's new Department of Agriculture at Dublin Castle. However, Griffith maintained that the only value of protectionism lay in its capacity to create a more balanced economy. True protectionism, he emphasised, 'does not mean the exclusion of foreign competition—it means rendering the native manufacturer equal to meeting foreign competition ... [by refusing to] see him crushed by mere weight of foreign capital'. Protectionism, therefore, meant maximising the potential benefits to be derivable from both domestic and international commerce in both an agricultural and manufacturing sphere.[102] As was reflected by his call for Ireland to become an agricultural-manufacturing nation, Griffith desired for Ireland to become a competitive trading nation. This necessitated breaking through Britain's protective trade wall that governed the economy of Ireland by dictating that Ireland could not trade outside the United Kingdom. To some extent, Griffith echoed Tory propaganda since the end of the Anglo-Boer War in calling for 'that unity of material interests which produces national strength': this was how he defined 'the policy of the National Council'.[103] Nevertheless, Griffith meant this in a purely Irish, rather than United Kingdom, context. Other minds were working in a similar, if somewhat different, direction.

Irish Tories had recently established an 'Ulster Unionist Council' to champion the idea of making local government representation the bedrock for their political organisation. As an extension of this trend, the old Ulster Party leadership represented by landowners like Edward Saunderson were being challenged by the likes of James Craig, the new MP for East Down. Craig identified far more with the empire as a purely commercial entity than with the British state, advocated tariff reform and, with the assistance of Belfast city council (first established in 1888), had attempted in vain to establish a Belfast Stock Exchange to prioritise local Irish economic interests.[104] Griffith claimed that the Sinn Féin Policy's 'hope lies in the future attitude of the Protestant democracy of Ulster'. He expressed a hope that it would soon reject 'the bloated plutocrats and hungry lawyers whose Protestantism was confined to beating the Orange drum once a year' and join with his National Council and Crawford's party in realising that all Irish workers 'have been sold by English parties without any material gain to the country'.[105] In making these arguments, he was clearly hoping to make some inroads upon Craig's political support base.

Robert Lynd, a popular Belfast writer and essayist from a Presbyterian background, agreed with Griffith's perspective. He wrote a pamphlet for the National Council in which he cited Griffith as the best possible political guide for northern workers. Lynd noted that while many Ulster Protestants were being encouraged to point to the rapid growth of Belfast from a small town into a major city as an indication that Ireland was well governed, 'no true Orangeman, I am sure, will consider a thriving Belfast anything but a small compensation for a dwindling and decaying Ireland'. Furthermore, as recent developments had shown (namely, Craig's failure to establish a viable Stock Exchange in Belfast), Belfast's commercial success was not at all dependent upon local entrepreneurial ability but rather a total servitude to more powerful London-based firms, thereby potentially bringing about Belfast's ultimate economic decline.[106] The Dublin Tory author Standish O'Grady similarly suggested that Griffith's policy should encourage all Irish Tories to 'shift their ground': 'they can only oppose the Constitution of 1783 by proclaiming themselves a foreign garrison. They cannot oppose it as Irishmen.'[107]

Griffith placed much emphasis upon the question of Ireland's harbour, port and dock boards. He noted that these port authorities were currently refusing to publish annual returns of goods imported solely because London firms' shipping agents governed them. However, he suggested that it was potentially in their power to work with the county councils in calling for the restoration of Irish customs authorities.[108] 'To bring Ireland out of the corner and make her assert her existence in the world', Griffith also argued that an effort should be made to encourage the Dublin Stock Exchange and the banks of the country (principally, the former 'national bank', the Bank of Ireland) to end their unionist policy of directing all Irish capital to be invested in British stock rather than in industries within Ireland.[109] Griffith also protested that of the £250,000 subscribed to the Irish Party over the past decade 'not a shilling of that money was expended during all those years by the Parliamentary Party in explaining to the Irish people how they were overtaxed, in outlining any policy for them to follow in the matter, or even in assembling them to consider the question'.[110]

Some of Griffith's concerns were echoed by A.W. Samuels K.C., the successor of W.E. Lecky and predecessor of Edward Carson as the MP for Trinity College Dublin. He was also president of that college's Statistical and Social Inquiry Society of Ireland. This society's journal had subscribers in universities throughout Europe and North America. Samuels similarly maintained that the question of the management of Irish finances 'require earnest consideration on the part not only of those who interest themselves in economic problems or take part in the administration of Ireland, but also of every person who, as public man or private citizen, dwells in or has to do with this country'.[111]

Samuels maintained that 'the system of subvention of the local needs of Ireland and Scotland, inaugurated in 1888 [in conjunction with the English local government act of that year], is neither constitutional nor financially sound'. This was because 'the basis upon which the percentages of 80 per cent for England, 11 per cent for Scotland and 9 per cent for Ireland were fixed has never been explained, and the figures and calculations upon which it was established have never been disclosed.' In the absence of the office of Vice Treasurer of Ireland (abolished by Gladstone in 1872), no means of appealing for financial fair play for Ireland even existed. Instead, all Irish revenue was included within that of the United Kingdom and only a maximum of 9 per cent of such revenue could ever be reinvested in Ireland. While some English politicians maintained that the respective populations of each country justified this arrangement, Samuels argued that this 'is not in accordance with constitutional right or fair play' as 'taxation should be so arranged as to fall equally—that is with equality of burden according to their resources—upon each of the three kingdoms … fairly applied to meet the particular needs of each of the three kingdoms'. If this was not done, then the existence of the Union could only be 'to the detriment of Ireland'. Therefore, Samuels suggested, there was a need to return to 'the financial principles [of equality between the kingdoms] upon which they entered that Union' in 1801; principles that had first been established or won during the later-eighteenth century by Grattan's parliament.[112]

Griffith's principle hope for the Sinn Féin Policy was evidently that this particular Irish Tory ('unionist') case could be adapted and made to serve Irish nationalist purposes through the medium of the National Council. However, although 75 per cent of the 6,000 individuals currently employed by the urban and county councils and poor law boards in Ireland claimed to hold nationalist sympathies, they equated this sympathy simply with loyalty to the Irish Party in opposition to all the Irish Tories' ideas. They were certainly not likely to embrace Griffith's idea of making a unilateral decision to act like 'a national civil service', as opposed to an imperial one, by joining the National Council because that would have inherently meant rejecting the Gladstonian politics of home rule to which the Irish Party leadership was committed. Meanwhile, in Ulster if not in Dublin, the Tories, being committed by party politics first and foremost to opposing the Irish Party, were suspicious of any 'nationalist' scheme, no matter how well it was justified, because of the majority Irish Party's closeness to the material interests of the Catholic hierarchy. In this way, a combination of misleading party-political nomenclatures in Ireland, Dublin Castle clientelism and sectarian attitudes was likely to sink the Sinn Féin Policy at its inception.

The Hungarian Policy of calling upon Irish MPs to abstain from attending the imperial parliament was justified as part of the new Sinn Féin Policy economically. Griffith claimed that as trading figures showed that Britain was claiming almost all of the yearly profits from Irish trading, it would be of infinitely greater value to Ireland than sending representatives to the imperial parliament to attempt to establish the identity of Ireland as a distinct economic and trading entity internationally by seeking to break the British boycott on direct Irish trade with the international community.[113] Tory opinion, represented by Craig and Samuels, was not so sure about Griffith's claim about the possibilities of international trade. For example, Samuels lamented that 'since 1825 there has been no records kept of Irish imports and exports' owing to the abolishment of separate customs boards for Ireland. Although Plunkett's Department of Agriculture would begin publishing during 1906 'for the first time a report on the trade in imports and exports at Irish ports', the reliability, as well as the source, of this information and what it actually meant for the economy of Ireland was totally unascertainable. This was because

> There is at present no means of accurately distinguishing from the colonial and foreign trade of Great Britain, the indirect colonial and foreign trade of Ireland which passes to and from Irish ports through those of Great Britain, especially Liverpool and London ... The consequence is that the total trade of Ireland with countries outside of Great Britain cannot be at present definitely ascertained.

This very uncertainty was Craig and Samuels' motive for continuing to uphold the Union. This mentality was reflected by Samuels' decision to accept on faith that the overall figures for British imperial trade were so positive that 'Irishmen, too often prone to pessimism', should think optimistically about 'the opening markets of today and of the years to come'. Furthermore, as 'by far the greatest part of our commerce is, and always will be, with Great Britain and care must be taken that this shall be developed and not diminished', it was not necessarily opportune 'to be looking on their country as an impoverished island' or to be considering the necessity of opening wider markets.[114]

Britain was the only country in Europe that could neither feed its own population nor provide the raw material for its manufacturing industries without imports. This was why Griffith was correct in pointing out that every European economy except Britain's (and, by default, Ireland's) encouraged the greatest possible degree of international trade without depriving their country's industries from protective tariffs. Protective tariffs were also *the* lever of negotiation in all contemporary international relations. In this way, ever since 1892, the French and Germans were eclipsing the British in economic power, forcing Britain to rely more on trade with its own colonies than trade within Europe (although this trend was also being emulated to a lesser extent by most other European nations). It was for this very reason, however, that Griffith's idea of developing an extensive Irish trade with the European continent—something that the British could not manage—could appear quite absurd. In addition, no matter how much tariff barriers to trade were erected or dismantled within Europe, the economies of all small independent European nations remained virtually co-dependent with the economies of their larger and stronger neighbours.[115] Partly for this reason, Irish unionists considered that an independent Ireland was not inherently necessary and an idea that was actually best dismissed altogether. In effect, alongside with the Irish Party, it was considered that Griffith's politics could not be profitable. As a result, Griffith's politics were not adopted and his personal profits remained slim.

Being an Irish nationalist, Griffith deemed Ireland to be politically backward due to its failure to grasp that every country's political and economic development was inherently rooted in resistance to any centralisation of power that was not in its own self-interest.[116] In making such arguments, Griffith was fully aware of the 'propagandist nature' of what he wrote.[117] An ideological bent existed within all aspects of (supposedly impartial) contemporary writings on political economy,[118] and it was Griffith's ideological nationalism which inspired his claim that he made the arguments which he did only because 'I could induce nobody else to say what I believed if left unsaid would cause the nation to rot.' Another reflection of Griffith's ideological nationalism, or indeed republican frame of mind, was his argument that 'the truisms of life elsewhere' had become 'novel doctrines in a country where the elemental rights of the citizen had ceased to be understood'.[119] To some extent, in keeping with the Young Ireland tradition of the 1840s, Griffith's patriotism was also essentially a matter of seeking to claim for Ireland a right to a national self-determination as strong as Young Englander Tories within England had once claimed for their own country. However, the dynamics to Irish party politics and, in particular, their material foundation, made it virtually impossible to advance such ideals beyond their first, or purely propagandist, base. The first five years of Sinn Féin's existence provided clear indications of why this would remain the case.

CHAPTER FIVE

The Stillborn Party: Sinn Féin (1906–10)

T.W. Rolleston, an Irish Tory patron of Horace Plunkett's cooperative movement, wrote to Lady Aberdeen regarding Griffith's Sinn Féin Policy that he believed 'unless the parliamentary movement can offer on its side a programme equally clear, honest and self-consistent, it must inevitably go down before its antagonist'.[1] This perspective reflected an appreciation for Griffith's capacity to engage constructively with Tory politics. As was being demonstrated by the career of William O'Brien MP, however, this was also a recipe for political ineffectiveness in Ireland. Griffith would promote his programme by arguing that 'the Unionist or the Parliamentarian need not be exceeded in patriotism by the Sinn Féiner. Of the nation they are equally units with equal duties and rights'.[2] This was practically an admission, however, that the 'unionist' and the 'parliamentarian' had no real need for a 'Sinn Féiner'.

The intended status of the National Council as a platform for defectors from all other parties necessitated that Griffith targeted all corners. Frequently, however, he ended up winning none because of the absence of a credible political leadership, or party base, for the National Council. Its chairman Edward Martyn (one of the 40 per cent of the Irish landed gentry who were of the Catholic religion) was an enthusiastic member of the landed gentry's Kildare Street Club.[3] He was widely considered to be a mere eccentric, with a greater enthusiasm for Our Lady's Choral Society and the Abbey Theatre than for politics. John Sweetman was a very wealthy and thereby influential individual, but he had little prospect of escaping from his semi-retired political standing. This was because the Irish Party and the United Irish League was irrevocably committed to ostracising him from public life. Party politics was definitely not Sweetman's forte. There was also the problem that the two planks in Griffith's platform—the Gaelic League and the Industrial Development Association (IDA)—not only represented myriad interests but their leaders also tended to dismiss Griffith as a man who was attempting to hijack these organisations for his own purposes.[4] This resistance prevented Cumann na nGaedhael from ever becoming a vibrant political movement.[5]

The Cork nationalists who initiated the IDA, Terence McSwiney and Liam de Roiste, read and occasionally contributed to Griffith's journal but politically they worked with Irish Party activists. These included J.J. Horgan (vice-president of the Cork Gaelic League) and J.P. Boland MP. These two men were responsible for persuading the Imperial Board of Trade in London to register the official trademark of the IDA (*Deánta i hÉireann*), thereby putting it on some solid political footing.[6] William O'Brien and T.M. Healy, each of whom had political connections with some small to medium-sized business owners, as well as Tory ('liberal unionist') landlords such as Lord Dunraven and Captain J.S. Taylor, gave the IDA some footing in Munster, while it also had the sympathy, if not the active support, of both the Ulster loyalist *Belfast Newsletter* and the managers of the Harland & Wolff shipbuilding firm in Belfast.[7] As Griffith hoped, the IDA planned to gather data on Irish industrial and natural resources. However, at its conferences it emphasised to Griffith's dismay that it considered agriculture as inherently Ireland's primary industry and that it had no desire to change this situation. This reflected the IDA's status as a British government-approved body.[8] Griffith's desire that Ireland could become an agricultural-manufacturing nation was inherently made impractical by the fact that a strategically planned import campaign would be necessary to facilitate this goal but the practical non-existence of Ireland as a distinct legal and economic entity gave Irishmen no basis upon which to build. There were also ideological reasons for the unpopularity of Griffith's programme.

The writings of Griffith's Irish contemporaries were essentially characterised by a prevarication between the options of seeking funding for state or voluntary (church-centred) bodies. Horace Plunkett championed the state-centred approach in his book *Ireland in the New Century*. Monsignor O'Riordan of the Irish College in Rome wrote a popular antithesis *Catholicity and Progress*. Cultural nationalists like George Russell dedicated their writings to both quarters. All, however, generally ignored the Sinn Féin Policy, which was deemed impractical because it was proactive in a way that was too contrary to both the government's plans and established practice.[9]

The fear of challenging the government encouraged most to remain silent or neutral in matters of policy, as if policy formation was inherently the sole prerogative of the imperial civil service as the Irish question in British politics unfolded. Reflecting this, most Irish writers focused almost exclusively on ethical considerations of modernist trends in education and their role in shaping a collective sense of values. No alterations of existing financial norms were either envisioned or proposed. For instance, in 'sufficiency indicating the general spirit in which I would have Irish education recreated', Patrick Pearse of *An Claidheamh Solus* (a supporter of voluntary education) was simply following a long-established trend in *The Murder Machine*, as in all his subsequent writings, by emphasising that 'I say little of organisation, or mere machinery. That is the least important part of the subject.'[10] To focus on ends and means, as Griffith had done and kept suggesting, would have entailed questioning the role of all existing financial institutions within Ireland, as well as the wealth of the Protestant and Catholic Churches, but nobody was prepared to do this. In this way, one might say that the dynamics of Irish party politics under the post-1886 consensus was as much a bastion of conservative inaction as Buckingham Palace and the Vatican.

The Catholic Church's mission to combat state control of education was facilitated by the semi-independent status of Dublin Castle's National Board of Education. This, in turn, formed the essential context for all the Gaelic League's activities. The league's status as a voluntary body reflected the bishops' desire for comparatively weak and dependent Irish public representatives, as well as the nature of the Gaelic League's relationship with the civil service. Indeed, its voluntary ethos (whatever influence notable league members had was supposed to be exercised only as individuals) was practically guaranteed by the fact that half the Gaelic League's membership was junior civil servants. On this particular question, Griffith was the victim of a common form of myopia. He fantasised that the cultural nationalism of Gaelic League civil servants could prompt them to collectively decide to act against the British state, as well as counter the corrupting legacy of party-political brokerage in civil service appointments.[11] However, their cultural nationalism was essentially a manifestation of their desire for promotion within this same British civil service, which had facilitated this particular trend.[12]

Griffith's National Council could acquire no funding from the Gaelic League. At the league's annual fund-raising events (usually held on St Patrick's Day), Stephen Gwynn, a Tory supporter of Redmond,[13] and Eoin MacNeill collected all the financial proceedings. Meanwhile, Griffith's National Council associates and would be co-promoters of the Sinn Féin Policy (Aldermen Tom Kelly and Walter Cole, Seamus MacManus, Edward Martyn, James Connolly and Henry Dixon) were confined to representing only the league's 'Cumann na Leabharlann' (Library Club) in an associated parade.[14] As such, Griffith was still in a comparable position to what he occupied as the twenty-two year old chairman of John O'Leary's Young Ireland League; an organisation then typified by many

Irish Party supporters as a group for 'harmless crazy bookworms'.[15] Griffith's conflict with the leadership of the Gaelic League was subtle but perpetual. It was illustrated best by his attempt to present a call by Douglas Hyde for the finances of the National Board of Education to be managed locally instead of by the Imperial Treasury as a Sinn Féin stance and the categorical refusal of Hyde (an ally of Archbishop Walsh on the National Board of Education) that this was case.[16] The failure of the National Council to appeal to the Gaelic League ensured that the most critical determinant of the Sinn Féin Policy's chances of success was the nature of the business community within Ireland.

The landslide Liberal Party victory in the 1906 British general election was a source of much enthusiasm to the Irish Party. Considering the Liberals as their allies, Redmond and his party would even hold a special Westminster banquet for Liberal Party leaders such as John Morley (Cabinet Secretary for India, formerly Gladstone's Chief Secretary for Ireland), Lord Loseburn (Lord Chancellor of England), Winston Churchill (Colonial Under Secretary) and Augustine Birrell (Chief Secretary for Ireland) to celebrate their return to power.[17] The business community in Ireland, however, continued to be primarily Tory in politics. This was reflected by the IDA's fortunes in Munster and Belfast. Nevertheless, the Irish Party invariably celebrated the fact that Irish Tories 'in the councils of the English Tory party are an ignored minority ... wholly unable to deflect its policy to the advantage of Ireland.'[18] This was the Irish Party's justification for believing that the Liberal Party would ultimately ensure their material triumph over the Tories within Ireland and in the process defeat the 'Protestant ascendancy'. In doing so, the Irish Party essentially downplayed the significance of the fact that the Tories had been the authors of the home rule policy even more so than the Liberals and the Liberals were the initiators of the constructive unionism policy in Ireland alongside the Tories.[19] Strange to say, this reality did not hurt the Irish Party. A matter that did hurt the Irish Party after 1906, however, was that the Liberals were opposed to the Tory policy of the National Education Board supporting the Gaelic League. As a result, the controversy surrounding the English education act of 1902 would return with a vengeance after 1908 when a Liberal government took up the Tory policy of establishing a 'national university of Ireland'. Griffith appreciated the extent to which this trend in the politics of education could work to the National Council's advantage.[20]

The true significance of these trends in Irish Party circles for the Sinn Féin Policy stemmed from Griffith's consequent need to deal with the Tory business community within Dublin. Although it puzzled some of Griffith's friends, business figures in Dublin City Hall (associates of Crawford) actually helped Griffith in producing his economic-nationalist analyses.[21] The Irish Party, having allied itself to the Catholic Church and its property interests, had neither influence with nor much interest in the fortunes of the Chambers of Commerce in Ireland, but the nature of the Sinn Féin Policy was such that these financial institutions were central to Griffith's programme. This was demonstrated by the first effort made to promote the Sinn Féin Policy. This was to call for the nationalisation of Irish railways; an idea that Sweetman first championed, on Griffith's behalf, at a meeting of the General Council of County Councils.[22]

In support of Sweetman's Irish Financial Reform League, during the late 1890s William Field, formerly the independent parliamentary representative of Griffith's YIL, had advocated the establishment of a new 'commercial party' in Irish politics that would make the nationalisation of the railways its first demand. Field noted that railway nationalisation had taken place throughout Europe, the Americas and the British colonies (indeed, everywhere except the United Kingdom) because 'if the state does not manage the railways, the railways will soon manage the state' due to their centrality to business. Both manufacturing and successful trading in manufactured goods required cheap transit. However, the current English directors of railway companies within Ireland were charging very high rates for transit within Ireland and offering very preferential rates to British merchant-shipping owners and importers, making 'commercial success unattainable' in Ireland except to British-based firms.[23] Similarly, a contemporary French observer noted that 'all the productive capacity of Ireland [for business] is made barren by this inverted form of protectionism', favouring a centralisation of the country's commercial interests within Britain and effectively making the ports of Dublin and Belfast and the connecting Irish railways mere extensions of the Chambers of Commerce of Liverpool and Glasgow.[24] In terms of political representation, this was essentially why T.P. O'Connor was returned for Liverpool rather than Dublin and John Ferguson made Glasgow rather than Belfast his political home.

Field noted that it was cheaper to ship goods between Dublin and Liverpool or London than it was to transport goods within Ireland. As a result, the commercial life of Dublin, Belfast and all other Irish cities had become completely divorced from each other. Instead, each was totally dependent on distinct and private business connections in Britain.[25] If Dublin, Derry and Belfast faced a perpetual challenge in surviving as significant trading ports, the port towns of Drogheda, Dundalk and Newry had already entered into a reputedly terminal decline. Galway had ceased to be a significant commercial centre during the 1860s after the British government closed and never reopened its American trading routes (well-founded rumours existed that this policy would soon be extended to Cork in order to better facilitate the commercial development of Southampton), while Limerick had barely survived as a commercial centre. This had occurred only because James O'Mara, a son of the treasurer of the Irish Party who would soon defect to Sinn Féin, managed to make Limerick joint host with London of his successful bacon factory (a fact that had already given Limerick a somewhat derogatory nickname—'pig city').[26]

To reverse these trends, James McCann, the Louth-born Chairman of the Grand Canal Company, had joined with Field in calling for the 'local nationalisation' of all Irish railways and waterways. In this way, the transport companies could begin working together in promoting a common economic policy that was based upon a consideration of purely Irish business interests. In defence of this idea, McCann emphasised that the much-lauded yearly agricultural produce of Ireland, although larger (under current circumstances) than its manufacturing produce, was actually quite small in itself. Directly mirroring the state of the national economy of Britain (of which Ireland was being managed as just a small part), the yearly agricultural produce of Ireland was totally insufficient to provide for the needs of the Irish population. Instead, they were fed mostly by mass-produced English consumable imports that were produced using Irish exports. Ireland's annual agricultural produce was also smaller than the capital raised annually by the Irish railways alone. McCann argued that the managers of Irish transport companies should take the lead in demanding a cessation of the over-taxation of their country and, in turn, demand a greater investment of all revenue collected in Ireland in local business enterprises, including the meat industry. This should be accompanied by a deliberate alteration of their rates to favour Irish over British traders, as the combined effect of the inherently interrelated issues of commercial transit and national taxation practices were the cause of all Ireland's economic woes.[27]

McCann, a Dublin MP much admired by Griffith, died suddenly in 1904,[28] but his ally Field (MP for St Patrick's Division, Dublin) had recently been elected to Dublin County Council as a member of the Dublin Port and Dock Boards. In this capacity, Field supported Sweetman's Sinn Féin motion before the General Council of County Councils in October 1906.[29] The timing of Sweetman's motion was influenced by the fact that English railway directors, having recently created 'Tourism Ireland' in Dublin, were championing the idea of nationalising control of all Irish railways in London as a means of securing a total English monopoly over the expected future rise of a significant tourism trade in Ireland.[30] Sweetman, a lifelong shareholder in J.T. Pim's Great Southern and Western Railway, maintained that while the current management of the railways was destructive to Irish business interests, placing them in the hands of the British government (an idea first touted during the late 1860s, when Sweetman was a member of the Liberal Party)[31] 'would also be detrimental to Ireland'. The solution Sweetman recommended was that the railway companies should be brought under one management 'subject to the control of some body representing the people of Ireland'. He suggested that 'the General Council of

County Councils could be made use of as such a representative body, if no other representative body were formed'.[32]

As Sweetman himself noted, a major stumbling block to his own proposal was that the General Council, a creation of Sir Thomas Henry Grattan Esmonde MP, acted just in an advisory capacity. It had neither law-making nor coordinating powers over the local government bodies or their finances. Sweetman believed, not unreasonably, that the General Council, by potentially representing all local government representatives in Ireland, was far more deserving of state funding than the Department of Agricultural and Technical Instruction, which owed its existence as a Dublin Castle cabal to a single politician who had been repeatedly defeated at the polls: Horace Plunkett.[33] Sweetman's proposed solution to the problem of the General Council's lack of authority was to send a copy of his resolution to every local government body in Ireland to recommend their support for his proposal. He suggested that the rates collected by the county councils each year could be used as security for a long-term purchase agreement with the railways provided that they were first brought under a central management rather than the present situation of a multitude of separate boards of directors.[34]

In common with the shipping companies, most very wealthy businessmen in Ireland had some share in the railway companies although they were generally owned more by English than by Irish shareholders.[35] In addition to the shipping companies, the membership of the railway companies' boards of directors overlapped greatly with the board of directors of the banks within Ireland. Many of these men also served as chairmen of the (Tory) Dublin Chamber of Commerce. This placed control of the most important financial institutions of Ireland into a very small number of people's hands. All these people were located within Dublin, not the Ulster Unionist Party's heartland of Belfast or the Irish Party's political heartland of the provinces. Their families also generally intermarried rather than risk any dispersion of their personal wealth.[36] Reflecting this, it was significant that although James McCann, a respected Dublin stockbroker, had been able to give his views on 'the economics of the Irish problem' to the Bankers' Institute of Ireland (a body recently established by Andrew Jameson, the Scottish director of the Bank of Ireland and an active unionist),[37] this had evoked no actual response from such quarters. The Sinn Féin Policy was widely perceived to have its greatest potential support in Dublin (hence the use of Griffith's writings by Kettle's UCD society as a template for its own counter-propaganda).[38] However, the fact that 'Dublin does not lead Ireland as Paris leads France' made the assumption of the political leadership of Ireland from a Dublin base or, indeed, the development of an Irish nationalist politics, a virtual impossibility.[39] This situation was essentially the direct result of the extant banking arrangements of the 1820s.

The abolishment of the Irish customs houses during the 1820s progressively weakened the significance of the Chambers of Commerce in Ireland. Inevitably, this had an impact on Ireland's political representation as well. Irish politicians were powerless to champion the commercial interests of these institutions, while Irish businessmen were equally powerless to assist politicians in mobilising effective platforms. This was why, for instance, William Dargan (1799–1867), the chief initiator of the Irish railway companies, at no stage maintained an association with any Irish politicians.[40] During the 1900s, the competing demands for championing an industrial exhibition of Irish industry or an exhibition of British industry within Ireland was made meaningless by the nature of the country's financial institutions.[41] Inevitably, it was the latter option that was chosen (during 1907) and this resulted in the creation of new imperial parks and monuments in both Dublin city and Kingstown (Dun Laoghaire) to celebrate the prosperity of imperial (London-based) merchant firms that operated in Ireland. This prosperity, however, neither had, nor was going to be, reinvested, or kept, within Ireland.[42]

The 1907 industrial exhibition in his hometown was a blow to Griffith's programme. Ongoing religious divides within the Irish business community also evidently discouraged the formation of new commercial parties in Irish politics. For instance, in Dublin, there were many noted Quaker business leaders in the city. One of the most well known, the bookseller Alfred Webb, was, to his own admission, 'very much in accord with the Sinn Féiners', if they would avoid certain dubious, i.e. IRB, connections.[43] Ever since the 1870s, however, the Quakers, as well as many Catholics, had been deliberately excluded from the city's Chamber of Commerce, whose members were almost strictly members of the Church of Ireland.[44] This reflected the irony of Dublin Tories' passive support for Griffith's propaganda. They evidently valued it only because it assisted their own arguments against the Irish Party. However, as Samuels' career showed, they did not have the courage of their convictions.

On the question of nationalising financial institutions, Griffith realised that to speak of state ownership when there was no separate Irish government was contrary to his own definition of the potential benefits of nationalisation. He viewed nationalisation as a principle of government that was not inherently a good thing but merely a matter that suited current Irish needs, to resist the process of British centralisation.[45] The many impasses the Sinn Féin Policy faced on the railways question essentially paled into insignificance, however, compared to the obstacles facing the Sinn Féin Policy of nationalising the banks. Griffith's approach to this question reflected a major weakness in his reasoning. Griffith usually spoke of nationalisation not as a policy that began at the apex of the Irish commercial world, namely the banks. Instead, he spoke of it as a policy that began at the lowest levels of municipal or county council government and could somehow, in time, be impressed upon commercial elites.[46] This was unreasonable, however, because of the nature of party politics and local government bodies as they operated within Ireland. In addition, his National Council was subsidised by as little as £500 a year (or sometimes far less). On such a budget, the best the National Council could do was to issue propaganda or—as would be attempted in the wake of the 1907 exhibition—publish yearbooks of relevant statistical information while patronising small-scale Christmas exhibitions of Irish-made goods.[47] The very small scale of such enterprises made Sinn Féin seem ridiculous to many people.

While Griffith ridiculed 'Irish conservatism' as the 'ostrich policy', supposedly shared equally by Irish Tories and the Irish Party,[48] Sweetman's advice to Griffith that it was not their responsibility as Sinn Féiners to present any direct party political opposition to the Irish Party was an idea that Griffith accepted in practice, even if the tone of his propaganda very often indicated otherwise.[49] Meanwhile, Sweetman's deeply conservative Catholicism and his shareholding in the *United Irishman* certainly made it an increasingly conservative organ on social issues at least.[50] Often, there was little positive for Griffith to focus on politically. This prompted the publication of editorials on minor subjects such as single products as part of the 'buy Irish' campaign of the IDA or localised quarrels at Gaelic League events that were chaired by priests unsympathetic to the UIL. Any time potential supporters were elected to local government, Griffith would simply repeat the idea of establishing a national council of 300 representatives and present the UIL rather cynically (owing to the knighting of some of its local government officials) as an organisation whose chief function was to save British loyalists from political extinction.[51]

Griffith renamed his journal *Sinn Féin* in April 1906 in an attempt to capitalise upon Douglas Hyde's successful US fund-raising tour for the Gaelic League and the fact that one of the promoters of Hyde's tour thereafter expressed a desire to invite a Sinn Féin speaker to America.[52] Griffith expected to be invited. Instead, he was bypassed because of some of those same dubious associations that repulsed Alfred Webb from Sinn Féin and that Sweetman simply did not understand.

Griffith continued to promote the anti-enlistment campaign as part of the Sinn Féin Policy. He now justified this campaign primarily on economic grounds, noting that Britain's imperial wars during the nineteenth century—on the continent, in the Crimea, in Sebastopol, in Afghanistan, in Egypt and in the Transvaal—had never been a direct concern of Ireland, yet the country was forced to contribute many millions of pounds to these war efforts despite the fact that 'every pound of that Irish gold could have been better spent in Ireland'.[53] Simultaneously,

Griffith protested that while the police forces in Britain were subject, both administratively and financially, to the control of municipal governments, the Dublin Metropolitan Police (DMP) and the Royal Irish Constabulary (RIC) were governed directly by Dublin Castle, which was not responsible to Irish municipal authorities, yet these same municipal authorities were forced to issue, collect and pay the taxes for the upkeep of these police forces.[54] These were effective criticisms of the dynamics of the highly centralised and unaccountable nature of the imperial administration at Dublin Castle. However, other men promoted the anti-enlistment cause in a very different manner.

In October 1902, to mark the end of the Boer War, obscure Trinity College students founded a new 'Dungannon Club' of the IRB. It called *openly* for the formation of an international alliance of secret revolutionary organisations along anti-British lines in supporting anti-enlistment: 'a section of Russia, Ireland, India and China have partly together struck on this new policy', which 'must be applied … outside Ireland'.[55] This propaganda essentially reflected the survival of the Victorian tradition of an overlap between the worlds of Irish imperial war-correspondent journalism, Fenian propaganda and British intelligence programmes. Mirroring developments during the mid-1880s,[56] it also led an Indian politician to call upon Griffith, ironically with a request for an introduction to the leadership of the Irish Party.[57]

The Dungannon Club had recently been extended beyond the confines of Trinity College. With some passive support from George Gavan Duffy, a prominent London barrister who was curious about Sinn Féin, P.S. O'Hegarty, a Cork-born clerk, launched this initiative. Acting on P.T. Daly's orders, O'Hegarty replaced the elderly figure of Mark Ryan as the London IRB lynchpin and demanded that P.N. Fitzgerald retire in favour of his own brother Sean O'Hegarty.[58] O'Hegarty's instrument to spread the Dungannon Clubs was Bulmer Hobson, a young Protestant Gaelic Leaguer from Belfast who was popular with local cultural nationalists and also maintained an association with Sir Roger Casement, a British Foreign Office official of Irish Party sympathies who acted as his political mentor.[59] Hobson was chosen in New York instead of Griffith to represent Sinn Féin in America partly because Patrick MacCartan, the Dublin correspondent of John Devoy's New York *Gaelic American*, noted that Griffith was a relatively poor public speaker.[60] For the most part, however, it was motivated by Clan na Gael's need to establish new intermediaries with the IRB.[61] Acting under P.T. Daly's direction, the IRB officially declared itself a supporter of the Sinn Féin Policy in April 1906 to facilitate Hobson's tour, yet it *rejected* Griffith's emphasis on the significance of the precedent of the Renunciation Act of 1783, whereby the imperial parliament was denied the right to legislate for Ireland.[62] This was an inconsistent position.

The fallout of Hobson's American tour was the establishment of *The Republic* (Belfast). This short-lived journal of the Dungannon Clubs maintained that Irish nationalists' battle should be 'not with England, but with the people of Ireland—it is the battle of self-respect ... against the moral cowardice, the slavishness, the veneration for any authority however and by whoever assumed—that have marked the people of this country for generations.'[63] Behind this republican moralising and revolutionary posturing, however, was a practical refusal to support Griffith in his desire to win Irish Party defectors over to the National Council (*The Republic* declared the Sinn Féin Policy's emphasis on local government representation to be futile).

One legacy of the Anglo-Irish consensus of 1884–6 was the rapprochement between the Irish Party and Dublin Castle actually coincided or perhaps even *led* to a rapprochement between the Irish Party and the IRB.[64] The latter moribund organisation had operated on an essentially caretaker executive since October 1902. This was financed on Mark Ryan's behalf by the equally elderly figure of Robert Johnston of Belfast. On the suggestion of Seamus MacManus (Johnston's son-in-law) in America, Johnston and his followers had tried to mobilise the Irish AOH organisation behind the Sinn Féin Policy instead of the Irish Party, but P.T. Daly responded by expelling Johnston and his followers from the IRB and also misappropriated American funding rather than let it reach Griffith's hands.[65] John Redmond, while keeping a close watch on Daly, employed F.B. Dineen, a controversial leader of anti-enlistment movement within the GAA,[66] to act as a Sinn Féin mole on behalf of the Irish Party.[67] This IRB obstructionism helped to ensure that Griffith was not able to capitalise upon the greatest political opportunity that came his way at this time, namely the possibility of many defections from the Irish Party to the Sinn Féin Policy after Redmond and Dillon gave their support to Chief Secretary Augustine Birrell's deeply unpopular Irish Council Bill of May 1907.

As a permanent settlement of the question of Irish self-government, Birrell proposed making the heads of a few select departments within the Dublin Castle administration open to public election. The Irish Party's more youthful members reacted by expressing doubt about the leadership ability and political judgment of the senior ranks of their party in their acceptance of this plan. In the recent past, John O'Donnell MP, general secretary of the United Irish League, had demonstrated some sympathy with the National Council idea, although the assistant secretary of the UIL continued to label it 'the Sinn Féin Humbug'.[68] Several prominent backbenchers now expressed a willingness to defect from the Irish Party to Sinn Féin.[69] The most significant of these was James O'Mara, a leading Irish businessman who was the son of the co-treasurer of the Irish Party alongside Patrick O'Donnell, the Catholic bishop of Raphoe. O'Mara had been expected by John Redmond to become a senior party member. Instead, he would soon resign from Westminster, choose to financially support Griffith in promoting the Sinn Féin Policy and encourage further defections from the Irish Party.[70] This necessitated a direct response from Redmond regarding the Sinn Féin Policy.[71] Meanwhile, John Dillon re-emphasised the necessity of strengthening the Irish Party's control over the press, noting to Redmond that 'I do not believe it is possible to maintain the Irish Party without some newspaper [the *Freeman's Journal*] in Dublin.'[72] Redmond himself judged that he had two challenges: first, the perpetual one to preserve Irish Party unity ('my chief anxiety ever since I have been Chairman of the Irish Party') and, second, to meet the general feeling in the country that 'a great effort should be made to get all of Ireland into one movement—O'Brienites, Healyites and Sinn Féiners—and that the Party is strongest and most representative body to do this'.[73]

The fact that Sinn Féin prioritised local government representation as its political platform led Redmond to blame the rate-collecting county councils for all Ireland's economic woes, including a failure to address the question of over taxation. Griffith retorted that 90 per cent of the taxes collected in Ireland stemmed from the Imperial Parliament's indirect taxation on goods and services rather than county council rates. He also emphasised that the revenue collected from indirect taxation in England was necessarily granted by law to the local authorities every year in order to improve the services of municipal authorities and to promote local business enterprises, but in Ireland this revenue went directly into the imperial exchequer with no legal provision for any return to Ireland. The local government bodies had no authority or say in this matter. As a result,

> The British tax gatherer sits in every dining room in Ireland and stands behind the counter of every public-house, grocery and tobacconists in the land…This has been done and is carried on under the direction and superintendence of an old gentleman living at Rathfarnham, outside Dublin, and known as Sir Robert Holmes. This man is the British Treasury Remembrancer in Ireland and the real governor of the country.[74] The Aberdeens and Birrells [the Lord Lieutenant and Chief Secretary at Dublin Castle] who loom so large in the public eye are merely the screen behind which men like Holmes carry on the financial plunder of Ireland, as are the three Englishmen, Pittar, Parry and Crawford, who rule the Custom House interdict upon direct trade between Ireland and the Continent. Ireland has got to realise who her real governors are and direct her blows at them.[75]

Griffith was here highlighting the often only nominal powers of the 'Irish' executive, as well as its departments, at Dublin Castle. This was due to extent of its subordination to the Imperial Treasury in London in all matters of governance; a situation launched by Gladstone's civil service reforms of the mid-nineteenth century.[76]

Redmond responded by ridiculing the idea that the Dublin Castle administration's policy was 'the financial plunder of Ireland' on the grounds that the British government had generously granted Ireland with various monies. Griffith pointed out, however, that 'every penny expended by the British Treasury in Ireland is raised out of Irish taxation' and that the land annuities were issued as long-term loans at significant interest rates, not as grants, despite the fact that these loans were only small fractions of the Irish revenue that should have been expended annually in Ireland regardless.[77] As a genuine example of a British grant, Griffith cited Gladstone's granting of £4,000,000 to the Dublin Castle administration during 1854 to offset the imposition of a special spirit tax he had introduced to define the parameters of the Irish liquor trade, but in return for this one-off payment Ireland had since paid to Britain £109,250,000 in spirit taxes.[78] The reason why business and banking practices in Ireland were doing absolutely nothing to improve the material welfare of the Irish people, Griffith emphasised, was that 'Irish capital is locked up in English savings banks and there is no movement [of that capital] to keep the people in Ireland.' He emphasised that 'if that money were brought into play in the country it would mean the revivification of Ireland, industrially and commercially',[79] but Britain simply did not want Ireland to ever have the slightest capacity to become a financial competitor.

Sinn Féin made its strongest political showing during 1907 in north Wexford, where Sean Etchingham's *Enniscorthy Echo* newspaper and Sir Thomas Henry Grattan Esmonde, the local MP, declared their support for Sinn Féin. Griffith responded by speaking in support of Esmonde's re-election at a rally in Enniscorthy that was attended by 5,000 people. Although he had given lectures in private halls, this was probably Griffith's first-ever experience of open-air public speaking. Esmonde himself did not attend. He sent a letter to Griffith, however, in which he stated that although 'how far … my opinions coincide with yours I do not know', he believed 'we are back to our position of 1885' because 'parliamentary agitation, as now conducted, has spent its force' and, in the process, 'freed the hands' of Irish politicians to adopt a different course. He declared himself in favour of the repeal of the Union, as did the local leader of the UIL, who wrote to Griffith that 'I hope sincerely that Sinn Féin as a rallying cry will have more reality and more tangible results' than the Irish Party's rally cry of 'home rule'.[80]

The speeches of the Sinn Féin speakers present reflected the nature of the nascent party's support. The local activist Robert Brennan focused upon the significance of Esmonde's statement 'as striking testimony from the inside' of the political bankruptcy of the Irish Party's position. Alderman Walter Cole emphasised that 'in putting forward a policy different from that which had been generally accepted as the policy of the Irish nation [the Irish Party] for the last generation [since 1885] they did not presume to claim for themselves any monopoly of patriotism'. Together with Sean T. O'Kelly (who spoke in Irish), Alderman Tom Kelly defined the purpose of Sinn Féin as being a more stalwart defender of Catholic interests than Redmond's party could possibly be at Westminster. The most significant speaker was C.J. Dolan MP, who stated that he could affirm from direct personal experience of the imperial parliament the absolute truth of what Griffith had been arguing for years in his journals. Dolan noted that if the Irish public 'believed the *Freeman's Journal* they would believe that the British Parliament hung attentive on the lips of the Irish members, but what really occurred was this':

> They would be given one day to discuss Irish business … but when the expected day arrived they found the English and Scotch benches were empty … [Westminster treats] Ireland's affairs and Ireland's representatives with contempt … I will not continue to be a party to a policy which can do nothing for Ireland, but which prevents her, by raising false hopes in her breast, from doing something for herself.[81]

Griffith himself emphasised that, contrary to popular belief, Parnell's years of significant activity in Westminster were confined to just '3 or 4 years … [c.1877-1881 when] he found the weak spot in parliament and used that spot. That weak spot is now removed'. Even when Parnell was at his most effective, however, the Irish Party was 'as powerless to prevent England passing evil legislation for Ireland as they were to compel her to pass good legislature'. This was why the Irish Party could not point to a single piece of legislation over the previous thirty-five years as its own creation. Indeed, bills introduced by Irish MPs at Westminster almost never reached a second reading. Emphasising that Parnell was as unpopular with the *Freeman's Journal* and the rest of the Irish press during his obstructionist days as Sinn Féin was during the present, Griffith argued that 'the flowing tide' was now with Sinn Féin as it was with Parnell in the maiden years of his political career:

> The evicted tenants carried out the Sinn Féin policy in the Land League days … The idea about the necessity of sending men to parliament to force concessions from the English parliament is contradicted by

history. When O'Connell started his movement and won [Catholic] Emancipation, there was no Irish Party in the British Parliament ... I have known members of parliament, honest and patriotic men, who went into it good Irishmen and who came back from the House of Commons ... [regarding] every measure from the point of view of the exigencies of English parties and not from the point of view of the Irish people ... [yet the public] were told that when the Irish members left parliament, they were leaving the battle ground.[82]

Griffith maintained that as soon as the Irish public withdrew its representatives from the imperial parliament and supported the anti-enlistment campaign against the British army, Britain would be forced to abandon the unequal Anglo-Irish relationship that was defining the Union and allow Ireland the status of an equal. Suggesting that there was 'nothing wild' about the Sinn Féin policy, Griffith argued that if 'the Gaelic League gives Ireland a firm foothold in true Irish nationalism', 'the Sinn Féin movement gives Ireland a firm foothold in true Irish politics' so that 'a few years hence, men will wonder at themselves at having ever looked to Westminster for Irish salvation'.[83]

After James O'Mara (MP for Kilkenny) resigned from parliament, some prominent Irish Party figures wrote to him expressing their opinion that it was a courageous thing to do.[84] This was because, as was the case with John Sweetman's resignation in 1895, what was possible for O'Mara was not possible for most other party members: lacking his financial independence, they could not afford to do without their parliamentary salary.[85] Resigning from parliament would have meant the end of their careers in more senses than one, while few had the good fortune of the popular nationalist leader William O'Brien to be married to a wealthy Russian lady who had saved him from bankruptcy on more than one occasion.[86] The fact that O'Brien's wife was also Jewish even made him the subject of anti-Semitic rants by Irish Party supporters.

There was also the issue of party discipline.[87] Refusing to tolerate any opposition, the UIL had already responded to the Sinn Féin challenge by using its influence to demote Esmonde and Sweetman from their positions as president and vice-president respectively of the General Council of County Councils.[88] O'Mara realised the difficulty of this situation. While he contributed money to *Sinn Féin* (which still made a loss, under Sean T. O'Kelly's management, of about £130 in its first year of publication),[89] he encouraged C.J. Dolan (MP for Leitrim) to adopt a policy of parliamentary obstructionism within the Irish Party instead of resigning. This was because Sinn Féin did not yet have a credible political organisation. This would have been a constructive political strategy. It was also in keeping with Esmonde's sense of the political situation. C.J. Dolan, however, decided to resign (not suddenly, for 'as you know I took a long time to make up my mind as to the wisdom of the Sinn Féin policy')[90] and seek re-election to parliament in Sligo-Leitrim as a National Council candidate. This was despite the fact that the National Council ('Sinn Féin') did not yet have a political organisation outside of Dublin city council.[91] This was a foolish decision.

Reluctantly, O'Mara offered the funding for Dolan's election campaign but Esmonde, in the name of common sense, backed off and instead appealed to the UIL not to follow Dolan's example.[92] As a result, when Tom O'Donnell, one of O'Mara's closest allies in the Irish Party, moved in favour of the withdrawal of the Irish Party from Westminster at a meeting of the UIL Directory, only four present voted in favour of the motion.[93] Redmond's chief agent to defeat Dolan's election campaign was P.A. McHugh MP, editor of the *Sligo Champion* and close confrere of AOH president Joseph Devlin, the young MP for West Belfast, who rapidly became the political leader of Catholic Ulster after Bishop O'Donnell, the Irish Party treasurer, lifted the church's ban on membership of the Ancient Order of Hibernians (hitherto known derogatively to most Ulster Catholics as 'the Green Order'). McHugh assured Redmond that Dolan did not have the slightest chance as the Catholic Bishop of Kilmore 'has nailed his columns to the mast in support of the party'.[94] This fact ensured that all UIL branch leaders, being parish priests, worked to defeat Dolan, who did not poll well.

Although Griffith had believed that 'the party—or at least the majority—will not consent to withdraw from Westminster', he had intended in the run up to the Dolan campaign that Sinn Féin would attend a conference of Irish Party backbenchers that Tom Kettle was planning to convene to discuss all future alternatives for the party.[95] This was potentially a great opportunity for Griffith to present his case. The passive sympathy for Sinn Féin of Laurence Ginnell's Independent United Irish League in the midlands and the call of William O'Brien's *Irish People* in Cork (probably the most influential provincial Irish newspaper) for the creation of a new political movement that would reflect popular opinion by incorporating Sinn Féin also reflected the existence of significant potential.[96] However, at National Council meetings, IRB activists P.T. Daly and Bulmer Hobson started arguing 'for some reason I can't understand that the present [National Council] constitution permits the whittling-down of the national demand' and argued against attending Kettle's conference.[97] Noting that this stance was definitely 'not calculated to do good', Griffith emphasised that 'the platform of the National Council is broad enough for all Irishmen—whether they be republicans or repealers—and to narrow as a small number wish to the former only would make the Sinn Féin movement impossible of achieving its end'. This was because it would prevent it from making a persuasive case to the Irish Party and other political interest groups to join its ranks.[98]

The death of John O'Leary in March 1907 had led to the amalgamation of Cumann na Gaedhael (of which he had nominally been president) with the Dungannon Clubs under P.T. Daly's presidency. Daly named this group the Sinn Féin League. After months of republican obstructionism, it was not until late in 1907 that this Sinn Féin League and Griffith's National Council amalgamated and officially became known as the Sinn Féin Party. The first Sinn Féin Party Executive consisted of Edward Martyn as president, John Sweetman and Griffith as vice-presidents, Aindrais O'Broin (Andy Byrne) as general secretary and Walter Cole and Sean T. O'Kelly as honorary secretaries. Its Dublin-centred focus was reflected by the subdivision of its National Executive (at 11 Lower O'Connell Street) into 'resident' and 'non-resident' members, the former consisting entirely of inhabitants of Dublin. As the influence of the National Council representatives in Dublin city council (totalling seventeen councillors) far outweighed the importance of the Dungannon Clubs, the Renunciation Act clause was kept in the party's constitution.[99] This fact was of far less significance, however, than Sinn Féin's failure to develop a party organisation that summer when it was needed the most thanks to P.T. Daly.[100]

To mobilise enthusiasms, Sinn Féin would soon boast, unrealistically, of having the support of 'one-fourth of the whole population, despite the opposition of the entire daily press and misrepresentation from nearly every quarter'.[101] Griffith would later claim, alongside new supporters such as Sean Milroy (an English-born nationalist activist in Ulster), that it was Sinn Féin alone that saved Ireland during 1907 from the debacle that was Birrell's Irish Council Bill.[102] The Irish Party's decision to withdraw its support from the Irish Council Bill was certainly wise and opportune, but this was evidently motivated by the state of opinion within its own party alone. For instance, the Dublin Irish Party MP Tim Harrington felt confident in typifying Griffith alongside P.T. Daly and Henry Dixon as 'the representatives and the agents of [the American] Clan na Gael' and, upon this basis, suggested that they had 'no real grip in the city'.[103]

Notwithstanding Griffith's claim that there was 'nothing wild' about the Sinn Féin Policy, it was practically revolutionary in its logic. For instance, Griffith had suggested that while the British treasury gave £2,000,000 every year to the Irish poor law boards on the condition that they buy all their workhouse supplies in Britain, the poor law boards (consisting mostly of UIL members) could simply ignore this provision and instead use this money to purchase Irish supplies to boost Irish businesses, in the process reducing unemployment and ensuring less Irish people would have to rely on poor law aid or else emigrate.[104] In effect, he was talking about launching an immediate economic war against Britain. People could admire such ideas in theory but nobody was prepared to support them in practice.

One achievement of Griffith's propaganda campaign was to re-highlight discrepancies in the Irish Party political tradition. For instance, as had been the case in the past, its publicity body in Britain, J.J. Clancy's Irish Press Agency (established 1886), was often prepared to publish rational critiques of British rule in Ireland, including damning Griffithite criticisms of the system of over-taxation.[105] This was done to influence British voters into believing in the justice of Irish complaints. However, specifically before an Irish audience (and under the watchful eyes of Dublin Castle), the Irish Party and its press never did this from 1885 onwards (this being a condition of the Anglo-Irish security consensus of 1884–6).[106] Instead, it simply celebrated the legacy of Gladstone as the first man to introduce the question of 'Irish home rule' into British politics as a reason for the Irish public to have faith in the party's inevitable future success.

Griffith absolutely hated this trend, believing (with good reason) that it was serving to deprive the Irish public of any true sense of the realities of British and Irish politics or, indeed, recent history. The extent to which Griffith kept returning to citing Gladstone's career (he suggested that Gladstone's only actual legacy was that 'every man, woman and child in Ireland is owed at the present moment £90 by the British Exchequer—money fraudulently taken from you and your parents since 1853')[107] was motivated by his felt need to provide a wake-up call to Irish Party supporters. It was also motivated by his idealistic dream that both Irish Tories and the Irish Party could come together under the umbrella of the National Council if they simply accepted the fact that 'there is one platform on which Ireland ought to and should unite … the platform of financial redress'. Maintaining that 'so long as Ireland sends representatives to Westminster' it was giving assent to its own economic exploitation, he suggested that 'our policy—to stop the plunder of Ireland' was one upon which 'the Irish unionists still profess their willingness to combine with Irish nationalists … but only a United Ireland can win it an early and complete victory.'[108]

Once again, however, Griffith was essentially talking about launching an economic war against Britain that nobody was prepared to support in practice. For instance, it was technically true that, by law, no article could cost any more in Ireland than it did in Britain under the Union of 1801. British customs had simply ignored this law ever since Whitehall abolished Irish customs in the 1820s. As a result, every single Irish consumer was being subtly and illegally exploited financially on a daily basis for the past eighty-five years.[109] Griffith's idea, however, of 'a united Ireland—unionist and nationalist—responding to England's refusal to do elementary financial justice to this country by a policy of abstention from excisable commodities…causing her to lose involuntarily the money she will not voluntarily refund'[110] was not likely to find any support. This was because although it was true that 'all the productive capacity of Ireland [for business] is made barren by this inverted form of protectionism' by Britain,[111] the modernisation of the monetary, transport and commercial worlds had followed precisely this dynamic ever since the 1820s (and would continue to do so until at least the 1970s).[112] Therefore, no living figure within the monetary or business world, as well as the civil administration, of Ireland had ever been accustomed to anything different. This may well have been an unjust situation, but it was one that Irish people had been so long accustomed to accepting as a fact of life there was no evident wish to change it.

In economic terms, the Irish Party represented a primarily grazing farming-community that had developed since the famine because of the rapid industrialisation of England and the resulting creation of a British market for Irish cattle. Its support from the business community was confined mostly to small enterprises of shopkeepers and publicans whose business revolved around a localised economy based on market towns and a handful of successful distilleries (excluding Sweetman's and one or two others, these distilleries were usually owned by Tories, including James Craig's Dunvilles Distillery).[113] Even if the sons of such families studied to be barristers, politicians or priests (as they frequently did), they still had no say or, indeed, any great reason to be concerned with international trading or imperial taxation practices. These matters remained the interest, if no longer a prerogative, of the members of the chambers of commerce of Dublin, Cork and Belfast. From the 1850s onwards, however, such men generally did not stand for political election. Usually Tory in sympathy, they had silently consented to Gladstonian imperial fiscal trends.[114] Meanwhile, the birth of an Irish Catholic middle class at this time was intrinsically linked to a willingness to derive whatever personal profits were to be had by supporting the development of London as Ireland's business capital and, in turn, letting all those whose livelihoods depended entirely on local Irish circumstances go to the wall. It was not for nothing that the Irish people developed the reputation internationally at this time as the least patriotic and most slavish, or peasant-like, of political communities.

In Belfast, men who were likeminded to Griffith could hardly risk supporting his desire 'to place England in the dock' on economic grounds. For instance, the Ulster Unionist Party shared Griffith's preoccupation with the findings of Tory government's Financial Relations Commission of 1896. They would never support the idea of financial redress to the degree that Griffith suggested, however. As this would have been tantamount to declaring an economic war on the Imperial Treasury, it was feared that any attempt to do so would result in punitive economic measures that, potentially, would undo those financial arrangements by which London had recently turned the small town of Belfast into a new city. Such punitive economic measures could also cripple southern Ireland's food and meat-producing firms for larger British traders. Indeed, it was hardly coincidental that Griffith's chief business allies, Walter Cole (a fruit merchant between Dublin and Liverpool) and James O'Mara (a bacon factory owner, with his business headquarters in Limerick and London), supported his idea of abstention from the imperial parliament but, like the Irish Party or (in practice) the Irish Tories, resisted supporting his taxation arguments.[115] This was because an economic war against Britain was a struggle that Irishmen could not possibly win. Why, therefore, did Griffith continue in pursuing such a seemingly futile course?

It would be hard to exaggerate the extent to which Griffith's political outlook was shaped by his status as a poor and lifelong Dubliner. The careers of his longest supporters in City Hall, Alderman Tom Kelly and the ex-Land Leaguer Jennie Wyse Power PLG,[116] would be defined by an attack of the city's housing and poverty problems.[117] These issues also preoccupied some ex-mayors of the city and budding economic analysts who likewise favoured major reforms of the Irish workhouse system.[118] Griffith was proud of them for producing credible Sinn Féin policy documents on these matters during the late 1900s.[119] Griffith himself, however, attributed the root of the existence of these Dublin socio-economic problems, which had shaped his whole life, directly to the imperial treasury's government of Ireland.

As a historical proof, Griffith argued that the Irish quit and crown rent which had been collected for the city's upkeep 'and had been used to provide Dublin with fine streets and sweep away the slums etc.' was misappropriated by the imperial treasury and 'used for the beautification of the English metropolis [London]' instead. This had frustrated, for example, a scheme of the Dublin Corporation during the early 1850s 'for the sweeping away of the Dublin slums, and their replacement by great streets and avenues', 'drawn up by Engineers and Architects of the Corporation … [and] unanimously adopted by the Dublin Corporation, then largely Conservative [Tory]'. This plan failed because when the corporation 'claimed from the English Government of the day the money due to Ireland for the Quit and Crown rents for this purpose', 'the Government refused to give it back'. Lacking any means of appealing this decision, the corporation's members not only abandoned such schemes for improvement but the corporation as well,[120] letting the city itself go to ruin. These monies were still technically the property of Dublin citizens each and every year, but the corporation ceased demanding its right to such funds from about 1858 onwards and, by now, they were almost completely forgotten about:

> This is the cause of the present state of affairs … It is owing to this that Dublin housing for the poor is in such a condition … The people should know this. *The World* [my italics] should know this, for England in her propaganda pointed to the Dublin slums

[compared by some contemporaries to the situation in Calcutta or Saint Petersburg] as a proof of Irish incapacity and corruption. The tables should be turned on her ... The corporation again should put this matter forward, claiming that stolen money ... showing that Dublin slumdom is the creation of English robbery.[121]

Griffith's distaste for the Irish Party was certainly partly inspired by its predominantly rural representation. If an Irish parliament ever came into being, Griffith desired that its urban representation would be increased at the expense of its rural.[122] Although not a political woman,[123] Griffith's fiancé Maud Sheehan, a fellow Dubliner, also resented the fact that the tenor of Irish politics under the Irish Party's electoral hegemony was often designed to 'make one think how dreadful we [Dubliners] were not country people' and so were somehow not deserving of consideration or perhaps even be considered as being truly Irish.[124]

By the beginning of 1908, Griffith had spent four years addressing the heart of Anglo-Irish relations in a direct and—at least during the Irish Council Bill controversy—particularly relevant way. R.M. Henry, an Ulster Tory academic in Queen's University Belfast and an associate through the Gaelic League, credited Griffith for having 'stamped upon every column he wrote his intense and vivid sense of truth' as well as a 'great gift of discerning what was essential and of holding to it without faltering'.[125] However, within months of the fading of the Irish Council Bill controversy, which had seemingly guaranteed that Sinn Féin would win many parliamentary supporters, the material dynamics underlying all existing forms of Irish party political networking (or ostracisms, as the case may be) had provided Griffith with no new supporters, or political associates, other than a few dozen IRB conspirators who liked to attend public nationalist lectures and who congregated around a tobacconist shop in Dublin city centre that had been newly opened by Tom Clarke, an ex-political prisoner (and former manager of the *Gaelic American*) who had recently returned from America.

Sinn Féin was being used for some ulterior motives. For instance, F.H. O'Donnell used the existence of the Dungannon Clubs within Sinn Féin as a cover for approaching the Austro-Hungarian government, falsely claiming to represent Irish revolutionaries while under the watchful eyes of the British Foreign Office.[126] Meanwhile, Sir Roger Casement's friend Bulmer Hobson was writing pamphlets which argued in direct opposition to Griffith's programme that the Sinn Féin Policy 'is in reality war' that necessitated physical violence and a 'simultaneous application in Ireland, India and Egypt'.[127] It would have been difficult to imagine a more absurd hypothesis.

Griffith did acquire a couple of notable new associates from the revolutionary underground at this time. These were Sean Milroy, who became a fellow student of the economic basis of Anglo-Irish relations, and Sean MacDermott, an ex-school teacher who replaced P.T. Daly as Sinn Féin's national organiser. MacDermott was a very energetic organiser who did all he could to network Sinn Féin's supporters into new party branches.[128]

During 1908, Griffith hoped to make his mark on the Irish university debate. He desired 'that a faculty of Irish studies be established in the university' and 'that degrees be instituted in agriculture and economics'. Most of all, he hoped that a single national university under strictly non-denominational management could be established to prevent north–south and religious polarisations from dominating Irish life. For this reason, Griffith welcomed the British government's idea of creating a national university under non-denominational management, but felt that the university bill would create problems by separating the management of the universities of Dublin and Belfast.[129] Understanding that the Catholic hierarchy's extant loyalty to the Irish Party had led to C.J. Dolan's defeat, Griffith also realised that the Sinn Féin Party needed a more effective president than the indifferent figure of Edward Martyn. He was glad, therefore, that John Sweetman, a man who knew the hierarchy intimately, agreed to become the new Sinn Féin president during 1908. Sweetman, however, reacted to the university debate in a manner directly contrary to Griffith.

Sweetman warned Griffith that he must not under any circumstances make arguments in the press that criticised the principle of denominational education.[130] Griffith wished that Sweetman would see that there were broader issues at stake with regards to university education, noting for example that 'Archbishop Walsh, I hear, disapproves of the Bill, but will not oppose it.'[131] These appeals fell upon deaf ears, however, because, unfortunately for Griffith, Sweetman was a lay Catholic obsessed with ideas of orthodoxy.[132] Equally, in deference to the bishops, Sweetman was highly fearful of taking any step that might shatter the unity of Ireland's Catholic political representatives. In warning Griffith that 'no party can succeed in Ireland to which the priests are actively hostile' and that 'anti-clericalism would destroy the Sinn Féin Party',[133] Sweetman clearly equated criticism of the principle of denominational education upon any grounds to be tantamount to an intolerable anticlericalism. Aside from suppressing James McCann's *Peasant*, Sweetman once even considered using his influence to have *An Claidheamh Solus* shut down when its editor Patrick Pearse (himself something of a religious fanatic)[134] passed a comment about Daniel Mannix, the president of Maynooth College, that Sweetman considered to be possibly non-deferential in its implications regarding the church's unquestionable right to have complete control of education.[135] For this very reason, Sweetman was no doubt being deadly serious when he warned Griffith that *Sinn Féin*'s days would be numbered 'if you make your paper, like Mr. [W.P.] Ryan's *Peasant*, an organ of anti-religious education'.[136]

As soon as the university question entered the limelight, Griffith received many appeals from a section of the Gaelic League, including some UCD students, to turn *Sinn Féin* into a daily paper that would support their call to make knowledge of the Irish language obligatory for entrants to the new university.[137] Although a sincere demand, this development was partly a mere political by-product of the Liberal government's past withdrawal of the National Education Board's support for the Gaelic League. Fr O'Hickey, the professor of Irish at Maynooth College, instigated this compulsory Irish demand, making him a temporary icon for many young Gaelic Leaguers. While his highly publicised adherence to this stance in defiance of his ecclesiastical superiors may have ultimately cost him his professorship, it served a different purpose politically. In particular, by causing debate on the implications of the exclusion of Queen's College Belfast and Trinity College Dublin from the proposed National University of Ireland to be silenced, it focused the public eye instead upon a man whose only public responsibility was to teach Irish to young Catholic seminarians. Considering that the Irish Party 'will do nothing unless a public opinion is moved in this matter' and that its inaction could augment divisions between the Dublin and Belfast universities by denying to the former the right 'of fixing its own courses and subjects of study',[138] Griffith took up the compulsory Irish demand to increase Sinn Féin's popularity with the Gaelic League. More fundamentally, however, Griffith saw this as a means of attracting 'Irish-American capital' to Sinn Féin in the light of the prior promises that were made to Hyde by the American universities.[139] This particularly annoyed Hyde, who wrote to John Redmond that 'I wish very much I could disabuse people's minds of the false impression that the Gaelic League is connected with Sinn Féin.'[140]

Seamus MacManus of Notre Dame University would soon bring the president of the American AOH to Ireland in an attempt to make a Sinn Féin sympathiser the new president of the Irish AOH in place of Joseph Devlin, the young Irish Party whip. Both Maynooth College and Archbishop Logue of Armagh, the Catholic primate of Ireland, were evidently quite sympathetic to the Americans.[141] Be that as it may, realising that the Catholic hierarchy were not enthusiastic about the compulsory Irish idea, Sweetman warned Griffith that the future of Sinn Féin would become 'precarious' if he adopted this stance. Sweetman also pointed out sound political reasons why the idea of founding a daily paper was misjudged, aside from the obvious fact (with which Griffith agreed)[142] that he would be unable to raise the necessary capital (£8,000):

> People largely take a daily paper for its general news and don't
> mind much about its politics. A sprightly weekly paper would

have more political influence than a daily paper with a small circulation. A body of men who could get letters into the ordinary daily papers, read by everyone [a tactic favoured by Sweetman himself],[143] would have more influence than a special daily organ which would only be read by the converted.[144]

Nevertheless, Griffith persisted with the idea of founding a daily paper. He launched a daily edition of *Sinn Féin* in August 1909 with the financial support of Seamus MacManus, despite the fact that the National Council was already in debt of £200.[145] It would only last for five months and caused Griffith to fall into personal debt.[146]

Griffith's motive in taking this gamble was the seeming convergence of several political opportunities. First, in the wake of the Dolan campaign, Griffith desired to appeal to Sinn Féin's potential new followers among supporters of the cooperative movement in the Connacht–South Ulster region. To this end, Sean MacDermott formed several Sinn Féin branches in this territory while the daily edition of Sinn Féin (which did not adopt a propagandist tone) published market news relevant to the sale of immediate consumables, such as dairy products, on the Irish market. This was the first time such material appeared in one of Griffith's journals and reflected the daily edition's status as an actual newspaper. It was sometimes printed in as much as 60,000 copies (hitherto Griffith's weekly journals generally had a circulation of only one or two thousand copies). Although this circulation figure had dropped to about half by the time the daily folded, the weekly edition of *Sinn Féin*, which continued, managed to increase its circulation to about three or four thousand copies and to thereafter sustain this readership.[147] This was an unprecedented level of exposure for Griffith's arguments.

A second reason why Griffith gambled in launching a *Sinn Féin* daily was that William O'Brien's political supporters in Munster, who were independent of the UIL and had won the support of Terence MacSwiney's Cork IDA, were making a direct appeal to Sinn Féin to amalgamate with their ranks. This raised the prospect of Cork and Dublin municipal politicians allying themselves to form a new political party.[148] Griffith sensed a real political opportunity in the fact that O'Brien's group were being equally critical of Redmond for failing to oppose a proposed Liberal government budget that, potentially, would increase existing levels of over-taxation in Ireland by as much as £2 million a year.[149] A third reason for Griffith's gamble in launching the daily edition of *Sinn Féin* was that the future of the National University of Ireland was still far from certain and both the general membership of the Gaelic League and much of the student population of the country were far from pleased about this fact. This was a readership that Griffith acquired through the burst of publicity surrounding the launch of the daily edition and which he managed to retain thereafter, more or less, for his weekly edition of *Sinn Féin*. While this weekly edition of *Sinn Féin* retained its propagandist tone, its contents changed slightly. In the manner of established commercial newspapers, it now contained more regular news items as well as popular features such as political cartoons and even photographs to broaden its appeal.

To a significant extent the stated editorial policy of the *Sinn Féin* daily, which identified itself as a national rather than a party organ,[150] reflected Griffith's temperamental unsuitability for party political journalism. It also betrayed a degree of naivety. To Griffith, witnessing individuals who were 'admitting in private conversation that I am right whilst in public they are alleging the contrary' was not an inevitable feature of the rat-race contest that is political life. Instead, it was a 'kind of dishonesty I had thought was confined to a dying form of Irish politics'.[151] The *Sinn Féin* daily collapsed at the time of the January 1910 general election. This occurred because the eleven independent Irish MPs led by William O'Brien, by joining with Redmond and the Irish Party, were able to hold the balance of powers in the House of Commons by opting to keep the Liberals in power in return for a promise to introduce another 'home rule bill'. As a result, O'Brienite and, to a lesser extent,[152] AOH interest in Sinn Féin virtually disappeared. Recently established small Sinn Féin branches in the provinces opted to join William O'Brien's new All-for-Ireland League instead when that body was established in March 1910.[153] Along with his sudden misfortune in being struck down with polio,[154] this played a very significant part in decreasing Sean MacDermott's interest in attempting to sustain a Sinn Féin party organisation.

After the plug was pulled on the *Sinn Féin* daily edition, Griffith was fortunate that some assistance was offered to help him deal with the resulting liabilities by both William O'Brien's political supporters and appreciative Gaelic Leaguers. This assistance also had a personal dimension. In November 1910, a testimonial was collected for Griffith to enable him to buy a new home in Clontarf (costing £300) and to marry Maud Sheehan after a six-year engagement.[155] Not all contemporaries appreciated this, however. Mary Kettle (wife of Tom, the finance spokesman of the Irish Party) claimed that many people (although not her own husband) felt that Griffith did not deserve a penny, as he had formerly written that 'there is not a member of the Irish Party who would not sell his father's bones or his mother's honour for place or pelf'.[156] Indeed, on the balance, Griffith's caustic pen probably won him a lot more enemies than friends.

Griffith considered himself very fortunate to have been able to marry the woman he loved.[157] It was evidently an appropriate match. Frequently referring to Arthur as 'my boy' with 'the sweetest disposition', Maud was a woman with a temperament that was as equally self-possessed and forthright, as well as difficult and unworldly, as her husband's.[158] They also had a mutual fondness for quiet and private, rather than gregarious or public, social habits, such as playing chess, listening to music, planting flowers and going for long walks.[159] Their union would be blessed with the birth of two children. If Griffith had little personal reason to complain by the end of 1910, however, he had still much to do to find greater acceptance in the Irish political world.

Hitherto, Sinn Féin was essentially a stillborn party because its policy had been virtually impossible to implement and so existed only on the level of propaganda. Be that as it may, Griffith's principal protest since 1904—that Irish politicians were being dangerously cavalier in ignoring the centrality of financial issues to the question of Irish self-government—became particularly relevant to political debate after 1910. This was because the demand for a new Government of Ireland Bill converged with a fiscal crisis. The framework of home rule was about to receive an unprecedented level of public exposure and definition. If there were any chance that Griffith would be able to make his voice heard in the resulting debate, it would undoubtedly rest in his capacity to highlight the devil in the details of Anglo-Irish relations and, in turn, win the appreciation of more established politicians for his arguments.

CHAPTER SIX

The Framework of Home Rule (1910–14)

The two principal British political parties—the Liberals and the Conservatives (Tories)—naturally espoused two different fiscal policies. This played a part in creating two different party-political attitudes regarding Ireland. In keeping with Gladstone's ideal, the Liberals desired that Ireland would be governed strictly in the financial interests of the British mainland by creating a colonial administration akin to that in Jamaica or New Zealand.[1] This was in keeping with treasury policy and so had virtually become an aspect of state that was necessarily accepted by all parties. At the request of Irish Tories, however, the Tories in Britain nominally espoused the greater investment of imperial funds in the government of Ireland to emphasise Ireland's formal status as an equal part of the United Kingdom.[2] Griffith considered the Tory policy as superior in principle but was also keen to point out that it was of no real benefit to Ireland because, on the whole, the Tories were regulated more by English than Irish considerations.[3] Tom Kettle, the finance spokesman of the Irish Party, agreed. Hence he claimed that 'there is one thing dazzlingly certain: in Irish finance, salvation is not of the Tories'.[4] The Irish Party's inability to shape a fiscal policy for Ireland was becoming a greater problem, however. As Griffith emphasised every week during the first half of 1910, the party's recent achievement of the balance of power in the House of Commons only served to highlight this fact. To keep the Liberals in power, the Irish Party accepted a budget that increased existing levels of over-taxation in Ireland (approximately £3 million a year) by a further two million pounds. This led to political condemnation not only from the (Tory) Dublin Chamber of Commerce but also from various potential Irish Party support bases such as all the commercial Irish farmer, licensed trader and hotelier associations in the country.[5] As a result, the exploitative elements to the fiscal management of Ireland could no longer be ignored by Irish politicians.

In reaction to this situation, some Ulster unionists pointed to the status of Tom Kettle as 'a marionette' of the Catholic hierarchy as proof that 'our Catholic countrymen do not really understand patriotism—that, in fact, the Catholic Irishman's idea of patriotism is simply the apotheosis not of his country but his Church'.[6] The status of the Catholic Church as an institution that was inherently independent from all states naturally made it completely indifferent to all economic matters except in so far as how it affected itself and, in particular, its independent communal responsibilities, such as the financial management of schools and hospitals. William O'Brien's willingness to give voice to the business community's criticisms of Redmond for refusing to acknowledge this fact was important because the Irish Party could not deny its relevance (hence Griffith's typification of O'Brien as 'Mr. Redmond's conscience').[7] However, the Irish Party itself simply rebuked these criticisms by arguing that it was totally unfair that 'The Party' (and according to its rhetoric there could only be one 'Irish' party) was being asked to conceive of ideas regarding finance or to 'make provisions for the future' because this was 'an error ... which casts the onus on the wrong shoulders. Not we, but the [Liberal] Asquith Ministry, are the Governors of Ireland.' Although temporarily an ally of the party, O'Brien was also ridiculed as an 'inconsequential man' for questioning whether or not the Irish Party was right in 'entrusting the whole financial future of Ireland to a secret treasury tribunal'.[8]

Erskine Childers, a Liberal Party imperial theorist, not only supported this Irish Party stance but also offered his assistance in defining it; a move that the party welcomed. Redmond was currently promoting the idea that Ireland's great destiny in the new twentieth century was to work with the diplomatic channels of the Catholic Church to assist in the better development of Anglo-American relations for the greater good of the British Empire worldwide.[9] Reflecting this, Childers championed what he described as 'the political Liberalism of the Church'. This was not a reference to liberalism, but rather the extent to which Rome was prepared to support this thrust of British foreign policy.[10] Childers admitted that the Irish Party's politics did not allow for any strategic economic thinking or planning specifically for Ireland, as the 'Irish members [of parliament] have not the elementary motives for advocating economy or even sufficient motive for far-seeing and constructive statesmanship on Irish matters'. Furthermore, 'the large majority are conscious of this fact...The mental habit of Ireland is to look outside her own borders for financial doles and grants and to completely disassociate expenditure from revenue.'[11] From the British point of view, this was the inevitable positive result of Liberal government policy regarding Ireland ever since Gladstone's imperial treasury reforms of the mid-nineteenth century.[12]

Ignoring the original terms of the Act of Union between the Three Kingdoms, Childers was absolutely categorical in defining Ireland as a colony ('we must build on trust or we must build on sand') and maintained that this was why the Irish Party must be supported.[13] He also noted that the justification for the idea of colonial home rule was 'a very old one and a very well-tried one in the history of the Empire'; namely 'to throw on a people the responsibility for their own fortunes' to help them 'understand the extent of its own powers and limitations'. Childers believed that this was the best way to encourage the Irish, of their own accord, to eventually mature from their present status as a colonised inferior race into becoming true imperialists that realised that the economic interests of Ireland's 'mother country', Great Britain, were the greatest safeguards of liberty in the modern world.[14]

Griffith's differences with Childers were fundamental on an economic level. He believed that not unless Irishmen had the power to formulate an economic policy purely in Ireland's interests, even if this was sometimes contrary to Britain's, 'we must remain poor and powerless':

> This condition of affairs renders our position unique in Europe. The study of economics with a view to their application to our needs and wants has never been encouraged in the Ireland which gave a father to modern political economy in Cantillon[15] ... Since Isaac Butt was Professor of Economics in Trinity College seventy years ago the national application of this half-science has been neglected in Ireland.[16]

All MPs accepted equally that the impact of British foreign policy developments on the imperial treasury's policy regarding Ireland must necessarily be accepted perpetually. This meant that for all intents and purposes (public posturing notwithstanding) all Irish Protestant 'loyalists' essentially held the exact same political perspective as the Catholic Irish Party. This was reflected by the fact that Irish Tories were now abandoning the Buttite idea that Ireland was still technically a distinct political and economic entity under the original terms of the Act of Union.[17] Tom Kettle generally emphasised the significance of the fact that David Lloyd George, the Liberal Chancellor of the Exchequer, was envisioning creating a costly new social welfare system and was even prepared to consider limiting the vetoing power of the opposing House of Lords to facilitate this. The Tories were unenthusiastic about this idea. However, both the Liberals and the Tories were naturally wholly united regarding the long-feared threat of German naval supremacy; a threat which had now become a reality and needed to be provided against financially. As a result, from the winter of 1910 onwards, the sole determinant of British governmental policy regarding Ireland became to maximise the potential Irish contribution to the costs of British imperial defence and, in particular, the exigencies of a seemingly necessary (and covert) British war mobilisation (a development that Griffith would later claim had already been underway, in the expectation of an Anglo-German War, as early as 1907).[18]

The disputes regarding Lloyd George's proposed budget led to the holding of a second British general election during 1910, which saw the balance of power virtually unchanged in the House of Commons. It resulted in a significant shift in political debate regarding Ireland, however. Earlier that year, Griffith had judged that Sinn Féin had no need to contest the elections and that Redmond's unwillingness to support William O'Brien in opposing a budget that clearly could cripple Ireland financially must be politically damning for the Irish Party. In turn, Griffith expected the birth of a tradition among Irish politicians of engaging in strategic economic thinking or planning specifically for Ireland.[19] However, that winter the British treasury claimed—in a complete turnaround from figures revealed earlier that year[20]—that a very serious deficit now existed in the Irish contribution to the Imperial Exchequer which needed to be remedied and that this alone had to become *the* basis of all considerations of future political initiatives regarding Ireland. This announcement was made simultaneously with Prime Minister Asquith's sudden declaration than he intended to introduce a 'Government of Ireland Bill' a year hence based entirely upon this principle of fiscal management.

To Griffith's dismay, the Irish Party accepted these claims uncritically. In turn, the idea was touted to create Irish volunteer forces for the sake of the British war effort. Hobson's creation of a new IRB journal *Irish Freedom* was one response to this trend.[21] Its most significant manifestation, however, was Childers' recommendation to the British government the raising of Irish Volunteers, such as were already being publicly advocated in Ulster, precisely because the treasury had now supposedly proven beyond doubt that Ireland was 'costing more to govern than it subscribes in revenue and therefore contributing nothing in money to the expenses of the army, navy and national debt' at a most critical time. Childers also suggested that such Irish Volunteers should be maintained perpetually until such time as 'the return of Ireland to the position of a contributing member of the Imperial partnership' was made feasible, however long that may take.[22]

To justify the Liberal Party's stance on Irish finances, Childers was highly critical of past Irish Tory calls for increasing public expenditure in Ireland. He argued that it was an intolerable disgrace that the extraordinary poverty of Ireland was forcing Britain to pay out more money on insurance and old-age pension benefits than could reasonably be expected, as well as to subsidise by means of what he typified as a kind of 'state socialism' bodies such as the Congested Districts Board.[23] To put an end to this waste of British money, Childers, who had an invincible faith in Gladstonian fiscal doctrine, claimed that it was self-evident truth that 'the growth of the Liberal [Party] principle of government as applied to the outlying portions of the British Empire...support the principle of home rule for Ireland' along a definitely colonial line, akin to South Africa, Malta, Jamaica, Newfoundland or New Zealand. A federal solution akin to the dominion constitutions of Canada or Australia must necessarily be ruled out for all time because Ireland's close proximity to Britain would mean creating a new United Kingdom federation of parliaments purely for the benefit of the Irish, which was an absurd notion. Therefore, a colonial government linked to the United Kingdom by means of a form of external association was, in his view, the best solution for the Empire.[24]

In response to this British debate, Griffith was alive to the seeming impossibility of creating federal parliaments for the United Kingdom.[25] This was why he had argued in favour of a return to a debate on the original terms of the Union and, in particular, the principle of Anglo-Irish equality, stemming from the Irish constitution of 1783, that it embodied.[26] Hitherto, this had been an aspect of Irish Tory debate. A.W. Samuels K.C., who held an unofficial status as the finance spokesman for Irish Tories since the mid-1890s, continued to protest very strongly against Liberal fiscal policy regarding Ireland up until November 1910. Now, however, he suddenly changed his views. This occurred because Edward Carson, Samuels' successor in TCD politics, had just assumed the parliamentary leadership of the Irish Tories at Westminster and demanded that Samuels abandon his prior emphasis on economic matters.[27] Instead, at the request of the English Tory party, Carson deliberately diverted debate on the framework of home rule completely away from the essence of the issue, which was finance, onto questions of religion or even a supposed inherent threat of Irish lawlessness.

This initiative of Carson's was facilitated partly by a UK-wide debate at this time upon the cultural legacy of the British Empire. As Sweetman noted, within this debate, the Irish Party was being 'openly imperialistic' but 'the people do not seem to mind'.[28] Griffith's response to this debate was to argue that the Empire was a culturally alien concept in Ireland—a perspective then championed by many *Irish Freedom* contributors—but nevertheless the central role of British foreign policy in shaping Irish politics, both past and present, could not be ignored.[29]

Griffith argued that the brief period in history when Ireland exercised some real political and fiscal autonomy (1783–5) had been made possible only because developments in British foreign policy had made England temporarily powerless to combat an Irish determination to resist an English economic absolutism over the British Isles. According to Griffith, British foreign policy had impacted on Ireland since 1794 not in the manner of colonial evolution posited by Childers. Instead, Britain had sought to scare Irish politicians into surrendering more completely to English economic absolutism through political subterfuge. Frequently, this was done by forming and sustaining revolutionary undergrounds in Ireland to assist Whitehall gather foreign policy intelligence abroad and, occasionally, to cause uprisings in Ireland itself so that the public would look to Britain for protection. Notwithstanding his own republican background, Griffith maintained that this was a central dynamic to British governmental policy regarding Ireland ever since the days of William Pitt and was still the role of Ireland in British foreign policy in the present day.[30] This meant that Irish politicians could be absolutely certain that, as the next major European war approached, the British government would again promote sectarian disturbances in Ulster, in order to polarise Ireland's political representatives along religious lines, and use so-called revolutionaries during wartime to both cause a self-defeating rebellion in Ireland and to perform espionage work among Britain's continental and north American enemies. If history was not to repeat itself endlessly, Griffith argued, it was absolutely essential that those politicians who wielded most control over the wealth of Ireland made a definitive stand against English economic absolutism now. For this reason, Griffith appealed primarily to Ireland's self-styled 'unionists' to call for the creation of a coequal 'Anglo-Hibernian Empire' (an idea influenced by Samuels' TCD predecessor W.E. Lecky)[31] under a dual monarchy as the price for Ireland's support of England in the forthcoming European war with Germany.[32] Only if Irish Tories accepted the Sinn Féin Policy of an Irish economic nationalism, Griffith argued, could the ever-repeating cycle in Irish history of the exercise of English economic absolutism over the British Isles and the inevitable result of constant Irish political instability, perpetuated cheaply by Britain by means of revolutionary undergrounds, be finally and definitely broken.[33]

Griffith's provocative thesis was unique and it was meant to justify his claim that the Sinn Féin Policy provided the only possible means of ever advancing the ideal of Irish independence. Instead, however, it merely provoked a response from C.H. Oldham, a stalwart of the Statistical and Social Inquiry Society of Ireland. In the recent past, while president of the Rathmines School of Commerce (1900–8), Oldham had been a stern critic of Irish-Ireland attitudes towards industrial revival but on subsequently becoming professor of commerce at UCD he was generally considered to be a passive sympathiser with Sinn Féin.[34] Oldham rejected Griffith's provocative thesis on the grounds that the English Privy Council actually controlled all Irish legislation from 1495 until 1793. He emphasised that no English government had ever compelled Ireland to pay it taxes or to contribute to imperial expenditure prior to the Union of 1801, but the Irish parliament of the day, which Griffith had falsely presented as nationalistic, had always volunteered to do so anyway. According to Oldham, it was not William Pitt and the French War of 1793–1815 that had led Ireland into such a damaging position financially, but rather the fact that England's own system of financial regulation during that period was slightly chaotic. This had prompted fiscal miscalculations, such as that Ireland could afford to contribute a higher percentage of all British revenue each year than it actually could. This frequently bankrupted the country. This was why 'the Articles of Union' were 'waste paper so far as finance is concerned' but Britain had been content with these arrangements 'for at least as long as Ireland has yielded a net profit'.[35]

Although he had a different perspective on history, Oldham agreed with Griffith regarding the present. He supported Griffith in arguing that nobody could realistically claim there was a deficit in Ireland's contribution to British imperial treasury.[36] Oldham emphasised that while Britain was now complaining of a loss of £1.5 million over the past year, Ireland was still paying £3 million more every year than it could afford. He estimated that, to date, Ireland's true revenue paid into a common British treasury under the Union had exceeded what was expended locally by about £330 million, 'which I call the British profit out of the Union'. Therefore, 'the Irish nation must be incapable of learning any lesson from its past history' if it was not prepared to demand a comprehensive financial tribunal *now* to establish a regime of strict fiscal justice in the government's management of Irish finances. In a remarkable expression of optimism, Oldham even argued that the current situation could have 'no element of permanence more than any other swindle can have'. Without seeking to provoke the Irish Party, he also intimated that any debate upon the idea of home rule must be made by Irish political representatives to reflect that fact.[37]

This necessitated a response from Tom Kettle. In the light of Oldham's argument, Kettle now admitted that the Union, as it has developed, had led to the financial plunder of Ireland in violation of the original terms of the Union;[38] that no audit of the sources of British treasury claims regarding Ireland was possible and thus its claims regarding deficits could never be trusted;[39] and that Parnell and the Irish Party, in 'an offence to national dignity', had accepted Government of Ireland Bills by which an Irish parliament would hold no fiscal autonomy, thereby ensuring that 'our position will be merely that of an employee, doubtless not without remuneration … [which] may be irresistible'.[40] Nevertheless, Kettle still maintained that the only stance possible of Ireland on fiscal affairs was that of John Redmond. This was three-fold: to seek recognition that the only question raised by financial matters was a purely ethical or moral one; to raise the question of whether existing provisions for the financing of education in Ireland was morally justifiable on a politico-religious level compared to the situation that existed in England; and to see what might arise in the future from Lloyd George's recent suggestion to establish an Irish Development Fund.[41]

Griffith had recently called for 'a council on finance' to be established in Ireland.[42] Unlike Oldham, Griffith argued that a root of Irish financial problems was that banking practices in Ireland were doing absolutely nothing to improve the material welfare of the Irish people.[43] As a solution, Griffith had called for the establishment of a proto-national bank in Ireland, or else for 'the public bodies in Ireland' (such as the county councils) to persuade 'the existing banks … [to] play the part of national banks' by threatening to otherwise withdraw their accounts. In this way, without necessarily breaking with the (sterling) gold standard based on the gold reserves of the Bank of England, the liquidity of Irish banks could become localised within Ireland, rather than tied up in investments in British government stock, in turn encouraging the banks in Ireland to cease their longstanding practice of being 'willing to lend the money of the Irish people for British [business] purposes but not for Irish ones'.[44] To promote this idea, Griffith had launched the Sinn Féin People's Bank Limited during 1909 with some moral support from Terence MacSwiney's Cork IDA. Griffith promoted this bank by suggesting that it 'is successfully combating usury and offering equal inducements to depositors with those offered by the British Post Office Banks [a government-owned bank and the main holder of most ordinary Irish citizens' private savings] with the distinct advantage … that Irish money is available for Irish purposes only.'[45] Subsequent efforts to promote debate on banking in Ireland were quickly silenced, however.

During January 1910, an attempt was made to revive the Irish Financial Reform League that had been suppressed on the reunification of the Irish Party ten years previously but this initiative was crushed within a month.[46] That summer, to coincide with the relocation of the Sinn Féin Bank from Lower O'Connell Street to a new party headquarters at 6 Harcourt Street,[47] anonymously published articles that sternly criticised the Irish banking situation appeared in the *Statist*, a London economic journal. These raised a few eyebrows in high political circles and consequently John Dillon, the Irish Party leader, was determined to discover and silence the culprit. It appears to have been Griffith.[48] Meanwhile, the suppression of the Irish Financial Reform League, combined with the proposed Liberal Party budgets, led the Dublin Chamber of Commerce to argue that 'the Chancellorship of the Exchequer has fallen into evil hands'.[49] As some Irish bank directors were members of the Dublin Chamber of Commerce, Oldham and Griffith's idea of establishing a financial tribunal might have provoked a political response at this time if the will was present. However, the attention of the Irish Party, representing the majority of Irish politicians, was focused elsewhere.

In addition to its continued commitment to the Anglo-Irish security consensus of 1884–6, the Irish Party's determination to boost its profile specifically among voters in Britain resurfaced at this time. This was attempted by the publication of a highly publicised biography of John Redmond (written by his own cousin and publicised by Childers) to celebrate the supposed arrival of the Irish Party leader as a central figure in British political life. This book did not question Redmond's standing as *the* political representative of nationalist Ireland even though it quoted him proudly boasting that Irishmen could not survive economically for even a month if the country's politicians did not rely entirely on Britain for direction.[50] Combined with most Irish politicians' reliance on the church, this trend was why Childers celebrated that 'the strength and beauty' of 'the idea of home rule', as well as 'the vital energy on which its fruition depends', was both 'impossible to kill' and would soon 'place Mr. Redmond among the number of those who have saved the Empire from the consequences of its own errors'.[51]

Despite Griffith's best efforts, the Sinn Féin People's Bank had little more than a nominal existence as a cooperative bank. His concern with usury was in line with a broader trend within the Irish cooperative movement. This was the prevalence within rural Irish society of corrupt 'gombeen men' who acted as exploitative moneylenders; a trend made possible due to the comparative unwillingness of the Irish joint-stock banks to issue loans of Irish money to Irish people. As an ethical solution, Fr Finlay of UCD and Sir Horace Plunkett's Irish Agricultural Organisation Society had invited some English agricultural bankers to set up their businesses in Ireland. In turn, these Englishmen won the support of the Congested Districts Board for their businesses. This resulted in the creation of a federation of agricultural credit societies in Ireland after 1900, but these had already begun to disintegrate by 1909.[52] Griffith's hope to apply the principle of cooperative banking to both a rural and urban community environment was connected to his idea of establishing a joint 'agricultural and manufacturing union' in Ireland;[53] a goal which had been attempted, in vain, by republican Land Leaguers such as Thomas Brennan, Matthew Harris and Michael Davitt during the 1880s. This idea floundered once again after 1909 because William O'Brien's Munster-centred attempt to prioritise the business interests of market towns was little more than an effort to heal a longstanding Tory–Irish Party divide in Cork city council that had developed during the mid-1880s and which had governed his actions, as well as that of his old Cork fenian friends, ever since that time.[54]

Along with his ongoing efforts to establish contacts with Irish businessmen living abroad,[55] Griffith deemed the Sinn Féin Bank to be an initiative that was worth sustaining, no matter how disappointed he was at its results. Co-managed by Alderman Tom Kelly and his brother, the Sinn Féin Bank had a very small clientele that consisted almost exclusively of poor Dublin workers that were attempting to survive a contemporary housing crisis.[56] With minimal capital it could not be a competitive threat to well-established financial institutions, let alone a proto-national bank, although the establishment of new financial bodies could serve to challenge existing business practices of older institutions. Reflecting this, late in 1910, Griffith would add to his proposed Sinn Féin programme the idea of 'the foundation of a National Land Bank, subsidised to complete land purchase' agreements. His idea here was to ensure that the British government would not have exclusive regulatory authority over this process and to encourage the Irish banks to look more sympathetically upon the demands of tenants for favourable terms.[57]

Griffith's idea that the Irish county councils could promote the Sinn Féin Policy by threatening to transfer their accounts from the existing banks if the latter did not begin investing in Irish concerns did not win support from such quarters. The only cooperation with Sinn Féin (in the broadest possible sense) offered by the county councils related to the Gaelic League. This was the county councils' decision to promote the idea of compulsory Irish for matriculation to the National University of Ireland (NUI) by subscribing funds to the NUI to persuade it to accept this principle. This decision was made in June 1910, to take effect three years hence, during the same week as Sinn Féin (inspired by Alderman Kelly's opposition to the anti-Catholicism of the British coronation oath) worked to ensure Dublin city council would not pass a resolution expressing sympathy with the British Royal Family upon the death of King Edward VII.[58]

There was little or no appreciation for Sinn Féin within the NUI. Although Oldham, a distinguished graduate of TCD who was now at UCD, had been bold enough to express Sinn Féin-like dissatisfaction with Irish economic circumstances, Griffith was very disappointed by the general lack of initiative of NUI staff in such matters:

> When the National University was founded we hoped for something from that institution. It has a professor of political economy and a professor of national economics and a number of lesser instructors of the popular mind. Is it premature to ask when these gentlemen will begin to realise that there is a relation between economics in a university and the people outside?[59]

Griffith believed that the root of this lack of initiative was that the NUI's staff, reflecting Archbishop Walsh's chancellorship, were too concerned with trying to assume a personal social status to rival that of the employees of the historically more prestigious (and Church of Ireland owned) Trinity College. This was leading to appointments being chosen more on the basis of personal friendships, clericalism and party political influence rather than actual academic vision or merit. Although Griffith fully agreed that the NUI needed to aim to become 'a popular university', he deemed its manner of attempting to achieve this goal as fundamentally mistaken.[60] In turn, he judged that the mental outlook of the university and its staff was far too inward looking and self-congratulatory to be truly benefiting Irish society; hence, most of its graduates were still choosing to emigrate.[61] The NUI was only a nominally non-denominational university. The Catholic hierarchy, reflecting Archbishop Walsh's chancellorship, were generally allowed to act as significant political players behind the scenes, while both Trinity College Dublin (which remained in Church of Ireland hands) and Queen's University Belfast (which was governed largely by Presbyterians) remained separate institutions, thereby helping to cement north–south and religious political divisions on the island with the full support of Ireland's political and religious representatives and, of course, the British government, which funded the universities.[62] This was why the British government's decision, acting on the advice of Edward Carson, to treat the Irish question after 1911 purely in terms of religious demographics was a tactic that it could assume to have had an inherent Irish approval.

If Griffith's ideas were often interesting, they still disqualified him from being accepted by Ireland's professional classes. Gaelic League stalwarts Eoin MacNeill and Douglas Hyde not only considered Sinn Féin to be a complete non-player but had also acquired NUI professorships by playing ball politically through maintaining a working political relationship with both the Irish Party and the Catholic hierarchy. By contrast, Griffith, rather like Patrick Pearse of *An Claidheamh Solus*, had been left in a very precarious position, both financially and in terms of his career prospects. Reflecting this, John Sweetman decided to resign as president of Sinn Féin early in 1911 because Griffith had intimated his intention to do the unmentionable; namely, to begin criticising the religious communities in Ireland for ignoring the economic consequences of their purely selfish actions.[63] The withdrawal of Sweetman's support increased Griffith's financial difficulties in sustaining *Sinn Féin*. Griffith appealed in vain to Sweetman to reconsider his decision to resign,[64] while by the summer of 1912 it would become necessary for Griffith to consider mortgaging his newly acquired home solely to keep the paper alive.[65] Nevertheless, he stuck to his guns in promoting his Irish nationalist ideas.

While a party still nominally met under Griffith's presidency, the new Sinn Féin Party headquarters now served as little more than a lecture theatre for a rapidly declining party membership. Reports of branches dissolving were received regularly, although those who remained took some interest in Griffith's exploration of the theoretical possibilities of an Irish meat trade opening with the European continent, amongst other ideas.[66] However, even Griffith's principal supporters at this time, M.J. O'Rahilly (managing director of *An Claidheamh Solus*) and Eamon Ceannt (a fellow senior Gaelic Leaguer), did not actually make Sinn Féin their vehicle for holding public demonstrations. Instead, they chose to work with Sean MacDermott's new United National Societies Committee.[67] Although it did not involve an actual political opposition, this reflected a seemingly deliberate IRB boycott of the Sinn Féin organisation at this time. Around the same time as Sweetman decided to resign, the Dublin IRB distanced itself from Sinn Féin while the Cork IRB leader Sean O'Hegarty officially resigned as the local leader of Sinn Féin.[68] It is likely that IRB as much as Irish Party activists did not appreciate the arguments that Griffith had made recently regarding the role of the British Foreign Office in Irish history.

A great peculiarity resurfaced in Irish political debate at this time after Edward Carson organised a monster protest demonstration of Belfast Orangemen against the idea of Irish home rule on supposedly 'constitutional' grounds. There was both a logical and a disingenuous side to this stance. The logic in Carson's stance rested on the claim, rationalised by many British constitutional lawyers, that tampering with the Union in any way in the immediate wake of the Parliament Act of 1911 was far too sudden and radical an initiative to be contemplated. Indeed, the spirit of the 'unwritten constitution' of Great Britain dictated that the full legal implication of the restriction of the House of Lords' right to veto legislation was something that could not be realised for very many years. Upon assuming the leadership of the English Tory party in November 1911, Andrew Bonar Law, a Canadian-born advocate of economic protectionism for Britain, encouraged Carson to claim that the Tories would be acting in the true spirit of the constitution by establishing an Ulster Provisional Government, backed up by Irish Volunteers, if a Government of Ireland Bill was passed three times by the House of Commons purely in order to sabotage, or dismiss the constitutionality of, the same bill. This claim could not be disproved because the constitution was a superior principle to that of party politics, while advocates of this viewpoint could never be coerced into adopting a different position; at most, they could be persuaded to think differently through party political debate.[69] The cleverness and underlying purpose in this Tory stance was that by raising the issue of volunteer forces (and, by implication, the patriotic duty of facing the German menace) it established a political unity with the Liberals regarding Ireland and financing imperial defence. The disingenuous side to Carson's stance was that it was sold to large sections of the general northern Irish public—most of whom were naturally incapable of understanding the provenance to the issue—as a question purely of defending the Protestantism of the British constitution against a supposed Catholic menace. This was a totally nonsensical claim that Carson, who was a histrionic character notwithstanding his great professional legal talents,[70] could attempt to propagandise, although it required an effective local champion. Somewhat bizarrely, James Craig was the man chosen to fill this role.

There were actually some parallels in the lives of James Craig and Arthur Griffith. Both men were the exact same age and stolid characters who had been in South Africa. Both men had advocated non-sectarian education, tariff reform and voting-rights for women when few others in Ireland did. Though neither were good orators nor university-educated men, each were known for their capacity to impress through making solid political statements of fact that were unaffected by party-political prejudice.[71] The root of the great difference in their lives, or careers, was wealth. While Griffith had lived in the slums of Dublin, Craig was the son of a millionaire whiskey distillery owner (Dunvilles). In an attempt to acquire an aristocratic social status, his father had purchased his own landed estate ('Craigavon') and, although a Presbyterian (as were Griffith's northern cousins), encouraged his son James to marry an English woman who was politically well connected in high Church of England (aristocratic Tory) circles. On Carson's suggestion, English Tories now picked Craig to lead an Ulster-centred agitation and to coordinate a tighter Church of Ireland–Presbyterian alliance through the Orange Order. This raised a personal conflict for Craig.

On a purely personal level, Craig identified far more with the empire as a purely commercial entity than with the British state or the nominal Protestantism of its constitution. Indeed, the defining basis of James Craig's unionism was similar to Arthur Griffith's nationalism. This was a reasonable fear that home rule as envisioned by the Liberal Party (turning Ireland into a colonial fiscal entity) could lead to complete economic ruin and social chaos for Ireland. Having played a part in launching an abortive effort to create a Belfast Stock Exchange, Craig knew from first-hand experience that he and the rest of the Irish business community were in the precarious position of being 'mastered by and not master of circumstances and events'. Feeling this to be unavoidable, however, he now simply did whatever he was told by his English Tory paymasters.[72] An alternative political trajectory for northern businessmen to that which was being laid out for Craig was represented by the career of the Rt. Hon. Thomas Lough MP, the successor of the first Ulster Unionist leader E.J. Saunderson (1837–1906) as the Lord Lieutenant of Cavan and a politician admired by Griffith. Although now nominally a London Liberal MP, Lough continued to live in Cavan, was a supporter of the cooperative movement (his brother owned the largest agricultural cooperative in Ulster) and had written the most 'devastating exposé' of Anglo-Irish economic inequalities, *England's Wealth, Ireland's Poverty* (London, 1896).[73]

Saunderson himself, a colonel of Scottish descent and major landowner in Armagh, had formerly led the protests against the over-taxation of Ireland. Saunderson's reaction to once being defeated in a parliamentary election by Joseph Biggar (an Ulster Presbyterian republican, founder of the Land League as well as a son of the then chairman of the Ulster Bank) had led him to take a very controversial move, however. This was to revive the Orange Order (an organisation that Saunderson had previously ridiculed as a body of pitifully ignorant men and social riff-raff) and turn it into a serious political organisation that was led by the landed gentry, not just in Ulster but also in Scotland, purely in order to suppress the Land League.[74] Saunderson's legacy remained during the Edwardian era when the Ulster Unionist Council attempted to put down Land League style agitations among Ulster Protestant dissenters (led by T.W. Russell and Thomas Sloan) through the medium of the Orange Order. In turn, this forced Craig's Belfast contemporaries to adopt a 'highly defensive unionism', which was both 'embattled and carefully patrolled'.[75] Lough entertained no such insecurities, however. Ignoring Carson's hysterical claims about imaginary threats to the Protestantism of the British constitution, Lough argued that the fate of any Government of Ireland Bill must be 'decided largely on its financial proposals'. He believed that all Ulstermen must take a stand based not on any sectarian grounds but rather an Irish economic nationalism. He was adamant that the Irish Party's willingness to accept a Liberal Party measure which would leave control of customs and excise, or four-fifths of all Irish revenue, in the hands of the imperial parliament, while having an Irish parliament established and subsist purely on just one-fifth of all Irish revenue (namely the country's existing local government rates) could only make a very bad situation infinitely worse. This made it an absolute imperative that a commercially minded Irish party took an immediate economic nationalist stand on the basis that Ireland was currently 'hopelessly handicapped in conducting its commerce' solely because of the abolition since 1823 of the operations of a separate Irish customs house.[76]

In common with Lough, Griffith emphasised that the economy of Belfast was inherently tied in with that of the rest of Ulster, which not only had a far less urban population than Leinster, and less valuable agricultural holdings than either Leinster or Munster but, along with Connacht, it had the highest county-by-county emigration figures of any Irish province.[77] Griffith also emphasised that Ulster was not at all notable for successful local business enterprises; a viewpoint substantiated by modern historical research.[78] Furthermore, as economic realities rather than religious differences determined the true quality of life in Ireland, Griffith believed that the trend of allowing Belfast to become a trading port and business centre for English and Scottish rather than (northern) Irish entrepreneurs, while the rest of the country was governed as if it was an inherently pre-industrial economy (excepting the distillery trade), was only proving detrimental to Belfast. In particular, Belfast could never have become the home of constant social strife (completely unlike the rest of Ireland) and it would never have experienced great riots every time significant national legislation was announced if it really was the home of prosperous and contented citizens.[79] The true problem facing northeast Ulster, Griffith maintained, was that it had never been given a chance to become integrated into the economic life of the rest of Ireland. This was why the new city of Belfast had essentially been left to drift in its own distinct world of political uncertainty, characterised by suspicion, defensiveness and localism.

Griffith's attitude regarding the potential of Carson and Craig's new movement was sceptical. He typified Carson as a man who was being paid fees in London to whitewash a Liberal government that he was only pretending to want to overthrow. Meanwhile, Griffith deemed the newly adopted semi-histrionic stance of Craig's Belfast-centred circle of politicians to be 'amazing for men who are reputed to be in business hard-headed'.[80] Partly owing to Griffith's friendship with Lindsay Crawford, formerly editor of the *Irish Protestant* and leader of the Independent Orange Order (who later, in support of Griffith, founded the Canadian branch of the Irish Self-Determination League),[81] Griffith did not believe that Carson and Craig could succeed for very long in using the Orange Order in the manner which the English Tories were directing them. This was because Griffith expected that, as had occurred during past several general elections (he was fond of citing events as far back as 1828, 1868 or the pro-Irish independence Orange convention of 1873), the Orange Order would soon split up into conflicting sections and witness 'a semi-socialist party emerging out of Orangeism, which in the towns is far more socialist than any other section of the Irish population'.[82] As an extension of this reality, Griffith also expected that franchise increases in the future would ensure that the myth of a separate Ulster question would soon disappear. This was because an extension of voting rights to the working classes would bring about an inevitable liberation of northern Protestants' vote from 'obsequious deference to the squire': 'what landlordism was in the old days in Ireland the present generation can scarcely realise'.[83]

While a prominent Ulster Tory who took an interest in Griffith's writings 'has sent me a good deal of accurate information heretofore',[84] Griffith's only public champion in Belfast hitherto had been Robert Lynd, a popular essayist. In the past, Lynd had argued that his fellow Ulster Presbyterians should recognise their political brother in Arthur Griffith and his Sinn Féin Policy and, in turn, cease to follow the lead of English Episcopalians. To Lynd's mind, these titled high Anglican individuals were men who hypocritically popularised the idea 'that everything national in this country is sheer Popery' and whose disingenuous supporters in Ulster, on retiring from public life, inevitably 'had some honour of office conferred on him in return for his services as England's agent and purveyor of lies to the Irish Protestants'.[85] Although the economic mistreatment of Ireland by Britain had been a founding premise of the Ulster-centred Irish Tory movement in the past, future political leaders (and, indeed, some future historians)[86] of this movement no longer referred to this fact. This development took place quite quickly. This prompted Griffith to begin criticising the stance of the Church of Ireland.

In the wake of Carson's political initiative of September 1911, the Synod of the Church of Ireland (which invariably sat in Dublin) argued that home rule would be 'a degradation of the status of Irishmen' due to their losing a voice in the management of 'an army, a navy…[and] the power to defend their shipping and their ports'. To this, Griffith retorted that 'if it be a degradation to the status of Irishmen that they should be thus restricted in College Green, it is a degradation to the status of Irishmen that they should now be so restricted from Westminster': currently, Irishmen had no authority over shipping, ports or national defence. Griffith suggested that the Church of Ireland was failing in its duties to Protestants throughout Ireland by uncritically echoing the sentiments of the alien political world that its Anglican equivalent within England inhabited.[87] Griffith's response to Carson's new self-consciously Protestant movement was to argue that they were being manipulated by 'the choice between Irish patriotism and English party' every bit as much as Kettle's Roman Catholic followers. In defence of this argument, Griffith noted that 'it is no political secret that the majority of the English Tories [Carson's current supporters] were prepared to adopt Home Rule' and if the Tories rather than the Liberals had introduced the Government of Ireland Bill 'no Synod of the Church of Ireland would be invited to condemn it' by the state church in Britain. Griffith typified the level of political confusion that existed within the Ulster Protestant community in this matter as yet another example of how a failure to analyse political questions rationally had developed within Ireland solely because 'measures affecting Ireland have been, and are still, mainly judged in Ireland not by Irish standards but by those set up for us by English party'. Increasingly, in the case of Ulster Protestants and most members of the Church of Ireland nationwide, this meant the propaganda of the Conservative Party within England.[88] Since the inception of Sinn Féin, Griffith had argued that this trend was a contributory factor to the situation whereby Irishmen were losing the perception necessary to develop a clear 'national standard of comparison and value' and so begin formulating rational political policies in their own best interests.[89]

While Griffith had always criticised the Irish Party for seeking to prevent the Irish population 'from indulging in any reflection on their country's position', he now began claiming that this 'superhuman devotion to the cause of the Loaves and Fishes' was also coming to define the politics of the Ulster Party. Griffith's accused both parties of failing to realise that the reason why Ireland was the only country in Europe with a perpetually declining population, having lost 'one-third of the Episcopalians and one-third of the Presbyterians as well as one-half of the Irish Catholics' in recent times, was their refusal to accept 'the cold truth—that whether Ireland be Catholic or Episcopalian or Presbyterian' mattered not in the slightest to Britain so long as it had its own way with the economy of Ireland. However, Griffith's conclusion from this premise, that Ireland 'will be devastated in its people and in its trade so long as what is termed the "British Empire" is England—and nothing but England',[90] could also be used as a persuasive case *against* an Irish economic nationalism.

Griffith would soon grow very disillusioned with Irish Protestants' stance. He suggested that 'A.W. Samuels … is all dumb as oysters now' because 'for him, Mum's the Word'. He also argued that while Archbishop Plunket of Dublin, who had protested against the over-taxation of Ireland in 1896 and was later honoured by a statue on Kildare Street, 'was a unionist but an Irishman', his successor as the Protestant Archbishop of Dublin, Dr Bernard, was merely 'a timeserver and a West Briton' because he refused to take such a stance. Not surprisingly, this led Dr Bernard to write a strong letter of protest to Griffith's publication.[91] Meanwhile, although Samuels would ultimately attempt to revive some of his economic nationalist arguments after Carson abandoned his TCD parliamentary seat, he was very quickly retired from politics altogether upon being requested by Dublin Castle to act instead as its legal advisor and, in turn, necessarily maintain a deliberate silence on the economy.[92] Carson's success in removing the economic dimension to the debate on home rule was facilitated equally by Liberal Party intellectuals. Taking as their premise that the constitution of the Union had changed irrevocably with regards to Ireland from its original form, they issued propaganda that spoke abstractly of the probable evolution of a 'new Irish constitution' without any reference to financial realities, thereby intentionally masking the purely economic thrust behind the government's current intentions for Ireland in the same manner as Gladstone had formerly done.[93]

* * *

When Asquith's Government of Ireland Bill was introduced in parliament in April 1912, exactly like its two predecessors of 1886 and 1893, it was drafted entirely on the basis of the British treasury's alleged recent discovery of shocking deficits in the Irish contribution to the Imperial Exchequer. Ignoring Sweetman's appeals not to criticise the bill in case this might hurt the Irish Party,[94] Griffith argued that, just like the previous bills, it was highly doubtful the proposed

Irish parliament could survive if the bill passed in its present format because it would be completely unable to meet either the economic interests of 'unionist workingmen and manufacturers' or of 'southern industrialists' due to its inability to regulate the economy.[95] In opposition to the stance of Childers and Kettle, Griffith maintained that not only could nobody vouch for the claim that Ireland was costing more than it was contributing to the Empire, but it was also highly disingenuous for the Irish Party to associate the costs of the UK-wide pension and insurance acts with the Government of Ireland bill because they were, or should be regarded as, entirely separate matters.[96]

Describing many of the bill's provisions as measures which 'inside the four corners of constitutional liberty no defence can be made',[97] Griffith also extended Ulster Unionists' past republican-minded critique that home rule meant 'taxation without representation' by arguing that the existing Union was equally unconstitutional for similar reasons. In particular, the British parliament's power to withhold supplies to the monarchy was the entire basis of the British constitution ever since the seventeenth century. However, neither the existing Irish administration nor its political representatives in parliament were allowed such powers, either under current circumstances or under Asquith's proposed bill. This would ensure that, as before, 'in the case of a financial dispute … the British government will argue with the Irish government's purse in its pocket'. This left Irish politicians with no means of querying whatever figures the British treasury produced for them. If this situation was not changed now, Griffith maintained that it was inevitable that political conflicts between Britain and Ireland would continue forever into the future:

> It is puerile to say that such a conflict can never take place because Home Rule will lead Ireland to entertain feelings of friendship for Great Britain. Friends and lovers, as well as foes, differ on questions of fact and finance. If, for instance, England were engaged in a serious war tomorrow, it is certain she would demand a monetary contribution from Ireland. It is probable that an Irish parliament begotten in the image of the party that calls the home rule bill a final settlement would willingly subscribe such a contribution. But it would desire to fix the contribution on a scale such as Ireland could afford and it would have no power to do so.[98]

Griffith argued that in all issues of financial justice or political liberty, Asquith's proposed bill, like Gladstone's before it, 'not only guaranteed England against the obligation of fulfilling these engagements, but provided that Ireland should ensure her for all time against having to fulfil them'.[99] The proposed establishment of a Joint Exchequer Board with a permanent British majority would not alter the Imperial Treasury's control of Ireland: 'Englishmen will collect our taxes, Englishmen will bank our taxes, and Englishmen will give back out of them what *they calculate* we are entitled to … it is practically in its power to bankrupt Ireland' at any time it wished and so perpetually hold the entire Irish political community to ransom.[100]

In addition to the inability of the proposed Irish parliament to control the expenditure of revenue, Griffith pointed to its powerlessness to grant licenses to any Irish businesses as well as its legal inability to reform the current Irish administration, which both Griffith and the Secretary of the Imperial Home Rule Association argued was costing the Irish public over £1 million more than was necessary every year. These factors were practically guaranteed to bankrupt Ireland. Griffith maintained that unless Ireland attained the right to control taxation with its own exchequer, to raise an army, to make trade treaties with other countries and to set up its own consular representation abroad, it could have no independence.[101]

In September 1912, to coincide with Ulster Tory unionists' religiously based Solemn League and Covenant against the idea of home rule, calls for the partition of Ireland and exclusion of the entire 'Protestant' province of Ulster from the workings of the Government of Ireland Bill began to be championed aggressively in public. Griffith had been forewarned of this development. In May 1912, an Ulster Tory informed Griffith that the Liberal Party leaders Winston Churchill and Lloyd George were going to persuade John Redmond and the Irish Party to accept partition on religious grounds as the price for establishing an Irish parliament.[102] By September 1912, they had indeed persuaded Prime Minister Asquith that this was the correct policy to pursue, sooner or later.[103]

This development reflected the political strategy favoured by Henry Wilson of Longford, a leading political–military adviser to Churchill (himself a Liberal who, from his family background, had strong English and Irish Tory connections). Although a proverbial 'southern unionist', Wilson was now a firm supporter of the Ulster Tories in politics. It was Wilson's belief that if Lloyd George, as Chancellor of the Exchequer, could get the Irish Party to accept the principle of partition as the price for British political parties being willing to pass the Government of Ireland Bill, this would actually ensure that the bill could never be a workable measure and no real devolution of powers to Ireland could ever take place.[104] These developments effectively proved that Redmond party's holding of the balance of power in commons was politically meaningless or, at least, a matter of absolutely no relevance to the government of Ireland. The terms of the Government of Ireland Bill was a subject for the two principal British parties to settle between themselves. Public manifestations of polarisation on the subject were merely a deliberate charade to manipulate voters and mask the true financial intentions of the British government regarding Ireland.[105]

Griffith continued to voice such criticisms of the bill, as well as the three parties' public posturing on the matter, up until July 1913, when 'now that this bill is outside the possibility of improvement we have done with it. Henceforth it is no concern of ours.'[106] Indeed, to his own admission, Griffith could only be a completely powerless critic on the subject matter. He lamented the fact that

> The people of this country have been mistaught to equate home rule with repeal of the union and will probably continue to do so until some form of home rule is law. We cannot condemn a home rule scheme for not being that which it is fundamentally impossible for it to be. We can only condemn those who have confused home rule and restoration of the Irish parliament in the popular mind.[107]

Not surprisingly, Griffith's arguments were not popular with Irish Party supporters. The very fact that Griffith had been prepared to engage in old Irish Tory-style criticisms of the Irish Party—that if it failed to question the financial implications of the proposed home rule bill, then he hoped Ireland's self-styled 'unionists' would work to 'maintain this country's dignity' by doing so[108]—was sufficient to make him seem not only irrelevant but even a quite obnoxious and untrustworthy figure to large sections of the Irish reading public. In the meantime, Griffith's personal fortunes continued to slide downhill.

By 1913, the dwindling sales of *Sinn Féin* had forced Griffith to take up other work. This would include being the principal history lecturer for the Gaelic League in Dublin; a job that F.H. O'Donnell, another censorious critic of the Irish Party,[109] held for the Gaelic League in London. As this paid little, Griffith began writing series for other publications. This included a history of post-famine Ireland that was written for William O'Brien's *Free Press* (Cork) and republished twice.[110] Griffith also contributed to the *Evening Telegraph* a serial history of the contribution of past members of the Royal Irish Academy and Royal Dublin Society, as well as various clergymen, to the Irish language revival.[111] Just prior to beginning this series, Griffith had also written to the *Irish Book Lover* championing the idea of the late Alfred Webb of creating a dictionary of Irish biography.[112] He also wrote a very general series on Ireland for the *Southern Cross* (Buenos Aires), a journal founded by Griffith's old Irish–Argentinean friend William Bulfin, which partly reflected Griffith's inclination to draw direct contrasts between the experience of Ireland and that of all other nations.[113] Finally, Griffith began producing his own editions of the writings of the chief Young Irelanders of the 1840s, including both reprints and compilations of selected journalism. Starting with a new expanded edition of John Mitchel's *Jail Journal* (Dublin, 1913), Griffith produced four such books over the next five years. With good distribution by M.H. Gill & Son, they sold quite well.[114]

Sinn Féin grew closer editorially to *An Claidheamh Solus* during the summer of 1913. Unhappy at his own deliberate marginalisation by Hyde and MacNeill, its editor Patrick Pearse now proposed to Griffith to form a joint-editorial policy with *Sinn Féin*.[115] As M.J. O'Rahilly, the managing director of *An Claidheamh Solus*, was now active primarily in Sinn Féin,[116] as was Eamon Ceannt (a frequent contributor to both publications), Pearse's suggestion made some sense. To some extent, Griffith seems to have gone along with this idea. He now began focusing less on economics and more on the Gaelic League's cultural nationalist obsession with the supposedly all-consuming (and undefined) concept of 'anglicisation'; a favourite subject of Pearse, which was used as a cover for issuing (largely ineffective) criticisms of all and sundry. Griffith accused Douglas Hyde, the Gaelic League president, of encouraging the league to be as inactive as possible in order to appease a procrastinating Irish Party. Although he was indeed loyal to Redmond, Hyde was angered by this attack. He maintained that the fact Sinn Féin's policy was 'incompatible' with his own was actually beside the point. The real issue, Hyde suggested, was that it was simply not the right of Griffith, who had no direct responsibility for the league, to criticise those for whom the league 'means everything' and who had to balance considerations regarding the financing of Irish education about which mere critics like Griffith were either unaware or unappreciative.[117] Meanwhile, if Griffith was deflated by his failure to impact on the home rule debate and the dwindling sales of *Sinn Féin*, the very sudden outbreak in September 1913 of an industrial dispute in Dublin on a scale never witnessed before (or, indeed, ever to be witnessed again) would throw him very much on the defensive in justifying the relevance of his political worldview.

Griffith was first subject to stern criticism from labour quarters around the same time as the IRB temporarily boycotted Sinn Féin in the wake of the publication of *Pitt's Policy*. In September 1911, while Carson launched his Belfast-centred movement, James Larkin launched a popular *Irish Worker* newspaper in Dublin with funding from a nascent English labour movement. In this journal, Larkin immediately began denouncing Griffith as 'scum' who 'knows as much about politics and economics as he does about the Irish worker, which is nothing'. Misleadingly typifying Sinn Féin as a sinister attempt by rich Irish capitalists to stop 'the world-wide upward movement of the toilers of the earth', Larkin mocked Griffith because of his personal bankruptcy (arising from the failure of the *Sinn Féin* daily) and challenged him directly to stand as a municipal candidate for any labour ward in Dublin against the Irish Party if he required proof of how much the Irish working classes detested his politics.[118]

The rationale to Larkin's politics was the existence of a common labour market in Britain and Ireland under the Union. Therefore, Griffith's critique of the Union inherently made him an enemy to Larkin.

Sinn Féin's record as the party most committed in Dublin City Hall to tackling issues of urban poverty meant that any new labour party in Dublin would have to make winning over its supporters a basis for establishing its own political organisation. By joining with the ex-Sinn Féiner P.T. Daly in promoting the Irish Transport and General Workers Union (ITGWU), Larkin would succeed in making workplace conditions for labourers the basis for a new agitation, although Larkin too focused upon attempting to find influence within Hyde's deeply conservative Gaelic League.[119] Regarding 'my old friend Arthur Griffith', James Connolly was arguing by the autumn of 1913 that while 'new labour' socialists could be permitted to sympathise with the cultural nationalism of Sinn Féin, they could never be allowed to support its politics as 'its economic teaching … appeals only to those who measure a nation's prosperity by the volume of wealth produced in a country, instead of by the distribution of that wealth amongst its inhabitants.'[120]

Without a credible Sinn Féin party organisation, Griffith could only respond to this challenge in print. This he would do fairly reasonably, if quite ineffectively. Larkin's *Irish Worker* had called for strikes as soon as that journal was established in September 1911. By contrast, Griffith had judged at that time that strikes could only 'set the country back a little' but, as they were bound to fail, 'the eventual result will be good … in opening the eyes of the Irish workmen to the manner in which Englishmen and adventurers are exploiting them.'[121] During the sudden labour dispute of September 1913, Griffith maintained that 'it is the right of every Irishman willing to work to be secured a fair living in his own country' and that 'the right of labour to a fair share of the joint product of labour and capital is clear and undeniable'. Griffith also argued, however, that 'in any pitched battle between capital and labour with no intervening force, capital must always win'. On the same basis, Griffith emphasised that while a strike was often useful as a 'weapon of defence', 'as a weapon of offence [the form Larkin's ITGWU strike took] it is useless'.[122]

Griffith was unsympathetic to Larkin's strike of September 1913 for this and other reasons. Noting that English labour politicians had funded Larkin with £5,000 to launch a massive industrial strike on the basis of ITGWU labourers' workplace conditions in Dublin, Griffith argued that this was not only inopportune but also neither these English labour financiers nor Larkin himself were prepared to accept any responsibility for 'the hardships he has encouraged his Dublin victims to endure'.[123] Griffith's belief in the principle of government intervention in economic development made him prioritise making the machinery of local government a basis for action. He argued that the solution for workers' hardship in Dublin lay less in the workplace environment (the sole basis of Larkin's strike) than in the combination of their living conditions and the relationship between employers and City Hall. Griffith argued that the Sinn Féin Party's councillors in City Hall could remedy all the latter problems, if only they received greater support, and that current labour activists were 'no worthy descendants of the old Dublin trade unionists' (he cited the activities of his father's generation during the 1860s) in not desiring to attain influence over municipal government policy through seeking election to City Hall. Griffith found this approach somewhat inexplicable, as this goal was much more attainable now than it was fifty years previously.[124] Around this time, James Connolly was being lauded in the Irish Party's *Freeman's Journal* for suggesting the establishment of arbitration courts between employers and employees as a solution to the industrial dispute. Regarding this, Griffith noted that Sinn Féin had suggested this exact same policy in both 1907 and 1909 but neither the ITGWU nor the employers had either listened or responded at that time simply because of the Irish Party's political boycott of Sinn Féin.[125]

The timing of Larkin's strike, which provoked lengthy riots, served to completely paralyse Dublin politically at the exact same time as the new Ulster Volunteer Force formed their own Provisional Government. Ironically, this was done on the basis of a completely false claim that home rule would subject them to a disloyal Catholic executive. The British government also introduced a ban upon any further commercial transits between Ireland and the United States around this time, thereby potentially paralysing the economic life of Cork, Limerick and Galway cities.[126] The actual impact of Larkin's strike on Dublin commercial life was minimal, but it was quite damaging to some nationalist politicians. For instance, William Martin Murphy had recently been elected as the first (modern) non-Tory chairman of the Dublin Chamber of Commerce. It was under Murphy's chairmanship that the Bank of Ireland made its first effort (also during September 1913) to coordinate the business practices of all Irish banks by means of a standing committee.[127] However, Murphy's simultaneous willingness to chair employers' associations that were ready to lockout striking labourers allowed Larkin to make him his target. He funded 20,000 workers in Dublin to strike (by far the largest, as well as the strangest, industrial strike in Irish history) on the single motion that 'Murphy must go!', as he did indeed go as the chairman of the Dublin Chamber of Commerce a couple of months later, to be replaced by yet another Tory unionist. A further irony of Larkin's short-lived strike was that it would later be celebrated as a founding event for modern Irish labour politics despite its absence of precedents or antecedents, as well as the fact that Larkin's own union, the ITGWU, actually came to the Griffithite conclusion that Larkin had always been more of a saboteur than a sincere champion of its interests and, like P.T. Daly, had actually misappropriated its funds.[128]

At the time of Larkin's strike, Dublin Tories began arguing that increases in Irish deposits in the Post Office Savings Banks and Joint Stock Banks were proof of Irish prosperity and the inherent value of the common British and Irish labour market. In response, Griffith repeated his argument that too much of this capital was being invested in British government stock rather than Irish business (a claim that was inherently true with regards to the Post Office Savings Banks, a state-owned bank, if less so with the Joint Stock Banks), but he could not offer any great practical justification for his idea of nationalising the banks.[129] Indeed, the fate of the new Irish banks' standing committee was very likely to be sealed by whatever financial settlement was being determined by the Government of Ireland Bill. On this level, a fact that certainly did not fare well for any opponent of partition was that the man who would prove to be Ulster Tories' most amenable, if not the most personally sympathetic (being a Liberal), ally in government was the same politician who had actually inspired the Parliament Act, namely David Lloyd George, the Welsh-speaking Chancellor of the Exchequer.[130] The prerogatives of the British treasury continued to remain supreme in all matters relating to the government of Ireland. Meanwhile, having been politically embarrassed by Larkin's strike (no matter how unsuccessful or counter-productive that strike may have been), Sinn Féin's self-styled Chancellor of the Exchequer with the Welsh name, Arthur Griffith, was struggling more than ever to justify his own policy.

In response to debate on the labour question, Griffith published a manifesto in October 1913 in which he sought to justify various claims. This included that 'Sinn Féin is a national, not a sectional, movement'; that 'the one force in material affairs stronger than capital' was 'the nation'; and that, according to his favoured definition of nationhood, a nation 'cannot afford that any one of its sections should be enslaved by the other'.[131] This was the obvious value, to Griffith's mind, in a nation's self-government. There was certainly a deep political irony, however, in the fact that this cultured and intelligent manifesto on the nation was written mostly in the first person.[132]

Correctly emphasising that the idea of internationalism was as old as civilisation itself, Griffith argued that modern labour activists' complete ignorance of this reality had led them to mistake as visionary prophets of the future quaint old writers such as Karl Marx, Ferdinand Lassalle or Pierre-Joseph Proudhon. Griffith argued that these men were romantic and conservative neo-feudalists in their response to the growth of the modern nation-state. In response to the debates on the 'social question' (the urbanisation of peasant labour) that had begun with Saint-Simon during the 1820s, these strictly upper-class and university educated men had suggested that 'the Salvation of Humanity is to be found … [in] a revival of feudalism with the state instead of the noble as all-provider—wherein the subject is relieved by a benevolent despotism from the exercise of his personal initiative and the discipline of personal responsibility'. Griffith emphasised, however, that 'whether capital begot labour in the beginning or labour begot capital, without the wedding of capital and labour we cannot have production. We cannot slay the one without destroying the other'. Therefore the romantic, or nostalgic, argument of Marx and other post-Napoleonic era writers on the means of production 'has no truth at its base' because it is 'not capitalism, but the abuse of capitalism, [that] oppresses labour'. The essential question or challenge, therefore, was not the withering away of the nation and the state but rather for the former to begin better regulating the latter, this being the value of a modern nation-state.[133] Griffith was adamant that 'the labour problems of Ireland' were not solvable by 'quack remedies' funded from England, but rather 'are to be solved through a study of the conditions of countries near akin to ourselves—countries such as Denmark, Norway, Romania and even Serbia'. Upon this basis, he questioned 'are they facts for a *National* University to be proud of' that this reasonable perspective, of what could be learnt from other countries, was being completely ignored, or even held up to ridicule as a popular subject for laughter, in Ireland?[134] It is quite possible that many Irish contemporaries would have considered Griffith's arguments in this regard as quite reasonable. Nevertheless, reflecting a longstanding trend, they won him no more supporters.

* * *

During November 1913, while Bulmer Hobson worked in Dublin to persuade Eoin MacNeill to establish an 'Irish Volunteer Force' to rival the 'Ulster Volunteer Force' (this allowed the British government to falsely claim the existence of a threat of civil war in Ireland), Lloyd George persuaded the rest of the British cabinet that the Government of Ireland Bill should nominally be passed the following year, but its implementation delayed indefinitely on the grounds that some northern counties must be permanently excluded. He also persuaded Redmond to decide how many northern counties should be permanently excluded from the workings of the Government of Ireland Act purely on the basis of an analysis of the size of the Catholic and Protestant populations in each county.[135] Reflecting this, after agreeing definitively to the principle of the excluding northern counties in March 1914, Redmond engaged in a deliberately protracted debate at a conference at Buckingham Palace, summoned by King George V himself, that presented Irish religious demographics as the sole basis for the future government of Ireland. This Buckingham Palace conference—the terms of which inherently made it impossible of achieving any resolution—was designed to ensure that although the bill passed for the third time in Commons in May 1914 its enactment was delayed. Indeed, the conference was postponed indefinitely the day the expected European war began that August. The following month, as the Government of Ireland Act was nominally being placed on the statute book, Roger Casement, although he had been the advisor to John Redmond in the management of the Irish Volunteers,[136] announced from America his intention to organise an Irish resistance to the British war effort,[137] and was soon reported publicly to be consorting with Germans.[138] If, as Griffith had predicted, what he had termed as 'Pitt's Policy' had once again won the day, the Irish public was completely powerless to prevent this from happening.

Griffith ignored the Buckingham Palace conference because he remained sceptical regarding the possibility of the British government being able to use religion as a justification for partition. He argued that 'there are few outside the lowest state of Orangeism who believe for a moment that Protestantism would be in any more danger under an Irish than it is under an English government', and that 'no one is unaware that sectarian feeling today is infinitely less bitter now than it was' when the home rule movement was first established, 'not by Catholics but by Protestants', forty years previously.[139] Griffith maintained that when Britain's 'Liberal government gives Catholics JPships and small government situations' and 'Tory governments confer these favours on Protestants', Irish public opinion should realise that neither political party favoured either religious community any more than the British civil service was particularly concerned with the Muslim or Buddhist religions. Rather, 'both actions have just the one aim—to keep Ireland perpetually divided against itself'.[140] By such time as Redmond accepted partition in March 1914, Griffith was not only arguing that Irish MPs should reject the proposed Government of Ireland Act, but was also making the claim that 'unionist Ulster cannot cut itself adrift from the rest of Ireland without, if the rest of Ireland so wills, suffering enormous loss'. This was because Ulster was, in reality, no more a self-contained area than was Munster.[141]

Griffith's response to the formation of the Irish Volunteers was almost non-committal.[142] He noted that 'it enables Irishmen to realise one of the highest duties of citizenship—the defence of the country and the right to bear arms' and he would soon join the movement to express appreciation for its citizen-soldier ethos.[143] However, he was against the idea that it should ever become an opposition movement to the Ulster Volunteers. This was because

We do not believe that Ulster unionists are any more in earnest today in their threats of armed resistance to the English government than they were in 1828 or 1868. National union is desired and sought by every Irishman who intelligently loves his country and every section and party should and ought to be willing to concede much for its attainment.[144]

Likewise, Griffith was opposed to the idea that the Irish Volunteers should ever be considered as a weapon against the British government:

> If all able-bodied Irishmen armed, even then, the event of a conflict with England would be very uncertain. There is always the British fleet ... [while] the best volunteer movement that can grow up on Irish soil today will neither in numbers, armament or leadership be equal to the British army ... We know that to start with the assumption that this movement is going to deliver Ireland quickly from her political ills is mischievous. What it is going to do, if it be guided manfully, is to put a public opinion with backbone in it into the country; to make men more conscious of their duty as citizens; to associate the ideas of order and discipline with the idea of liberty; to bring the manhood of Ireland in touch with realities, and to make it clear-seeing and fearless ... As to what a volunteer movement may develop into in time—whether the sword may unite where now the tongue divides; whether the comradeship of arms may beget a comradeship of purpose in North and South ... we cannot prophesy. But these things may be so, and a National Army strong enough to hold Ireland for the Irish be eventually evolved.[145]

Within a couple of days of Griffith publishing this editorial, however, the British government proclaimed the importation of arms and ammunition into Ireland. This created a sense of belligerent defensiveness among many volunteers.[146]

Redmond's acceptance of partition in March 1914 coincided with several politically engineered spectacles that were designed to both excite Irish public opinion and facilitate wartime defence budgets. These included a supposed British army 'mutiny episode' at the Curragh in opposition to the idea of home rule (although, in reality, it was well-known that home rule involved increasing the army's defence budget), while subsequent gunrunning by the Ulster and Irish Volunteers were, in each case, facilitated by British navy personnel.[147] These developments effectively served to silence Griffith's perspective on arms-bearing as a purely Irish civic matter long before *Sinn Féin* was suppressed by Dublin Castle in August 1914 according to wartime press censorship laws (the Defence of the Realm Act) that would actually remain in place in Ireland until July 1921.[148]

Just prior to *Sinn Féin* being suppressed, Griffith had spoken out clearly regarding what he saw as the issues raised by the outbreak of war:

> Ireland is not at war with Germany. She has no quarrel with any continental power. England is at war with Germany and Mr. Redmond has offered England the services of the National Volunteers to 'defend Ireland'. What has Ireland to defend and whom has she to defend it against? Has she a native constitution or a national government to defend? All know that she has not … all know that Mr. Redmond has made this offer without receiving a *quid pro quo*. There is no European Power waging war against the people of Ireland. There are two European Powers at war with the people who dominate Ireland from Dublin Castle. The call to the Volunteers to 'defend Ireland' is a call to them to defend the bureaucracy in that edifice.[149]

While 'a base attempt is made by our slavish press to evoke in Ireland not a pro-Irish but an anti-German sentiment', Griffith maintained that nationalists' duty was not to side with England unless 'it withdraw the present abortive home rule bill and pass in the same space of time a full measure of home rule', or, 'in the alternative, let a Provisional Government be set up in Dublin by Mr Redmond and Sir Edward Carson, and we shall give it allegiance'.[150]

In September 1914, partly in reaction to Casement's action in New York, Eoin MacNeill established a rump body of the Irish Volunteers as a means of rejecting Redmond's leadership of the vast majority of that movement. With moral support from Bulmer Hobson, Redmond had successfully encouraged them to enlist in the British war effort. Like Griffith, MacNeill opposed this move. The latter maintained that nationalists' duty was to ensure that a real measure of home rule would be secured and, in turn, partition avoided. While it had a national membership of roughly 10,000 men, however, the capital of MacNeill's volunteers was little more than that of Griffith's old National Council: approximately £1,500.[151] Perhaps more than anything else, this reality illustrated the complete success of the British government in imposing its desired framework for home rule between 1910 and 1914.

Most Irish Party supporters were accustomed to a generation of misleading press reporting that had presented 'The Party' as being not only the embodiment of the 'Irish nation' but also as being at the very heart of all British political developments. The latter idea was something that Redmond's supporters had tried to promote since 1910 to an even greater extent than before. As a result, Irish Party supporters were encouraged to see contemporary events—from

Carson's initial Tory posturing up until the Buckingham Palace conference—as evidence that 'the Irish crisis had brought Britain to the brink of civil war' and that violence, or the threat of violence, had become the Empire's only remaining defence against Irish Catholics' irresistible challenge to the British constitution.[152] This, however, was essentially a complete misreading of the political situation and a total reversal of the actual power basis of the Anglo-Irish relationship. For this reason, the Irish Party was partly responsible for creating a deep 'crisis of popular expectation' in Ireland at this time.[153]

As in Gladstone's day, financing imperial concerns was the government's only real priority in shaping Irish policy. This political situation had never changed. The policy framework of home rule that had been spelt out by Erskine Childers for both the Liberals and the Tories in 1911 fully reflected this.[154] At no stage was Ireland within the top dozen priorities of the imperial government, while the country's politicians (including the leaders of 'The Party') had only ever individual roles to play in debating the empire's interests.[155] As one historian has noted, this was essentially why Griffith's comment regarding the government of Ireland bill '"if this is liberty, the lexicographers have deceived us" was completely beside the point'.[156] It was also why James Craig and Edward Carson could take up the individual administrative responsibilities, offered to them by Lloyd George's cabinet during the war, as the Treasurer and First Lord of the Admiralty respectively, without making any real switch in political emphasis.[157] The local political organisations of the Ulster as much as the Irish Party counted for little in these considerations.

Over the next four years Griffith would make numerous efforts to break through what he would famously term as a 'paper wall' of wartime press censorship. His Sinn Féin enterprise was in danger of reaching new heights of absurdity, however. He identified strongly with MacNeill's volunteers while continuing to focus on economic affairs. However, the very fact that the Irish Volunteers in no sense represented either the wealth or the property of the country meant that Griffith's attempt to champion a national economic perspective had become partly divorced from its essential context, namely the actual management of the country's financial institutions and its political consequences. Therefore, any rise in the popularity of Sinn Féin's propaganda through the medium of the Irish Volunteer movement could serve to mask that its actual political potential—originating in its capacity to embrace propertied Tory as much as Catholic nationalist opinion—was now in danger of falling into a very steep decline. Indeed, the failure to establish a national council on finance during the period 1909–12 did not bode at all well for the future of Irish nationalism.

CHAPTER SEVEN

The First World War and the Reinvention of Sinn Féin (1914–18)

Although he was without power or authority, Griffith was well suited to offer an independent critique of Ireland's response to the First World War. Aside from his experience studying the economic relationship between Britain and Ireland, he had been analysing the performance of the small nations of Europe for the past decade. In addition, his familiarity with developments in South Africa ever since the Boer War[1] also gave him a vantage point to critique the politics surrounding Herbert Kitchener, a native of Co. Kerry who was formerly the British chief of staff in South Africa and was now the supreme British military commander. Griffith's initial response to the outbreak of the First World War, however, was simply to organise a public anti-war demonstration to emphasise that Sinn Féin stood for 'neither King nor Kaiser but Ireland'.[2] This represented an informal political alliance with Eoin MacNeill's Irish Volunteers, stemming from the latter's embrace of the Sinn Féin Policy of anti-enlistment. MacNeill never had and never would hold Griffith in a high regard, however.[3] This anti-war demonstration also brought to fruition a trend that had been evident since the autumn of 1913, which was to return Griffith closer to the political orbit of the IRB.[4] The dynamics of this little understood world would play a significant, if not a decisive, part in bringing about a reinvention of Sinn Féin during the First World War.

Typified by some historians as 'an underground party'[5] and by others as 'a political school',[6] perhaps the greatest illustration of the true nature of the

IRB's political world was its leadership's perpetual connection with Irishmen abroad that had the political outlook, or even careers, of international war correspondents.[7] Since 1902 the IRB had operated purely within the Gaelic League (for all intents and purposes, an Irish Party managed organisation) and, therefore, its existence was virtually forgotten. T.M. Healy, who had been almost as knowledgeable as Davitt of its internal affairs (he was essentially the IRB's defence lawyer since 1884),[8] was surprised to discover during 1915 that the IRB still existed.[9] This was because it was widely understood in Irish Party circles ever since the Special Commission of 1888 that it was being wound down with encouragement from Michael Davitt and William O'Brien.[10] The publication of *Irish Freedom* (initially financed by the septuagenarian John Daly)[11] did not represent a revival of the IRB: Bulmer Hobson actually sided with Redmond on both the issue of the Irish Volunteers and the introduction of wartime press censorship.[12] Tom Clarke and Sean MacDermott, IRB treasurer and secretary respectively, responded by ignoring Hobson's Dublin IRB organisation, which consisted of a few hundred men (two-thirds of the entire remaining IRB membership), as well as all those whom P.T. Daly had promoted in the past (effectively, the other third of the organisation's ranks, led by Denis McCullough, the IRB's nominal president). Instead, they resolved to attempt to create an entirely new IRB organisation within the ranks of MacNeill's Irish Volunteers while, owing to his status as Redmond's chief critic, Clarke invited Griffith to act as a propagandist on behalf of the new organisation.[13] Griffith accepted Clarke's offer but only conditionally.

Although the IRB was a strictly autonomous organisation according to its own rules, the American Clan na Gael frequently ignored this prerogative.[14] Partly for this reason, Griffith did not trust the IRB very much and his own response to the political challenge posed by the outbreak of the war would be characterised by a few false starts. He refused to join the IRB's new executive or to support Clarke's idea that the volunteers should actually plan a rebellion, which he deemed a counter-productive idea. Indeed, very soon the latter ambition caused several of the IRB's most determined activists to be arrested.[15] William Sears of the *Enniscorthy Echo*, a long-term journalistic ally, had already formed the *Irish Volunteer* in defence of MacNeill's stance, and Griffith indicated to Clarke that he would also be willing to act as a propagandist on behalf of the Irish Volunteers and, in doing so, could facilitate the IRB's desire for a new nationalist propaganda campaign. Griffith did not believe that Clarke and MacDermott could find any support for their idea of a rebellion but expected that, in return for his assistance, they would keep him informed of their plans. His own idea was that the best way Ireland could capitalise upon the European war was to seek independent representation at whatever peace conference concluded the war, if that were possible.[16]

To coincide with the first annual convention of the Irish Volunteers in October 1914, Griffith launched *Eire-Ireland* on Clarke's behalf. This was an initiative that he justified as a necessary act of defence for the Irish Volunteers, 'which the prostitute daily press of Ireland will, in so far as it does not suppress, attempt to misrepresent and distort'.[17] As an example of this, Griffith noted that those who were expressing opposition to the idea of a Militia Ballot Act (a form of conscription) being introduced in Ireland were already being labelled in the government-controlled press as 'cowards'.[18] It was inevitable that press censorship would be introduced during wartime. However, Griffith would proclaim in *Eire-Ireland* that, not the law, but 'ignorance, cowardice or corruption may variously be assigned as the explanation of this attitude of the daily press'.[19] This was not an effective editorial policy and attacks on *Eire-Ireland* would soon ensure that it was short-lived.

The Lord Mayor of Dublin Thomas Sherlock (a former stalwart of Dublin literary societies) and AOH leader J.D. Nugent (who formerly prevaricated between supporting Sinn Féin or his own closest friend John Dillon) both claimed to have proof that the minority of Irishmen who were opposing war enlistment were in receipt of German secret service money; a claim that most Irish newspapers supported. In common with other volunteer officers, Eoin MacNeill was very casual in his dismissal of this attack,[20] which was possibly the best way to ridicule it. Problems immediately arose, however, because MacNeill was also a UCD professor. As a result, Archbishop Walsh, being the chief medium through which the British government funded higher education in Ireland owing to his status as NUI Chancellor, was called to task by the British government for the independent existence of MacNeill's volunteer movement. Therefore, the Catholic hierarchy was suddenly placed in a difficult political position.[21]

Griffith made exaggerated efforts to proclaim Irish neutrality regarding the war. However, in attempting a counter-offensive against the Irish Party's press,[22] he was prone to making arguments that could indeed be interpreted as being designed to muster sympathy for the Germans and their allies. For instance, contrasting the defence budgets and populations of each international power, Griffith suggested that England and France were the greatest militarists.[23] To discredit the Irish Party, he also emphasised that the axis powers represented Catholic Europe, or 'the last Catholic great power' that might be willing to defend the temporal authority of the Pope.[24] The British House of Lords soon took up the claim of Lord Mayor of Dublin regarding Germany financing the Irish Volunteers' press. This persuaded IRB activist Patrick Mahon, the publisher of *Eire-Ireland* (and formerly the publisher of *Irish Freedom* and the *Irish Worker*), that it would be inopportune to defy the censors any longer, prompting *Eire-Ireland* to cease publication on 4 December.[25] Although its final issue featured an advertisement 'look out for *Nationality*—edited by Arthur Griffith', this journal did not appear. This evidently occurred because Tom Clarke realised that a propagandistic dead end had already been reached.

Griffith's response to his inability to escape the wartime press censors was to launch *Scissors and Paste*. This publication lasted for little over two months and included no details of its editorship.[26] Without including a single editorial comment, however, its style betrayed Griffith's favoured satirical approach towards political journalism. *Scissors and Paste* reprinted carefully selected extracts from articles in various uncensored publications: Irish, British, American, Catholic and even Australian papers and journals. While their origin was clearly demarcated, Griffith invented new subtitles for each selection in order to hint how he would like these extracts to be read. This game with the censors ended in early March 1915 when the police seized the offices of *Scissors and Paste*. This quite probably occurred because of Griffith's failure to resist the temptation to place an advertisement in its last issue mentioning himself by name as the man who would be giving the annual 'Emmet Anniversary' public lecture (an event traditionally organised by the IRB) in a few days time.[27] Therefore, although Griffith's name was now becoming better known to the Irish public,[28] by the late spring of 1915 he had failed to make any constructive response to the war, aside from his decision (reflecting his *Scissors and Paste* experience) to keep scrapbooks of press cuttings on each European nation's wartime performance. He would draw upon this information in an attempt to understand a likely post-war political situation.[29]

Once it became clear that the war would not be short lived, a British coalition government was appointed during May 1915. This presented Griffith with a renewed opportunity to make his voice heard in Irish political debate. Hitherto, both leading figures within the Irish Volunteers, such as Patrick Pearse of *An Claidheamh Solus*, as well as passive sympathisers with that movement, such as Griffith's former patron John Sweetman, emphasised they felt no political hostility to John Redmond, even if they did not agree with his particular stance on the war.[30] The formation of a coalition government in Britain, however, raised an additional difficulty beyond the question of press censorship for Irish Catholics in expressing their attitudes towards the war because it practically negated the Irish Party's right to an independent voice altogether. All of a sudden, Griffith's prior argument that a different method of political organisation to the Irish Party was necessary became relevant to various parties. Growing political resentment regarding the stillborn Government of Ireland Act exacerbated this trend. This was evidenced by the demand of Dublin Corporation (still largely loyalist, notwithstanding its unanimous selection of John Clancy as mayor-elect earlier that year) that John Redmond speed up the implementation of the Government of Ireland Act by unilaterally convening an Irish parliament in Dublin.[31]

Another problem caused by the prolongation of the war was its role in preventing the Irish Party from fulfilling its responsibility of providing a voice for the Roman Catholic Church on Anglo-American relations within the British imperial parliament. This had become a particularly thorny issue because of America's neutrality and Britain's desire to persuade America to join with the Allies. The church could not afford to be associated with the pro-war effort for this very reason. It had to appear strictly neutral. By the spring of 1915, however, Redmond's ally Sir Roger Casement was already being cited publicly by the Tory London *Times* as a man who had 'a warm place in German hearts'.[62] It was also no secret that Casement had recently been associated with Devoy's *Gaelic American*; a publication that would be censored, for a time, by the American government for not adopting a strictly neutral editorial stance on the war.[33] As Devoy had not been an ally of Redmond since 1900 or 1902,[34] the United Irish League of America denounced Casement publicly for his behaviour.[35] Meanwhile, Casement's actions necessitated that the Church make an effort to prove that Boston, rather than Berlin, was the axis of Ireland's role in the Catholic world: the mere presence of American Catholic businessmen such as Diarmuid Fawsitt (formerly of the Cork IDA) at Irish Volunteer conventions was considered insufficient evidence.[36] Reflecting this, with the approval of American Catholic bishops, a definite shift in the political expression of Catholic opinion now took place in both America and Ireland. In doing so, trust was withdrawn from John Redmond and his associates.[37] As an extension of this trend, Irish Catholic leaders also made an effort to advertise, to a far greater extent than British Catholic opinion, their sense of solidarity with a Vatican-approved Catholic pacifist movement in Europe, led by Cardinal Désiré-Joseph Mercier of Belgium, in expressing principled opposition to all forms of war and military coercion.[38] To MacNeill's Irish Volunteers, whose recruitment posters depicted a lone volunteer guarding the Irish coastline under the benevolent protection of an image of the Sacred Heart,[39] Cardinal Mercier's movement represented their gallant allies in Europe and a truer representation of the politics of the Irish Catholic world than the actions of Redmond or, indeed, Casement.

The direct fallout from this development in Irish politics was the enforced resignation of Redmond's ally Douglas Hyde as president of the Gaelic League in favour of Eoin MacNeill and, practically speaking, a split in the Irish Party. Encouraged by the Irish Catholic bishops, Irish Party backbenchers now emphasised that they wished to see Ireland remain a rural and frugal society that was not only governed by Catholic family values and domestic cultural traditions but also complete immunity from the terrifying forces behind the current war between Europe's industrialised nations.[40] Reflecting this trend, William O'Brien's wing of the Irish Party soon began calling for Sinn Féin to be both revived and reinvented in order to give voice to these sentiments that the Irish Party's leadership was now incapable of doing (this issue determined the tenor of all electoral contests that would be held in Ireland that year) while T.M. Healy, the cleverest of all clericalist Irish politicians, began expressing enthusiastic support for MacNeill's Sinn-Féin-like promotion of the anti-enlistment cause as an expression of Catholic neutrality regarding the war.[41] This development suited the Catholic Church in both Ireland and neutral America and it also led to a shift in contemporary debate on Ireland's relationship with the European continent. Hitherto, academics had often compared Ireland's relationship with Britain to Belgium's relationship with France. It had been suggested, for instance, that Irish–Belgian parallels existed on the basis of their mutual desire for denominational education systems against the British–French insistence on state-controlled education, as well their co-dependent, yet supposedly positive, business habits in their industrial relations with their more powerful neighbour.[42] This perspective was now altered, however, to an exclusive focus on the Catholic factor, as represented by Cardinal Mercier and the Irish Volunteers.

Due to the recent departure of Tom Kettle for the warfront (where he would meet a tragic end, reputedly while still in search of 'the secret scripture of the poor'),[43] Archbishop Walsh needed new lay political allies to give voice to the church's stance. For this reason, he chose Joseph Mary Plunkett (son of papal count G.N. Plunkett, then director of the National Museum of Ireland) and, to a lesser extent, the Sinn Féiner Sean T. O'Kelly to act as lay intermediaries with Monsignor O'Riordan's Irish College in Rome. This was done to ensure that the Pope would fully understand and sympathise with the political predicament facing MacNeill's Irish Volunteers in maintaining its anti-enlistment and pro-Cardinal Mercier stance.[44] Allies were also sought among talented Gaelic League activists within MacNeill's volunteer movement, most notably Eamon DeValera.[45] DeValera seems to have kept watch for Archbishop Walsh on the activities of Tom Clarke's IRB circle, as well as the activities of Casement;[46] each of which were being funded by the American Clan na Gael, albeit according to strictly separate channels.[47] These developments during 1915 marked both a revival and an extension of the initiative of Daniel Mannix, formerly president of Maynooth College and now an archbishop in Melbourne, Australia, in throwing his weight behind Griffith's Hungarian Policy during 1904–5 in an effort to advance diplomatic considerations of the Roman Catholic Church beyond what the Irish Party was capable of doing. This now became a critical factor in redefining and boosting the appeal of Sinn Féin.

As an economic nationalist party under Griffith's presidency, Sinn Féin had faded into obscurity ever since 1911 and now had an only nominal existence. Griffith's personal popularity at this time, however, was boosted by the fact that the longstanding mutual hostility between Griffith and supporters of the Irish Party had recently overflowed into direct conflict. Redmond's supporters perpetually mocked the failure of Griffith's journals by labelling him as the arch practitioner of a 'mosquito press',[48] which presumably would soon be squatted out of existence. Irish popular opinion no longer particularly appreciated this attack on Griffith, however, because numerous other efforts were now being made in the press to give a voice to the stance of MacNeill's Irish Volunteers. This reality, combined with ambiguities in some sections of the Irish business community's attitude towards the war, gave Griffith a window of opportunity to launch a new journal during the autumn of 1915.

Herbert Pim, a moderate unionist and prominent member alongside the Bewley family (owners of Bewleys' Oriental Cafes since the 1840s) of the tight-knit Quaker business community of Dublin and Belfast, decided to publish some propaganda nominally in support of Sinn Féin through launching his own short-lived journal *The Irishman*, with offices in both Belfast and Dublin. The Irish Party was highly sceptical of Pim's activities and as he was an associate of Andrew Jameson (an arch-Tory director of the Bank of Ireland) his initiative was probably viewed as another example of the Tories promoting Sinn Féin as a purely cynical exercise. However, as Pim was a man of wealth and formerly a noted sympathiser with the UIL, he could not be as easily ignored or dismissed as Griffith. Pim also had a significant connection with MacNeill's Irish Volunteer movement because a family firm was its accountant.[49] Privately, Griffith also had very little time for Pim, 'my well-meaning but feather-headed friend', because (as would be represented by the title of some of Pim's publications) he was an unrepresentative spokesman in championing Sinn Féin and was also guilty of exaggerating its programme in such a manner that was likely to hold it up to ridicule.[50] Pim's adopted pseudonym in attempting to convince the public that he was now a champion of Irish nationalism, 'A. Newman', also did little to inspire confidence. Nevertheless, after the surprising success of John Devoy in organising a monster Dublin funeral procession for Jeremiah O'Donovan Rossa of New York (an event for which Griffith contributed to the commemorative booklet),[51] Griffith was able to launch a new publication with Pim as his assistant-editor. Unlike *Eire-Ireland*, *Nationality* was very much a Sinn Féin publication. It is unclear who exactly financed its publication (historians have generally assumed that it was the IRB) or how it escaped the wartime press censors,[52] but it seems likely that this development had something to do with Pim's influence in the business world.

Nationality made a determined effort to link the existence of the Irish Volunteer movement with Sinn Féin's economic nationalist policy. During its six months in print, each editorial and front-page commentary focused exclusively on economic affairs. Griffith contrasted Redmond and Carson's stance twenty years previously, when they had united under an independent (Parnellite/Tory) banner in protest against the over-taxation of Ireland, to their current stance, being united in support of a war that was exponentially increasing the over-taxation of Ireland, which had allegedly already bankrupted the country.[53] Pim himself adopted a contrary perspective.[54] Meanwhile, emphasising that 'Ireland is being taxed for this war', Griffith also argued that the motive of England and, indeed, every other war combatant, in promoting conscription was far more economic than military. In particular, Griffith suggested that the introduction of military law was a pre-emptive means to enable business leaders to contain the industrial troubles that they knew would follow the inevitable great economic disruptions caused by a major international war.[55]

Griffith argued that the year 1916, being the centenary of the amalgamation of the exchequers and the twentieth anniversary of the Financial Relations Commission report, should become the first year in Irish history when the Irish people would take the lessons of the country's economic history to heart and resolve to launch an entirely new Irish nationalist politics based on the principle of self-determination.[56] As 'the fraudulent manipulation of figures' upon which the whole 'home rule sham' was based was 'drafted to provide that the Irish should be so tightly fettered financially and commercially that they could never move forward', Griffith suggested whenever people sang 'God save Ireland' in the country they should be singing neither out of frustration nor a desire to fight militarily, but rather to express a resolve to find definite political means of averting both national bankruptcy and personal destitution for the majority of the country's inhabitants.[57] As an example of this ongoing problem Griffith noted that London bankers were currently being assisted by the legal profession in investing all Irish wartime savings purely for their own ends and that war taxation was now costing every Irish family approximately £20 additional expenses every year.[58]

Nationality attracted some notable contributors around the same time that the English press began labelling Sinn Féin as the root of all vocal opposition to the British government in Ireland.[59] However, Griffith's determined efforts to revive the economic debates of 1911 evidently meant little to most contributors and readers compared to the fact that *Nationality* now essentially became *the* vehicle for the growing number of critics of state censorship and the operations of the Defence of the Realm Act in Ireland. This led to a significant boost in the circulation of Griffith's journal,[60] and he did fairly well in appealing to this readership. Griffith intelligently dismissed pro-war propaganda—that it was a 'war for Christianity, civilisation and the small nationalities'—by emphasising that all Europeans had heard this nonsense countless times before ever since the Congress of Vienna a century earlier.[61] As additional proof of how the Defence of the Realm Act 'operates against the use of logic in Ireland', Griffith pointed to the wartime appointment of a London *Times* editor as the new editor of the *Irish Times* and the subsequent dismissal of all its old staff for being independent-minded Irish Tories.[62] Griffith viewed this as symptomatic of an enhancement of a timeless English policy to 'build a wall of paper around this island'. 'On the outside of it she wrote what she wished the peoples of Europe to believe of the Irish'; namely, that they lacked the intelligence necessary for any sustained effort (such as conceiving of economic regulations necessary to the practice of self-government) but, holding life cheap, they could at least make 'good soldiers' or 'murderers'. 'On the inside' of the paper wall, England wrote 'what she wished the Irish to believe of Europe' by closing off all meaningful communication (particularly business communications) between Ireland and the European continent or, indeed, the Americas.[63] To Griffith's mind, breaking through this 'paper wall' was not a mere propagandistic exercise: it was essential to the possibilities of the development of an Irish nationalism.

Griffith's longstanding criticisms of Irish Party activists for taking Dublin Castle jobs achieved particular currency during the war. This was because members of the Irish Volunteers were continually being arrested for simply speaking on public platforms whereas a half-dozen leaders of the Irish Party, alongside a half-dozen leaders of the Ulster Party, were simultaneously earning a £1,500 bonus to their annual parliamentary salaries of £400 a year for promoting army recruitment in Ireland.[64] Only one Irish representative at Westminster, Laurence Ginnell (the former leader of the independent UIL), was prepared to speak in parliament in protest against these weekly arrests of Irish Volunteers.[65] Griffith himself was fairly active as a public lecturer at this time, alongside Patrick Pearse.[66] That neither man was arrested was probably because neither *Nationality* nor *An Claidheamh Solus* were explicitly associated with the Irish Volunteers; a probable intention of Sean MacDermott.[67] In addition, alongside a revamped *Catholic Bulletin* (edited by a *Freeman's Journal* defector J.J. 'Sceilg' O'Kelly), they were now virtually the only Irish journals that were ready to assist the Catholic hierarchy in protesting about the refusal of the Irish Party's press to publish the clergy's pacifist letters in the Irish press. This not only gave British journalists and politicians a free rein to denounce the Irish church for refusing to endorse the Allies' war effort, but also necessitated that the bishops look outside Ireland (for example, to American forums or by making direct appeals to Rome) to allow their voices to be heard.[68]

The essential context of these developments was the same politics that had partly governed Redmond's actions in the past and, indeed, continued to do so to a significant degree; namely, the role of the Catholic Church in Anglo-American relations.[69] Griffith, however, often published sensationalist propaganda that presented the issue at hand in misleading, or at least populist, Catholic terms, namely a supposed freemason conspiracy against the Vatican.[70] As much as any political commentator, Griffith was capable of opportunist mud throwing. A direct impact of these trends on Irish politics was the emergence of Fr Michael O'Flanagan, an American priest recently brought back to Ireland by Archbishop Walsh, as both a platform speaker in support of Ginnell as well as a lead writer for Griffith's journal. In *Nationality*, Fr O'Flanagan offered critiques of the war, as well as British foreign policy, across the whole globe.[71] Meanwhile, the alleged censorship being imposed upon the Catholic Church found an impractical reflection in its peculiar impact upon Patrick Pearse. The editor of *An Claidheamh Solus* voluntarily began producing an exaggerated (almost messianic) prose regarding a 'spiritual nation' in an attempt to give symbolic, or literary, expression to what was occurring politically within Catholic Ireland. In a literary sense, this was an inspired prose that found an appreciative audience but, being a literary rather than a political man, this was essentially the full extent of Pearse's political thought:[72] outside the debate on schooling, there was little that Pearse either could or actually desired to contribute to Irish society,[73] although various personal factors had drawn him closer to the revolutionary underground's orbit.[74]

By early 1916, some in the Irish Party felt that the party needed to tone down its enthusiastic pro-enlistment stance. Although both America and the Roman Catholic Church were still in favour of total neutrality in the war, John Redmond had recently promoted a British war loan effort in the United States at the direct request of the British Foreign Office.[75] Deeming this to be a big mistake, John Dillon now called for an end to Irish enlistment and worked to secure a promise from the British cabinet that full conscription would not be introduced into Ireland.[76] As it was universally known that the Irish Party no longer had any influence with the British government, however, this was a case of 'too little too late'. The decision of Cardinal O'Connell of Boston to call a major American convention in support of the Griffithite idea of promoting Ireland's claim to full independence at whatever peace congress concluded the war was an illustration of this reality.[77]

Tom Clarke decided early in 1916 to organise a rebellion regardless of circumstances. This was a development about which Griffith was evidently kept in the dark,[78] as the Irish Party may have been, although the fact that the Admiralty, the War Office and British Foreign Office knew of this intention for an Irish rebellion (evidently via the American Foreign Office)[79] and would do nothing to prevent it would indicate that Redmond, being an employee of the Foreign Office, as well as Edward Carson and James Craig of the Admiralty, understood fully what was taking place and literally did nothing to prevent it.[80] This may be explained by the fact that an Irish rebellion would be one sure means of enabling both the British government and the two Irish political parties (the 'Irish' and 'Ulster' parties) to vindicate their politically self-defensive claim ever since September 1914 that all Irish opposition to the Allies' war effort was a German-funded conspiracy. Roger Casement was the lynchpin to this strategy.

During March and April 1916, Griffith made a somewhat abortive effort to hold a Dublin Mansion House conference on the theme of the over-taxation of Ireland. He also wrote editorials claiming that the government's forthcoming wartime budget would be catastrophic for Ireland.[81] Simultaneously, he gave public lectures to the Dublin Irish Volunteer battalions in which he celebrated their recent success in recruiting and suggested to them that they were a manifestation, 'after a lapse of 130 years', of the economic-nationalist Irish Volunteer movement of the 1780s.[82] According to Sean T. O'Kelly, Griffith learnt of the intentions for a rebellion only a couple of days before it occurred and therefore shared in MacNeill's sense of betrayal by Clarke and MacDermott for keeping him in the dark.[83] Prior arrests and increasing threats of suppression by Dublin Castle were most definitely goading the volunteers.[84] During the Easter week rebellion of the Dublin volunteers, Griffith abandoned his newspaper office and spent the week seeking to confer with Eoin MacNeill in an effort to draft a joint statement regarding the rebellion.[85] Meanwhile, Pim wrote an editorial for *Nationality* (which was subsequently suppressed by Dublin Castle) in which he practically justified the rebellion as an act of protest against a British army circular that called for the immediate arrest of all members of the Irish Volunteers, Sinn Féin and the Gaelic League.[86] This circular (which reputedly was printed in Count Plunkett's home) had been received by Alderman Tom Kelly, Sinn Féin's leader in City Hall, and read out before the corporation a whole week before the rebellion. At the time Kelly, as well as MacNeill, believed it was forgery that Dublin Castle leaked in an attempt to provoke a rebellion.[87] Certainly, the impromptu manner of both the rebellion and the casual, almost hesitant, manner in which its various leaders (most of whom had no interest in the IRB's nominally republican ideals) became involved,[88] made it a similar act to many past rebellions in various European capital cities. Like the European republican rebels of 1848, these Irish rebels resolved to simply man barricades, proclaim an ideal and then defensively hold those barricades for as long as was possible.[89]

To the rebels, the seizure of the General Post Office was partly justified, on a practical level, both as a means of preventing communications both within the city and between the city and the Curragh. However, the Dublin rebellion, having involved insufficient forces, was not essentially a military act. The General Post Office was the Irish headquarters of the British Government's Post Office Savings Bank, the chief holder of Irish citizens' private savings. It was also the institution with which the Sinn Féin People's Bank had been intended to compete. The rebels also occupied the headquarters of the Hibernian Bank.[90] This may indicate that the Dublin volunteers were drawing their own conclusion from Griffith's economic nationalist lectures. The IRB's republican proclamation was drafted in the home of Jennie Wyse Power, the treasurer of the Sinn Féin Party, whose husband John (a newspaper editor in Dublin for the previous thirty years, old IRB activist and long-term friend of both Griffith and Clarke) had long been well known in Dublin for his anti-royalist attitudes.[91] Although nominally rebelling on behalf of the IRB (partly to vindicate its 'Fenian dead'), Clarke and MacDermott, who was formerly chief organiser of the Sinn Féin Party, evidently wished that the rebellion would be associated with Sinn Féin. Reflecting this, it was claimed that they wished that Alderman Kelly, treasurer of the Sinn Féin People's Bank, alongside Griffith and Sean T. O'Kelly, would become the leaders of a provisional Irish republican government *if* the rebels could hold out long enough to establish such an assembly. In the IRB's revolutionary tradition, this was a logical stance.[92] However, O'Kelly (whose court-martial would be prevented by Archbishop Walsh and who resigned from the IRB thereafter) would never give credence to this idea.[93] More significantly, Archbishop Walsh himself claimed that the rebellion was simply the result of the postponement of the Government of Ireland Act and the ensuing breakdown of the political process ever since the previous summer (stemming from the negation of the Irish Party's independent voice) and the resulting manoeuvring of all Irish politicians in an attempt to compensate for this fact.[94]

The writer James Stephens also argued that there was a definite association between the Dublin rebellion of 24–29 April 1916 and Sinn Féin.[95] If so, this was more on the level of ideas than of organisation. While the Sinn Féin Policy (or, more specifically, the National Council platform) held the allegiance of one-sixth of the membership of Dublin City Hall during John Sweetman's Sinn Féin presidency of 1908, eight years later its representation was confined to just three city councillors.[96] Of these men, only one (W.T. Cosgrave who, like Griffith, was a mutual friend of John MacBride and Thomas MacDonagh) held rank as a senior volunteer who fought in the rising. Although he shared Tom Kelly, J.W. Power and Griffith's preoccupation with assisting the poor of Dublin (as a native of James Street, he had long known of it first hand), Cosgrave was best known hitherto as an efficient administrator and respected organiser of committees in City Hall. It was this reputation alone that saved him from execution for taking part in the rebellion.[97]

The Dublin rebellion of 1916 was deeply controversial because it was associated with two directly conflicting goals. On one hand, it gave expression to the undercurrent of resentment that had long existed among the unutilised political talent within the Gaelic League and which was now beginning to surface via the Irish Volunteers.[98] This reality reflected its actual status as a rebellion and an event that isolated circles of volunteers nationwide tended to view as having being made in their name. On the other hand, it achieved the ambition of Whitehall, John Redmond and Edward Carson to portray all opposition to the Allies' war effort as a treasonable act of sedition. The latter development was facilitated by Sir Roger Casement's arrival in Ireland with German firearms despite his total opposition to a rebellion (he immediately surrendered himself to the police).[99] Casement's action made the rising presentable as an inherently pro-German rebellion. Furthermore, as he was a nationally and internationally famous figure, the publicity that would be generated by the joint British and Irish public appeals that Casement not be executed had a significant political fall out. It was also unique. The Irish public made no appeals for clemency for any of the rebels.[100]

A fall out of the Dublin rebellion was the immediate imposition of martial law, leading to the imprisonment without trial in Britain of most leaders of the Gaelic League, the Irish Volunteers and Sinn Féin (including, of course, Griffith). Due to their continued imprisonment, this would be a source of deep political contention for a whole year after the rebellion. More so than the executions (which ultimately evoked a similar public response as those Manchester executions of 1867 which had inspired the 'God Save Ireland' national anthem), this development became the basis of the Irish public's response to the fall out of the rebellion. In particular, although a political prisoners question had begun with the arrests of the Irish Volunteers during the summer of 1915, it was the suspension of Habeas Corpus in the wake of the April 1916 disturbances that made it a deeply contentious issue. Henceforth, the British government attempted to define Irish nationalism according to the terms of Casement's so-called 'German Plot'. Catholic Ireland, lay and clerical, considered this as a grotesque case of political misrepresentation, designed only to justify the mass arrests. While this united priests and people to a greater extent in their desire to rebuke the government's perceived hypocrisy, a template had effectively been set that trapped both the Irish Volunteers and Sinn Féin into a repeating political cycle, namely arrests and a resulting struggle for recognition of political prisoner status. Aside from providing an excuse to revive the IRB, practically speaking this made the entire political world and potential of both the Irish Volunteers and Sinn Féin subject to the management of a team of crown defence lawyers who were centred in London and were also engaged with the government in the debate on the legality of introducing conscription.[101] It also made the shared experience of internment in prison a motive for many political figures' subsequent actions.

Griffith was extraordinarily close to the rebellion. He was one of only a handful of people who knew virtually all the men who were executed for their part in the rising personally. He reacted 'with unusual emotion' when he learnt from his prison cell in London (where he was held after the rising) of the executions: 'something of the primitive man awoke in me. I clenched my fists with rage and I longed for vengeance.'[102] Indeed, like many other Irish contemporaries, Griffith soon turned into an emotional sympathiser with the rebellion *after* the event. This was partly the rebels' motive. Shortly before his execution, MacDermott explained to a friend in prison that 'we hoped to push the ball up the hill high enough for others to push it up the whole way after us'.[103] The general Irish public's reaction to the rising, however, was shaped less by whatever idealism that the rebels may have felt—Sisyphus' impossible goal was hardly an inspiring *political* ideal—than by the simple fact that the Irish experience of the First World War was mostly indirect. This was certainly true for all sympathisers with the Irish Volunteers. While the great loss of life on the European continent was a major concern of the families of recruited soldiers, the Irish public did not witness their suffering, just as Zeppelin bombings of civilian populations (terrifying events that Griffith would experience while imprisoned in London)[104] were completely unknown in Ireland. Instead, the introduction of severe martial law in reaction to a student-like Dublin rebellion became the lens through which a great deal of Irish public opinion perceived the political meaning of the war precisely because it was this martial law that made militarism visible from their front door steps for the first time, as if Ireland had somehow become something of a war-zone itself despite the absolute peace that reigned in the land. This paradox created significant political tensions and actually inspired more people to join the Irish Volunteers in an attempt to act as a peaceable citizens' defence force in opposition to the suspension of the right to trial before imprisonment.

Hitherto, the Irish Volunteer movement had encompassed a multitude of perspectives that were united according to its politically justifiable and non-seditious ethos of civil defence, namely guarding the Irish coastline for the British government at a time of international war. In the wake of the introduction of martial law, however, it suddenly acquired the ethos of civil defiance.[105] This not only increased its members' sense of political self-importance (they could now claim to be community leaders of some sort) but it effortlessly and unwittingly turned the volunteer movement into a public expression of that political mentality which the IRB had hitherto attempted to instil into Irish society purely by stealth; namely, that the *sans culottes* of Irish society should become a committed citizen–soldier polity who were proverbial brothers in the IRB's 'virtually established republic' in opposition to the martial law of a distant monarchical government.[106] In this way, a cult of the 1916 rebels was born to a significant degree.

Desiring recognition as a political prisoner, Griffith deliberately engaged in rebellious activities in Reading gaol. Together with fellow Sinn Féiners Walter Cole, Ernest Blythe and Sean T. O'Kelly, he burned a copy of the Government of Ireland Bill and on being subsequently brought before a prison committee Griffith (who also refused to shave for so long as he was in prison) 'told them they did not exist for me and that I did not recognise either them or the British Government'.[107] Arthur Lynch, an Australian-born republican and former pro-Boer commando (by now the British army's principal recruitment officer within the Irish Party's ranks) spoke in favour of a general amnesty for all the Irish prisoners that November, using Griffith's case as a prime example. Griffith was actually angered by this, however, having a letter smuggled out of prison to state that he in no sense wanted special treatment, or for the Irish Party to act on his behalf 'as they know how much I detest them'.[108] Having been interned rather than subject to trial, Griffith was released from prison that December. As a result, he was able to arrive home in Clontarf to greet his wife and children on Christmas Day morning. The political prisoners issue continued long afterwards, however, and became a significant basis for political mobilisation.

The publicity surrounding Casement's case allowed his defence lawyer George Gavan Duffy to create a prisoners' aid association, known as the Irish National Aid Association (it soon expanded its title to include the phrase 'Volunteers Dependants Fund'), in London during the summer of 1916. This soon spread to Dublin where Fred Allan managed the local organisation up until June 1917, when the last of the senior prisoners were released.[109] These included Eoin MacNeill, the nominal leader of the volunteers, and two figures who, like Sean T. O'Kelly, escaped court martial and execution, namely the Countess Markievicz and Eamon DeValera. None of these figures was happy about the IRB's ongoing influence in the Irish Volunteer movement and wished to see it disbanded. The IRB's survival was facilitated partly by Allan's decision to surrender the reins of the Irish National Aid and Volunteers Dependants Fund to Michael Collins, a young successor to Tom Clarke as IRB treasurer who had been selected for the position by Clarke's widow. Collins was released from prison in December 1916 alongside Michael Staines, the most senior-ranking volunteer to surviving the rising.[110] Echoing developments after P.W. Nally's prison death in 1891, the friendship that had formerly existed between John Dillon and Thomas Ashe, a senior ranking volunteer who died in prison from force-feeding, seems to have assisted Collins in acquiring insider information from UIL figures regarding the operations of the police at Dublin Castle.[111] This may indicate that Irish Party–IRB networks, stemming initially from the non-confrontational O'Brienite–Fitzgerald stance of the mid-1880s and culminating in P.T. Daly and Bulmer Hobson's anti-Griffith stance in the late Edwardian period, had continued uninterrupted throughout the First World War. Whatever the case, any continuity in Irish political organisations after the rebellion mattered little compared to the British government's utilisation of the rebellion to advance its own framework of home rule.

The most significant fall out of the Dublin rebellion was the British cabinet's decision to appoint David Lloyd George, the Chancellor of the Exchequer (he would be appointed Prime Minister that winter), as the head of a new government committee on Ireland. This committee announced in June 1916 that the Government of Ireland Act would be introduced in Ireland according to a definite plan for partition, permanently excluding six northern counties, while it was also announced that the conscription question would not be dropped. From prison, Griffith judged that Lloyd George's efforts to push forward the questions of partition and conscription would probably 'tend to unite those whom it was meant to further divide'.[112] However, it actually led to a further split in the Irish Party's United Irish League. An anti-partition group in Ulster known as the Irish Nation League was formed. It received a political boost around Christmas 1916 when the release of Count Plunkett and Griffith from prison coincided with the death of the MP for North Roscommon James O'Kelly, an old founder of Parnell's Irish Party and lifelong friend of John Devoy.[113]

With the support of Fr Michael O'Flanagan (curate of Boyle, Co. Roscommon) and some Catholic bishops, Count Plunkett expressed support for the Irish Nation League and announced his intention to stand for O'Kelly's vacant seat. As Plunkett's son had been executed for his part in the Dublin rebellion, the count presented himself as a protest candidate who had no intention taking his seat alongside the Irish Party if he was elected. Sensing an opportunity, Griffith endorsed Plunkett's campaign on behalf of Sinn Féin. Plunkett's success in February 1917 enabled Griffith to revive *Nationality* with financial assistance from James O'Mara, whose son Stephen (who represented the third generation of the O'Mara business dynasty) simultaneously became the treasurer of the Irish Nation League. The latter body refused to ally itself with Sinn Féin, however.[114]

Reflecting Griffith's newly found fame (an anonymous biographical pamphlet on Griffith would soon be produced),[115] the front-page header of the new edition of *Nationality* bore a large subtitle 'edited by Arthur Griffith'; the first time his name featured so prominently on one of his journals. During and after his imprisonment, Griffith remained convinced that attempting to secure representation as a small nationality at whatever peace conference concluded the war should be Ireland's sole concern. This was notwithstanding the fact that it was absolutely clear to him that, even if Irish nationalists secured a strong representation, 'we are not going to get all we need'. Instead, an essential propaganda purpose would be served: whether they gained entry to the peace conference or not, Irish politicians could

> Stand on the stairs and harangue the world outside … to unmask a hypocrite [Britain], educate Europe and clarify the mind of a lot of silly Irish people who believe Ireland has a duty to look after other people's affairs and not to attend to her own.[116]

If this was far from a practical programme, the fissures within virtually all political organisations since May 1915, combined with the fear of conscription, an ongoing rancher dispute in rural Ireland and the expectation of urban labour disputes arising from the industrial impact of the war, made any new catch-all political programmes generally appealing to the Irish public at this time. As a result, the traditional Irish Party rhetoric of loyalty to 'The [One] Party' lost a little of its hold. Beginning in Cork City,[117] Sinn Féin now began to win some support for implementing the platform that Griffith suggested.[118]

Even by his own standards, Griffith now became merciless in attacking the Irish Party, who 'dominated Ireland by corruption and intimidation for years past'. Portraying it as the party that had cheered when the 1916 rebels were shot, Griffith argued that

> Not until they approved that government's execution of Irish patriots and sought to aid it in partitioning Ireland as it had partitioned Bengal ten years before did the Irish people fully realise that the party they had trusted and supported exceeded in treachery and corruption that party … which 116 years ago sold its country and constituents by voting the Act of Union for England's pay and rejoiced it had a country to sell…So far as the gold and aid of English governments can resuscitate and rehabilitate the Seventy [Irish Party MPs], that gold and aid will be given. It would be imprudent to underrate the hidden strength behind this mass of corruption and unwise to delay in organising the strength of the now resentful people.[119]

While Griffith maintained a reasonable focus upon the government's fiscal policy as the determinant of political events, his propagandistic instincts also led him to emphasise social disruptions in the country, emphasising wartime food shortages (as big an influence on public attitudes at the time as the conscription threat),[120] inflated prices and, indeed, arrests.[121] The context of the latter was certainly not any offensive military campaign by the Irish Volunteers.[122] Rather, it was the involvement of rural members of the volunteers in Laurence Ginnell's anti-rancher agitation. This agitation was inspired by the fact that the Land Act of 1903 had never been a particularly workable measure for either landlords or tenants, notwithstanding the (politically-motivated) claims of Tom Kettle's circle of UCD academics to the contrary. Although the Irish Party had opposed Ginnell's agitation ever since its inception in 1906 that opposition now became militant among both Irish Party supporters and unionist landowners, led by Viscount Midleton in Cork, who demanded arrests and accused Ginnell's followers of sectarian animosity.[123]

The motive behind these reactions was the fact that the British government's postponement of the Government of Ireland Act similarly postponed indefinitely a necessary reconsideration of land law. Potentially, this allowed the tenantry the opportunity in the interregnum to attempt to impose their own terms on landowners;[124] a class that now included many Irish Party supporters. This disruptive development had a knock-on effect on urban areas. This formed a backdrop for industrial disputes that similarly were not governed by any militancy among activists, but rather the disruptive economic impact that the First World War had upon an already totally divided economy.[125] Oldham's explanation of this division was accurate. This was that the dynamics of economic development within Ireland had made manufacturers and farmers direct competitors with each other in seeking aid from Britain rather than economic allies in their relationship with Britain, thereby separating the rural and urban economies from each other.[126] So long as this remained the case, there could be no distinct economy of Ireland, nor could one reasonably speak of the existence of an Irish nationalist politics. This was why Griffith's employment of a strict national determinism in his arguments as the basis of 'true political economy'[127] did not reflect either business or labour thought within Ireland to any significant degree. It was Griffith's hope, however, that the Sinn Féin Party could soon remedy this situation.

Griffith's idea of abstaining from Westminster politics remained unpopular in Ireland. The Irish Nation League championed the idea of representation at a post-war peace conference and denounced the Irish Party as being beyond hope (it had 'misled the country' and 'sacrificed opportunities') but it did not rule out seeking representation at Westminster because it was considered that the challenge of creating an effective new political organisation required a very careful testing of the waters.[128] Eamon DeValera was likewise very hesitant to accept the idea of directly opposing the Irish Party at the polls. This was because he was far from sure upon what platform any new party should be based and judged that Griffith's Sinn Féin Policy of opposing Britain economically was 'irrelevant' and tended 'to alienate a number of Irishmen'.[129] The question of political leadership was also problematic. Neither Plunkett nor Griffith, who had always sought to find suitable spokesmen for his policy, was considered prospective party leaders. Plunkett was actually in favour of the complete disbandment of Sinn Féin, not just the IRB. In the face of this impasse, Fr Michael O'Flanagan formed a few new branches of Sinn Féin on his own initiative and organised a party convention without the prior consent of Griffith as the party's president in an attempt to create a new tenor for Sinn Féin.[130] A far more critical factor in determining the future of Sinn Féin, however, was the stance of William Martin Murphy and his *Irish Independent* newspaper.

The British government's decision in May 1917 to introduce a new franchise bill to enfranchise most men, as well as women over the age of thirty, was practically guaranteed to make as deep an impact on political arrangements in Ireland as did the franchise bill of 1884 (it was this measure that first allowed Parnell's party to secure more than a marginal political representation). Griffith suggested that the Irish Party would desire to delay, or even prevent, the implementation of a new franchise bill, fearing its consequences.[131] Just as Gladstone had launched negotiations between Parnell, Archbishop Walsh and Dublin Castle to stage manage the impact in Ireland of the 1884 franchise bill, Lloyd George proposed launching a convention of all Irish parliamentary representatives at Trinity College Dublin under the chairmanship of Sir Horace Plunkett of Dublin Castle's Department of Agriculture and Erskine Childers to stage manage Irish politicians' reaction to the latest enfranchisement. Invitations to attend were sent to all parties, including Sinn Féin.[132] The Prime Minister intended that the implementation of partition was to be a subject of discussion. With the support of three Protestant bishops, the Irish Catholic hierarchy actually made a public declaration against partition in seeming deliberate defiance of Lloyd George, even though Archbishop Walsh simultaneously wrote to the press emphasising that it would be 'living in a fool's paradise' to deny that the partition question was already settled because of the formation of the British cabinet's Irish government subcommittee in June 1916: 'the mischief has been already done ... the country is practically sold.'[133] Griffith liked to claim otherwise,[134] as did William Martin Murphy, who made the *Irish Independent* the leader of an anti-partition movement.

Murphy scored a political coup against Horace Plunkett and Erskine Childers by attending their Irish Convention and thereafter highlighting the complete lack of freedom of debate allowed to its participants. By championing the idea of demanding greater political autonomy (including fiscal autonomy) for Ireland than was on offer under the Government of Ireland Act, Murphy and the *Irish Independent*, which became the top-selling newspaper in the country, gave a tremendous boost to Sinn Féin.[135] Griffith soon boasted that the circulation of his weekly organ *Nationality* 'now exceeds that of any journal published in Ireland except the *Daily* [i.e. *Irish*] *Independent*'[136]—a very remarkable and sudden change in Griffith's career as an editor and journalist—but he essentially owed this development entirely to Murphy's initiative. The *Irish Independent* was the most popular newspaper to Sinn Féin's newly found supporters. Prior to Murphy's death in June 1919, it even nicknamed itself as 'the generalissimo of Irish newspapers' on the basis of its effective leadership of the post-1917 independence movement in Ireland,[137] which was opposed by all other Irish newspapers with a national circulation. In this sense, if it was not for Murphy it is doubtful that Sinn Féin could ever have become an increasingly popular party during and after 1917.[138]

The United States' decision to enter the war in April 1917 due to Germany's opening of a military treaty with Mexico and simultaneous launch of submarine attacks on American commercial transports to Britain played a major part in determining the war's outcome. In Ireland, the US entry into the war played a significant role in giving a boost to demands for alternative forms of political representation. With assistance from the Irish National Aid Association and Volunteers Dependent Fund, a political prisoner (Joseph McGuinness) was narrowly returned as an abstentionist (nominally Sinn Féin) candidate in Longford in early May. During this campaign, the hitherto unknown figure of Michael Collins, echoing theatrical old IRB election tactics, literally burst into a Sinn Féin meeting uninvited and announced that any abstentionist candidates should be run on a republican ticket.[139] This idea was not accepted (Collins had no position within Sinn Féin) but Maurice Moynihan, the old founder of Sinn Féin in Kerry and a long-term supporter of Griffith, championed it on the grounds that 'the United States did not join this war for the purpose of re-establishing on a firmer base the tottering thrones and effete monarchies of Europe' and, therefore, republicanism was bound to become the future basis of a post-war peace conference. Moynihan suggested that the Irish Party and all Irish politicians should be focused upon this reality. The war had supposedly been fought for the small nationalities of Europe and many of these were expected to become republics after the war, as 'the age of monarchy is rapidly passing into history'. Therefore, it would be foolish not to present Ireland's desire for self-government in a similar light.[140] Around this time some British imperialists actually began championing the idea of an Irish republic, albeit for a different motive.

Captain Stuart Stephens' *The Repeal of the Union Conspiracy, or Mr. Parnell and the IRB* (London, 1886)—an English Tory publication which was nicknamed in British secret service circles as 'the Black Pamphlet'—had cited the Irish republican ideal negatively for the sake of the ensuing *Times* inspired British government commission, whereby the Irish Party renounced all its alleged Irish nationalist tendencies during the Land League days.[141] Thirty years later, however, Stephens suggested in the *English Review* that in the post-war challenge of reconstructing the imperial economy, establishing an Irish republic 'within the British Empire' could be a feasible and peaceable solution. This prompted Eoin MacNeill to write to the *English Review* in support of Stephens' seemingly paradoxical idea.[142]

MacNeill's motive, as understood by Griffith, was to champion the principle that 'whatever form of government, whether it be the Greek form of republicanism or the Gaelic form of monarchy, a freed Ireland might choose for herself, it is obvious that the interest of an independent Irish state would direct her to live in peace with her nearest neighbour'. Therefore, MacNeill welcomed the fact that Stephens had argued that any 'objection to the independence of Ireland from the English military point of view' was unsustainable. Griffith's own take on this reality was that 'a completely independent Ireland would live in peace with England, whereas a fettered Ireland never can'.[143] Unlike MacNeill or Griffith, however, Stephens did not oppose the government's plans for partition. His republican suggestion, therefore, was evidently meant exclusively for a future 'Southern Ireland'. As the creation of a written and federal constitution for the United Kingdom was impossible, if there were to be two Irish parliaments under a partition settlement, one of the parliaments would have to be excluded from the United Kingdom altogether according to a colonial, as opposed to federal, principal of imperial government. As Childers had noted in 1911, this parliament could only retain its connection with the United Kingdom, as well as the Empire, by means of an alternative form of 'association' to what was the norm in 'the external relations of the Dominions'.[144] At least in theory, a British republic of Southern Ireland could attain this goal.

Among most new Sinn Féin supporters there was great uncertainty, at both the level of propaganda and party organisation, as to whether challenging the Irish Party should be viewed as an end in itself or whether the state of the country's entire political representation was a question that was potentially growing dangerously out of hand. This paradox was reflected best by the nomination of DeValera as a Sinn Féin Party candidate for East Clare a month after his release from prison in June 1917. Griffith celebrated DeValera's return, suggesting that he was 'a man with the mind and capacity that Ireland will need at the Peace Conference—the mind and capacity of the statesman'.[145] As DeValera was a trusted confidant of Archbishop Walsh, however, the Catholic Church strongly supported DeValera's candidacy without actually rejecting the Irish Party. This was not well appreciated by the Irish Party leadership at the time, which judged if any Sinn Féin victory should occur 'the blame for the defeat ... will lie on the bishops and the priests who split the National vote',[146] but as far as the church was concerned, a rise of Sinn Féin did not necessarily represent an eclipse of the Irish Party. This was its great difference with Griffith, who refused to attend Horace Plunkett's convention less as a means of allying himself with the Catholic bishops in making a tactical refusal to cooperate with Lloyd George than a means of encouraging the Irish public to reject all of what Horace Plunkett's political career represented; namely, the British government's economic policy, accepted hitherto by both the Irish and Ulster Parties, that agriculture must inherently be Ireland's only indigenous industry.

Prior to the war, Irish economic commentaries had emphasised that government statistics regarding the wealth and annual trading figures of the United Kingdom were absolutely no indication of economic or trading circumstances for Ireland and the very great material challenges that were facing inhabitants of both town and country, often leading to emigration.[147] Horace Plunkett's Department of Agriculture had been ridiculed for its very expensive and seemingly useless work (such as producing grossly unreliable and politically motivated statistics regarding agricultural trade),[148] while Griffith had argued that the Irish public should not believe Plunkett when he claimed to have insider cabinet knowledge that Lloyd George only had Ireland's best financial interests at heart.[149] Griffith's efforts to sustain these arguments during the war had generally gone unnoticed, however.

Although Lindsay Crawford, Griffith's old friend (now in Canada), would claim that the Dublin rebellion of 1916 was economically motivated,[150] virtually no contemporaries (including Pim, who soon withdrew his support for Sinn Féin)[151] shared this perspective or championed Griffith's claim from October 1915 onwards that the Irish Volunteers were primarily an economic–nationalist movement. This was hardly surprising. A nationalisation of Irish finances would have totally disrupted and potentially undermined the wealth of Catholic Ireland alongside that of every other Irish interest group. The ambition of NUI Chancellor Archbishop Walsh to maximise future British funding for Irish education had essentially no different motive to the protest of Pearse's circle of Gaelic Leaguers (many of whom took part in the rebellion) that a shift in British financial management of Irish education had taken place, from positive discrimination in favour of promotion of the Irish language to a reversal of this stance.[152] Neither the Dublin rebellion nor its aftermath essentially altered this consensus.

The (mostly unionist) business community had ridiculed Griffith's justification of the Irish Volunteers' anti-enlistment stance as an economic matter. They questioned Griffith's sanity in overlooking the fact that neither the British government nor Irish businessmen of any political persuasion could ignore the economic context of the war. Characteristically, Griffith retorted to this argument that 'sane people in Ireland are those who realise that 2 and 2 make 4, and who cannot be persuaded by bribery or coercion to declare that they make 3, 5, 7 or 9 as the exigencies of British exploitation demand'.[153] War or no war, Griffith maintained that the essential question was that the Government of Ireland Act on the statute books was nothing more than 'a penal act against Irish finance'.[154] He maintained that Lloyd George's proposed Irish Convention was nothing more than a ruse to disguise this fact. However, the extent to which Griffith had been prepared to attack literally *everybody* (including W.M. Murphy)[155] in print during the period 1913–16 may not have lent much credence to his arguments to contemporaries.

Under the Government of Ireland Act, all taxation in Ireland was to be collected by the British customs authorities and the British Board of Inland Revenue. In turn, this was to be sent to the imperial treasury where a five-man 'joint exchequer board', consisting of two Irish and two British nominees and a chairman appointed by the British cabinet (thereby securing a permanent British majority), were to decide how Irish taxes were to be spent. Under such circumstances, Griffith argued, 'the authority of the Irish parliament in College Green will not exceed the grocer at the corner'.[156] At any time it pleased, the British parliament could continue to implement commercial restrictions to secure a permanent monopoly in Ireland for British-based firms, necessitating in turn that Irish businessmen would have to make London their headquarters. While Carson and Redmond's supporters, in defence of the British government's policy, had always deliberately ridiculed Sinn Féin (not least owing to the small-scale of its Aonach na Nollaig) as a simple-minded protectionist movement for a handful of products, Griffith pointed out that this propaganda deliberately misrepresented Sinn Féin as inherently protectionist in order to mask the sound reasoning of its economic nationalist strategy:

> The question of the control of customs is not a question of whether Ireland will or will not adopt a tariff against England. It is a question of whether Ireland is to remain forever subject to the fiscal policy that a majority of the British parliament may at any time pursue

without concern for Ireland's interests ... Eighty years ago England
pursued the most rigidly protective policy in Europe. Ireland was
forced to pursue the same policy without regard to whether it
suited her or not. Sixty years ago England reversed her fiscal policy
and Ireland was forced to do the same. Years hence England may
return to protection, and if Ireland is in the same position ... she
will be forced to do the same ... The question of customs is not—
let us repeat and emphasise—a question of raising tariffs against
England. It is a question of preventing Ireland from having her
fiscal policy upset every time a new fiscal doctrine appeals to the
English electors as good for England.[157]

Griffith argued that Lloyd George had played a deliberate game of 'playing
Southern Irishmen off against Northern Irishmen and then hypocritically
lamenting that the Irish nation is not unanimous'.[158] Irish Party and Ulster Party
representatives both accepted that the existing Government of Ireland Act was
irreversibly on the statute books and were now supposedly united, at Lloyd
George's request, in speaking at Trinity College about the principle of dominion
government or 'colonial home rule'. Griffith argued, however, that this was being
done in order to prevent Irish, British and international (especially American)
public opinion from understanding that the Prime Minister's Government of
Ireland Act on the statute book was actually a complete negation of this principle.
A dominion government, Griffith noted, would have absolute control over
customs and excise; the right to raise and control an army and navy; the right
to enter trade treaties with all nations; freedom from the British national debt
and the right to decline to participate in any of England's wars—'large and useful
measures', representing 'independence within the British Empire'—but none
of these rights was granted by the Government of Ireland Act. For this reason,
Griffith argued that the 'unity' of which the Ulster and Irish Parties now spoke
at Trinity College is 'but a name for the mask of English statecraft', under which
'Ireland is forced to cheer her own degradation and her own proposed mutilation'
by championing a deliberate ignorance of constitutional facts. Griffith noted
that if any believers in 'home rule' had ever existed in Ireland hitherto, Irish
and Ulster party representatives would have been perpetually taking dominion
constitutions, adapting them to Irish circumstances, and putting them forward
as an Irish claim. This had never been done, however, so 'apparently the idea that
Ireland should really possess as much power as even a British colony was too big
for their grasping'.[159]

Griffith called upon all supporters of the Irish and Ulster Parties to refocus
on the meaningful debate on the actual fiscal relationship between Britain

and Ireland that had taken place during 1911 prior to Horace Plunkett and Lloyd George's success in silencing the issue. He pointed out that English merchant shipping owners' exclusive control of the Irish trading circumstances (determining transport and, in turn, customs costs) governed economic realities in northern and southern Ireland to the exact same extent and, therefore, no reasonable person could possibly deny that the economy was inherently the sole basis of their shared experience. Griffith also suggested English merchants' control of transport and customs costs was also the real cause, rather than wartime shortages, of rising coal and food prices in Ireland.[160] He argued that a sound reason for Ulster politicians to reject 'a leader like Sir Edward Carson' was that it was 'well known to those engaged in Ulster trade' that, at present, 'Belfast is governed by the British coal and iron ring, which has a tight grip on the industries of the north.' Carson, being 'surrounded on one side by Bonar Law, the head of the Scottish iron trade, and by Londonderry, the great coal owner, with Lord Rhondda [a Welsh coal industrialist and Lloyd George's Minister for Food Control] in the rear', could never 'be expected to secure the economic independence of Ulster. That is a task which waits on other hands.'[161]

At this time, Carson and his new southern unionist ally Viscount Midleton of Cork were dining with British army generals in Dublin's Kildare Street Club and calling for the imposition of martial law throughout Ireland as the only solution to all the country's problems. By contrast, Thomas Lough, who would have been a more natural successor of Edward Saunderson as the leader of the Ulster Unionist Party, was joining with Sir Thomas Henry Grattan Esmonde in speaking out in support of Griffith's arguments against the impact of wartime taxation on Irish economic interests.[162] That this argument did not receive wider currency, or publicity, was partly due to Lloyd George's success in using the Irish Convention to divert attention away from his *actual* policy regarding Ireland, which was to secure greater control of the country's banks in order to better enable him implement partition without disrupting the economic provisions of the Government of Ireland Act.

With Lloyd George's encouragement, at the same time as DeValera's highly publicised East Clare election campaign, the London City & Midlands Bank (later known as the Midlands Bank) purchased the Belfast Bank. This was quickly followed by the purchase of the Ulster Bank by the London County & Westminster Bank. These developments went largely unnoticed by the general Irish public. Even Griffith evidently failed to notice them until the autumn of 1917.[163] Concurrently, C.H. Oldham was appointed by UCD as its new 'chair of national economics'. Although he had been a pivotal figure in highlighting discrepancies in the Anglo-Irish economic relationship during 1911, to Griffith's dismay, upon the outbreak of the war Oldham practically became a mouthpiece for the arguments of Plunkett's Department of Agriculture; a body regarding which Griffith noted that 'particulars must be known to it' but 'it carefully keeps them hidden until it is too late. Meanwhile the British government, which knows the facts, is putting into force a policy of partition already'.[164]

During the war, Oldham began arguing that Ireland's century-long unemployment and emigration problems 'seems to be drawing near its end' due to wartime recruitment and the impossibility of actually emigrating during wartime. He also suggested that the economic logic of the European war, as well as trends in international trading, seemed to favour an even closer integration of Irish with British business interests in the future, especially in the areas patronised by Plunkett, such as the export of livestock.[165] While Griffith deemed Oldham to be 'a most estimable man' and to be infinitely better suited to the UCD chair than his predecessor Tom Kettle, 'who knew a great deal about English literature and nothing whatever about economics of any kind',[166] he deemed Oldham's appointment at UCD to be a terrible mistake. This was because 'he instructs his pupils that Ireland is an economic complement of Great Britain' and 'that political misfortunes and social instability are the chief factors in the economic decadence of Ireland' rather than the actual economic impact of British legislation. Like Oldham, Griffith maintained that every aspect of Irish trade 'requires careful investigation'. However, Griffith argued that this was being 'carried on in a haphazard fashion, without regard to the interest of the producer or the consumer' in Ireland. This was entirely contrary to the idea of teaching national economics.[167]

Griffith's claim that the question of the banks 'requires more careful examination than has yet been given to it'[168] by the general Irish public was echoed at this time by R.C. Kelly, K.C., a director of the National Bank. Speaking before the Social for the Statistical and Social Inquiry of Ireland, Kelly protested that not until the latter stages of the war, when the disturbing prospect was being raised of the Irish banks being completely bought out by recently amalgamated British banks, 'not to bring money here but to take money from Ireland' (just as had occurred after the end of the Napoleonic Wars), was any consideration being made by Irish economic analysts that the temporary economic bubble created by the war had masked much more fundamental problems in the infrastructure of the economy of Ireland ('the denationalising of our banks and annexing of their resources') which had temporarily been forgotten about and were now potentially about to grow much more acute.[169]

Griffith's distrust of the British government is understandable if one considers that the Government of Ireland Act was drafted on the basis of an alleged deficit (£1.5m) in Ireland's annual contribution to Britain when the country's revenue was approximately £10 million a year, whereas Britain's wartime management of the economy of Ireland had necessitated since 1914 the withdrawal from the country of surpluses ranging up to from £23 million a year to meet the costs of the war effort.[170] This reflected the fact that both southern Irish farmers and northern industrialists had to increase production very significantly to meet the needs of the war effort, leading to a commensurate increase in Irish banks' level of investment in British government stock in London. Many individual businessmen no doubt profited from the war venture.[171] Griffith was not blind to this. He argued that, under current circumstances, Irish and Ulster Party supporters could no longer 'plead a desire for the prosperity of Ireland as the ground of his unionism, though he might plead a desire for his own personal prosperity at the expense of Ireland'.[172] Similarly, he judged that 'not the country but the banks are doing well out of the increase in deposits' and that the simultaneous raising of the prospect of their absorption into British banks 'is dangerous and unsatisfactory'.[173]

The integration of the Irish banks' business activities with the British war effort was a matter that Griffith could only critique in the manner of a student observer rather than a master analyst of the financial world. This was because, as always, he could only draw upon whatever information that the banks themselves chose to make public.[174] On this basis, Griffith was highly critical of the Munster and Leinster Bank for keeping very little of its money within Ireland;[175] credited the National Bank for having a financial position 'of great strength', although 'we are not told the relevant extent of its business in Ireland';[176] and criticised the Hibernian Bank for losing money in foreign investments.[177] Without formally speaking in favour of the nationalisation of the banks—an objective that he no doubt realised was unattainable—Griffith re-emphasised that:

> Banking is the key to industry, and until Ireland can secure control over her banks she cannot be said to possess the golden key of the future. The resources of our people, as indicated by savings deposited in the banks, are ample to develop our commerce when they are duly applied to that purpose.[178]

Banks could only survive by engaging in profitable enterprises, however, and Griffith's own critique of the Hibernian ('it would be interesting to know how much money the bank has really lost in foreign investments ... at all events it would be better to have the money lost in Ireland than abroad')[179] unwittingly highlighted a reason why the banks did not have much confidence in the Irish business market. This was also why the banks' Irish shareholders, who (as Griffith well knew)[180] were generally receiving very limited dividends, were not issuing demands to the banks' directors to risk taking such action.[181]

Over the next few years, all Griffith's weekly publications frequently printed statistics summarising the assets of all Irish banks, critiquing or appraising their performance somewhat neutrally according to any rise or fall in their deposits, and repeating the claim that once these assets were applied for Irish purposes the country's problems could begin to be addressed.[182] This material was published alongside Griffith's claims that any rebellion against British rule must be economic, not militaristic, in nature, and that a London-centred Irish financial world was effectively conspiring against a realistic Irish economic nationalist alternative.[183] As he had done since 1915, the British government's 'victory fund' or 'war loan' fund-raising campaign was a matter that Griffith critiqued by suggesting that whatever figures the Chancellor of the Exchequer produced in this matter relating to Ireland would no doubt be as unreliable as whatever figures were produced prior to the war: 'England shall collect 15 shillings in every pound sterling of Irish revenue, and shall herself keep the books and fake them.'[184] Griffith's deliberate denotation of the Sinn Féin Party's own fundraising campaign as Ireland's 'victory war fund' was an attempt to highlight to all party supporters that the Sinn Féin policy was, first and foremost, an attempt to reject British management of Irish economic interests.[185]

If Griffith's claims regarding the limiting effects of British legislation were justifiable, to a significant degree it was the practice of Irish financial institutions that he was faulting first and foremost. They feared that if opportunities to invest in profitable British governmental or commercial businesses became more limited, they would suffer financially. This development could, in turn, further decrease whatever limited capital they had available to invest in Irish business. As Dublin more so than Belfast was still essentially Ireland's banking capital, Griffith continued to stand by his conviction that 'unionist Ulster cannot cut itself adrift from the rest of Ireland without, if the rest of Ireland so wills, suffering enormous loss' in a self-governing Ireland.[186] To continue making such arguments after the banking developments of 1917, however, was naïve and, on a political level, deeply controversial. This was possibly why many new Sinn Féin activists did not risk championing Griffith's economic nationalist ideas.

The purchase of the Ulster Bank by the Westminster Bank in October 1917 coincided with a nominal redefinition of the Sinn Fein Party's objectives as well as an alternation of its executive. Griffith willingly stepped down as president of Sinn Féin in favour of DeValera,[187] who was simultaneously granted the presidency of the Irish Volunteers by MacNeill. The party subsequently decided that while it would attempt to champion the ideal of an Irish republic at future international peace conferences—the adoption of a republican demand being deemed necessary solely to attract *some* American and international attention to Ireland—whatever form of government an independent Ireland might ever take in the future must be a matter that was left entirely open.[188] Reflecting this, in his opening speech as the new leader of Sinn Féin, DeValera adopted a more Catholic as well as a more militant tone than Griffith. If the former stance echoed the legacy of John Sweetman, the latter was deemed necessary by DeValera if only to prove his own suitability to become the new president of the Irish Volunteers. The changes in the Sinn Féin Party at this time were more a matter of organisation than of policy, however.

Three new figures (Fr O'Flanagan, Countess Markievicz and Count Plunkett) became vice-presidents of Sinn Féin, alongside the veteran figures of Arthur Griffith, Sean T. O'Kelly and W.T. Cosgrave (recently elected as an abstentionist candidate for Kilkenny). Long-term friends of Griffith in Sinn Féin, such as Alderman Tom Kelly, Robert Brennan and Jennie Wyse Power, remained the party's directors for elections, but this responsibility was now taken on more by newcomers such as Fr O'Flanagan who, in the absence of a chief whip (this was not a parliamentary party), was effectively the party's chief organiser. The latter trend was encouraged by the simultaneous appointment of Bishop Fogarty of Killaloe, the Catholic bishop for DeValera's electoral constituency, as the Sinn Féin Party treasurer. This was essentially a preliminary step to the decision of another Catholic bishop, Bishop O'Donnell of Raphoe, to resign as the treasurer of the Irish Party. O'Donnell's decision motivated the resignation of Joseph Devlin of west Belfast (the AOH president) from the Irish Convention and partial distancing of himself from the Irish Party, of which he had previously been chief whip.[189]

The O'Mara business dynasty in Limerick, who had been co-treasurers with Bishop O'Donnell of the Irish Party since the late 1880s (notwithstanding James O'Mara's partial siding with Griffith in 1906), now began working with Bishop Fogarty.[190] This represented, on a very real financial level, the transference of Catholic financial support away from John Redmond to Eamon DeValera. It also led to a sudden transformation of Sinn Féin from an organisation with very little funds to an actual political party that was not short of money.[191] Reflecting this, its immediate focus was less upon the formulation of policy than the mere establishment of party branches in order to create a new political party. Just like the former branches of Redmond's party, these were usually convened and chaired by parish priests.[192]

Over the next six months, Griffith toured the country fairly regularly to address new Sinn Féin party branches in the counties Cavan, Waterford, Donegal, Tyrone, Clare, Tipperary, Kilkenny, Roscommon, Mayo, Offaly and Limerick.[193] *Nationality* presented the idea of Irish representation at the post-war peace conference as the most realistic and constructive alternative to the Prime

Minister's Irish Convention at Trinity College. However, Griffith's journal could not mask how the course of events was seemingly validating the government's sectarian handling of the Irish question. For instance, while the Church of Ireland favoured the Irish Convention solution, the Catholic Church did not.[194] Meanwhile, the only international attention being granted to Ireland at this time was coming from Catholic prelates within the British dominions. This group was led by Archbishop Mannix of Melbourne, who was describing Sinn Féin as a new Catholic party to replace the Irish Party, and defined its anti-conscription and pacifist stance, inspired by Cardinal Mercier, as the sole basis of its politics.[195]

Attempts made by Sinn Féin in early 1918 to return some of Griffith's associates for northern constituencies failed;[196] namely, Sean Milroy for East Tyrone and Patrick MacCartan for Armagh. Griffith had intended that the latter would take a lead instead in making an appeal to President Wilson in the United States.[197] Meanwhile, Griffith's myriad attempts through *Nationality* to validate his Sinn Féin policy in purely political and economic terms evidently did not influence the public mind very much compared to the Catholic Church's championing of Sinn Féin as a monolithic, or one-dimensional, anti-conscription party. The defining moment of this agitation occurred when the government introduced a conscription act in April 1918. This prompted the hierarchy, partly at DeValera's bidding, to summon the Irish Party leadership to Maynooth College and the convening of a major Dublin Mansion House conference under a new lord mayor, Laurence O'Neill of the United Irish League.[198] At this event, Griffith stood as a nominal leader of the anti-conscription campaign on a seemingly equal level with John Dillon of the Irish Party, William O'Brien of the All-for-Ireland League, Thomas Johnson (a deeply committed, albeit essentially clericalist, leader of a newly formed Irish Labour Party), DeValera and the inevitable T.M. Healy. The resolutions adopted at this conference were subsequently drafted into a statement by Mayor O'Neill and sent to President Wilson in the United States.[199] Concurrently, Griffith was nominated as a Sinn Féin party candidate for East Cavan. The priest who selected Griffith's candidacy (a Fr O'Connell P.P.) made no attempt to hide what policy he was expected to represent:

> This union of the priests and people of East Cavan in an unanimous selection of Mr. Griffith is but a reflex of the union of the whole priesthood and people of Ireland manifested throughout the country to resist conscription by the most effective means in their power.[200]

Although they were now nominally united with Sinn Féin on the anti-conscription front, Irish Party stalwarts did not welcome Griffith's selection. The

Freeman's Journal labelled his selection as a parliamentary candidate to be a gross act of 'political indecency'. John Dillon, who had succeeded the recently deceased Redmond as Irish Party leader, said he would 'fight to the bitter end' rather than see Griffith attain any personal victory, claiming that his entire career was based upon propagating lies.[201] Meanwhile, Edward Carson, who had succeeded in getting the British Labour Party to support Plunkett's Irish Convention, repeated his claim (supported by Captain Stephen Gwynn of the Irish Party) that Griffith was being funded by the German secret service. *Nationality* responded by intimating that it was Carson who knew about British secret service matters in Germany and elsewhere while dismissing the context of his actions as an 'elaborate felon-setting of Mr. John Devoy in America',[202] designed to counter Sinn Féin's intention to look for American support. Indeed, if such an effort was to be made, it was well known that Devoy's *Gaelic American* newspaper and his associates on New York city council would be the first port of call.

The ensuing electoral contest in Cavan would prove to be the bitterest struggle between the Irish Party and Sinn Féin to date. The fact that the leadership of both parties felt it necessary to visit the constituency several times to speak in favour of the respective candidates was certainly an illustration of its seeming importance.[203] The British government evidently deemed the matter important too. On 18 May 1918, it issued a proclamation against Sinn Féin and subsequently arrested both DeValera, who was on his way to addressing a Cavan meeting, and Griffith on the basis of an alleged German Plot led by one of Casement's former associates.[204] Griffith was arrested at his home on 24 May and then placed on a British navy boat at Kingstown (Dun Laoghaire). He was then deported to Gloucester jail while being denied the right to communicate with either the general public or his own family.[205] As a result, Griffith was denied any part in either organising or deciding a policy for the Sinn Féin Party thereafter. Over the next year, Fr O'Flanagan was the party's acting president while Eoin MacNeill and Alderman Tom Kelly were nominally his chief assistants but MacNeill tended to view the latter as a political lightweight, who was 'easy to persuade' and thus not an authoritative figure.[206]

Nationality would claim that 'the English government has been too late in throwing Arthur Griffith in prison' because he had 'left behind him imperishable records to guide us' as well as 'a personal example of inflexible rectitude to inspire us'.[207] The development of Sinn Féin since 1916, however, had been an essentially *ad hoc* process that had only very partially reflected Griffith's ideas. To some extent, by the time of Griffith's arrest, Sinn Féin was being reinvented, under the impetus of the First World War and with the Catholic hierarchy's all-important support, as a replacement party for the Irish Party without making a formal commitment to *any* policy other than to oppose conscription (its shared policy with the Irish Party) and to seek an international audience (its principle difference from the Irish Party, albeit a relatively slight one to the Church), not least to undo Redmond's past mismanagement of Irish Catholic organisations in the United States. Meanwhile, the audience for Griffith's economic ideas, including his critiques of various financial institutions and their practices, had been confined to readers of specific columns in his journals.

The underlying framework of home rule still remained essentially unaltered by 1918, the only difference being the British government's public announcement after May 1916 that it was modifying details of the Government of Ireland Act to facilitate partition according to a definite twenty-six county and six-county framework. Several attempts would be made, not least by Griffith himself, to resist this consensus over the next three years. However, under the continued operations of the British government's Defence of the Realm Act—which allowed for both state censorship and military arrests in Ireland from September 1914 right up until July 1921—it often proved very difficult for Griffith and, indeed, most other Irish contemporaries to judge if, or how, any of their efforts were either failing or succeeding.

CHAPTER EIGHT

The Launch of Dáil
Eireann (1918–19)

Griffith's East Cavan campaign was the first post-Irish Convention parliamentary by-election to be held and it involved nearly every prominent nationalist politician from both the Irish Party and Sinn Féin.[1] It was a bitter contest that lasted a few months (April–June 1918). Its capacity to polemicise opinion was reflected by the decision of the Ulster unionist leader Lord Londonderry to offer his support to the Irish Party candidate,[2] while the extent of Irish Party hatred for Griffith was such that the Catholic hierarchy considered for a time withdrawing his nomination altogether.[3] Griffith only learnt of the positive ultimate outcome (he won about 60 per cent of the votes cast) through reading belated reports in British newspapers. This was because he was denied the right to receive any visitors in prison or to see any Irish newspaper until August 1918.

The fact that Griffith was in prison may have helped him to secure a large vote because of the extent of public outrage at the number of recent imprisonments without trial. Meanwhile, several of his canvassers were arrested and the Home Office blocked all his attempts to write letters to his constituents and the press. In his private letters, Griffith (who had not felt sure of victory) typified his return and that of each Sinn Féin candidate as an Irish expression of support for 'that right of national self-determination [US] President Wilson advocates [since January 1918]'. Indeed, Griffith claimed that support for Sinn Féin showed 'that Ireland supports the doctrine of self-determination for small nations' everywhere. Somewhat unrealistically, he hoped that British opposition to this idea would soon make President Wilson more sympathetic to Sinn Féin's stance than to that of the Ulster unionists on the question of partition if the question of Irish self-determination were successfully brought to his attention.[4]

Viscount (later, the Earl of) Midleton of Cork assumed the responsibility of leading the unionist position within Ireland at the time of the East Cavan campaign (Carson would soon announce his retirement from politics). Although Midleton had been a fellow advocate with Carson of coercion in Ireland, he now emphasised that he was completely against partition on economic grounds.[5] Reputedly, Midleton took this course on the suggestion of Scottish Bank of Ireland director Andrew Jameson (also owner of Jameson's Distilleries) in an effort to prevent the triumph of Irish separatism.[6] It is unlikely that such fears were quite so prevalent, however. Such fears of 'separatism' were less an expression of genuine insecurity (such as the existence of a national security threat) than a simple fear of losing a capacity to master the course of Irish politics. Midleton boasted the support of 'the largest commercial interests in Dublin', including Lord Iveagh's Guinness Breweries and Jameson's Distilleries, and now spoke of the necessity of creating a 'secure business environment' for specifically Irish interests and emphasised the importance of placing the principle of 'country' (Ireland) before 'party' (the spoils of party political privilege) in championing any declared opposition to partition. In doing so in name of an Irish unionism, Midleton dissuaded many businessmen from considering supporting Sinn Féin's efforts to establish a similar platform in the name of an Irish nationalism. Furthermore, in suggesting that Britain's wartime over-taxation in Ireland (including various new income taxes) had hurt the great Irish landowners the most,[7] Midleton also sought to reaffirm the traditional Tory–Irish Party socio-economic divide as a basis of political allegiances. This was likely to produce an expected reaction in the run up to the December 1918 general election.

Midleton's action may be said to have highlighted how little Griffith's ideas, if attractive on paper, had a capacity to mould party political allegiances in Ireland. In common with William O'Brien, Griffith had always argued that any depletion of Irish wealth could only be harmful to the country's interests, generally irrespective of the degree to which it was unpopular Tories who owned most of that wealth. This was why the Irish Party, being party-politically opposed to the Tories, often ridiculed O'Brien and Griffith as fools who were acting as mouthpieces for 'landlords and cranks'.[8] The stereotypical 'nationalist' view of 'unionist' critics of the Irish Party was that they were a peculiar Anglo-Irish class of men who 'always owned property, shares and businesses in Britain and Ireland—without thinking much about the difference'.[9] However, this perspective overlooked a fundamental economic fact that both Griffith and O'Brien had always refused to ignore; namely that what was true for wealthy Tories in this respect was equally true of every single property, business and

Plate 1. Griffith's birthplace at 61 Upper Dominick Street, photographed before its demolition by Dublin Corporation. (National Library of Ireland, O'Luing papers)

Plate 2. The earliest known portrait of Griffith (aged twenty-six).

Plate 7. Jennie Wyse Power (1858–1941), a suffragette and treasurer to the Sinn Féin Party. The IRB's infamous republican proclamation of 24 April 1916 was written and signed in her home because of her husband's long-term association with Tom Clarke's political friends.

Plate 8. Arthur and Maud Griffith as newly weds sitting in the back garden of their home in Clontarf (1911). Note Griffith's orthopaedic boots. The couple had not been able to afford to marry during their previous six-year engagement. This house was a wedding gift to them from William O'Brien's political supporters within the Gaelic League. By 1912, however, the home was already partly mortgaged due to financial pressures. (National Library of Ireland, Griffith papers)

share owner in Ireland—completely irrespective of individuals' party politics, religious affiliation or social status (high or low)—due to the very nature of the country's financial institutions. This was why the Irish Tory critique of the Irish Party–Liberal alliance maintained a fundamental relevance and why Griffith and O'Brien had been determined to make it the unifying 'all for Ireland' basis for an Irish nationalist debate. The very fact that London banks directed the economy of Ireland theoretically made the Sinn Féin Policy a reasonable means of attaining Irish nationalist goals, but its impracticality seemed overwhelmingly self-evident to most contemporaries. London's economic authority over Ireland was deemed unbreakable.

The development of modern party-political traditions (governed by party whips) in Britain and Ireland in the post-1884 period had witnessed a political challenge to landed elites in both countries. This had represented not a birth of democracy but rather a promised birth of a new professional class who would broaden the parameters of existing patronage networks in the worlds of finance, education and politics.[10] The principle source of Irish divergence from this British norm—a concentration of Irish capital in the increasingly unprofitable commodity of land—lay in the comparative absence of any class to replace the traditional role of landowners (by now, almost exclusively Tory in politics) as those men who were best positioned to both understand and extrapolate for the wider Irish public how the golden rule was truly affecting the development of political society.[11] This trend remained of paramount importance throughout the 1910s. For instance, during the fiscal debates of 1911, the only party outside of Griffith's Sinn Féin and William O'Brien's All-for-Ireland League to protest that 'Ireland in fiscal or commercial matters is doomed always to be treated badly or disregarded' by Britain, as well as to call for a government-commission in the matter, were Irish Tory peers (future allies of Midleton) in the British House of Lords. Their unilateral efforts at this time to open up new profitable transatlantic trading roots with Canada in both Galway and Dublin had won support from the Canadian Prime Minister and members of a few Irish Chambers of Commerce, but this project was strangled at its inception by British peers (both Liberal and Tory) on the grounds of the legal non-existence of Ireland as a separate economic unit.[12]

In an age of party politics, it was hardly surprising that Irish Party supporters would frequently accuse this wealthy minority of Irish Tory businessmen or landowners of contemptible arrogance in claiming to be able to unilaterally speak on behalf of Ireland, as if they inherently knew what was best for 'the country', and likewise accuse Griffithite and Fenian propagandists, being reputed Frankenstein by-products of dated Tory nation-state ideologies among the poor,[13] of the same vice. However, the Irish Tory critique that the arrival of party politics as a key factor in the brokerage of British wealth would never result in the birth of an Irish nationalism, let alone the Irish Party's dream of an expected '*el dorado* of government jobs and pensions',[14] because the country was suffering from fundamental infrastructural problems that were keeping the country poor had a great deal of validity to them. No general election could potentially have stimulated greater debate in Ireland on these realities than the first general election to be held under (almost) universal suffrage, which was due to take place in the winter of 1918. Griffith was unable to make any input, however, because he was kept in Gloucester Jail up until March 1919.

Under the acting presidency of Fr Michael O'Flanagan (who was now also the 'foreign affairs' spokesman of the party),[15] Sinn Féin's 1918 general election campaign was fought using a relatively sectarian platform. As acting editor of *Nationality*, Seamus O'Kelly maintained that 'if we are treasonable' in the British government's eyes, this was because 'in Cromwell's days and since we have been largely Papists in Ireland'.[16] In deeming the Irish Party as untrustworthy, election flyers called upon the voting public to 'follow the lead of the bishops' by supporting Sinn Féin, which was typified as not only the last remaining guardian against Orange business ascendancies and Redmondite warmongering in Irish life but also as the only Irish political party that sincerely 'wish you a holy and happy Easter'. Reflecting the iconic status of the imprisoned figure of DeValera as the official president of both Sinn Féin and the Irish Volunteers, Sinn Féin convention tickets now showed rifles crossed under the volunteers' emblem initials 'F.F.' (Fianna Fáil) and called, rhetorically or not, on the voting public to 'smash the fraud' of an Ulster parliament.[17] Little or no mention was made of economic matters either in its election literature or at party meetings, however. Under the circumstances, it is not surprising that historians of the post-1917 Sinn Féin Party have typified it as an ideologically incoherent party.[18] Certainly, in adopting a political stance that expressed nothing more than a claim to an inherent entitlement to power, the new Sinn Féin Party repeated the example of the Irish Party, whose supporters' naïve belief that the electoral eclipse of the Tories in Britain during 1906 would be permanent had only strengthened this tendency.[19]

Midleton felt entitled by the outcome of the Irish Convention to champion the ideas of Westminster retaining complete control of all customs and security matters in Ireland and a strong (and non-elective) Irish upper house being established to represent the propertied and business communities (he presumed that elected Irish politicians could not come from such sections of society) with both extensive vetoing powers as well as a right to sit in the British House of Lords. Opposition to this programme had come not from the Irish Party majority under John Redmond, whose death virtually coincided with the close of the Irish Convention and for whom Griffith wrote a surprisingly neutral obituary, suggesting that it was up to future historians to judge him.[20] Instead, it came from Patrick O'Donnell, the Catholic Bishop of Raphoe and a former Irish Party treasurer who would succeed Michael Logue as Primate of All-Ireland in 1924 and was traditionally an ally of John Dillon in politics.[21] Midleton interpreted this as meaning that the church was now concerned primarily about a perceived negative impact that the home rule settlement might possibly have upon the financial regulation of Irish educational institutions, including the NUI, a church prerogative.[22] A reason to draw this conclusion was that Dillon was willing to support William Martin Murphy in expressing criticism of the Midleton-inspired conclusions drawn by the Irish Convention. Dillon's actual motivation at this time, however, was to draw Sinn Féin closer to the Irish Party's traditional political stance.[23]

After the highly personalised East Cavan contest had finished and Griffith was silenced in jail, Laurence O'Neill, the United Irish League mayor of Dublin, worked with Fr O'Flanagan, the Catholic bishops and John Dillon (with whom DeValera, an old admirer of the Irish Party, had been more than willing to share anti-conscription platforms)[24] in selecting Sinn Féin candidates for the 1918 general election. Irish Party involvement in this process was done in the name of preserving 'national unity' in terms of Irish political representation. This also involved persuading a nascent Irish labour party not to contest the election and it was essentially a direct extension of the Maynooth College inspired platform for the anti-conscription convention of April 1918.[25]

Reflecting Archbishop Walsh's stance on the formation of Lloyd George's Irish Situation Committee, from June 1916 onwards Fr O'Flanagan had been fully accepting of partition, arguing that

> The island of Ireland and the national unit of Ireland simply do not coincide … National and geographical boundaries hardly ever coincide … If we reject home rule rather than agree to the exclusion of the Unionist Party of Ulster, what case have we to put before the world? … I agree that the 'homogenous Ulster' of the unionist publicists is a sham and a delusion. But if there be no homogenous Ulster how can there be a homogenous Ireland? A more accurate description of Ireland for the past 200 years would be an economic and social duality.[26]

Fr O'Flanagan was here highlighting that the idea of the existence of a united Irish nation in the past was essentially a myth (when had such an entity ever existed?). This was contrary to Griffith's claim that 'to assent to these things would not be to come to an agreement with Orangeism but to surrender to it and make an Irish parliament so impotent that thereafter Orangeism would be justified in asserting that home rule could not benefit the country'.[27] However, there was nothing essentially incongruous with Fr O'Flanagan's stance in Sinn Féin's adoption of a nominally republican platform after October 1917. This was precisely because the latter was justified according to the goal of seeking an American audience; in effect, making an effort to re-establish the platform of the Church as an intermediary in Anglo-American relations that had been broken down solely because of Redmond's over-enthusiastic championing of the British war effort in a neutral America during 1915.

Reflecting this, O'Kelly's *Nationality* (which refused to criticise Dillon for assuming a directing role over the Sinn Féin Party, notwithstanding his well known hatred for everything that Griffith stood for) cited Pope Benedict's appreciative response to the American president's proposed peace programme for Europe by suggesting that this indicated that close parallels existed in the Papacy's and the American Republic's definition of true freedoms which, once allied, 'will give a new impetus to civil liberty the whole world over'.[28] Similarly, Hugh Saunders Blackham (who often called himself 'Aodh de Blacam'), a London-born writer and (Protestant) Christian-Democratic journalist, began theorising about potentially positive Irish, British and American connections in this specific field of Catholic thought and, as an extension of this, published *Towards the Republic* as a justification of Sinn Féin's potential political role.[29] Simultaneously, 'Friends of Irish Freedom' conventions were being held in the United States under the chairmanship of three American Catholic cardinals, Cardinal Gibbons of Baltimore, Cardinal Farley of New York and Cardinal O'Connell of Boston, who made appeals to Sinn Féin in Ireland to find a common cause with them.[30] An alternative rationale for raising a republican demand continued to be championed by the IRB, however, and this would find some reflection in the tenor of the resolutions adopted at the Sinn Féin Ard Fheis of October 1918.

The Victorian IRB organisation had often attempted to popularise republicanism by nominating political prisoners for parliament who would be disqualified if elected; a tactic last adopted in John Daly's case during 1895. Harry Boland, a gregarious man (like his father before him, he was the leader of the Dublin GAA), repeated this example upon becoming one of the Sinn Féin Party's secretaries during the summer of 1918. He persuaded Bishop Fogarty, the Sinn Féin Party treasurer, to nominate as many political prisoners for parliament as was possible. In turn, this gave the IRB treasurer Michael Collins, as leader of the prisoners' defence association, a significant role to play in Sinn Féin for the first time.[31] While the party leaders were in jail, the Sinn

Féin Ard Fheis resolved in October 1918 that 'it is the duty of every member [of Sinn Féin] to join the volunteers'; referred to the state as 'I.R.' (the Irish Republic); claimed, totally falsely, that the IRB's republic 'proclaimed in Dublin in the Easter of 1916' had already been 'acknowledged by many of the powers of Europe'; and referred to the National Council of Sinn Féin as 'the provisional government of Ireland' or 'the Irish republican parliament'.[32] This was in keeping with the IRB tradition of issuing pre-emptive propaganda in seeking to mobilise enthusiasms, but the attitude of the Sinn Féin Party towards republicanism was rather more ambivalent than such statements indicated. For instance, although he had intimated a willingness to embrace the very dubious republican stance on the British imperial constitution that had been suggested by Captain Stuart Stephens,[33] Eoin MacNeill, the acting vice-president and effectively the lay leader of Sinn Féin, had recently equated the Sinn Féin platform with the legacy of both Daniel O'Connell and the history of the Irish Party without making any reference to Griffith's economic nationalist programme or, indeed, republicanism.[34]

The IRB's espousal of republicanism, in common with Griffith's (he may never have formally left the IRB)[35] in the past, was usually a simple matter of championing the citizenship–slavery dichotomy that appealed to so many nineteenth-century nationalists and radical democrats. This was a brand of morality with an exactitude that often appealed to writers and volunteers but, even if it echoed a political idealism, it was usually branded as a deep folly in Ireland because it could prompt the adoption of very simplistic, almost militaristic, forms of political analysis:

> Are we all prepared to do our duty as citizens of a free country? The statement that the Battle of Waterloo was won on the playing fields of Eton may cause a smile, but it is true—as true as the statement that the battle of Ireland's independence was fought and will be won in the Gaelic League, Cumainn Sinn Féin and drill halls of Ireland [the IRB's recruiting grounds] … The overthrow of the Westminstrels is no guarantee that we are prepared for freedom.[36]

This style of propaganda began to appear regularly in *Nationality* after the untimely death of Seamus O'Kelly in mid-November 1918. After O'Kelly published an article that was critical of intended Dublin celebrations for the British army on Armistice Day (11 November), armed government forces raided the offices of *Nationality* and O'Kelly, being a very sensitive man of frail health, actually died of a heart attack, aged just thirty-eight. Griffith was deeply upset when he heard this news in prison.[37]

The editorship of *Nationality* now passed to J.J. Burke, a Liverpool-born IRB activist. Until recently, Burke had been a sub-editor of *Young Ireland*. This was originally a children's journal, owned and edited by Aodh de Blacam, that during 1918 was turned into a nationalist weekly, owned and edited by Michael J. Lennon B.L., an old personal associate, if not quite a political associate, of Griffith's. Somewhat unusually, Lennon was both the son of one of James Carey's former 'Invincibles' and a religiously minded barrister who particularly admired de Blacam as a Christian–democratic thinker. By contrast, J.J. Burke was a former friend of Thomas Ashe and Pierce McCann (a Sinn Féin leader who would soon die in prison) who had joined the Irish Volunteers in 1915 and played a small part in the 1916 revolt, having been (alongside Michael Collins) part of a contingent of IRB men in England who left for Dublin at this time. Burke was almost completely unknown, however, outside of IRB circles.[38] In this way, the Sinn Féin weekly fell under the IRB's influence, or direction, just prior to the 1918 general election.

Although he accused the Irish Party of preaching 'a gospel of futility' and of being 'an Irish Expeditionary Force to Westminster', Burke praised de Blacam's attempt to equate American republican and Catholic conceptions of liberty and suggested that as an extension of this 'we can oblige Mr. [John] Dillon [the leader of the Irish Party at Westminster] by hoisting the Stars and Stripes alongside the flag of the Irish Republic'.[39] Burke was grossly opportunistic, however, in his attempt to manipulate Catholic majority sensibilities. For instance, in response to Archbishop Walsh's somewhat disingenuous claim that the Church had ceased to support the Irish Party 'thirteen or fourteen years ago',[40] Burke claimed that 'the very existence of the Catholic Church will be endangered' if Irish representation was not completely withdrawn from Westminster. He also accused Irish Party supporters not only of 'blasphemy' in criticising Sinn Féin but also of 'threatening us with "Ulster" plantations in Munster, Leinster and Connacht', 'the overthrow of the Catholic Church in Ireland' and attempting to 'stone' Fr O'Flanagan as well as giving 'the kiss of Judas' to the Irish republican cause.[41] Alongside this nonsense, he also justified the selection of incompetent political prisoners to unseat economic nationalists such as William Field, who would lose his seat to the imprisoned Countess Markievicz, purely on the grounds of their past refusal to condemn the European war.[42] Curiously, while Field had formed the Hibernian Insurance Company in 1908 and remained a member of the Dublin Port and Dock Boards,[43] Collins' IRB circle launched the 'New Ireland Assurance Company' during 1918, partly to finance their own concerns (including to attempt to import and distribute arms from the Dublin docklands) while Collins himself would adopt the name 'William Field' for all his secret IRB correspondence.[44]

The end result of the December 1918 general election—the return of seventy-three Sinn Féin members (mostly political prisoners who were disqualified),[45] twenty-six unionist candidates and six Irish Party candidates—was certainly striking. For instance, in Connacht, little-known Sinn Féin candidates often out polled Irish Party stalwarts with careers dating back to the Plan of Campaign by an almost 10–1 majority. The involvement of Cardinal Logue of Armagh, the Catholic Primate of Ireland, in picking Sinn Féin candidates in agreement with Eoin MacNeill of UCD and John Dillon of the Irish Party was celebrated by *Nationality* as evidence that these election results were nothing less than 'Ireland's declaration of independence'.[46] This bold public propaganda belied the fact, however, that the Sinn Féin vote was mostly a protest vote designed to express dissatisfaction at the previous thirty months of coercion and arrests. It did not empower nationalists in any direct way. In addition, as the European war was now concluded, a completely new and uncertain political situation, internationally and nationally, was sure to emerge.

On the level of domestic UK politics, uncertainty loomed large. Cardinal Logue understood that the British government desired to engage in a 'clever play to keep the Irish question floating', leaving 'Sinn Féin, Carsonism and Socialism … [to] fight each other over the unfortunate fate of Ireland' with nothing to gain on any side.[47] An additional reason to consider that Sinn Féin's recent victory could prove to be pyrrhic and short lived was that great diversity in public opinion was still an undeniable reality. For instance, those Irish Party supporters who had cooperated with the church and John Dillon in engineering Sinn Féin's political victory were privately very unhappy that, as election time approached, they had been overly demonised by the clergy for having a poor record previously on the question of conscription.[48] This split the proverbial nationalist vote to a far greater extent than the Irish Party had intended and the unexpectedly great extent of the party's subsequent loses (which was probably exacerbated by the British 'first past the post' system) created a strong backlash of resentment, including within the NUI.[49] Together with the opposition of Midleton's party, this might be said to reflect Sinn Féin's lack of meaningful support among the professional classes.

The sense of excitement in Sinn Féin over recent successes reflected a popular belief that a significant new political departure had taken place. In some respects, however, it simply represented a political rebirth: like the Irish Party at its inception during 1880, the new Sinn Féin Party included many lower-middle-class journalists; was ready to consider adopting defiant stances in the politics of education and land-law reform; had an enthusiastic sense of Catholic solidarity; and a seemingly revolutionary wing through having IRB supporters. However, its influence with the professional classes was, at yet, negligible. This

Achilles heel of the party was camouflaged to some extent by the willingness of Laurence O'Neill, the UIL mayor of Dublin, to allow the Sinn Féin Party to hold that national assembly it had promised at its recent Ard Fheis. Symbolically, this assembly was held at the same site as the Irish Party's initial meeting of 1880; namely, the mayor of Dublin's private residence (the Mansion House) on Kildare Street. Sinn Féin founder Alderman Walter Cole of Dublin celebrated this event by writing from prison to Thomas Martin of London that 'when the few of us met in the Metropole *that* day 14 or 15 years ago we hardly dreamed to see *this* one so soon, did we? Congratulations that we have lived to see it come'.[50] However, as Sinn Féin was neither a complete nor essentially a parliamentary party the question of what this assembly gathered in the Dublin mayor's private residence (for fear of breaking the law, it was never even granted the right to sit in Dublin City Hall) could actually achieve was far from certain.

On the same day as this meeting (21 January 1919), Midleton proposed that all those who supported partition should be excluded from the Irish Unionist Alliance, which styled itself as an organised body of Irish business leaders and landowners. This led to a split in that association. Midleton and southern Irish peers withdrew to form an Anti-Partition League, while Lord Farnham of Cavan, the Ulster unionists' chief spokesman in the House of Lords, assumed the leadership of the rump Irish Unionist Alliance.[51] Farnham believed that partition could not possibly work economically if the full nine counties of Ulster were not included in the proposed Northern Ireland statelet. For voicing this sense of insecurity or concern, however, he would soon be forced to retire.[52] This was a clear indication that, notwithstanding London's purchase of the Belfast and Ulster Banks and the degree to which property and church leaders were willing to comply with Westminster's intentions, the economics of any proposed partition settlement was still an issue that was far from decided.

Griffith, who managed to retain his health in prison,[53] was returned unopposed for East Cavan during the December 1918 general election. He was also returned for North-West Tyrone. Being a champion of women's suffrage for many years, he was glad to learn that 'one nomination paper was exclusively filled by women'.[54] However, as the prison censors continued to prevent him from having any letters published in the press he remained unable to communicate with any of his constituents.[55] Nevertheless, on learning from a prison visitor on 23 January 1919 of the holding of a Sinn Féin convention two days earlier Griffith was able to hastily draft a proposed programme in a couple of hours and have it smuggled back to Dublin. This programme was certainly ambitious, but it also demonstrated a sense of realism.

Although judging that 'the Dáil Eireann is admirable', Griffith believed that it was particularly important that 'the Dáil should not commit itself to any scheme that it does not feel can be worked out with its present resources'. In particular, instead of making grandiose proclamations of being a provisional republic, it should realise the importance of building up its platform of support in a slow and methodological fashion ('first things first'). For instance, 'the intention to secure control of the local bodies is most important' as if the Dáil, a would-be parliamentary assembly, did not have authority over the county councils, urban district councils and harbour boards of the country, then it could have absolutely no governmental authority whatsoever:

> The power of these bodies vary but are in all cases important ... Full return of goods imported and exported from Ireland can be probably made available [from the Dublin Customs House] through securing these boards ... [creating] ... power large [enough] to dominate and direct the Department of Agriculture [at Dublin Castle, which] can be secured for Sinn Féin. This is a matter of vast importance to the agriculture, fisheries and industries of the country.[56]

Griffith suggested that the Sinn Féin Policy goal of directing local government bodies (and, in turn, reforming the poor law boards in a Scottish fashion) should be entrusted to sympathetic legal minds such as Eamon Duggan and George Gavan Duffy, the Four Courts secretary Henry Dixon and Sinn Féin's political followers in local government (especially in Dublin, Limerick and Monaghan), each of whom could help the party envision new local government legislation. In addition, 'the application and if necessary the revision of the National Civil Service scheme put forward by Sinn Féin eight or nine years ago should be considered. In connection with this H. Mangan, City Accountant of Dublin [Corporation], who had much to do with its drafting, might be consulted'. Griffith believed this initiative could also be used to create a Dáil authority over the local government judiciary bodies. Nevertheless, Griffith clearly did not envision any major alterations to the existing legal system:

> Lawyers like [Eamon] Duggan etc. can explain the working of the Arbitration Act under which these Courts have power ... [and this legislation] should be copied and the courts carefully constituted, with several guiding rules established, after an investigation of the present working ones.[57]

As a first step towards allowing the Dáil to begin to conduct business, Griffith emphasised that 'it is necessary to secure the cooperation of a bank'. He judged, probably simply due to the size of their assets (the Sinn Féin People's Bank had very little capital), that 'the National or the Munster and Leinster would be the best':

> The inducement that would have them is in the power of the County Councils etc. If we control these bodies we can offer the bank, which agrees to help in this matter, the whole banking of the public funds passing through the hands of the Committee. [James] O'Mara and others of the businessmen, with [Lorcan] Robins of Westmeath and Bank Managers favourable to us, ought to discuss the matter.[58]

Another inducement for the banks to cooperate with Sinn Féin and the Dáil would be for them to establish reliable business connections. Although any hope of sending of consular representation abroad is 'probably not practicable now', sympathetic businessmen, such as Patrick Moylett of Ballina, Co. Mayo, should try to gather groups to travel to France, seeking to establish new Irish business connections, while 'existing men in other countries might be utilised'. In this Griffith was evidently more preoccupied, or at least more familiar, with the European than the North American business environment:

> Gerald O'Loughlin in Denmark may be thoroughly relied upon. William Dunne in Norway [is] equally able and reliable … As to French politicians, George Barry and Denys Cochin, more or less royalist and Catholic leaders, are powerful, especially the latter, and the former is very sympathetic. Lucien Milleroye [a former lover of Maud Gonne], the nationalist, is a fairly strong man and sympathetic. See Victor Collins, Stephen McKenna etc. [Irish journalists working for English language Parisian newspapers] about French politicians—see them separately. The ecclesiastics [Irish bishops] should know much about D Cochin. See Mgr. O'Dogherty of Omagh [a founder of the Irish Nation League] about this.[59]

In its first meeting at the Dublin Mansion House (it would take a couple of months before the assembly would meet again), the Dáil had issued a general declaration of independence and 'an address to the free nations of the world'. This was done in preparation for one particular initiative. The previous two Lord Mayors of Dublin (Laurence O'Neill and Thomas Sherlock, both of the United Irish League), accompanied by Sean T. O'Kelly, representing the Sinn Féin Party, and P.T. Daly, representing the new Irish Labour Party, were sent to Paris in an attempt to meet President Wilson (who had been granted the freedom of Dublin by O'Neill) prior to the beginning of the Versailles Peace Conference.[60] Not surprisingly, Griffith also judged the Parisian peace conference to be the first priority and a far more important issue than securing the release of political prisoners (including himself). He also believed, however, that employing 'a reliable statistician is essential' if any such international appeals or addresses were to be made. This was because it would be necessary to draw meaningful international parallels. He believed that the Dáil should try 'contrasting Ireland, Czechoslovaks and Poland'. In addition, 'there ought to be a covering letter to each separate state or nation recalling Ireland's associations with it'.[61]

Regarding the Parisian situation, as 'the passport barrier will be worked very probably by [French Prime Minister] Clemenceau ... against Irishmen or non-naturalised Irish-Americans' arriving in France, Griffith believed that the Irish-American 'Friends of Irish Freedom' organisation (which included ex-Sinn Féiners Patrick MacCartan and Diarmuid Lynch) should be contacted to secure the assistance of 'men from America of high standing'—preferably senators from both the Democratic and Republican parties—in making an appeal for an Irish delegation to be heard. Griffith also believed that the current American wife of Seamus MacManus in Notre Dame University, being 'a granddaughter of the Liberator of Venezuela', could attempt 'to secure the sympathy of the small South American States which are at the Peace Conference' for Sinn Féin. As the United States was currently aspiring to assume greater directive economic influences over these small South American states (a foreign policy initiative actually first launched by Patrick Egan, formerly the Land League treasurer),[62] this may have been a reasonable idea. Owing to the great importance of the United States to the Peace Conference, Griffith also believed that the Dáil should work closely with the Friends of Irish Freedom regarding domestic American politics in order to better appeal to President Wilson. To this end, Griffith suggested contacting the US labour leader Samuel Gompers who had begun his political career in New Jersey alongside J.P. MacDonnell, an ex-Dublin IRB labour activist.[63] Most of all, in every public pronouncement by the Dáil,

> Our attitude should be that Wilson is a sincere man striving to give effect to his programme of freedom for all nations and struggling against all the forces of tyranny, imperialism and lusty world power, which are seeking to dominate the peace conference ... Continue to strengthen his hands until he—if he ever does—yields up his own programme. Up the present he has stood up to it ... [but] his position is one of serious difficulty.[64]

Finally, while making all these efforts, Griffith believed it would be essential that the Dáil would not be 'provoked by the Castle gang' ('when their provocation tactics fail, they will fail') and equally

> It should keep well before the people the fact that the reason why great schemes which commend themselves to the nation cannot be worked at present [i.e. in the short term] is the existence of English government in Ireland … However desirable any scheme should be of improvement for the country, the Dáil should only apply what it is in its power at present to apply … [therefore] it would not be advisable either to go into the details of an Irish Constitution at present: just keep the straight question of Irish independence first.[65]

Although it was written within just two hours, Griffith's programme was certainly the most detailed plan yet to appear before Sinn Féin's national assembly. It certainly reflected his political experience. One of the first people to read the programme was actually DeValera, who was able to resume the presidency of Sinn Féin in early February 1919 after having being rescued from Lincoln Jail by Collins' IRB aides.[66] DeValera did not know what to make of Griffith's plan, however.

DeValera had never been involved in drafting, or considering, any programme for government and had no thoughts, as yet, of a provisional government. Instead, he was preoccupied entirely with his own personal moral responsibility as president of both Sinn Féin and the Irish Volunteers. In this regard, DeValera noted that 'my advice to the people of Ireland would be precisely that of Cardinal Mercier to the Belgians' during the recent war, which was to adopt a position of passive rather than active resistance to the ruling power. DeValera felt certain that 'honest men everywhere will understand the position' of Sinn Féin only if it allied itself fully with the Catholic hierarchy in Ireland in seeking to persuade Cardinal Mercier to call for an international inquiry into the state of Ireland, thereby countering British Catholics' emphatic claims, which were being made in both London and Rome, that the cardinal's anti-conscription politics during the First World War was in no sense related to the current Irish demand for political independence.[67] Such competitions between Irish and British Catholic influence at Rome had been a prevalent feature of Irish politics ever since the days of Cardinal Paul Cullen and had been a particularly important backdrop to the establishment of the Irish Party's political identity during the mid-1880s.[68]

Specifically regarding Griffith's programme, DeValera wrote to Cathal Brugha, the nominal acting president of the Dáil, that he believed the Dáil was so weak that it was best to ignore its existence entirely. Instead, DeValera proposed to grant the responsibility of directing Ireland's case 'to *one* person for supreme direction'. This was Fr Timothy Corcoran, the Jesuit editor of UCD's *Studies*, whose fitness for this task DeValera judged to be 'beyond question'.[69] Corcoran was currently a member of the Viceregal Commission on Intermediate Education and had supported John Redmond during the First World War. More significantly, Corcoran was professor of education at UCD; a position he would hold until his death in 1942. In this capacity, he had responded to the imprisonment of his UCD colleague Eoin MacNeill and his expulsion from the Royal Irish Academy in the wake of the 1916 rising by attempting to regroup the Catholic education movement, hitherto led by MacNeill on Archbishop Walsh's behalf, under a newly defined Sinn Féin banner.[70] Supported by the *Catholic Bulletin* (edited by 'Sceilg'), this circle was also determined to remove the IRB, which was blamed for the 1916 rising (which had potentially jeopardised the entire fortunes of the Catholic education movement), from all Irish political organisations; hence DeValera's call upon Brugha, hitherto an IRB member, to demand its disbandment,[71] although it seems that Brugha was not very willing to comply with this.[72] DeValera requested that Brugha maintained absolute secrecy regarding the arrangement surrounding Fr Corcoran so that no one in the Dáil should ever know about it, with the exception of Eoin MacNeill who could be counted upon to ensure that 'the political side closely cooperate'. Meanwhile, Fr Corcoran's capabilities as an advisor on church diplomacy made DeValera 'much easier in my mind' as to whether or not it would be possible for Irishmen to make any international appeals.[73]

DeValera's decision to bypass Griffith's Sinn Féin programme entirely was understandable. Although John Dillon had worked with MacNeill and the Catholic bishops in selecting the Sinn Féin candidates for the 1918 general election, the Irish Party—having many years experience of informed debate on international relations in the Imperial Parliament—retained its complete scepticism regarding Griffith's claim that Ireland could someday acquire a voice in international relations as an independent nation. Noting that 'history affords a complete answer to the Sinn Féin claims', the Irish Party emphasised that it was 'well-settled international law' that 'independent sovereign states at war alone can enjoy the rights of belligerents' and that 'belligerents only can be present at a peace conference', but no country had recognised Ireland to be either an independent state or a belligerent. Furthermore, even if, in theory, a Sinn Féin spokesman secured a right of access to the Peace Conference,

Great Britain will get up and point out to America, France, Italy and Belgium that he represents Sinn Féin Ireland, which had for its gallant allies Germany and Austria—the Sinn Féin Ireland that refused to aid the Allies in the fight … Are they going to desert Britain, their ally, for Sinn Féin Ireland … Need anyone ask what the Allies answer will be?[74]

DeValera might be typified as occupying a position somewhere between Dillon and Griffith at this time. He understood the logic of Dillon's stance, yet he believed that the Sinn Féin Party, under proper direction, could find a more satisfactory solution than the Irish Party if it attuned itself more fully to the Catholic bishops' diplomatic influence in Rome, London and especially the United States (symbolised by Cardinal Gibbons' recent 'Friends of Irish Freedom' conventions in the United States). DeValera was also no doubt fully conscious of the concerns regarding the financing of Irish education that were held by Archbishop Walsh as NUI Chancellor; a position to which UCD allies of the archbishop (who was by now 77 years old and in ill health), including Fr Corcoran, were ready to appoint DeValera as his successor, if the British government approved.[75] DeValera's entry point into Irish politics during 1914–15 was similar to Fr O'Flanagan's[76] and a political mission of his career would be to balance the prerogatives of church diplomacy with the question of Irish self-determination; a challenge which, probably more so than any other figure in Sinn Féin, he was well equipped to tackle.

Nationality had interpreted the result of the December 1918 election as meaning that Sinn Féin's 'leaders must be released … not as a favour, but as a right'.[77] The Sinn Féin prisoners were indeed released from prison in early March 1919. On returning to Dublin, Griffith concentrated on assuming his responsibilities as an elected representative and member of the Dáil. As this meant postponing resuming the editorship of *Nationality*, Sean Milroy assumed responsibilities as sub-editor to make Burke focus more on reviving an economic nationalist commentary. Meanwhile, the first order of business for Griffith was coming to a decision how to square the Sinn Féin programme, as well as the Dáil's nominal republican objectives, with the current national and international situation.

Griffith believed in common with DeValera that 'the present occasion is scarcely one in which we would be justified in risking the lives of the citizens'.[78] Ever since 1917, isolated and predominantly rural Irish Volunteers circles had been occasionally involved in scuffles with landowners or the police.[79] This had two contexts. First, the volunteer had a lack of firearms. This made some units willing to perform arms raids without authority from the movement's national leadership.[80] Second, there was the socio-economic issue of the longstanding dispute regarding land law. This was an issue that was liable to grow tenser now that the European war had ended and thousands of unemployed ex-British soldiers, some of whom were willing to join the volunteers, had returned from the front to their farms. It soon became clear to Griffith, therefore, that if the Dáil were to establish its authority it would have to tackle the land question.

To this end, the Dáil recruited an assistant-secretary of the Department of Agriculture and Technical Instruction, Diarmuid O'Hegarty, who had worked for almost a decade with T.P. Gill (who still directed Dublin Castle's department on behalf of Horace Plunkett) and consequently knew all its business. O'Hegarty, who had joined the IRB upon siding with the Irish Volunteers against Redmond's National Volunteers, became a very professional 'cabinet secretary' for the Dáil (a model of government being pioneered by Maurice Hankey in Britain), while due to his closeness to representatives of the financial establishment he was nicknamed by Boland and Collins, with a sense of humour worthy of Tom Clarke,[81] as 'the parson'.[82] Also recruited from Dublin Castle's Department of Agriculture was its wartime advisor to the British army on food control, Robert Barton, a long-term associate of Plunkett's who was appointed as the Dáil's own 'minister for agriculture' (by contrast, the Sinn Féin Party's former food control advisor, the Irish-American Diarmuid Lynch, had been forced by Dublin Castle to flee the country the previous year).[83] These formalities could mean little, however, if the Dáil did not find a banker. It could not.

Michael Collins, hitherto the Dáil's nominal minister for 'home affairs', was appointed as the Dáil's 'minister for finance' with the responsibility of finding an appropriate banking solution. This was probably done because he was a former employee of both a stockbroker firm and the Post Office Saving Bank in London with some experience also of working for an American financial institution in London[84] (although some historians have claimed that Collins worked briefly for the Imperial Board of Trade).[85] Griffith assumed the responsibility of 'minister for home affairs'; a title that notwithstanding its connotations of policing and justice practically meant the minister for establishing a platform to begin implementing the Sinn Féin programme. The Dáil's dependence on existing civil service personnel inherently made it a cog within the greater wheel of the Dublin Castle administration just as much as it was an attempt to begin governing the operations of that greater wheel. This was the very nature of Griffith's proposed Irish nationalist experiment. The question remained, however, whether or not the Sinn Féin Party would be prepared to take the gamble of attempting to spin this particular wheel and what this could actually achieve.

If it was to be launched successfully, the Dáil required a defence to justify the idea of creating a national governmental administration from a local governmental base. This meant that propaganda was important as well as funding. On the latter basis, DeValera justified abandoning the Dáil at the very first meeting he chaired for the sake of going on an American fund-raising tour; an idea Griffith supported.[86] Meanwhile, a 'ministry for publicity', led by the London Catholic Desmond Fitzgerald, was created to defend the Dáil in the press. As the international press agency regarding Ireland was regulated by Britain, the nature of this challenge was such that the activities of various Irish businessmen on the continent whom Griffith knew and were now placed in communication with a nominal 'foreign affairs ministry' (led by Count Plunkett) could, in reality, do nothing more than offer very limited assistance to Fitzgerald's publicity ministry.[87] The most notable Dáil envoys appointed abroad were Sean T. O'Kelly and George Gavan Duffy, who worked initially in Paris (at the time of the Versailles conference) and then in Rome, but outside the church's Irish Colleges in these cities they had no real bases for their work.[88] Furthermore, the winning of support from such church channels represented only a very small coup for Sinn Féin because the Irish Party had practically been responsible for first establishing such networks, as well as Irish political contacts with the new American Catholic universities (which, aside from John Devoy, would provide DeValera with his only real base for his American tour), in the past.[89] O'Kelly and Duffy's failure to gain entry to the Versailles conference, or to acquire a private audience with President Wilson, was deemed by the mainstream Irish press as proof that Sinn Féin had already irrevocably failed, prompting John Dillon to boast that the Irish Party would soon be revived. Meanwhile, the new Chief Secretary at Dublin Castle was claiming publicly that the IRB was 'the whole Irish problem', allegedly being both the progenitor and basis of the Dáil as well a medium for encouraging lawlessness in response to the arrest of a few Sinn Féin troublemakers.[90] As Michael Collins, the sole regulator of the Dáil's finance department, was also the IRB's treasurer, he may have had a point.

It was up to Griffith to prove that the Dáil was being established as a truly workable institution (Brugha would prove an administrative ally in this regard)[91] and not as a mere propagandistic exercise. However, as Griffith was well known to be a journalist (and quite a controversial one), public faith in this idea may not have been particularly strong. Indeed, if Griffith was often an adept critic, the idea of his being able to establish and run an Irish government all on his own initiative may have made as much sense to some contemporaries as the idea that the editor of the London *Times* could single-handedly do all the work of the British imperial cabinet if only he got the chance. A clear indication that the new Sinn Féin Party was not very enthusiastic in its support of Griffith's counter-state programme, represented by the establishment of Dáil Eireann, was that only 60 per cent of Sinn Féin branches in the country bothered affiliating themselves to that party's national executive. Of that 60 per cent, only 3.5 per cent subscribed any membership funds during 1919 while very many branches established prior to the general election triumph of 1918 also never paid up any membership fees for that year.[92] Meanwhile, repeated calls by *Nationality* for Sinn Féin Party branches to remain active all the year around, not merely to repeat the old UIL example of meeting only at election times under the chairmanship of the local parish priest,[93] were simply ignored.

While *Nationality* always threw a positive slant on the Dáil's mission it never refrained from pointing out whatever it deemed to be problematic circumstances, including the fact that the Dublin Castle administration would still be able to collect over £35 million revenue annually in Ireland for the British government until such time as the Dáil's programme succeeded in its entirety.[94] Although Griffith rightly emphasised the practical issue of resources above all else, the columns of *Nationality* and the minutes of Dáil Eireann provide a clear contrast. The former expressed the propagandistic ideal of Irish potentialities and the latter reflected the bare reality, akin to former meetings of the central branch of Sinn Féin,[95] of a handful of would-be governmental committees being set up that operated on a minimal budget but nevertheless passed resolutions expressing a resolve to take constructive steps to begin an administrative takeover from a local governmental base.[96] The alleged potentials of the Dáil, as intimated by *Nationality*, are worth examining first.

The state of the financial world in Ireland was a constant subject of examination in *Nationality*, the editorship of which Griffith would eventually resume that summer.[97] It maintained that while people in Ireland were 'used to hearing much of "poor Ireland" from a former school of politicians', thanks to the birth of the Dáil 'a fact, we believe, is now revealed for the first time to the people of Ireland'. This was that the Irish banks were only using 3 per cent of its total deposits from the Irish people (approximately £46 million) to accommodate its own Irish customers in loans, deliberately withholding any substantial loans to Irish traders, entrepreneurs and private individuals, while investing most of the remainder (£44.5 million) in Britain. Arguing that 'this is the real cause of Ireland's so-called poverty', *Nationality* re-emphasised the original Sinn Féin Policy that 'any scheme of reconstruction which is undertaken must have as its primary object the retention of this money in Ireland'.[98] It was upon this basis of a need to repatriate the country's sterling assets that it highlighted what were considered as Irish potentials both with regards to international relations, i.e. the potential birth of an Irish foreign policy, and the possibilities for the internal development of a sound infrastructure for strong business and good government.

Griffith has sometimes been defined by historians as having been a narrow-minded man, mostly due to the perception that nationalism can breed xenophobia or racism: 'despite the imposing array of statistics and parallels with which he impressed or bewildered his readers, Griffith was a narrow nationalist.'[99] However, his comparisons of Ireland with other nations were not essentially rooted in a racial ('anti-British') or simplistic geographical nationalism but rather a desire to highlight what could potentially be done. For instance, he emphasised that the gross exchequer returns of Ireland and Sweden during 1919 were identical (£35 million). As the latter was able to use such monies to become not only the most successful state in Scandinavia but also to create and sustain perhaps the most dynamic and well-trained civil service on the whole European continent, Griffith suggested that it was not unrealistic to assume that Ireland had some potential of its own.[100] He identified the internationalist focus of post-1918 American bankers as a dynamic that was opening up new markets. The ability of Australia, a 'pre-war pastoral country', to capitalise upon this trend particularly impressed Griffith, transforming itself suddenly into 'a manufacturing exporter' focused upon the European market for the first time.[101] As an extension of this, Griffith considered that the combination of Britain's huge war-debt to the United States with the fact that Ireland was still Britain's principle trading partner,[102] meant that Ireland, if it was allowed *genuine* economic freedoms by Britain for the first time in its history ('we have burst through the wall of paper England built around us—we have still to burst through the trade wall') *should* be able to become a significant third-party to the Anglo-American economic relationship, not least by eventually developing its own independent trading relationships with America, Italy, France and Japan.[103] These arguments were made alongside traditional Sinn Féin arguments such as that 'a permanent market' for Irish cattle existed in at least two European countries (Germany and Italy) and a potential market in at least one other (Denmark), while there was also a possibility of reviving various historic Irish trading-routes. These included the French market for Irish dairy and woollen products (closed since the 1680s), the Iberian market for various luxury Irish consumables (closed since the 1780s; once this trade even had a South American dimension, going as far back as the 1680s) and the more recently closed (i.e. since the 1860s) American market for Irish fish.[104] To Griffith's mind, exploring the possibility of exploiting these potential opportunities was Dáil Eireann's reason for existence.

Identifying theoretical possibilities was one matter but convincing Irish businessmen, or indeed their British business–political magnate masters, of their relevance was quite another. From his public speeches (being preoccupied in the Mansion House, Griffith generally confined his direct interaction with his

Cavan constituents to holding occasional monster rallies), one could certainly cite some unrealistic claims that he made in a generally unsuccessful effort to mobilise business enthusiasms. These included the assertions that 'there is not enough English gold in the London treasury to buy East Cavan'; 'in eight months Ireland, emancipated and erect, has advanced nationally fifty years' and 'the Irish question is today a world question'.[105] Likewise, Griffith's sense of excitement at the thought of Ireland reaching potentially unlimited American markets sometimes led him to make ridiculous assertions ('Ireland commands the [gateway to the] Atlantic').[106] Meanwhile, his desire to minimise Irish nationalists' perfectly understandable fear in challenging the two principle business magnates on the island (Lord Iveagh of Guinness Breweries and Andrew Jameson of Jameson Distilleries/Bank of Ireland) sometimes led him to make remarks that were so flippant as to be downright silly:

> We notice that the protest of the sober judgment of the organised unionists against Ireland's recognition as an independent [trading] nation was moved by a Guinness and seconded by a Jameson.[107]

Griffith's desire to develop an Irish fishing industry was a deep-seated aspect of the Sinn Féin's programme that, not surprisingly, attracted Patrick Moylett, the chief businessman in Ballina, Co. Mayo (Ireland's 'salmon capital'). It also led to the creation by Griffith of a Dáil ministry of fisheries, which was motivated by the fact that the fishing industry was completely underdeveloped in Ireland, being less than 4 per cent of the size of that in Britain (and not generally in Irish businessmen's hands either) despite the fact that the Irish coastline was unaffected by any landmass boundaries, as well as far longer than that of England or Scotland. This ministry was not popular, however, and many contemporaries dismissed Griffith's idea that the fishing industry in Ireland should be at least as developed and competitive as that of Britain as unrealistic. Commentating on the lack of public interest in the idea and the banks' unwillingness to support it, Griffith once quipped in response that all the fish in the seas along Ireland's coastline, as well as in its internal lakes and extensive river networks, must be guilty of the same alleged bias as himself: they were 'anti-British' fish, 'with the possible exception of the cod', and so all consideration of their physical existence had to be denied in the name of political decorum.[108]

A remarkable feature of Irish life in this context was that the large farm owners who dominated southern Irish political representation under the Irish Party frequently opposed the arrival of any new economic interest group in politics: this could upset the 'one party' political norm that the Irish Party had almost grown accustomed to accepting as an inherent fact of Irish life. Another remarkable fact in this context is that the banks in Ireland, being directed from London, actually declared that fisheries could not possibly be a sound financial investment in a country with a geography like Ireland and, of course, all Irish businessmen necessarily had to follow the banks' dictates.[109] Griffith's ideas may have been made impractical in the light of established business norms. They were not necessarily unrealistic, however, in terms of possibilities for development, if such possibilities were allowed. The great flaw, of course, in all Griffith's arguments regarding potentials was that they were inherently based on the precondition that it could first become possible for Irish money to be invested in Ireland purely for Irish purposes. This was a completely unrealistic hope. Furthermore, even the making of this suggestion inevitably led to an aggressive counter reaction. This came not just, or even primarily, from the British public sector or 'state' but, most potently of all, from the private sector.

Nationality published articles each week for well over a year covering, in serial fashion, all forms of taxation and how they impacted on the general economy as well as the public and private sector in Ireland. Simultaneously, it called for the Irish public to break the total monopoly held by English insurance companies within Ireland; another source of many millions of pounds perpetually leaving the country. While this may have inspired the formation of the Irish National Assurance Company (which, in turn, prompted the City of Dublin Assurance Society to announce its intention to begin investing some of its funds in Ireland for the first time in its history), several rival firms were now established that had no registered offices, addresses or prospectuses but were evidently established solely in the hope of fooling gullible Sinn Féin supporters and discrediting genuine Irish efforts to establish such companies.[110] Similarly, when some Sinn Féin supporters such as Eamon Duggan (formerly of the Estate Duty Office) and Joseph McDonagh (formerly of Inland Revenue) formed business consultancy firms to advise the Irish public on taxation matters in support of Griffith's goals, firms that were clearly not at all reliable were established immediately thereafter as intentionally disreputable rivals.[111]

By far, however, the greatest opposition to Sinn Féin's goals from the private sector stemmed from English shipping syndicates. Despite resistance from some Irish shareholders, these were succeeding in securing the complete shareholding of Irish shipping companies one-by-one, thereby ensuring 'our exporters and importers [will be] entirely at their mercy' and that the necessary first step towards Irish independence, namely the development of international trading routes centred on Irish ports, was growing increasingly unlikely.[112] Partly in response to a long-term campaign in *Nationality*, the Irish Cattle Traders Association (still led by William Field) attempted to purchase a major Dublin steam line company during the summer of 1919 only to find that it preferred to sell out to a powerful English syndicate for £36,000 *less* than what the Irish traders offered.[113] A similar sale agreement appears to have taken place in Cork. Local TDs who were long-term associates of Griffith and active in the IDA (namely Terence MacSwiney, Liam deRoiste and J.J. Walsh), as well as Austin Stack (chairman of the Tralee & Dingle Railway and an assistant Dáil minister) were all silent in this matter, which was quite probably facilitated by whatever interest rates were on offer in private bank loan agreements. Griffith himself emphasised that the biggest problem this raised was the English syndicates' ability to grasp all existing lines of transport must necessarily prevent the creation of any new Irish shipping firms at a time when all first-world countries were creating several. This development will 'seriously affect the future position of our country as a trading nation' by ensuring that future Irish firms, if ever established, could never compete because of the absence of a financially-supportive commercial transport system.[114]

Determined to have something positive to report, Griffith pointed to the recent establishment of a single American shipping line (under a nominally 'Irish-American' ownership) between New York and Dublin. Although, as Griffith admitted, this was the *only* one of sixty new American shipping lines including an Irish port in its trading routes (all others viewed Liverpool as inherently the only port to deal with for matters in anyway related to Irish markets), Griffith nevertheless suggested that it was a potentially positive sign for the future.[115] Indeed, the *only* positive development Griffith could cite as an example of a *real* direction for a future Irish foreign policy (Griffith essentially ignored the focus of his compatriots on church diplomacy) was the (still largely Tory) Dublin Chamber of Commerce's expression of appreciation for the work of Michael MacWhite, an old Edwardian Sinn Féin colleague of Griffith's, in forming a Franco-Irish Society in Paris to open up new business connection between the two countries. Reflecting this, over the next two years, MacWhite would send almost weekly reports regarding his efforts to Griffith's newspapers, which were reprinted in the hope of stimulating public belief in the Dáil.

These reports in *Nationality*, citing Irish potentials, fitted into the category of propaganda that was supportive of the Dáil. The actual proceedings of the Dáil were unknown to the general Irish public, however. This may not have been an entirely bad thing for its leaders. This was because the most the Dáil could actually do was usually to vote to allocate small amounts of funds and personnel to various committees that were formed to promote the Sinn Féin Policy. Furthermore, both this initiative and the volunteers who assumed the leadership of these committees (for instance, a department of fisheries, a department of forestry and a commission on industrial resources) were generally confined to the party's pre-1914 membership,[116] quite possibly because these were among the very few men in the new party who had joined out of a belief in the practicality of its economic goal of an independent Ireland. The latter initiative (the commission on industrial resources) was actually taken by Griffith solely to put pressure upon the IDA (which Griffith had hitherto encouraged, in vain, to start focusing on American markets) to begin cooperating with the Dáil.[117] Like most professed nationalist sympathisers in the country, however, this was something that the IDA (a British-government approved body whose existence was regulated by the Imperial Board of Trade) always refused to do or, at the very least, would never formally do.

Among the party's latest recruits, there were some who *did* call upon the Dáil to launch a national taxation-reform campaign to deal with the question of imperial over taxation, including Joseph MacDonagh (a Tipperary TD). The younger brother of Thomas MacDonagh and Pearse's successor as headmaster of St Enda's College, MacDonagh had recently worked for the Board of Inland Revenue and called for more efficient administrative practices by the Dáil.[118] However, when Griffith was queried in the matter of taxation by MacDonagh he had to admit that, while the finance minister (Collins) was considering the question of income taxes, 'they had no proposals at the moment'. Griffith also noted regarding the 'real taxation' issue of customs and excise revenue (the greatest source by far of state revenue) that a campaign to deal with this issue could be faced with insurmountable obstacles. Meanwhile, W.T. Cosgrave, as minister for local government, answered similar questions by emphasising that these were issues to be dealt with 'as soon as the Irish Government was in a position to function'.[119]

The Dáil not only had no standing with any bank (hence its hope to establish a new one) but its total financial resources (approximately £25,000) could only last a very short time even under its, as yet, very limited programme for government. The Dáil's absence of financial support made a 'national loan' scheme necessary. Regarding this, Collins noted that 'upon this loan the whole constructive policy of Dáil Eireann depends'. Evidently anticipating a very limited response, however, Collins noted that 'even if nothing came of this movement…the loan would be redeemed'. His simultaneous and almost inexplicable reference (beyond the fact that he was also IRB treasurer) to 'redeeming the Fenian bonds' (historic funds held by a British-owned bank in New York that John Devoy had failed to acquire in 1885) may well have done little to inspire confidence among potential Irish investors. Nevertheless, as fund-raising was of paramount importance, the launch of a national loan scheme (with Bishop Fogarty, James O'Mara and DeValera as its official trustees) simultaneous with a proposal to establish an agricultural loan bank (to be managed by Collins and agriculture minister Robert Barton, whom Griffith noted to DeValera 'has turned out exceedingly useful')[120] was the most significant initiative to be taken by Dáil during 1919. Indeed, by August, it was showing some signs of becoming a determined administration.[121]

Notwithstanding legal complications surrounding the idea of issuing bonds, DeValera's American tour was fairly successful in collecting funds. Griffith encouraged him to persevere in this work as 'I am fully convinced that your presence in America with the presidential election in the offing is our greatest asset', while 'so long as you hold Irish-America, what they can do to us here is non-effective'.[122] Typifying the nature of his own work as seeking 'unofficial recognition of the republic',[123] DeValera agreed with Griffith that it was worth ignoring Horace Plunkett's dubious recent claim to be in favour of dominion status for Ireland instead of the Government of Ireland Act on the statute books (as this was nominally a seditious stance, nobody believed that Plunkett was sincere).[124] DeValera also requested that Griffith keep providing him with statistics and information to use for his propaganda campaign.[125] In this, DeValera expressed a willingness to address the two issues that Griffith prioritised; industrial development and the League of Nations experiment.[126] His public speeches also demonstrated a clear sense of realism, however. In particular, DeValera emphasised that even if it was true that Ireland had always been governed in a commercially exploitative manner by Britain, it was equally true that 'the big nations have never been willing to give back what they have grabbed'.[127] This reflected a divergence between DeValera and Griffith's sense of the political situation.

Nationality was very enthusiastic about DeValera's tour and was largely responsible for propagating a DeValera personality cult. From this basis, it soon began considering what it typified as the most fundamental foreign policy question Irishmen should be considering; namely, the relationship of Ireland with the Anglo-American world. Griffith's public declaration that 'the Irish question is today a world question' reflected his tendency to be carried away by this enthusiasm.[128] He emphasised the eclipse of London as 'the world's financial centre' and, from this basis, suggested that 'across the Irish Sea today, we are witnessing the convulsions of a slowly dying Empire ... An Empire is passing as Carthage and Rome passed ... The coming Empire of the world is America.'[129]

Emphasising that 'it is a fundamental of English policy to destroy any country that attempts to compete with her in sea-borne commerce', Griffith argued that Britain had plotted a war against Germany ever since 1907 for precisely this reason but, as the War Office's plans had miscalculated and it ultimately required American intervention to win the war, 'America has taken England's place as the creditor nation of the world.' Furthermore, every European nation, as well as several American and Asiatic powers, now owed billions of dollars to the United States and none more so than Britain. As Britain was now America's debtor and 'America is challenging far more formidably than Germany did England's monopoly of the sea', Britain would never be able to reverse this trend and 'that automatically means the end of England as a great power':

> England without supremacy on the sea is a second-rate European state ... England's statesmen understand this ... England's people do not ... England cannot fight America; she cannot compete with America; she cannot pay America—she still thinks she can trick America. The League of Nations Covenant as it stands is her trick. And today Ireland is doing more than all the remainder of Europe to prevent that trick succeeding.[130]

This was how Griffith justified DeValera's American tour. However, as *Nationality* itself had already noted, whatever potentially positive consequences that the adoption of Wilson's proposed 'League of Nations Covenant' had at Versailles, this was almost totally negated by the inclusion of a clause stating that action on behalf of a victimised small power could only be taken if all the major powers agreed. This logic marked no new departure from those long-established norms of European diplomacy that had led to the First World War in the first place.[131] The claims of Griffith's *Nationality* that DeValera's American tour would attract the world's attention to this flaw in the League of Nations proposal was essentially an extension of its prior editorial policy of claiming that 'unless Ireland is free, the world will not be free', and 'the plain people of the world march with us' in this understanding.[132] This perspective lacked a fundamental balance, however. Indeed, contrary to the common historical argument that 'Griffith was a narrow nationalist'[133] the essential basis of his political myopia was this tendency to make a wish the father of his thought. In this sense, the criticism of him that he adopted the stance of a 'publicist rather than an intellectual'[134] was justifiable. Reflecting this, DeValera would soon have to begin reminding Griffith that his capacity to assist Ireland in any diplomatic sense was actually extremely limited to the point of being almost non-existent.

Griffith was keen to claim that economic advantages for Ireland could arise from American involvement in a post-war reconstruction of Europe. In particular, he considered that major disruptions of European markets as a result of the war could lead to new market openings for Ireland. This could possibly lead to 'extensive pooling arrangements' or 'inter-allied agreements' regarding 'the staple [agricultural] products of our country' far beyond the existing confinements of the British market. Griffith judged that because the victor states of France, Italy and Britain had suffered just as much as had Germany and

Russia in the recent war, 'a great gulf in history' was opening, making 'American merchants, or rather their banking organisations', a key determinant of the future. Furthermore, as the population of Europe was now five times greater than it was a century previously, 'a long, troublous period' was certainly coming across the whole of Europe far more unsettling than in the post-French Revolution or post-Napoleonic periods: 'the soil is the same, the extent of arable surface is the same. But there are four times as many people to be provided with the means of livelihood'. Under such circumstances,

> All these nations are looking to America to help them out of their difficulties. We are perhaps fortunate in Ireland in having no national or commercial debts [he was here temporarily forgetting about the Land Commission]. The Irishmen who will not support today the financial independence of his country is worse than a rogue—he is a fool ... England's commercial debt to Ireland is ... [a] secret carefully guarded in the bosom of the bankers. It is known, however, that England has borrowed heavily from our banks ... Happy is the nation today that has no debts. But it will take the united efforts of the best minds and the best wills of our country to save her from the perils which Europe has to face today.[135]

Griffith believed that the combined fact of Britain's colossal war debt to the United States and Britain's great dependence, to date, on assuming control of the Irish food market for its own needs had created a market leverage point whereby Irish businessmen could potentially begin persuading the banks in Ireland to abandon their longstanding policy of not lending money in Ireland 'beyond a certain fixed point' (i.e. only for small enterprises). Hitherto, the banks in Ireland had taken 'no account of the possibilities of future development' beyond the tradition set after the amalgamation of the British and Irish exchequers in 1816 of 'taking the savings of the Irish people and permanently investing them out of the country' in the hope of securing a larger dividend on their investments. However, Griffith suggested that post-war circumstances might present a very convincing argument to the banks to begin adopting a different perspective:

> Here the speculative element enters, and it is [or should be] the privilege of the public and not the banks to speculate on the possibilities of the future, to take risks with their profits. It may be good policy for banks to get the public to take the financing of industries out of their hands ... [as] the banks in Ireland

are crippling themselves as well as the country with English mortgages. Let us contrast the policy of the American banks. They are steering a great campaign for foreign trade. Many of them have formed special foreign trade departments. These, of course, perform the ordinary functions of advising their customers…but they do much more to help the American exporter. They show him how to ship his goods, they even find customers for him, and they keep him well posted in foreign demands, tariffs, freights and necessary details.[136]

If this was too adventurous an idea for Irish bankers, Griffith noted that all the city banks in Britain were currently selling shares in their business to raise money specifically for the concerted purpose of redeveloping local industries in the wake of the war. He questioned why it was that the Irish bankers, who claimed to be so attuned to British economic realities, refused to ever consider doing the same in Ireland? From this premise, Griffith concluded rather cynically that 'we await with interest any better proposals for helping industry in Ireland with the several hundred millions of pounds of which the banks in Ireland have the guardianship'.[137] Not surprisingly, however, the Irish banks, being regulated by the Bank of England, chose to remain completely silent. Like the rest of the Irish business community, they acted as if Dáil Eireann did not exist precisely because, in a commercial sense, it did not.

These press statements of Griffith on the banks, made while acting president of the Dáil, were printed only a couple of days before he formally announced to the general public for the first time (in late August 1919) that the Dáil would be forming its own agricultural loan bank, supported by a national loan from the general Irish public. This policy was no doubt intended by Griffith not only to challenge Horace Plunkett's Department of Agriculture but also to pressurise the existing banks in Ireland into changing their business practices.[138] A probable indication that this was considered a troublesome development by the British government (or, at least, one worth safeguarding against) is that in early September, around the same time as the imperial treasury began implementing its own reforms for the United Kingdom, Dublin Castle suppressed *Nationality* and proclaimed Dáil Eireann, together with the Sinn Féin Party, the Irish Volunteers and the Gaelic League, as an illegal organisation. This forced the Dáil out of the Dublin Mansion House and to become a totally underground administration. Griffith's response was to claim that the British government had acted purely out of a fear of the Dáil's capacity to do 'constructive work … to develop Ireland's social, political and industrial life for the welfare of the whole people of Ireland'—a capacity that justified its claim to act 'as the supreme national authority'.[139] To some extent, however, the damage had already been done.

Through *Nationality*, Griffith had recently sought to alert the Irish public to what he typified as the coming of a new international economic order to which Ireland would have to adapt: 'the economic life of today does not permit the isolation of a people'.[140] Regarding the challenge of meeting the British government's intended treasury reforms (Lloyd George had declared an intention to increase public expenditure across the United Kingdom), Griffith re-emphasised his belief that as 'money spent in a country by an external power must of necessity be subject', it would be necessary to resist 'false measures of bribery cloaked as reconstruction which are about to be offered [by Britain] to decoy the Irish people from the path of independence, security and integrity' in favour of the government's century-long policy of British economic protectionism within Ireland.[141] What was the use of making such arguments, however, when members of the Dáil or Sinn Féin could not even speak in public without being arrested?

In addition to this muzzling of the Dáil's 'TDs' (renegade MPs, as far as the law of the law was still concerned), *Nationality* was not only silenced but also never revived. In response, Griffith used its capital to attempt to buy out Michael J. Lennon's *Young Ireland*. This effort was only partly successful. Griffith became a major shareholder in *Young Ireland*, which remained in print for another three years. However, he could neither assume its editorship nor use it to the same extent to propagate his economic nationalist ideas. The combination of Griffith's shareholding and the transfer of Milroy and Burke from the editorial team of *Nationality* to *Young Ireland* (joining and, to a slight extent, counterbalancing the influence of the religious-minded editorial team of deBlacam and Lennon) brought the latter journal closer to *Nationality*'s previous editorial stance. However, although it adopted a similar format, it was still a very different type of journal, being most notable for its populist and overtly religious sensibilities. It was not essentially the effective adjutant to the Dáil's campaign that *Nationality* had been. Griffith would never again assume the editorial chair of an Irish newspaper. His career as a journalist was now effectively over.

The outlawing of the Dáil had a number of impacts. Collins was determined to keep the 'national loan' scheme afloat but, as he informed DeValera, this was proving increasingly difficult due to police vigilance.[142] Meanwhile, completely irrespective of the nominal existence of the Dáil, the declaration of the Sinn Féin Party, the Gaelic League and the Irish Volunteers as illegal organisations was a very provocative and coercive measure that increased the nationalist community's determination to adopt a defiant stance; a fact that may be said to have worked to the Dáil's advantage in the long term.

Another issue was the relationship between the Sinn Féin Party and the Catholic Church. To coincide with the launch of DeValera's American tour at the beginning of July 1919, Cardinal Logue and the entire Irish Catholic hierarchy had issued an official pronouncement. This criticised the British government for making needless arrests; argued that the Irish people, if they followed the wise counsel of Cardinal Mercier, would ultimately find their just reward; and claimed that 'no body of Irishmen can be more profoundly interested than the Irish bishops in any scheme that would satisfy the legitimate aspirations of Ireland'. At the same time, it noted that 'an unredeemed wrong in Ireland' had necessitated that they 'speak out in the hearing of the world' before the American public. As the American Catholic hierarchy now welcomed DeValera, the Irish Catholic hierarchy expressed 'our profound gratitude' to the Americans for 'so nobly espousing the cause of Ireland at this turning point in her history'. Not surprisingly, however, the bishops did not speak in favour of Dáil Eireann (it made no reference whatsoever to its existence) or, indeed, any aspect of its governmental programme. The closest the hierarchy came to doing so was in its reference to the extent to which 'money is being poured out as water across the channel':

> If we ask back a little of the huge overcharge paid out of this country, to put life into our [the Church's] starved systems of education, the cry comes from the Castle that the remedy is to add to the rates. Every day the air is charged with rumours about unsettling such parts of the public administration.[143]

This was partly an anticipation of the British government's intended treasury reforms of September 1919. It was significant, however, primarily because the church was expressing the very conservative belief that any significant financial alterations in the public administration in Ireland, as operated by Dublin Castle, would be unsettling. The Sinn Féin Party's lack of support for Griffith's counter-state programme may partly be explained by this very fact. This also raised the prospect that if Griffith's counter-state programme was somehow promoted successfully by the underground Dáil it would not take too long before the church would throw its weight behind a counter-balancing and perhaps more realistic initiative. This reality would ultimately play a significant part in determining the history of Dáil Eireann as an underground administration.

CHAPTER NINE

Dáil Eireann as an Underground Organisation (1919–20)

Dáil Eireann only met eight times between September 1919 and July 1921. In each instance, this was done surreptitiously either in a Dublin hotel room or else in the private residence of Walter Cole (Griffith's closest personal friend in politics) with little more than a couple of dozen members in attendance.[1] Where the respective authorities of the Dáil and Sinn Féin Party began and ended was not always clear. For this reason, one Irish historian has described the Dáil at this time as a champion of a 'primitive and one-dimensional politics' because it was 'an assembly that was little more than a forum where the representatives of Sinn Féin could talk to themselves' with 'no opposition to be persuaded or convinced' and no supporting civil service administration worthy of the name.[2] Others have typified the Dáil as a revolutionary government. Certainly, it was an attempt to maintain an underground administration of some kind in support of Griffith's counter-state programme for the Sinn Féin Party. Not all Sinn Féiners were necessarily prepared to support Griffith's goal of setting up a counter administration to Dublin Castle, however. For instance, the outlawing of Sinn Féin and the Dáil in September 1919 prompted the practical withdrawal of Fr O'Flanagan and Eoin MacNeill from the former, temporarily leaving Griffith as acting president of both bodies.[3]

This had two results. First, there was a definite radicalisation of the party's nominal programme. In November 1919, Griffith ordered all Sinn Féin Party members to prepare for the 1920 local government elections with the goal of assuming control of the financial resources of these bodies once elected. This was to be done to ensure 'the expenditure of the rates raised in Ireland inside Ireland'. Simultaneously, they were to set an example by pledging their allegiance to Dáil Eireann as the national government, once they were elected. With the support of party secretary Patrick O'Keeffe, Griffith also issued election literature which claimed that once the Dáil assumed complete control of the public finances of the country it would introduce various initiatives, including a grants scheme to enable the working classes attend university and to use local governmental rates to establish more technical schools in Ireland. Those in Limerick, having been denied funding by Dublin Castle's Departure of Agriculture and Technical Instruction, were already looking to the Dáil for support.[4] This reflected a long-term trend. Mechanics Institutes were closing down, while some of Griffith's old YIL cohorts such as William O'Leary Curtis and Louis Ely O'Carroll (president of Kevin Street Technical School), both barristers of strong nationalist sympathies (reputedly they were IRB men during the 1890s), had long struggled to promote their technical education institutes. Dublin Corporation generally served as their only defender in the face of both clerical indifference and some Dublin Castle opposition, even from Plunkett's nominal department of agriculture and 'technical instruction': the idea of a technical education being a higher education was slow to take root in Ireland.[5] Griffith desired that the Dáil would speed up this process, however. He also promised that the Dáil would finance the development of those industries in Ireland that manufactured goods 'under trade union conditions' and instigate major changes in the Irish health services. In addition to the longstanding Sinn Féin goals of the 'abolition of unsanitary houses and areas' and 'the provision of meals and proper medical and dental inspection for children attending schools', the Dáil would ensure 'the fosterage in healthy homes of orphaned children' by doctors and nurses acting purely under the county councils' management instead of the existing arrangement sustained entirely by voluntary organisations of the religious orders.[6] Desire for reform was not necessarily strong in Irish society, however. The formation of the Dáil, with its intention of forming an independent Irish state with its own civil service, had already inspired the creation of oppositional Catholic secret societies to combat the 'ultra nationalists' in Ireland, or all those who were prepared to look beyond the simple question of 'faith and fatherland' and relying on the Church to provide for all social services, including education and health.[7]

To further his goal of reforming the medical service, Griffith had formed a Dáil 'public health committee', led by doctors Kathleen Lynn and Richard Hayes. This worked with the Housing Committee of Dublin Corporation, led by

Alderman Tom Kelly of Sinn Féin, to improve access for all poor urban workers to medical treatments and supplies. On 11 December, however, Alderman Kelly was arrested for promoting this work. He was subsequently imprisoned without trial in Wormwood Scrubbs prison in England. Dublin Castle persuaded City Hall that Kelly should not be allowed to resume his duties whenever he was released; a tactic that also used in the case of the arrest of the corporation's secretary Fred Allan, by now the administrative leader of Sinn Féin, as well as secretary of the Dáil's 'courts', in William Field's Blackrock–Dun Laoghaire local governmental constituency.[8] Kelly's arrest coincided with the first of several raids, or sackings, of the small Sinn Féin People's Bank that funded his activities. This development led ultimately to this bank's collapse in early 1921, following the assassination of its manager David Kelly.[9] This indicated that Dublin Castle was not simply prepared to risk allowing the Sinn Féin Bank, hitherto a very small concern, become a beneficiary of either the Dáil's attempt to assume control of the public finances or its separate loan scheme, while, perhaps surprisingly, at DeValera's request, no effort would be made by the Sinn Féin Party to revive this bank during 1921.

A second consequence of Griffith's assumption of the acting presidency of both the Dáil and Sinn Féin was the launch of a major British propaganda war to discredit both organisations by describing them as terrorists. This stance could only be justified by referring to their alleged association with 'the IRA'. As was reflected by *An tOglach: The Official Journal of the Irish Volunteers* (edited by Piaras Beaslai, a son of the leading Liverpool Catholic journalist of the day and a friend of Griffith), 'the IRA' was never the name for the Irish Volunteer movement.[10] Nevertheless, this non-existent body soon loomed as large in the press under the continued operations of the Defence of the Realm Act (this gave Dublin Castle the right to control the press) as non-existent 'Fenians' had in the wake of the suspension of the right of habeas corpus in Ireland during the mid-to-late 1860s.[11] This represented a politically motivated British attempt to portray a false picture of the Irish Volunteers as the entire basis of the nationalist struggle in Ireland.

Non-TD members of the volunteer movement had recently been requested to swear allegiance to the TDs' authority as vested in the Dáil.[12] The purpose of this action was to officially assign the responsibility to the Irish Volunteers, which was 'hitherto an independent body',[13] of assisting the Sinn Féin Party in implementing its programme at a local governmental level; a task that was directed from within the Dáil by Griffith, as minister for home affairs, and Cosgrave, as minister for local government. This was to be done by assuming the communal responsibilities of resigning members of the police forces (who were to be peacefully boycotted) as soon as Sinn Féin began assuming the reins of local government itself. At the same time, the Irish Volunteers, acting strictly as a civil defence force, were to work to ensure that the British authorities did not deprive the Irish population of foodstuffs or medical supplies as a coercive measure. This was, in effect, the principal responsibility of Cathal Brugha, the Dail's defence minister, and a summation of the entire responsibilities of the volunteer movement.[14] A deliberately misleading British propaganda tradition of referring to 'the IRA' and Dáil terrorism was launched in the wake of the January 1920 urban local government elections in Ireland, however, precisely because it was from this time onwards that Sinn Féin Party's declared intent to begin assuming the control of the public finances of Ireland first surfaced as a serious political issue. To counter this trend, British propaganda portrayed Sinn Féin as the sole aggressor and pointed to 'the IRA' to vindicate this perspective. The affect that this had upon the self-perception of ordinary volunteers is unknown, but as the British government had regulatory authority over the press it may well have coloured judgments to a significant degree.

Griffith's ambition that the Dáil could take control of the public finances did receive a boost during the January 1920 elections. Sinn Féin candidates, nominally running on this ticket, received an equal percentage of first preference votes to the unionist business leaders who effectively controlled the governments (or purse-strings) of all Irish cities.[15] However, not until the rural local government elections could also be held (these were intentionally delayed until June by Dublin Castle because it was expected they would result in a huge Sinn Féin majority) could Sinn Féin possibly consolidate its claim from this basis a right to control of the public purse. On the advice of the Irish Party, Dublin Castle had introduced a proportional representation electoral system just prior to the January 1920 elections in the belief that this would serve to highlight that Sinn Féin had got slightly less than 50 per cent of the votes cast in December 1918 (roughly 70–75 per cent of the electorate had voted) and, therefore, it had supposedly triumphed at the polls only because of the British majority vote ('first past the post') system. This initiative essentially failed, however. Griffith had actually been a champion of proportional representation electoral systems ever since 1912, believing that they served to minimise oligarchic practices in politics.[16] Writing to De Valera, who likewise deemed the results of these local government elections as critical to the fortunes of his campaign in America,[17] Griffith typified the electoral results of January 1920 as an indication that the Irish public 'have implicit confidence in your leadership' and 'are pledged to the Republic'.[18]

To sustain public confidence in the national loan scheme (which would be floated outside of Ireland as well, especially in America under Harry Boland), Griffith had recently claimed on behalf of the underground Dáil that 'perfect arrangements' had been made to ensure that the British government would never be able to seize its capital.[19] This was an exaggerated boast, however. The attempt to seize control of the public finances of Ireland was inherently the responsibility of all members of Sinn Féin nationwide, at least according to those who believed in the Dáil's existence. Meanwhile, the national loan campaign was the specific responsibility of Collins, as finance minister. Neither scheme could have much basis without a supporting bank within Ireland. This was not available, while the Sinn Féin Bank at 6 Harcourt Street was far too easy a target for the police. Collins' response was to seek the advice of Art O'Brien, a wealthy figure with contacts among English cooperative bankers. O'Brien had recently set up a 'London Office' of the Dáil in the private home of a sister of Roger Casement, which was located just across the road from the private home of the British Home Secretary.[20] His London Office also became a communications hub for secret IRB couriers, directed by Diarmuid O'Hegarty, who attempted to distribute a single-sheet *Irish Bulletin*, produced by Desmond Fitzgerald and edited by Frank Gallagher (formerly editor of William O'Brien's Cork *Free Press*),[21] from November 1919 onwards to all Dáil 'envoys', i.e. unofficial consuls, abroad in an attempt to counter the influence of entirely negative British press reporting internationally.[22] No real solution to the banking problem had been found, however, by such time as the British government effectively led a counter attack against Sinn Féin.

In February 1920, the Imperial Treasury appointed a new team of administrative experts to Dublin Castle, led by Sir John Anderson, Alfred 'Andy' Cope and A.P. Waterfield. Their job was to immediately begin implementing partition: the passage of the new Government of Ireland Bill, just introduced in Westminster, was considered a preordained conclusion.[23] Simultaneously, a bizarre and unauthorised attempt by a handful of Irish volunteers, directed by Ernest O'Malley, to repeat the example of the Phoenix Park murders was used by Dublin Castle as a justification for the revival of the British intelligence unit and military curfew in Dublin that was launched in the summer of 1882. Almost immediately, this led to the arrest of most Sinn Féin leaders, as well as (allegedly) the seizure of the complete rolls of the names and addresses of the membership of 'the IRA', in Ireland's deposed capital.[24] Collins' response to this establishment of a British intelligence campaign was controversial. He arranged the execution of Magistrate Alan Bell, a founder of the British intelligence system created in Ireland in 1882, on the grounds that Bell was about to seize the Dáil's funds, which Collins had recently risked lodging under various false names in Irish banks, all of which remained totally loyal to the British government.[25] To prevent their seizure, Collins would subsequently bank these funds, with Art O'Brien's assistance, under false names in various London banks, although this would ultimately create some problems for the Dáil in reclaiming this money because of the unorthodox bookkeeping involved.[26] This was anything but a perfect arrangement, but it was perhaps the best that could be done under the circumstances.

At the time of the imposition of the British military curfew in Dublin, Griffith was in London speaking, at O'Brien's request, at a rally at the Royal Albert Hall that was organised to demand the release of Tom Kelly and all other Irish political prisoners.[27] This demonstration was organised by the Irish Self-Determination League of Great Britain, a recently established body that was led by a popular Liverpool labour city councillor P.J. Kelly (who first met Griffith during the 1890s). Its national organiser was Sean McGrath, a long-time associate of Collins.[28] As an organisation, it effectively replaced the small Sinn Féin movement that was established by Sean Milroy in Britain during 1918. This was done when it was realised that propaganda on behalf of the Dáil rather than a Sinn Féin party-political organisation in Britain was what was needed.[29] Its fortunes reflected how little interest there was in Irish nationalism in Britain, however.

There had been a long tradition of Irish-born citizens in Britain embracing radicalisms, including republican radicalisms not necessarily connected with the IRB.[30] A political expectation existed in Britain that P.J. Kelly would some day follow the example of T.P. O'Connor (MP for Liverpool since 1885, now the father of the House of Commons and an Irish-born legend in British radical circles) in running for parliament.[31] O'Connor's political leadership over the Irish community in Britain was essentially broken during 1914–15 when, together with the *Catholic Herald* (the leading Catholic newspaper in Britain, edited by Charles Diamond, a former Irish Party MP and leading English Catholic journalist ever since the 1880s),[32] he aggressively promoted John Redmond's National Volunteers. This became Michael Collins' entry point into politics and was what prompted Art O'Brien to join the IRB with a view to promoting a rebellious 'Irish Volunteer' breakaway group.[33] O'Brien and Collins thereafter opposed the *Catholic Herald* regarding the political organisation of the Irish in Britain, while this newspaper responded by waging a bitter and relentless propaganda war against Sinn Féin, which (after 1918) was known in many English and Scottish Catholic circles as 'the Sin Fiends' and blamed for all civil unrest in Ireland.[34]

T.P. O'Connor survived in British politics only through identifying with a nascent labour party, while Collins and O'Brien sided with Griffith in typifying all British labour organisations as being characterised by complete indifference to Ireland. The truth of this assertion may be seen in the fact that although it attracted a very large membership (far larger, for instance, than any previous Irish Party support body in Britain), the Irish Self-Determination League of Great Britain received absolutely no support from labour or indeed any other section of the British political community.[35] The only interest in Britain in anything to do with Ireland after 1918 came from a small minority of Scottish cultural nationalists who, ultimately, could only find a political outlet in a nascent labour party. On Art O'Brien's advice, Griffith surreptitiously offered Dáil funding to the Scottish National Committee (later, in 1924, known as the 'Scottish National League' and then, in 1933, as the 'Scottish National Party') when it began passing resolutions during 1920, with the support of the still extant Davitt-inspired Highlands Land League, expressing sympathy for the idea of 'the establishment of independent Gaelic Republics in the two sister nations of Scotland and Ireland'.[36] This reflected a very marginal legacy going back to the days of John Ferguson, an influential late Victorian Scottish republican politician,[37] who, incidentally, was also almost solely responsible for keeping Young Ireland and IRB books in print for the reading public in late-nineteenth-century Ireland.[38] It was an accurate reflection of just how little interest in Irish nationalism existed in Britain, however.

It is against this backdrop that the decision of Erskine Childers to transfer his allegiance from the Liberal Party and the Irish Party to Sinn Féin at this time should be understood. Whitehall's new Labour Ministry employed both Childers and his friend John Chartres to readdress the Irish question in the light of the post-war reconstruction of the British economy.[39] After 1918, British labour activists had begun adopting 'anti-imperialist' (i.e. anti-war) rhetoric in reaction to mass unemployment for ex-soldiers. In turn, this prompted British political leaders, in an effort at appeasement, to begin speaking of the existence of a new benevolent 'commonwealth' as opposed to a warmongering 'empire'. While leading historians of the British Empire have typified the usage after 1918 of this commonwealth nomenclature as intentionally misleading 'bullshit',[40] Childers, a life-long advocate of liberal definitions of the Empire, nevertheless believed that it offered a new way to define 'the Irish question'. In the pro-British labour *Daily Herald* (a paper which would attempt, in vain, to interview Griffith), Childers argued during 1919 that all Irish political disorder was the result of very similar labour problems as existed in Britain, stemming from post-war demobilisations.[41] The common labour market under the Union in Britain and Ireland had been the basis of Larkin's strike of 1913 and the British Labour Party's support for Edward Carson's stance regarding the Irish Convention of 1917 and it now became a basis for Childers' arguments. The Irish Labour Party's unwillingness to support the Dáil reflected the economic strength of the Union and if Sinn Féin stood apart from this reality, it did so on essentially two different grounds. First, to Griffith, this was due to the desire to create an independent Ireland with its own distinct government, economic regulations and labour conditions. Second, to the church and perhaps to the Catholic majority, this was due more to a lack of enthusiasm or perhaps even an opposition to labour politics in general. In the wake of the imposition of the British military curfew in Dublin during February 1920, however, Childers changed his tune and launched a different propaganda campaign. This was done in the *Daily News*, a historic London radical paper whose Parisian edition was formerly, at the request of the British secret service, the author of the entirely misleading, yet very influential, 'dynamite war' propaganda of the mid-1880s regarding how the funds of the suppressed Land League were supposedly being used.[42]

Childers now focused entirely on the theme of 'military rule in Ireland'. While the Dáil (including, of course, Collins) emphasised that it was not at all an aggressor, Childers claimed that the essence of the Irish conflict was entirely military in both its origins and its nature. Upon this basis, he now declared himself a sympathiser with 'republican Ireland', which he explicitly equated with Catholic Ireland.[43] By this time Childers and Chartres had already offered, through the medium of O'Brien's London office, to defend (or perhaps one should say 'define') Sinn Féin from a purely labour political perspective.[44] In the wake of the labelling of the Dáil and Sinn Féin as terrorist organisations, Griffith decided that Childers could serve a different purpose. In particular, as Childers was a famous figure within high British political circles, Griffith requested that, if he was serious in seeking to assist the Dáil, he should begin working with Art O'Brien in propagandising the justice of the Dáil's cause specifically among British parliamentary politicians. Childers welcomed the chance to work for the Dáil's publicity office (run by Desmond Fitzgerald). Rather than addressing himself to British politicians, however, Childers concentrated on having his *Daily News* articles (which ran from March until August 1920) republished as a top-selling pamphlet. *Military Rule in Ireland* not only ran through several editions in Ireland, it was also circulated widely in Irish-America and translated into French and Spanish editions, thereby making it (quite possibly) the most widely read publication on Ireland that year worldwide, everywhere *except* Britain.[45] This was not what Griffith had requested, but nevertheless the Dáil's publicity office generally viewed it as a successful venture.

Although he had the reputation of a propagandist himself, this was not essentially Griffith's concern during 1920. He let the *Young Ireland* journal run its own course and viewed preparation for the intended local governmental takeover of June 1920 to be all-important. Just prior to his departure for America, DeValera had cited Griffith as practically the guide for the Dáil 'in outlining what should be their attitude in matters of industry and commerce' and in 'working out schemes for meeting the exact situation in which they found themselves',[46] but no matter how much, or how little, faith the Dáil had in Griffith's leadership, he could neither predetermine the course of events nor guard against effective British counters. The reaction of the Irish Banks Standing Committee to Westminster's introduction of the Government of Ireland Bill would be the most telling example of this.

In preparation for the rural local government elections of June 1920, the Irish Banks Standing Committee (directed largely by Andrew Jameson of the Bank of Ireland) ruled in May that all pre-existing loan arrangements for Irish local government bodies, as well as for the Irish universities, schools, churches, hospitals and charities (the financial worlds of Catholic and Protestant Ireland), should be maintained. However, any attempts to open new business-loan arrangements, or accounts, after May 1920 would be subject to punishing interest rates to make it inequitable for any Irish institution to decide to alter their pre-existing business arrangements.[47] In addition to refusing to make any long-term loans to Irish local governmental bodies and businesses, the Irish banks' guiding business principle remained to offer poorer interest rates on both loans and deposits to all significant customers than were on offer from banks in Britain, thereby making it inequitable for any major Irish capital holder (such as a large business or an institution) not to either seek their loans or invest their funds in Britain. The sole exception to this general rule was to offer more favourable interest rates to private (non-corporate) depositors who had a purely personal wealth of at least £25,000 (the equivalent, in modern terms, of being at least a millionaire). Loans, or advances, made between the banks themselves, as well as to the most senior bank officials, were also deemed worthy of special or more favourable treatment.[48]

In this way, resistance to any change in the management of Irish finances was firmly entrenched. For the same reason, although Jameson had recently voiced his concern to the British government regarding the growing influence of Griffith's economic nationalist ideas,[49] rumours of Sinn Féin sympathies (stemming from a willingness to strike) among the recently established 'Irish Bank Officials Association (IBOA)', a trade union for lesser bank officials (this included assistant branch managers, tellers and clerical staff), was only a very mild source of anxiety to the Irish bank directors who essentially occupied an unassailable position. In March 1920, the IBOA were persuaded by the bank directors to recognise the new Labour Ministry established by Whitehall, as well as Sir James Campbell (later Lord Glenavy), the Crown's recently appointed Lord Chancellor in Ireland, as the arbitrator of its disputes.[50] A nationalist rebellion from such quarters was unlikely, if not impossible.

It was hardly surprising that the Irish Banks Standing Committee decided to facilitate Lloyd George. This was done by expressing its full agreement with the proposals of the London-owned Belfast Bank (increasingly associated politically with James Craig) that the regulation of banking in Ireland must remain completely outside the control of the two proposed parliaments to be established under the Government of Ireland Act. This goal was facilitated by an agreement that all clearing arrangements (i.e. settlements for all capital transactions between the Irish banks) must be made exclusively through drafts that were drawn in Belfast directly on a London bank.[51] This was designed to insure that the financial world of London continued to regulate all Irish financial matters, but now via Belfast rather than Dublin; a development which, under partition, could give Northern Ireland pre-eminence over the economic interests of Southern Ireland due to Belfast's practical status as a regulator of all southern Irish banks' major business, on London's behalf.

The political impact of these secret developments just prior to the June 1920 local government elections played a large part in determining Sinn Féin's fortunes thereafter. They were also responsible for creating a greater sense of security within the Irish Unionist Alliance regarding the viability of Whitehall's plans for partition. Only major private shareholders and account holders in the banks could possibly have had an inkling of what was taking place. Meanwhile, it seems clear that Griffith and most Sinn Féin supporters simply did not know these details. Since the Dáil was driven underground, Griffith had allocated funds to enable the appointment of ministers as substitutes for arrested men; stressed the importance of continuing to support the goal of setting up an agricultural loan bank and local government courts; championed the work of the Dáil's consuls abroad; and noted regarding British coercion that 'there are some members whose health would not stand the strain', but 'there are others who must retain their liberty to carry on the work of the Dáil'.[52] This reflected Griffith's ambition that so long as the Dáil held out, ultimately the British government would have to deal with it on its terms. The injustice of military curfews and other aspects of British coercion made the Irish public increasingly sympathetic with this idea. However, a rude awakening was essentially awaiting all those stood by this hope without realising what priorities had been set by the country's financial institutions.

When the Dáil met in late June 1920, Griffith celebrated Sinn Féin's success in the district and county council elections and pointed to the fact that, despite British coercion, this was the most significant meeting the Dáil had yet to hold. Griffith announced the closure of the Dáil loan scheme (which had collected £290,000) and decreed the establishment, under Robert Barton, of a land bank, which would use the Dáil loan as capital. He also decreed the establishment of Dáil courts. Reflecting widespread fears that the latter initiative could be abused, Griffith emphasised that 'no claim ... shall be heard or determined by the Courts of the Republic unless by written licence of the Minister for Home Affairs' or his department.[53] To this end, a supplementary justice department was established.

Although nominally led by Austin Stack, it was actually led by a distinguished barrister Kevin O'Shiel, Sinn Féin's most notable recruit from the former Irish Nation League.[54] O'Shiel would be appointed by Griffith as the Dáil's official land commissioner and was largely responsible for facilitating the establishment of the Dáil's own arbitration courts that summer. Together with Eamon Duggan, he secured the support of a handful of other legal figures, including some (such as P.J. Ruttledge) who had, until very recently, been champions of the absolute British loyalism of the Irish legal profession.[55] If a seeming boost for the Dáil, however, this represented only a very minor coup. Like the IBOA, the Irish law clerks that campaigned for higher wages during 1919–20 ignored the existence of the Dáil, as well as its 'arbitration courts'. The handful of barristers now supportive of the Dáil remained a very small minority who had essentially been drawn to Sinn Féin simply because of the need for legal representation for the many men who had been arrested for having opposed the conscription movement of 1918.[56]

A significant addition to the Dáil's personnel at this time was Kevin O'Higgins, who was appointed as a substitute minister for local government for the imprisoned W.T. Cosgrave. At the time, Collins was toying (in theory) with the idea of introducing an income tax at a lower rate than the British government's rate to win the loyalty of the Irish public, while he also supported Ernest Blythe's idea of the Dáil setting up its own, state-run, 'import and export company'. Joseph MacDonagh and Eoin MacNeill welcomed this idea while it was also proposed that the Dáil should begin investing its funds in secure Dublin Corporation stock.[57] By contrast, O'Higgins immediately focused attention on the practicality of the scheme of securing control of the public finances. He agreed that 'at first sight it would seem that the straight thing to do was to break with the English Local Government Board immediately'. However, he also stressed the need for 'a commission of experts … to enquire into the possibility of carrying on local administration without financial aid from the English Government'. In particular, it needed to be clearly understood what 'would enable councils to meet altered financial conditions, if it is decided to break with the English Local Government Board'.[58] In effect, he was indirectly highlighting the problem of the banks' unwillingness to oppose the British government. The reaction of many prominent TDs to this debate indicated that their attitude to local government was governed less by considerations of finance, or indeed the theory of Griffith's counter-state programme, than the mere ambition of the Dáil being able to hold out against the British propaganda war. For instance, Terence MacSwiney typified the decision not to recognise the British courts as simply a question of 'playing for position', and suggested that 'it was now for the British Local Government to make the next move'. By contrast, Cathal Brugha argued that if either the Dáil or the British administration decided to withhold or alter rate payments, 'chaos' would ensue that might well prove only counterproductive.[59] In other words, reform or change was not necessarily what either TDs or their constituents had in mind: they were simply waiting for the British government to reopen negotiations.

The Sinn Féin Party's resounding success in the June 1920 local government elections provided the impetus for many RIC men nationwide not only to resign from that force but also to vacate police barracks. This essentially became the moment of the Irish Volunteers' rise to positions of significance as community leaders. In addition to recruiting resigning RIC men, local units subsequently burnt down many of these abandoned barracks in order to prevent their reoccupation by hostile forces. To some local nationalist communities, this development was as surprisingly welcome as some kind of Irish military victory. As Kevin O'Shiel noted, it also provided the basis for a subsequent public endorsement of his work to set up the Dáil's own arbitration courts at a local governmental level.[60] As this seeming disappearance of the RIC's moral authority occurred in conjunction with Sinn Féin's resounding success in county council elections, the morale boost this generated not only promoted many volunteers to look upon themselves as co-leaders with Sinn Féin of the nationalist enterprise, but led both parties to grow in appreciation of each other. However, as both Brugha and Collins lamented, the expectation in the Dáil that the volunteers could now assume the moral responsibilities of the RIC as a police force was often frustrated by a lack of professionalism and, as O'Higgins would later note, a basic reason for this was finance: the RIC had always been a well-financed force, while the Dáil simply did not have such resources.[61] This reality allowed opponents of the Dáil to launch an effective propaganda campaign from the summer of 1920 onwards that portrayed the Sinn Féin movement as an instrument of lawlessness.

It might be noted that the reaction in Westminster when a single Irish speaker in the House of Commons mentioned in passing the Dáil's declared victory for its national loan campaign was general laughter. This was because the Dáil's funding was still only 1 per cent of what the Dublin Castle administration was still withdrawing from Ireland annually in revenue and only 3 per cent of what the British government was still *spending* in Ireland annually as part of its regular public expenditure to sustain the Dublin Castle administration.[62] Meanwhile, despite intelligence warnings from Collins that *agent provocateurs* were at work and no offensive actions must ever be taken by the volunteers in Ulster,[63] attempts at arms raids were performed there.[64] In conjunction with the largely symbolical burning of barracks elsewhere in the country, this development was cited by Ulster Tories as a justification for the unilateral establishment of special constabularies in Ulster as well as Orange riots and pogroms of Catholic workers in both Derry and Belfast, both of which led to over a dozen deaths.

The shooting of a Lisburn RIC man following the death of Cork mayor Tomas MacCurtain was widely denounced as an alleged 'IRA' vengeance shooting; a claim that was absolutely denied by Collins and Bishop Fogarty, both of whom supported Griffith in publishing statements in which he attributed all the violence, particularly in Ulster, to secret machinations within Dublin Castle, arming and paying unemployed men specifically for the purpose of either committing outrages or provoking riots and then blaming this on nationalist politicians.[65] Griffith's claim was evidently true. When British foreign secretary Lord Grey queried the Prime Minister regarding this situation, Lloyd George noted that such tactics 'had from time immemorial been resorted to' in Ireland by the British government, while the cabinet secretary Maurice Hankey (also the director of British military intelligence), after conferring with the new leaders of the Dublin Castle administration, noted in his diary that 'the truth is these reprisals are more or less winked at' as a cheap and handy way of manipulating the Irish political situation and, in particular, British and Irish public opinion.[66]

As the situation in Ireland grew more tense Horace Plunkett's call for an imperial settlement of the Irish question won increasing support, including from Irish Catholic peers, NUI academics and the former Sinn Féin sympathiser Sir Thomas Henry Grattan Esmonde.[67] This occurred not least because it was reported that Lord Grey, the British foreign secretary, was willing to raise the question of Irish self-determination with President Wilson while he was in the United States to discuss the new League of Nations project. The Irish Party sent T.P.O'Connor, whose wife was the daughter of an American Supreme Court judge, on a complementary American mission (O'Connor's fourth such American tour since 1902) and he was reported, in some quarters, to be receiving a far greater audience with the business community and established American politicians than DeValera.[68] The significance of these trends was not lost upon educated Irish opinion. While the Defence of the Realm Act and sensational burnings of empty police barracks were sufficient to make a large section of the Irish public mistakenly believe that domestic political matters had changed greatly at this time, the situation in Britain and America, unlike that in Ireland, was not governed by state censorship. Therefore, a realistic assessment of the situation of Ireland in the light of Anglo-American relations was generally considered the best guide to future developments.

Griffith never lost an opportunity to claim that 'a tremendous amount of progress has been made' in forwarding the struggle for Irish self-determination abroad and that his ministry, particularly (although by no means exclusively) after the suppression of the Dáil, 'considered that the centre of gravity [of their efforts] lay in the United States' with DeValera's attempts to influence American opinion. Regarding Lord Grey's mission, Griffith's retort in defence of the

Dáil was to call on the Irish public to ignore the significance of his actions, claiming that he was making a futile attempt to appease American opinion due to Britain's wartime debts. He believed that 'the general feeling in the States is absolutely on the side of Ireland' and that, so long as the Dáil held firm in the stance it had taken, by the time of the next American presidential election, it would be possible for DeValera to make 'the recognition of Irish independence the prime issue in the next election of the US president'.[69] Not for the first or last time in his career, however, Griffith was surrendering too much to his own propagandistic instincts and, in the process, making highly unrealistic claims in defence of his political aspirations. Many in Ireland understood this. So too did DeValera.[70]

The opening months of DeValera's American mission during the summer of 1919 had been an impressive display of the ability of the Friends of Irish Freedom, led by Cardinal O'Connell of Boston, to organise opportunities for DeValera to address a couple of lesser US state assemblies on the east coast (e.g. Massachusetts) and to thereafter go on a lengthy nationwide lecture tour.[71] By the beginning of 1920, however, the only option left for DeValera to promote his goals was to seek to expand Sinn Féin's fund-raising potential specifically through the medium of the American Catholic press. To place this question in context, it is worth noting that while successful American (Catholic) bankers such as Eugene Kelly of the Emigrants Savings Bank had been willing in the past to act as a treasurer of Irish Party support bodies in America in the name of developing positive Anglo-American relations,[72] no American financial institution was prepared to invest in the Dáil.

The *Gaelic American* was of no use to DeValera. Notwithstanding his relative fame, John Devoy's brand of Sinn Féin journalism was essentially as unique to the New York political world, including its municipal politics, as Griffith's journalism had been to that of Dublin. Its take on Anglo-American relations did not reflect the issue of church diplomacy. Its need, stemming not least from its wartime conviction, to champion a purely American perspective on the issue of the League of Nations, combined with its fierce criticisms of DeValera's suggested analogy between Ireland and Cuba, prompted DeValera to look elsewhere for support from February 1920 onwards. This was a decision that Griffith appreciated, sooner or later.[73] While employing Boland as his secretary, DeValera entrusted Joseph McGarrity, a very wealthy hotel and liquor dealer in Philadelphia, and John Finerty Junior of the Chicago *Citizen*, son of the former president of the United Irish League of America,[74] with the job of looking after the Dáil's fund-raising mission.[75] However, as the Dáil had been outlawed, like the controversial American funds of the Land League (which were likewise collected solely through newspaper appeals and, ultimately, secretly banked in

Paris due to the Land League being outlawed in Ireland), DeValera could never legally bank in Ireland whatever funds he collected in America. This created a long-term problem.[76]

In his letters to DeValera, Griffith could not advise him well on diplomatic matters. Instead, he merely forwarded him news as well as information for propaganda purposes. He also forwarded addresses, including a lengthy 1920 St Patrick's Day address, to reassert the Dáil's absolute faith in the eventual success of DeValera's diplomatic mission.[77] By now, however, DeValera had grown tired of this situation. He realised that outside of Catholic diplomatic channels, Ireland had no real options open to it. This was reflected near the outset of his tour by his meeting various New York socialites, centred around the figure of Sir Shane Leslie, who thought they could utilise the Catholic bishops to persuade public opinion to support the British position regarding Ireland, but DeValera advised Griffith that it should be possible to counteract this trend.[78] This was his top priority. Writing to the Dáil cabinet in April 1920, DeValera judged that its most important priority must be to ensure that no antagonisms could ever develop between the Roman Catholic Church and 'the Irish people'. Such an eventuality, DeValera believed, could only have 'disastrous results':

> I can conceive of scarcely anything worse for the Church or for Ireland than that the idea should grow among the young men and women of Ireland that the Church is simply playing the policeman for the British Government. The feeling of bitterness and resentment on account of the action of Rome on 'Fenianism' [in the United States—a probable reference to Devoy's propaganda] and on the 'Plan of Campaign' [in Ireland] has not yet completely disappeared, though it is disappearing rapidly through the influence of the Church's support during the past few years [i.e. since 1915]. Anything that would help to revive again the notion that the Church is on the side of the big battalions would be a calamity. All the good work that has recently been accomplished would be completely undone … The position now is in many respects closely analogous to the position at the time when conscription was threatened … Under God nothing so much contributed to the saving of the Irish people on that occasion as the bold uncompromising action of the Irish Bishops. They saved Ireland and they endeared themselves and the Church to the Irish people more than ever before. If His Holiness should deem it wise to make any pronouncement, I would entreat with all my soul that it be of the same bold and unmistakable character as that

of the Irish Bishops in the case of conscription ... This memo, written purely from the point of view of the situation in Ireland, is reinforced by taking into account the position here in America.[79]

This perspective of DeValera led him to view Sean T. O'Kelly and George Gavan Duffy's missions to the Vatican, seeking to counter British Catholic influence there, as being of the utmost political importance.[80]

By contrast, Griffith appealed to DeValera not to abandon the goal of seeking an audience with President Wilson. By the summer of 1920, however, DeValera was certain that 'the greater part of my usefulness here is over': he was now having difficulty in finding an audience with even a single American congressman and thus could in no way compete with Lord Grey's diplomatic influence.[81] Although, as Devoy noted, Irish-American influence was not large,[82] many members of the Friends of Irish Freedom judged that the weakness of DeValera's mission was partly his own fault. This was because he ignored their advice about the need to understand American politics. He even approached the issue of church diplomacy on the basis of his concern regarding the role of the church in British or Anglo-Irish relations, not American politics, thereby echoing the past example of John Redmond. This caused some American Catholic bishops to join with South Carolina Baptist politicians within the Friends of Irish Freedom in denouncing DeValera as an enemy of republican political freedoms and 'a foreign potentate'.[83] A note of desperation may perhaps be read into DeValera's suggestion that British rule in Ireland should henceforth 'be fought by the hunger striker'. He argued that 'the worldwide publicity which this form of protest [soon to be employed by Terence MacSwiney] will give will be the nearest we can go to securing intervention', while 'the work which is being done in Ireland towards making the Government function as a *de facto* government is advancing our cause, even here, more than anything that could be done by our friends in this country'.[84] Evidently, Ireland's diplomatic mission was, for all intents and purposes, already dead.

The foremost illustration of the Irish desire to appeal to American opinion during 1920 was perhaps Kevin O'Shiel's *The Making of a Republic* (Dublin, 1920). This was an examination of the American struggle for independence that suggested a parallel for Ireland in a manner akin to Griffith's *Resurrection of Hungary* thesis and Devoy's *Gaelic American* propaganda (itself, a product of Irish-American Fenian journalism going back to the days of John Savage).[85] O'Shiel noted that the Americans 'became "Sinn Féiners"' to win independence in the face of American Tory opposition to their right to economic freedoms; suggested that Americans had a reason to support Ireland now; and argued that a clear moral could be drawn by Irishmen from the Americans' historic republican example:

> It is foolish to expect always a high standard of zeal and unselfishness from a whole people, even in the noblest of causes. Enthusiasts often forget that they are dealing with flesh and blood, which is the most fitful and most changeable composition on earth. Had the great Washington despaired of his ill clad, badly-disciplined, mutinous and famished troops, nobody would have blamed him, but what would have become of the United States? … An academic belief in liberty is well enough, but it will never set free a country. What is wanted more than anything else is that deep-rooted conviction which controls superfluous talk and guides the energy of the oppressed towards the performing of great deeds. The palm of freedom is for the brave, the patient, the serious and the industrious.[86]

In theory, Griffith's belief that the American situation was far too important for DeValera to abandon his efforts to contact President Wilson had some slight justification. For instance, Maurice Hankey, the British cabinet secretary, judged at this time that

> The primary and original cause of our troubles in the East from Egypt, through Palestine, Mesopotamia and Persia to India, is President Wilson with his fourteen points and his impossible doctrine of self-determination. The adoption of this principle at the peace conference [in Paris] has struck at the very roots of the British Empire all over the world from Ireland to Hong Kong, and has got me into a hideous mess.[87]

However, the only willing audience DeValera and Griffith had won to date had essentially been freelance British journalists. It was through this channel that DeValera's sole diplomatic idea in the United States—that Ireland could become a neutral and independent state within a protective British military zone, in a manner akin to Cuba's relations with the United States, if its independence as a republic was first acknowledged—had found an audience.[88] It was also through these press channels that appeals were made, in vain, to Griffith to come to an understanding with the British government during the summer of 1920.[89]

In late July 1920, an actual Liberal Party MP (Alfred Davies, who addressed Griffith as a 'brother MP') sent a personal invitation to Griffith to open negotiations with Lloyd George on the promise that 'the government, I am certain, will give you anything except a republic. I have spoken to many members of the House [of Commons] and they one and all suggest to the Government that you receive Dominion Home Rule.'[90] This occurred on the same day as the Dublin Chamber of Commerce made a surprise declaration against Westminster's intended Government of Ireland Act, favouring instead 'a measure of complete self-government'. This occurred despite the fact that the Dublin Castle administration was currently (albeit secretly) laying the groundwork for a Northern Ireland government, complete with its own civil service administration and Public Record Office ready and waiting.[91] For the latter reason, one might presume that this act of the Dublin Chamber of Commerce was a mere ruse promoted by Midleton and Jameson. On the other hand, it may also have been caused by what was perhaps the single greatest coup that the Irish Volunteers ever achieved. Purely on W.T. Cosgrave's initiative, the volunteers had seized the financial records of Dublin Corporation for the Dáil's local government department, thereby bringing the commercial world of Dublin under the direction of Cosgrave's department to a significant degree.[92] Cosgrave, for one, believed that the goal of the Dáil replacing the authority of the British Local Government Board in Ireland was well underway at this time.[93]

Not surprisingly, Griffith was aware that the raising of the question of dominion status when an entirely contrary piece of legislation (the Government of Ireland Act) was being settled in Westminster was a ruse by the British government. On this basis, his intended reply to Lloyd George's secret intermediary was to state that the Dáil would not accept any proposal 'to negotiate a treaty of peace between the two nations' until the British government first recognised the Dáil's status as an actual government. To undermine the influence of the propaganda of Horace Plunkett's Irish Dominion League, Griffith also rejected claims that Dublin Castle's coercive tactics were no different than those of any other European government in dealing with the great social upheavals, or labour unrests, that had taken place in the wake of the war. This idea was defended by Griffith on the grounds that 'Sinn Féin is not socialist, individualist, Bolshevist or capitalist ... there are no "moderates" and no "extremists". All stand together on the common election manifesto of December 1918.'[94] This was the political mantra throughout 1920 of *Young Ireland*, a weekly journal that Griffith partly owned. The seemingly indisputable visual evidence of the great disturbances in Ulster was encouraging others to accept a contrary idea of Sinn Féin, however.

The issue of Dáil unity and the Dublin Chamber of Commerce's surprise announcement was soon overshadowed by an action taken by a section of Belfast

Corporation in reaction to the recent pogroms whereby, it was claimed, over 5,000 people lost their jobs. Some Belfast city councillors now called for 'a commercial boycott of Belfast' and appealed to businesses to 'immediately withdraw all accounts from banks having their headquarters in Belfast and transfer them to banks with headquarters in other parts of Ireland'.[95] The Dáil was a little divided on this issue.

Sean McEntee and Paul Galligan, the TDs for Monaghan South and Cavan East, supported this idea, while Ernest Blythe and Arthur Griffith, the TDs for Monaghan North and Cavan West, completely opposed it. Blythe did so on the grounds of his belief that 'the basis of every trouble in the north was sectarian', not economic, in nature. By contrast, Griffith opposed the idea on the grounds that a boycott 'would be an admission that Belfast was outside Ireland'. He argued that the real issue was the need for the Dáil to assert that 'the imposition of political or religious tests as a condition of industrial employment in Ireland' was illegal. Griffith's motion to this effect was carried by all, including Terence MacSwiney whose last action before his arrest later that month was to propose the formation of a commission 'to inquire into English organised opposition to the republic' and to see 'how far the objections of the people of Belfast and the corner counties to an Irish Republic may be met'. Fellow Cork TD Liam deRoiste argued that 'economic penetration' by the Dáil into the commercial world of Belfast 'was the solution of the Ulster question', but he was adamant that this should be negotiated by consensus, not boycotts.[96]

Sinn Féin subsequently published flyers emphasising that the Dáil had decreed that 'the imposition of religious or political tests as a condition of industrial employment is illegal' and that the Dáil's fight 'is a fight for all the people of Ireland, irrespective of creed, class or politics'. Reflecting this, it was argued that 'every man of Irish birth should get a chance of becoming a loyal citizen of the Irish Republic and of earning an honest living in Ireland', including, of course, all the inhabitants of Belfast.[97] As such, the Dáil refused to instigate an economic boycott of Belfast. However, the Belfast Corporation party that demanded it persisted in launching the scheme anyway. This was accomplished with support from sections of the Labour Party, which still resolved to remain outside the Dáil not least owing to its belief in a common labour market with Britain. Some local Dublin businesses also support the boycott.

In mid-September, Griffith's response to this situation was to appoint a representative of the Dáil (Michael Staines) to supervise this situation;[98] a fact that would lead some to mistakenly assume, or rather claim, that Griffith and the Dáil had authorised such a boycott.[99] This was not true. The Dáil simply had a complete inability to prevent such a boycott and thereafter sought to keep tabs upon the situation. Its powerlessness was partly because of its lack of influence over a labour party that not only retained its independence from the Dáil's authority but also, as an extension of this very fact, continued to be influenced by its British counterpart and was willing to launch strikes accordingly. Likewise, business firms who held their accounts in London often deliberately acted in defiance of the Dáil's wishes. Once again, the private sector in Ireland was proving to be anything but an ally of Dáil Eireann. The idea of promoting fiscal reform for the sake of creating an independent Irish government was not widely supported. The British propaganda campaign regarding alleged 'IRA' atrocities was deliberately tied into a propaganda campaign associated with the Belfast boycott, which was now used to illustrate the nature of Dáil terrorism. This promoted some contemporaries, as well as future historians,[100] to overlook the more central issue of the actual nature of the Sinn Féin Party in Ulster.

In the provinces, clear-as-day economic realities behind what was often known as 'parish pump politics' were generally sufficient to convince most Sinn Féin Party members how they should stand, irrespective of Dáil decrees. The Ulster leader and organiser of Sinn Féin, who was the responsible for the return of Griffith, Collins and DeValera (amongst others) for northern constituencies, was Eamon Donnelly, an ex-AOH member. Once a prison officer in Armagh city, he had some small business contacts across north Connacht, the midlands and south Ulster. As P.A. McHugh had been (and, indeed, Joseph Devlin continued to be), this made Donnelly alive to the politico–religious polarisation of attitudes that existed amongst Connacht and Ulster businessmen, from the shopkeepers of Sligo, Boyle, Letterkenny or Monaghan towns to the larger merchants of Derry, Belfast and Newry. He would remain a lifelong opponent of the idea of partition but, as was reflected by the role of priests in Griffith's nomination for Cavan (Griffith's own Protestant relatives in Cavan opposed him politically),[101] there was a lack of real business allies for Sinn Féin in the province, although the Dáil loan scheme did find one notable business supporter in Monaghan.[102] As impressive as Griffith's economic nationalist objectives could appear on paper, therefore, they had no real practical meaning at a constituency level. Little or no provincial bank directors had ever intimated any real willingness to support them and, consequently, it made little or no sense to any section of the business community. Reflecting this, while Sinn Féin in Ulster, under Donnelly, did not support the Belfast business boycott and pledged its allegiance to the Dáil, it was powerless to put into effect any meaningful response of its own. This allowed propagandists to ignore the issue of the actual basis of Irish nationalist political organisations in Ulster altogether, and to date, it has remained an uninteresting subject to historians.[103]

The Dáil's meetings in August and September 1920 were among its most impressive. Among the novel proposals its members came up with at this time was to form an 'Economic Council' for all of Ireland.[104] Henry Harrison, a well-known

Ulster Protestant and former MP who was decorated for his service during the First World War, later became a notable critic of the economics behind the idea of partition (he would ultimately be awarded with an honorary doctorate by Trinity College, partly for his statistical examinations of the Anglo-Irish relationship).[105] During the autumn of 1920, however, Harrison actually argued in favour of Midleton's Anti-Partition League and Plunkett's Irish Dominion League uniting to persuade the British government to negotiate an Irish settlement exclusively through their organisations and to ignore the existence of a supposedly phantom Dáil.[106] This may well indicate that *if* the Dáil had not been driven underground a year previously (and in turn subject to a harmful propaganda war), its capacity to unite Irish public opinion behind a constructive political programme might have found much greater appreciation during 1920 than it actually did.

The British Prime Minister was receiving warnings at this time from William Wylie, Dublin Castle's chief land-law advisor, that Griffith's policy was actually beginning to succeed at a local governmental level.[107] For this reason, when British foreign secretary Lord Grey obliged Horace Plunkett in early October by writing to the *Times* suggesting the introduction of dominion home rule in Ireland, a British cabinet row ensued. Lloyd George demanded that the foreign secretary withdraw his press statement.[108] The Prime Minister's policy remained, in the cabinet secretary's words, simply to 'establish a parliament in Ulster, and if S. Ireland refuses to establish a parliament … occupying the ports only, and collecting then the customs and excise duties' for all of Ireland.[109] So long as the Imperial Treasury's complete authority over the economy of Ireland was retained—an authority that would have been lessened greatly by *actual* dominion status—the British cabinet was evidently not too worried if the establishment of a Southern Ireland parliament, even such as was envisioned by the Government of Ireland Act, was postponed. In the meantime, Griffith's attempts to assume control over the public purse in Ireland and to force Britain into recognising the Dáil's authority were simply not to be tolerated.

As an underground administration, the Dáil's ability to manage financial issues could not be very effective. The loan scheme reflected this. For instance, Griffith attempted at this time to acquire the Dáil loan funds that had been collected in America but this could only be done by stealth. £75,000 of the £500,000 that Griffith requested was, in fact, received by the Dáil, via Clan na Gael agents in Berlin,[110] but as Dublin Castle had an intelligence agent within Collins' finance department,[111] it was no doubt aware of these actions.

Griffith's goal in acquiring these funds remained the creation of an agricultural loan bank. Doing so would create the expectation in Ireland that the Dáil, *not* the British parliament, would be the author and financial regulator of all future Irish land law legislation. This goal was made impractical, however, by the fact that the Dáil had to look to Art O'Brien and Robert Barton's English business friends to find an administrative solution to the challenge of forming such a bank. Their principal such associate was Sydney Parry, an English cooperative banker, rubber plant owner in Africa and cousin of Roger Casement. Parry had joined O'Brien's 'Casement branch' of Sinn Féin in London.[112] He was also a friend of Lionel Smith Gordon, an Oxford-educated son of an English peer who, after being a teacher of economics in the University of Toronto, became interested in the principles of cooperative banking and farming and wrote several notable books on the theme. Smith Gordon first became associated with Robert Barton during 1912 when both were prominent members of Horace Plunkett's Irish Agricultural Organisation Society.[113] Under the management of Lionel Smith-Gordon, an Agricultural Loan Bank was tentatively established during the autumn of 1920 with a founding capital of £250,000 drawn from the Dáil loan scheme. It could not act extraneously to the existing banking system in Ireland for very long, however.

Initially, the Dáil's bank sought to establish a basis for its inter-bank loans and security for its investments through Parry's English cooperative bank and its associates, including a cooperative bank in Berlin, for whom Robert Briscoe, a Dublin-born Jewish businessman, acted as an intermediary for the Dáil. Briscoe was acting on Collins' direction. The very involvement of Collins as well as some members of the American Clan na Gael in this work would lead some future historians to assume that Briscoe was engaged in securing armaments.[114] However, the actual context of this German activity was simply the joint efforts of Collins and Devoy, as treasurers of the IRB and American Clan na Gael respectively, to find a secret means of forwarding American funding to the Dáil.[115] This system was soon disrupted, however.

In October 1920, DeValera decided to sever all connections between the American Friends of Irish Freedom and the Dáil and requested that Harry Boland sever all connections between the Clan na Gael and the IRB. This caused the Clan na Gael to split so that Devoy's leadership could be formally rejected. Boland had been the IRB's president (a position he had assumed upon the arrest of Sean McGarry) when he first arrived in America, in July 1919. After DeValera and Devoy quarrelled in February 1920 over the former's Cuban analogy, however, Boland practically acted as DeValera's personal secretary in all matters and worked to undermine Devoy's influence in the Clan. Devoy deemed this as unfortunate. He typified Boland as a man of great courage but with the weakness that 'he was not a man of intellect'. This not only made him 'wholly devoid of political judgement' but also allowed DeValera to manipulate him, effectively turning him into his personal valet, or slave: 'DeValera owned his soul.'[116]

Devoy's differences with DeValera stemmed not least from DeValera's alleged inability to understand the United States' stance on the League of Nations.[117] Neither this nor the Cuban analogy was the real root of the conflict, however. It was primarily an issue related to the management of the Clan na Gael. Devoy's relative political savvy stemmed from his forty-year career in the New York press world, its relationship with many American political organisations and his dealings with Irish politicians ever since the days of Parnell, *not* his leadership of the Clan na Gael. The latter was an organisation which Devoy himself had long understood could not do anything for Ireland except to attempt to fund the IRB for whatever purposes the latter organisation alone required: the Clan could never take any revolutionary action itself because 'we knew there were many British spies in the organisation who would reveal what we were doing and enable the British government to take prompt measures to stop us'.[118] Boland did not understand this fact and DeValera sought, through Boland, to manipulate the Clan to his own ends.

Joe McGarrity, who now founded a rival Clan na Gael organisation against Devoy, encouraged Boland to believe that an extensive and direct arms importation scheme from America to Ireland could be launched.[119] This was naïve in the extreme. It also reflected a paradox in McGarrity's career. Although a respected and well-read figure in the Philadelphia Catholic community (this was the initial root of his friendship with Patrick MacCartan),[120] the history of McGarrity's involvement in Clan na Gael was governed by actions that were almost always contrary, whether intentionally or not, to whatever limited objectives that the IRB could pursue in Ireland.[121] This mattered nothing to DeValera. He acted on the understanding that the *Gaelic American* had not supported his personal intentions for the Dáil loan scheme in America and, therefore, Devoy's circle should not be allowed to interfere in that matter. He also feared, quite reasonably, that Collins would not find a means to securely bank the American funds.[122]

Collins fully understood the IRB and Clan na Gael were separate organisations and the latter's only responsibility was to finance the former's wishes. This led Collins to question the wisdom of Boland's actions, even if he had to trust in Boland as the IRB's eyes and ears in America.[123] The IRB would never again succeed in establishing a working relationship with the Clan na Gael. The timing of Boland's decision was also rather unfortunate for Collins. This was because it virtually prefigured an upsurge in successful British actions against the Dáil. Collins nevertheless took comfort from his belief that 'it is quite plain that the situation is causing them concern, and that all is not so well as the Imperial spokesmen would have us believe'. Curiously, however, Collins pointed to the situation abroad, in British international relations, rather than in Ireland itself as the basis for this claim.[124] This reflected a misdirected attention on his behalf.

Like DeValera, Griffith did not view Irish revolutionary organisations as being of the utmost importance. He had recently suggested to DeValera that American city corporations should be requested to finance the rebuilding of Irish towns that were sacked by British auxiliaries in a similar manner as they had financed the rebuilding of French towns that were destroyed during the European war.[125] This reflected his desire to encourage American investment in Ireland. Meanwhile, it was Griffith's responsibility to make an official Dáil response to the death of Terence MacSwiney in late October after a seventy-four day hunger strike in Brixton jail. MacSwiney's action did far more than any other single episode to attract sympathetic international press attention to Sinn Féin. Before such an audience, Griffith commemorated the death of his old friend very emotionally, arguing that it was a manifestation of the fact that Irishmen's unrivalled capacity to endure suffering would ensure their ultimate triumph.[126] However, lest Sinn Féin win the propaganda war between Britain and Ireland (this seemed possible, briefly, in the wake of MacSwiney's death) Lloyd George authorised a dual onslaught upon the Dáil, one propagandist, the other military, from which it was unlikely to recover.

In early November 1920, Dublin Castle instigated an intense policy of military raids and court martials, including executions. Michael Collins' response would prove deeply controversial. Drawing upon the full extent of his information from within Dublin Castle, Collins ordered the shooting of fourteen suspected intelligence agents in Dublin. However, this led in turn to the immediate execution of two of Collins' closest friends and the inflicting of an India-style punishment beating upon unarmed Dublin citizens, when twelve random people were shot dead in Croke Park. During the attack on Croke Park, Griffith and his family were out for a Sunday walk and heard the shooting. On returning home to Clontarf, a boy was waiting at his front door and advised Griffith not to stay at home that night. He left at once but as he travelled in the direction of the city centre, seeking a safe house, he was caught, arrested and brought to Mountjoy prison.[127] Thanks to 'Bloody Sunday', the Dáil had lost its acting president within a matter of hours.

The private diary of cabinet secretary Maurice Hankey, who was also the director of British military intelligence, indicates that Collins' 'Bloody Sunday' killings hit their intended target.[128] This factor was irrelevant, however, compared to 'the troubles' that followed over the next three to four months. For the first (and essentially the last) time, the Anglo-Irish conflict seemed to take the form of a military conflict, thereby validating the British propaganda war regarding Dáil terrorism. This was evidently Whitehall's intention. Its motive was that its

Government of Ireland Act was now being passed through Westminster and, therefore, inciting Irish resistance was seen as a means to discredit the Dáil's policy of non-cooperation with Westminster as much as was possible to the British, Irish and international public. Simultaneously, the British cabinet attempted to launch negotiations with the Dáil through various covert channels. The foremost of these were Fr O'Flanagan, who dealt primarily with Alfred Cope, the new assistant under-secretary at Dublin Castle, an unidentified Sinn Féin negotiator named 'Lynch', and an old associate of Griffith, Ballina businessman Patrick Moylett (who, like Lynch, dealt directly with the British cabinet).[129]

Moylett would later publish an account of his actions at this time.[130] He indicated, not entirely honestly, that he was requested to seek a compromise on behalf of Galway City Council, where he had business interests and where British auxiliaries had recently instigated severe blows against Sinn Féin. He argued that his action was not controversial because of two factors. First, as a co-director of the Dáil's 'Import and Export Company', set up on Blythe's suggestion months previously (which Brugha had utilised for arms importations), Moylett was aware, as was Robert Barton (the Dáil's minister for agriculture), that the new Dáil bank was being 'framed and registered under British laws' to prevent its suppression,[131] although it seems that this action was not actually taken until the spring of 1921 (several months later). A second reason why Moylett did not consider his actions as controversial is that he had informed Griffith when he had first contacted the British government during the summer of 1920. Griffith gave Moylett no credentials to negotiate, however. In mid-November, however, Griffith did lead Moylett to understand (and pointed him to a Manchester *Guardian* interview he gave on the subject) that, if he was talking with the British government, he should let them know that 'a truce and a conference, unhampered by preliminary conditions, between representatives of the British government and representatives of Dáil Eireann ... could be speedily arranged'.[132] This was an indication that Griffith felt that the Dáil had now advanced sufficiently in establishing its authority that the opening of peace negotiations in search of a negotiable settlement could soon be opportune.

Collins assumed the role of acting president after Griffith's arrest. He felt that Moylett was overstepping his authority by claiming to have official credentials as a negotiator and, therefore, was playing into the hands of the enemy.[133] The essential issue here was the potential that existed for the British government to take advantage of these single would-be intermediaries with the Dáil to claim a subsequent right to draw up preliminary conditions before making any actual, or official, instigation of negotiations with the Dáil by formally recognising its authority. That this was the British government's intention was indicated by Cope's success in persuading Fr O'Flanagan to express approval for his idea of initiating negotiations with the Sinn Féin Party via Australian Catholic bishops. These men had no standing with Dáil Eireann. Nevertheless, it seems that Eoin MacNeill expressed full approval for this initiative, which began with the Welsh Earl of Denbigh, a leader of the Catholic Union of Great Britain.[134] Archbishop Patrick Clune of Perth, Australia, succeeded in interviewing many Sinn Féin leaders in early December. Collins protested to Clune that he considered his actions to be 'entirely dishonest' and stated that he wanted the archbishop to make it known to the general public, as much as the British government, that the Dáil was ready for defensive military action if need be. This was a defiant stance that Collins justified as a necessary evil to prevent the Dáil from being completely bypassed, or manoeuvred into a totally subordinate position. Collins was receiving indications that a peace agreement was indeed in the process of being reached.[135]

In Mountjoy prison, Griffith managed to keep in touch with Collins through sympathetic wardens. He met the archbishop and re-emphasised the Dáil's desire for peace. However, Griffith cut off all discussions with Clune once he demanded that the Irish Volunteers surrender their arms as a preliminary step towards negotiations.[136] Thereafter, Griffith went on a hunger strike to express his sense of solidarity with the ever-rising number of Irish Volunteer prisoners who were doing the same.[137] He also drafted a statement to emphasise what he considered as the falsity of British press reports, which were claiming a deep division and serious conflict of opinion now existed amongst the Sinn Féin leadership. Griffith maintained that, now as ever, 'the [Dáil] ministry acts as a unit in international relations and no member of it has acted or will act ... without the knowledge and concurrence of his colleagues.' While 'Ireland desires to live in peace with all nations without exception', 'Ireland will not accept subjugation in any form in the false guise of peace.'[138]

A particularly strange occurrence took place just prior to the launch of these negotiations involving clerical intermediaries. This was a great arson attack on the Liverpool docklands. This area was the basis of the electoral support of the Dáil's one British political supporter, P.J. Kelly, who was duly arrested on the charge of organising the arson attack. A monster British labour protest demonstration on Trafalgar Square soon necessarily led to Kelly's release and the abandonment of the charges.[139] Nevertheless, a campaign of inexplicable and meaningless outrages (for instance, the burning of isolated farm houses) took place thereafter throughout northern England (from Lancashire to York) that continued incessantly well into the following spring. All of these were attributed by the British press to 'the IRA' (supposedly acting under the direct direction of the Dáil cabinet in Dublin) and were used to justify literally hundreds of arrests. This included Sean MacGrath, the leader of the Irish Self-Determination

League of Great Britain, while the barrage of arrests upon all Irish organisations in Britain actually forced Art O'Brien to begin cooperating with the police to some extent.[140]

Although Collins had proposed to MacGrath the formation of Irish Volunteer units in Britain as early as October 1919,[141] there is no evidence to link either man with the British arson campaign of early 1921 which had the result of negating many of Collins' old networks. This prompted Collins to judge that he (or, one might say, the IRB) was now a spent force in so far as he could assist the Dáil's defence ministry.[142] Furthermore, although it seems that Rory O'Connor, a friend of DeValera and best-man at Kevin O'Higgins' wedding, *may* have been the nominal leader of the Irish Volunteers in Britain during 1921,[143] it is unlikely that this trio approved of the arson campaign either. A clue regarding its provenance is that Maurice Hankey seemingly knew of the initial Liverpool attack before it even occurred.[144] A possible indication why this was the case lies in Moylett's claim that Griffith once told him that Richard Mulcahy had theoretical blueprints for an attack on various English docklands that he once lost to Dublin Castle during a police raid on his Ranelagh home. This was something to which he (Moylett) personally decided to draw London's attention,[145] although there is no indication in Mulcahy's papers that he ever ordered such an attack. Reputedly, Brugha was in favour of the idea of outrages in Britain (although this remains uncertain) but was persuaded against carrying it out.[146]

DeValera returned to Ireland on the same day (23 December 1920) as the Government of Ireland Act, which formally established both Southern Ireland and Northern Ireland, became law. Since the previous summer, around the same time as he gave up the idea of attempting to contact President Wilson, DeValera had conferred frequently in America with Archbishop Mannix of Melbourne. It was understood by international Catholic journalists that Mannix was in the United States at the direct request of Lloyd George, irrespective of the British play of prohibiting the archbishop from visiting Ireland on his return to London (where he would remain in conference with Church leaders and, to a lesser extent, the British government, up until March 1921, when he left for Rome).[147] DeValera professed to be willing to work with Mannix because the Catholic Church was an inherently independent institution with its own diplomatic powers. This meant that Mannix was essentially a free agent, no matter what the British government asked him to do.[148] Furthermore, it was precisely because DeValera anticipated that the British government would soon attempt to resolve the Irish situation through placing an emphasis on church diplomatic channels that he considered that the Dáil had to be fully prepared for this eventuality by having as strong a rapport with the church as was possible. For this reason, although DeValera dissuaded Fr O'Flanagan from continuing the peace negotiations, he only censured rather than expelled him from Sinn Féin for having bypassed the authority of the Dáil. Similarly, on resuming the leadership of the Dáil cabinet, DeValera sought to persuade all its members that Mannix, being a former president of Maynooth College, would always speak in defence of the total independence of Irish Catholics and their bishops in their relations with the Vatican. Therefore, any attempt to mobilise British and international Catholic opinion against them would fail because Britain could never force the Catholic Church to become a party to any settlement regarding Ireland with which it did not approve.[149] In effect, DeValera was maintaining that the very independence of the church was a factor that could now give the Dáil some leeway in pushing forward its demands for autonomy without necessarily having to accept the terms of the Government of Ireland Act passed at Westminster, thereby giving it the time and space to search for a different and more satisfactory settlement.

To a significant extent, the history of the Dáil as an underground administration was now over. By the time of Griffith's arrest, whatever departments the Dáil possessed had established their operational procedures to essentially the fullest extent that was possible under the circumstances. In the months ahead, they would not progress much further beyond the level of the appointment of additional clerical staff to facilitate more effective departmental reporting. Reflecting this, on being requested to call a meeting of the Dáil in mid-January 1921, DeValera and, in turn, all members of the Dáil focused on the issue of the truce negotiations.[150]

In his own estimation and that of most TDs, no member of the Dáil was better equipped than DeValera to negotiate with the church. Reflecting this, he was essentially entrusted to lead an effort to chart an independent negotiating position for the Dáil between the British government and the church. In doing so, one might argue that DeValera sought to shift the goal posts of the Dáil's ambitions. The irony this ultimately presented, however, was that it was Griffith who would be given the responsibility, after his release from prison, of running with the proverbial ball. This was despite his relative lack of familiarity with the political developments that occurred during his nine-months imprisonment.

CHAPTER TEN

The Search for a
Negotiable Settlement
(1921)

During Griffith's imprisonment (November 1920–July 1921), Dublin Castle executed twenty-three Irish Volunteer prisoners without trial; British auxiliary police forces assassinated the elected Sinn Féin mayors of Cork and Limerick; and vindictive British forces completely ransacked Cork city centre and imposed martial law throughout Munster (making the possession of a weapon a capital offence, punishable by immediate execution) in response to a single ambush of a dozen British soldiers in Kilmichael, Co. Cork, which was the only attack made upon British forces in Ireland. This was what became known euphemistically as 'the troubles'.[1] At its heart was the irony that Dáil Eireann had never made any secret of its peaceful intentions as well as its desire to negotiate an agreement with the British government. Nevertheless, the British government sanctioned such draconian actions by Dublin Castle while simultaneously seeking to arrange a settlement with Sinn Féin through old Irish Party networks and the Catholic Church with a view to ignoring the Dáil's existence entirely.[2] This reflected Britain's belief in its inherent right, as well as its own ability, to impose its desired political settlement upon Ireland without reference to the expressed will of the majority of Ireland's elected politicians.

Due to its financial power, Britain was also able to win its propaganda war regarding Ireland at this time. Arthur Balfour persuaded the humanitarian and international Red Cross organisation in Geneva, which was a very popular pacifist movement right across Europe in the wake of the First World War and, for many, an inspiration for the League of Nations project, to officially label Dáil Eireann as a terrorist organisation. This was proof that not only had Ireland failed to break through what Griffith termed as 'the paper wall' of British state censorship but that all the Dáil's would-be diplomatic envoys abroad had failed completely in their mission. A significant illustration of the fall out from this development is that when the esteemed English author G.K. Chesterton desired to echo Griffith's protests the previous summer by blaming the British government for orchestrating every act of violence in Ireland and thus being the only true 'terrorist', he found it necessary to publish his critique as far away as Canada.[3]

The arson campaign within England was what perpetuated this propaganda situation during the first half of 1921.[4] It led Cardinal Bourne of Westminster, the leader of the Catholic Church in Britain, and the Irish Party leader John Dillon to state that British cooperation with Sinn Féin must be delayed until all outrages (for which Sinn Féin was not even responsible) were first denounced.[5] The arson campaign also encouraged the British public to sympathise with the British cabinet's uncompromising stance. The Catholic Union of Great Britain, which had translated and published Cardinal Mercier's writings for the English reading public, strengthened this campaign by publishing material that emphasised that the Catholic Church enjoyed complete liberty of action under the British government in Ireland, with the additional bonus of generous annual state grants to Maynooth College, and therefore it had no reason whatsoever to tolerate any opposition to the British state by the Irish public.[6] Count Plunkett felt betrayed by this stance and it led him to write almost theological letters of protests to Cardinal Bourne.[7]

The Dáil's actual activities were almost completely unknown to the general Irish public, not just the international community, because it had been forced underground. This worked to Britain's advantage. After Westminster passed the Government of Ireland Act in December 1920, Whitehall was able to announce in February 1921 that it would soon appoint Edmund Talbot (Lord Fitzalan) as the first Catholic Viceroy in Ireland ever since the reign of James II (1685–1689). This was a decision that displeased Edward Carson (who formally announced his political retirement) but greatly pleased the Vatican. It also focused the eyes and ears of everyone from the English cooperative banker Sydney Parry to the former National Volunteer leader Maurice Moore (who had formerly employed Erskine Childers as his secretary in promoting the British war effort) to the South-African British diplomat General Jan Smuts on Rome.[8] Meanwhile, southern unionist business leaders, led by Midleton and Jameson, who funded the British auxiliary forces via the Bank of Ireland, were demanding that they 'be accepted as *the* mediators' by both Lloyd George and Sinn Féin in reaching a final political settlement.[9] This reflected their desire to exercise complete control over whatever financial settlements were reached regarding Ireland. It may also be said to have reflected the extent to which Griffith's ideas had become a common bond between the Dáil cabinet and those Irish Volunteer circles in the provinces and, indeed, the cities, that bore the brunt of the auxiliaries' ire. Nevertheless, it was widely believed that the context of the respective activities of the Dáil and Irish Volunteers differed: were the Irish nationalist public really committed to Griffith's ideas of complete self-government or were they simply preoccupied with resisting coercion? With the support of a sympathetic Irish member of the British House of Lords,[10] DeValera would later typify the challenge that this particular debate provoked as a question of proving the Dáil's moral authority as a guardian of peace, but this was a peace that nevertheless could only be established 'by ordeal'.[11] Reaching terms for an appropriate settlement was an uphill battle. Reflecting the status or preoccupations of the church within Ireland, however, DeValera continued to focus on church channels rather than the question of Irish finances in the search for a solution.

Even though Plunkett's title of 'foreign affairs minister' was nominally given to the imprisoned Griffith, DeValera practically abolished the Dáil's foreign affairs ministry in early 1921 after ordering the Dáil not to meet with representatives of any foreign governments, especially the United States.[12] Instead, Robert Brennan was given the title of 'under secretary for foreign affairs' who was not to deal with anyone in the Dáil, or its cabinet, except DeValera himself. In turn, working in conjunction with Archbishop Mannix of Melbourne and acting on the advice of Fr Corcoran S.J., DeValera would supervise the progress of the crucial diplomatic mission at the Vatican. To this end, Art O'Brien was encouraged to disband his London Office (DeValera suggested that he take up the Irish publicity cause in Spain instead),[13] while on the suggestion of P.J. Little's Irish circle in South Africa, it was proposed to organise a 'World Conference of the Irish Race' to be held a year hence in Paris (and possibly also in Montreal, Canada—Kathleen Hughes, an Englishwoman in Canada, was initially made the secretary of this entire project) with the support of the English-speaking Catholic diasporas of Australia, South Africa and the north and south American continents. This 'World Conference' was to become the entire focus of the Dáil's international work henceforth.[14] The sole exception to this system lay in the question of the United States.

The job of Irish publicity in America had already passed (ever since October 1920) into John Finerty and Joseph McGarrity's hands with crucial support from Robert Ford's New York *Irish World*.[15] Nevertheless, the secret courier system favoured hitherto by Boland and Collins to maintain Dáil contacts with America could not be entirely disbanded. This was because the American Clan na Gael continued to exist, notwithstanding the severance of all its connections with the IRB in Ireland.[16] To accommodate this factor, John Chartres, formerly of the British Labour Ministry, was appointed by DeValera to Berlin to supervise and deal with all those American emissaries that might attempt to get into contact with the Dáil by means of that clandestine system Collins and Boland had devised the previous summer in an attempt to forward funds from the Dáil loan scheme in America to the Dáil itself.[17] Frank Fahy, an old Gaelic League stalwart who now worked for the Dáil's education department, was mystified by the way the financing of Dáil departments now seemed to be partly regulated from Berlin (Collins too was encouraged by DeValera to work through this channel).[18] In reaction, Fahy coined a popular expression in Dáil circles at this time: 'who the hell is John Chartres?'[19] Meanwhile, Collins himself was growing increasingly sullen and despondent, protesting that 'certain members of the hierarchy are being worked to make the position worse and worse for ourselves with a view to making the settlement for England more easy and the terms offered [the Government of Ireland Act] appear more magnanimous'.[20] In response, DeValera expressed appreciation for Collins' past work under extraordinarily difficult circumstances—circumstances that evidently necessitated unusual responses[21]—but he maintained that this type of work would no longer be necessary. While censuring him for 'Bloody Sunday', DeValera also requested that Collins continue to act as finance minister.

DeValera's belief in the absolute necessity of Irish politicians relying on the Catholic Church was seemingly validated by the role of the Irish church in making the most constructive response to the 'paper wall' problem. A Mansion House Relief Committee that was regulated by the Irish Catholic hierarchy, rather than the Dáil, was established and it succeeded in getting the Pope's approval for a new Irish 'White Cross' organisation that would emphasise Sinn Féin's actual status as victims of coercive terrorism, thereby countering Britain's success in getting the international Red Cross to label the Sinn Féin Party as terrorists. With the church's approval and under the secretarial management of a recently retired British army major (who was also a cousin of Erskine Childers),[22] the White Cross succeeded very quickly in raising five times more funds from the general Irish public (£1.5 million) than the Dáil's loan scheme had done.[23] The White Cross also wrestled authority away from IRB activists over their chief cover body in public life to date, namely organisations for the relief of political prisoners (this was a matter over which Collins still retained a strong sense of personal responsibility, although the Catholic religious orders had and would continue to do most in terms of actually visiting and consoling the prisoners).[24] These developments echoed the work of a previous and not dissimilar Mansion House Relief Committee in collecting far more funds at short notice, as well as providing more influential political leadership to Irish nationalist organisations, than the original republican-directed (and self-styled provisional government of the) Irish National Land League forty years previously.[25] As there had been no alterations in the management of Irish finances, the socio-economic dynamics of Irish political representation had not essentially changed greatly in the interregnum.[26]

If the Irish White Cross effectively advertised the peaceable intentions of Sinn Féin, there was also the question of advertising its capacity for government. To this end, Timothy Corcoran S.J. (also professor of education at UCD) formed *Cumann Leigheacht an Phobail*, under DeValera's presidency, to publish lectures on government that were to be given at the Dublin Mansion House.[27] In doing so, DeValera and Corcoran bypassed the entire Dáil ministry, both past and present. The responsibility of defining the prospects of Irish economic development was given to the elderly medieval historian Alice Stopford Green (formerly a Liberal Party propagandist)[28] and her cousin Edward Stopford, another Church of Ireland figure with connections to the financial establishment,[29] supported by Erskine Childers. Green was an opponent of Griffith's economic nationalist programme, considering that his Irish nationalism could have no appeal to anyone except to some sections of the urban working class.[30] The challenge of defining all questions of local government administration was given to James MacNeill, a former leader of the Indian civil service in London and a brother to Eoin MacNeill with some support from Sir John O'Donnell, an Irish Catholic peer in the British House of Lords who had been associated with Horace Plunkett.[31] The responsibility of considering the question of agriculture, defined mostly according to the notion of cooperative farming, was given to Fr Michael O'Flanagan and Fr Tom Finlay S.J., formerly a president of Horace Plunkett's agricultural society and an economic advisor to the Irish Party. The responsibility of analysing all question of labour politics, as well as the supposedly central role of Christianity in defining all issues of public order, was given to two Jesuit priests.[32]

The launch of *Cumann Leigheacht an Phobail* in March 1921 was essentially a manifestation of Irish conservatism and no doubt provided a clear signal to concerned parties that the republican radicalism of the Dáil hitherto, as represented by Griffith's grandiose visions of reform, was not to be taken too seriously. In effect, it reflected the need of Sinn Féin to square its ambitions not with a blueprint of complete Irish self-government but rather with the practical connotations of the Government of Ireland Act. The launch of *Cumann Leigheacht an Phobail* coincided with several notable developments. These included the British auxiliaries' success in suppressing Griffith's small Sinn Féin People's Bank. No attempt was ever made to revive it. Simultaneously, Andrew Jameson formed the Irish Businessmen's Conciliation Committee that, with Midleton's support in Cork, would work from March 1921 onwards to negotiate an agreement between DeValera and Dublin Castle.[33] Also at this time, Erskine Childers was appointed as the Dáil's new 'publicity minister' despite the fact that he was not a member of that assembly and had never even stood for election in Irish politics (although he would do so successfully that summer). The first Dáil committee on education was also formed at this time. It consisted of Fr Corcoran and Eoin MacNeill and, in keeping with the church's concern with the intermediate education debate, focused exclusively on the question of financing secondary schools.[34] Another significant development at this time was the expansion of the directorship of the Dáil's National Land Bank and the resulting recognition of that body by the Irish Banks Standing Committee. Hitherto its directors had been the Dáil ministers for agriculture and trade (Robert Barton and Ernest Blythe), but the new directors appointed at this time were men who, with the nominal exception of Childers, had no connections with the Dáil. These were James MacNeill, James Douglas (an Ulster Quaker who also helped to manage the Irish White Cross) and Sir Henry Grattan Bellew (a Galway peer in the British House of Lords).[35] Reflecting this, in March 1921, Lionel Smith Gordon, the manager of the Dáil's bank, effectively acknowledged the economic reality of partition ever since December 1920. He noted that the 'Belfast banks, which are much more under the influence of English and Scottish conditions', were following the positive post-war example of the American banks in 'not rigidly insisting upon' a need for ample collateral security before making loans to businesses in an attempt to revive the post-war economy, but this was not being done in the rest of Ireland: 'the time may have come for more vigorous development in Southern Ireland but to a large extent the old traditions stand in the way.'[36]

As a former English entrepreneur with much experience of the private sector and who had now offered his services to the Dáil, Smith Gordon had no particular axe to grind. This essentially made him a neutral figure in assessing the relevance of the Irish economic nationalist programme that had been championed by Griffith and his finance minister Collins. Smith Gordon accepted Collins' view that the key determinant of policy formation must be the Irish public itself: 'Irish men and women as private individuals must do their share to increase the prosperity of the country.'[37] From this premise, he argued that it was up to the Irish public to demand that the Irish banks change their business practices regarding how they invested the Irish public's money. Echoing Griffith's past arguments, Gordon noted that it was indisputable that Irish banks' total reliance on English markets for their investments makes it 'harder for an Irishman wishing to promote or develop an Irish industry to borrow £5,000 than it is for an Englishman in good standing to borrow twenty times the sum' for the exact same purpose in Ireland. Although this had been viewed in the past as a positive means of sustaining small business enterprises as the backbone of an indigenous urban economy in Ireland, in practice, Gordon pointed out, this had 'the direct result ... to make emigration inevitable' because:

> Trade and money go hand in hand, and it is equally true that people follow trade ... No nation which exports its money to the detriment of its own industry can be surprised if the people also leave it. They have, in fact, no practical alternative.[38]

In other words, small-to-medium business enterprises were insufficient to sustain a national economy but this was precisely how the economy of Ireland had been managed hitherto to make it a labour provider for Britain. From his many years of first-hand experience of the English manufacturing industry and 'the large distributive farms in England' (the beneficiaries of southern Irish meat producers), Gordon also argued that the Irish public should realise that their sole value to the economy of the United Kingdom was that they were considered by the entire British private sector purely as 'a field for exploitation'. As an extension of this, English businessmen 'regard every effort to start independent industries in Ireland as an impertinent menace to themselves, to be resisted by any possible method':

> They want to keep this country a market which they can flood with their surplus goods, and it must be a source of satisfaction to them to find that we are willing to assist them in this object by sending them money to invest in extension of their own business instead of keeping it to invest in business of our own.[39]

He considered that perhaps the greatest fools in this regard was the Irish Party's traditional political support base of the grazing farming communities of Munster and Leinster. Echoing the past analyses of Griffith and the septuagenarian William Field, Gordon highlighted the fact that the role of English shipping monopolies in determining all transport costs (including those of the associated railways) and in turn the state's customs and excise policies was causing every single producer on the Irish agricultural market, as well as every urban consumer of commodities in Ireland, to be exploited on a daily basis. Even if 'the importance of this has been to some extent obscured of late by war conditions', Gordon believed that 'with the reopening of the world market it is likely to become painfully obvious' once more that:

The surrender of practically all cross-channel shipping into foreign hands has resulted in placing Irish manufacturers and [agricultural] producers practically at the mercy of the [English] buyers for so long as the same people who buy the goods can fix the cost of carrying them, which the *producer* has to pay, the theory of the open market by which Irish farmers in particular set so much store is practically a fiction ... The Irish stock raiser exports thousands of beasts every year for which they are paid the live weight of the meat. The beasts are resold in England on a basis that gives [English cattle traders] a profit ... the whole by-products [of the butchered, processed or packaged meats] are simply a present from Ireland to England; a present that we subsequently buy back from them at a price dictated by themselves. The result of this process is to deprive Ireland not only of a very large proportion of the reward properly due to the stock raisers but of a valid source of employment.[40]

So long as this situation continued, Ireland was only a food producer for the British agricultural industry but it had no such industry itself. In turn, no money could be made available from this agricultural business for reinvestment in Ireland that could allow Irish market towns to develop into business centres or cities in a comparable manner to how similar market towns had already become cities in the rest of the United Kingdom and Europe, providing full employment for their citizens or, at least, ample scope for economic development. The lack of provisions for financial returns to the local, or municipal, governments in Ireland under the 1898 act only compounded this problem.

Like Griffith, Gordon essentially recognised that a complete revolution in the management of Irish financial institutions was not likely. He could also acknowledge the degree to which existing banks were 'well conducted institutions'. Unlike Griffith, however, he focused more upon the question of depositors' attitudes than purely political factors. For instance, he emphasised that 'by far the greater part of the £200 million lying on deposit in the Irish joint stock banks represents the accumulation of small savings of people who cannot afford to take risks and who have no knowledge of the complications of the investment market'. He believed that Irish farmers in particular were 'suspicious of investments' and were also not 'greedy for [earning] high interest rates' on their deposits. Gordon agreed with Griffith, however, that the Irish bank–shareholding public *should* begin looking beyond the question of the purely personal dividends due to them and start acting like the bank–shareholding public of all civic-minded peoples in the world in demanding that the banks' share capital and reserve funds simply must not be invested in a way that could do their own country harm. Such a development would first necessitate that the Irish public 'arrive at quite a new point of view—the attitude that a bank is a national institution with a national objective' and thereby start thinking like Irish nationalists. Gordon predicted that 'if the Irish public were to insist upon making such an inquiry', it would shatter the false notion that Ireland was 'a miserable country with no money or opportunities for investment or development' and, in turn, opportunities for providing employment for its citizens. Furthermore, 'I venture to say that the results [exposed] would be profoundly unsatisfactory to them—and also to the bankers, who measure their success by the amount of deposits they are able to attract.'[41] Initiating such a process could thereby lead to a realisation within Ireland of the necessity of reform according to the principles of an Irish nationalism.

The true motive and significance of the British state censorship in Ireland under the extant Defence of the Realm Act was essentially its ability to mask the reality (which Griffith's suppressed *Nationality* had formerly highlighted) that a sell-out by Irish shareholders to British shareholders was being encouraged throughout the commercial world, especially in the transport and banking industries, from 1917 onwards. This was being done in order to facilitate Whitehall's plan to make partition the instrument for preserving the existing, economic basis of the Union throughout the length and breadth of Ireland. The Irish preoccupation with protesting regarding political arrests—a process that was typified by some Sinn Féin publicists as 'four glorious years' in the history of Irish nationalism—actually reflected the success of the British government's strategy of misdirecting Irish public attention away from this economic fact. Commenting on this development, Gordon believed that 'the temptation offered to the shareholders by the offer of large premiums on their shares' if they did sell out to British concerns was being accepted in Ireland mostly because it was believed that it simply would not be possible to resist this demand: now, as before, 'the superior investing power of the English public enables them to do whatever they wish with Ireland'. Accepting, or adjusting to, this reality was seen as the open secret of Ireland, or Irish life, regarding how to truly prosper in society. Nevertheless, Gordon believed that it might still yet be possible for the Irish public to resist this trend in British history if they began to spread some awareness within Ireland that 'if Ireland is to build an economic life ... commensurate with the position she hopes to occupy among the nations ... she must have a banking system of her own based on definitely national aims'. This would necessitate creating a strong Irish government that believed in the necessity of creating a state-directed economic policy, whether for an intermediate period of time or else in perpetuity:

> This can only be done by one of three methods ... The bank must have an actual state backing [he cited Germany as a role model here, 'where definite industrial and trade banks have been established with the approval and backing of the state'], or it must be of a cooperative nature (so that the capital is variable and the dividends strictly limited)[42] or finally, its shareholders must have so much interest in the question of industrial development that they are prepared to provide the bank with ample capital at a moderate rate of interest ... Of all the critical problems which the country has to decide in the course of the next few years, not the least critical is that of the attitude of the people will adopt towards their banking institutions and the use through them of their money.[43]

Sean Milroy, Griffith's appointee as the Sinn Féin Party's official spokesman on solving the dispute over partition, had championed similar arguments to Smith Gordon's in *The Case of Ulster* (Dublin, 1919). Remarkably, however, this had not evoked an interested response from any section of the Irish public; a clear indication that, in economic matters, the general Irish populace remained unionist in their thinking. One reason for this was the tradition, as represented by the Irish Party, to equate the nation with Catholic interests that had no particular interest in the concept of political self-determination beyond the level of control of education. Reflecting this trend, DeValera's appointed Joseph MacRory, the Catholic bishop of Down and Connor (and later the Catholic Primate of All Ireland), as Sinn Féin's new spokesman on partition. This coincided with a massive surge in financial support for the Irish White Cross. However, following the example of King George V's 1914 Buckingham Palace conference on Ireland, Bishop MacRory's preoccupation was solely with the sectarian dynamic behind northern social troubles, arising from the existence of competing education systems, and he had no interest whatsoever in any economic issues on a national level beyond the question of the management of schools and hospitals.[44]

After the death of Archbishop Walsh in April 1921, DeValera accepted the nomination of Timothy Corcoran S.J. and Michael Hayes to become Walsh's successor as the next NUI Chancellor. This would give DeValera, the Sinn Féin Party leader, the responsibility for financing Irish higher education (with the exception of Trinity College) outside of Northern Ireland on behalf of the British government, as well as to maximise financial support for the NUI within the private sector.[45] In terms of his own career, this was a prestigious achievement for

DeValera that boosted public appreciation for his status in political society very significantly. Indeed, it would not be an exaggeration to claim that DeValera now enjoyed a respect across the full political spectrum comparable to that formerly enjoyed by John Redmond and Archbishop Walsh. This development contrasted greatly with both the experience and political vantage point of various IRB leaders since February 1921. Now that the republican agitation and their own organisation had all but been defeated, such men expected to wake 'up some morning to find ourselves members of the civil population, with peace made and our occupation and our power gone. Then I'll go back to the poorhouse and I suppose you'll start selling collars again.'[46]

Acting on the advice of Erskine Childers and General Jan Smuts of South Africa, DeValera began concentrating at this time upon theoretical solutions to Ireland's difficulties; in particular, the question of finding a suitable constitution. Smuts' sympathetic advice was rooted in 'my belief is that Ireland is travelling the same painful road as South Africa'. In particular, as the dynamics of the imperial economy could not be changed Smuts believed that DeValera's ambition that the partition dispute could be resolved constitutionally was unrealistic and that his best hope instead was to concentrate on attaining 'a free constitution for the remaining twenty-six counties' as a stepping stone to further developments.[47]

During April 1921, DeValera began secret meetings with Lord Derby, until recently the British secretary of state for war, regarding the best means of ending the Anglo-Irish conflict.[48] As explained to Art O'Brien, DeValera approached these discussions on the premise that even 'the most conservative British statesmen ... acknowledged the right of the British Dominions to secede should they choose to exercise it'. If Britain was to offer Ireland *true* dominion status, therefore, there was a possibility of working 'in the direction of an independent *friendly* state with at least a guarantee of neutrality from us'.[49] A quagmire in these Anglo-Irish debates was DeValera's preoccupation with the fact that the dominions were 'part of the British Empire of *their own free will*'. However, in the 'unwritten constitution', or common law traditions, of British law, the dominions were essentially an evolved form of colonial government, being granted additional powers by Westminster over time whenever it best suited the economic or political interests of the rest of the Empire: they had not chosen to enter the Empire 'of their own free will' but had been both created and evolved as part of it. To the British government, this was inherently *the* basis of the constitution of Ireland.

DeValera had another source of constitutional advice in the Jesuits. The Catholic tradition of canon law was far more theoretically compatible with the common law traditions of countries such as the United Kingdom, Spain and even the United States than with the republican constitutional tradition in Europe, which favoured codified rather than common law practices and traditions. This was precisely because canon law, like the common law tradition, inherently emphasised the centrality of the spirit of the law above the letter of the law. In the Catholic tradition of thought, a mere written constitution was no guarantor of liberty. This was why the European republican tradition was generally viewed by the church as an outgrowth of the Napoleonic tradition of the forcible imposition of the structures of a modern nation-state, regardless of circumstances or the consequences.[50] A separate Irish constitution could be evolved upon the basis of existing British law, however, by using the Catholic tradition of canon law as a theoretical framework. DeValera was attracted by this idea, and it was also understood by George Gavan Duffy, the most senior legal mind associated with the Dáil.[51] Not surprisingly, Lord Derby had no interest in Catholic canon law. He recognised, however, that DeValera's willingness to accept the relevance of existing British law to any possible Anglo-Irish constitutional settlement provided a basis for a future Anglo-Irish agreement. For this reason, discussions continued and conditions for a peace agreement were soon finalised. The republic may have been dead but the ideal of establishing an Irish constitution—itself, a semi-republican concept—was still alive and kicking.

During the May 1921 general election candidates were returned for both the Northern Irish and Southern Irish parliaments that were legally established on 23 December 1920. Sinn Féin willingly ran its candidates in these partition-based elections just as much as did the Ulster Unionist Party. However, as a means of advertising to the general Irish public its intent to continue to claim greater constitutional rights than was on offer under the Government of Ireland Act, Sinn Féin boycotted the idea of immediately forming a Southern Irish parliament. DeValera was granted the right by Lord Fitzalan, the new Catholic Viceroy for Ireland, to meet James Craig in Dublin the week before these elections. A strange precursor to the peace agreement that followed was an invasion of the Dublin Customs House by an Irish Volunteer force that was under the command of Oscar Traynor. These men deliberately burnt various Irish companies' registers as well as the financial records of Ireland's harbour bodies before the DMP arrived to arrest them.[52] These were the very financial records that contained the business and trading information upon which Griffith's Sinn Féin Policy and, indeed, the Dáil's prior economic–nationalist strategy, necessarily had to be based. This self-destructive act virtually undid the coup of the volunteers a year previously in seizing the financial records of Dublin Corporation for the Dáil. It also occurred around the same time as the Businessmen's Conciliation Committee arranged a deal with the Sinn Féin Party that became known as 'the truce'. Evidently, therefore, an implicit condition of that 'truce' was that the desire advertised by Griffith hitherto, namely to fundamentally alter or undo the economy of the Union in Ireland, was now to be abandoned by Sinn Féin.

As W.T. Cosgrave would note, the proverbial truce agreement 'took a definite shape'. As was reflected by Griffith's own unwillingness to support the idea of Irish Volunteer disarmament as a precondition to Anglo-Irish negotiations, since the previous winter the volunteer movement was coming to be 'known popularly, though erroneously, as the "Irish republican army" [IRA]'.[53] This was an inaccurate name not only because it was not an official title. It was erroneous because the truce agreement was based on the understanding that the volunteers would henceforth be allowed to *assist* the RIC and DMP in policing responsibilities by means of liaison arrangements between the two forces. Hence, as Dublin Castle noted, from June 1921 onwards, 'in each county the representative of the IRA [Irish Volunteers] is in direct liaison with the County Inspector [of the RIC]' with a view to coming to a joint decision regarding any breaches of the peace, 'locally as they arise'. In doing so, they acted under the central authority of a committee headed by Under Secretary Alfred Cope at Dublin Castle on behalf of the British Home Secretary, while 'the closest cooperation between the police and IRA' existed everywhere. This was a decision that was reached with the approval of the entire membership of the Dáil and the Irish Volunteers, including, of course, the leadership of DeValera, as Dáil president, Cathal Brugha, as the Dáil's defence minister, and Richard Mulcahy, the leader of the Irish Volunteers.[54]

This development was essentially a logical summation of the prior strategy of the Irish Volunteers of attempting to assume the policing responsibilities of the RIC, albeit according to a dynamic whereby the existing British administration was not necessarily going to be supplanted totally. The only slight resistance to this trend existed in one of two parts of the country 'which are old strongholds of the Irish Republican Brotherhood',[55] which, being a secret entity, inherently presented something of a wildcard; a fact that, increasingly, did not make it popular with anybody. The fact that the IRB was a political rather than a military organisation, however, meant that its slight obstinacy, which might be more accurately typified as disgruntlement, counted for comparatively little. As its acting leader Michael Collins would note, the truce agreement meant the permanent defeat of the aspiration for an explicitly republican settlement;[56] hence, the disgruntlement of those who were most responsible for instigating that idea.

Alfred Cope, the recently appointed Under Secretary, had hitherto been a very senior customs official.[57] This was Lloyd George's motive in appointing him to Dublin Castle and making him the basis of the truce negotiations. These began during the winter of 1920 with the *Freeman's Journal* and Irish Party activists (who supported the economic principles of the Government of Ireland Act) and were made viable by DeValera's entry into negotiations in April. As a result of the truce, Griffith was released from prison on 11 July 1921. Having spent the previous nine months incarcerated, he had a little difficulty adjusting to the new political circumstances. DeValera was to meet Lloyd George in London on 14 July and he asked Griffith and Plunkett, the Dáil's nominal 'foreign affairs' ministers hitherto, to travel with him. Griffith was not allowed to take part in the negotiations, however. Instead, he was to act as a publicist on behalf of the Dáil's negotiating team with the British press in London. Reflecting this, when queried by the British press whether he would be willing to come to an agreement regarding 'the two great issues' for Britain, naval security and free trade, Griffith replied that all issues should be covered if a treaty was agreed, but he would tolerate no 'confidence tricks' from the British government as:

> The Irish representative who would permit his hands to be tied in any way by the British Cabinet before he sat down to negotiate with it would be as helpless as the fly in the spider's parlour and less deserving of sympathy. It is obvious that there can be no settlement unless as the outcome of an unfettered conference, and if the British Government does not want an unfettered conference, it does not want a settlement—it is only playacting in the hope of deceiving the world.[58]

DeValera soon returned to Dublin on the understanding that he would continue to negotiate with Lloyd George by correspondence. Although this was nominally supposed to be a governmental (or even an 'inter-governmental') matter, this correspondence was almost simultaneously published by Erskine Childers, the Dáil's publicity minister, as part of a publicity campaign that celebrated the supposedly ever-growing authority of Dáil Eireann in the wake of 'the truce'; a fact that played a significant role in influencing public attitudes.

The launch of a new Dáil publicity campaign was made possible by the lifting of both the military curfew in Dublin and martial law in Munster. Coming immediately after this seeming end of the Defence of the Realm Act, it was a development that was celebrated greatly. In addition to DeValera's seemingly defiant correspondence, Childers published various pamphlets and documents that detailed the work of Dáil Eireann and its departments to the general Irish public for the first time. These were reproduced in Griffith's *Young Ireland* in serial form under the title 'The Work of the Republic'.[59] This coincided with self-consciously celebratory activities, such as boosts in fund-raising by the Sinn Féin Party and many public marches and drills by the Irish Volunteers (a.k.a. 'the IRA') in all Irish town squares. This development was made the basis for launching an advertising campaign in all newspapers for a fresh recruitment drive to that force. *Young Ireland* essentially reflected the understanding of Collins, however, that this latest volunteer recruitment drive could, at best, simply duplicate the past (by now much depleted) strength of the 'IRA' with no possibility of any greater long-term results than what had already been achieved. However, this was not at all clear to many of those who joined the Irish Volunteers for the first time in the midst of the celebratory fanfares of the summer of 1921.

Griffith was a little shocked and displeased that Childers had effectively risen to become the private secretary and chief political advisor to the Dáil's president.[60] This was because he knew that Childers was not a supporter of the Sinn Féin Policy of altering fundamentally the economic basis of the Anglo-Irish relationship. To Griffith's mind, this was tantamount to being an opponent of Irish nationalism. However, the basis of the Dáil's mission had now essentially become to find an answer to Childers' own personal conundrum. This was to find an alternative basis for Southern Ireland's relationship with Britain to what was the norm in the external relations of British dominions. The truce was practically based on the premise that the economic terms of the Government of Ireland Act were set in stone. For various reasons, however, this was not clear to many contemporaries. For instance, during the summer of 1921, on behalf of Dublin Castle, Cope practically claimed to all members of the Irish nationalist public with whom he came into contact that 'we are defeated';[61] a claim that was joyfully repeated to all and sundry in the months ahead. However, the British were only claiming a moral rather than a political defeat and it is worth noting what was the precise reasoning behind that claim.

Thus far, only semi-professional English auxiliaries had been sent to Ireland to join the staff of the demoralised regular Irish police forces, which were staffed (beyond the officer class) primarily by Irishmen. British military involvement had been confined exclusively to the field of political intelligence (certainly not military intelligence), the situation in Ireland from 1919–21 having been, in this sense, absolutely no different to what it had been perpetually between 1882 and 1904. The only 'defeat' of British prerogatives that had occurred stemmed from a single meeting of the British cabinet's Irish Situation Committee in London during June, after the King opened the Northern Irish parliament. It was an embarrassment to Dublin Castle and to Cope to have to report that the King could not likewise open a Southern Irish parliament, but instead was supposed to have to sit around waiting until Dublin Castle could begin fully implementing the Government of Ireland Act in Dublin. So that the King could avoid having to procrastinate, it had been considered during June to begin utilising the British army in Ireland for the first time. Reflecting this, the British cabinet was fully prepared to consider executing every member of Dáil Eireann immediately and also set an example to the general Irish public by shooting at least 100 random Sinn Féiners every week thereafter; trifling operations to carry out in a military sense. Even all the opponents of sending the army into Ireland for the first time believed that all the leaders of the Dáil, including the imprisoned Griffith, must be tried for treason some day for having defied the King's wishes, with Balfour alone dissenting to suggest possibly implementing 'transportation [including penal servitude for life] rather than hanging as a punishment' following their inevitable conviction.[62] Such are the ways of monarchical governments, especially when they were at the centre of a political Empire, and this was the reality behind both 'the truce' and the political situation during the summer of 1921. It was purely for publicity reasons that the British cabinet decided against adopting this particular approach to finding a quick-fix solution. In principle, they had no objection to the idea.

A deep paradox regarding the so-called 'truce agreement' was that the many Irishmen who had been involved in negotiating various peace agreements between Dublin Castle, Jameson's Conciliation Committee and the Sinn Féin Party prior to Griffith's release from prison in July 1921 privately knew about this state of opinion in Dublin Castle and, in turn, the British cabinet. However, they could not state this to the general Irish public. This was because the proud citizen–soldier enthusiasms of many ordinary volunteers and Sinn Féin Party activists nationwide in resisting the Defence of the Realm Act ever since 1914—which they had correctly interpreted as an effort to reduce them to political silence—had not only become an end in itself, in terms of political mobilisation, but was also very many contemporaries' abiding sense of the meaning of the recent struggle. Irish politicians could not deny this. Although a military conflict had not taken place, the perpetual visibility of armed men, both auxiliaries and volunteers, on the streets—a development to which the Irish public were unaccustomed[63] and did not like (hence the anti-conscription vote of 1918)—made many people *feel* like they were in the midst of such a conflict. The ultimate illustration of this Irish political mentality would be the collection of political recollections of thousands of non-military personnel under a 'military history' umbrella term many years later.[64]

The absolute highlight of Sinn Féin's campaign from a publicity point of view had been the focusing of the international media's attention on the return to Cork of Mayor Terence MacSwiney's body for a proud funeral cortege by the local Irish Volunteers/IRA in full uniform. This event had also been perhaps the ultimate expression of the paradox in Irish attitudes towards militarism. It was an event that was captured by international press photographers and reproduced in newspapers around the world. From such photos, one can see that standing only a couple of feet away from 'the IRA' of Cork—a supposed circle of great militants who would soon be directed by Liam Lynch (until recently, a British army private)[65]—are British forces who are policing the streets for the same 'IRA' to enable these volunteers and would-be nationalist rebels march in MacSwiney's honour without creating too great a traffic disturbance.[66] In other words, the British forces were still in absolute control of law and order. However, public pride in MacSwiney's defiant nationalist stance led many Irish people to view themselves as occupying a higher moral ground, as if the power relationship between British and Irish forces was the converse to what it was in reality.

The public stance regarding 'the truce' in Ireland was both understandable and justifiable in an Irish party-political context. With its manifold political advisors in Ireland, Dublin Castle could understand this. However, other British government officials could not. For instance, H.A.L. Fisher, the most distinguished historian in UK universities at the time (he was also the UK's minister for education and an aid to Balfour in Geneva), typified the publication of DeValera's seemingly defiant public letters to Lloyd George (these were published as if the Irish occupied a position of equal, or even superior, strength, militarily or morally) as an act that was 'scarcely consistent with sanity': 'if it had proceeded from any foreign government, we should certainly be entitled ... to overcome any promptings of military prudence' and simply wipe all these Irish politicians off the face of the earth.[67] This 'childish folly' of the Irish was made tolerable to Whitehall only because Lord Fitzalan, the Catholic Viceroy at Dublin Castle, together with Alfred Cope, his assistant under-secretary, repeatedly assured the British cabinet, via Catholic Church channels, that they knew from first-hand knowledge that 'DeV and Co. do not mean to fight again' while both Cardinal Logue, the Catholic Primate of Ireland, and Bishop Fogarty, the Sinn Féin Party treasurer, were likewise assuring Dublin Castle that 'things will come right, if time is given'.[68]

Robert Barton and Art O'Brien, in acting as DeValera's intermediaries with the British cabinet, emphasised that DeValera's published letters were only propaganda 'intended to educate the British public as to what Sinn Féin stood for'. However Whitehall interpreted this as a cowardly refusal by DeValera to admit in public that he had already agreed to reach a settlement with the British government purely on the latter's terms. The days of issuing propaganda or making any attempt to alter the political balance were already long over.[69] In response, Cope advised the British cabinet that they needed to take into consideration the fact that DeValera 'is not master in his own household'. Furthermore, he noted that while 'the point seems to us trifling' and was rooted entirely in 'a characteristic Irish refusal to face the hard facts of the situation', the members of the Dáil cabinet were 'all hypersensitive' regarding 'the form of the invitation' to negotiate. This was because they 'do not wish to be regarded as paupers accepting a gift, but as equals entered into a negotiation and making a bargain'. By the beginning of September 1921, however, the British cabinet decided 'to tell DeValera quite briefly that the British government does not propose to restate its position' on the impossibility of abandoning the Government of Ireland Act, but 'if the Dáil is of the opinion that any useful purpose would be served … send plenipotentiaries'. If any political rupture came, the British government would strengthen Northern Ireland's military garrison, keep control of customs and excise across the whole island and simply ignore Sinn Féin in Southern Ireland which, it was judged, 'would de-popularise the Sinn Féin government'.[70]

DeValera now realised that he had no time left to procrastinate. He informed the Prime Minister that 'we have had no thought at any time of asking you to accept any conditions precedent to a conference'. This was the complete opposite of what the public statements of DeValera that were published in Irish press by Childers had claimed. At the same time, however,

> We request you … to state whether your letter of Sep 7th is intended to be a demand for a surrender on our part, or an invitation to a conference free on both sides … If the latter, we readily confirm our acceptance of the invitation and our appointed delegates will meet your Government's representatives at any time in the immediate future that you designate.[71]

The Prime Minister still did not budge. He would not do so until cabinet secretary Maurice Hankey, the director of British intelligence, sent him an intelligence communication on 27 September regarding 'Irish intentions at the Conference, if it takes place'. This had 'reached me from a lady who is herself a Roman Catholic and in close touch with the highest English and Irish Roman Catholic leaders. I am not at liberty to mention her name, which is well known to you.'[72]

Hankey noted that DeValera had decided on the following political strategy. A delegation would be sent to attempt 'to squeeze the Prime Minister to the utmost possible' but 'then to say that they can agree to nothing without the consent of the electorate'. At this point, 'the ecclesiastical authorities [the Irish Catholic hierarchy] are then to intervene and strongly advise acceptance of the Government's proposal'. Thereafter, 'the leaders will accept the advice and agree', but '[De] Valera and the other leaders have to save their "political faces"', by opposing the agreement and, in turn, presumably acting as a form of loyal opposition to those who accepted the agreement.[73] This satisfied the Prime Minister that the situation had been resolved and all that remained was to finalise details.[74] The following day, he sent an invitation from his holiday home in Gairloch, Scotland to DeValera to send plenipotentiaries and to begin negotiations on 11 October; an invitation that was immediately accepted.

The inequality of the Anglo-Irish negotiations that followed was predetermined. Irish deputies who would oppose the agreement stated publicly that they knew the compromise had already been reached in September 1921, if not earlier, while Collins viewed the compromise as having begun with the peace agreement of June–July.[75] Even as the London negotiations were taking place, extensive secret British political intelligence work regarding Ireland was still being performed in Dublin.[76] DeValera appointed plenipotentiaries on 14 September, two weeks before they were even requested, and at the last meeting of the Dáil to be held until after an agreement was signed.[77] If equal negotiations between governments had been possible, the Irish team of plenipotentiaries probably would have directly reflected the authority and personnel of the Dáil's ministry. This would have placed DeValera as the head of the delegation, Brugha occupying the defence portfolio, Collins the finance portfolio, Stack the justice portfolio and Griffith the foreign affairs portfolio, in each case supported by an appropriate team of legal experts or senior civil servants, *if* such personnel was available. It was not. Instead, the Irish delegation would consist of a grand total of just five men.

Griffith was appointed by DeValera to head the delegation with the support of two legal experts, Eamon Duggan and the London-Irish solicitor George Gavan Duffy, who was currently assisting J.H. MacDonnell, Art O'Brien's solicitor, in legally representing all Irish political prisoners in Britain.[78] Collins was also preoccupied with the political prisoners issue. As a result, DeValera asked him to handle the entire defence portfolio, not his cabinet brief of finance. In practice, this 'defence' issue simply meant dealing with the question of arranging a mutual amnesty between British and Irish forces; an issue that had been progressing since June-July.[79] The final member of the team of plenipotentiaries was Robert Barton, until recently the 'minister for agriculture'; an office that had been re-titled by DeValera as 'minister for economic affairs'. Barton could potentially speak on financial affairs, but it appears that he was given no specific brief by DeValera. Excepting for a small clerical staff headed by Diarmuid O'Hegarty, which would concentrate on forwarding communications to Dublin,[80] these five men had no support. However, Erskine Childers, supported by John Chartres, would practically become the unofficial sixth member of the delegation by virtue of his being allowed by the relevant British negotiators (Winston Churchill and F.E. Smith, better known as Lord Birkenhead) to take a direct part in those defence negotiations which had the imperial connotation of naval security, this being a question that was a little beyond Collins' comprehension.[81]

Griffith no doubt understood that he would have to reach a settlement. As both W.T. Cosgrave and Kathleen Clarke noted, the inherent inequality in the negotiations led DeValera to give direct personal advice to Griffith that, unfortunately, he would have to assume the role of a scapegoat, to a greater or lesser extent, and this was a reality that Griffith accepted.[82] As was reflected by his informal brief 'to squeeze the Prime Minister to the utmost possible', Griffith had the ambition, however, to maximise the powers of the Dáil. Later on, Gavan Duffy believed that Griffith was also very conscious of the reality that if an agreement was not reached, the British government could 'appeal over our heads ... to expose the weakness of the really national elements' and that this could also cause the Dáil's management of the Irish Volunteers to get out of hand, as 'the military mind is the same in every country ... they think of nothing but their own particular end and cannot be brought to consider the political consequences of their proceedings'.[83] However, there is no indication that Griffith was particularly concerned with any issue relating to the volunteers until quite late in the negotiations.

Griffith's negotiating team arrived in London with no fanfare. This differed very significantly from the situation in July when a High Mass was said for DeValera's delegation, which was thereafter greeted by cheering London-Irish mobs. On that occasion, Griffith was carried on the mob's shoulders from the cathedral doors all the way down a main thoroughfare to a waiting cab. The rest of the Southwark Catholic community had not been so impressed, however. A totally sincere request was made to their bishop to have St George's Cathedral re-consecrated after Irish 'sin fiends' had supposedly desecrated it from having crossed its threshold.[84] Reflecting this, in October, no member of the London Catholic clergy would be seen in the presence of the Dáil's delegation. Although accompanied by Bishop MacRory, no High Mass was said in their honour either, while the British press claimed that the delegation looked nervous.[85] Journalists were completely avoided and a private residence of no official or diplomatic meaning was used as their base (later, the delegation would receive a massive bill for alleged property damage, caused by cigarette burns, spilt wine and the like).[86] The night of his arrival, Griffith telegraphed his wife that he wanted her with him.[87] Maud, who had written many passionate defences of her husband to the prison authorities during his two years of imprisonment,[88] duly arrived.

Griffith and Lloyd George had never met before and their initial impressions of each other are worth recording. The Prime Minister was surprised by Griffith's unemotional manner, a quality that he deemed untypical of Irishmen, and his laconic speech in a strange Dublin working-class accent. Meanwhile, Griffith was surprised that the Prime Minister, who was secretly known in British cabinet circles to be a philanderer, still looked like a very young man, having 'a smooth face, showing no lines on it' despite the fact that he was almost ten years Griffith's senior. On mentioning this in passing to his wife the following morning, Maud suggested that the British Prime Minister 'must have an easy conscience'. To this, Griffith immediately responded 'he has no conscience!'[89] As close as the Griffiths were, politics was one subject that they did not discuss together.[90]

According to one British source, Griffith's opening statement to the British delegation was a defiant one that 'we feel that from the days of Pitt onwards it has been the policy of this country to keep Ireland in a subordinate position'. This took Lloyd George by surprise because it seemed to disregard a prior Irish acceptance of the original proposals that were sent to DeValera on 20 July for a British settlement 'that the Irish people may find as worthy and as complete an expression of their political and spiritual ideals'. DeValera had also totally accepted in mid-September that 'His Majesty's Government cannot recognise formally or informally, directly or by implication, an Irish republic.'[91]

Surviving shorthand notes of Griffith gives an indication of how he approached aspects of the negotiations. Rather than raising the specific issue of a republic, his goal was to win 'full recognition of the existing power and privilege of [the] Irish parliament [Dáil Eireann]'. This meant 'every appointment [must be] solely on authority of Irish Cabinet. Britain should have no more [executive] right of appointment'. Griffith also maintained as a right that 'Irishmen [are] to determine whether the new powers [under any Anglo-Irish agreement] shall be … administered by a single Irish body or be taken over separately by N.[orth] & S.[outh].'[92] This idea of creating 'a single Irish body' that was unaffected by British executive power was evidently the basis for Griffith's hope to bring James Craig into the negotiations in an effort to resolve the partition dispute. However, the British government had effectively ruled out this option already the previous summer.[93] It considered partition as a permanent fixture or, at the very least, a done deal.

Reflecting the dynamics of post-war British politics and, in particular, the new British labour ministry with which Childers and Chartres had formerly been associated, from the outset of the negotiations the British negotiators sought to convince Griffith that the Empire was being in the process of being reinvented as a more benevolent 'Commonwealth'. Griffith's notes indicate how he attempted to respond to this. He argued that in a true 'community of nations', 'Ireland's status should be equal to that of Britain' and this would have a number of consequences. First, as the 'King holds his position by a purely parliamentary title' and 'the British parliament may abolish the monarchy', it 'follows that equality of status would make it [possible] for the Irish parliament to abolish the monarchy in Ireland'.[94] As this was true, Lloyd George quickly changed the subject.

Reflecting Midleton and Jameson's negotiations with Sinn Féin up until June 1921, the Prime Minister would cite the existence of a southern Irish unionist population against Griffith, noting that he already understood from prior negotiations with Dublin that the Irish wanted to 'provide safeguards for the representation of minorities, especially in the Second Chamber [elective house], not less effective than those afforded by the Government of Ireland Act 1920'. Griffith, who had not been a party to the truce negotiations, absolutely denied this, however. He stated that the Dáil's cabinet had only agreed that southern unionists could potentially be nominated to seats in a first chamber (a senate or upper house) of an Irish parliament but they had absolutely no chance of winning seats in the elective or legislative chamber and could never be simply nominated to that assembly. Griffith was adamant that there could never be any compromise upon this point.[95]

On the question of defence, Griffith focused on the realistic question of costs. Lloyd George emphasised that the first British condition for any agreement was that Ireland recognised the 'common concern of both countries in the defence of their interests on land and sea'. Upon this basis, the British were demanding that 'the Royal Navy *alone* shall control the seas around Ireland'; that this right 'should be accorded by the Irish state in Irish harbours and in the Irish constitution' and that Britain should also 'have all necessary facilities for the development of defence and of communication by air'. As Ireland had no navy or air force of its own, Griffith essentially sidestepped this question by focusing on the question of territorial forces. As the Dáil had 'no money' and could not afford a large army, Griffith stated that Britain could, by negotiated agreement, play a part in regulating the size of Irish territorial forces (including its voluntary forces), provided that the Irish territorial forces were not legally subordinate to Britain. Meanwhile, in fulfilment of Ireland's broader defence obligations to Britain, Griffith suggested that the Dáil could 'make a small naval contribution' in the form of funding.[96] While he desired that there would be 'no English land, sea or any force' in Irish territory, instead of arguing in favour of total neutrality Griffith argued that Ireland, if it had dominion status akin to Canada, 'may help in war' or it 'may not'. What was essential, Griffith considered, was that it was fully recognised that it was a matter purely for Ireland and not for 'the English ministry of F[oreign] A[ffairs] and the English Cabinet to decide when and how "the defence of interests is a common concern"'.[97] Griffith's reasoning here reflected a slight difference from DeValera in that he was focused more upon the purely practical or financial aspect of the defence, or 'neutrality', question. He would not allow himself to be diverted from this reality by purely theoretical considerations. Indeed, it was hardly surprising that it was on the question of the economic basis of the Anglo-Irish relationship that the negotiations soon began to hinge.

When the Prime Minister emphasised the issue of an Irish contribution to the British national debt (a claim upon Irish monies that even T.P. O'Connor considered unfair and excessive),[98] Griffith emphasised that 'none of the dominions has any share of Britain's debt'. However, evidently owing to the ongoing existence of Gladstone's land annuities schemes (which, of course, were regulated by the Irish banks on behalf of the British government), Griffith seems to have come to the conclusion quite quickly that a figure for Ireland's contribution to Britain's national debt was something that would probably have to be established rather than a principle to be rejected outright.[99] This might be said to have been a serious and somewhat unavoidable weakness in Griffith's negotiating position. By contrast, when the Prime Minister demanded that Ireland could not alter or restrict the flow of commercial transport between the two islands or pass any protective duties, Griffith was adamant that Ireland could not make a law to this effect. This was because it needed control of customs and excise on 'many goods such as teas, sugars and tobaccos, which Ireland would necessarily have to import'. In addition, 'we might have Irish goods to export to such countries' and, if so, 'return cargos' (possibly meaning independent Irish control of merchant shipping companies) 'would be necessary' to facilitate this.[100] A definite stumbling block had now been reached in the negotiations. This was because the British government's purpose in partitioning Ireland was essentially to ensure that the imperial treasury's control over Irish revenue, initiated during the period 1816–1824 and reinforced by Gladstone's mid-to-late Victorian initiatives in terms of imperial fiscal policy, would not only be retained but also strengthened as much as was possible. Although he had first been persuaded to enter politics by Michael Davitt, Gladstone was Lloyd George's role model in all matters relating to the government of Ireland.[101]

Lloyd George's response to Griffith's demand for an ability to regulate Irish commerce was to ask to meet Griffith privately regarding the interrelated issues of the economy and partition on a Sunday night. Although this was a day on which no negotiations had been planned, it was a request to which Griffith conceded. At this private meeting held outside of Downing Street, Griffith refused to budge on the issue of the Dáil having powers to manage the economy of Ireland. It was at this point of the negotiations that the British Premier, nicknamed 'the Welsh Wizard', demonstrated his great cunning in negotiations. He requested to know that if 'Irish demands were met' on economic matters, could Griffith give him assurances regarding all British concerns in relation to Irish attitudes towards the commonwealth, the crown and naval defence. Griffith intimated that he might be prepared to move in this direction. This apparently satisfied the Prime Minister and the meeting ended amicably. A day or two later, however, Lloyd George requested that Griffith make a statement *in writing* of what they had discussed in private. Perhaps foolishly, on 2 November, Griffith drafted such a statement for the Prime Minister, which the latter, with the help of a little trickery, subsequently used to his advantage.

Griffith's original written statement emphasised that the financial relations between the two nations must be fundamentally adjusted and he was prepared to let this adjustment 'rest in the hands of an agreed arbitrator'. In turn, 'provided I was satisfied on other points', he would be 'prepared to recommend a free partnership of Ireland with other states associated within the British Commonwealth, the formula defining the partnership to be arrived at in later discussion'. He would also be prepared, on the condition of 'the recognition of the essential unity of Ireland', to recommend that the British navy be provided with some Irish coastal facilities 'pending an agreement similar to those made with other Dominions providing for the assumption by Ireland of her own coastal defence'. Regarding 'the North East of Ireland', Griffith stated that he believed its 'existing parliamentary powers' should 'be derived from us and guaranteed, if it is thought necessary, by you'. Griffith had never supported, but hitherto could not stop, the Belfast boycott, and thus he stated regarding the north of Ireland that he had no wish that its 'industrial life should be hampered or discriminated against in any way'. However, 'on no account could I recommend any association with the Crown or the Commonwealth if the unity of Ireland were denied in form or in fact'.[102]

In his previous communications with DeValera, Griffith had emphasised that he was attempting to persuade the British government that 'the six counties should be allowed to choose freely whether they would be in North or South'. He interpreted Lloyd George's action in arranging a private meeting as meaning that the Prime Minister would work to draw Craig into the negotiations at Griffith's request, in which event 'we shall have gained essential unity and the [remaining] difficulty we shall be up against will be the formula of association and recognition'.[103] Lloyd George did meet with Craig, but he would do so completely independently from the Irish delegation. In turn, he forwarded misleading reports to Griffith who, reporting back to DeValera, evidently fell into the trap of thinking that a proposed 'Boundary Commission' mentioned by the Prime Minister could take a form akin to a national plebiscite.[104]

The British cabinet was occasionally prepared to acknowledge to itself that 'our Ulster case is not a strong one'.[105] As Childers noted, this was because Ulster 'was not an economic entity but a historic name'.[106] There was no history to the proposals for partition other than the manner by which the economy had been handled specifically since the period 1911–17. Griffith considered the British cabinet to be 'remarkably ignorant' of the true state of life in the north of Ireland.[107] He also believed that if he could enter into direct negotiations with Craig a mutual settlement between north and south could be achieved. In response to Griffith's focus upon the idea of an all-Ireland council of finance, the British government cited the existence of Dáil courts against him. As these were established in the name of rejecting any vestige of British authority, the British cabinet could not now sell the idea to Westminster, or the general British public, of an all-Ireland body being set up in a jurisdiction under which such bodies were nominally into operation. As this argument made sense, Griffith felt that he had to take this idea into consideration.[108]

Tom Jones, the assistant British cabinet secretary, claimed that Craig was initially open and favourable to the idea of an all-Ireland council of finance being established, but Craig quickly reversed this stance on discussing the matter with Churchill and Birkenhead (the Lord Chancellor).[109] At their insistence, Craig became preoccupied instead with arranging the transfer of full operational control of the RIC in Northern Ireland from Dublin Castle to Stormont. Simultaneously, Craig insisted that he not be drawn further into the negotiations and requested that the fact of his correspondence with the Prime Minister regarding the negotiations with Griffith must not be made publicly known, let alone published, until after negotiations with the south were concluded.[110] This was a request that was followed. Griffith and his delegation were not treated with equal respect, however.

Up until mid-November, Griffith was preoccupied with the fact of Craig's withdrawal ('he had become more intractable as a result of the people he had met here in London') and coming up with alternative proposals to the 'tentative suggestions' that were being presented to the Irish delegation.[111] Matters then changed quite suddenly and definitively.

The Prime Minister surreptitiously distributed his own printed copies of Griffith's letter of 2 November. These excluded both the final section on partition (stating that he could not accept the Crown without Irish unity) as well as Griffith's remark that the 'existing parliamentary powers' of the north east of Ireland were 'to be derived from us and guaranteed, if it is thought necessary, by you'.[112] The Prime Minister did this in order to create a widespread belief that Griffith had surrendered to all the British government's demands, not least regarding the Ulster question, and this had a curious impact on the reports subsequently made.[113] The belief that Griffith had compromised the Irish delegation very quickly reached politicians outside the negotiations, both British and Irish, as well as the press of the Irish diaspora and the Dáil's envoys on the European continent. This occurred precisely because an alleged circular on the negotiations, intimating a total Irish acceptance of all Britain's demands, appeared on the front page of the *Daily News* (Childers' favoured outlet during 1919) on 19 November.[114]

Deciding that the moment had come to force the negotiations to a speedy end, Lloyd George became adamant that the only basis under which a new 'boundary commission' could be established was the same as that which all Irish political representatives had previously agreed to at the King's 1914 Buckingham Palace conference. This was that the question of partition was a purely social one that must be defined and resolved according to religious demographics alone. Reflecting this, Tom Jones claimed the boundary commission idea actually originated with Edward Carson,[115] who no doubt knew that such an arrangement could solve nothing and was purely a ruse.

The Irish plenipotentiaries, already thrown off balance by the actions of the press, were also suddenly brought to the House of Lords, where Sir Gordon Hewart, the Attorney General for Britain, stated that there was a real possibility of war if they did not reach an agreement very soon. This was done on the same day (22 November) as Stormont began assuming some policing responsibilities. In turn, a draft agreement document was simply given to the Irish delegation.[116] As Eamon Duggan recalled, all of a sudden, 'the Cabinet [in Dublin] knew, and we knew, because we had got a week's notice, that we would have to give a yes or no answer on a certain day'.[117]

The Anglo-Irish negotiations had thus far lasted for little over a month. Purely on the Irish side, the only slight sign of a problem had been a temporary dispute regarding DeValera's seeming alteration in late October of the brief of the Dail's negotiators, intimating to them that if a break in negotiations was deemed necessary this should be done on the question of the Crown rather than partition (their initial brief). The delegation was uncomfortable about this because it was both a negation of DeValera's prior acceptance of the dominion status proposal and it was also a denial of the fact of the delegation's status as plenipotentiaries.[118] This dispute passed quickly, however, because it was not a definite stance on DeValera's part. In late November, however, DeValera acted suddenly in a disruptive manner. Around the same time as Tom Jones wrote to John Chartres in Berlin regarding the British attorney general's action, DeValera wrote to Harry Boland in America that an actual 'war' was forthcoming because of the impossibility of any Irish acceptance of a place for the Crown in a political settlement. Almost simultaneously, DeValera threatened Richard Mulcahy and the entire existing leadership of the Irish Volunteers/IRA with dismissal and spoke of forming a totally 'new army' in their place.[119] This created a particularly tense situation upon the Irish delegation's return to Ireland.

Griffith had evidently been quite confident regarding how the negotiations were going up until late November. After his trip to Dublin at the end of the month, however, he returned to London 'labouring under a deep sense of crisis'.[120] There were a number of reasons for this.

Knowing that altering the wording of a clause within any British agreement could not possibly alter the source of that agreement,[121] both Griffith and Collins argued that DeValera was being unrealistic on the issue of the Crown: attempts to champion the idea of external association without an oath to the Crown had been tried and immediately shot down. Griffith felt that Childers was a particularly bad influence on DeValera in his capacity as an advisor in these matters. This was understandable. A good example of Childers' approach can be seen in his response to the British government's initial proposals of 20 July 1921. He immediately wrote a lengthy treatise on the matter for DeValera, referencing all the defence implications of various constitutional models that the great world powers employed on different continents. He did so notwithstanding his simultaneous acknowledgment that it 'was quite logical' to regard the Irish Volunteers ('the IRA') simply as 'a mere local volunteer reserve under British control'.[122] In matters of theory and practice, Childers was not a good advisor.

DeValera's concern regarding the Crown was probably influenced by his awareness (notwithstanding his own moral opposition to oath-taking of any kind, which he deemed to be a denial of free will)[123] that the volunteers' past republican oath, by its very nature as an oath, would be held dear by many. Therefore, it could be personally dangerous to call upon men to break it. Although the volunteers' oath had been to the authority vested in the Dáil as a parliamentary assembly alone, Griffith certainly understood this mentality very well. Unlike DeValera, Griffith himself had gone on hunger strike in prison during December 1920 to express his sense of solidarity with the Irish Volunteers. However, Griffith believed that DeValera's current idea of creating a 'new army' if Mulcahy determined to keep the volunteers loyal to whatever settlement the plenipotentiaries might have to sign on behalf of the Dáil was dangerous to the point of pre-empting civil war. Griffith could not understand how DeValera refused to acknowledge this. The manner in which DeValera attempted to justify his stance to himself was not all that convincing either.[124] However, it is hardly surprising that many others beside DeValera felt that there were serious problems with the draft agreement. This was precisely because there were.

The idea of a truce becoming permanent and thereby becoming a basis for a treaty was implicit in the working title of the draft agreement: 'articles of agreement for a treaty'. Reflecting this, most of its provisions related explicitly to the implementation of defence and security arrangements with a view to accomplishing a mutual amnesty for British and Irish forces in the recent conflict and establishing new such authorities in Ireland, partly as an extension of the agreement of June–July 1921 and partly as an extension of the proposed constitutional settlement itself. To many, including the British government, this was evidently the essence of the matter. By contrast, Griffith placed emphasis upon the idea that the right to establish a distinct, written Irish constitution upon the model of the constitutions in the dominions, whereby sovereignty was recognised to reside primarily in the state's own citizens, was the best guarantor of Irish liberties. This seemed to mean the achievement of full dominion status and, in turn, economic and political freedoms. However, it was asserted to in the agreement that this was a right that it would take a full year to establish. Herein lay the problem. This meant that the terms of the proposed constitution was a matter to be determined by ongoing political negotiations in the interregnum. This involved a very great deal of uncertainty. If they signed the agreement, the Irish were essentially committing themselves to an agreement without knowing if the desired end result would actually be achieved, let alone become a workable measure, a year hence. In particular, what would happen to that proposed 'treaty' if the British accused the Irish of breaking the agreement (or, indeed, vice versa) in the meantime due to some violation of the truce by some volunteer or auxiliary? Would the entire Anglo-Irish agreement simply disappear into thin air? It appears that it was primarily for this reason that neither Robert Barton nor Gavan Duffy was at all enthusiastic about the idea of signing the draft agreement. By contrast, Griffith and Collins' greater willingness to sign stemmed from a belief that such ongoing political negotiations should be able to accomplish their desired purpose.

Griffith would generally refer to the proposed deal as 'the peace agreement'. As an example, both he and Collins evidently believed alongside Bishop MacRory that Lloyd George's promise to issue directions to the northern assembly to reach a good relationship with the Dáil, *if* the plenipotentiaries signed the agreement, was sincere.[125] This was indeed a logical perspective if dominion status was truly being offered. Meanwhile, Collins placed a great deal of importance on the promised mutual amnesty of the agreement whereby, conceivably, all Irish volunteer prisoners (and there were still many hundreds imprisoned in Britain) would be released from prison and, in turn, allowed to either retire or to resume their volunteer activities as some kind of political victors by acting in the service of an independent Irish government.[126] Be that as it may, it might be argued that neither Griffith nor Collins should have been blind to the fact that Lloyd George was still pressing the delegation about the British government's wish that the Dáil accommodate the southern unionist population.[127] In their private discussions, these unionist businessmen practically considered themselves as a party to that agreement which, in fact, only plenipotentiaries of Dáil Eireann had a right to sign, precisely because of their role in negotiating the initial truce.[128] This was an unofficial status that the British cabinet, or treasury, was effectively willing to grant to them in practice. This did not bode well for Griffith's intentions for the agreement.

Although Griffith returned to London with an unaltered brief as a plenipotentiary (namely, a complete freedom to sign an agreement), he did so shouldering a very great anxiety: could a split Dáil vote on an Anglo-Irish agreement potentially result in a split army instead of merely creating a loyal parliamentary opposition, and, in turn, inherently debilitate the Dáil in negotiating the constitutional terms with Britain that it desired? Burdened by this preoccupation, Griffith requested to see Tom Jones, the acting British cabinet secretary, alone at midnight on 4 December, and 'spoke throughout with the greatest earnestness and unusual emotion' for a whole hour about his desire for peace above all else. His motive in doing so was partly a desire to capitalise upon the British government's desire to close an agreement quickly by making as many conditional Irish demands as was possible at short notice: '"this is our first attempt", said A.G., at "secret diplomacy"'. For the most part, however, 'the upshot of the whole talk' was the Griffith's great fear of some kind of ensuing civil war in Ireland destroying all of what the Dáil had been attempting to achieve ever since 1919.[129]

Emphasising that 'there is much distrust' in Dublin because of a 'fear that if the "treaty" is signed they will be "sold"' to the southern unionists, Griffith noted that the Irish plenipotentiaries were being 'told that Sinn Féin has surrendered much ("The King" and "Association with the Empire") and got nothing to offer the Dáil in return'. Griffith 'pleaded—this was the burden of our talk' that, to resolve the situation, the Prime Minister needed to 'get from Craig a conditional recognition, however shoddy,[130] of Irish national unity in return for the acceptance of the Empire by Sinn Féin' or else the plenipotentiaries could not 'carry more than about one half' of the Dáil in support of any agreement. From this moment, Griffith effectively made the mistake (if, indeed, he had any alternative) of relying on Britain to resolve Irish difficulties, as was reflected by his appeal to the Prime Minister, through Jones, to 'help us to get peace' by secretly 'have a heart to heart talk' with Collins, who equally wanted to avert a split army and for the truce to remain permanent. This problem was essentially a direct result of the British Attorney General and DeValera's talk of an impending war. Griffith believed that Collins could establish a disciplined national authority over the Irish Volunteers/IRA ('90 per cent of the gunmen will follow Collins') but *only* if all future conflict was avoided.[131]

Jones' response to Griffith's plea was to arrange the suggested meeting between Collins and the Prime Minister the following morning, while Griffith was requested to meet the King. Jones' own additional piece of personal advice to the Prime Minister, which was not heeded, was that 'I think Craig should be sent for. Peace with Ireland is worth that effort with Craig.' He also believed that the revival of a coercive policy in Ireland could undermine the government's popularity in Britain and it might also undermine the government's efforts at Washington where cabinet secretary Maurice Hankey (the man whom Jones was temporarily deputising for) was shouldering the far more important responsibility for the British government of settling the future direction of Anglo-American relations.[132]

Griffith's pleas did result in some very slight gains for the Irish plenipotentiaries. Hitherto, Griffith's belief that an agreement could enable the Dáil to assume regulatory authorities over the economy of Ireland had yet to receive any guarantee. Lloyd George had thus far only engaged in a game of nudges and winks with him on that matter while continuing to express his belief that no customs barriers should exist between the two countries. The Prime Minister now reluctantly consented, however, to the principle of allowing the Irish control of customs and excise,[133] quite possibly because Griffith intimated that the Irish would, in return, not necessarily attempt to impose customs duties on specifically agricultural exports.[134] This agreement, although informal, was to become the basis for what Jones would later describe as 'the spirit of the bargain with the South'.[135]

Reflecting the common law basis of the British constitution, a 'bargain' was essentially the inherent nature of any possible Anglo-Irish agreement. Griffith and the rest of the Irish plenipotentiaries signed a revised draft of the presented agreement in the early hours of the morning of the 6 December; the time deadline they had been given a week before. It could (and would) be argued that a valid criticism of the action of Griffith's delegation was that they had allowed themselves to be rushed into signing. It was also true, however, that DeValera's brief to them in September had emphasised that they must sign an agreement after having made an initial effort to squeeze the British Prime Minister to the utmost possible. This is precisely what Griffith did.

Under the agreement, Northern Ireland had the right to decide not to be a part of the proposed Irish Free State administration within a month of the agreement being signed. The provisions in the agreement relating to Northern Ireland reflected a significant fiscal ambiguity. Although 'the settlement of the financial relations between Northern Ireland and the Irish Free State' was to remain entirely open, it was stated that safeguards should exist to ensure that the Irish state's fiscal policy would not unduly affect 'the trade or industry of Northern Ireland'.[136] This may well have been read by the Irish delegation as a simple extension of Griffith's belief, shared by most of the Dáil, that no discrimination against northern businesses should ever take place. Furthermore, if Dublin attained dominion status, it would make sense for Belfast to desire to come within its economic orbit. This was an eventuality that Griffith and Collins expected. However, by virtue of the fact that Northern Ireland, under the extant Government of Ireland Act, was to have no fiscal autonomy of its own but instead exist purely as part of the economy of the United Kingdom, this provision virtually meant that the Irish state's fiscal policy must not negatively affect the trade and industry of the United Kingdom as a whole, as defined purely by Whitehall. In this sense, Griffith's belief that a recognition (on paper) of full constitutional freedoms as a dominion should allow Ireland real economic freedoms as well as harmonious north–south relations may have blinded him to the fact that a likely consequence of the agreement would be that no matter what type of constitutional liberty the proposed twenty-six county Irish state was ever to adopt (including, in theory, a republican–style written constitution of some kind), the actual economic identity of the state must remain that of Southern Ireland for so long as Northern Ireland was in existence. Subsequent developments would prove just how determined the financial regulators of Ireland were to impose this particular consensus prior to the Irish Free State's possible birth in December 1922.

Griffith would argue that if the drafting of a new Irish constitution could proceed unimpeded, due to the maintenance of the truce, this could lay the basis for greater constitutional and economic liberties for Ireland than it had ever enjoyed before. One might well argue that Griffith had done remarkably well as a negotiator in facing a formidable British imperial cabinet, virtually alone and with minimal support, despite facing an almost preordained political conclusion. However, the fact that the agreement, even if conceivably a political victory for Ireland, was not generally seen to be a moral victory partly doomed Griffith to acquire that mantle which the international (mostly British) English-language press had already attempted to ascribe to him in the wake of the British government's sly press leaks of November 1921. This was that he was the man who had supposedly been single-handedly outmanoeuvred by Lloyd George and, in the process, was solely responsible for both betraying an Irish ideal of freedom ('the republic') and, in the process, signing away Ireland's freedom.

CHAPTER ELEVEN

Securing an Anglo-Irish Agreement? (1922)

The Anglo-Irish agreement of December 1921 was a very accurate reflection of the actual political situation that Dáil Eireann had faced throughout the whole previous year. It involved formal recognition that the Southern Ireland parliament, as established by the Government of Ireland Act of December 1920, needed to be convened. However, this was now to be done according to the principle that dominion status had formally been granted to Ireland for the first time, solely as a result of the agreement that Griffith had negotiated and signed. This was to become the basis, under that agreement, for the creation of the Irish Free State in December 1922 with its own written, albeit not formally republican, constitution.

No matter had been resolved definitely as a result of the agreement, however. Instead, an alternative trajectory for developments had simply been provided for. Unionists did not welcome this fact. This effectively made them the chief anti-treaty party. In addition to their well-publicised opposition to the ineffective and essentially meaningless Boundary Commission idea (itself, a deliberate ruse of Sir Edward Carson),[1] there was the unpublicised reality that 'we were parties to the *Agreement* [Midleton and Jameson's peace pact with DeValera in June 1921]. We never were parties to the *Treaty*'.[2] The British cabinet had signed that treaty without Irish unionists' prior agreement. Theoretically, this meant that if a dominion parliament were to be established in Dublin, the Dáil cabinet would be, by far, the greatest authority in the land. This would mean that it would have the power to make political decisions, such as Griffith's desire for full fiscal autonomy or to break through the 'trade wall' prohibiting Irish trading outside the United Kingdom, that would greatly disrupt and inherently undermine all the established norms upon which

Irish unionists' power was based hitherto. This was a fact of Irish politics at this time that was very often overlooked, however, due to the public obsession in the south with the issue of swearing oaths. The initial authors of such oaths, the IRB, reflected an alternative perspective. With Collins and Kathleen Clarke's approval, many IRB veterans would not formally support or vote for the Anglo-Irish agreement, simply in order to express their republican political sympathies. Equally, however, they would not seek to sabotage it, the most common response being to adopt a personally neutral stance while accepting a need to promote the peace, preferably in a manner conducive to the egalitarian or republican sympathies of the parish-pump radicals from which they had formerly derived their support.[3]

Notwithstanding his great desire for the release of all Irish Volunteer political prisoners (a goal covered by the mutual amnesty section of the treaty agreement), the perspective of Michael Collins, the acting leader of the IRB, on the treaty agreement was essentially an extension solely of his responsibilities as the Dáil's minister for finance. He would argue that:

> Irish men and women as private individuals must do their share to increase the prosperity of the country. Business cannot succeed without capital. Millions of Irish money are lying idle in banks ... If Irish money were invested in Irish industries, to assist existing ones, and to finance new enterprises, there would be an enormous development of Irish commerce. The Irish people have a large amount of capital invested abroad [in Britain]. With scope for our energies [options for self-government available under the treaty agreement], with restoration of [business] confidence, the inevitable tendency will be towards return of this capital to Ireland. It will then flow in its proper channel. It will be used for opening up new and promising fields in the country ... [and] it is for the Irish people to take advantage of these opportunities. If they do not, investors and exploiters from outside will come in to reap the rich profits which are to be made [just as British unionists had formerly done] ... A prosperous Ireland will mean a united Ireland. With equitable taxation and flourishing trade our North East countrymen will need no persuasion to come in and share in the healthy economic life of the country.[4]

This reflected Sinn Féin policy since 1905. It was also Griffith and Collins' justification for arguing that the establishment of the Irish Free State would mark the death of Irish unionism, including the Irish Parliamentary Party (or Gladstonian) political tradition of actively promoting complete economic dependence on Britain. Simultaneously, it would mark the birth of a self-governing Ireland that not only *could*, for the first time, but also *would* make the economic well being of Irish citizens the inherent basis and motive of Irish policy formation. However, a great obstacle to championing this perspective was the provenance of the truce agreement of June 1921. In addition, there was the question of the actual nature of opinion within the Sinn Féin Party itself, as it had developed since 1917.

Jameson's conciliation committee that organised 'the truce' with Sinn Féin had stood for the retention of the unionist principles of the Government of Ireland Act. This included the principle that control of banking in Ireland must lie entirely in London and remain completely outside the hands of the governments of Northern Ireland and Southern Ireland. Would this principle still apply in an Irish Free State? The ultimate determinant of this question would be the opinions and, in turn, the activities of Ireland's political and business representatives.

Ever since October 1917, the treasurer of the Sinn Féin Party was no longer Jennie Wyse Power (in whose home the republican proclamation of 24 April 1916 was signed) but Bishop Fogarty, the Catholic bishop for DeValera's own electoral constituency in Clare. The church did not favour any great changes in financial institutions' practices. Furthermore, the secret strategy decided upon by DeValera in September 1921 to stage manage both the establishment of an Anglo-Irish agreement and the subsequent creation of an opposition movement to that agreement was based on the principle of keeping the Sinn Féin Party intact under his leadership and in favour of an anti-treaty stance. As Bishop Fogarty explained to the Catholic Viceroy (who, in turn, explained this to Churchill), this opposition to the Anglo-Irish agreement, to be manifested through the Sinn Féin Party, was to take the form of a purely personal sympathy with DeValera's oppositional stance 'not so much on political grounds as with sympathy for him in his misfortunes' in having to step down as leader of the Dáil.[5] No contradiction was seen to exist with this stance in the nominal retention of the Dáil under the presidency of Griffith who, indeed, would receive a letter of congratulations and expression of hopeful belief in his capacity to govern Ireland in peace from Pope Benedict XV shortly after the agreement was accepted by the Dáil.[6] As such, this arrangement essentially reflected nothing more than the Catholic Church's adherence to the very simple principle of retaining a sense of Catholic social cohesion within Irish political society. That was its responsibility. Its practical connotation, however, was to minimise appreciation of the economic nationalist arguments that Griffith and Collins favoured and to encourage Irish political mobilisation under a very different banner. This would dictate the form that the debate of Sinn Féin TDs on the treaty agreement would take. Economic questions were deliberately overlooked.

Another factor of significance was the question of Ireland's relationship with the international community. The treaty agreement stated that this was, henceforth, to be based upon the dominion status principle underpinning the constitutions of Canada and Australia; themselves, partly the initial creation of old Ulster Catholics.[7] However, ever since the Irish Party and British Catholics had mounted an anti-Dáil propaganda campaign during the winter of 1920–1,[8] DeValera and the Irish Catholic hierarchy had already committed themselves to the idea that the church was to become the basis of Ireland's relationship with the international community. The commitment of DeValera, with the Irish bishops' full support, to seek to mobilise international Catholic opinion under the mantle of a unifying Parisian 'World Conference of the Irish Race' to be held in January 1922 was still extant. It also fed into the Anglo-Irish understanding reached in September 1921 that a form of Catholic opposition to the Anglo-Irish agreement that was about to be signed would be both tolerated and facilitated.[9] Partly from Sir Shane Leslie's advice regarding DeValera's Catholic support base in New York,[10] Churchill was well informed of the meaning of these developments.[11] They were reflected by Countess Markievicz's action on the very same day as the Anglo-Irish agreement was signed by Griffith (6 December) in sending a coded message via Art O'Brien in London to Archbishop Mannix of Melbourne (codenamed 'the managing director') that opposition to the agreement was about to be organised through the pre-arranged international channels.[12] By making an Australian archbishop a director of this campaign, such an anti-treaty agitation could potentially maximise the relevance of Childers and Gladstone's past desire to make Ireland a similar British fiscal entity to the hitherto purely agricultural entity of New Zealand.

This 'Irish Race' convention idea was essentially a purely propagandist exercise, however. It was also liable to be burdened by unrealistic public expectations ('the diaspora and the Irish in Ireland were simply working to different agendas') yet it nevertheless formed *the* basis upon which DeValera and Sean T. O'Kelly sought to define their stance regarding any potential Anglo-Irish agreement for at least a couple of years.[13] Aside from meeting the supposed necessity of enabling the church to resume its proper place in Anglo-Irish relations, implicit in this DeValeraite approach was an understanding that was reaffirmed by the terms of the Anglo-Irish agreement itself; namely, that the question of creating an Irish constitution was inherently going to be a matter for the long haul. No written Irish constitution existed hitherto—not even a proposed draft of a republican constitution[14]—and, under the agreement, the constitutional question inherently could not be settled until at least December 1922.

Many Irish contemporaries were inclined to view this entire question of settling an Irish constitution with great impatience, or even scepticism. Churchill's desire to impress the British cabinet's impatience in this whole matter upon the Irish public via the Dublin Castle administration ('speed it up if you can') also contributed to this process.[15] This was unfortunate because it eclipsed Irish public appreciation of the fact that a positive consequence of treaty agreement was that it enabled Irish constitutional experts, most notably Hugh Kennedy, to now *begin* acting as aides to George Gavan Duffy and Eamon Duggan in the Dáil in attempting to envision the creation of a distinctly Irish jurisprudence for the first time. This was an unprecedented and not insignificant development in modern Irish history. Purely in the short term, it also necessitated that an attempt be made to make other existing Irish constitutional leaders (most notably William Wylie, the loyalist draftee of British land law legislation in Ireland, and privy councillor Lord Glenavy) more sympathetic towards Dáil Eireann's political aspirations for self-government.[16] This was no easy task.

All political anxieties in Ireland at this time essentially stemmed from the single fact of Sinn Féin and Dáil Eireann's lack of support from the private sector in Ireland. All questions of republicanism, as well as the uncertain impact that any revised Anglo-Irish agreement could have upon the church–state relations, naturally paled into complete insignificance compared to the reality that so long as a settlement required ongoing negotiations and the existing situation since the truce (nominally dual administrations, even if working together by means of liaison committees) continued, the fortunes of every capital holder in the country had a question-mark hanging over their heads. This was precisely why the Bank of Ireland played such an important role in the truce negotiations. As an extension of this reality, both this bank and other business leaders, which included T.M. Healy (a co-director with Sweetman of the Great Southern and Western Railway), were made a party to the negotiations by the British, acting particularly in an advisory capacity regarding the likely impact upon property and business owners within Ireland of the RIC–Irish Volunteer arrangements.[17]

Griffith's Irish negotiating team were not informed about these developments. This was because it was known that it would be interpreted by Griffith as an intolerable insult to Dáil Eireann's claim to governmental authority. However, Gavan Duffy's awareness of Griffith's fear of the likelihood that the British government would 'appeal over our heads ... to expose the weakness of the really national elements'[18] betrayed his realistic understanding of a likely consequence of the private sector's lack of sympathy for the Dáil hitherto. More than anything else, it was also this reality that governed James Craig's reactions to the political situation.

In theory, Craig was willing to support the idea of an all-Ireland council on finance. He was fully aware that the *real* issue in Anglo-Irish relations was, in his own words, the 'claims for excessive payment of contribution to imperial taxation in years gone by etc.' This Gladstonian economic policy had caused great harm to the economy of Ireland, including the north. These were issues that preoccupied Griffith and Craig equally, the latter emphasising that 'I am quite willing to attend any conferences' with Dublin and London representatives on the question, *if* that were possible. However, Lloyd George 'in framing his agreement with the Sinn Féin leaders agreed to a "Boundary Commission" without taking me into consideration, and this has involved me in difficulties which I have not yet surmounted' in persuading the northern business community that they were not about to be subject to chaotic disruptions with probably no definite resolution: 'I should not like the same thing to happen again.'[19] This fear of disruption, not any fear of Sinn Féin economic or military supremacy (Sinn Féin had no powers of this kind whatsoever), was the root of Belfast politicians' anxiety.

Griffith had perceived during the negotiations that Birkenhead, whom he recognised as early as 1911 to be 'the cleverest of the younger Tory leaders',[20] owing to his very status as the Lord Chancellor, was the greatest obstacle to both his attempts to impress a sense of the reality of the Irish political situation upon the British cabinet and to get Craig involved in the negotiations.[21] In the days of the Irish Party, the financial aspect of Anglo-Irish relations had usually focused, at the request of the Catholic hierarchy, exclusively on the matter of the financing of education. This matter had long since been settled, however. For instance, H.A.L. Fisher, as Britain's minister for education, emphasised that the stipends for higher education arranged under the Government of Ireland Act (this would see £48,000 per annum provided by the imperial treasury to DeValera as the NUI Chancellor, and £30,000 per annum provided to Trinity College) should be unaltered under the new treaty arrangement.[22] This was not a source of contention. However, it was upon meeting Birkenhead that Craig suddenly decided to oppose the idea of an all-Ireland council on finance and follow the former's plans to maximise an Irish contribution to the economy of imperial defence by militarising the north.[23] It was also Birkenhead who dramatically ended the negotiations, not of course on the threat of war (there was no Irish army in existence, so to speak), but purely in opposition to Griffith and Collins' demand that settling the issue of the financial relations between Dublin and Belfast 'should be a matter for discussion between ourselves and the Ulster representatives'.[24]

Birkenhead and Churchill were extraordinarily close. Churchill's outlook was shaped by his paramount concern with financing from London the imperial defence of all the colonies worldwide in a tense post-Versailles atmosphere; the oil situation in Iraq (*the* question which he would soon use to topple Lloyd George); and Hankey's intelligence work regarding the potential dangers of a naval race between Britain, Japan and the United States (another matter in which Lloyd George upheld a different opinion).[25] These were Churchill's obsessions and they not only made him very impatient regarding Ireland, but probably also fed into his defensive mentality. For instance, even before the negotiations with Griffith began, Churchill had judged summarily that the entire essence of the issue regarding Ireland was that 'Sinn Féiners wish to lay their grasp' on the 'wealth of Ulster' but 'in this they will never succeed … should a civil war ensue Ulster will certainly be supported by the whole power of the British Empire.'[26]

It was Churchill who had already persuaded the imperial treasury to undertake the payment of new special police forces in Ulster 'as the nucleus of a military force to be used against the South should the need arise' in the event of an Anglo-Irish economic war.[27] This placed Craig in a very difficult position. He knew that Churchill's conception of life in 'Ulster' and, indeed, Ireland, was totally false but, at the same time, Craig faced a paramount difficulty in that the cost of even the most basic of regular communal policing in the north was a matter for which Northern Ireland, possessing no fiscal autonomy of its own, could never burden the costs.[28] Therefore, he had to follow suit with Churchill's demands.

The Prime Minister's play on the Boundary Commission, which revived the false Buckingham Palace Conference notion of religious demographics being the entire basis of the Irish question, had been motivated by his belief that 'no solution acceptable to both sides was possible'. His only real priority was to silence the demand for change as quickly as possible. This was his motive in getting the Irish to sign an Anglo-Irish agreement of *any* kind, irrespective of 'whether the treaty was an empty formula or not'.[29] The burden this created in terms of Irish politics was that Griffith and Collins were still emphasising the will for change above all else. However, many other politicians simply wished that the economic uncertainty facing the country would be resolved as soon as possible. To many, hugging to the economic principles of an Irish unionism, rather than creating an Irish nationalism, was the surest means of restoring such certainty. From this perspective, so long as Griffith continued to promote his programme for change, so long would the achievement of economic stability be postponed. This, not any question of violence, also shaped many contemporaries' negative perception of what Craig once described as 'the present IRA methods'.[30] Reflecting this, it was the economic instability of Ireland that motivated many contemporaries' lack of faith in the volunteers' capacity to work effectively with the RIC, let alone to supplant its authority as a responsible communal police force. This complicated the issue of the policing of Ireland and, in particular, how to mediate a proposed mutual amnesty for the recent conflict.

As the heads of the respective delegations that signed the agreement, Griffith and Lloyd George wrote to one another prior to the former's introduction of the document to the Dáil. In this correspondence, agreed principles were re-emphasised that (from the British side) 'we propose to begin withdrawing the military and auxiliary forces of the crown in Southern Ireland when the Articles of Agreement are ratified' and (from the Irish side) that 'every possible step will be taken to protect persons and property in the future'. The latter would also mean that 'on the setting up of the Provisional Government an Indemnity will be issued to all members of the British Forces and other officers of the British Government and also to all other persons who cooperated with them in any capacity whatsoever during the recent hostilities in Ireland in respect of any acts committed or alleged to have been committed by them, whether in Ireland or elsewhere [i.e. the arson campaign in England]'.[31] It was expected that this move would soon secure the release of all the pre-truce Irish political prisoners, numbering about 1,100 men, who were still imprisoned without trial in Britain.

The decision, reflected by Emmet Dalton's involvement in security negotiations,[32] to include British forces in the proposed amnesty agreement partly explains the British cabinet's decision to pass control of the Irish Situation Committee from the Prime Minister to Churchill's hands, as soon as the agreement was accepted on the Irish side. Churchill was prepared to release all the pre-agreement Irish prisoners, i.e. those arrested up until June 1921, but 'post-truce people' or any subsequent offenders were not to be included in this category. Churchill would also argue that there could be 'no moral justification' for the release of ex-British soldiers under any circumstances, as these men were inherently mutineers. As such, ex-British soldiers of any kind could not be included in the mutual amnesty provided for by the treaty agreement. However, this raised question marks over the careers of many an Irish Volunteer. Virtually all volunteers, even if they had never *formally* served in British forces (that is, if one ignores Childers' definition of the volunteers/ IRA as an inherently British force),[33] had been trained by and thereby had been closely associated with ex-British soldiers. This was reason enough for any volunteer to be anxious. In addition, several divisional commanders *had* been ex-British soldiers. For instance, a Munster volunteer appointed as a divisional commander around the time of the truce, Liam Lynch, was personally known to T.M. Healy, an Irish Volunteers' defence lawyer and now an advisor to Churchill, to have formerly been a British private.[34] In theory, therefore, the treaty agreement potentially meant that, if Churchill had his way, Lynch was doomed to be hanged for treason; a fact that no doubt partly motivated his leading role in attempting to mobilise volunteer opposition to that agreement.

The Dáil was to begin debating the Articles of Agreement on 14 December 1921. Having signed the document, Griffith's commitment to the agreement, which he generally referred to as 'the peace agreement', was now essentially total, although he would naturally emphasise his willingness to abandon it if voters rejected it.[35] His general attitude towards the negotiations had been that

> Views put forward in it are not crystallised by being put forward. The only thing that matters or is binding upon the parties that confer is their final agreement. Interim attitudes are wiped out by that agreement.[36]

That 'final agreement' could only come about once an Irish constitution became law in December 1922 and subsequently became the basis for an Anglo-Irish treaty between two states. This nature of the agreement was reflected by its very title: 'articles of agreement for a treaty'. From the inception of the Dáil debates, however, the unfortunate precedent was set of mistakenly referring to the agreement as a treaty, as if its terms were already set in stone. As the Dáil's president, it was DeValera who was responsible for setting this tone.

At the very outset of the Dáil debates on the agreement (which were usually chaired by either Eoin MacNeill or 'Sceilg'), DeValera emphasised that it had been decided in advance of sending the plenipotentiaries to London (i.e. in September 1921) that the whole cabinet would not take responsibility for the negotiations. Meanwhile,

> The plenipotentiaries had the responsibility of making up their own minds and deciding on it ... It was also obvious that the cabinet and the plenipotentiaries should keep in the closest possible touch. We did that ... the plenipotentiaries, acting in accordance with their rights, signed the treaty.[37]

With regards to the already widely publicised issue of a split cabinet on the agreement, DeValera noted that 'I am anxious that it should not in any way interfere with the discussion on the treaty, which the plenipotentiaries have brought to us.'[38]

Backbenchers protested that the entire Dáil cabinet had completely misled them about the fact that it was decided several months ago to conclude an agreement. In response, Collins emphasised that the delegation's credentials as plenipotentiaries was universally known since September 1921 and, therefore, the Dáil cabinet had never engaged in any act of deception. However, Eoin

MacNeill, supported by DeValera and Richard Mulcahy, ruled that 'the genesis of the present document' must never be discussed in public again.[39] Thereafter, in addition to banning any discussion on the origins of the agreement, MacNeill and DeValera introduced a ruling that all 'treaty' discussions henceforth were to be based entirely around a different 'document no. 2'. All TDs, as well as the Irish press, were equally forbidden from referring in public to any specific details of this 'document no. 2', which, it was intimated, did not involve an equal compromise upon republican principles to the signed agreement. In reality, it was one of the British cabinet's draft agreements of the previous autumn, redrafted by Childers, with DeValera's alternative oath wording included. It was *this* decision, not the signed agreement (let alone a 'treaty'), which subsequently became the basis of the division within the Dáil.

Although forbidden from referring to any details of 'document no.2' in public, Griffith defied MacNeill's ruling. He stated that he 'must refer to the substance of it' because it was an absolute lie that some men were standing 'uncompromisingly on the rock of the Republic'. Griffith emphasised that, long before the negotiations began, 'not once was a demand made for recognition of the Irish Republic' by DeValera's cabinet. It had been determined that the only question to be resolved was how to reconcile the British and Irish stances with honour, 'and I hold we have done it'. He noted that he signed the agreement 'not as an ideal thing, but fully believing what I believe now, as a treaty honourable to Ireland and safeguarding the interests of Ireland', while to speak of 'half-recognising the British King and the British Empire', as DeValera was now doing, was a meaningless 'quibble of words'.[40]

Griffith claimed that the introduction of 'document no. 2' was forcing the entire Dáil (not just the plenipotentiaries) to speak, act and vote under 'a handicap', namely, preventing them from fulfilling their proper duties and responsibilities as TDs. Changing the subject of the Dáil debates away from the terms of the actual agreement was risking the possibility of great public confusion and, in turn, much civil unrest: 'so far as my power or voice extends not one young Irishman's life shall be lost' by such means.[41] Similarly, Eamon Duggan would maintain that 'the whole Cabinet and the whole Dáil and the plenipotentiaries' had accepted the responsibility of negotiating an agreement with Britain and 'the responsibility that rested upon us that night in London has now devolved upon you'.[42] Griffith, Collins and Duggan maintained that this responsibility must not be sidestepped, although the two other plenipotentiaries, Robert Barton and (to a far lesser extent) Gavan Duffy, would not give this argument their full moral support. This would prove problematic.

To a significant extent, the real difficulty facing the Dáil had little or nothing to do with the proposed agreement but rather the issue of TDs' relationship with their constituents. The Dáil had been a one-party assembly but Sinn Féin, although it had created a constitution for its own party and another one for the Dáil, had never created a constitution for the Irish state itself because, thus far, it had no authority to do so. The party's defiant stance in Anglo-Irish relations also had two dimensions that coexisted ever since its October 1917 convention. On that occasion, Griffith, the outgoing party president, emphasised his belief that 'the England of 1917 is not the England of 1913 and the England of 1918 will not be the England of 1917' and, therefore, 'Sinn Féin will outlive Mr. Lloyd George and anything the English Government can do against it.' From this perspective, the economic decline of British imperial power on the international stage ever since 1892 was now being exposed in the post-war world, and this made the likelihood of Irish nationalists achieving their demands stronger than ever before. By contrast, DeValera, the incoming Sinn Féin party president, emphasised simply that

> I am a Catholic and I have never yet found the Catholic religion to be contrary to anything I hold in my mind or that commonsense dictates … I have certainly yet to find that the Catholic Church or any Christian religion is going to allow itself to be made a tool for the oppression of the country, a tool in the hands of the oppressor. I speak of this matter because we are a religious people, a moral people and we will do nothing that is morally wrong … some people talk of constitutionalism. Let them show me the constitution—a constitution that is acknowledged by the Irish people—and then I will legally obey that constitution. But if they have no such constitution, if the Constitution is of the foreigner, then I say it is a sacred duty on us to despise that constitution, to get rid of it and set up a legitimate constitution of our own.[43]

Since the inception of Sinn Féin, the appeal of republicanism (at one time, a popular form of egalitarian or revolutionary politics in Ireland, Britain and elsewhere, at least up until 1884) had been manifested on two principle occasions. In both instances, however, this had been done in an essentially indirect way. Most recently, this had occurred because of the need to appeal to an American and international audience in the run up to the Versailles Peace Conference, which was based on the idea of a coming international republican political order: hence the involvement of the United States and the birth of the German republic. This Irish stance on international relations, however, had been abandoned since December 1920, if not earlier.

A more longstanding and far more significant factor in creating an appeal for republicanism in Ireland at this time was the growing willingness of Irish Catholic opinion to reassert Daniel O'Connell's belief in the obnoxious nature of the royal coronation oath in Britain, which in deeming Catholicism a heresy made the British parliamentary oath of allegiance (hitherto accepted by all Irish parliamentarians) particularly repugnant. This Catholic perspective, rather than a republican egalitarianism or a republican constitutionalism, had been the motive of the Sinn Féin protests during the royal coronations of 1903 and 1910 and it was this Catholic perspective alone that DeValera now used to justify his opposition to the Anglo-Irish agreement of December 1921. Underpinning this approach was also DeValera's firm belief that neither the Catholic Church nor 'any Christian religion is going to allow itself to be made a tool for the oppression of the country'. Therefore, the Irish search for an appropriate constitution must be governed, first and foremost, by the desire to create a Christian–democratic ethos for the constitution or state, this being the chief motive of Irish politicians in being willing to chart a different course for their country from what were perceived to be British constitutional norms. Being a faithful Catholic, DeValera maintained that he had no inherent obligation to take 'oaths as regards forms of government', including oaths to a British king (as well as, presumably, any form of republican oaths). He also argued that he could also state as a moral certainty that the Irish people 'should be ready to go into slavery until the Almighty had blotted out their tyrants', even if this took for all eternity, rather than accept a situation whereby there was any need for prior British approval of an Irish constitution. Reflecting the fact that he had not been in Ireland when the Irish parliament introduced its own oath, he also claimed that his refusal under any circumstances to abide by political oath taking meant that 'I am probably the freest man here to express my opinion.'[44]

Michael Hayes, a NUI senator who recently appointed DeValera as NUI Chancellor (a job that DeValera formally took up on behalf of the British government on 19 December in the midst of the 'treaty debates'), questioned DeValera's assertion that the treaty agreement encompassed a 'peace with dishonour'. In response, DeValera maintained that the Irish control of education allowed for by the treaty agreement could be undone by a harmful 'spiritual penetration' that would 'kill' all 'Irish ideals' if an oath to the British crown remained a nominal feature of Irish political life.[45] The only way 'a proper peace' could be established, or all disputes between Britain and Ireland could be resolved 'permanently', DeValera maintained, was to be fully 'reconciled to that party which typified the national aspirations of Ireland for centuries' and whose guidance alone could ensure that the goal of establishing 'an independent status in international relations' need never be abandoned.[46] By this, DeValera meant the inherent diplomatic independence of the Roman Catholic Church, which, from the inception of the Dáil, DeValera and MacNeill judged, on the advice Fr Timothy Corcoran S.J. (now a leading anti-agreement propagandist), inherently presented Irishmen with their only possibly outlet for an independent voice in international affairs. DeValera's emergent anti-treaty party maintained that 'to be modern and democratic it is not necessary to be unchristian',[47] and not until an Irish constitution could be established to reflect these ideals should a (Protestant) British monarch be received in Dublin 'just as any other head of state was, in a friendly way'.[48] Upon this premise and in support of DeValera and Sean T. O'Kelly's stance, George Noble Plunkett, a papal count (he was also the British government's Director of the National Museum of Ireland), maintained that Griffith would soon discover that his unfaithfulness to this Christian–democratic ideology was 'not reconcilable with the conscience of the Irish people' and, consequently, 'Irish-Ireland' would 'soon know him no more'. Plunkett also stated that he personally looked forward to the day when, in God's name, all Irishmen would once again be forcibly prostrated and humiliated before the whole world, just as he imagined the rebels of 1916 had been.[49]

Griffith was particularly irked that DeValera, having initially ordered that no personal elements were to be brought into the debates, subsequently stood silently by while he was subject to character assassinations based upon such irresponsibly religious histrionics. Griffith retorted to Plunkett that 'you have ... set the idea that this generation is going to die and that the next generation is going to get something. That is not sanity, politics, or statesmanship'.[50] Old republicans in the Dáil—generally former IRB members—supported Griffith in this stance, and were also puzzled and shocked at the manner by which Plunkett misinterpreted the intent of the 1916 rebels. Plunkett's stance did reflect the reality, however, that the Catholic Church in Ireland could not yet come out publicly in support of the Vatican's approval of the British government's appointment of a Catholic representative of the King in Ireland (i.e. the Viceroy Lord Fitzalan) without risking a great loss in the church's popularity in Ireland (the cult of the 'martyred' 1916 rebels had had peculiar side-affects).[51] It was the political responsibility of DeValera's nascent 'anti-treaty' party to ensure this could not happen by carefully guiding the Irish public's understanding of the Anglo-Irish agreement in such a matter that would make the Irish population fully supportive of the church continuing to hold a particularly prominent place in Irish public life.[52]

Michael Collins was particularly irked by the way this anti-treaty position, with its explicitly Catholic underpinnings, was frequently and (to his mind) irrationally typified as a noble attack on all traitors to the republican cause. He did not see DeValera's obsession with the idea of creating a church-approved,

Christian–democratic, written constitution for the prospective southern Irish state as an issue of republicanism. Instead, like Griffith, Collins emphasised the principle of parliamentary supremacy over all. Although typifying himself as a man who was now in a no-win political situation, Collins stated that he wanted it to be remembered by all that when the British government sought through the medium of Australian Catholic archbishops (including self-styled 'managing directors') and Fr O'Flanagan (now a leader of the 'anti-treaty party') to compromise the Dáil while it was still wedded to a republican cause, he alone had stood up against the Catholic Church when it threatened to excommunicate all those who stood by the principle of the supremacy of Dáil Eireann as a parliamentary assembly: 'I took responsibility for that in our private councils. I take responsibility for it now, publicly ... I shall always like the men to remember me like that.' Aside from this public expression of his IRB credo, Collins emphasised that the Dáil had already compromised upon the full republican idea when it accepted the British government's invitation to negotiate, and that each and every member of the Dáil must now face this responsibility in a manly fashion:

> We shall be judged as to whether we have done the right thing in our *own* conscience or not ... Don't let us put the responsibility, the *individual* responsibility, upon anybody else. Let us take that responsibility ourselves ... and let us in God's name abide by the decision.[53]

Owing to the failure of the Dáil to defeat Britain in the field or to win any international recognition, Collins maintained that they should accept that it was membership of the British Commonwealth, not the diplomatic independence of the Roman Catholic Church (which, ultimately, only concerned and could only be of benefit to the Church, not to Ireland), which could give Ireland an actual diplomatic status for the very first time in the country's history. This was one that could grow over time:

> I do not recommend it for more than it is. Equally I do not recommend it for less than it is. In my opinion it gives us freedom, not the freedom that all nations desire and develop to, but the freedom to achieve it.[54]

Like Griffith, Collins also emphasised that the plenipotentiaries had not signed 'the final document ... as a treaty' but rather they signed 'on the understanding that each signatory would recommend it to the Dáil for acceptance' as an agreement that could become the basis of a future treaty.[55] This was a treaty that, once achieved, would have to be worked very hard upon if it was to achieve anything, that is the Irish public were actually sincere in their desire to determine their own political future.

This perspective failed to find a significant voice in the debates, however. For instance, Griffith claimed that the agreement had 'no more finality than we are the final generation on earth' and also noted that:

> Who was going to say what the world would be like in ten years hence? If they made peace with the English people now, that did not say they were for ever bound not to ask for more ... In the meantime they would move on in comfort and peace towards their goal.[56]

However, in the face of Griffith's emphasis upon the potential right of Irish politicians to assume a much-needed control over many matters, DeValera maintained that the 'common citizenship' principle mentioned in the agreement meant that no army or ministry could ever be established in Ireland that would be other than a British one. While this statement was greeted with much hooting in opposition, DeValera responded with perfect confidence that 'time will tell'. He emphasised that even if the Articles of Agreement was not viewed as a final settlement in Dublin it would be treated as such by Britain. This was because 'it cannot be one way in this assembly and another way in the British House of Commons' due to the latter's inherent superiority.[57] This was a practical admission of the Dáil's virtual status as the parliament of Southern Ireland ever since DeValera's peace negotiations began before the general election of May 1921. It also betrayed the political logic of the true reality that was behind the agreement itself; namely, that in return for the right now granted by Britain to Southern Ireland to create its constitution, no effort would be made to disrupt the Anglo-Irish economic relationship as it had existed under the Union.

According to DeValera, he altered the minutes for the final cabinet meeting before the plenipotentiaries signed the agreement in order to better substantiate his 'anti-treaty' party's stance; an action that he justified apologetically as a necessary evil in order to better manage the response of the general Irish public to the agreement, as well as their understanding of its meaning. While understanding and appreciating the root of DeValera's motivation, Griffith also maintained that it would be foolish to both 'deceive ourselves' and the general Irish public by now claiming, retrospectively, that 'Ireland had a republican government functioning all through Ireland' when 'you all know here that instead of governing throughout Ireland the utmost we could do was to hold, and to barely hold, the position we were in'. Asking both the Dáil and the general Irish public to always remember 'the facts of the situation', Griffith celebrated that British forces would be withdrawn from the country if the agreement were ratified.[58] He believed this would be the ultimate guarantor of peace.

In the light of the perpetual opposition to militarism in Ireland ever since the launch of the anti-conscription campaign, Griffith's emphasis upon the withdrawal of British forces was a question that could potentially have swayed the Dáil very much in favour of the agreement. DeValera knew this and feared its consequence in his efforts to establish an anti-treaty party. For this reason, Erskine Childers—once again, entirely ignoring the issue of a non-existent Irish defence budget—emphasised military and naval realities as proof that there could never be any equality of state power between Britain and Ireland; a debate that DeValera, Brugha and Mulcahy facilitated by censoring any discussion the Dáil's actual defence capacity.[59] This, in turn, led two plenipotentiaries Robert Barton and, to a far lesser extent, George Gavan Duffy to give implicit support to Childers' stance of refusing to acknowledge Britain's inherent military superiority by making very emotional speeches in which they stated that they had signed the agreement and would recommend its acceptance only under very great protest at the injustice of having to bow to a superior military force.[60] Observing this 'sabre rattling', on the economic advice of the Bank of Ireland, Dublin Castle (with the moral support of Sir Shane Leslie) anxiously advised the British cabinet to do nothing to jeopardise the plans of a military evacuation of the south and releasing the Irish prisoners, 'otherwise we play into the hands of Barton' in seeking to break the truce.[61]

Although Barton (incidentally, the one Protestant member of the Irish delegation of plenipotentiaries) would henceforth work directly for Childers in promoting an anti-treaty propaganda campaign, it is doubtful that he desired civil unrest in Ireland. Rather he simply desired to escape from his responsibility as a director of the National Land Bank as quickly as possible, favouring instead his purely personal project (to be supported by Emmet Dalton) of launching Ireland's first ever film studios with private London funding.[62] Be that as it may, his action set an unfortunate precedent. Most TDs used Barton's admission of being a reluctant signatory as a basis to emphasise their own individual credentials, focusing on whether or not they personally would have done the same if they had been plenipotentiaries. This was a pointless exercise which, in turn, became a popular pastime among the general Irish public: would 'you' have supported 'the treaty' if you were in the plenipotentiaries' shoes? As a result, personalities rather than the terms of the agreement became the subject of focus. This indicated a very deep lack of confidence in the capacity of the Dáil and, in turn, its plenipotentiaries, to make authoritative decisions. It also caused a sense of collective responsibility for the recent course of events to be partly abandoned. This was a fact that, not surprisingly, was not lost to the general Irish public and that many contemporary Dublin political cartoonists were far from shy in pointing out in a satirical manner.[63]

Eamon Duggan, the fifth plenipotentiary, emphasised in defence of the plenipotentiaries' stance that they had certainly not signed due to a fear of British militarism. This was because he and 'I suppose everybody ... have known it as long as I have been old enough to know anything ... [that] Britain militarily is stronger than we are ... we are not giving away any military secret when we state that'.[64] However, the agreement had already been characterised by a large number of TDs as nothing less than a militarily inspired 'treaty of terror' on the grounds of Barton's speech. In this respect, a very unfortunate sign for Griffith's political hopes was that fellow economic–nationalist minded TDs, as well as some of his oldest supporters, were among the vocal opponents of the agreement upon precisely this basis, with Joseph MacDonagh, for instance, suggesting that to accept this agreement was tantamount to accepting a British demand to surrender with their 'hands up!'[65]

The impact that this tenor of debate, which was reported across the national media, had upon some sections of Irish Volunteer opinion was probably significant. How were they now to perform their policing responsibilities, which they had carried out since July 1921, without feeling that they were liable to be labelled as some kind of traitors in the process? Reflecting this, in contrast to Kevin O'Higgins' statement that it was the responsibility of every democratically elected politician to represent the sizeable minority of their constituents who had opposed their election as much as the majority who had voted for them,[66] the Cork TD Sean O'Hegarty (incidentally, also the leader of the local IRB) would state that his personal status as 'a soldier' (Irish Volunteer) meant that there was inherently no question of him ever supporting the agreement. In protest against this 'negation of freedom', Griffith would emphasise that unless the volunteers remained loyal to the Dáil's decision-making authority and the electorate alone were given the opportunity to decide if the agreement was 'good enough', then 'the moral authority of Dáil Eireann ... is gone and gone for ever'.[67]

Although it was the members of Dáil Eireann alone who, acting on behalf of constituents, had the right to vote on the agreement, not the electorate, the idea had been touted since September 1921 to let the next general election (whenever that might be held) decide the issue. This effectively predetermined that the Dáil debates were less a vote on the articles of agreement for a treaty than a preliminary step to facilitate the intended rise of pro and anti-agreement political parties: hence its theatricality. When the Dáil voted in favour of the agreement by a narrow margin (64–57) in early January 1922, possibly out of pure relief, Griffith telegraphed his wife that a victory had been won.[68] This was hardly the case, however.

Griffith was never a good public speaker and, on the whole, he had been ineloquent not only regarding the agreement but also about his and Collins' vague claim, rooted in his ambitious hope to alter the economic bases of partition, that Craig could be persuaded to begin cooperating with the Dáil if the agreement was first accepted.[69] Griffith himself claimed that the introduction of 'document no. 2' meant that he could not make as strong a case in defence of the agreement as he wished: 'the President does not want this document to be read. What am I to do? What am I to say? Am I to keep my mouth shut and let the Irish people think about an uncompromising rock?'[70] This point naturally became less and less convincing as the debates wore on, however, while Griffith's growing reticence clearly reflected a realisation that his desire to avoid an evenly split house was not going to happen now, no matter what he said or did.

The very fact that Griffith could not prove that positive results would stem from the agreement was damaging.[71] Meanwhile, Eoin MacNeill's observation that there appeared to be a widespread impression in the Dáil that once they had to deal directly with Dublin Castle 'we will be overawed by these people, perfumed, in uniform, and dressed up in their court dress, and the rest of us will be all rubbing our foreheads in the dust before them, as flunkeys',[72] reflected a lack of confidence among TDs in their own ability to truly take over any of the reigns of government for the first time. Indeed, excluding Cosgrave and a handful of others, none had ever performed such responsibilities before. Instead, on the nomination of the Catholic bishops, they (including the intellectual NUI academics) had simply stood as parliamentary politicians to serve as illustrations of 'the union of the whole priesthood and people of Ireland manifested throughout the country to resist conscription by the most effective means in their power'.[73] Their careers were tied into the patronage networks operated by Catholic Ireland (namely, promotions made in conjunction with the Church's socio-economic influence), not any manifestation of an authoritative nationalist Ireland, and now their bluff had essentially been called. This was potentially embarrassing. Therefore, deliberate obfuscations, which were also rooted partly in a concern regarding how contemporary historians' would analyse their activities, regarding 'the treaty' characterised the subsequent behaviour of very many TDs.

An additional complication was reflected by Griffith's belief that if Sinn Féin split and failed to rally itself behind the agreement in order to make it a success, the influence of the Irish Party's old political networks (including NUI academics) would soon re-assert themselves and 'let back into Irish politics the time-servers, the men who let Ireland down before, and the men who, through weakness, not through dishonesty, would let her down again'. It was no secret that this body of opinion, which had sided with the British Government against the Dáil during the recent troubles, was determined to re-establish that consensus which had been the basis of their political power and remove Sinn Féin completely from the political scene. Therefore, sidestepping the responsibility of proving that Sinn Féin and the Dáil could make the agreement work could 'condemn the other young men to a fruitless struggle' and see a re-emergence of the troubles. Hence, Griffith pleaded with those TDs who opted *not* to attempt to take over the reigns of government to take care regarding how they spoke and acted as public representatives: 'do not save your faces at the expense of your countrymen's blood.'[74]

Griffith's call upon the Dáil not to welcome the old Irish Party's support networks back into the Irish nationalist fold was certainly not appreciated. Mary MacSwiney reminded Griffith that John Redmond was once 'the leader of the Irish race' just as much as DeValera was at present, and that her own personal status as a respected teacher in a fee-paying Catholic private school also meant that, completely unlike Griffith, she knew what she was talking about in such matters.[75] Professor W.F. Stockley, a doyen of Irish university politics since the days of Gladstone, took the anti-treaty side because he considered that the claims of Griffith and Collins—who, incidentally, he deemed far more 'anti-British' in their attitudes than the rest of the Dáil—to be honourable or trustworthy men could not possibly stand up in the light of their denigration of the legacy of the Irish Party.[76] Needless to say, Stockley was not speaking from a preoccupation with anti-conscription politics (that had been a dead issue since November 1918, even if anti-militarism was still a great public preoccupation) or old debates on unionism, but rather the relationship between the Irish Party and professional society in Ireland. Griffith, Collins and Cosgrave's very humble social backgrounds meant that they personally counted for very little in terms of the dynamics of Catholic professional society: in fact, they were not a part of that society at all. The Dáil was now supposed to continue, however, under Griffith as a working-class president. The Catholic middle classes did not necessarily favour this option and, consequently, some clearly favoured a revival of Irish Party traditions and using DeValera's Sinn Féin Party as the appropriate forum.

DeValera maintained that he was in no sense debilitating the Dáil by withdrawing his own supporters: the Dáil had been completely powerless all along. Griffith and Collins' fear that DeValera's withdrawal of support could undermine the necessary goal of making the truce permanent was rooted neither in a fear of British militarism nor opposition to the plans for a party-political system that had been made in September 1921. Rather it was rooted in their discomfort in DeValera's declared wish during November 1921 to create two armies. To their minds, this was a certain folly, not least because it could, directly or indirectly, lead to an Irish Party attempt to remove all Irish economic nationalists from the scene by force. Nevertheless, it was certainly an idea that could win *some* support due to the great uncertainty that existed in every parish in Ireland regarding the financing of even basic policing, let alone issues of national defence. For the most part, however, DeValera emphasised the principle of the constitution above all, arguing that it simply remained for him to see whether or not Irish constitutional lawyers were capable of meeting the challenge of drafting a constitution for the proposed Irish Free State that could meet all the necessary requirements.[77] From this self-styled magisterial standpoint, DeValera would offer his own particular brand of loyal opposition.

Within a week of the agreement being ratified by the Dáil, Griffith, as president, appointed a new Dáil ministry. Its personnel was as follows: Michael Collins—finance; Ernest Blythe—trade; George Gavan Duffy—foreign affairs; Patrick Hogan—agriculture and fisheries; Michael Hayes—education; W.T. Cosgrave—local government; Richard Mulcahy—defence; Joseph McGrath and Kevin O'Higgins—labour.

As chief signatory of the articles of agreement, Griffith also appointed a ministry for the proposed Provisional Government that was to take the responsibility of converting the administrative entity of Southern Ireland at Dublin Castle into the Irish Free State's administration or civil service. Its personnel was as follows: Michael Collins—chairman; Eamon Duggan—home affairs; Patrick Hogan—agriculture; Eoin MacNeill—education; W.T. Cosgrave—local government. Griffith decreed that the latter body was to have support from Fintan Lynch, Joseph McGrath, Kevin O'Higgins and 'such other persons (if any) as may from time to time be determined by the Ministers' of the Dáil, it being also accepted that 'persons other than members of the Dáil [such as Dublin Castle civil servants] might be co-opted on the Provisional Government and appointed on committees there under'.[78]

This arrangement had a number of connotations. All those who had no time for the Dáil tended to look upon Collins, being the chairman of the Provisional Government, as the effective political leader of the country because of his responsibility as chief intermediary with Dublin Castle. This was certainly true of those old *Freeman's Journal* and Irish Party supporters who wanted, just as much as Midleton, this Provisional Government to be based upon the unionist principles of the Government of Ireland Act that had been passed into law with the support of John Dillon in December 1920.

Griffith naturally claimed directive power over both ministries, due to the existence of Dáil Eireann. The appointments of Duggan, Hogan and Cosgrave to the Provisional Government recognised, however, that the critical areas of 'home affairs' (i.e. justice and policing) and local government were matters that *had* to be settled by means of working directly with the Dublin Castle administration. By contrast, the withholding of defence and foreign affairs portfolios purely for the Dáil parliament reflected Griffith's intention to make it *the* governmental basis of the future Irish Free State. This was also Collins' intention, much though the supporters of the Government of Ireland Act who now looked to the Provisional Government desired otherwise, and his dual responsibility as chairman of the Provisional Government and the Dáil's minister for finance provided the medium for attempting to find a satisfactory administrative solution.

While it was intended that the two education ministers would work in the closest collaboration with each other, this arrangement was quickly frustrated by Eoin MacNeill's decision, supported by fellow Gaelic Leaguer Frank Fahy, to resign from the education portfolio at Dublin Castle. This occurred after he was appointed to lead the Dáil delegation (which included Seamus Hughes, a fanatically socialist supporter of Griffith) at the 'World Conference of the Irish Race' in Paris. While MacNeill was critical of DeValera's attempt to boss the proceedings at that conference, his personal status as a representative of the bishops' educational aspirations, as well as his common bond with DeValera in the politics of UCD, evidently motivated his belief that he could not afford to be identified too closely with the Dublin Castle administration. This resulted in the appointment of Fintan Lynch in his place.[79] Before resigning, however, MacNeill, who pointed out to Gavan Duffy for the need of new consuls abroad, did achieve the positive coup for the Dáil of meeting the French Prime Minister in an official capacity. This prompted Griffith to enter into communications with the French consulate in Dublin and evidently, with Michael MacWhite's support, played a part in allowing Griffith to receive communications from the French and Canadian governments, noting the possibility of future trading relations if the Free State came into being.[80]

In addition to chairing all cabinet meetings, Griffith was willing to chair all meetings of a subcommittee to be 'formed to deal with matters of non-vital importance … [meeting] twice weekly'.[81] This reflected his desire to keep the Dáil ministry as proactive as possible. This ambition was undermined, however, by serious financial difficulties or complications. Stephen O'Mara (in New York) and Art O'Brien (in London) held the Dáil's funds, arising from the national loan campaign, but neither was willing to assist the Dáil any longer.[82] Furthermore, it was not until late February that the trustees of the Dáil's funds (Bishop Fogarty, O'Mara and DeValera) agreed to even meet with Griffith and Collins. Then, the decision was made that various American accounts should be transferred to American government banks in the names of the existing trustees, and that 'the new government to be set up in Ireland accept the financial obligations of Dáil

Eireann'.[83] In effect, this meant that DeValera's intent was that the Provisional Government alone should have control of the Dáil's finances at some later date. This incapacitation of the Dáil created a widespread impression that Griffith and his ministry were mere puppets and that Cope's administration, in conjunction with Collins as a nominal chairman of the Provisional Government, were the only real government in the country. This made Griffith's challenge of sustaining public confidence in the Dáil a very uphill battle indeed.

Griffith understood and respected the sensibilities of most of DeValera's supporters. He fully accepted that, simply for negotiating the agreement, he 'would have critics … whatever happened' and that most criticisms of the agreement made upon the basis of the oath of allegiance were 'honest'.[84] Although he did not consider it a priority, he himself had argued in the past that Ireland should have the right, if it so desired, to create a parliamentary oath of allegiance that reflected public religious sentiment.[85] He had also noted in the past 'the history of England does not record one instance of a Treaty made by that country with a weaker country which she observed when it became her interest to break it'.[86] This was partly why long-term readers of his, most notably Sean T. O'Kelly, were so puzzled by his seemingly unflappable belief in the agreement that he had signed.[87]

Another of his own arguments that could be cited against Griffith was his (realistic) assessment that 'to the Englishman, from the duke in his palace to the radical cobbler crying "damn the House of Lords!"' the idea of Ireland being 'an equal partner in the Empire with England' was totally unacceptable and repugnant for basic economic reasons to the point of its being virtually impossible to obtain.[88] Why then was he now seemingly expecting the Irish public to have faith in Lloyd George's goodwill? The answer to this question was that this was not actually what Griffith was either asking the Irish public to believe or what he himself believed would ever be necessary. This requires some explanation.

In the past, Griffith had criticised the fiscal implications of each of the Government of Ireland Acts in a similar manner to how Childers now criticised the defence implications of the Articles of Agreement. Griffith noted that even if resistance to English ascendancy within the Empire might ultimately develop among various British colonies to Ireland's advantage

> Ireland [under the Government of Ireland Act] is bereft of the powers of resistance which Canada, Australasia and South Africa hold … It is mere nonsense to believe that because England does not interfere with her colonial parliaments she will not interfere with an Irish parliament. Her colonies are thousands of miles away from her centre of government … Ireland is but two hours'

sea-journey from her shores. She is physically and fiscally naked
... No matter how extensive the powers a home rule measure
purports to confer on Ireland, these powers are illusory if an
unrestricted veto exists in the British Government [as it did under
the Government of Ireland Act].[89]

By contrast, Griffith noted that if *true* dominion status were obtained, sufficient
'fiscal and physical strength to oppose a veto' would exist in Ireland and real
independence would automatically flow from such a situation.[90] He believed
that this was now a definite basis of the Articles of Agreement, interpreting
the idea of common citizenship as implying equality of state power. Somewhat
naively, Griffith cited a private letter of Lloyd George as proof that Britain
was 'pledged now before *the world* [my italics]' to honour the principle of
Anglo-Irish equality. Such status, previously always denied to Ireland, would
mark 'the greatest revolution' in Irish history to date and motivated his own
acceptance of the agreement: 'It is a treaty of equality, and because of that, I
am standing by it.'[91]

On the surface, Lloyd George's cabinet treated Griffith's cabinet in precisely
such an equal manner in early 1922. However, while the Dáil was debating the
Articles of Agreement the previous December, the British cabinet had already
established a new 'Irish Situation Committee', consisting of treasury, war
office and colonial office figures, to determine the British government's policy
in carrying through the agreement and yet whose deliberations were deemed
'unsuitable for presentation to the Irish leaders [Griffith and Collins]'.[92]

This British cabinet sub-committee was very quick to find fault with the work
of Griffith's cabinet. Significantly, it emphasised that the Joint Exchequer Board
provided for under the 1920 Act to enable the transfer of treasury officials and
funding to Northern and Southern Ireland had been 'hard at work' hitherto.
However, Collins, acting on Griffith's direct orders, 'prohibited movements of
staff etc.' and caused the civil service reforms to be 'largely suspended'. This not
only 'severely curtailed' the attempt of the British Government to establish the
Joint Exchequer Board that was planned during 1920, but also made it 'very
hard' for 'the Northern Government ... to keep things going'. In the first week of
February 1922, Craig demanded that this be stopped. On Dublin Castle raising
this issue with Collins, however,

> He was inclined to argue that he did not recognise the Act of 1920,
> and in any event that the boundaries of Northern Ireland were
> subject to adjustment and that therefore the whole matter should
> be regarded as in suspense for the present.

Regarding this, the cabinet sub-committee emphasised that 'this, of course, is quite an untenable position' and that the Joint Exchequer Board provided for in 1920 had to be established fully.[93]

Similarly, one of the first actions of Griffith's cabinet was to propose that Dublin Castle's Local Government Board and the Local Government Department of Dáil Eireann should be amalgamated under the latter's authority. The question of suitable civil service personnel for this body was to be determined by the Dáil alone; namely, by a cabinet subcommittee consisting of Griffith, Gavan Duffy and Cosgrave.[94] This policy was also extended to the post office system of the country. Reflecting this, Griffith 'appointed as secretary [to the proposed amalgamated local government department] a former employee of low rank who was discharged after the 1916 rebellion because of his refusal to take the Oath of Allegiance' and a similar figure in charge of the post office department, with authority to assume complete control of 'the revenue department' (the Post Office Savings Bank) on behalf of the Dáil as soon as 'the position of the Provisional Government has been regularised by law'. Regarding this, the British cabinet's Irish Situation Committee argued that 'this, of course, is an intolerable position and quite unwarranted by anything in the treaty'. In particular, it was expected that it would create 'a state of things which, if not checked, may become serious', not least by shaking 'the [business] confidence of a large section of the community' who had no belief in the Dáil and who, in turn, would refuse to allow 'credit and prestige' to the Provisional Government if Griffith had his way.[95] Chastised for this action, the Dáil cabinet decided to postpone temporarily its efforts to amalgamate the local government boards.[96] Meanwhile Griffith, via Collins, was requested to report to London immediately regarding this situation, with the instruction that 'Kevin O'Higgins [a nephew of T.M. Healy], with whom we have discussed the whole position, will be able to give you further information' regarding what the British government's concerns were.[97]

The practical logic behind DeValera's assertion during the 'treaty debates'— that even if the Dáil did not consider the agreement as a final settlement it would be treated as such by Britain[98]—was now increasingly becoming evident. DeValera's action in his capacity as a trustee of the Dáil's funds reflected this. The DeValera who, in support of Griffith, proclaimed during 1919 that Britain's authority in Ireland was based upon commercial exploitation and 'robbery'[99] had not essentially changed his politics. However, his appointment as NUI Chancellor—a nomination that he accepted initially in the hope that it 'might be of public value and of help to our cause'[100]—almost certainly opened his eyes regarding the question of what politics could or could not sustain the confidence of the business and property owners of the land. This reality fed into the holding of a significant Sinn Féin Party Ard Fheis in February 1922.

Griffith hoped that this would serve as the opportunity to rally the party behind his plans for the Dáil. In doing so, Griffith was evidently unaware that the British cabinet's advisors had already determined within two days of Griffith's appointment of his cabinets that the question of his 'remaining outside' the Provisional Government was an issue to be watched, as was his wish to exercise powers as president of the Dáil; an institution 'which it is hoped [by Dublin Castle] to disestablish shortly'.[101]

At this Ard Fheis, Griffith emphasised that the Sinn Féin Party had pledged its allegiance to the Dáil at its previous Ard Fheis in November 1921 and that it should continue to do so. He argued that the terms of the agreement were in accord with articles of Sinn Féin's constitution, to 'deny the right and oppose the will of the British parliament and British crown or any other foreign government to legislate for Ireland'; to 'make use of any and every means available to render impotent the power of England to hold Ireland in subjection by military force or otherwise'; and to

> Give its undivided allegiance and entire support to Dáil Eireann, the duly elected parliament of Ireland, in the exercise of all its legitimate functions, and in all the steps it legitimately takes to maintain public order, to provide for national defence, to secure good government, and to promote the general welfare of the whole people of Ireland.

Expressing his belief that the Irish public were 'a people of great common sense' and that 'the Irish people were going to show a capacity, economically and politically, for the rebuilding of the nation', Griffith felt confident that they would fully appreciate the significance of the fact that the treaty was 'the first instrument' to exist in Irish history that would allow Ireland to assume 'full fiscal control' of its own affairs; that the country did not have this right under the previous Government of Ireland Acts; and that these new powers would enable Irish politicians 'to banish from their midst the miserable poverty they knew to exist in the country' and 'give them the power to deal with all the social problems that today could not be dealt with by them but were [still being] dealt with by an external and non-understanding country'. Griffith suggested that whoever 'would say to the Irish people they must not take this' opportunity, but instead 'must go back and fight an impossible fight', was providing bad advice. While emphasising that he 'had no other masters' than the Irish electorate and that he would still be fully prepared to reject the agreement if voters rejected it at the next general election, Griffith emphasised how it provided for 'the evacuation of Ireland after 700 years of British troops' and the establishment of 'equality with England, equality with all nations which form the Commonwealth and equal voice in the direction of foreign affairs' with a guarantee that the other commonwealth nations would join with Ireland to hold Britain accountable if it sought to break the new Anglo-Irish treaty that was in the process of being agreed.[102]

Griffith's arguments completely failed to persuade the Sinn Féin Party, however. Parish priests governed most of its branches and were in favour of DeValera's continued presidency of the party. DeValera himself emphasised at this convention that the only reason for the Sinn Féin Party's existence was to maintain that political unity which was represented by Catholic Ireland's united stance, both clerical and lay (including, of course, the Irish Party), against the British government's policy of conscription that took place in 1918; a unity that DeValera now claimed Griffith was only attempting to undermine. Upon being re-elected as president of Sinn Féin, DeValera maintained that it would be better if the party was split someday (Sean T. O'Kelly was currently testing the political waters for forming a new anti-treaty party) and even for there to be two different armies associated with it than for it to subscribe to 'a false unity', but that any such split, or even the holding of elections in Ireland, should be delayed either for a minimum of three months or until such time as a constitution for the proposed Free State was published.[103]

DeValera's point regarding the constitution was relevant to a significant degree, as it was only once such a constitution was published and accepted by the British government that the various issues that Griffith was *already* attempting to solve could even begin to be addressed. This was a shortcoming of Griffith's approach to politics at this time, albeit a perfectly understandable one. Alongside Hugh Kennedy, Griffith took the lead in defending proposed Free State constitutions in London (the first such constitution being presented in early March). In doing so, he made very strong claims in defence of Ireland's right, under the terms of agreement, to fashion a constitution that gave real economic and diplomatic powers to Dublin. A seemingly appreciative British cabinet withheld making any definitive response to these claims. To Griffith, this was an indication of consent to the principles he had outlined and that the matter would soon be settled. However, the reality was that the British cabinet withheld a definite response purely because it knew that 'departing from the spirit of the bargain with the South' would soon become necessary.[104]

Although, in theory, Griffith was absolutely correct in the claims he was making, in practice (in the Prime Minister's words) the rights he was claiming for Ireland as a potential dominion, namely to develop its 'own ideals of political, economic and social welfare', was something to which Ireland was not inherently entitled, as the dominions' rights in these matters was 'not based on theory but on experience'; namely, the degree to which Whitehall had first judged that they were entitled to, or that it was in everyone's best economic interests (primarily Britain's), that they begin to exercise these powers. Lloyd George delayed pointing this out to Griffith until June 1922.[105] Griffith immediately retorted to the Prime Minister that it was 'perfectly clear' that the rights he was claiming on behalf of the Dáil/Provisional Government to fiscal authority were unassailable,[106] but his own cabinet colleagues, while agreeing that Kennedy should raise the matter with the Lord Chief Justice of England, appear to have been slightly reluctant to consent to Griffith adopting such a defiant stance.[107]

The outcome of the February 1922 Sinn Féin Ard Fheis was a source of very great disappointment to Griffith, the party's founder, who was also author, as well as the chief extrapolator, of its never-appreciated programme for government. Although the party had not yet technically split, the fact that a struggle for control of the party's limited financial resources followed proved that its days were numbered. Furthermore, it had already become privy to a very bitter propaganda war thanks to Erskine Childers, the official 'anti-treaty' director of publicity.

To coincide with Griffith being called to London to account for his attempt to assume control over the British government's revenue department in Ireland for the Dáil, Childers (director of publicity for the Sinn Féin Party at Suffolk Street in Dublin) established the headquarters of his 'Republic of Ireland' press agency in the old Liberal Party heartland of Manchester. Although 'document no. 2' was merely a slightly revised copy of a paper on the constitution that was originally authored by the British cabinet, Childers' propaganda campaign was based upon the idea that this document 'leaves Ireland an Independent Republic'. Childers also argued that it would have allowed 'Ireland's honour to be saved' were it not that 'Arthur Griffith was already definitely committed to accept allegiance to the British crown' prior to his even going to London and so 'refused even to present it [document no.2]' during the negotiations the previous winter as 'an honourable alternative to the Articles of Agreement signed under threats of war in London'.[108] Also courtesy of The Republic of Ireland in Manchester, Robert Barton's top-selling *Truth About The Treaty And Document No. 2* maintained that, in Irish nationalist politics (upon which Childers was supposedly the greatest authority), Arthur Griffith had always been a man who was inherently 'committed to surrender' to Britain. Therefore, during the treaty negotiations in London, Griffith's 'presence was in any case valueless' to Ireland as a plenipotentiary.[109]

Griffith's response to this propaganda campaign was to persuade the Dáil cabinet to call for the dismissal of Childers and Barton from their positions as directors of the National Land Bank. This could only be done, however, if

DeValera (as a trustee of Dáil funds) also gave his consent, but this was not forthcoming.[110] Griffith also called a massive 'pro-treaty' rally at the junction of Dame Street and Grafton Street in the centre of Dublin. At this event, the largest open-air address of his career, Griffith denounced Childers, the anti-treaty director of publicity, as 'that damned Englishman' but the Dáil's president would be severely criticised by large sections of the Irish national media for making this supposedly 'racist' (anti-British) remark against the man whom the Irish Party formerly adopted as their chief ideologue. Addressing thousands outside of Trinity College, Griffith typified Sinn Féin's abandonment of his economic nationalist policy at Childers' request as being tantamount to saying that 'the best way to save the soul of Ireland was to get its body lacerated'. Noting that 'we have heard that doctrine in Ireland before', Griffith equated the stance of the so-called anti-treaty party, of ignoring all economic considerations, with that of the old (clericalist) Irish Party, which abandoned the urban working class as well as all economic ideals of Irish nationalism after 1886. Having spent over half his life living in inner-city tenements in the direst poverty, Griffith emphasised that

> I remember often hearing from some foolish people when I was young that the poorer the Irish people were the better the national spirit would be. That was an absolute fallacy. The poorer the people were the more dispirited they got and the more prosperous and the better off the people were the better their spirit was to meet and defy oppression ... [and any] encroachment upon their rights ... They had in Ireland ... been struggling for every little thing ... and in 25 years they had been able to do very little because they were without legislative power. They have legislative power now; they have absolute control over their own money; they have absolute control over every artery of their trade and commerce. It was absolutely at their disposal to use their taxation in what way they liked in the development of the country ... We have (pointing to the Bank of Ireland) that building from which the British Government evicted, 120 years ago, the legislature, and from that day the impoverishment, the degradation and the depopulation of Ireland began. Now the process has reversed.[111]

Griffith's claim to authority over Ireland's principle bank was sincere but actually a little misleading. Collins had been allowed by Dublin Castle to meet the directors of the Bank of Ireland in January 1922. At Griffith's bidding, Collins attempted to order them to finance the new Irish state with a view to this bank eventually assuming a status akin to an independent Irish national bank.[112] Hitherto, at the

Bank of England's request, the Bank of Ireland had invested all monies raised by the British state in Ireland in the Bank of England. Consequently, although a very provisional promise to cooperate with Griffith's finance ministry (or, at least, the Provisional Government) was offered by the bank's directors, resistance to change was its priority. This was manifested in a number of ways.

On a purely political level, Andrew Jameson of the Bank of Ireland was very much in favour of the withdrawal of British troops. He believed this was essential to an acceptance of the agreement.[113] In any event, these troops could serve elsewhere, including potentially Northern Ireland, while the costs (and importance) of territorial forces were far less significant to Britain than that of naval and air forces. Jameson, however, had made no secret to the government regarding his opposition to all of Griffith's past economic ideas.[114] Reflecting this, not long after Griffith's monster meeting outside the Bank of Ireland headquarters, the Irish Banks Standing Committee (secretly) reaffirmed its commitment to the decisions made during the summer of 1920 (including the financing of the NUI and all religiously-managed institutions such as the hospitals and schools). In addition to a formal implementation of a London-centric central clearing arrangement for all inter-bank transactions, it formally drew up a provision regarding fine trade bills (loans) for businesses that operated in Ireland. The Irish Banks Standing Committee sole definition of a person, firm or company recognised as being of sound financial standing was that it is domiciled in London.[115]

With the encouragement of Cope (himself a leading imperial customs official), Dublin Castle soon transferred from London experienced British treasury civil servants, most notably Joseph Brennan and J.J. McElligott, a former UCD graduate who edited the London *Statist*. This was done to regulate the work of the Provisional Government's proposed finance ministry, potentially making Michael Collins far less a director of economic policy on behalf of Griffith's Dáil than a mere tool to give a new finance department its public face. This was all done before the slightest transfer of powers to the Provisional Government was allowed. While historians have interpreted issues of staffing as a justification for this arrangement,[116] it had a definite political context as well. This was that the British government simply did not trust anyone except its own civil servants to be able to sustain public confidence in any government within Ireland. This had already been demonstrated in the case of Griffith's proposed local government reforms. The official that the British government had objected to on that occasion, supposedly on the grounds of being grossly unqualified, was actually a TD, former banker and assistant to the Dail's finance ministry, Lorcan Robbins.[117] Evidently, Robbins was not disqualified on the grounds of qualifications, skills, experience or an ability to sustain public confidence in good government. He was disqualified simply because he was an Irish nationalist. Hence, as the Catholic Viceroy of the King in Ireland noted gleefully, Griffith and Collins would soon 'realise [that] the art of government is more difficult than they expected'. This was because their desire to undo the past practices of English imperial administrators would inevitably be frustrated by the fact that 'this of course is exactly what every [government] official of any experience is' (including, of course, himself) and only the employment of such men could be acceptable to the British government or else the Irish would be accused of breaking the treaty.[118]

By March 1922, therefore, Griffith was in a very peculiar position indeed. He had submitted a Free State constitution to London, claiming fiscal and diplomatic autonomy, and it faced no objections. Indeed, he had not yet been given any direct indication from Whitehall, Dublin Castle or the banks that his interpretation of the treaty agreement was not being accepted. Furthermore, although it had not formally supported the Dáil prior to 'the truce', the *Irish Independent*, which prided itself on being a progressive business journal owing to its innovative work to develop the advertising industry, was generally supportive of the arguments of Griffith's *Young Ireland* (still edited by Milroy and Burke) that the treaty agreement presented the only way forward for Ireland, both economically and in the matter of partition (represented by the Boundary Commission idea).[119] Meanwhile, on 10 March, DeValera wrote to Griffith from the Sinn Féin Party headquarters on Suffolk Street regarding their mutual deep concern in updating the country's electoral registers for a forthcoming general election. In doing so, DeValera unequivocally addressed Griffith as the 'President of the Republic'.[120]

Behind the scenes, however, London was making definite arrangements for keeping its complete control of both monetary policy and all civil service reforms in Ireland. Meanwhile, by late March, developments had taken place that threatened to drown all Griffith's political hopes in the Liffey. This occurred essentially because of the accumulation of numerous unresolved issues that all parties outside the Dáil had little or no confidence in its ability to resolve, not least because it had no authority over such matters. These included ongoing threatened strikes by the Irish Transport and General Workers Union. This was a development that, aside from the British labour party, their actual employers, who were not sympathetic to the Dáil and whose transport companies straddled both jurisdictions in Ireland, may actually have encouraged. The temporary suspension of a central authority with complete control over all issues of law and order also encouraged some robberies in rural Ireland by people who sought to take advantage of this situation.[121] The most damaging problem of all, however, was the resumption of troubles in Belfast during February.

Collins had been forewarned of this, noting to the Prime Minister that he had learnt at Dublin Castle that attacks were being planned on northern nationalists and that 'this action can only be carried through under cover and by support of your troops'.[122] Collins was not granted the dignity of a reply, however. Instead, over a hundred shootings, all of which were attributed by British politicians to anonymous 'IRA' forces, took place in Belfast the following week, which in turn was used by the British cabinet as justification for placing Belfast under martial law (Craig, of course, simply had to go along with this), the militarisation of the north and to accuse the Dáil of instigating the northern troubles. This was a sure means of counteracting the Dáil's efforts to assume regulatory financial authority, even if this was potentially the Dáil's legal right. In addition, as was the case under the old Union with Ireland, the policing of Northern Ireland under the new Union (the Government of Ireland Act) was an issue that, by law, had to be kept entirely under the military's authority, not elected politicians, such as Craig and his Ulster Unionist Party in their fancy new Stormont buildings, or indeed the local government bodies (the latter principle being the legal and fiscal situation regarding policing throughout Britain).[123] In this way, all Irish politicians' attempts to assume and carry out the responsibilities of government were still being practically held to ransom by subtle uses of British militarism.

The British cabinet knew—it had already been planning for this eventuality during 'the troubles' with the full cooperation of the Irish Banks Standing Committee—that the dynamics of partition could be used to prevent any attempts by Griffith to disturb the norms of the existing economy of the United Kingdom of Great Britain and Ireland by using the north to destabilise the whole of Ireland politically. This was considered as a necessary alternative to using punitive economic blockades against Southern Ireland to force it to obey London's economic will because Dublin could potentially hit back by denying Britain its perpetual need for Southern Ireland's agricultural exports.[124] This was precisely why, having already presented the dominion option to Dublin, most members of the British cabinet were not blind to the potentially 'unpleasant' consequences of the fact that 'Southern Ireland has privileges denied to the North' to exercise, at least *in theory*.[125] To some extent, this was a reality that Griffith hoped to be able to capitalise upon not least by persuading Craig that Dublin could be a more natural and beneficial economic ally of Belfast than London. In the face of this peaceable ambition, however, stood a century-long legacy of business habits in Ireland that not only served to facilitate London's ambitions but also made London seem as the only guarantor of accepted or established fiscal norms throughout Ireland. It should not be forgotten that southern unionist figures such as the Earl of Midleton still viewed themselves not only as the key power brokers in Ireland, but also as a party to an agreement that, in fact, only plenipotentiaries of Dáil Eireann had signed.[126] Churchill certainly granted them this unofficial status, which effectively originated with the fact that it was *they* who (on behalf of the British government) had arranged the peace agreement with DeValera during the early summer of 1921 that had led to the sending of plenipotentiaries in the first place.

Griffith necessarily sought to accommodate Midleton's political circle owing to their extant authority over the Irish banks. However, he perpetually refused to concede to their demands, forwarded to the Dáil using Darrel Figgis as an intermediary, for authority over an Irish legislative assembly. These demands were made concurrently with Griffith's negotiations with London regarding a Free State constitution and included Midleton's plan for the establishment of a non-elective senate strong enough to counter the power of the Dáil as a legislative assembly.[127] This would mean that the Dáil could not introduce any economic reforms with which unionists did not agree. This is why Griffith refused to compromise with Midleton.

Financial matters aside, outside of purely Sinn Féin circles, Midleton's circle could also claim to have some *moral* authority due to the fact that the former Irish Party had accepted its ideas for an Irish constitution, with an upper house stronger than the legislative assembly, at the 1917 Irish Convention. While the authority of Dillon's party over the press had been lessened to a significant degree (during 1919 the party lost partial control over the *Freeman's Journal*, which now supported the 'Provisional Government' but not Dáil Eireann),[128] it had played an influential role, alongside the Catholic Union of Great Britain, in demonising Sinn Féin ever since the summer of 1920. In addition, its influence with the grazing or wealthier farming community in Ireland was still significant. Reflecting this, the old 'moderate unionist' community, represented by the likes of Sir Horace Plunkett, were still influential commentators on Irish affairs. Plunkett still ran the Department of Agriculture at Dublin Castle and the organ of his Irish Agricultural Organisation Society (the *Irish Homestead*) soon renamed itself as the *Irish Statesman*; a not inaccurate reflection of its own sense of self-importance. To some extent, the defection of Robert Barton from the Dáil's ministry for agriculture *gave* Plunkett's circle such importance. Partly for this reason, Lionel Smith Gordon, the manager of the Dáil's National Land Bank (who hoped to promote the Dáil's ambitions regarding markets in the United States), felt that Sinn Féin's failure to declare its support for Griffith's economic policy in February 1922 was virtually a catastrophe for the Dáil that must set back its economic ambitions for at least a decade.[129]

These were reasons why DeValera's chosen manner of offering his loyal opposition to the Dáil was considered problematic by some of Griffith's supporters. Not least of these was W.T. Cosgrave, who felt that the evident, even if not a formal, split in Sinn Féin was being used as an excuse by 'so-called businessmen' not to place their trust in the Dáil and even to deliberately encourage disorder in order to persuade others (by bribes or otherwise) to do the exact same.[130] The only initiative in any way connected with the Dáil that the Irish Banks Standing Committee *did* decide to fund during 1922 was a proposed housing committee.[131] It seems, however, that this occurred only because William Field (on behalf of Dublin Corporation) had already persuaded the Dublin Chamber of Commerce, then headed by Jameson, to support such a scheme, once an opportune moment arose, during early 1919.[132] The Society for the Statistical and Social Inquiry of Ireland seemed to imply that this scheme, along with reforming the poor law boards in line with a British governmental report of 1909, should be the full extent of the preoccupations of 'a patriot parliament … in the twenty-six counties known as Southern Ireland' during 1922.[133] To some extent, this may been seen as an indication that grandiose ambitions for reform neither had nor did exist much further beyond the confines of revolutionary-minded cabinet of Dáil Eireann.

Within Sinn Féin circles, DeValera generally professed not to have abandoned the Dáil's former ambitions by sidestepping its cabinet. To *other* sections of Irish political society, however, the reality that DeValera now stood outside that cabinet was reason enough to welcome the very fact of his political independence. Reflecting this, political friends of Fr Tom Finlay and Alice Stopford Green drew the following contrast between Griffith and DeValera's retrospective popular appeals during March 1922. With his dogmatic claims that Ireland required many fundamental reforms, Griffith was typified as the embodiment of 'the stubbornness of a stone on two legs'. If he had power, he had no popular appeal. By contrast, it was suggested that 'how could the historians of the future ever understand from anything he had said the influence of Mr. DeValera over his past and present colleagues unless someone had noted the disarming friendliness of his eyes?'[134]

This assessment, published by the southern unionist *Irish Times*, reflected the fact that nobody could accuse DeValera of forcing anybody to do anything during 1922. In such a deeply conservative political society as that of Ireland, the very fact of DeValera's apparent powerlessness and inaction allowed him to maintain a benevolent persona. Furthermore, the perpetual threat of British coercion, which was nothing inherently new in Irish society, allowed DeValera to pose as an iconic figure that was being marginalised due to unnatural outside influences.[135] By contrast, Griffith would increasingly face the burden of being accused from *all* directions of defying established Irish political consensuses purely out of his own 'stubbornness' in pursuing a course of action that nobody really wanted. This would prove to be his downfall.

CHAPTER TWELVE

The Survival of Dáil Eireann (1922)

Numerous interrelated political factors made the survival of Dáil Eireann, in any shape or form, far from certain during 1922. The predominant feature of the anti-treaty propaganda campaign, which was officially directed by Erskine Childers from February 1922 onwards, was to emphasise the Dáil's powerlessness to act as a parliament. This placed every member of Griffith's ministry under very considerable strain because it made the Irish public as unappreciative as possible of their efforts to facilitate, in the Dáil's own interests, a transfer of powers from Britain by means of the Provisional Government. The latter was a body that anti-treaty unionists, led by Midleton, still hoped would become the basis of a parliament of Southern Ireland under the Government of Ireland Act if the treaty arrangement, providing for an Irish Free State with powers to trade outside the United Kingdom (i.e., the Union), could be destroyed. Meanwhile, every effort by Griffith's cabinet to accommodate the Childers–DeValera body of anti-treaty opinion was not so much welcomed by the latter but rather 'interpreted as a sign of weakness' to be capitalised upon.[1]

Another factor that did not help Griffith was the reporting of the British press, which was also read widely in Ireland. The perpetual British press criticisms of the DeValeraite 'anti-treaty party' while treating the matter of the government of Ireland as a question that was now permanently settled rather than an issue that was only now beginning through a civil service takeover reflected a form of wish-fulfilment regarding the legacy of the Government of Ireland Act that, with the support of Midleton's party, was likely to come true.[2]

Apart from playing upon this fact, the rationale adopted by the DeValeraite party in defending their own stance was weak, however.

Childers and Barton's effort to champion the idea that 'document no. 2 [which was authored by the British cabinet] ... leaves Ireland an Independent Republic'[3] was not only totally unconvincing but also completely false. This was precisely why Sean T. O'Kelly's subsequent effort in March 1922 to form a new Cumann na Poblachta party in opposition to Griffith's ministry purely in order to defend 'the existing republic'[4] was not allowed by DeValera to get beyond the drawing board stages, particularly after this stance was denounced by the Irish College in Rome as insane.[5] Be that as it may, many supporters of this section of anti-treaty opinion attempted to popularise the idea of upholding the legitimacy of a defunct ministry against the very parliamentary assembly that had given it birth. This was an ideologically monarchist and anti-democratic idea that, remarkably, actually played a significant part in shaping Irish public attitudes. Henceforth, it would not be uncommon for commentators—admittedly, either ignorant or deliberately disingenuous ones—to speak of legitimism as the basis of republicanism.[6] This was done as a means of discrediting all talk of the credibility of a republican ideal in Ireland as much as was possible by deliberately associating it with a completely anti-democratic stance. That this could occur at all, and it did occur very easily indeed, was proof that Ireland continued to identify primarily with British rather than European or American political systems or traditions, let alone any form of indigenous Irish political tradition. Not surprisingly, John Devoy of New York was alive to this reality. In aggressively supporting Griffith and Collins' defence of the republican principle of parliamentary supremacy above all, this old unrepentant fenian typified DeValera as a typical Spaniard who, along with his politically ignorant priests, was leading an anti-democratic counter-revolution in the most approved Mexican or Latin American style by attempting to set up a tin-pan dictatorship in the name of a bogus *Il Presidente*.[7] In Ireland itself, however, few could understand how anyone could possibly typify a 'leader of the Irish race' or 'the national leader' (both monarchical ideas) in such disparaging terms or, indeed, be so willing to distinguish between priests' unquestioned wisdom as moral advisors compared to their practical weaknesses as political advisors. Instead, most were content to accept the simple idea that a republican should henceforth be defined as anyone who said 'nay' to a treaty settlement that it was actually intended to keep, in one form or another.

The Dáil's ambition for a smooth and peaceful transfer of powers was frustrated by policing problems and, in turn, the revival of press censorship. This occurred as a result of a specific series of events. Regarding policing, in keeping with Griffith's initial Sinn Féin ideals, Dáil Eireann wished to completely undo the anti-democratic situation that existed under the Union whereby the police were unaccountable to the public in Ireland, though not in Britain; a situation perpetuated by the (as yet) unreformed local government legislation of 1898. Reflecting this, ever since Mulcahy had signed the peace agreement with General Macready in July 1921, the Dáil's home affairs legal experts, such as Eamon Duggan and Kevin O'Shiel, were working to facilitate a situation whereby the existing liaison arrangements between the Irish Volunteers and the RIC would become the basis for the creation of a new, demilitarised and accountable Irish police force. This was an advantage, from the Irish side, to 'the truce', and was a fundamental aim, or basis, to both the Dáil's counter-state programme ever since 1919 as well as the reformist work of Griffith's ministry regarding local government in the early spring of 1922. However, it also presented a huge logistical challenge that required time to resolve.[8]

It was intended by Griffith's Dáil cabinet that 'all volunteers would be given the chance of joining the regular army or police force' of the new Irish state.[9] This was to be done once the British territorial forces and RIC vacated their various barracks, but this process was frequently delayed. For instance, the RIC's deliberate delay in evacuating Templemore Barracks, which was intended by Griffith's Dáil to serve as a headquarters and training grounds for its unarmed guardians of the peace or 'Gardai', was looked upon with much suspicion by Munster Irish Volunteers, who were anxious about their own career prospects.[10] Partly as a result, although Griffith's cabinet was drafting legislation to give generous salaries and pension arrangements to every member of the Irish Volunteers that would swear to continue to uphold the Dail's authority as either regular police officers or soldiers,[11] the Dáil's decision to postpone the holding of Irish Volunteer conventions until the home affairs ministry first had the necessary administrative bases in place (this included establishing parliamentary authority over local government courts) to provide such beneficial arrangements to the Irish Volunteers was not widely appreciated within its ranks.[12] Instead, deep doubts regarding the Dáil's abilities to meet these logistical challenges created an atmosphere of suspicion. If Childers' propaganda campaign encouraged this trend he was not essentially its author. As it was widely known that the Dáil had no money, it could reasonably be asked how the Dáil could possibly provide for such reforms or salaried personnel. Was the general Irish public really to believe that the unionist Bank of Ireland, which had formerly funded the 'Black and Tan' auxiliaries, would now be willing to finance this new arrangement? Could it be that Irish society was about to witness the birth of 'Green and Tans' instead?

Craig and the north of Ireland had their own distinct policing problems. As if to absolve the British government from Collins' proof of Dublin Castle's treachery during February, Churchill offered in late March to create a peace pact document, bringing both Collins and Craig to London to sign this document, whereby, it was promised that normal policing facilities would be facilitated in Belfast and its environs by the British government. Churchill also promised that Westminster would pass the Irish Free State (Agreement) Act under which very substantive powers were to begin to be transferred to Dublin as early as late-July 1922. However, during this very moment of Collins' absence from Dublin, with DeValera's support, Oscar Traynor set up a new anti-treaty 'IRA Organisation' in Dublin that, although it expressed an unwillingness to fight, nevertheless expressed total opposition to the Provisional Government and all that it stood for.[13] This would mean that no transfer of powers could take place. For precisely this reason, upon Collins' return, Churchill could perpetually point to Dublin, not to Belfast or to London, as the root of all disruptive political behaviour. In the process, this would inherently leave Griffith and Collins without any proverbial leg to stand on in their defence if they should ever seek to call foul on the British signatories to the Articles of Agreement again.

The formation of the IRA Organisation seemingly represented the birth of a permanent partition within the Dáil's former support basis, increasing the likelihood of Irish nationalists scoring an own goal in the near future. Nevertheless, it is quite possible that these potential complications could well have been resolved amicably and Irish Volunteer unity maintained were it not for the role of propaganda in fuelling suspicion. A significant development here related to the press. Although its most recent employees included republican sympathisers (including Desmond Ryan), there was still no love lost between the *Freeman's Journal*, the old Dublin Castle organ, and all those who sympathised in any way with Griffith's ideals. Reflecting southern unionist opinion, the *Freeman* invariably praised the existence of the Provisional Government as a basis for renewed Anglo-Irish solidarity (this actually made Collins something of a celebrity to old Irish Party supporters) without giving much credence to the existence of Griffith's Dáil cabinet (where Collins' loyalties actually lay). In the wake of the volunteer dispute over its postponed convention, the *Freeman's Journal* office was (inexplicably) ransacked. Thereafter, it made the very strange move of appealing to Griffith and the Dáil for financial compensation for damages.[14] This event was relatively meaningless in itself. However, it was used as an excuse by Alfred Cope at Dublin Castle to absolutely insist on the restoration of state press censorship. This was a familiar burden that Irish society had suffered ever since the 'great war' and had been greatly relieved to have avoided, to a significant extent, ever since the truce. As Cope was the chief British instrument for establishing the Provisional Government at Dublin Castle, however, Collins had to respect his wishes. His solution was to appoint Piaras Beaslai, editor of *An tOglach*, as a press censor.[15] Collins believed that Irish Volunteer control over this arrangement would be sufficient to make it palatable enough for the Irish public to tolerate while simultaneously sustaining public confidence in the Dáil. However, to a significant extent, it had an opposite affect because press censorship of any kind naturally fuelled suspicions regarding the intent of government. This idea was deliberately used thereafter by Childers to misinterpret the Dáil's decision to postpone volunteer conventions.

Not without reason, contemporaries generally equated Irish Volunteer unity with two different, albeit hitherto complementary, factors. First and foremost, there was the issue of the volunteers' loyalty to the Dáil's minister of defence and president (currently, Richard Mulcahy and Arthur Griffith); and second, the bonds of friendship among its officer corps that had been sustained not least by the IRB and its former role in imbuing its officers with republican sympathies. Both these factors were now called into question, however. The question of the IRB became a matter that anti-treaty propagandists (and, to a lesser extent, pro-treaty propagandists) increasingly sought to turn into a particularly contentious issue. This occurred for one specific reason.

At the time of the Sinn Féin Party Ard Fheis, Harry Boland, a republican opponent of the terms of the treaty agreement, had brought Joseph McGarrity to Dublin to publicly promote the idea that he had secretly touted to Collins the previous year. This was to restore the historic connection between the American Clan na Gael and the nationalist movement in Ireland.[16] This connection, traditionally sustained by the IRB, was one that Boland himself was formerly responsible for breaking completely on 18 October 1920, at DeValera's request. It was also a connection that Collins was largely indifferent to the idea of restoring: 'You know there is no feeling at home now of looking to America in the way former generations look to Westminster.'[17]

In common with John Devoy (the very old, now effectively retired, Clan na Gael founder, who informed the Dáil cabinet of DeValera's efforts to manage the Dáil loan funds in New York),[18] Collins realised that any potential issue of American financing now revolved entirely around the Dáil, not secret revolutionary organisations. Similarly, during the treaty debates, Collins had suggested that the fact of the Dáil's prior failure to receive any recognition of the Irish republic in America was reason enough to kiss the Clan na Gael goodbye.[19] Boland, however, had spent the last three years deeply involved in Clan circles in America. Acting under McGarrity's direct influence, he championed the opposite viewpoint. DeValera, to whom Boland was fanatically loyal, had also advised him the previous November (while Boland was still in America) that the formation of a 'new army' might well be necessary and, in doing so, DeValera was evidently calling for American financial assistance.[20]

Boland had tried, in vain, to make Collins support the idea of allying the IRB with McGarrity's completely new 'Clan na Gael' organisation in March 1921 and he would do so again in February 1922. He interpreted Collins' indifference as a sign neither of the IRB's organisational independence (the right, always conceded historically by Devoy, to expect the Clan to fund only the IRB's wishes—this, for instance, was Devoy's sole motive in accepting Tom Clarke's call for funds for a rebellion in January 1916)[21] nor that the Clan na Gael was no longer important. Rather, Boland interpreted this situation as evidence that the IRB Supreme Council was somehow guilty of treachery.[22] In reaction to this frustration of his hopes, with McGarrity's support, Boland used $60,000, kept in the Merchants Bank in Washington D.C. in his own name as 'the property of the Irish Republican Brotherhood', to finance Oscar Traynor, Liam Lynch, Rory O'Connor and Liam Mellows to form a new 'army'.[23] Boland's intent ('I have not the slightest hesitation in placing the money at their disposal') was his belief that

> Their action will undoubtedly bring things here [in Dublin] to a head and I for one am optimistic enough to think that the Army by its desire will bring the Free Staters to a reasonable frame of mind. If anything can compel them to draft a constitution, it is this action of the Army ... The Army has taken a decisive step towards maintaining the Republic ... You know how hard I worked for unity but I realised that there can only be unity on the basis of no compromise of the National Honour.[24]

With this single impulsive action, Boland was essentially responsible for creating the IRA Organisation. The action it took—which Boland thought as a good means to compel the Dáil to draft a written constitution (although it had already done this, two months previously)—was no less than to occupy the Four Courts in Dublin and, in turn, seek to negotiate both army and Dáil unity purely on its own terms.[25] These terms, on Liam Lynch's advice (who wrote to Boland that 'I wish to thank you for your cooperation in this matter'),[26] included 'payment [of salaries] ... which has been denied by the MD [Mulcahy, Minister for Defence]'; the 'cost of maintenance of barracks etc. at present commanded by the IRA'; and the 'evidence which would prove that the Beggars Bush GHQ have employed ex-British soldiers or Black and Tans—such as that alleged at Limerick and Templemore'.[27] In other words, Irish Volunteer anxiety regarding their career prospects, as well as their doubts (or impatience) regarding the possibilities of the Dáil implementing the planned salaried employment and mutual amnesty scheme, led them to go on strike against the Dáil's ministry of defence. This could hardly be described as a patriotic act. However Boland, after three years in America, misinterpreted this action as a potential means of 'maintaining the Republic'.

Although the new IRA Organisation was essentially a trade union for Irish Volunteers, Boland's ultimate intention in this matter was to create a 'new SC [IRB Supreme Council]'. This was a body for which he had been president before leaving for America ('were it not … you were a colleague of mine on the SC I would have hesitated longer ere I handed the money over') and ambitioned to lead once again, but

> I have had so many sad experiences of low tactics and dirty suggestions during the past six months that I am very anxious to secure that my action in regard to the monies shall not be 'twisted by knaves to make a trap for fools'.[28]

However, Boland's actions (not for the first time)[29] were extremely foolish. In his absence (and, indeed, even prior to his absence, if he had the intelligence to realise it), the IRB had been little more than a fraternity among volunteer officers whose chief goal and achievement, practically speaking, was simply to sustain *An tOglach* as a morale-boosting Irish Volunteer journal and operate secret couriers to facilitate the operations of the underground Dáil (the flashpoint of Collins' ordering the shooting of intelligence agents was a very isolated event). However, the police crackdown on the IRB's activities in the winter of 1920–21 had rendered it completely impotent as an organisation by February 1921. The truce and, in turn, the treaty agreement had led to the promise of release of many of its members from prison, if peace was maintained. Most members of the IRB (which had, in total, about 3,000 members; a relatively insignificant number) had experienced all this. Boland and Lynch had not.

Boland's action coincided with a dispute regarding the funds of the Sinn Féin Party, which were temporarily frozen,[30] as well as the unpopular decision whereby Piaras Beaslai, editor of *An tOglach*, was appointed as a state press censor. Boland's $60,000 may be said to have bought support for his initiative (other monies were not available) and it also suddenly made him an authoritative figure in the Sinn Féin Party headquarters at Suffolk Street. This raised a peculiar irony, however. Boland's funds had officially belonged to the IRB and yet it was now used for a propaganda campaign whereby, quite simply, the IRB was blamed for everything.[31] If Boland saw this as a means of achieving his own little organisational coup, it was responsible for creating an extraordinarily confused situation, not least because as the IRB was a historic and secret organisation it was the perfect scapegoat for adopting a misleading propaganda campaign. Not surprisingly, Childers would literally jump at this opportunity. The IRB's final organisational circular of 12 December 1921—which encouraged every member to make up their own minds regarding the treaty agreement in their own

311

peaceable way—was now misinterpreted in many different ways. The two most common ideas propagated was that Collins had used the IRB to secretly bribe men to 'betray the republic' by accepting the agreement ('jobs for the boys'—not that there were actually any jobs to be had) and that the IRB traitorously considered its own historic republican oath of membership (the 'virtually established republic' theory of 1848)[32] as something separate and perhaps even something somehow superior to the Dáil's oath of allegiance or that which each, supposedly more plebeian, volunteer had once taken.[33] If anyone in Irish society wished to take revenge on the IRB for having organised the 1916 rising, they now had a perfect opportunity of doing so. As a corollary of this, as was reflected by the tone of many anti-treaty flyers that bore slogans such as 'Arthur Griffith downed Redmond for looking for home rule. Poor Redmond!',[34] if any former Irish Party supporters wanted to take revenge on Griffith, they could now potentially appeal successfully to arms to secure this objective.

The organisational structure of DeValera's Sinn Féin Party, for which Childers was chief propagandist (Childers was also a party to the arrangements surrounding Archbishop Mannix),[35] was such that the Catholic Church was almost inherently a key broker in solving political disputes in Ireland via the parish priests who governed many Sinn Féin branches. As was reflected by Kevin O'Higgins' dismissal of the relevance of the Boland charade ('a faction fight between two letters of the alphabet'), the Dáil cabinet also generally subscribed to this idea. The officially neutral stance of the Irish diocesan church (the bishops and parish-based clergy) regarding the treaty agreement won the approval of Catholic bishops of Irish descent throughout the United Kingdom and the English-speaking Catholic diaspora worldwide.[36] In doing so, the church had proved its unwillingness to be made a tool of politicians and not to allow its proper communal responsibilities as a church to be perverted in any way. Meanwhile, as was reflected by the state of opinion in the Irish College in Rome, the anti-treaty stance of the monastic church (the religious orders, with responsibilities for international church diplomacy) had clear limits. Reflecting this, DeValera's St Patrick's Day speeches about 'wading through Irish blood' would soon cause him to be called to task by Archbishop Byrne of Dublin. Griffith was now receiving death threats from 'the IRA' should he speak before a public meeting in County Sligo (convened by the local mayor) on the grounds of DeValera's latest intimations that Griffith had somehow traitorously overstepped his authority in having signed the treaty agreement;[37] a manifestly false idea. The volunteers in north Connacht were led by Thomas Derrig who, at the suggestion of Ernest O'Malley (a volunteer well-known in British army circles and a southern divisional commander since February 1921), now sided with Liam Lynch's group that occupied the Four Courts on the very same day of Griffith's arrival in Sligo.[38] As minister for defence, Mulcahy ordered Griffith to travel to Sligo with an army presence. This was an idea that upset Griffith, who maintained that 'Dáil Eireann has not authorised and will not authorise any interference with the right of public meeting and free speech.'[39] He could not overrule the decision, however. Furthermore, he was persuaded by Mulcahy to draw up his last will and testament in the expectation of his sudden death. In this, it was later revealed, Griffith included a political remark: 'let the people stand firm for the Free State. It is their national need and economic salvation'.[40]

The calls for Griffith's assassination led to a secret conference conveyed by Laurence O'Neill, still the mayor of Dublin. This brought Griffith and DeValera together to debate matters with Archbishop Byrne of Dublin at the latter's Drumcondra palace a week before a synod of the Catholic bishops was due to take place at Maynooth 'with a view to coming to some agreement whereby order might be maintained in the country.'[41] Although the Catholic Viceroy believed that Archbishop Byrne was very firm with DeValera in calling upon him to make greater efforts to maintain the peace,[42] Griffith himself did not believe that this meeting had any satisfactory conclusion other than to call for more public Dáil sessions. It was intended that these would be held in the council chamber of University College Dublin (to be chaired by Eoin MacNeill) rather than the Mansion House, with tickets made available for forty visitors, 'twenty tickets to be at the disposal of the President and twenty at the disposal of Mr DeValera TD'.[43] It was also decided, however, that 'in addition to the ordinary police arrangements for the Dáil session a military guard would be also provided'.[44] The very fact that a general strike against militarism was launched, with the church's moral support, by the Labour Party the day before the planned meeting made the Dáil suddenly look particularly defensive, however. A particularly tense situation had arisen, therefore, by the end of April 1922.

As late as mid-March, as was reflected by Griffith's success in presenting a draft Irish Free State constitution before the British cabinet in London, the ideal of consolidating the authority of Dáil Eireann by expanding upon its past work was still live and vibrant. By the end of April, however, increasingly its mere survival was actually far from certain. This uncertainty was reflected by the fact that while Stormont had successfully decreed on the same day as the Dáil's 'treaty debates' began that it had the right to dissolve any local government bodies that were not obeying its legal jurisdiction,[45] four or five months later the Dáil itself, being subject an overwhelming obsession with a secular theology of swearing oaths (of both the civil and uncivil kind), still could not be sure of the allegiance of a single local government body within its own nominal jurisdiction. If this partition within southern Irish political representation was not remedied, then it was liable to dictate the outcome of all political alternatives and leave all Irish political representatives, north and south, with a very painful situation indeed.

At the Drumcondra conference, DeValera denied having any authority over the new IRA Organisation.[46] Few people believed this in the light of his ongoing willingness to rely on McGarrity and Boland's support (although he kept a slight distance from both during the early part of 1922).[47] However, the paucity of funds for Irish nationalist organisations—a somewhat deliberate situation in the light of DeValera's recent action at the Ard Fheis—made public opinion more tolerant of prevarications at this time, as if every political action was necessarily dependent on a prior British acceptance of an Irish constitution. To DeValera's sympathisers, the press censorship issue added to the perception, born at the time of the initial Dáil debates on the agreement, that his biggest problem would be the absence of a sympathetic press.[48] By contrast, DeValera's critics felt that he was guilty of attempting to take advantage of the church's independent status. In particular, if the church had acted true to itself and the bishops' neutrality was politically unimpeachable, DeValera was essentially attempting to claim the same status for himself, as he was every bit as much a Jesuit (and enjoyed the same diplomatic immunity) as his advisor Timothy Corcoran, acting distinctly from but in parallel with the diocesan church without undermining the overall integrity of that union which is Roman Catholic Church, involving (international) monastic and (national) diocesan churches.

The Belfast riots of February 1922 had not only been used as a reason for the British government not to release the pre-truce prisoners but they also created a new bevy of political prisoners. More than anything else, it was this political prisoners issue that allowed Childers to attain both respect and a position of leadership in anti-treaty/IRA circles. A year previously, as the Dáil's publicity minister, Childers had denounced Dáil consuls for failing to appreciate that the Crown (as far as he was concerned) was not something 'English' but rather a sovereign principle of international justice worldwide.[49] Now, however, with the aid of some rich Englishwomen of professed communist sympathies (including a sister of Lord French, Fitzalan's predecessor as Viceroy at Dublin Castle),[50] Childers founded a new amnesty, or prisoners' relief, organisation in Dublin. With the support of Maud Gonne (who had initially written to Griffith in support of the agreement but now, emerging from eighteen-years retirement, opposed it), Childers persuaded the Cumann na mBan women's organisation to make this political prisoners issue *the* central basis of an anti-treaty agitation.[51] This agitation, which actually became a basis for (in peace time) an unprecedented political mobilisation of Irish women,[52] was as significant a factor in shaping Sinn Féin Party activities as Boland's action precisely because it had much funding. Meanwhile, money was something that Griffith's ministry had not.

Although he promised fair play to all sections of society, generally speaking Griffith believed that to uphold public belief in the Dáil it was necessary that it did not rely too much on the assistance of unpopular politicians. This was an attitude that some republican anti-treatyites, by styling themselves as a watchdog of the Dáil lest it associate with non-republicans, encouraged. This attitude could be taken a little too far, however. For instance, Griffith turned down an offer from Sir Horace Plunkett, an internationally well-known figure, of Dublin Castle's Department of Agriculture to do fund-raising work for the Dáil in America. Choosing a Belfast publican Denis McCullough (albeit with some assistance from T.A. Smiddy, a noteworthy Cork professor) to do this work instead was a poor choice of alternative.[53] Such decisions may partly explain why the provisional promise made by the Bank of Ireland to work with the Provisional Government had yet to produce any positive results for the Dáil. Griffith and Collins actually chose to look elsewhere. By the beginning of May, this initiative had raised £200,000—a not insignificant sum to be in the hands of Irish nationalists but certainly not enough to sustain any governmental body— while requests were also made that the trustees of the Dáil funds (DeValera, Bishop Fogarty and Stephen O'Mara)[54] loan the Dáil cabinet £28,000.[55] This was no more or no less than what the Dáil had operated on from 1919–1921 and Griffith and his finance minister, with a naivety all their own, may well have been so accustomed to this situation that they did not fully realise its inadequacy for promoting their declared goals. For the most part, however, their preoccupation was with simply sustaining the Dáil until such time as Britain would recognise its status as the Irish parliament by a transfer of powers. Only then could the Dáil count on the support of the country's financial institutions.

Other aspects of the Dáil's relationship with the private and public sector in Ireland betrayed the legacy of its Sinn Féin Party antecedents, with a tendency to seek solutions in personal loyalties alone. The strength of DeValera's (or, rather, the Irish hierarchy's) Irish White Cross relief organisation the previous year lay in the very fact of its non-party status: it did not refuse money from anywhere, irrespective of politics, and it had no formal association with Dáil Eireann.[56] Childers' 'Irish Republican Prisoners Defence Fund' now succeeded in acquiring White Cross funding and simultaneously requested funding from the Dáil's finance ministry. Believing that such actions were mere attempts at propaganda coups, however, the response of Griffith's cabinet was to refuse requests for Dáil funding (an offer of money from McGarrity was also rejected), seek to have the 'White Cross money allocated' elsewhere, or 'failing this, the matter be exposed'.[57]

If such resolutions perhaps betrayed some of Griffith's deep-seated journalistic instincts in defending his own corner, they were inherently justified according to the reports being received from Richard Mulcahy, the defence minister.

Contrary to popular belief, it had always been Mulcahy, never Michael Collins of the IRB,[58] who had been and was still in charge of the Irish Volunteers and determined all matters relating to 'the army'. His reports to Griffith's cabinet were of such a nature, however, that Griffith could be forgiven for making knee-jerk reactions. For instance, on 10 April, Mulcahy announced dramatically that 'a definite military policy was in operation … by irregular troops'.[59] Three days later, however, Mulcahy reported contradictorily that 'the military situation is well in hand'. Shortly thereafter he suggested that perhaps matters should be let run their own course, presumably without any direction from the ministry of defence whatsoever.[60] An added complication here was that the matters of White Cross relief, policing and 'the army' all fed into concerns regarding the situation in Ulster, where the Belfast boycott continued to be a matter that both pressurised the Dáil and remained totally outside of its own control.

It should not be forgotten that the Dáil had never supported the boycott of Belfast businesses, which originated with local Belfast politicians.[61] It was only because this boycott campaign was launched and sustained regardless of the Dáil's wishes that the Dáil thereafter appointed a junior minister to supervise the matter, as it could not afford to be seen to be completely indifferent to a disruptive social situation of such great public concern. The Dáil's boycott official neither could nor did do anything more than report on the matter, however. This was true of both Griffith's initial appointee (Michael Staines, who resumed this responsibility in 1922) and DeValera's appointee during 1921, Joseph McDonagh. The latter, a supporter of the idea of industrial cooperatives, actually came up with proactive plans to resolve the situation in Belfast in a purely economic manner, but these were completely ignored by DeValera's cabinet because non-interference in the north was considered a given.[62] This reflected the deep irony of the inclusion of the Belfast boycott in the discussions between Craig and Collins in both January and March 1922. While the outcome of these meetings were reported in the press as if it was in the Dáil's or Stormont's power to make or break the boycott (Craig and Collins 'agreed' that it should stop),[63] the boycott continued regardless simply because its directors determined that it should. Neither Craig nor Collins ever had any authority in this matter. The logic of the Belfast boycott was simply the wish of the private sector in Ireland to enforce partition and, in particular, the logic of the Government of Ireland Act, whereby no Irish parliament could have any authority over the economy. Cosgrave, who was in a position to know about such matters, was absolutely certain that it was 'so-called businessmen' who opposed the Dáil that deliberately encouraged such social and economic disorder in Ireland in order to persuade others, by bribes or otherwise, to likewise oppose the idea of an Irish parliament ever having directive powers.[64] This was the surest way of destroying the promise inherent in 'the treaty'. Public acceptance of the formation of the IRA Organisation as a trade union for Irish Volunteers also reflected this trend of opinion regarding labour politics in Ireland, which Childers also encouraged.

From the spring of 1922 onwards, the Belfast boycott committee issued requests to the Dáil for financial compensation for its activists as well as direct army involvement in the north.[65] Neither of these things either could be or ever were offered, however. Mulcahy proposed that the best that could be done was to send a team of journalists to Belfast to launch a counter-balancing propaganda campaign (this proposal was dismissed), while Collins believed the large number of Catholic workers being forced south could possibly be accommodated in abandoned workhouses along the border.[66] This was as much as could be done. As in the case of railway and docklands strikes, the Dáil had no authority in such matters. Dáil appeals to the Labour Party for assistance regarding the strikes were rejected. The Labour Party also refused to have anything to do with the Provisional Government.[67] This was a probable indication that both business and labour leaders in Ireland had no real time for the Dáil and simply wished for the return of pre-1919 political circumstances (the end of the Sinn Féin 'Irish nationalist dictatorship'), as well as the consolidation of both the Government of Ireland Act 1920 and the economic bases of the Union, as soon as was possible.

In response to repeated demands by the Belfast boycott committee for Dáil support for its activities, Griffith's cabinet did meet some of its representatives on 21 March. On this occasion, the Belfast delegation produced an intelligence communication received from Art O'Brien in London regarding an alleged plot of the British army for the complete re-conquest of Ireland through Belfast. This was meant to incite the Dáil into attacking the north and so effectively commit a political suicide.[68] Churchill was making provocative noises about the Ulster boycott as well. This persuaded Griffith during late March that Mulcahy's prior idea of launching a publicity campaign regarding the situation in Ulster, advertising issues such as 'the excessive numbers of British troops in the North East', 'the financing of the Specials' and 'the bona-fides of the British Government in carrying out the terms of the treaty' (in particular, in the matter of keeping the peace) *might* be given support, but no action regarding the situation must be taken 'until after the passing of the Irish Free State Bill through the British House of Lords'.[69] It would be too risky to do otherwise before such an eventuality.

When Collins and Craig signed Churchill's so-called 'peace pact' in London on 30 March, Griffith had considered that this removed the burden from the Dáil of having to deal with the northern situation, while 'time must be given to see if that agreement will be honoured'.[70] Northern and Southern Ireland had not been at each other's throats during the recent political conflicts, however, nor had Collins and Craig ever been at 'war'. Instead, disturbances had simply been engineered to incite public opinion as much as possible and so limit the likelihood of 'the passing of the Irish Free State Bill through the House of Lords' from ever occurring. Cope would claim that this was 'the work of hooligans on both sides' of the border rather than official government forces, north or south,[71] although it undoubtedly had financial support from more powerful figures than mere street-corner 'hooligans'. It may well have had support from Dublin Castle itself or else disgruntled British military figures.

If not exactly popular, Griffith was progressively earning much respect in Ireland at this time by keeping a steady head and promoting strictly responsible actions, despite much provocation.[72] Initial moves to create the basis of a Free State civil service were supposed to be facilitated by London during April 1922. Not surprisingly, this was to begin in the all-important matter of finance. A spirit of cooperation or progress was difficult to maintain, however. For instance, Joseph Brennan, London's transfer to the finance department of the Provisional Government, embarrassed Michael Collins (and undermined greatly his old support networks) by instigating legal proceedings (in Collins' name, both as Chairman of the Provisional Government and the Dáil's finance minister) against Art O'Brien for not summarily surrendering all the Dáil funds that he held. Although Griffith's cabinet had already expressed a desire to replace O'Brien in London, this was an unpopular move that almost persuaded George Gavan Duffy, a long-term friend of O'Brien, to resign from the Dáil cabinet in protest.[73] It made absolutely no allowance for the fact that O'Brien, like many an anti-treatyite, evidently wanted to be sure that the Irish Free State, with a constitution representing genuine autonomy (it was not generally believed that this could ever be achieved), would first be established before allowing Dublin access to such resources. Collins himself evidently believed, or at least desired, that these matters could be settled amicably over time, through personal consultation, without resorting to such legal threats.[74] The action of civil servants in such matters was perfectly understandable, however.

An Anglo-Irish political conflict, as well as a conflict in political cultures, had long been sustained by the fact that, under the Union, the Irish could never receive whatever government they might be said to have voted for, or to ever enter a government except perhaps as a purely individual (non-party) constituent (this being the option that Carson and Craig took during the First World War). In contrast to British politicians, therefore, Irish politicians had no direct experience of government or of working closely with civil servants. The Irish Party–Dublin Castle alliance established during 1886 was nominally supposed to moderate this trend by introducing party-politics into the making of civil service appointments, although this merely served to further corrupt an already unrepresentative model of government. After 1918 the perception still existed among British government officials that Irish politicians inherently constituted 'a colourful crew', who somewhat humorously chose as 'their "leaders" …. [a] gallant, proud, mad, collection of gangsters, poets, patriots, bigots, adventurers, opportunists and political schemers', little or none of whom supposedly knew what governance, nationhood or independence actually meant.[75] Specifically during 1922, a significant factor in augmenting this conflict in perspectives was that while many Irish politicians focused on the goal of achieving an ideal constitution, British civil servants invariably focused on blunt actualities of administration. For instance, Griffith hoped during April 1922 to be able to settle the matter of establishing an autonomous customs and excise office in Dublin for the proposed Free State, but the secretary of the department of customs and excise in London wrote that, administratively, much needed to take place before the formation of a Dublin office could even begin.[76] London was not satisfied that Irishmen could run a civil service.

Churchill was not particularly impressed by the Dáil's evident willingness to allow a professedly anti-Provisional Government force occupy the Four Courts. However, he did not demand action against such men. This was because the Four Courts 'IRA' officers in question all had legal representation from respected Kings' Councillors regarding their salary claims.[77] Rather, Churchill's immediate response was simply to request that the efforts being made to establish new forces of law and order in Ireland would begin to be addressed in a more realistic, administrative manner. Hence, on 2 May 1922, Churchill wrote to Cope at Dublin Castle that

> You should do everything in your power to persuade Mr. Collins to draw arms from the British Government [the British forces to be withdrawn from Ireland],[78] which has a large surplus … There is, of course, no power to prevent the Provisional Government making purchases abroad, or in England if they insist on doing so … but only after you are assured that these weapons will pass directly into the hands of the Provisional Government and not be snapped up on the way. If it is decided to insist on this importation, report to me what [transport] arrangements are being made.[79]

Churchill's report, while realistic in an administrative sense, also reflected the reality that the whole matter of the withdrawal of past forces and instigation of new ones had not progressed very far. As late as May 1922, for instance, Midleton and the Earl of Cavan (chairman of the British cabinet's defence subcommittee for all Ireland) managed to ensure that there were still four British battalions in Cork, who were due to be relocated to Ulster.[80] The placing of the finance department of the Provisional Government on sounder terms during April would facilitate such options as Churchill suggested. However, Collins would prioritise instead the issue of negotiating with Boland and others for maximising a unity of purpose amongst TDs and Irish Volunteers. This was not necessarily the best practical option, and it led to the 'faction fight between two letters of the alphabet' becoming the focus of attention once more.

Ever since Boland had taken his unusual initiative, the IRB was progressively manoeuvred into being revived as an organisation with a view to virtually acting as a trade union for all volunteer officers and, in turn, securing 'army unity'. Some Dáil cabinet members, such as Kevin O'Higgins, naturally realised that this was a potentially problematic development because armies do not have their own trade unions. However, on a purely political level (as cabinet minutes show), Griffith welcomed anything that might resolve inner conflicts in the volunteers.[81] Collins was reported in early May to have been 'quite cheerful and feels pretty confident' about the success of old IRB networks in resolving difficulties (Kathleen Clarke played a key part in this).[82] Boland also felt that the goal of army unity had been virtually achieved, and so 'am quite happy with the present situation':

> The whole game is now in the hands of Mr. Collins. We shall see how he will act. I, for one, would like to think that he will direct all his actions towards the Republic. I cannot say that I doubt him; yet I am uneasy as to his intentions. Our only safeguard is the Army and I am happy, indeed, to report that unity has been secured and in so far as it was possible to safeguard the Republic we have succeeded. As a result of the union I will be in a position to secure the return of the money given the IRA. I will have it lodged in the name of the two members of the SC [IRB Supreme Council] pending a convention, after which I will hand it over to the new SC. I am very proud of the fact that the Clan money saved the situation and am sorry that there should have been any uneasiness amongst the members of the Executive as to my disposal of the money.[83]

Dublin Castle 'took Collins to task' regarding his willingness at this time (early May) to speak publicly about the treaty being a 'stepping stone' to a republic. Regarding this, Cope noted that

> He [Collins] said that he has faith in the treaty and that when it gets going the people will be satisfied with it. He says that everyone

must agree that Ireland is nearer a Republic than she was before the treaty and in that respect the treaty is a stepping-stone. But he is not out for a Republic any more than Smuts is. If having worked for the treaty the Irish people wants a Republic then the position would have to be dealt with. He says ... that no one can place a limit to the march of a nation and that the leaders of all countries stand in the same position. And so on. He thinks that some of us are misrepresenting his intentions or do not appreciate his difficulties sufficiently ... [Regarding the Irish constitution] I am not sure that the King's Representative will get a very prominent place in it ... [but] don't get alarmed.[84]

The essence of the difference between Collins and Boland as the two rival IRB leaders was the former's emphasis on the potential of political evolution to satisfy republicans and the latter's almost instinctual judgment that 'our only safeguard is the army'. They both assumed that the IRB Supreme Council, as the republican–Sinn Féin element to the Irish Volunteer movement ever since 1913,[85] was the ideal vehicle for managing the concerns of soldiers of republican sympathies. However, some segments of the volunteer movement now viewed 'the IRA' not as a nickname (certainly not for an IRB 'rank and file', although that was an origin of the nickname) but as an institution in itself and so resented the very existence of the IRB; a secret organisation with a dubious anticlerical reputation to many Catholics. The relationship between Boland and Collins also reflected conflicting priorities in the history of recent Irish republicanism.

Boland had a strong sense of family tradition. He was proud that, in his own words, his father James, a Dublin IRB leader in Parnell's days, was a man who 'had to ... fly away because he believed in a Republic' and whose mother was a cousin of Thomas Kelly, a Galway-born American soldier whose claim to fame was to depose James Stephens, who opposed any futile attempts at insurrection, and force an abortive attempt at an IRB rebellion to take place in 1867.[86] Boland was proud of these facts, but they reflected a legacy of hare-brained attempts at conspiracies that proved only counterproductive; the negative legacy of which had earned the republican underground the (partly justifiable) reputation of being a tool of the British secret service and inspired, at the request of the Catholic hierarchy in Ireland, the Vatican to declare, as part of the church's official teachings, that the 'American or Irish society called Fenians' must be denounced alongside 'those sects called Freemasons, Carbonari or any other kinds of sects which either openly or privately plot against the Church or legitimately constituted authorities'.[87]

Collins had not the same political lineage as Boland, although his close friendship with Moya O'Connor Davies, the daughter of the founder of the IRB Supreme Council in 1868 and niece of the IRB leader in Parnell's days, was a factor that brought him into the republican fold.[88] The IRB's Proclamation of the Irish Republic (written when less than ten per cent of adult males had a right to vote), a founding charter of the IRB Supreme Council, had set a tone for subsequent Irish radicalism in Parnell's days:

> We have suffered centuries of outrage, enforced poverty and bitter misery. Our rights and liberties have been trampled on by an alien aristocracy who treated us as foes, usurped our lands and drew away from our unfortunate country all material riches … The real owners of the soil was removed to make room for cattle … while our men of thought and action were condemned to loss of life and liberty … All men are born with equal rights … We therefore declare that, unable longer to endure the curse of monarchical government, we aim at founding a republic, based on universal suffrage, which shall secure to all the intrinsic value of their labour … We declare also in favour of absolute liberty of conscience and the complete separation of Church and State … We intend no war against the people of England; our war is against the aristocratic locusts, whether English or Irish … Republicans of the entire world, our cause is your cause. Our enemy is your enemy. Let your hearts be with us. As for you, workmen of England … avenge yourselves by giving liberty to your children in the coming struggle for human freedom. Herewith we proclaim the Irish Republic.[89]

Between the disestablishment of the Church of Ireland in 1869 and the accession of Edward VII in 1901, Irish republicans had helped launch many initiatives—the world's first-ever amnesty movement, the cultural nationalist Gaelic Athletics Association and the Young Ireland Society (the progenitor of the Anglo-Irish literary movement), the Irish National Land League, the political organisation of the Irish in Britain and the Irish Parliamentary Party. However, the ultimate net result for Ireland from British politics during this period had been a slight Irish deviation from the UK-wide land law reforms (this would see Irish land purchase agreements whereby a fraction of Irish revenue was re-offered to the country as long-term loans at high interest rates) and the survival of a demoralised Irish Party that was almost wholly dependent on their one influential ally in government circles (T.P. O'Connor), whose only ultimate return investment in Ireland was the importation of Irish editions of those newspapers he had founded for the working classes in northern England, *The Sun* and *The Star*.[90] The rise of the Irish–Ireland movement during the Edwardian era reflected the resulting disenchantment.

The effort on 24 April 1916 by the last surviving remnants of the IRB (Tom Clarke and Sean MacDermott) to occupy the General Post Office in Dublin—an institution which was managed by Moya O'Connor Davies' Welsh husband—in order to issue a fresh republican proclamation to the Irish public was welcomed by Michael Collins who, having initially entered politics to overthrow the political leadership of T.P. O'Connor (a future Labour privy councillor) over the Irish in Britain, sought in the wake of the treaty agreement to combine the appeal of the Irish–Ireland movement with the Irish republican tradition of thought in *The Path to Freedom* (Dublin, 1922). As Griffith's finance minister, Collins championed Griffith's ideal that 'the keynote to the economic revival must be development of Irish resources by Irish capital for the benefit of the Irish consumer' and the repatriation of Ireland's financial assets abroad.[91] He also argued, in light of the republican perception that 'slavery still exists … today in Ireland', that

> The complete fulfilment of our full national freedom can … only be won when we are 'fit and willing' to win it. Can we claim that we are yet fit and willing? Is not our country still filled with men and women who are unfit and unwilling? Are we all yet educated to be free?[92]

P.S. O'Hegarty maintained that, in seeking to resolve the army dispute with Boland, Collins successfully championed similar ideas to restore unity and sustain confidence in the idea that all Ireland's political problems, including potentially partition, could be resolved by the assumption of regulatory authorities by an Irish government under the treaty agreement.[93] Boland's surviving correspondence presents a different picture, however. While Boland did not appreciate the tendency of much anti-treaty propaganda to attempt to make a scapegoat of Griffith ('damn it, hasn't Griffith made us all!'),[94] his reaction to seeing a draft to the proposed Irish constitution (this occurred in late June) was outright hostility for one reason alone, namely a belief that the inclusion of monarchical paraphernalia would serve to 'disenfranchise republicans':

> The constitution of the Irish Free State is worse than the Treaty … Those who will continue the fight for the republic will have a harder task than those who have preceded them, as any effort to gain the

independence of Ireland will be treason against the constitution of the country[95] ... AG [Griffith] said the constitution was evidently all that Mick [Collins] wished it to be, namely: an instrument that could be accepted by republicans without dishonour to their principles ... [but] the British ... in the meantime had handed the Irish Constitution over to their experts to work their will upon it and make Ireland safe for the Empire. How well the British succeeded the enclosed 'Irish Constitution' will show ... The best men and women in the land are defeated ... Mr Collins can have a parliament of suckers who will only too happy to swear oaths as King George may require [but] ... I feel like 2 cents ... God alone knows what the outcome will be ... I can't understand the minds of Mick and Griffith ... I will end this hurried letter with the hope that you will not be discouraged by the story it tells. Keep the Organisation [IRB] intact.[96]

Griffith's paramount concern with achieving fiscal autonomy for Ireland, i.e. real independence, was essentially the motive behind all his actions. For many contemporaries, however, this evidently mattered less than the issue of what form the Irish constitution would take on paper. It was largely for this reason that the occupation of the Four Courts was viewed (and even respected) by many Irish contemporaries not as a mere demand for the payment of volunteer salaries (which it essentially was), but as a symbolical representation of the need for Irish politicians to hold firm on the question of the constitution. As a general election approached, however, the belief grew that republicans and their obsession with perfect written constitutions should no longer have the right to delay the settlement of Irish political difficulties. This was less Griffith's concern, however, than the issue of the need to keep Dáil Eireann, not the Four Courts or indeed any other authority, as the locus for all Irish political developments.

In preparation for the intended attendance of anti-treaty deputies at the Dáil on 26 April, Griffith supported the idea of a public plebiscite on the issue of the constitution being launched but 'the offer of a plebiscite and two further offers of election' was 'refused by Mr DeValera'.[97] As it was Mulcahy rather than Collins who managed the issue of army unity, cabinet minutes present a very different picture of the issue of army unity negotiations than IRB correspondence indicates. Griffith himself favoured the idea that the Dáil cabinet accept 'the reception of a delegation of army officers'.[98] However, when Griffith ruled that 'the army officers who have been in conference on the situation and who wish to address the House be now received', this was overruled by Mulcahy and O'Higgins who wanted the matter to be kept strictly private and not to involve the whole cabinet.[99] Indeed, although what Mulcahy described as a 'truce' between the competing volunteers was agreed,[100] the exact terms of this agreement was evidently not revealed to Griffith's full cabinet. Surviving correspondence of DeValera indicates why this was the case.

Mulcahy judged that Sinn Féin Party unity under DeValera's presidency was necessary to maintain IRA unity. This was the origins of the agreement in mid-May that both pro- and anti-agreement deputies would nominate themselves on the one ticket or 'panel' ('Sinn Féin') in the next general election, which, it was proposed, would be held in mid-June. Due to their mutual reliance upon IRB circles, Collins, and particularly Boland, liked to think of themselves as the authors of this unity scheme (sometimes referred to by journalists as the Collins–DeValera pact) but this was not the case. DeValera himself claimed that the pact was based entirely upon a private understanding reached between himself and Richard Mulcahy, the Dáil's defence minister, that DeValera, as president of Sinn Féin, should henceforth be given complete political authority over the IRA,[101] not Griffith, the Dáil's president or even his cabinet.

Reflecting this trend, one of Churchill's intelligence agents met DeValera in secret in Dublin. He understood that DeValera actually had no interest in the election pact whatsoever, but instead wanted to force the British to engage in direct military intervention in Ireland sometime in the near future to defend the Provisional Government against an IRA under his own nominal command, believing that this was the only way to win greater party political approval for his own anti-treaty stance in the future.[102] If so, this was very irresponsible on DeValera and, indeed, Mulcahy and O'Higgins', part.[103] However, there was a practical dimension to this stance as well.

DeValera's prior action in February, ruling that the funds of the Dáil be kept in the names of the existing trustees (who now stood outside the Dáil) and that 'the new government to be set up in Ireland accept the financial obligations of Dáil Eireann' at a later date,[104] reflected the understanding that, for the treaty agreement to work in any fashion, the Provisional Government *had* to be the fulcrum of development and that the re-institutionalisation of the Dáil upon that basis would soon become necessary. In this sense, the attempts by Griffith and Collins to jealously guard their cabinet's current authority could potentially jeopardise the whole agreement by delaying this process unnecessarily. Indeed, the British Government would soon judge that both Griffith and Collins had been guilty of procrastination and being uncooperative.[105] By contrast, DeValera's efforts to sustain prospective Dáil finances and retain the loyalties of anti-treaty Irish Volunteers in an independent fashion could serve to facilitate a transfer of powers by relieving all prospective Dáil cabinets from the burden of having to play the Boland–Collins game of seeking to retain a party-political (or other) platform that would not turn old friendships into animosities. In effect, these 'brothers in the republic' were valuing personal factors above all else, particularly the realities of administration, and so were not making very wise political decisions.

Griffith did not welcome the panel idea for two reasons. First, he felt that it was practically a negation of the relevance of the Dáil as a parliamentary assembly at the expense of DeValera and Childers' strategy in manipulating the Sinn Féin Party. Second, he resented the fact that the agreement was presented to him virtually as a *fait accompli*. He did not know about its provenance and played no part in its establishment. His wife's assertion that he felt that Collins had betrayed the cabinet in making the pact agreement behind his back would indicate that Griffith knew little more about the matter than what the newspapers were saying.[106] Griffith did not believe the panel idea was necessary for 'army unity' and was confident that the army did not present an insurmountable problem. This was because he believed that there was absolutely no public will in Ireland for violent conflict of any kind, certainly not purely for the sake of a choice of wording in a parliamentary oath; an oath that politicians would have to take before performing, in either case, the *exact same* responsibilities of government: 'If the Irish people say … fight for that, I would say to them that they were fools but I will stay in the ranks. But the Irish people will not do that.'[107]

What this perspective of Griffith's essentially ignored, however, was that the issue of the oath had the potential to create conflict less because of the choices facing parliamentarians than the choice facing Ireland's prospective defence forces. Many prospective members of such forces were not prepared to swear allegiance to an authority that could not pay their salaries and was in danger of going up in smoke. The willingness of the men in the Four Courts to rely on the Crown lawyers to defend their case reflected the fact that the sooner that the Dáil and its courts were disbanded, the better were the chances of the Four Courts men receiving redress of their grievances; a fact that may explain their willingness to toy with the idea of encouraging the British to engage in direct military intervention in Ireland in the near future with a view to reasserting Dublin Castle's authority.[108]

In public, Griffith argued that 'there had been no personal ill-feeling' between DeValera, Collins and himself. One of his reactions to the pact proposal was to suggest that it might refocus minds of the question of the partition of the island. In this matter, Griffith re-emphasised his belief that all 'wanted to get the present Unionists of Ulster for a United Ireland'. Griffith believed 'that could be done', but 'if it could not be done, they were not going to coerce them':

All he asked of his colleagues and comrades was this—that they accept, whatever their principles and views might be, the expressed views of the Irish people, and whilst holding to their own views, not to do anything to obstruct those who decided to go by a different path to achieve the same result. I want unity in Ireland but I also want peace with England.[109]

Panel or no panel, Griffith also felt justified in continuing to voice his beliefs regarding the socio-economic basis of the emerging two rival parties in nationalist Ireland.

Speaking at Dundalk in preparation for the general election, Griffith once again compared the tactics of DeValera's party to those formerly adopted by Redmond's party. This was to refuse to take any actions that might upset the British financial establishment, letting other parties (principally the Church and the unionists) do all the political thinking for them and proverbially knock on the head anyone who disagreed with this consensus regarding the dynamics of Irish public life. Griffith repeated that he had 'fought against the late Irish Party for years' because 'no politicians, no body that the people elected and gave their confidence and help to, had a right to turn around and dictate to them their business'. Their claims that the Irish public had no other options open to them were always false, Griffith believed. In particular, if unionist party-political restrictions stemming from imperial parliament majorities, combined with unnatural monopolies of power within Ireland itself (represented by the highly centralised nature of the Dublin Castle government), may have made this trend possible in the past, Griffith emphasised his belief that this would soon no longer be the case. This was because, for the first time in Irish history, 'there is but one sovereign and supreme power in Ireland and that was the people'. As an extension of this fact, 'it was for the people to say whether they would have the treaty or not ... deciding [by election] whether the men who signed the treaty or the men who said that the treaty gave away something were right or not.' Griffith maintained that the Dail's plenipotentiaries 'gave away nothing' on the grounds that they had facilitated Ireland's move from 'being in a subordinate position to England' to one of being 'on equal terms with England'—an unprecedented achievement in Irish history and an unprecedented strength—with a 'chance now of standing on an equal footing with other peoples' as well:

Under the treaty they had signed, they should realise that they stood [i.e. could stand] as a nation amongst the nations of Europe ... they stood free and recognised amongst them; they were masters in their own house ... What was the world going to say to them when they were offered a free opportunity of proving their capacity to govern themselves and a capacity to make good if they were afraid to take the opportunity?

The anti-treaty party, Griffith maintained, was daunted by the fact that Ireland 'had 150,000 unemployed at the present time' and simply did not believe that Irish nationalists would be able to assume the right to direct the country's financial institutions, rather than the unionists. This was why, in their desire to shirk the challenge of getting the country on its feet economically, they were also attempting 'to humbug the people' by stating that what they must do was 'to go on with the fight' militarily, when they all knew that what this actually meant was the Dáil losing all its current powers in the process.[110]

In contrast to Griffith, the British cabinet was inclined to view the panel idea (the attempt to hold an 'agreed election' with no contests, although this had been the nature of most general elections held in Ireland ever since 1886) as an attack on southern unionists, which might be said to have included the old Irish Party and labour. Regarding this, Churchill noted that

> It seems to me absolutely necessary to tell Griffith on Monday that we will have nothing to do with such a farce, nor will we pass any act of parliament creating the Free State or according a permanent status to the Irish Government on such a basis. We cannot consider that the Treaty is being fulfilled unless the Irish people have a full free opportunity to express their opinion.[111]

In the light of his own opposition to the panel idea, Griffith certainly did not need to have this explained to him.

The reaction of James Craig, who always kept a weather eye on Dublin opinion, to the proposed 'election pact' is worth noting. He had to take an interest in this matter because the date for elections—both north and south—still had to be agreed with Dublin by the 'cooperation of cabinets'.[112] His own cabinet believed that 'the proclamation of the IRA and IRB' as illegal organisations would facilitate the abandonment of the panel arrangement and, in turn, the possibility of Dublin–Belfast talks (under the supervision of London), although he remained firmly opposed to the Boundary Commission idea being a subject of discussion because this was an impractical programme.[113] This latter view may be seen as evidence that Craig was a considerably more sensible, or honest, politician than Sir Edward Carson of Dublin or John Redmond had ever been: religious demographics were not the basis of partition. London's financial management of Ireland was the determinant.

Many people in the south actually had a similar perspective to Craig specifically with regards to the election pact. This was due to the fact that 'people are afraid to make their views known to each other' for fear of being attacked by 'so called IRA soldiers' if they spoke in public; a fact that led them to judge that 'this Free State Government [which was not yet in existence] seems to have no power' to protect their right to free speech.[114] This might be said to have been an unfortunate side product of the obsession of Sinn Féin politicians with 'army unity'. This seemingly not only made 'the IRA' the most important issue, but also made it possible for it to claim to be the *only* important issue in Irish life at this time or, at least, convince themselves of that idea, for at least so long as the opera at the Four Courts continued.

The minutes of Griffith's cabinet partly indicate why this situation was essentially allowed to come about. Notwithstanding Griffith's distaste for the election pact idea, his cabinet had been holding out, to some degree, in favour of the idea of some anti-treatyites (who professed to be incredulous that the Provisional Government was not currently carrying out 'all executive functions') of establishing a coalition government of pro and anti-treaty parties. This was to be based on a common understanding that the Dáil 'is the supreme governing authority in Ireland ... derived solely from the people of Ireland'. This idea of a coalition was made impracticable, however, by the demand of anti-treatyites that they should have an equal right not only in the determination of the appointment of government personnel (an idea tolerable to Griffith's cabinet) but also *sole* right in the matter of appointing defence personnel (this was deemed impossible).[115] In this debate, DeValera's anti-treaty party were guilty of confused thinking. DeValera and his followers claimed that revising the constitution of the Dáil, which was a parliamentary assembly, would be tantamount to revising the constitution of the Irish state.[116] These were separate matters, however. A constitution for the state was only in the process of being drafted for the first time.

Griffith reported that the idea of a coalition government had broken down by mid-May. Some pro-treaty TDs, such as Joseph McGuinness, still felt that the election panel idea would actually symbolise 'the indefensible right of the Irish people to free election' as 'every or any interest is free to go up and contest the election against the National panel'.[117] While Griffith expected the panel and coalition government ideas 'would lose us the confidence of people' and Mulcahy was certain that such a coalition 'would not be favourable to our relations with England', Collins reported that after discussing the matter with DeValera that he also 'does not think much will come out of it' as 'DeValera would not agree' with its principle either.[118] This raises the question of why did the panel idea ever receive a nominal public approval by TDs at all?

Mulcahy's advice as defence minister was once again evidently the key determinant. The belief that it was the 'position in [the] north', over which the Dáil exercised no control, that was 'largely responsible for [the] situation in South' of increasing political disorder among volunteers ('mutiny conditions') sustained the idea that some extraordinary measures were needed to restore order. Upon this basis, it was judged 'that [the] pact makes for military unity and control'.[119] Equally, however, this pact was something to uphold only in 'the spirit in which [it] was made' for as long as was necessary.[120] In terms of strategy, the Dáil cabinet made a poor decision on 24 May, which was directly contrary to Griffith's strategy hitherto but in keeping with Mulcahy's sense of political situation. It was decided that publicity was needed 'to explain origins of situation—use of military by civic power against Catholics' in Northern Ireland and that the proactive action of launching a 'press campaign in Ulster' was needed.[121] This provoked a very confrontational response from Churchill that soon led matters to spiral out of control.

Lloyd George privately felt that the willingness of Henry Wilson of Longford, an old friend of Midleton, Churchill and the Earl of Cavan, to provoke civil unrest in Ulster ever since February 1922 purely to destabilise the Irish political situation was no longer either a cost-effective or a productive strategy. For this reason, both the British Prime Minister and his acting cabinet secretary believed that it would soon become necessary to forcibly remove Wilson from the scene, placing the direction of the British army in Ulster under less partisan control, as Wilson was doing all in his (considerable) power 'to embroil *us* on their side against the South and get us back into a pre-treaty situation. This is incidentally playing DeValera's game too.'[122] As the British cabinet wanted to avoid the expense of sending troops into Ireland at all costs and was not prepared to let Wilson force them to do so, in addition to removing Wilson from the scene it was decided to try to force Collins, one way or another, to abandon his goal of army unity in the south.[123] This was attempted by adopting a particularly hostile attitude to Dublin regarding the proposed constitution of the Irish Free State.

On 1 June, Lloyd George wrote a very hostile letter to Griffith in which he argued that the Irish constitution he had submitted was solely responsible for creating a 'very grave situation' that was 'wholly inconsistent with the Treaty'. He maintained that Griffith had failed to understand that the rights he was claiming for Ireland to develop its 'own ideals of political, economic and social welfare' was something to which Ireland was not inherently entitled, as the dominions' rights in these matters was 'not based on theory but on experience';

namely, the degree to which Whitehall had first judged that it was in everyone's best economic interests (primarily, the United Kingdom of Great Britain and Northern Ireland) that they begin to exercise these powers. For this reason, the British Prime Minister claimed that he was now entirely justified in demanding any alterations to the Irish constitution that he felt necessary and that Griffith, having signed the agreement, was obliged to comply with all his demands.[124]

Griffith replied that the British Prime Minister was totally mistaken. He emphasised the fact that when a draft of the constitution, 'in all substantial particulars in the form now presented', was presented in the first week of March, no Crown official had objected to it. For this reason, Griffith argued that the British cabinet was clearly allowing itself to be unduly influenced in their attitudes by recent political disturbances, or 'the atmosphere which seems to have gathered from the course of events'. He maintained that it was 'perfectly clear' that the Dáil had acted fully within its rights under the Articles of Agreement in fashioning the constitution as it stood. Furthermore, if any claim were ever to be made otherwise by London, legal proof would have to be offered in defence of this claim.[125]

Griffith was correct that the British cabinet was being disingenuous in protesting about the proposed Irish constitution. As the British cabinet secretary noted, the Free State constitution presented no 'insurmountable difficulty'. The 'more serious trouble' related to Wilson, the British army in Ulster and the attempt of southern unionists to force British military intervention in Ireland as their favoured means of protecting their own economic hegemony.[126] The latter issue had become of immediate importance to Midleton's circle. This was because it was on 27 May 1922 that the (nominal) legal entity of Parliament of Southern Ireland officially ceased to exist. This meant that the Provisional Government, under Collins, now officially had the legal right to recognise and establish a parliament for the proposed Irish Free State. This, of course, would be Dáil Eireann.[127] Reflecting this, Dáil Eireann was already being referred to as 'the provisional parliament [of the Irish Free State]' by such time as a proposed constitution of the Irish Free State, which was yet to be formally accepted by Westminster, was published in June.[128]

Griffith and Collins were brought to a Downing Street conference on 31 May, the same day as the Royal Ulster Constabulary was officially established, and were unjustly held accountable, on southern unionists' advice to London, for recent disturbances in Belfast. The Earl of Midleton, who (almost secretly) retained British battalions in Cork, and J.K. Bernard, the provost of Trinity College Dublin, both judged that Collins had not 'kept faith' to his responsibilities as chairman of the Provisional Government. This reflected their realistic fears that Collins intended the Dáil to be a more powerful institution than the Parliament of Southern Ireland under the Government of Ireland Act. They protested to Churchill that Collins 'intended this all along' and thus was untrustworthy. By contrast, Griffith was considered to have been 'honest in his attention' to any issues they might ever have raised, although he was considered unimportant because he occupied the supposedly meaningless position as president of the Dáil.[129]

The significance of this body of southern unionist opinion (which also directed all the banks in Ireland, which straddled both jurisdictions) in determining British government policy in Ireland, north and south, should not be underestimated. Just as Sir Henry Wilson, the director of local defence in Northern Ireland, had been a relocation from Longford (his birthplace), it was the Earl of Cavan, not any 'Northern Irish' figure, who chaired the British cabinet's secret defence subcommittee on (all) Ireland.[130] Not surprisingly, both Griffith and Collins denied having any responsibility for recent disturbances in Northern Ireland. However, Churchill told Collins that he had secret information (allegedly from Mulcahy's general army headquarters at Beggars Bush, Dublin) that 'the IRA' was responsible for all outrages in Ireland and Northern Ireland in particular; that Collins himself had no authority over the army; and that 'there can be no question of any enquiry [being made by Griffith and Collins] into those operations which have been carried out by the military command at the express order of Her Majesty's Government'.[131]

At the request of his southern unionist Irish friends, Churchill was clearly attempting to force a confrontation. On 4 June, on the basis of an alleged 'IRA' attack in County Fermanagh, the British army actually crossed the border of Northern Ireland to occupy the town of Pettigo, County Donegal. As the leader of the Dáil Eireann government, Griffith issued protests regarding this. The facts Griffith presented in defence of his case (i.e. absolutely no Irish involvement in such border instances) were deemed correct by no less a British military authority than General Macready.[132] This may well explain why the British Prime Minister was growing anxious.

On 8 June, Lloyd George wrote a long letter to Churchill pleading him 'not to be tempted' by 'precipitous action, however alluring the prospect may be' in attempting to achieve their desired political settlement in Ireland. The Prime Minister believed it was not fair to Dublin for Churchill to continue to support Henry Wilson's false claims that the Dáil was behind any outrages committed within Northern Ireland. These irresponsible actions were motivated only by Wilson's belief that the survival of Northern Ireland was dependent entirely on military rather than political or economic factors (Craig's non-existent policing budget essentially explained his willingness to tolerate Wilson's political attitudes in this regard).[133] Churchill held firm, however, for one particular reason. Cope was advising him that his personal threats to Collins, both on 31 May and subsequently, were starting to have their desired affect. Collins now feared that 'the firing of a single shot by an irresponsible would have most serious results' and feeling that he had absolutely no control over the situation, was more ready to look to Churchill for a solution.[134] On learning this, Lloyd George would also throw his weight behind Churchill's strategy. This may have partly motivated by the fact that his political survival was now in question (he would resign as Prime Minister in October). Lloyd George's former status as a radical meant that, in the post-war political world, 'the man who had won the war' (as he was formerly known) was destined to be sidelined to the political wilderness and labelled as a 'great outsider' because his willingness to promote American financial investment in Britain would turn Churchill, an absolute opponent of this idea, into that national icon which, at least temporarily, Lloyd George had formerly appeared to be.[135]

Griffith was also feeling the pressure. The decision of Griffith's cabinet to take a firm stand regarding the northern situation and to publish a 'skeleton constitution' (London was insisting that this would be done before any general election) was motivated by a determination to prove that the Irish had kept to their side of the bargain, not only regarding the treaty agreement but also with regards to the preceding truce ('the situation [is the] same of July last').[136] However, the cabinet was also showing signs of crumbling under increasing pressures to the point of actual serious division.

Although all agreed that 'no troops of any kind to be sent into N.E.' and Griffith and others felt that the Pettigo incident was essentially an attack on the Irish state, Mulcahy's still often contradictory defence communications, based on an unknown intelligence, now somehow seemed to substantiate British claims of ambivalent Irish intentions: 'we are approaching army unity in the south', 'border war started by irregulars', 'must secure withdrawal of irregulars'.[137] Griffith now started taking a much firmer line against Mulcahy regarding what the latter termed as his ongoing work with 'the irregulars'. He was showing signs of being DeValera's stooge. When Mulcahy read news about agreements being reached regarding army unification—how many such 'agreements' were necessary?—Griffith now objected to a 'majority on the other side of army council' being granted special favour by Mulcahy, as this amounted to a surrender of parliamentary control.[138] While Mulcahy claimed that this was 'a temporary settlement', Griffith now demanded that there must be a definite undertaking by all army personnel on all sides 'not to turn arms against people', 'to support any government elected by people' and to recognise that 'if any attempt made to interfere with independent candidates [normal electoral and governmental procedure] our full military strength to be employed'.[139] If the Dáil surrendered its claim to control over the army, it would be surrendering its right to survival as a parliamentary government.

Mulcahy continued to pursue a very strange course of action, however. Indeed, during Griffith's subsequent absence in London on the matter of the constitution,[140] actions were taken as if the Dáil cabinet was now suddenly bent on self-destruction. At cabinet meetings of 9–12 June, Mulcahy actually reported that he was in favour of organising 'incendiary attacks' in Belfast and that he had the agreement of the Four Courts men in this matter. He would also postpone further army unity negotiations until 'after [a] coalition [government]' was first formed.[141] This was tantamount to a rejection of the entire policy of the Dáil hitherto, which had been nothing if not consistent. As a result, Gavan Duffy professed a willingness to resign from the government. In the light of DeValera's claim to authority (via Mulcahy) over 'the IRA', Mulcahy's actions at this time also seemed to substantiate the British Prime Minister's judgement regarding the entire Pettigo situation that 'Henry Wilson and DeValera are behind this' in desiring to precipitate a conflict that would force the British army to re-establish its authority throughout Ireland.[142] This would have been consistent with the Government of Ireland Act of 1920. However, it was not consistent with the Articles of Agreement for a Treaty, which established the principle of Irish control over policing and defence in Ireland for the first time in modern Irish history.

The publication of a draft constitution at the time of the general election was considered too hurried and inopportune a move by some cabinet members. If what Boland indicated was true, Griffith was not entirely happy about this situation either.[143] It is against this light that the election results of mid-June should be seen. Historians have generally typified this election as having resulted in the return of 58 pro-treaty Sinn Féiners, 36 anti-treaty Sinn Féiners and 34 non-Sinn Féin representatives.[144] As this election was held in the middle of a very confused political situation, however, its results were inherently inconclusive. Furthermore, the very issue of the panel arrangement was proof that the idea touted in Dáil cabinet circles in September 1921—that it should be possible for various political parties to emerge peacefully by the time of the next general election—had not been possible to achieve. Indeed, this would not be essentially possible to achieve for another five years. The reason for this was the very fact that, aside from the question of the ongoing dispute regarding an Irish constitution (none had yet been officially accepted by Westminster), it had not yet been possible to establish a regulatory financial authority in Ireland. Under the circumstances, party politics could inherently have no meaning beyond the level of a single, or common, 'national' platform.

One significant manifestation of this reality was the increasing sense of desperation of Michael Collins, the Dáil's finance minister, regarding the lack of political progress being made. Although he was the politician who held perhaps the greatest responsibility for securing the transfer of powers from the Provisional Government to the 'provisional parliament' of the Irish Free State (Dáil Eireann), his judgment of the entire Irish political situation would soon be summed up in a desperate plea: 'what can we do?'[145]

One of Churchill's secret informants regarding Collins' intentions was Hazel Lavery, the American wife of Sir John Lavery, who introduced himself to Dáil circles by means of New York political organisations during the early stages of DeValera's 1919 American tour (his wife later befriended Collins through first befriending Moya O'Connor Davies).[146] A serious blow for the Dáil in defending itself from the unionist anti-treaty propaganda campaign occurred on 22 June. The British cabinet's decision that Sir Henry Wilson must be removed from the scene 'at all costs'[147] came true: he was shot dead on the streets of London on the very same day as the Dáil had intended opening a new public parliamentary session in Dublin to celebrate the establishment of its authority.[148] Two ex-British soldiers were arrested and blamed for the killings. Lloyd George claimed, however, that they had documents upon them linking them directly with Rory O'Connor's 'IRA' group in the Four Courts, as well as 'IRA' men who were supposedly planning to commit terrorist outrages throughout Britain (in subsequent trials, documents relating to past arson attacks in Britain during the spring of 1921 were produced in support of these claims).[149] The Prime Minister now felt entitled to issue an order to Dublin Castle that Collins, as chairman of the Provisional Government, must remove O'Connor's men from the Four Courts 'without delay' if a Dublin government was ever to be allowed to be established. Lloyd George argued that a mandate had been established to do so after the recent general election results and he emphasised that the British government 'are prepared to place at your disposal the necessary pieces of artillery which may be acquired, or otherwise to assist you as may be arranged'.[150] Simultaneously, Mulcahy began demanding that immediate military action must be taken against Irish soldiers in Clonmel; a call Griffith rejected.[151]

Griffith's response to Lloyd George's action was to call an immediate meeting of the Dáil cabinet. He issued a demand to the British Prime Minister for access to all the documents that he claimed to have regarding the Wilson incident before the Dáil would issue any 'official' (governmental) reply.[152] This call was ignored, however, because the British cabinet had dealt with Griffith hitherto solely because he was chief signatory of the Articles of Agreement: they had never yet officially recognised the Dáil. Meanwhile, Collins himself did not even attend this meeting of the Dáil cabinet. Instead, he withdrew into personal isolation. In response to a call upon him by Lady Lavery to realise that it was 'a time for statesmanship', Collins poured his heart out to her regarding what he saw as the difficulties that he faced. This information, of course, went straight to Churchill:

> Things have been dreadful but with God's help all will not be lost. The latest tragedy is awful. I have prayed this morning—*prayed*—that we may be shown some way out of it all—some way to end the awful happenings. *What can we do?* … Our opinion here is that the men [shooters of Wilson] acted entirely independently. It is said that they are both ex [British] soldiers. What you said in your letter about the 'inevitableness [sic]' is correct … I don't know what I can do now. I keep saying to myself that if they [anti-treatyites] had all met me in the same spirit of peace and cooperation that I met them, that we would win the whole feeling to our side; I felt at the time that they wouldn't and couldn't see where we were drifting to, and now I suppose the outrage and counter-outrage must go on forever … We *are* going to put an end to the Four Courts opera and what it means—if we can't we must face our *own* end. But it is not by force only we can do it. We are stronger after the election—a little only—but we are stronger in that we have got rid of the dual administration business, and that is an immense gain. We can go forward now without being hampered by the catch cries of the old opposition.[153]

In asserting that 'we have got rid of the dual administration business', Collins was evidently referring to the end of the legal existence of the Southern Irish parliament on 27 May 1922 and the resulting emergence of Dáil Eireann as the provisional parliament of the Irish Free State (it had adopted this title on its own headed paper by 26 June).[154] He believed that this meant that the authority of the Dáil to act as *the* government of Ireland was now firmly established. Reflecting this, Collins' response to the British government's call for action against the Four Courts was to officially resign from his responsibility as chairman of the Provisional Government (a less meaningful post in the wake of the disestablishment of the Parliament of Southern Ireland). In doing so, Collins effectively severed his political connection with Dublin Castle, which, as far as the *British* government was concerned, was still the government of Ireland. This was essentially why the Dáil's action at this time would prove so controversial.

While the logic of political events clearly indicated that the Dáil was to become the recognised parliament in Dublin, Westminster had not yet granted it such recognition and would not do so until the political situation in Ireland was deemed satisfactory. Collins' resignation from the Provisional Government was therefore not only premature but also an intolerable, or even an illegal, act as far as London was concerned. Griffith, who never had any connection with the Provisional Government, clearly approved of Collins' strategy and quite probably authored it. Collins requested the approval of Griffith's Dáil alone for his assuming the leadership of whatever armed forces that its defence minister (Richard Mulcahy) could now muster. It was Alfred Cope, the Under Secretary at Dublin Castle, who ordered the British artillery and the Four Courts was bombarded by Emmet Dalton on 28 June. This effectively instigated an armed conflict between an executive-less Provisional Government and anti-treaty forces. Michael Collins, as commander-in-chief of Dáil Eireann's new 'National Army', would seek to end this conflict as quickly as possible by attempting to negotiate a truce purely between this new authority (Dáil Eireann's National Army) and anti-treaty forces, bypassing Dublin Castle and the Provisional Government as much as was possible.[155] This was precisely the rationale Griffith adopted. He issued as many statements as possible stating that the National Army recognised the governmental authority of the Dáil Eireann parliament alone; that both were pledged to recognising the sovereignty of the Irish people; and that Dáil would be ready to reconvene as a public parliamentary assembly in a few weeks time, once this brief and unfortunate conflict had ended.[156] As far as the British government was concerned, however, Griffith was seriously jumping the gun. In doing so, he had prompted Collins to do the same.

DeValera's response to the firing on the Four Courts was to issue a 4 July statement to the Irish diaspora worldwide labelling Griffith and Collins as military dictators.[157] Meanwhile, Churchill expressed delight at the instigation of armed conflict in Dublin. With regards to 'the question of who ordered it', Churchill noted that 'my disclaimer in the House of Commons' should be sufficient to cover Cope and the British administration at Dublin Castle from any criticisms and 'we shall certainly adhere to that position'. Promising Cope a knighthood for his action, Churchill stated that the 'entirely new situation' created by the outbreak of southern Irish hostilities and death of Wilson would relieve the United Kingdom of all responsibility to deal with problems on the island of Ireland and, in turn, allow the British government to concentrate on much more important matters, such as the oil situation in the Middle East.[158]

To Robert Brennan's befuddlement but to his own personal amusement DeValera thereafter engaged in the largely symbolical action of enlisting alongside Childers as a private in the 'anti-treaty IRA' within the Sinn Féin Party's Suffolk Street headquarters.[159] Feeling that he had won his propaganda war, DeValera was essentially satisfied. He had no great desire to become engaged in the troubles that followed but instead essentially adopted the position of waiting for the cessation of a conflict that, as its instigator Alfred Cope (a natural ally of the southern unionists within the Dublin Castle administration) knew only too well, no member of the general Irish public actually wanted.[160] This was not reflected by Erskine Childers' subsequent propaganda war, however.

To try to motivate the anti-treaty IRA Organisation to fight and to justify his own misleading propaganda since 1920 that the Irish question was an entirely military one, Childers founded a publication entitled *Republican War News*. In itself, this title was a complete negation of the peaceful and democratic Irish definition of the republican demand for national self-determination hitherto.

Childers launched an anti-'Griffith and Collins' propaganda campaign immediately upon the firing upon the Four Courts. Aside from attempting to destroy Griffith and Collins' claims that the Dáil and its associated National Army represented the principles of popular sovereignty (this was done not least by claiming that the National Army were merely 'Black and Tans and British soldiers dressed in Free State uniform' and emphasising DeValera's membership of the IRA),[161] Childers claimed in the weeks before Griffith and Collins' deaths that both men really only had the support of *one* body of opinion: the secret society of the IRB. Claiming that 'this war is not a war for the security of the people; it is a war for the supremacy of the IRB', Childers argued that the IRB 'care nothing for the people or its will' and aspired to be 'the only lawful civil government'. Typifying its members as having the mentality of 'a military dictatorship', Childers not only highlighted that the IRB was 'denounced for three generations in the pastorals of the Irish bishops' but also suggested that 'Commandant General Oliver Cromwell' stood in spirit alongside Michael Collins and his 'contemptible soldiers': 'would Christ approve such a party?'[162] As Cromwell was prepared to execute political legitimists (i.e. monarchists) in order to defend the principle of parliamentary sovereignty over the army and other matters, Childers *may* have had a point, at least in the light of the debates upon the course of English history with which he was so familiar. Childers' propaganda team would even blame the convenient scapegoat of the IRB for the death of its own leader Harry Boland.[163] He also published political cartoons by Constance Markievicz (who had better claims than Mrs Lavery to be an aristocrat) that portrayed Griffith as having always been a Union Jack waving British imperialist who had only ever wished to wade through republicans' blood, and now, reflecting this, was supposedly sending National Army soldiers out in the middle of the night with orders to assault and physically abuse DeValera's wife and children.[164]

Shortly after the onset of the armed conflict in Dublin, Griffith was virtually incapacitated by a strange and severe attack of tonsillitis (this left him temporarily speechless and gave him breathing difficulties) as well as a partial nervous breakdown and thus required serious medical attention at Saint Vincent's Hospital. By mid-July, Griffith realised that the Dáil would not be able to meet later that month. Reflecting this, his last public statement (made in writing) was to note that he had decided to postpone reconvening the Dáil from 28 July until 12 August 1922.[165] He would not live to see that date, however. The previous day, he dropped dead suddenly in Saint Vincent's Hospital after getting out of bed in an effort to go to the Mansion House to arrange the proposed Dáil meeting. Examined by his old friend Dr Oliver St John Gogarty, Griffith was reported to have died of a brain haemorrhage.[166]

Griffith's death was both a deep personal shock and a political setback for Collins, who had now lost that leader who gave his own political stance some meaning. After attending Griffith's funeral on 16 August, a distraught Collins decided to spend a day resting at the Laverys' residence in Greystones, County Wicklow (this had sometimes also been used as a home for DeValera during the spring of 1921). This might not have been a wise decision. On 18 August, on his way from Greystones to Dublin, Collins' car was ambushed in the Belfield–Donnybrook area (not exactly a republican stronghold, in terms of voting patterns) and thirty rifle shots passed through the windows. This led to the incapacitation of the driver. Thereafter, a bomb was thrown directly at the stationary vehicle. Collins was very lucky to have survived this assassination attempt and when 'I recounted the incident at a government meeting last night ... apparently it was not of sufficient interest for publication.'[167] Collins death three days later under similar circumstances was reported to be a freak accident and Dublin Castle certainly encouraged all Irish public servants to adhere to that position. Collins' near (or perhaps actual) success in drawing up the terms of an independent National Army truce with the IRA in County Cork just before his demise was soon forgotten.[168]

As the position of chairman of the Provisional Government had been left vacant by Collins' resignation in late June, W.T. Cosgrave (who had taken over Collins's responsibility as the Dáil's finance minister upon the formation of the National Army) was ordered by Dublin Castle to fill this position on 25 August, six days before the Royal Irish Constabulary was formally wound up outside of Northern Ireland (although, Cope emphasised, 'there has been and still is a lot of underground [police] work going on').[169] It had still not been possible to reconvene the Dáil since 22 June.

Mulcahy's orders in late July that the Dáil court system must be disbanded was an unpopular move and a reversal of prior cabinet policy[170] that led both George Gavan Duffy, the minister of foreign affairs, and Eamon Duggan, the minister for home affairs, to resign from the cabinet (a decision Duggan formally took in early September, although he later would perform some work as a parliamentary secretary).[171] This meant that no Irish signatory to the Articles of Agreement for a Treaty was still in a position to stand by it. However, Churchill had already attempted to assure Mulcahy, through Cope, that 'we shall not require the signatures of living men' to continue in the set political course.[172]

Cosgrave was determined to step into the breach left by Griffith and Collins' deaths. He reconvened the Dáil on 9 September and was elected as its president in place of Griffith. Griffith and Collins had been in favour of creating a position of 'Commissioner of the British Commonwealth', to be appointed with the assent of the Dáil executive, as the representative of the King in Ireland instead of a Governor General (the title used for such offices in India).[173] However, Kevin O'Higgins, the new home affairs minister, proposed appointing T.M. Healy (his uncle) to the position of Governor General. Healy's status as both a political veteran and lawyer perhaps made him qualified for such a task. However, Healy's actual activities during 1922, being both a secret intermediary between the Dublin and London banks and a man whom Cardinal Logue, the Catholic Primate of All Ireland, was hoping would soon re-enter Westminster to represent Ulster Catholics' interests and grievances,[174] reflected how little Griffith and Collins' preoccupations had been in tune with those of this section of Catholic opinion in Ireland. If Cosgrave recognised this, he did so only to a degree.

Cosgrave was not only determined that the Dáil would survive but also that it would receive greater political recognition as *the* essential basis for the implementation of the treaty agreement. This meant getting both the Dáil *and* Westminster to vote in favour of the proposed Irish Free State constitution as soon as possible. Serious resistance to this idea was offered, however.

During September 1922, Lionel Curtis, who had performed similar work for Lloyd George at Dublin Castle as Cope had done for Churchill, virtually requested that the Dáil abandon the idea of having an Irish constitution altogether. This was reflected by the fact that he sought to persuade Cosgrave that the treaty agreement, by recognising the precedent of the Government of Ireland Act of 1920, was much more important than any issue of establishing an Irish constitution. Cosgrave insisted, however, that both his cabinet and the general Irish public wanted to have an Irish constitution as 'their own creation' and that this was their absolute *right* under the treaty agreement.[175] While Curtis obliged in forwarding this communication to London, Midleton's circle of southern unionists reacted during September–October 1922 by holding meetings with the Dáil cabinet that demanded that Cosgrave have the Irish constitution completely redrafted to accept the principles that the Irish and Ulster Parties had agreed to (and which Midleton had personally envisioned) during the Irish Convention of 1917–18. This meant creating a senate consisting of self-nominated southern unionist business leaders and property owners who would be granted supremacy of power over the legislative assembly. Midleton had two reasons to expect that this settlement could be forced upon the Dáil: first, the precedent of DeValera's peace agreement made with southern unionists in June 1921 (in theory, this had saved every member of the Dáil from immediate court martial and execution)[176] and second, the current role of Midleton's ally, the Bank of Ireland, in making loans to the National Army in the midst of the present conflict; a support that he could threaten to withdraw as a bargaining tool. Evidently, the anti-treaty party had proved completely victorious.

Cosgrave had absolutely no bargaining powers at his disposal. His reaction to this situation was simply to emphasise the principle of democratic self-determination that Griffith had stood for and to claim that just as Griffith had promised fair play to all,[177] it was the responsibility of all business leaders to act in good faith and, thereby, accept the fact that Irish voters *had* expressed approval for Griffith's policy repeatedly since 1918. Cosgrave's willingness to order the Dáil to vote to approve of the Free State constitution in late October, irrespective of Westminster's inaction in this matter, and thereafter to issue a warrant for the National Army's arrest and execution of Erskine Childers (the anti-treaty propaganda campaign had recently called for the execution of every member of Dáil Eireann)[178] was also a sign that the pro-treaty party was not going to completely disappear from Irish politics without some kind of resistance being offered. Ultimately, both Lord Iveagh of Guinness Breweries and Andrew Jameson of the Bank of Ireland conceded in mid-November 1922 that they should allow the Free State to be established, rather than be accused of 'breaking the treaty'[179] or face ongoing hostility from the Irish electorate (Guinness would soon do much to revive its own popularity by launching its first-ever, brand-marketing advertising campaign). This was the signal to Westminster to pass an act that December which recognised both the Articles of Agreement for a Treaty and the Dáil's constitution as the basis under which the Irish Free State was now to be established.

The Dáil, having approved of its own constitution that October, had to pass its own law subsequent to Westminster's act. This recognised the continued legal relevance of pre-existing British law, including the Government of Ireland Act of 1920 which had established the jurisdictions of Southern Ireland and Northern Ireland, but it also established the right of the former to establish its own independent constitution, as a dominion within the British Empire, known as the Irish Free State. This meant that Southern Ireland was no longer a part of the United Kingdom but instead was externally associated with it, while the Act of Union now applied directly within Ireland only with regards to Northern Ireland.[180] Dublin unionist opinion, represented by Guinness and Jameson, accepted this arrangement, as did Belfast unionist opinion, represented by Craig (although he still held firm in his opposition to the Boundary Commission idea). However, Cork unionist opinion, represented by Midleton, *never* would. Midleton refused to ever recognise 'the Free Staters' because he considered that the passing of an Irish Free State constitution into law, in *any* shape or form, to have been an irrevocable political defeat.[181] This was reflected by the fact that the representation of his political allies, such as Baron Glenavy (Lord Chancellor of Ireland in 1920), was now inherently confined (at best) to the Free State senate, without power over the legislative assembly. This was what Griffith had intended.

Dáil Eireann had survived, but only just. Anti-treaty propaganda, which denied the legitimacy of the Dáil, took two forms thereafter; one somewhat mild (this being represented by the Midleton school of unionist 'contemporary history' writing)[182] and the other somewhat more damaging by virtue of its being far more direct.

The combination of the order for the disbandment of the Dáil courts by Mulcahy in July 1922—a move opposed by some Dáil court officials partly for salary reasons[183]—with the appointment, on O'Higgins' suggestion, of a Governor General was used thereafter as the basis for a new anti-treaty propaganda campaign. This was based entirely upon a claim that the 'Third Dáil', meaning that assembly which Cosgrave convened on 9 September 1922 (and which anti-treaty deputies refused to attend), was an inherently illegitimate political assembly. This meant that it must be destroyed and denied all public recognition. This argument was championed on the basis of an alleged great compromise upon the principles of the 'First Dáil' (January 1919–June 1921) and the 'Second Dáil' (June 1921–September 1922). Cosgrave's release from prison of all those arrested during recent conflicts (11,000 men would be released during 1923)[184] did little to dissuade this body of opinion, which was sustained not least by Childers' posthumous gift to Irish political society *An Phoblacht* (as *Republican War News* was renamed after April 1923).

Cosgrave's solution to this difficulty was to prioritise one issue above all: to prove the reality of the Dáil as a government and to win public approval for its governmental authority by legislating as much as was possible in the interests of the Irish people.[185] In doing so, he was actualised by a sense that he was following directly in Griffith's footsteps in championing 'the real policy of Sinn Féin',[186] which had been permanently abandoned by February 1922 (if not earlier) by a different party that now bore that name. Cosgrave considered that Griffith had not only authored and developed this policy to its fullest degree, but he had also *led* the implementation of this policy between 1919 and 1922. Indeed, Griffith's ministries (April 1919–November 1920, January 1922–August 1922) had carried out the bulk of Dáil Eireann's proactive work hitherto.

Regarding Griffith's work in this regard, Cosgrave judged that 'in all his efforts he was actuated primarily by a steady realism' and a tremendous work ethic. Through these qualities, 'he had led his movement to the eve of success', not least by convincing the Irish public that Irish nationalist goals *were* truly worthy of support and could actually be achieved. This was done while simultaneously earning the personal respect of almost all sections of Irish public opinion by showing that, in his relationship to the Irish polity, he was both a 'noble and devoted servant' and a true citizen. Upon this basis, Cosgrave judged with regards to Griffith and his achievements that 'an autonomous Irish State remains as his best monument'.[187]

CHAPTER THIRTEEN

Conclusion

To some extent, Cosgrave's effort to ascribe an entirely positive legacy to Griffith's career was appreciated by many who came to be associated with Cosgrave himself as an Irish party-political system first evolved, during the 1930s.[1] Favourable treatment was granted to Maud Griffith, if not to Griffith's siblings, in terms of a government pension.[2] However, as many people were displeased with Griffith's apparent legacy. This is hardly surprising. When he died, the country was in a terrible and seemingly unsolvable mess, both politically and financially. In one of the last statements attributed to Michael Collins, he was reported to have said that Ireland was still in a financially solvent position before hostilities broke out in late June 1922 but now this was no longer the case. Childers and others sought to place the entire blame for this upon Griffith and Collins themselves.[3] Ambivalent attitudes also existed within Britain.

Griffith had argued that he stood for Irish economic freedoms and peace with England. The latter perspective fed into all the necessary British obsequies, such as the issue of formal condolences, which followed his death. However, the privately held view of many London figures that Griffith was a 'sour-bellied anarchist'[4] betrayed the reality that Irish economic freedoms had a potential to disrupt the British economy far more than the United Kingdom was simply prepared to allow. Essentially, any alteration of norms purely for the sake of Ireland was equated with anarchy. This was the reality of Irish politics, especially between 1919 and 1927 and it attained its greatest flashpoint during 1922. It also governed the careers of all TDs to a greater or lesser extent; most of all, for Dáil cabinet members. If Griffith and Collins could potentially be accused of having botched the efforts to resolve the thorny issues of the constitution and finance, DeValera and Mulcahy could equally be criticised for having failed to find a solution to the problems of

Plate 9. Election card for Griffith during the East Cavan contest of June 1918. (National Library of Ireland, Griffith papers)

Plate 10. The 'Sinn Féin People's Bank Limited' at 6 Harcourt Street had a twelve-year history before its suppression in March 1921. Reflecting the unpopularity of Griffith's ideal of an Irish takeover of the country's financial institutions, no effort was ever made to revive it. *Irish Independent* (1921)

Plate 11. Griffith being celebrated after the end of nine-months imprisonment (November 1920–July 1921) he received for leading Dáil Eireann. The summer of 1921 marked the peak of Sinn Féin's popularity. *Daily Mirror* (1921)

Plate 12. In London with Mark Ryan, Eamon Duggan and Bishop Joseph MacRory while preparing to negotiate an unpopular and virtually preordained Anglo-Irish agreement (October 1921).
Daily Sketch (1921)

Plate 13. Waiting in vain for the train to start: a frustrated Griffith on his way to Sligo (April 1922). Nationalisation of the railways was one of Griffith's plans to combat general poverty by promoting an infrastructure for business and employment in Ireland.
Irish Independent (1922)

THE GLITTERING GATES

ST. DAVID LLOYD GEORGE : " In you go."
ARTHUR : " Righto, it'll be heavenly."
MICHAEL : " I'm a bit doubtful, but I'll try
it for a while."
EAMONN : " I'll go below ; it may be easier
to get out ! "

Plate 14. This contemporary political cartoon represented the common perception that the treaty agreement was an arrangement with an insufficient grounding, thus making it a potential death trap for Irish politicians. *UCC Multi-text*

Plate 15. Shots fired over Griffith's grave following his burial (August 1922). On the left looking pensively into the grave is Michael Collins, Griffith's former finance minister. The last leader of the IRB alongside Harry Boland, Collins seems to have been the only National Army officer at the graveside to keep his head uncovered as a mark of respect. In Boland's opinion, 'Griffith made us all'. (National Library of Ireland, Griffith papers)

Plate 16. Ida Griffith and Nevin Griffith (a future barrister) photographed around the time of their father's death. (National Library of Ireland, Griffith papers)

" The President—God Help Him!"

Plate 17. A *Dublin Opinion* cartoon representing the difficulties that Griffith
faced during April 1922. W.T. Cosgrave would express the opinion
that Griffith died primarily due to overwork and stress.
Dublin Opinion (1922)

Plate 18. A portrait of Griffith by Leo Whelan R.H.A. that was unveiled
in Leinster House on the occasion of the 25th anniversary of the
formation of Dáil Eireann (21 January 1944) by Bishop Fogarty, the
former Sinn Féin Party treasurer. This was one of three portraits of
'Founders of the Dáil' that was commissioned by a committee that
consisted of W.T. Cosgrave, Joseph McGrath, Richard Mulcahy,
James Montgomery, T.F. O'Sullivan and Senator Barniville. The other
portraits were of Michael Collins and Kevin O'Higgins.

policing and defence. However, all were subject equally to the same overarching difficulty that made these apparent failures almost inevitable: the dichotomy that existed between the economic logic of the Government of Ireland Act and the constitutional liberties that were supposed to be allowed to Ireland by the Articles of Agreement for a Treaty.

What was christened by the Englishman Erskine Childers and would later be termed by all Irishmen as 'the Irish civil war' was essentially an economic fall-out from business and banking leaders' extant commitment to the Government of Ireland Act despite the fact that the vast majority of elected Irish politicians had recently rejected that settlement as undemocratic and inadequate to the point of being unworkable. If the perception that individuals such as Midleton and Jameson (an Englishman and a Scotsman respectively) were effectively able to hold the entire of Ireland's political representation to ransom in this way had some validity, it was also true that they were able to 'get away with it' not essentially because of any constitutional or security matter but rather because the business norms that they were associated with were simply too deeply entrenched in Irish life to be altered, let alone overcome, in such a short space of time. Irish control over the public purse in Ireland had never been allowed hitherto, and in June 1922 Churchill likewise determined that 'if necessary we shall collect our [the British Government's] money by a special levy on Irish goods or by a seizure of Irish customs'.[5] This reflected the vantage point of the British state. However, the Irish private sector had also supported this principle of British control of Irish finances for a very long time and excepting Griffith and his supporters, comparatively few within Sinn Féin had ever exhibited a true determination to alter this situation. Partly for this reason, historians have often been reluctant to ascribe much significance to the history of Dáil Eireann between 1919 and 1921.[6]

If one particular issue was denoted as the key determinant of Griffith's career, then it might be said to have been the common labour market that existed in Britain and Ireland under the Union. If not quite as much as the presence of the Government of Ireland Act on the statute books the common citizenship principle in the Articles of Agreement for a Treaty served to sustain this situation, which had created the dynamic whereby London was made the business capital of Ireland. This was a matter that was at odds with what Griffith was attempting to achieve. In common with other champions of serious economic reforms for Ireland, he favoured the nationalisation of Irish financial institutions not because he viewed this as an inherently good thing (in fact, he was inclined to hold an opposing viewpoint, at least in theory), but because he believed that the initiation of a state-directed economy policy for Ireland itself was an essential stepping-stone to localising Irish wealth within Ireland for the sake of developing a monetary policy that could protect and develop the economic well being of the Irish population. He was not alone in such attitudes.

John Busteed, a UCC economist, judged shortly after Griffith's death that Ireland's public figures needed to outgrow a legacy of the Irish Party by starting to engage in strategic economic thinking. In aggressively defending Gladstone's legacy for the Empire, the Irish Party had argued that ideas of protectionism and free trade were somehow mutually exclusive rather than inherently co-existing and fluctuating concepts, both in theory and in practice. The continuation of this trend of thought in the Ireland of the 1920s led Busteed to surmise that, evidently, 'in Ireland, we are not very interested in the cyclical fluctuations of trade; we probably do not believe in them; we are more anxious to prove that the country is going to the dogs or that it has a beautiful future in store.'[7] As in the Irish Party's days, many continued to view Irish nationality as a purely cultural construct. Meanwhile, in defence of Griffith's reformist intentions, UCD economist C.H. Oldham argued that 'the people that is unable to properly use statistics is not yet capable of self-government' and that the 'educational value' of drawing statistical comparisons with corresponding small European countries to Ireland, as Griffith had single-handedly attempted to do in his journalism ever since 1905, 'would be enormous'. This was because:

> 'We cannot really form a correct opinion about any subject of Irish economics unless we make a study of Irish life through the difficult language of comparative statistics ... In the past the province [nature of university appointments] of an Irish statistician [including Oldham himself] had been to supply just those Irish figures that were needed to complete the totals for the United Kingdom. Then, whenever comparison had to be made with foreign countries, the unit for comparison was never Ireland but always the United Kingdom ... [Drawing purely Irish comparisons with] other European or dominion countries ... will be an absolutely new departure in Irish statistics; it will carry the minds of the Irish people into regions of thought hitherto unknown to them. I do not mean that their knowledge of other countries will be enlarged by such comparisons; I mean that their knowledge of Ireland itself will dawn for the first time upon their intelligence with a quite novel significance.'[8]

This had always been Griffith's argument. In his day, to emphasise these points necessitated a forthright critique of the combination of cultural nationalism and political (i.e. economic) unionism that had defined the Irish Party's politics. This had, in Griffith's view, been responsible for propagating the myth of inherent Irish poverty and ignoring potentials for specifically Irish economic developments while silently acceding to the wealth of the country being invested almost exclusively outside of the country by the country's banks.

Despite the expected constitutional right of the British dominions to enter into their own trading treaties, the Irish Free State was not actually allowed to trade outside the United Kingdom, i.e. the Union, or the Empire, up until the Balfour Declaration of 1926. The assassination of Kevin O'Higgins in the wake of his winning recognition of this right (this prompted Cosgrave to commemorate O'Higgins alongside Griffith and Collins) would indicate that this right alone, upon which Griffith had placed so much emphasis as a necessary step towards Irish economic freedoms (the initiation of Irish customs policies were almost inherently meaningless without first securing this right)[9] and to which unionists were, by definition, inherently opposed, was considered by many contemporaries as *the* pivotal factor to the political life of the whole time period. This reality also essentially explains why law and order not only broke down in Ireland during 1922 but also did so to a far greater extent than it had between 1916 and 1921.

DeValera's supporters sometimes attempted to propagate the idea, or else genuinely believed, that (in Childers' words) all who fell during 1922 did so 'as a result of the accursed instrument signed in London on December 6th'.[10] However, there was no essential link between the treaty agreement and the fact that deliberate efforts were made from June 1922 onwards not only to facilitate many bank raids (a case of 'take the money and run' that sometimes took the form of 'an inside job')[11] but also to sabotage all the country's railway networks (why were men funded to do this?).[12] In addition to being a necessary handmaiden to the introduction of a tariff policy regarding commercial transits in Irish ports, Griffith had seen Irish railway nationalisation as essential for the development of an internal infrastructure for Irish business nationwide in conjunction with the Irish county councils and city corporations by bringing Irish market towns and cities together for the first time to serve a common economic strategy, determined in Dublin. Echoing the past arguments of Field, McCann and Sweetman, Lionel Smith Gordon, chairman of the Dáil's bank, had also suggested in 1921 that, in theory, such a development could soon see Irish market towns develop into dynamic agricultural–manufacturing cities, just as similar agricultural market towns had already done throughout Britain and the European continent. However, as a result of the sabotage of all Irish railways during 1922–1923, the banks decreed that the London Midlands and Scottish Railway, which was controlled and financed by the London Midlands Bank (which had already purchased the Belfast Bank during 1917), must be employed to finance the rebuilding of Irish railways. Essentially as a result, all railways within the jurisdiction of the Irish Free State became amalgamated under a single director to be appointed and controlled by this same British railway (managed by the London Midlands Bank), thereby giving British businessmen effective control of the infrastructure of all Irish business.[13]

Intentionally or not, this was essentially an achievement of 'the IRA Organisation', born in March 1922 as a trade union for Irish Volunteers and, to some extent, crystallised as an organisation after the outbreak of hostilities in June 1922, and the possibility of developing a commercially viable Irish transport industry for the sake of promoting indigenous Irish businesses and, in turn, opportunities for employment within Ireland itself, suffered as a result.[14] As the economy of Ireland continued to serve a primarily British purpose, most of Ireland's market towns were no more developed by the 1960s than they had been during the 1880s and the internal infrastructure for business and employment in Ireland, as envisioned by Field, McCann, Griffith and Sweetman, was not to be. In this sense, what would be typified as 'the Irish civil war' of June 1922–April 1923 was essentially a manifestation of how willing the private sector, with some encouragement from the British state itself, was willing to finance disturbances in Ireland simply to ensure that the London-centred dynamics of the economy could not be altered. For a long time, many in Ireland suspected that this was actually a reason for the existence of so-called republican undergrounds in the country. On this level, it is also worth remembering that although many typified the 1922 conflict, with Childers' encouragement, to be a case of 'the IRB versus the IRA' (or even the Irish Volunteer leadership versus its own rank and file), the IRB had initiated a tradition of a UK-wide Irish revolutionary underground in the Victorian period and its history proved just how easily it could be manipulated into competing sections for ulterior political motives. For this reason as much as its organisational weakness (if it contained remarkable men, IRB members who excelled in their actions generally did so in a purely individual capacity), it would be problematic to overestimate the importance of the IRB to the history of the time period.

Of course, sabotage was not inherently the dynamic of resistance to the idea of the formation of an Irish state-directed economy. The common labour market between Britain and Ireland was reason enough for many, including labour politicians, to be indifferent to the idea of economic development within Ireland itself. The Irish population's principle employers, beyond the level of the small-to-medium enterprises that were associated during the Edwardian era with William O'Brien's political followers, were British employers. Childers' success in launching a tradition of IRA–Marxist analyses of labour politics in perpetual opposition to the idea of an Irish state-directed economy was made possible by this underlying dynamic. Indeed, a sensible and profitable political choice for many Irish individuals and institutions to make during 1922 was to 'oppose the treaty'. Whether this was done under a nominally 'unionist', 'labour', 'home ruler', 'republican', 'Christian–democratic' or some other banner was essentially completely beside the point: for many, hugging to the economic principles of unionism rather than endeavouring to envision and implement the economic principles of an Irish nationalism made sense. Therefore, resistance to change was welcomed and the potentials Griffith identified in the treaty arrangement were negated. To a significant extent, this was inevitable in the light of its provenance during the summer of 1921. In this sense, perhaps the most fascinating question raised by Griffith's life and career is the whole question of Irish conservatism. Did Ireland, by necessity, have to be a land without reform?

Ten years before the outbreak of hostilities, the necessity of establishing an all-party council on the management of Irish finances to remedy the many serious economic problems for Ireland caused by the Union over the previous eighty-five years was a cause that was championed not only by Irish economic nationalist commentators such as Griffith, C.H. Oldham, William O'Brien, William Field and Thomas Lough but it was also a political desire of James Craig's supporters in Belfast and a concept that was validated, more or less, by both the Primrose Commission and Royal Economic Society in London. Despite Griffith's best efforts and Craig's deep concerns, however, the possibility of reform in the management of Irish finances to begin to suit Irish needs was suspended for good because London did not want to have to alter its priorities for the sake of (any part of) Ireland. As in 1886, a 'Government of Ireland Bill' was its instrument to achieve this goal but the inclusion of the principle of partition within that bill soon effectively guaranteed its achievement precisely because it prevented the re-establishment of the principle of recognising the existence of Ireland as a distinct economic entity.[15] On this level, the relevance of the economic debates of 1911 to the political situation of 1920–22 and, indeed, thereafter, was essentially paramount, but historians have seemingly been loath to admit this because of the legacy of partition. It is clear, however, that fiscal dependence on Britain, which the Government of Ireland Act was meant to guarantee by denying Irish parliaments the right to regulate Irish banks, could have a damaging effect on the evolution of party politics in the Irish Free State precisely because it made the formation of any true party-political policies on the economy very difficult. This was Sean Milroy's protest in Irish politics between 1922 and 1927; a protest which was made in defence of Griffith's programme, with the support of Griffith's widow, but was opposed by the banks, who forced Cosgrave to suppress Griffith's Young Ireland in December 1922.[16]

Milroy argued that after Westminster accepted the constitution of the Irish Free State in December 1922, Cosgrave should utilise the Dáil's powers to persuade all the banks in the country to accept their responsibility to act in support of the Dáil's governmental authority, not least by repatriating the country's sterling assets with a view to investing more in Irish than in British business concerns. This was necessary so that the Dáil could prepare to meet the great challenge that all modern democracies faced; namely, the worldwide trend ever since the mid-nineteenth century of the migration of rural labourers to towns and cities to provide them with much needed livelihoods. It was essentially this dynamic that had created all modern political parties in Europe and their divergent fiscal policies, while the failure to answer this challenge hitherto had created the dynamic of perpetual Irish emigration, primarily if by no means exclusively to the urban centres of Britain.[17] This goal was not implemented, however, because Cosgrave's hands were tied. Milroy's equal emphasis upon the fact that the banks within Ireland straddled both jurisdictions but were located primarily in the south (a fact that he believed could do away with any northerners' belief in a value of, let alone any possible need for, partition in an entirely peaceable and mutually beneficial fashion once a state-directed economy policy was employed in Dublin)[18] explains why Cosgrave's hands were tied. The Government of Ireland Act could not be ignored. Therefore, it had inherent supremacy over the rights of the Irish Free State to pursue its own economic policy. This meant that the Irish Free State retained the economic identity of Southern Ireland and the British mainland remained the principal business centre to which Irish labour necessarily gravitated.

Milroy was essentially correct that the right to freely pursue such policies as he described had been Griffith and Collins' motives in accepting the Articles of Agreement for a Treaty. This was the premise of his 'national group' in Irish politics, formed during 1923. Cosgrave requested that this 'national group' disband during 1924 (this was misleadingly justified by some according to a cover story regarding the IRB and the newly instituted Irish Defence Forces)[19] but this was not essentially his own choice. This was reflected by Cosgrave's reaction to Milroy's subsequent denunciations of the fiscal commissions of 1926–27 that led to the decision to allow the Bank of England alone to continue to manage the Irish state's exchequer account and to control a newly established Irish pound (featuring a portrait of Lady Lavery): in sympathy with Milroy's views, Cosgrave 'promoted' him to the Free State senate.

The Cumann na Gaedhael organisation, founded in 1923, was not essentially a political party but rather, like the Parnellite grouping of the 1890s, a movement that sought to refocus Irish political interest groups in the wake of a recent crisis. It also had the responsibility, as was reflected by the Ministers and Secretaries Act of 1924, to attempt to create the basis of an Irish civil service. The formation of an Irish party political system was delayed until 1927 precisely because it was not until then that the basis of the state's governance was actually determined. In the interregnum, Milroy was not making arguments based on some impractical or ideological belief in nationalisation purely for its own sake, much though he focused on the question of the choice of civil service personnel. He produced sound evidence that a majority of the private sector in Ireland actually favoured such economic reforms as Griffith envisioned, involving a much greater degree of state-directed economic development with a focus upon purely Irish considerations.[20] For this reason, historian Joe Lee has judged that

> 'The government did not reject Griffith's doctrines following a searching examination of the facts. It simply substituted for one set of unproven assumptions, based at least on some attempt, however perfunctory, to wrestle with the evidence of economic history, an alternative set of unproven assumptions based on no historical evidence at all.'[21]

Griffith's 'doctrines' were based on the common-sense principle that no government can possibly provide either employment for its citizens or provide for their welfare unless it sought to create a basis for a distinct labour market within its jurisdiction and to prioritise the same. This was contrary to unionism, but it was not contrary to logic. As O'Higgins was aware, however, Griffith did engage in propaganda that could make his nationalist arguments less convincing. For instance, his willingness to consider the significance of American investments in Europe as a potential determinant of monetary policies (this predated J.M. Keynes' espousal of such ideas)[22] was nothing if not an illustration of his determination to envision all potential future options for reform. The arguments of *Nationality* during 1919 were actually inconsistent and, therefore, often unpersuasive for precisely this reason, however.

The need for changing banking policy was the one consistent factor in Griffith's arguments at all times. The Dáil's formation of its own bank reflected this intention. Regarding this question of banking, Lee has argued that 'it was not necessary to import capital for Irish industry. There was adequate capital in the country. The problem was, as it had long been, how to mobilise it ... It was risk capital and entrepreneurship that Ireland lacked.'[23] Entrepreneurship and all business activity, however, were entirely dependent upon what enterprises that the banks themselves were prepared to risk supporting. In this respect, the ongoing determination of Irish banks to label the idea of nationalisation, in any field of business, as a potential economic disaster and to confine Irish business exclusively to the level of small-to-medium enterprises with very limited rights to capital investment reflected a determination to maintain London as Ireland's business capital at all costs. This was a conscious decision that the banks made and that Irish businessmen, in turn, necessarily had to follow.

The past arguments of the post-1896 Irish Financial Reform League have a certain historical significance here. Outside the United Kingdom, state-directed economies (with control over banking) *were* the norm. The British divergence from this norm stemmed primarily from the role of the government of the City of London, the principal base from which London financiers sought to direct government policy, in shaping Westminster's response to its own particular imperial challenge and how that challenge had evolved ever since the need to finance its first truly imperial wars arose during the eighteenth century.[24] The Victorian myth of the inherent supremacy of private over public enterprise was a peculiarly British one, designed to match specific British political circumstances, but nevertheless, Irish banks, before and after 1922, retained this same logic as virtually a gospel economic truth, while partition effectively cemented this same idea. This trend naturally played a large part in determining the dominant features of professional debate within Ireland; hence the dismissal of Griffith's ideas. As no Irish businessman was allowed support by Irish banks beyond the level of the smallest enterprises, any businessman in Ireland who wanted to establish a commercially potent enterprise, i.e. one on a larger scale that could serve as a major employer, needed to make Britain his home, if he had not done so already.

Tom Kettle once claimed that the 'open secret of Ireland' was that Ireland was a nation whereas the actual 'open secret' that everyone knew was that Kettle and company had not only accepted the economics of the Union but also secretly encouraged the Irish middle classes to accept the fact that adapting to a London-centric economic world was the 'secret' means to attain unimpeachable wealth and influence within Ireland. The churches had done this just as much as anyone who had more than a minimal capital within Ireland, including most institutions. In the Irish Party's day, encouraging this process was seen to be the best guarantor of the cultural health of 'the nation' or the economic security of the Irish people. If this meant limited opportunities for development, it was nevertheless seen as a guarantor of stability and most Irish politicians subscribed to this quintessentially conservative standpoint.

The very fact that both Smith Gordon and Collins touted the idea during 1921–1922 that the Irish bank shareholding public needed to take the lead in demanding a change in Irish banking policy reflected an awareness that, as in Britain, the private sector was generally considered in Ireland to be a more pivotal determinant of political events than the state itself and that the Irish public would not welcome a government that was interventionist to the extent Griffith had intimated. In theory, if the private sector had enthusiastically supported Griffith's goals, then the possibility of reforming the Anglo-Irish economic relationship very much in Ireland's interests could have developed, although the perpetually coercive policy adopted by the British government no doubt played a large part in discouraging the majority of the private sector from ever considering championing such reform because it could well prove to be entirely counter-productive in the face of a probable British reaction. For instance, there can be little doubt that if Craig had allied himself with Griffith during 1922 Churchill would have responded by metaphorically breaking his legs. Both during and in the wake of the propaganda wars of 1920–1922—born as a result of Dáil Eireann's revolutionary attempt to assume control of the public purse in Ireland by the means of local government—this issue was often associated by propagandists in the British press with an alleged 'IRA' terrorism, although this was certainly not the origins, or basis, of what was known as the 'Ulster Unionist' political tradition.

If an Irish nationalism was ever truly vibrant as a political movement, then there can be little doubt that any of the aforementioned economic nationalist commentators (including potentially Griffith himself, if he had taken the bait to become a MP) would have been employed as the Irish Party's finance spokesmen instead of Tom Kettle, a spokesman for the Catholic hierarchy. It was essentially the very fact that this never occurred which in their own estimation necessitated that Belfast politicians always reject the whole debate on 'home rule'. Contrary to Kettle's propaganda, this was not because they were 'Orange bigots' or defenders of a Protestant ascendancy (although, if representative, the secretive response of Dr Bernard to the treaty agreement was arguably a poor reflection of Irish Protestants' level of patriotism) but simply because the manner by which the Irish Party had championed the idea of 'home rule finance' actually made no sense whatsoever. For instance, if the problems that ultimately faced Northern Ireland were serious, they could only have been made much worse if they were compounded by an acceptance of economic logic that had governed the Irish Party's politics in the past, ignoring all economic matters entirely except in so far as they affected denominational education. Be that as it may, the course of Irish politics during the mid-1920s would ultimately have a strange affect upon how the history of Griffith's lifetime would be written, causing many unionists to actually seek to revive the reputation of the once hated Irish Party as much as was possible.

How Griffith would have reacted to the economic challenges of the mid-1920s is naturally unknown, but currency concerns may have overruled options. In

Britain, Churchill's decision to rely on an almost archaic gold standard principle for the pound sterling—the recent collapse of Dutch banks, not just Churchill's detestation of the idea of growing fiscal dependence on America, may partly explain this tendency—certainly made the Irish government very hesitant to champion economic reforms of any kind,[25] and it is worth remembering that, in the earliest days of Sinn Féin, Griffith did not consider an Irish breakaway from the British gold standard as absolutely necessary. Furthermore, if Griffith would have responded in a very similar manner to Milroy to events at this time, whatever choices that would have been open to him would have been the exact same as that which faced all other Irish politicians, stemming from the fall out of the banks' extant and seemingly irrevocable commitment to the Government of Ireland Act and the consequent undermining of the ideal of the Dáil directing an economic policy for Ireland. In this respect, Griffith and Collins' belief that the maintenance of peace in Ireland until the Irish Free State Act first passed the British House of Lords in December 1922 would be necessary if their political strategy was to work undoubtedly had a great deal of validity, and the political motive and economic significance of events between June 1922 and April 1923 was essentially to negate that plan. Griffith's take on the significance of the 'treaty debates' also have a historical significance here. He had emphasised that regardless of whether or not the Dáil had been able to retain a republican oath of allegiance or to create a nominally republican constitution, it would face the exact same challenge and responsibility of government as a parliamentary assembly; namely, attempting to mediate with the existing private sector by creating a new public sector. He had searched hard for choices in creating a strong public sector in Ireland that was in favour of nationalist reformism but choice was essentially the one thing that Irish governments did not have open to them after 1920.

The inability of the Dáil to alter pre-existing business norms on almost any level was perhaps best illustrated by state's balance of payments. The annual revenue of the Irish Free State for each of its first ten years of existence (averaging £25 million a year, with approximately £26 million a year spent in public service expenditure)[26] coincided almost exactly with the £1.5 million deficit that the British treasury (very dubiously) calculated in 1911 and that Childers had maintained, with the Irish Party's full support, must become the founding premise of all future governments in Ireland until such time as it may suit London to reassume such responsibilities itself (the latter was an option to be kept open, even it may never actually prove either rewarding or necessary to pursue).[27] This extraordinarily neat result in perpetuation of an imperial consensus of 1911 occurred despite the very great alternations in Irish revenue that occurred both during and after the First World War (which often saw Whitehall collect from Ireland a surplus of over £20 million a year) and the economic impact of partition (including depriving Dublin of all northern revenue) precisely because of an absolute continuity in a London-directed banking policy in Ireland. This was the ultimate proof of Sinn Féin's failure. It was also the most probable reason why Childers offered to shake the hands of a (soon to be permanently dismissed) cadre of National Army officers before he faced their firing squad in November 1922: he knew that he had already won and they had lost. From February 1922 onwards, the Sinn Féin Party practically adopted the Irish Party's economics as its own.

Reflecting this trend, the approach of DeValera's majority party to economic questions would be characterised by the adoption of a few surface initiatives without desiring to make any alteration to the banking infrastructure of the state.[28] A significant illustration of this reality was the career of Sean Lemass, a Dubliner of humble origins who, perhaps more so than most well-known politicians in the history of the post-1922 Irish state, shared Griffith's no-nonsense approach to political problems and a similar temperament. During the 1930s, old (soon to be deceased) allies of Griffith such as Tom Kelly and Jennie Wyse Power welcomed Lemass' attempt to launch a construction industry to solve Dublin's housing problems and promote employment.[29] This would earn Lemass' party the Dublin working-class vote. However, the new instrument used—the Industrial Credit Company—was, just like the Agricultural Credit Company (launched in 1927 to replace the Dáil's disbanded National Land Bank), based in London,[30] thereby reflecting the legacy of the Irish Banks Standing Committee's decision made in June 1922 regarding the necessary basis for all sizeable future Irish business initiatives; a decision that was taken without the knowledge or indeed any reference to the Dáil.[31] Later, Lemass would also oversee a government that would launch initiatives such as free secondary school education in Ireland. If all of these initiatives still fell far short of the reformist policy Griffith had originally envisioned for the Dáil of 1919–1922 once it assumed control of the public purse, remarkably Lemass' mere willingness to consider that reform might possibly be a responsibility of an Irish government would lead some future Irish historians to typify him as an 'enigmatic patriot' or even a 'democratic dictator';[32] the same bizarre labels that were applied to Griffith in 1922.

Party politics in Ireland after 1927 was polarised not least by labour difficulties that Childers had formerly counted upon to achieve his objectives. Later, twentieth-century historians would refer to 'a crisis in popular expectation in Ireland' and typify this as something that was born during the mid-1910s and that was defined by rival cultural nationalisms that were supposedly associated with British armed forces and 1916 rebels.[33] In reality, however, this 'crisis in popular expectation' was an issue that was born a full decade later (it was simply not known during the mid-1910s how events would ultimately turn out) once it was realised across the entire island that a practical deprivation of financial autonomy was seemingly leading to 'the final shipwreck of the nation', even if not many agreed with Milroy that this was a consequence of having acted in 'direct conflict with the teaching and doctrines of Griffith'.[34] Many preferred instead to point to the labour concerns regarding demobilised soldiers as symbolical of the situation the country faced. Although this question had the exact same economic (and, in turn, governmental) connotation irrespective of whether it was applied to Irish soldiers who had fought in the First World War or to Irish Volunteers who had once stood in defence of the Dáil,[35] a myth would develop from the ongoing labour tensions over this issue that a potential *coup d'etat* situation existed. However, there were essentially no such dangers involved at all. The Catholic hierarchy certainly perceived this,[36] not least because, unlike some Irish politicians, it never lost sight of the ongoing relevance of the arrangements made in September 1921 for the evolution of an Irish party politics.

This strange situation essentially occurred because, from 1927 onwards, the dynamics of party politics in the Free State was now defined exclusively by the DeValeraite stance on 'the treaty'; a trend that would be encouraged by the formation (with its financial headquarters in London)[37] of the *Irish Press*. Notwithstanding the DeValera–Mulcahy alliance of 1922 and the administrative problems that it involved, the idea that the breaking or making of political oaths was the root of all Irish political difficulties was championed relentlessly, as if Ireland would somehow have experienced no political problems whatsoever were it not for what Childers had described as 'the accursed instrument signed in London on December 6th'.[38] Others then attempted to present the converse argument. This merely served to substantiate this same one-dimensional focus, however (the treaty itself, apart from the intent to reform policing, had involved no real issue other than the right to create a written Irish constitution; a right from which, Griffith and Collins expected, a freedom to pursue new economic policies would develop). Most Irish people were not blind to the fact that this squabble was an attempt to obfuscate the source of the problems arising from the economic norms born during the mid-1920s, even if few realised that DeValera had delayed forming his own political party (Fianna Fáil) and recognising the 'legitimacy' of the Dáil until the British government had first determined, during 1926, that the state of the civil service in Ireland was now satisfactory.[39] In this, DeValera essentially had no choice, however, because this was the political logic upon which the peace agreement of June 1921 had been based. Although nicknamed as 'the truce', this was actually the initiation of a liaison agreement between the Irish Volunteers and the R.I.C. with a view to potentially disbanding the latter, if an Anglo-Irish agreement was reached. The delay in implementing that agreement or settlement, purely due to the unwillingness of the country's financial institutions to rally themselves behind the Dáil, forced DeValera to enter a prolonged political stasis, however, and to receive blame for disturbances just as much as the Dáil itself rather than its true author; namely, the British and Irish private sector. This created what might have been described as DeValera's and, indeed, Mulcahy's 'political cross' to bear.

DeValera's deliberate choice to encourage the Irish public to subscribe to Childers' propaganda regarding 'the treaty' for the remainder of his very lengthy career would earn him the reputation in some quarters of being concerned primarily with own self-justification. This was not quite true. There was a link between his stance and the arrangements made in September 1921 to facilitate a Catholic opposition to the forthcoming Anglo-Irish agreement, and a key factor in this arrangement from the Irish side was the question of the formation of a satisfactory (Christian–democratic) national identity for any prospective Irish state. The significance of the impact of this question upon the evolution of Irish politics should not be underestimated. It would play a large part in determining the tenor of future constitutional debate, as well as how Griffith's life and times would be interpreted by future generations. Therefore, having treated the issue of the activities of Griffith's supporters in the wake of his death, we must now turn to the question of the continuities in Irish life before and after Griffith's death in an attempt to provide an overall assessment of his career.

Historians have been inclined to associate an obsession with issues of national identity with a resulting lack of economic vision and typify this as one of the salient features of Irish life ever since 1922.[40] From this perspective, public opinion was so long conditioned in Ireland to seeking to construct a national identity tale to bolster cultural self-confidence, with appropriate iconic personalities to match, that both conceiving of and performing the responsibilities of government was a task to which even some of the best minds of the country were poorly conditioned. This may have been a legacy of the Irish Party's political journalist MPs at Westminster, from A.M. Sullivan to William O'Brien and beyond, who, with the support of the Catholic Church, had sought to construct an Irish national identity to bolster cultural self-confidence in Ireland in preparation for Gladstonian home rule; a measure that would have involved no Irish fiscal autonomy whatsoever but would have to helped to sustain the localised educational, or 'cultural', autonomy that already existed under the Union but could potentially become threatened, in the long term, by the ever-growing process of British state secularisation.[41] This trend also created a political continuity between the Irish Party and the post-1917 Sinn Féin Party, at least amongst those who spoke of the importance of the Irish language above all else.

Owing to its deep conservatism, this trend has often been associated with the Catholic Church and its education system in Ireland, as if priests, not politicians, were the authors of Irish conservatism. However, the essential choice of political conservatism was one that could only be made by the lay professional classes themselves. Fundamentally, it was the economics of the Anglo-Irish relationship that had always determined what choices, if any, could be made. The combination of the British government's financial support for Maynooth College ever since 1795 with its discrimination (by means of new Irish banks) against Irish business enterprises ever since the 1820s may have turned priests within Ireland into political activists and even spokesmen on financial matters to a far greater extent than may have ever been merited, but this was essentially a fallout from the British state's policy in Ireland more so than a manifestation of a temporal perversion of the church's intent. Furthermore, irrespective of the wealth and conservatism of the church, it had limited economic concerns beyond the fields of education, health and property: as a church, it had no reason to be unduly concerned whether or not Ireland ever became independent or not, except in so far as this may have impinged on its own welfare, and thus some nationalist politicians tendency to rely on the church to substantiate their own particular stance may perhaps be said to have created its own particular problems.

DeValera's attitudes may have been the most illustrative of the political temperament of the Dáil's membership on the question of prospective church–state relations. The church had facilitated his stance on the Anglo-Irish agreement of December 1921, yet DeValera had not accepted the suspicious attitude of secret Catholic fraternities regarding the idea of new Irish ministries of education or health being established, maintaining in the earliest days of the Dáil that while 'they had not yet an education or public health [ministry]…they should add them if they found it necessary'.[42] He would also not be prepared to listen to conservative Catholic theorists who questioned the value of the welfare state during the late 1930s, having initiated (together with Sean T. O'Kelly, his finance minister) the conversion of Irish deposits in the post office savings bank in London into government securities with a view to enabling the formation of a welfare policy in Dublin, albeit one whereby the longstanding relationship between the post office savings bank, the welfare state and the economics of the Anglo-Irish relationship remained constant.[43] DeValera's attitude towards partition was the same as that of the Catholic Church. He believed that the establishment of a Christian–democratic constitutional ethos for the Irish Free State could appeal to northern Protestants by making Ireland the most religious-friendly of modern European political societies. In this, however, he failed to realise the reasons why northern businessmen and, in turn, northern politicians had always opposed Kettle's way of thinking: religious matters were considered entirely separate and secondary to the whole question of the potential economic mismanagement of Ireland. The context of this proverbial unionist mindset would alter after the mid-1920s, however, when attempts would be made to use the history of Griffith's lifetime anachronistically to justify various contemporary stances on the economy, not least by referring to the debates on national identity.

The first and perhaps the most abiding example of this trend occurred during the mid-1920s when Stephen Gwynn, a former Gaelic League leader and now a leader of the National League party, launched a propaganda campaign claiming that 'Redmondism', an hitherto unknown concept (John Redmond himself would not have understood its meaning) meant simply to denote the potential that was resident in the old Irish Party, not only 'provides' the answers to all Ireland's political problems but 'proves' that Griffith was completely wrong in all his political attitudes *and* that his backwards-looking 'protectionist' economy policies were directly responsible for all Ireland's problems and lack of economic vision.[44] Within this politicised school of historical writing has also been a determination to label Griffith as an author of 'brilliant fulminations' in the cultural–nationalist world of letters alone,[45] rather than a serious political figure. In making such arguments, Gwynn was acting in line with the dynamics of the southern and northern Irish economy under the Government of Ireland Act and, therefore, his view was both personally rewarding for this own career and progressively came to permeate many sections of Irish society. His brother Denis Gwynn also attempted to substantiate this theory of 'Redmondism' by writing an appropriate contemporary history and he would be rewarded by DeValera by being appointed as first professor of modern Irish history at University College Cork. By the 1950s this trend had created a peculiar dynamic.

In the wake of the Republic of Ireland Act of 1949, elderly Irish Party figures within the universities propagated the idea that Griffith literally had to be dragged kicking and screaming into abandoning his elitist monarchist politics and accepting their republican majority viewpoint after 1917.[46] This very misleading idea was essentially propagated for one specific reason. During 1949, T.K. Whitaker had announced that about £150 per head of the Irish population of state assets was still invested purely in Britain and that in order to meet the challenges of the post-Second World War world, if the Irish state was to survive, it would have to attempt to repatriate some of its sterling assets, turn its eye towards American investments in Europe and meet the educational challenge of creating a more industrialised workforce.[47] Some people honestly considered that this made Whitaker some kind of visionary. Partly due to this reputation, he would ultimately replace DeValera as NUI Chancellor in 1975. However, Whitaker's post-1949 arguments were precisely what Griffith and in turn Collins, as Griffith's finance minister, had argued were necessary in the wake of the First World War as both the economic policy and the very reason for the establishment and existence of Dáil Eireann. In their day, this was seen also as a means for Ireland to catch up with the rest of Europe and to enter the modern world as a distinct nation. Evidently, however, this reality had been completely forgotten in the interregnum. There were several interrelated reasons for this development.

There has been perhaps no more destructive influence upon the development of a historiography of twentieth-century Ireland than the propaganda launched by Childers in the wake of the Four Courts bombardment. This equated the single issue of the relationship between the faltering of a party political pact and the challenge of possibly sustaining the Dáil by means of a coalition with a claim that 'Free State' and 'Republican' armed forces had now come into being and were 'at war'. The pact was not an issue of 'war', however. It related only to the holding of a single general election. Its faltering represented, at most, a failure to consolidate that agreement reached in September 1921 regarding how the development of a party political system for any Irish parliamentary government should come about at the time of the next general election. It was the uncertain economic situation facing the country that created this problem. Just as some proverbial 'unionist', 'home ruler', 'labour', 'republican', 'Christian–democratic' or some other interest group might find it advantageous to 'oppose the treaty', a similar dynamic could likewise motivate people to 'support the treaty'. This was a purely party-political scenario, however. Nevertheless, even those scholars who have attempted to conceptualise a framework for analyses of the evolution of an Irish foreign policy have typified an 'Irish civil war' as the founding event of the modern Irish polity,[48] notwithstanding the obvious fact that no country, let alone a foreign policy, can be based upon a civil war, either in theory or in practice.

That this level of confusion can arise in historical studies is undoubtedly a legacy of the almost perpetual state press censorship that existed in Ireland between 1914 and 1923, which was inherently designed to create a false sense, by means of the press itself, regarding what was actually taking place in the country on an economic and, in turn, a political level. The development of the Sinn Féin Party in the wake of its rejection of Griffith's policy during February 1922 is perhaps the ultimate illustration of how this atmosphere of suspicion, which was deliberately created by Dublin Castle in conjunction with the banks, could lead to political alignments that had little or nothing to do with that 'treaty' which was supposedly so important in determining the nature of all Irish political behaviour. A significant determinant of this dynamic was that representatives of those businesses and Irish institutions (including educational ones) whose capital was invested in Britain naturally did not want any efforts to be made in the direction suggested by Griffith (or, later, by Whitaker, after 1949). Consequently, they naturally wanted to control any efforts that may be made in this direction by attempting to confuse public understanding of the nature of various political interest groups in the country.

J.J. 'Sceilg' O'Kelly moved from being the chief *gaelgoir* of the Irish Party's and Dublin Castle's *Freeman's Journal* in the early days of Sinn Féin to being the chief propagandist of a Pearse cult in the *Catholic Bulletin* after 1916,[49] and, ultimately, the leader of the 'post civil war' Sinn Féin Party without ever essentially altering his politics, which was that of a Catholic educationalist who used the Gaelic League as his favoured medium for maximising Catholics' influence within the civil service. To uphold DeValera's stance that the terms of an oath of allegiance was absolutely central to the survival or destruction of an Irish national identity, Sceilg defined republicanism as an absolute detestation of the legacy of the French Revolution of 1789 and a wholehearted identification with Archbishop Walsh's justification of the Church's support for DeValera's American tour of 1919–1920: that at least in the American republic, if not in most European countries, politicians were not ashamed to assert along with Ireland that 'In God We Trust'. Furthermore, Sceilg declared that he had a divine duty to the whole of Irish society to set the historical record straight for all time. This was to uphold that the idea that the IRB were not the founders of the ideal of 'the republic' but they had been its arch-betrayers (in 1922) and had supposedly illustrated their willingness to betray it even before its inception because Griffith's ideal of Irish economic equality with Britain proved that he was a reactionary British monarchist and perhaps even an untrustworthy Catholic.[50] Some historians, concerned with the possibility of a decline in appreciation for denominational education in Ireland, have celebrated Sceilg's legacy as a brave upholder of a 'republican' ideal that was supposedly represented by the 1916 rising and have argued that this is the essential basis of the Irish state's national identity that must be preserved at all costs.[51] However, there can be no doubt that Sceilg's politics, which led him to *always* deny the legitimacy of the Dáil, were motivated by the old Christian–democratic (anti-statist) tradition of thought of that conservative body of Irish Party opinion for which Gwynn had now effectively assumed the unofficial status as an economic spokesman.

To those Cumann na nGaedhael supporters during the mid-1920s who represented Griffith's rather than Gwynn's ideals, Sceilg's brand of politics was perhaps the ultimate illustration of how DeValera had botched his own particular strategy in attempting to prepare for a regrouping of all Irish nationalist interest groups in the wake of the expected implementation of the Articles of Agreement for a Treaty in December 1922. DeValera certainly facilitated Sceilg's movement. Aside from attempting to deny the reality that the Irish state was founded in

December 1922, one example of this was the formation of a National Graves Association. Its job was to run Sinn Féin local history societies to propagate Sceilg's version of history and also to parade all the graveyards in the country where old IRB rebels may have been buried, presumably to keep a nightly watch in case Griffith, Collins, Devoy and company ever came back and needed to be run through the heart with a stake. Sceilg's party of republican ghostbusters need not have worried, however: the Fenian dead were well and truly dead.

A barrister who wrote a very noteworthy biography of the most well-known Irish Catholic barrister of Griffith's youth also wrote a study of this peculiar aspect of twentieth-century Irish political culture and suggested that it represented a social malaise of unknown origins.[52] However, this is not a credible argument. The perspective championed by the post-1922 Sinn Féin Party has self-evidently governed many aspects of both Irish historical studies and public commentaries,[53] and it had deep historical roots precisely because it was rooted in the same cultural–nationalist tradition that had sustained the Irish Party and would ultimately play a significant part in shaping the constitutional ethos of the Irish state. Some examples of this reality are worth noting.

David Sheehy, an old Irish Party leader since the late 1880s who had represented the views of the long-celebrated (or, at least, self-celebrated) UCD circle of literary intellectuals represented by the likes of the Sheehy Skeffingtons and Cruise O'Briens, became a daily communicant during 1922 in the hope that the ridiculous Irish (economic) nationalist policy and unholy ethos intended by Griffith and Collins for the Irish Free State would soon be no more,[54] and in doing so he was essentially acting no differently than Sceilg or indeed those who wrote epic verses for *Poblacht na hEireann War News* during December 1922, celebrating Childers as Ireland's greatest 'martyr' alongside other former British political luminaries such as Roger Casement. There was a reason for this. As it was known in Irish Party circles that the economic provisions of the Government of Ireland Act were set in stone as far as the country's financial institutions were concerned, any attempt by Griffith and Collins (and both men fully advertised their intentions in this regard) to revolutionise this system could potentially have involved tearing up the entire existing arrangements for the financial management of the country's universities, schools, hospitals and churches, along with virtually everything else (including Ireland's food producing market for Britain). Did anyone actually want this? Would they actually prefer to prevent it?

Just as had been the case during the British government's attempt to sideline Irish economic nationalist debate between 1911 and 1914 (most particularly during 1913), from the 1920s onwards the old Irish Party supporter, who often represented Ireland's meat producers for Britain, and the urban labour activist who claimed to draw inspiration from the internationalist ideas of

Larkin could still find a common economic cause in opposing the idea of an Irish economic nationalism by attempting to manipulate the private sector. That such a development, opposing (or even ridiculing) statist thinking in an Irish context, came to be associated with a terminology of republicanism after 1922 might be typified as one of the most peculiar manifestations of political nomenclatures in the entire modern history of Western Europe precisely because republicanism (including its pro-independence varieties) is inherently a state-centred conception of politics. Indeed, if the Irish polity was more in favour of a republican politics than it apparently seemed to have been then Dáil Eireann would probably not only have introduced republican-minded laws such as compulsory military service in the Irish Defence Forces but also be willing to treat all Christian–democratic, or other, critics of state-centred political philosophies, such as parliamentary (i.e. Dáil) supremacy over all, as second-class citizens or, possibly, even worse. This was not essentially the manner in which an Irish political society had evolved, however. Many historians have sought to explain this reality by referring to 'an Irish parliamentary tradition' or 'an Irish constitutional tradition' that supposedly long predated the birth of the Irish Free State.[55] However, what they are essentially describing here is the simple fact that Ireland has always been a common law country and one that, since Victorian times, has been preoccupied with issues of church–state relations; in particular, defending Christian–democratic values against state encroachment.

Strictly speaking, one cannot refer to 'an Irish constitution' or an (internationally recognised) 'Irish parliament' prior to 1922. Griffith played a significant part in creating both, as well as that National Army from which the Irish Defence Forces, which equally swore to uphold the authority of Dáil Eireann, emerged. However, within Irish political society and cultural commentaries (including academic and historical ones) there has always been a refusal to espouse such a perspective. This may be for fear to be seen to be championing an understanding of Irish life that is inappropriately too state-centred and thus contrary to the Christian–democratic identity of an intentionally weak Irish state. The sense that the Irish polity rejected all that Griffith stood for in 1922, just as the Irish Party had always done, may also have encouraged such a perspective. Whatever the case, it has had the affect of creating historical narratives that are essentially based upon a denial of the origins of the Irish state with a view to giving ample expression to the anti-statist mentality that has governed Christian–democratic as well as labour politics in Ireland, as elsewhere.

As intimated in the introduction of this book, if the European tradition of monument building means anything in terms of the culture of Irish society then it would seem to indicate that if one applies the old adage that history is written by the winners to an Irish context then Griffith must be typified not as a man who achieved his objectives but rather as the greatest loser of twentieth-century Irish history. Reflecting this legacy, the debates of well-informed Irish academics and politicians upon the economic legacy of the local government legislations of 1888 and 1898; the economic significance of modifications in Irish banking policy; the outbreak and development of First World War; the initiation of American investment in Europe after 1918; the formation of Dáil Eireann in 1919; and the relative economic significance of the Government of Ireland Act as opposed to the potential present in Articles of Agreement for a Treaty; have not aroused any interest from the historians of Ireland. Instead, historians have chosen to focus, in the Sceilg tradition, on the question of how to commemorate what has been described as 'the dead of the Irish revolution' as the basis of an Irish national identity.[56] This was a 'revolution' in which, as noted in the introduction, Griffith has been typified as the supreme 'counter-revolutionary' figure,[57] notwithstanding the fact that he was virtually the only Irish political figure during 1922 who was still talking about a forthcoming 'greatest revolution in Irish history' that Dáil Eireann was in the process of setting in progress.

Similarly, what is now being defined by historians as 'the Irish revolution' might be described instead as 'a British convolution' as it is supposed to have begun with Henry Asquith, by his introduction of a Government of Ireland Bill in Westminster in April 1912, the subsequent rise of volunteer and regular territorial forces (these two developments were inherently directly interrelated) for the sake of the First World War and to have been both defined and concluded as a purely military matter. Historians have also equated this militarism, especially from 1916 onwards, with a then non-existent organisation called 'the IRA' (which was not founded until 1922); an interpretation that has been patronised by British historians worldwide and has evidently has become the basis of the Irish state's national identity as well.[58] Such historical interpretations, however, are not only a flat denial of the logic employed by contemporary Irish political and business leaders but also of the fact that anti-militarism was the predominant tone of Irish electoral politics throughout the entire time period, not just during the 1918 general election. This was also true of all aspects of the defensive campaign adopted by Dáil Eireann after 1919. This was a campaign in which the Irish Volunteers, which first acquired an 'IRA' nickname in the British press during 1920 after Dáil Eireann was labelled as a terrorist organisation for its opposition to British control of Irish finances, endeavoured to act as a peacekeeping and nascent Irish police force at a local government level to encourage the reform or disbandment of the militarily governed R.I.C. in favour of the idea of creating an unarmed Irish 'gardai'. In this sense, the Irish Volunteers also had an anti-militarist ethos, while it was also the argument of most Irish nationalists from 1915 onwards that any defence forces for an independent Irish government would have no desire to become involved in international wars but instead support the concept of international peace-keeping; hence, the Dáil's attraction to the League of Nations idea.

If an 'Irish revolution' can possibly be said to have taken place during this time period of history at all, then it essentially began with the formation of Dáil Eireann as a parliamentary assembly and provisional government during 1919 (as represented by its declaration of independence, which was sent around the world) and reached its conclusion with the financial settlements of 1926–1927. This represented the summation of all unilateral Irish efforts, no matter how hesitant, to take control of their own destinies during this time period. Dáil Eireann—not a non-existent organisation called the IRA—was the progenitor as well as the essential basis of this agitation. By contrast, the Sceilg tradition of attempting to turn the Dublin rebellion of April 1916 (an event in which the Irish Party and Ulster Party's leaderships were complicit, via the personages of Redmond and Carson) into a retrospective 'independence day' has most certainly created a deep irony in Irish historical studies because this event had no essential context outside of the First World War (excepting perhaps the rather marginal history of the IRB). The same was not true, however, with regards to the establishment of Dáil Eireann or indeed its ultimate survival; the latter goal being the sole reason for the proverbial citizen–soldier polity of *that* time to have existed. This was also the true origin of the Irish Defence Forces, although the strength of the Marxist–IRA tradition of labour politics or analysis, launched by Childers, has been such in historical studies that to acknowledge the existence of an Irish army has actually been treated by many a historian as an almost ideologically fascistic idea, as if it were an attempt to deny the existence of the common labour market between Britain and Ireland. As university historians are themselves civil servants, one might be tempted to conclude that this trend of thought indicates that Dáil Eireann itself actually refuses to acknowledge the existence of Dáil Eireann as the government of Ireland while the Irish Defence Forces considers that it has no possible reason to exist.

Aside from the Irish Christian–democratic desire for a weak state, the explanation for these seeming paradoxes may lie partly in the relationship between the private and public sector in Ireland and, in particular, how little this has actually changed in some respects ever since the nineteenth century. The economy of Ireland remained more unionist than nationalist in nature. As an extension of this reality, common misconceptions in Griffith's day regarding Irish politics have continued to shape many historical studies to this day. For instance, Irish historical professors still argue that it was in the great Irish Party's power to make or break each successive British government and such governments, even such as that of Lloyd George, also supposedly fell purely because of 'the Irish question'. These claims have been rooted in a belief that if the Tories had not 'played an Orange card' against the Liberals from the mid-1880s onwards Ireland would have attained all its political desires.[59] This, however, is a fallacy rooted in a failure to understand that each British government rose or fell depending on its fiscal policy for Britain; a question in which Ireland (let alone 'orange cards') was non-existent as a distinct factor, no matter how much the Irish Party worked to make the United Kingdom a better place for its Catholic subjects. Just as T.P. O'Connor ultimately survived in British politics only through identifying with a labour cause, the only interest in Britain in anything to do with Ireland after 1918 came from a small minority of (non-Catholic) Scottish nationalists who, likewise, tended to find their only outlet in British politics in a nascent labour party. William O'Brien and Redmond's success in holding a very slight balance of power in Commons in 1910 (the development that led to the celebratory erection of a statue of Parnell on O'Connell Street) was no more a significant event in British politics than T.P. O'Connor's return for a single parliamentary division in Liverpool during 1886. Are Irish historians to base their understanding of modern Anglo-Irish relations and, indeed, the whole of modern Irish political history, on a belief that T.P. O'Connor was virtually the uncrowned king of Britain? In the logic employed in virtually all Irish university historical textbooks on the politics of the time period, however, he occupies precisely such a position, even if he is not mentioned by name.

A critical factor in the creation of such narratives has been the twentieth-century 'Marxist' mentality whereby dialectics on 'the course of history' are viewed as a necessary tool for winning a political battle for societal control. This may be said to have exercised a very unfortunate influence on Irish historical studies, not least because before 1938 there was no real body of scholarship on the subject at all and so the inherent starting point for historical scholarship (the beginning of research) was almost immediately eclipsed by a Marxist end point (an ideological argument). This trend was first made evident in the contribution to Irish historical studies of British Commonwealth historians who shared the preoccupation of London *Times* during the inter-war years (specifically from the formation of the British ministry of labour in 1918 onwards) in claiming that the hitherto unknown figure of Karl Marx, a briefly influential, albeit always marginal figure, in 1848 revolutionary circles, was now somehow suddenly a sovereign presence in determining the international and internal relations of every country of the globe; a perspective that was read *backwards* into an interpretation of the history of Ireland under the Union, especially since 1886, and the development of Anglo-Irish relations by Nicholas Mansergh, the British government's choice to head studies in the British universities of the challenges facing all the commonwealth countries (especially South Africa and India) and a political advisor to DeValera.

Without doing any historical research, Mansergh cited Marx, Lenin, Mazzini and a few English statesmen as the sole authorities on Irish life; claimed that to admit that an economic interpretation of Irish history under the Union is possible is to assert 'that the class struggle alone was fundamental'; and that 'Griffith's ambition … was to make Ireland a Gaelic Manchester' (ironically, Manchester was where Childers' anti-Griffith organ *Poblacht na hEireann War News* was published) and so he was dismissed by Irish political society, under the leadership of James Larkin, as a man whose ideas appealed only to the reactionary middle classes.[60] Regarding this thesis, it has recently been argued that Mansergh's 'unrivalled scholarship' and 'pioneering brilliance' have made his writings absolutely 'essential … for the understanding of nineteenth and early-twentieth century Ireland' and particularly 'an indispensable guide to relations between Britain and Ireland from the home rule crisis [1886]' onwards. His reputation as a historian is particularly 'secure' for all time because 'Mansergh's great strength as a historian was his passionate conviction that history was not merely about the "past" … [but] the relating of "history" to the violent [?] politics … of contemporary Ireland.'[61] Mansergh's writings, however, were essentially no different from those of the Earl of Midleton who, shortly before Mansergh, was labelled (in London) as 'the greatest living authority on Ireland' because he used an interpretation of modern Irish history to justify his overall interpretation of contemporary Irish politics and his extant desire to manipulate the Irish private sector into opposing the principle of Irish self-government;[62] a manifestly ideological exercise that, by its very nature, essentially denies the possibility of Irish historical studies at all by inherently defining it according to a perpetual present agenda.

If British writings on Irish history frequently betray an inappropriate, or insufficient, context for analyses, a curious by-product of the usages of history to sustain a cultural self-confidence tale in Ireland ever since the Irish Party's day is that few within Ireland itself outside churchmen, or even church historians, have been inclined to probe any deeper into the dynamics of Anglo-Irish relations under the Union than surface debates on national identity.[63] This did not necessarily guarantee improvements in historical understanding. For instance, one church historian (Emmet Larkin, who was also a student of Anglo-American relations) judged around the time of DeValera's death in 1975 that the terms of the concordat worked out between Parnell, the Catholic hierarchy and British government during the mid-1880s, which was created to deal with the potential problems arising from the fact that half of adult males were in the process of being enfranchised for the first time, was not only still extant but was also essentially the entire basis of the Irish political and legal system. This argument was justified as follows. With regards to politics, it was judged that this concordat in Anglo-Irish relations had saved Ireland from both 'the tyranny of the general will' and 'the politics of dissent' by creating a 'politics of consensus' that 'made an important contribution both to the making of democracy meaningful and to the survival of representative institutions'. This consensus 'was real ... because none of its constituent elements, the "bishops", the "party" or the "leader" was a law unto itself and none had the power to impose its will on the others'. Meanwhile, with regards to the legal question of a possible Irish constitution, the destruction of Griffith's pro-treaty party in 1922 and the promotion of DeValera's anti-treaty stance was necessary on the grounds that 'it was much easier to begin the return to the politics of dissent from within the framework of the politics of consensus than it would have been from the tyranny of the general will'. The great importance of keeping all Irish political developments, including the expression of dissent, 'within the framework of the politics of consensus' established during 1886 was fully understood by all Catholic professionals (be they academics, barristers or medics) as the condition of their employment, and 'that agreement, and the resulting consensus, in fact, has been fundamentalised in the [1937] constitution of the Irish State, and is basic to the politics characterised in Ireland today by the effectiveness of its democracy and the success of its representatives institutions in preserving and guaranteeing liberty'.[64]

Even though the church certainly had a part to play in Anglo-Irish relations, as well as in Anglo-American relations (including in so far as this related to Ireland; this being the dynamic that led to Redmond's downfall and necessitated DeValera's US tour), what Larkin was essentially describing here was the critical role of the Catholic Church in both creating and maintaining a sense of social cohesion in Ireland as well as in championing Christian–democratic ideas in politics. In turn, public representatives, including both elected politicians and professionals such as barristers and academics (including historians), were encouraged to both give expression to this consensus and, in the NUI tradition, to find answers to Ireland's problems as much as was possible in Catholic theories of social justice.[65] This may conceivably have been well and good in terms of the ethics of Irish public life, but if one accepts Lee's view that 'Catholicism had no place in the value system of financial capitalism',[66] then the question must surely arise for Irish historians: what was Irish public representatives' value system in terms of the management of Irish finances?[67] Was the establishment and development of a Christian–democratic value system considered the only goal for Irish politicians to achieve or the only potential reason for an Irish parliament ever to exist?[68]

The church's desire, with DeValera's support, to ensure that whatever written constitution Ireland might acquire after December 1922 would accurately reflect both the common law traditions of Ireland as well as those Christian–democratic political traditions that had been evolving in Ireland ever since the 1880s was essentially representative of Irish public opinion.[69] This was indicated by the fact that this preoccupation was shared not only by DeValera's anti-treaty party and the church, but also by the proverbial pro-treaty party beyond the level of the economic nationalist minority represented by the likes of Griffith and Collins. Indeed, the prevalence of Catholic educators in DeValera's professedly peace-loving anti-treaty party and the consequent complete unwillingness of pro-treaty NUI academics to criticise their stance was not at all coincidental.[70] DeValera's claim that he only had to look into his own heart to know what the Irish people wanted was later deliberately misinterpreted by some who felt he went a little too far in demonising the opposition in 1922. There can be little doubt, however, what this temperamentally conscientious (and, in turn, highly sensitive) politician actually meant: the Irish people did not want to live in a Godless state.[71] Both the treaty agreement and the IRB's constitution nominally stood for a complete (i.e. legally enforced) separation of church and state, but DeValera maintained that he was 'too trained in English democracy to sit down under a dictatorship'.[72] What 'English democracy' or 'dictatorship' he (or, indeed, his advisor Childers) was actually referring to here might have completely mystified some of his contemporaries. However, his remark was essentially a reflection of the validity of the aforementioned church history thesis in terms of its influence upon that section of Ireland's professional classes who, like DeValera himself, were educated in private Catholic schools and consequently believed that the survival and growth of a nascent Catholic governing class in Ireland rested upon one particular dynamic.

Although he may have claimed that in standing by the Church he was standing in line 'with centuries' of Irish opinion, in practice DeValera was simply standing by that consensus which Larkin identified as having been arranged during the mid-1880s and so had played a part in governing Irish public life ever since DeValera's own childhood. Henceforth, the equal relevance of the Catholic Church to Irish life as the relevance of the Church of England to English life was practically given a political seal of approval by 'English democracy', at least according to the political self-understanding of that body of Catholic professionals that had been represented by the Irish Party and who chose, partly at his own disingenuous request, to celebrate Gladstone's legacy upon precisely that basis. Irish historians still study and, indeed, even celebrate Gladstone's legacy for Ireland purely upon this same perception.[73] Those in Ireland who had resented that consensus after 1886, including Griffith, did so because they did not approve of the financial and, in turn, political connotations of Gladstone's *actual* governmental policy for

Ireland, which (contrary to Irish Party rhetoric) was upheld by the Tories as much as the Liberals (this is also why Churchill, with Lloyd George's support, relied upon this dynamic in an attempt to manipulate Anglo-Irish relations during 1921–1922). It was for this very reason that Griffith stood outside what Larkin described as 'the politics of consensus' to a significant degree. Many contemporaries understood this reality, while Griffith's friends sometimes acknowledged this as well, even if, when acknowledged publicly, this was often done obliquely, even in verse,[74] due to a fear of backlash arising from Catholic sensitivities to criticism.[75] That these sensitivities existed at all essentially had a peculiar origin. To the Catholic Church within Ireland itself, the simple fact that Gladstone (an avowed Christian) had overseen the disestablishment of the Church of Ireland in 1869 was a reason to view the significance of his career in such a very simplistic and positive light. The tradition of Catholic private schools in Ireland in perpetuating the idea that *this* was the basis upon which a governing class for Ireland had developed essentially reflected their skewed or, at least, limited sense of history, however.

The concept that Emmet Larkin described as 'the politics of consensus' was less a concrete political reality set in stone in Griffith's day than a deep-seated aspect of Irish political culture. In particular, the mere thought of any forcible break with the consensus upon which the Catholic professional classes in Ireland had attained and would continue to seek to extend their influence from the 1880s onwards was generally equated by this same section of society with an intolerable form of injustice. It is precisely for this reason that many of DeValera's contemporaries and, in turn, historians (in the present day, most notably John Regan, who used Childers' *Poblacht na hEireann War News* as the basis of his interpretation of 1922)[76] always typified the treaty settlement as a virtual 'counter revolution' against the inevitable direction that Irish political society was taking ever since the establishment of the Irish Party's hegemony in 1886. One reflection of this reality can be found in the arguments of Maynooth College historians that 'only a handful of ideologues expressed reservations' regarding this political impetus (and if there is one thing that Catholic and Protestant societies hate equally—be this in Ireland, England or indeed anywhere—it is 'an ideologue'), and, that specifically within the Catholic majority, this supposed ideological perversion of being dogmatic advocates of a political nationalism had generally occurred only among 'fenian' men who (like Griffith and Collins) had 'progressed' no further than a primary school education within the Catholic education system and, in turn, Catholic professional society.[77] This mentality has also found affirmation in the tradition of contemptuously referring to Griffith as a mere 'tabloid nationalist',[78] as well as in the continuity in Catholic professionals' mocking assertions, ever since the Victorian period, that the 'bould fenian men' were a mere laughable side-product of politically irrelevant cultural nationalist debates among the poorer (non-professional) classes.[79] Irish Catholic society was, in this sense and in its preoccupation with family connections, very aristocratic in its social values, perhaps reflecting the ethos of the hierarchy as the proverbial 'princes' of the church as much as the historic legacy of Irish involvement in British politics or, indeed, a prevalent ambivalence throughout Europe, including during the interwar years, regarding the merits of egalitarian or 'democratic' values.

The whole question of church–state relations was where especially strong continuities with the Irish Party political tradition existed. The argument of clericalist Irish Party MPs during 1886 in defence of their acceptance of Gladstone's virtual concordat for Ireland that 'to deprive the clergy influence in the State necessary means to deny the Church supervision over the morals of the people'[80] (this was also the basis of their denunciations of all their critics as Orange bigots) would not necessarily have seemed out of place in the Irish political discourse of the 1920s and 1930s or, indeed, thereafter. DeValera's determination to replace the Free State constitution with an explicitly Christian-democratic one (this objective, incidentally, was facilitated by two of Griffith's former supporters)[81] won much public approval during the 1930s and, indeed, long afterwards. The very emphasis on detail in the 1937 constitution essentially reflected the involvement in its drafting of the Jesuits who, as an Oxford University Jesuit explained to his UCD audience, partly intended the Irish constitution to serve as a role model text for Catholics in all other common law countries, such as the United Kingdom and the United States, in countering liberal political agendas by emphasising the vibrancy of Christian democratic thought.[82] One might say that it was partly as an extension of this trend of thought that, by the 1950s and 1960s, a higher percentage of Ireland's university graduates were acting in the service of the church (whether abroad or at home, as missionaries, clerics or educators) than in the service to the Irish public by means of the state.[83] Meanwhile, emigration continued to be a predominant feature of Irish social life and a keynote to the economic management of Ireland by London. More recently, if the trend of Ireland's university graduates seeking careers primarily in the church has dissipated, the exact same trend of the emigration of Ireland's professional classes, as much as its regular workforce, has continued, while the ethos of the state's education system and, in turn, the Irish civil service has changed comparatively little.

The chosen national identity of the Irish state, reflected in the statue of the pre-historic Fenian dying a perpetual and agonising death for the eternity in the GPO, was rooted partly in the fact that under Sweetman (1908–1911) and later DeValera's presidencies of Sinn Féin (1917–26), the taking of any political move that might potentially shatter what was considered to be the unity of Ireland's Catholic political representatives was virtually a taboo and deliberately frustrated at every turn. This was the reason for the virtual non-existence of the Sinn Féin Party under Griffith's presidency (1911–17; the era of the associated 1916 rising) and why its opponents after 1917 had considered Sinn Féin most controversial in the era of radicalisation brought about during Griffith's later acting presidency of the party (September 1919–November 1920). The persistence of this polarity of opinion reflected the paramount influence of the Irish Party, a party for which Griffith never made any secret of his hatred and vice versa.

At their most extreme, it is not difficult to see how such animosities coloured many contemporaries' perceptions of the meaning of the proverbial 'civil war' conflict of the 1920s. For instance, the satirical plays of Sean O'Casey, a former IRB man, not only highlighted the great poverty in Irish society and political leaders' complete indifference to it, but also expressed dissatisfaction with the tenor of mainstream Irish nationalism, suggested that the so-called 'IRA' had turned the Green, White and Orange tricolour, established by fanatical republicans of 1848 and cherished in some IRB circles, into Green, White and Yellow (White and Yellow being the colours of the Vatican). By contrast, Childers' *Poblacht na hEireann War News* had argued that the IRB was not only 'imperialist' (a claim based on the allegation that Collins was implementing Churchill's will), as Griffith supposedly was, but had similarly been 'blessed' by James Craig's 'Orange' Northern Irish government.[84] In support of this latter claim, DeValera actually maintained during the winter of 1922 that the IRA was a manifestation of God's will.[85] His paranoid suspicions that the IRB was somehow still a hovering presence in Irish society for at least another fifteen years partly motivated his later demand, after his re-entering the Dáil, for a fundamental reform of the Defence Forces (at least on the level of personnel),[86] and, ultimately, his installing explicitly religious features into Defence Forces flag protocol to represent, symbolically, the supremacy of the Christian preamble to his popular Irish constitution of 1937 above all else, even the constitutional office of President.[87] By contrast, in directly associating the question of arms bearing with religion, some of DeValera's critics wondered if he had perverted people's sense of religion in Ireland to the point of launching a 'devil era' in Irish politics.[88] In adopting such stances, however, DeValera had only done whatever Childers had previously advised him would be absolutely necessary for him to do.[89]

A less extreme and perhaps more representative example of the meaning of the conflicts of the 1920s to contemporaries was the debate surrounding Sean Milroy, who was secretary at the Mansion House to receive all persons who were trying to call on the Dáil on business from February 1922 onwards. Milroy played a part in contributing to animosity by repeatedly typifying Griffith's critics in *Young Ireland* as a party of men who simply congratulated themselves on being Ireland's 'spiritual' defenders, claiming to be proud of their country's great material poverty, moral sanctity and willingness to entertain an impossibly unworldly ideal (common only to Marxists and the most eccentric of Catholics) of the withering away of all state authority while doing absolutely nothing to help the Dáil combat high unemployment and emigration, eradicate Dublin slumdom or persuade northern industrialists to find common economic interests with the south so a mutually beneficial relationship could develop. This was the tone of *Young Ireland* throughout the late spring and early summer of 1922. To the Irish–Ireland majority, however, and this included Irish Volunteers ('IRA men') who were of a more middle-class (including Catholic university-educated) social status than Griffith, the employment of such arguments were equivalent to waving a red flag at a bull. This was because they were seen to echo Sir Horace Plunkett's prior and much-hated (particularly in Irish Party circles) typification of Catholicism as a socially degenerate educational force on a purely economic level, not least due to the aristocratic social structure of the Church itself.

In the light of these trends, it is perhaps not surprising that Irish historians have recently judged that Griffith as a historical subject presents 'an awkward memory' because his life and times represents 'a past that no longer seems to suit'[90] and so he has been necessarily 'airbrushed out of Irish history'.[91] Evidently, Griffith was in his own day and somehow remains to this day a very offensive little man indeed. Meanwhile, a former Irish Taoiseach has judged after a lifetime of reading academic Irish histories that 'our schools of political and economic history do not seem to me to have cross-fertilised in a productive manner, and this has left even the best of our political histories of modern Ireland somewhat one dimensional'.[92] This 'somewhat one dimensional' nature of even the 'best of our political histories of modern Ireland' may be seen in the evidently felt need of some of Ireland's top historians to draw conclusions regarding the nature of politics in modern Ireland in the light of the fictional writings of James Joyce, John McGahern or W.B. Yeats,[93] as if Ireland exists only in the realm of cultural identity studies, or 'a fiction of improvement';[94] a trend that has perhaps been encouraged ever since the 1990s by the fact that Irish historical studies have been effectively superseded as an academic study by a racial form of 'Irish studies', patronised by British and Catholic universities worldwide. A combination of an obsession with national identity debates and the weakness of the economy of Ireland may possibly have engendered a very shabby form of historical studies indeed. Perhaps one may say that the chief significance of these trends lies in their role in creating a false amalgamation of the themes of political history (including economic history), literary history and even religious history as one single literary theme: Ireland. If comprehensible, such writings by their very nature limit historical understanding of each of the three, essentially separate, components by refusing to treat and develop analyses of each theme as a distinct subject.[95]

The issue of a church-approved national identity for the Irish state evidently influenced thinking relating to the economic management of Ireland to some extent. For instance, Oldham's successors as UCD economists George O'Brien and Patrick Lynch, a graduate of Cambridge, both subscribed to the notion of Ireland being an inherently and almost exclusively agricultural economic entity, as well as a conception of contemporary Irish life that was rooted in the same historical–political consensus as was established by Irish Party journalists during the mid-1880s. For instance, Patrick Lynch, UCD's top economist during the 1950s and 1960s, deemed it particularly important for all policy-makers and scholars to realise that:

> 'Middle class leadership in Ireland had been firmly established by Daniel O'Connell [1775–1847] … the roads towards political and social progress … had united his people around a single issue, Catholic Emancipation'.[96]

This was a direct expression of the sense of history and national identity espoused by Irish Party MP journalists and clergymen specifically from the mid-1880s onwards. Now, it was being accepted, almost a century later, as virtually a fact that, in some sense, should govern the present. However, as significant and as brilliant an individual as O'Connell was, the idea of the existence of a politically strong Catholic middle-class in O'Connell's day was actually an invention of mid-1880s Irish Party journalists to describe the expected hope of the arrival of a new political reality in their *own* day. Only 1 per cent of adult males had a right to vote at late as 1848, after O'Connell's death, and the British claim to have enfranchised some middle-class individuals in 1832 was simply a claim to have enfranchised some members of those sections of society who, like O'Connell himself, either owned landed estates or extensive property without having a formal aristocratic title or else operated within the hitherto unappreciated world of business. As a result, 1832 marked a significant growth of the principle of London financiers determining government policy. The attainment by Catholics of the right of political representation in the British imperial parliament was a significant political event but its context has often been misinterpreted.

Another issue of national identity formation for the Irish state that could seem to preclude historical understanding was the ideal of 'the republic'. This was a notion that, in Ireland as in most countries, was frequently a nebulous concept due to the appeal that such terminology had, or even still has, to simply denote the broad idea of 'liberty'. Between 1919 and 1922, an ideal of 'the republic' naturally became associated with the challenge of forming a written Irish constitution, although not many evidently placed the same value as Griffith did upon the challenge of not only creating such a constitution but also utilising it as a buffer against British economic and, in turn, political manipulations. Instead, this ideal was consciously associated with an Irish Christian–democratic tradition, not least by DeValera (this being a logic behind his political pronouncements from October 1917 onwards).

This ideal of a constitution was a novel, if hardly strictly contemporary, development. The basis of the revolutionary republican tradition in Europe ever since 1848 had been the ideal of creating written constitutions to guarantee political liberties for a populace at large against the influence of unaccountable monarchical governments. In an Irish context, the IRB Supreme Council's creation of its own organisational constitution in 1868, which also included a provision that the organisation's armed members must obey its unarmed members 'lest anarchy supplant liberty', was a curious reflection of this tradition of thought, as well as their awareness of the American example. However, it was not a mainstream feature of Irish life. Reflecting this, Irish Catholic professionals who had no time for these 'Fenian bastards'—and this is how IRB rebels were termed during the 1860s and thereafter—pointed to the 'liberal constitutional monarchy' ideal of the unwritten British constitution as superior to the sort of political chaos that frequently surfaced in would-be republican countries like France.[97] This was an intelligible argument and an idea that many Protestant Tories upheld as well. However, Catholics' chosen manner of championing this ideal, in an attempt to contain forever the influence of republicanism, created a potential paradox in Irish political discourse. This was the idea that a dichotomy existed between the employment of 'constitutional methods' (a meaningless adjective, beyond the sphere, perhaps, of the activities or mental pursuits of constitutional lawyers) and any potential, or would be, law-breaker under the Crown. This idea was employed not only as the basis of Irish Catholic political discourse in the Irish Party's day but it was also used as the interpretative framework for Irish historical discourse during the twentieth century after the establishment in 1938 of a joint north–south association of professional Irish historians with DeValera's support.

The founders of this school of professional Irish historians were graduates of the Institute of Historical Research at the University of London and professed a desire 'to nurture a new generation of rigorously trained historical scholars' in Ireland just like themselves.[98] On a methodological level, they undoubtedly did much valuable work, particularly with regards to earlier periods of Irish history.

However, specifically with regards to the history of Griffith's lifetime and the history of Ireland since the Union of 1801 the astounding trait of the work of all these scholars was their almost strict reliance on the terms of reference formerly used in Irish Party political self-definitions in their own historical analyses. For instance, from the mid-1880s onwards, William O'Brien MP (whose popularity in Ireland always stemmed from his great activism rather than his actual arguments)[99] and many other journalists earned notoriety for their verbal acrobatics in attempting to describe the operations of all contemporary political and cultural forces in modern Irish society as one single dynamic. This was done through adopting an improvised rhetoric that most contemporaries deemed to be a tiresome form of verbal diarrhoea. In this journalistic world, to refer to political concepts such as the existence of advanced nationalist battalions in the press in impregnating the physical forces of constitutionalism against the revolutionary impetuses of fenian moral forces, or any potential variation in the usage of such terms, was supposed to make some literal sense. Notwithstanding their status as 'rigorously trained historical scholars' of the Institute of Historical Research at the University of London—a noted centre for rational and economic historical analyses of the modern world—the association of professional Irish historians used this terminology as *the* basis, or terms of reference, for their own analyses of the political history of Ireland ever since the Napoleonic Wars; studies that were also of note for excluding all economic analysis to political developments. This example continues to be followed to this day. As an extension of this trend, historians have deemed any Irish critics of the British state ever since 1848 as individuals who were inherently either terrorists,[100] or men who, like Griffith, must be considered solely as having been activists in the cultural–nationalist world of letters alone as advocates of a literary 'separatism' (separate from true politics). This trend may even partly explain why the ambition to write a political biography of Griffith championed by Milroy and others up until 1938 was ultimately superseded by a Fine Gael patronised publication that, echoing Gogarty's purely personal memoirs, portrayed Griffith in much the same light as its poet author: a quintessentially Edwardian man of letters.[101]

The historiography of the Union itself can certainly serve to limit understanding of Griffith's life and times. Griffith was essentially a more perceptive analyst of the dynamics of that Union than subsequent generations of British and Irish historians have been prepared to admit, but it had always been a subject for hot debate. Some trends are worth noting. James Bryce of Belfast earned the reputation of being the greatest constitutional thinker in either Ireland or Britain during Griffith's lifetime because of his deep and sympathetic analyses during the mid-1880s of the constitutional tradition that underpinned the American federal republic. Later, this earned him the position as the British consul to the United

States. Shortly before he died, however, Bryce judged that the historical profession as it had developed since the mid-nineteenth century in Britain was largely to blame for all the strife in Ireland in the wake of the Government of Ireland Act of 1920 by having propagated competing British and Irish cultural nationalisms for the past couple of generations under the mantle of the Union as it had operated within Ireland.[102] After 1886, this was done with the support of contemporary Irish Protestant and Catholic MPs without ever making any rational analyses of the basis of that Union or engaging in constitutional thought. J.G.A. Pocock, one of the leading constitutional historians or republican intellectuals of England in the present day, has also identified a conundrum in the fact that it was not until the 1990s that some historians of the British state began to conceive of the notion of a 'Four Nations' historiography. While this was done solely to attempt to understand the potential meaning of the prospects of devolution, it reflected the inherent Anglocentric mentality of all historical studies ever written of 'the isles' hitherto. To raise this perspective means questioning accepted truths regarding British national identity, however, and perhaps not surprisingly there has been a very strong counter-reaction against this latter trend.[103]

The labelling of Irish nationalism or any Irish criticisms of the Union as a merely cultural and inherently anti-liberal phenomenon was a deep-seated feature of both political debate and historical studies ever since Bryce's youth. This was essentially *the* reason for the satirical tone of Griffith's Irish nationalist journalism. Griffith was also correct in identifying the dynamics by which this process both came about and was continually propagated. Britain's response to the French revolutionary and Napoleonic Wars (this led not only to the enforced Union with Ireland in 1801 but also the economic reforms of 1816–1824) necessarily became *the* basis for the subsequent expression of national identity in Britain; in particular, the need for a positive (or 'liberal') definition of its own empire against the (allegedly) purely militaristic nature of the Napoleonic Empires. As Griffith was fully aware, it was this dynamic above all else that essentially shaped the career of Gladstone, who became a monumental figure of nineteenth-century British politics primarily through his success in simultaneously justifying British foreign policy as a purely economic construct (the supposed opposite of the continental brand of imperialistic 'tyranny') while, not least through founding an appropriately titled new party, propagating a new national identity for the United Kingdom as the world's premier 'liberal state'. If inclined to resent this partial appropriation of their mantle as the traditional custodians of British national identity, the Tories nevertheless fully appreciated (Gladstone, after all, was originally one of their own) its necessity in justifying the imperial enterprise to the British public. Reflecting this, Gladstone's post-1866 definition of any question of British reform within Ireland—the 'liberal state' versus the 'fenian threat'—became an ever-growing aspect of British journalism and contemporary historical writing on Ireland after 1869 and, to *this day*, it has formed *the* interpretative framework for British academic studies of modern Irish history.

During Griffith's lifetime, the challenge that this created for all Irish public figures lay in their inherent difficulties in ever voicing an independent perspective without immediately being denounced, even by the historical profession within the universities, as an enemy of 'the liberal state'. A significant example of this trend was that it was exclusively in those moments of their career when they occupied a purely independent (non-party) political standing that post-1886 Irish Party figures such as Redmond and Davitt were free to highlight the flaws in 'the liberal state' myth. This was done not least by pointing out a fact that no Westminster MP subject to a party-whip could afford to do; namely, that there had not been a single year since the earliest days of the Union that Ireland was not subject to unique coercive legislation that was completely unknown in the rest of the United Kingdom.[104] Irish historians' complete unwillingness to draw attention to this fact has resulted in Irish state-funded historical studies that have typified all forms of criticisms of the British state in Ireland ever since 1848 as a manifestation of terrorism, ignoring the fact that, in Davitt's day, mere activism in political circles in Ireland was often deemed as a suspect form of 'fenianism' (a conveniently generic, albeit meaningless, term: 'physical force' was another such term that was used) and even T.P. O'Connor, the future 'father of the House of Commons', was labelled as an Irish terrorist suspect by police forces during the late 1880s.[105] The attempts by Irish political contemporaries to describe this strange situation they faced may have been ineffective, but they have certainly had a peculiar impact on the writing of modern Irish history. For instance, a thematic survey written during the 1990s summarised all existing literature about Griffith and, as a result, among the themes employed was 'the shadow of Synge' and 'the great debate' between 'constitutionalism' and 'physical force' (lest there be any confusion, it is important to point out that the nature of legal jurisprudence and the laws of physics are supposed to have completely different meanings in Ireland than they do for the rest of humanity).

This trend may be said to reflect Irish historians' uncertainty regarding how to treat the question of militarism (a.k.a. political violence) as a historical subject matter precisely because of specific broader trends in historical studies. For instance, British historians are fully capable of recognising that, in modern history, Britain has militarily invaded almost 90 per cent of the countries of the globe,[106] but are evidently incapable of recognising that militarism has never been a prominent feature of Irish life. Not only has Ireland itself never launched a military invasion (not unless, perhaps, one counts an apparent sixth-century invasion of northern Britain), but there has been, properly speaking, no military conflict on the shores of Ireland ever since the imported English civil wars of 1640 and 1690 respectively. Nevertheless, according to Irish university textbooks (which are invariably written by Northern Irish academics) the theme of 'war' has been a perpetual feature exclusively of Irish life (though, of course, not of liberal British life) ever since 1798.[107] The lack of Irish regulation of the private sector in the country ever since 1816 may have stimulated confrontations or, at least, rivalries between communities in Ireland, but it should not have resulted in the destruction of historical reason.[108]

The ongoing paramount concern in Ireland ever since the 1880s with national identity debates would eventually come to be associated in the 'two Irelands' with a reliance upon the iconographies of the volunteer forces first established during 1913, but this very development may be said to actually show up the inadequacies of all such narratives for understanding the dynamics of the time period. Indeed, the preoccupation of many historians with the iconography of, or imagined security threats posed by, what have often been typified, retrospectively and falsely, as 'paramilitary bodies' during this time period belies the fact that the members of such organisations were often the least aware of all contemporaries of economic trends in the country; a reality that would be reflected in most of their subsequent efforts, published or unpublished, at recollections of this period.[109] As far as Childers was concerned, however, the idea of creating volunteer forces in Ireland did have an entirely economic motive, for London, as part of an overall imperial plan to finance a forthcoming European war; no more and no less.

Recruitment drives in Ireland, for volunteer and subsequently regular territorial forces (these two developments were inherently directly interrelated), were not much different from those adopted during the 1910s in the rest of Britain or Europe, whereby aristocratic social leadership[110] and, to some extent, religion was used as a motive. The latter factor was precisely why attitudes towards the war in Irish Volunteer circles shifted dramatically after the initial German outrages in Belgium gave way to the rise of Belgium as a centre for a Catholic pacifist movement. Meanwhile, a great irony in Carson's utilisation of a Solemn Covenant for his initial recruitment drive was that, although he was an Anglican loyalist, he was echoing the historic example of Scottish Presbyterian Covenanters who actually rebelled against the Crown's prerogatives by expressing principled opposition to all ideas of war and, of course, state churches. The overshadowing and suspension of this issue by the war represented the great political significance of the latter, but when the war ended so too did the essential purpose of the volunteer forces. In other words, they were not an issue of perpetual significance. However, the question of the management of Irish finances self evidently was, as Craig understood better than many and would quite possibly have been understood at large in Ireland were it not for the state censorship that was the Defence of the Realm Act.

An important factor regarding understanding the context of the history of the Irish Volunteer movement is that the British political mentality that underpinned the summary judgments of the cabinet's Irish Situation Committee between 1916 and 1922 was essentially no different to cabinet thinking between 1879 and 1886. The common denominator was an absolute faith that the mere employment of the paper blueprints for imperial administration, which were, in turn, founded not least upon Gladstonian fiscal policy for the Empire, was an infallible guide in maintaining 'the liberal state', even if this 'liberalism' meant imprisoning hundreds of Irish public figures without trial for expressing dissatisfaction with a single piece of legislation (as in the autumn of 1881), being ready, in theory, to consider the execution of all elected Irish politicians (as in the summer of 1921) for suggesting that Irish public finances might not inherently be a matter solely for the British government to dispose of, and subsequently attempting to bribe Irish politicians to renege on their past political stances (as in the *Times* Commission, launched in conjunction with the British local government reforms, of 1888) or to turn against their own people. During both periods, extensive political intelligence work was carried out in Ireland and it is a particularly unfortunate consequence of the Childers myths propagated between 1920 and 1922 that historians worldwide have, for one reason or another, been encouraged to falsely interpret this political intelligence work as a military intelligence situation; an interpretative framework for twentieth-century Irish history that has been both used and promoted by academic historians in Canada and Cambridge.[111] Part of the interpretative difficulties some historians have faced here evidently stem from the fact that military personnel were frequently assigned to do police work in Ireland, especially in conjunction with the Resident Magistrate System designed in 1881,[112] but this did not alter the nature of that work: political intelligence. Conversely, this was also true with regards to Collins' work in attempting to protect and promote the Dáil's finance ministry. The stationing of British troops in Ireland under the Union had, in itself, been a cost-measured process, designed to relieve communities in Britain itself from the 'tyrannical' financial burden of supporting a standing army and so sustain the English self-perception that they were living within a 'liberal' political society.[113] This reality had played a part in shaping the government of all Ireland prior to the treaty, but after the formation of the Free State it applied only to Northern Ireland.

Many of the aforementioned trends in historical studies completely negate Griffith's sense of the political situation during his own lifetime. This may explain the fact that, although his name has featured in many a history book, historical studies of Griffith, or his ideas, have actually been very rare. In the fifty years after his death, none were essentially completed. In his day, the Irish Party at Westminster necessarily ridiculed Griffith as a static thinker in order to express opposition to his ideas: such is the norm of party-political mud throwing. This was often an effective campaign too precisely because of the great sales of Griffith's initial book (1904) and relative lack of wide readership for his subsequent journalism (1905–1917). This made him something of a one-man band prior to when Archbishop Walsh issued his fatalistic warning in May 1916 that Ireland had literally and irreversibly been 'sold'. It should come as no surprise to historians, however, that Griffith was essentially no different than any economic or political commentator in history in that his ideas were certainly not static, just as the economic world is never static. When the first studies of Griffith were written during the 1970s, however, both subscribed to the old Irish Party idea of Griffith being a static thinker.

A pioneering study by a historian in the University of Ulster argued that 'the economic policies advocated by Arthur Griffith are too well known to require recapitulation here; all that needs to be said is that he was a protectionist through and through.'[114] The labelling of Griffith as a protectionist by mere virtue of his reference to such ideas was ironic. In synthesising critiques of the Union in an attempt to create a single platform for all who wished to undo the inequality of the Anglo-Irish relationship, Griffith had adapted the protests of unionist economists who emphasised that Anglo-Irish economic equality was promised under the original Union of 1801 but had been progressively abandoned ever since, *and* the arguments of a handful of Dublin nationalist MPs who understood that Gladstone's model for devolved government in Ireland from 1886 onwards would only maximise the existing great inequality of the Anglo-Irish relationship by prioritising even greater protectionism for exclusively British economic interests within Ireland. Griffith's intended basis for his Sinn Féin Policy—a National Council comprising both local government and national politicians that would attempt to reverse all these trends by prioritising exclusively Irish interests in a competitive manner—may have failed to materialise prior to 1914, but the very formation of Dáil Eireann in opposition to Westminster's prerogatives was an implementation of the National Council idea. This was governed by an economic nationalism, *not* a simple protectionism, which under the Union could, of course, only mean unionism.

The second study of Griffith's ideas completed during the 1970s, written by a professor of British history in the University of Tasmania, also subscribed to the notion of his being a static thinker. Echoing James Larkin's tirades on behalf of the British labour party during 1911, it was argued that the entire significance of Griffith's life and times was best summed up by an anonymous London-

Irish critic who once wrote of Griffith's contribution to Irish life that 'it is this futile rubbish which plays the game of the West Briton'.[115] This study won much critical acclaim from many British and Irish academics, although its author later admitted that 'objectivity is difficult to achieve' in writing about Griffith precisely because, somewhat paradoxically, over fifty years after the subject's death, 'Irish politics are still to some extent based on the polarisation of attitudes to the treaty' that is associated primarily with his name.[116] Having to write for such a reading audience meant that balanced historical scholarship on the subject matter was not essentially possible.

During the twentieth century, the conditioning of Irish universities to serve a Christian–democratic purpose, as was reflected by the British government's establishment of the NUI under Archbishop Walsh, often encouraged would-be Irish civil servants, or those who *had* to consider state-centred solutions to a greater or lesser degree, to seek their professional training in Britain, especially Cambridge, as they had always done under the Union. One consequence of this was the tendency of both Irish academics and university-educated politicians to understand the dynamics of their country's history according to the evolution of the British imperial paradigm. This may explain the tendency born during the late 1940s to define Irish historical figures such as Daniel O'Connell, Thomas Davis and Arthur Griffith in the light of the contemporary debate on Mahatma Gandhi,[117] and the tendency ever since the Suez Canal crisis of the 1950s to define the history of Ireland purely according to the dynamics of decolonisation. For instance, an Irish-speaking civil servant in Dublin who attempted a biography of Griffith at this time did a lot of good research yet could offer no interpretative framework for his (Griffith's) life other than to suggest that 'the era of decolonisation was beginning'.[118] The paramount influence of Erskine Childers, who first coined the notion of the Irish civil war, in shaping Irish political self-understanding in his day and, indeed, the influence of his arguments in defining the parameters of all Irish historical writings on the period 1912–1923 to this day, is essentially a manifestation of this same trend. During 1921–1922, DeValera tended to rely on Childers' 'expert advice' for the exact same reason as Redmond had; namely, his greater familiarity with the full spectrum of considerations that underpinned British foreign policy. Essentially, DeValera believed that he could learn from Childers. In turn, popular conceptions of various issues such as Irish neutrality were founded upon Childers' reasoning instead of Griffith's emphasis upon the hard facts question of balancing budgets for small-scale defence forces in an optimum manner to complement the country's overall political strategy in promoting its own economic well being.[119]

As an Irish nationalist, Griffith argued that Ireland needed to look outside the United Kingdom, i.e. the Union, to understand its place in the world.

Nevertheless, this has prompted most twentieth-century Irish historians to label Griffith in the same light as the Irish Party had critiqued him: he was 'a narrow nationalist'.[120] This inability of Irish politicians and academics to conceptualise Ireland's distinct relationship with the world, either economically or intellectually, during 1911 was why Childers had celebrated the legacy of the British Empire (an inherently liberal legacy, to his Gladstonian mind) in creating a framework of home rule to perpetually contain inferior races and slavish populaces such as the Irish.[121] It was also essentially why those close to Griffith were a little puzzled, as well as slightly bemused, by the inability of some post-1916 Sinn Féin propagandists to understand his ideas: 'to many minds Arthur Griffith must appear as incomprehensible as the Sphinx'.[122]

Griffith's political vision for Ireland was based upon a firm belief in the positive options that exist for smaller states to pursue their interests in their own original manner. This was not because he was a visionary or a particularly exceptional individual. Indeed, as a firm believer in a republican concept of citizenship Griffith took umbrage at any attempts to place such labels upon him or anyone else. In Cosgrave's opinion, this was what made Griffith 'a true representative of the Dublin working man' who 'had a real and intimate sympathy with the people in their aspirations' and so 'was always in touch with reality'.[123] Griffith's belief in Ireland's potential stemmed from what seemed to him a self-evident fact: Ireland was not a country that, either in terms of its required defence forces or in terms of potentials for its own economic development, necessarily had to preoccupy itself greatly with issues such as the naval balance of power in Singapore, Washington, the Mediterranean or Buenos Aires. It could be much more rewarding for Ireland to engage in pursuing its own independent trading arrangements, with countries great and small, and to engage in mutual exchanges of ideas and goods with other small European countries that had similar material interests and governmental challenges to Ireland itself in developing its own models of government, including many options for civil service reforms.

Some continental writers on Ireland in Griffith's day were puzzled by Irishmen's seeming complete disinterest in such concepts despite their claims to be nationalists. More recently, a professor of economics in Brussels has argued that modern-day historians' perception of the economy of Ireland ever since the eighteenth century has been characterised by very strong discontinuities and uncertainties in analyses and he came to the conclusion that this was perhaps primarily due to the arbitrary manner in which Irish exchequer returns to and from the imperial treasury were both calculated and implemented after 1817.[124] Privately, Robert Giffen (in 1886) and Hugh Childers (in 1894) would not have denied this assertion regarding the arbitrary management of Irish finances, although no British treasury figure ever dared to admit publicly the relevance of Oldham's arguments during 1911. Nor have Irish historians ever been ready to give any credence to Griffith's arguments.[125] Griffith was an 'amateur', i.e. non-salaried or non-professional, yet well-informed, figure in all Irish economic debates and his attempts to draw political conclusions from this basis were not widely appreciated: Redmond's followers' success in typifying Griffith as a simple-minded protectionist for sellers of Aran sweaters in the west of Ireland was a declaration of his political irrelevance and historians have accepted this consensus.

Partition has certainly encouraged the perpetuation of such analyses. Paralleling the judgments of southern Irish civil servants, once they began writing their own histories Northern Irish civil servants would deem Craig to have been a political failure because of his supposed lack of economic vision and initiative in governing Northern Ireland,[126] largely unaware that he lacked directive powers in such matters. Meanwhile, Carson was sometimes labelled as a 'conflicted political soul' or a depressive neurotic who nevertheless made the sound decision to accept Gladstone's policy for Ireland, which was 'necessary, just and disastrous—all at the same time' in its role in preserving the Union in Ireland for all time.[127] Seeking answers in history to the root of these issues led many Belfast scholars to emphasise the supposed perpetual relevance of politics in Parnell's day,[128] if only because it was judged, falsely, this was the paradoxical situation in which Northern Ireland now seemingly found itself and they needed to explain or rationalise. This seemingly reflected a conscious decision *not* to focus upon the economic basis to Irish political debates at that time when the question of partition was actually raised. These were debates that underpinned Craig's sometimes ambivalent attitude towards seeking similar constitutional rights to what Griffith was demanding, although he considered, or perhaps one should say fully realised, that the situation was too unsettled and risky to warrant making such a move; hence his continued commitment to the partition programme.[129]

What Emmet Larkin would typify as 'the tyranny of the general will' could be better described as the potential for social and political chaos arising from economic disruptions. Northern and southern Irish politicians feared this situation equally, but rather than combining forces to find an ideal solution they were encouraged to eye both each other, as well as the political communities within their constituencies, with jealously, resentment or suspicion, as they competed for influence on a relatively petty (almost parish based) economic level; another reflection of a disconnection between the world of Irish politics and the management of Irish finances. This may seem to indicate that modern Irish society, in its desire for prosperity, was never really convinced that promoting an ideal of self-government was the answer to its desires. Most of all, however, it essentially reflected a problematic continuity of the post-1886 situation; namely, the deliberate turning of party politics (itself, a new development) into an instrument of clientelism or brokerage, exacerbating a historic tradition in Ireland (common to all British imperial colonies)[130] of making politics a mere dispensary for private patronage networks, even within the civil service.[131] This was not an example of plutocracy at work so much as a deliberate curtailment of the potential relevance of party politics as an instrument of change through parliament, as well as the perpetuation of a corruptible model of governmental administration.

It is worth remembering that both the Sinn Féin Party and the Ulster Unionist Party were founded simultaneously in reaction to the fact that the Irish local government act of 1898 had done nothing to remedy these problems. For Griffith, this was seen to be debilitating to the goal of Irish industrial or economic development, and for inhabitants of Belfast, this was a concern partly due to concerns about local policing (the largest riots to date in the history of that city took place during 1886) and the lack of Irish jurisdiction over that matter. It is not difficult to see how the troubled history of what became known as the 'two Irelands' during the twentieth century reflected the persistence, as well as further evolution, of these exact same problems; all of which, as A.W. Samuels noted, could partly be traced back to the inequalities in the Union that first became glaringly evident (especially for Scotland and Ireland) in treasury reports published to mark the passing of the British local government reforms of 1888. Childers may have celebrated the tradition of establishing imperial economies and weak governmental administration throughout the British Empire in creating profitable yet, if necessary, easily abandoned annexes to Whitehall, but the connotations this had for Ireland has often been overlooked due to the tendency of scholars to reference British government debates exclusively and, in the process, ignoring Irish political debates and circumstances entirely, whenever addressing what has been not too accurately referred to as the evolution of an Irish constitutional tradition.

Historians of the southern Irish state have been as reluctant as those of the northern Irish state to consider the question of the economics of partition, although Mary Daly's brief retrospective reference to Griffith's ideas was apt while describing the economic history of the Irish state between 1922 and 1939. She noted that 'Griffith contemplated with equanimity a fundamental restructuring of the banks and stock exchange to assist an Irish industrial revival', but the longstanding existence of a common currency, integrated banking and transport systems, as well as a common labour market between Britain and Ireland after 1816, meant that the existing system 'could not be dismantled without pain'.[132] This was self evidently true. The extent to which it governed all political option that faced Ireland in the wake of the Government of Ireland Act of 1920 is a subject matter that scholars have generally refused to examine, however, just as much as many politicians during the 1920s and 1930s evidently desired to evade that particular question.

Daly's argument (in 1994) that an obstacle to Griffith's goals lay in the fact that the existing system 'could not be dismantled without pain' is essentially an accurate reflection of the economic history of the Irish state since 1949 or, more particularly, after 1969, when the first efforts were made by the southern Irish state to repatriate its sterling assets with a view to launching a distinct monetary policy.[133] What it essentially ignores, however, is that this goal was not possible at all during 1922. The consensus after the passing of the Irish Free State Act of December 1922 and prior to the 1960s was simply, in DeValera's words, that 'we can pass a law at any time to control the banks or to sever parity with sterling. We can do all these things. It is merely a question of whether it is wise or unwise to do them.'[134] However, the extant Government of Ireland Act of 1920 indicated that it was most definitely unwise to attempt this, precisely because, as DeValera knew better than most, this is what caused the upheavals of 1922–1923 and made Griffith and Collins' strategy impossible. Consequently, attempting the same again could only be self-destructive.

The definition of Irish history according to cultural debates on national identity alone practically ignores the reality that while the Irish state acquired the right to its own constitution—whether this was Hugh Kennedy's slightly liberal Free State constitution of 1922 or Gavan Duffy's slightly illiberal but more comprehensive and popular Éire constitution of 1937—the economic identity of the Irish state was conditioned to remain that of Southern Ireland. The necessity of cooperation between Dublin and London to facilitate the transference of sterling assets to Dublin after 1969 was opposed by many sections of the British and Irish private sector just as they had opposed Griffith and Collins' plans in 1922, but, this time, it was the northern Irish rather than the southern Irish population who suffered the most from this reality, up until the economic relationship between Britain and Ireland became regulated by Éire's entry into a European Monetary Union in 1994. A publication patronised by the Irish Banks Standing Committee highlighted an underlying dynamic of this situation during 1984 when it acknowledged that the Anglo-Irish economic relationship had *always* encouraged the Irish banks to follow a similar trajectory to British banks, but according to a dynamic whereby economic policy was kept approximately twenty to twenty-five years behind whatever was the contemporary dynamic in Britain.[135] Hence, for instance, the challenge identified by Whitaker in 1949 not only reflected a broader British response to the trend of American investment in Europe after the Second World War, but it would also not start to be implemented in Ireland until the early 1970s. Similarly, in 1922, Griffith had seemingly won recognition of the idea behind the Financial Relations Report of 1896, that Ireland was deserving of 'a distinct position and separate consideration', but while the treaty agreement practically acknowledged this principle in law, it did not guarantee significant freedoms to act upon that basis in practice. Count Plunkett's vision during 'the treaty debates' of lost generations in Ireland may have been macabre but it did perhaps have a context in terms of this disconnection between Irish politics and Irish finance. Similarly, while Griffith and Collins viewed the issue of partition as a question of the possible exclusion of six northern counties from Ireland and attempted to act upon that nationalistic political understanding, in practice what partition actually meant, economically, was the exclusion of twenty-six counties from the United Kingdom and the persistence of an opposition to any moves to break an indirect British control over the economic direction of Irish life.

If there were to be any chance that Griffith's policy could have succeeded in 1922, banking policy would have had to change. All breakdowns in law and order in history have a primarily economic context. The supreme and most debated example in history is perhaps still the long-term impact upon the entire European political order and economy caused by Louis XVI's inability to create a French national bank. Griffith's failure, through no essential fault of his own, to create an Irish national bank that could enable the Dáil to begin regulating the Irish economy clearly underpinned both its failure to command political allegiance and the Irish disorder of 1922–1923. It also partly doomed Griffith to be labelled as a figure of a disturbing era ('the civil war') that was best forgotten. A focus on attracting international business and investments in Ireland has led some to typify the modern-day economy of Ireland as an 'extremely open economy',[136] but, as reflected by the independent status of the Central Bank of Ireland ever since its initial formation in 1943 to deal with the economic disruptions caused by the Second World War, state regulation of financial institutions in Ireland is a principle that has never yet been possible to promote (even if nationalisation became a common factor to post-1945 European life)[137] as a means of ensuring that the citizens of the country itself remained the first priority, no matter how open or closed the economy may ever have been at different instances.[138] This could have peculiar consequences.

The first governor of the Central Bank of Ireland, from 1943–1961, was Lord Glenavy of the British House of Lords, the son of the man whom Griffith had to fight to prevent him dictating his unionist terms to the Dáil between 1920 and 1922 (this had included giving non-elected unionist senators powers of veto over the legislative assembly; a plan that Cosgrave barely managed to defeat in December 1922). Glenavy had completely contemptuous attitudes regarding both the general Irish public and all Irish government ministers, who he deemed to be 'cretinous slobs who pass for people of intelligence in Ireland'.[139] Yet such a man had absolute regulatory authority over all Irish financial institutions and, in turn, businesses, due to the extant Government of Ireland Act of 1920 on the Irish state's statute books (during the 1950s Northern Ireland actually began to outperform Éire economically, possibly partly due to a greater investment of Irish capital in the north by the Irish banks). Subsequent central bank governors, such as Maurice Moynihan and Patrick McGowan, were Irishmen who (unlike Glenavy) wrote intelligent studies of banking and sympathised with the Irish populace at large,[140] but they inherently occupied similar professional responsibilities as a direct result of partition.

Griffith's expressed hope in January 1916 that the new year—being the centenary of the enforced amalgamation of the British and Irish economies (1816) and the twentieth-anniversary of the Financial Relations Report (1896)— would lead to the birth of a new Irish polity that would base its understanding of the country's best interests upon an Irish nationalist understanding of the dynamics of the country's economic life and its potentials for evolution was perhaps novel. Perceptions of both he and his contemporaries have often been distorted, however, due to the economic legacy of partition. One instance of this may be said to be a supposed 'resurrection of Michael Collins'[141] in Irish historical discourse during the 1990s according to sometimes very misleading interpretations of his career.[142] Meanwhile, reflecting a prior interpretation of Collins' intentions in a 1970s study of the department of finance,[143] a recent history entitled *Freedom to Achieve Freedom* has emphasised the idea of an absolute continuity between the Irish Party's politics and a supposed intended and ultimate ethos of both the Irish Free State and Éire. It was argued that the Irish Party 'envisioned a highly centralised administration' (namely, the existing administration of Dublin Castle under the Union) while its willingness to withhold all funding for local government and to have no particular desire for the creation of an infrastructure for business or industry in Ireland, or to reform education according to this need, laid the basis for the enlightened agricultural economic policies of Fianna Fáil and Fine Gael in this direction during the early years of the Irish state, whereas Griffith and his followers never had any specific values to promote in terms of good government, nor did their ideas ever reflect 'economic reality'.[144] This may seem to reflect a deliberate writing of both the goals and the idealism that underpinned the initial formation of the Dáil out of history altogether, although the Irish party political divides born in the wake of Griffith's death naturally had material connotations and these reflected the legacy of prior conflicts between the Irish Party and Sinn Féin; conflicts in which it was the Irish Party tradition that clearly triumphed and gave birth to all modern Irish political parties, including the post-February 1922 incarnations of Sinn Féin itself. This might have been predicted.

Collins' often quoted assertion that the Free State arrangement potentially 'gives us freedom, not the freedom that all nations desire and develop to, but the freedom to achieve it' was a finance minister's statement of continued loyalty to Griffith's programme for government. It was less 'economic reality' (a static and thereby essentially false concept) than a restriction of freedom of choice that put an end to that programme, at least in the short term, and stopped Griffith and Collins dead in their tracks. This was the reasoning behind the Irish state's erections of memorials to both men (as well as Kevin O'Higgins) during the mid-1920s, and, ultimately, the erection of a half-complete column over Griffith's grave to mark the passing of the Republic of Ireland Act of 1949 to symbolise the fact that an ideal of an independent Ireland with genuine economic freedoms had been launched and, even if half the Irish population may not have appreciated this, it was an ideal that was not going to go away either.

Although it was a question that ultimately did not become paramount in European life until after the Second World War rather than the First World War, the question of the viability of small, yet economically competitive, independent states is a significant theme to twentieth-century history. Griffith's devotion to exploring that paradigm to the maximum in the interests of Ireland does seem to merit that Irish historians consider him much as he desired to be considered by his own contemporaries: a good Irish citizen, no more and no less, if not necessarily an extraordinarily talented one.[145] To this day, however, it is accepted wisdom throughout the Irish universities and much of Irish society at large that 'a dark shadow' was cast over the whole of Irish society from the 1920s until the 1950s solely because of the influence of Griffith or his isolationist and backwards-looking protectionist economic policy.[146] Griffith cast no shadow, however. P.S. O'Hegarty's description of the history of the Dáil between 1919 and 1922 that 'in three years a thing happened that ought to have taken three generations'[147] was a reflection of both the breadth of the aspirations of that assembly—the belief that the Irish Free State already had full economic freedoms was extant when O'Hegarty wrote in 1924—and the fact that the nature of its aspirations was such that it *might* actually take three generations to accomplish its initial vision. There is a curious historical coincidence here.

The 'trade walls' that Griffith sought to break down included securing Irish access to European and American markets (he directed the IDA's attention to these matters, as well as to the trend of American investment in Europe) and to advertise for Irish businesses the world over. Today, the IDA has many offices operating in every corner of the globe to promote Irish businesses and international investment in Ireland,[148] but although this body was established simultaneously with Griffith's launch of the Sinn Féin Policy in 1905, it lay dormant for almost two-thirds of a century due to difficulty in repatriating Ireland's sterling assets with a view to launching a distinct monetary policy. The idea of directing its attention abroad (beyond the United Kingdom) and facilitating such a focus by means of a planned monetary policy was Griffith's, however. Perhaps one may say that Griffith's historic 'paper wall' analogy presents something of an irony here. The only 'paper wall' still in existence today is, perhaps, in people's heads with regards to understanding the chronology of Irish history, due to the extent to which that subject has been used in the past to validate arguments regarding the present (including national identity myths) without focusing on the realities of statehood and economic matters as a basis of political history. As late as 2008, it has even been suggested that this dynamic has meant that a school of historical studies upon modern Ireland cannot yet be said to be truly in existence.[149]

The Republic of Ireland Act of 1949, if best known for marking the birth of an Irish foreign policy (as represented by the new responsibilities assigned to the Irish Defence Forces), gave rise to the first efforts made ever since 1922 to address a challenge that Griffith had identified as absolutely necessary to meet in order to redress the highly centralised nature of Dublin Castle's government under the Union; namely to create a more beneficial relationship between central and local government in order to create an administrative basis for economic development within Ireland itself. This belief motivated all Dáil policies between 1919 and 1922, although it was an idea that was sidelined thereafter until the creation of the Institute of Public Administration in Ireland in the 1950s.[150] This initiative may have reflected a perception that the state of the Irish civil service hitherto was inadequate. At least reputedly, the primary focus since 1927 had been simply the employment of self-satisfied *gaelgoirs* in defence of a sacrosanct national identity without entertaining any ideas of reform. This was no doubt a simplification. Amongst such sections of society, however, Griffith's infamous dictum that 'no law or series of laws can make a nation out of a people that distrusts itself' essentially had a purely cultural nationalist or 'Irish-Irelander' meaning in terms of the churches' politics of education. To Griffith himself, however, it had a definite economic or political meaning in terms of the necessity of establishing an agreed, permanent and dynamic platform for reform: a 'national council' with its eyes focused entirely upon the future while also necessarily possessing a sound conception of the country's economic past.

It is argued here that there are a number of reasons why Griffith may seem to have been 'airbrushed out of history'. First, there is the simple fact that the Irish state (though not the Irish parliament) was founded in December 1922 and he predeceased it. Furthermore, this foundation was only a beginning: the subsequent evolution of the state, as Griffith himself predicted, followed its own trajectory in meeting the demands of an unknown future. Second, there is the reality that Griffith's career in politics and, in turn, his arguments in defence of the treaty arrangement were based upon the defence of economic options that, in fact, were not *made* available. Ultimately, on an economic level, if not on a constitutional level, there was no 'treaty' and if the British cabinet ensured this by breaking the spirit of the agreement it made with Griffith, it was also evidently the case that its claims that there could be no business confidence in the type of government the Dáil was envisioning, up until Griffith's death, was partly substantiated by the fact that, ultimately, virtually no section of Irish society, whether out of fear of British coercion or genuine inclination, was prepared to facilitate its goals. On an economic level, Irish society practically chose *against* political independence by its own actions and as neither the British government nor the Irish public were prepared to facilitate 'the treaty' as Griffith understood it, ultimately he seemed to have left no legacy behind him. Similarly, in their recollections of him, both W.T. Cosgrave and Sean T. O'Kelly could not understand how Griffith, a quintessentially working-class figure, would ever be typified as an anti-labour figure, but the trajectory of the economy of Ireland practically sealed his future reputation in that regard.

Reflecting on the economic history of twentieth-century Ireland, Joe Lee noted that DeValera's constitutional reforms of the 1930s 'meant nothing in the real world of finance' and so were not as paramount in determining the course of Irish life as has often been assumed.[151] It was also true, however, that Griffith represented an ideal of Irish economic freedom that was not practicable during his lifetime. In particular, if his ideas were divorced from their context soon enough to ensure that they were largely forgotten, it is also true that the Irish political community itself rejected them, at least in the short term, and built the basis of a southern Irish state upon a basis that was more in line with British economic norms and based, for all intents and purposes, upon the economics of a Union of which the country was no longer a part. This was an expected outcome to many, which was essentially why, in a party political sense, the meaning of the conflict that broke out in June 1922 to many contemporaries would be that pro and anti-agreement parties had virtually developed by default upon that understanding. To many if not all contemporaries, both seemed to act upon the understanding that the possibility of the Dáil unilaterally determining the course of future events had grown too slim to bank upon. This was precisely because the principle of Ireland being a distinct economic entity was not possible to either recreate or establish.

A matter that has affected Griffith's historical reputation somewhat unjustly is the popularity of DeValera's constitution. This popularity stemmed not least from its removal of those monarchical paraphernalia that Boland had feared during 1922 would serve to 'disenfranchise republicans', but Childers was essentially successful in convincing a large section of the Irish public to forever associate these unpopular issues primarily with Griffith's name or his 'legacy'. However, it must be recognised that the constitution of Éire was itself based upon the same treaty agreement that Griffith had signed, which had won for Ireland the right to create such a written constitution. In this sense, the treaty did facilitate the quintessentially republican *idea* of creating written constitutions, albeit according to a dynamic that fitted with common law traditions. The Éire constitution enabled the Irish polity to combine these two legalistic concepts in a unique manner that could be a source of public pride. In its final act, however, DeValera's constitution also recognised, just as had the treaty arrangement upon which it was based, the continued relevance of all applicable British common law (Ireland remained a common law country), while the common citizenship principle was also retained; a fact that would not change even with the application of an 'official description' to Éire as 'the Republic of Ireland' in 1949.[152] In this sense, as Cosgrave noted, the Irish Free State-Éire was essentially 'an autonomous Irish state' if not quite an independent state in the traditional sense of that term (the boundaries of the state and its economic management did not match) and Griffith may have overestimated the extent of the liberties that he believed he had won for Ireland in that regard. At the same time, however, if the basis of international relations may have changed significantly since Griffith's day, his conception as to how to defend national interests in a perpetually fluctuating international economic environment did have some sound theoretical grounding by placing national self-interests first. This was a sound conception of independent statehood in any age.

Griffith's instinct that led him to view Europe rather than Britain or indeed (the Irishmen who, as British citizens, had left for) the United States as a necessary fulcrum for developing Irish potentials may be said to represent one more of this ideas that may seem to have had greater relevance in a very different age to his own. Perhaps, like his own charitable description of John Mitchel, Griffith may be typified as a man whose very independence of thought made him an individual that was inherently independent of intellectual fashions and so was capable of being 'a century out of date, back and forward', in terms of his perception. To Griffith's mind, this was a good definition of an ideal prototype of Irish citizen. This reflected his status as a preacher of ideas, which may perhaps, as in the case of Michael Davitt, have been his truest legacy. Like 'the father of the Land League', Griffith launched a political programme but material dynamics, such as his own relatively humble social status and long standing socio-economic bases to political mobilisations within Ireland, did not make him, or his own 'class', its ultimate beneficiary, while it was also true that their programmes were never implemented in full. For the most part, however, as an Irish nationalist Griffith stood for one simple concept. This was his defence of common-sense political logic against the peculiar censorships engendered by empires that had controlled Irish life hitherto. This made him a quite popular figure after 1915. He had always believed that this barricade to Irish development would continue to exist until it would dissolve naturally after Ireland attained economic freedoms and, in turn, an ability to provide for its own people. The fact that the history of his lifetime has remained, for many, a source of contention, or else has been treated as a subject of deep political controversy (as if it were a matter of current affairs), is perhaps an indication that such a development has yet to truly occur or that many of the same questions of nationalist reformism that preoccupied Griffith somehow remain particularly relevant.

Notes

INTRODUCTION

1. Michael Laffan, 'Arthur Joseph Griffith (1871–1922)', *Dictionary of Irish Biography*, 4(Cambridge, 2009), 286.
2. G. Doherty, D. Keogh (eds) *1916: the long revolution* (Cork, 2007); John Regan, *The Irish counter-revolution* (Dublin, 1999).
3. W.T. Cosgrave, 'Arthur Griffith (1872–1922)', *Dictionary of National Biography 1922–1930* (Oxford, 1937), 367–368.
4. Adam Zamoyski, *Holy madness: romantics, patriots and revolutionaries* (London, 1999), xi.
5. Gary Owens, 'Nationalist monuments in Ireland, 1870–1914: symbolism and ritual', in Gillespie, Kennedy (eds) *Ireland: art into history* (Dublin, 1994), 103–117.
6. Justin Wintle (ed.) *Makers of nineteenth century culture 1800–1914* (London, 1982), xxi.
7. Pamela Pilbeam, *Republicanism in nineteenth-century France 1814–1871* (London, 1995); Eric Hobsbawm, *The age of revolution 1789–1848* (London, 1962).
8. Harold Perkin, *The rise of professional society: England since 1880* (London, 1989).
9. Paul Kennedy, *The rise and fall of the great powers: economic change and military conflict from 1500 to 2000* (New York, 2001).

CHAPTER ONE

1. T.S. Cuffe, a historian of Dublin, to *Sunday Independent*, 17 Aug. 1930.
2. NLI, Minute Book of the Leinster Debating Society, Ms 19935, minute for 28 Nov. 1890.
3. From the 1850s onwards the imperial treasury refused to grant Dublin Corporation, which had only recently admitted Catholics, its right to the quit and crown rents it paid annually nominally for the city's own upkeep. Meanwhile, to avoid a new income tax, which was made more stringent for Ireland than for England, Dublin businessmen frequently left the country altogether and re-established their businesses in London, leading to a decline, by means of a domino effect, of both smaller city firms as well as demands for the services of the city's tradesmen. Sinn Féin pamphlet no. 3 (Dublin, 1907), pp 3–4; *Sinn Féin*, 25 Oct., 8 Nov. 1913; *Nationality*, 18 Dec. 1915, p 2.
4. Griffith's parents, who were both natives of Dublin, married in St. Mary's Pro-Cathedral on 14 May 1860 (NLI, Register of Marriages St. Mary's Parish, pos. 9159) and lived initially in rented accommodation on Mabbot Street, which was close to their parents' homes on Gloucester Street North (later 'Sean MacDermott Street') and Langrish Place (off Marlborough Street) respectively. These streets were slum areas of Dublin city centre at the time. Jacinta Prunty, *Dublin slums 1800–1925* (Dublin, 1999), 105–107, 338; Mary Daly, *Dublin: deposed capital* (Cork, 1984), 279–280. Arthur himself was born on 31 March 1871 in a tenement dwelling at 61 Upper Dominick Street and baptised as 'Arthur Joseph' two weeks later in St. Michan's parish church on North Anne Street (NLI, Catholic baptismal register for St. Michan's Parish, Dublin, pos. 8832). His uncle Joseph Griffith lived in a nearby tenement on 46 Mecklenburgh Street and fathered a child out of wedlock while a temporary inmate in the South Dock Union during 1863. Griffith's mother Mary

Whelan (whose family worked in the building trade) acted as the godmother to Joseph's child when he married the mother Marcella Connolly who, as Marcella Griffith, acted as godmother to the fourth child in Arthur Griffith's household, Frank Henry, who was born on 5 January 1874 at 61 Upper Dominick Street. (NLI, Catholic baptismal register for the South Dock Union, within St. Paul's Parish, Arran Quay, pos. 8836, entry 29 April 1863; Catholic marriage register for St. Mary's Parish, pos. 9160, entry for 23 December 1863; NLI, Catholic baptismal register for St. Michan's Parish, Dublin, pos. 8832, entries for January 1874).

5. The eldest child William George (Bill) Griffith was born in 1865 and left for England in his teens. He worked at various times as a labourer, chef, barber and army corporal. The second eldest Marcella Griffith (1866–1900) died of tuberculosis while living in a Capel Street tenement. NLI, M.J. Lennon papers, Ms 22,293 (1). Bill Griffith, who married and had a small family, returned to Ireland around 1919.

6. T.S. Cuffe, 'Journalism under difficulties: Arthur Griffith's early struggles', *Irish Press*, 6 January 1936. Cuffe knew Griffith's father who, he noted, worked for a time as a house decorator and was an acquaintance of Fr. C.P. Meehan, a priest who had been associated with the Young Ireland movement. T.S. Cuffe, 'Arthur Griffith and William Rooney', *Father Matthew Record* (March 1947).

7. Michael Lennon, later a manager of one of Griffith's publications, understood that this led the father to spend some time abroad, in Britain and even America, in the five years between his marriage and the birth of his first child. NLI, M.J. Lennon papers, Ms 22,293 (1).

8. Mary Daly, *Dublin: deposed capital* (Cork, 1984), 76.

9. Sarah Ward-Perkins (ed.), *Select guide to trade union records of Dublin* (Dublin, 1996), 90. Arthur Griffith Senior represented this union in a few meetings with employers during 1865. The minute books of this union, the Dublin Typographical and Printers Society, are held by the Irish Print Union on 35 Gardiner Street, Dublin 1.

10. *Citizen and Irish Artisan*, 7 June, 14 June, 26 July 1879. The editor and publisher of *The Citizen and Irish Artisan*, which existed from 1876 until 1880, was William Hastings, who ran a printing firm on 30 Great Brunswick (later Pearse) Street. Only copies of this journal from 1879–1880 appear to have survived. It sympathised with the Irish National Land League in so far as it was also ready to embrace the cause of the urban working class.

11. Mary Cronin, *Country, class or craft?: the politicisation of the skilled artisan in nineteenth-century Cork* (Cork, 1994).

12. *Citizen and Irish Artisan*, 7 June, 14 June, 26 July 1879.

13. *Citizen and Irish Artisan*, 21 June, 19 July, 18 Nov. 1879.

14. 'The cost of living', *Sinn Féin*, 20 Sep. 1913.

15. Michael Lennon, who attempted to write a biography of Griffith while working as a circuit-court judge in the 1930s, noted that Griffith's life could not really be understood without taking into full consideration his Victorian upbringing as a working-class inhabitant of the economically depressed city of Dublin. NLI, M.J. Lennon papers, Ms22293 (1).

16. Many of Griffith's Sinn Féin arguments were echoed by A.W. Samuels K.C., a successor of W.E. Lecky and predecessor of Edward Carson, as MP for Dublin University. See, for instance, A.W. Samuels, 'Some features in recent Irish finance', *Journal of the Statistical and Social Inquiry Society of Ireland* (1907), 1–40.

17. Griffith was a keen handball player, a frequent and powerful swimmer and also enjoyed taking long walks. NLI, M.J. Lennon papers, Ms 22, 293 (9) - Maud Griffith to Lennon, 1949.

18. Griffith referred to his drinking habits and participation in 'smoking concerts' while a member of the Leinster Debating Society. NLI, Ms19935 (minute book) and Ms3943 (society journal), articles written by Shanaghagh (Griffith), 22 Feb. and 3 Mar. 1889.

19. Griffith's first day at school, on 29 May 1876, had been at St. Mary's Convent School on King's Inn Street, a girls' junior school to which junior–infant schoolboys were also admitted. Two years later, on 10 June 1878, he was transferred to a recently established Christian Brothers school for boys at St. Mary's Place, while on 21 November 1881 he went into fourth class in the Christian Brothers school on Great Strand Street (which his father had once attended) to complete his primary school education. NLI, Lennon papers, Ms 22,293 (1), (2). The firm of William Underwood, 'printer and nautical stationer', occupied the same building (12 Eden Quay) as one of the largest merchant steamship companies in Dublin. In this capacity, the young Griffith would be sent on regular errands to various businesses across the city, as well as to the Freemasons Hall on Molesworth Street. He received additional training as a compositor at an associated firm run by Jane Underwood, who operated her own small printing firm at 5 Herbert Place, a side-street off Baggot Street. *Thom's Directory* (1882–84).

20. The Griffith family were tenant farmers in the region of Redhills, County Cavan. During the era of Catholic Emancipation, this Protestant family disowned Griffith's grandfather because he converted to Catholicism upon his marriage. He subsequently moved to Dublin, where he found work as a printer. Pilib O'Mordha, 'The Griffiths of Laurelhill, Co. Monaghan, and associated families', *The Clogher Record*, XIV, 4 (1993), 111–124.

21. NLI, M.J. Lennon papers, Ms 22,293 (2). St. Paul's Academy was a well-established secondary school on Arran Quay whose students were generally encouraged to do matriculation exams to enter the Catholic University. Griffith was allowed to use its library but no evidence exists to indicate that he sat an intermediate school examination. The employer in question was T.D. Sullivan MP, owner and editor of the *Nation*.

22. Owen McGee, *The IRB* (Dublin, 2005), 84–85, 108–110, 117–119, 137–138, 146–147, 160–163. Associated with this society was a poet Rose Kavanagh who edited the *Irish Fireside*, a literary magazine for youths whose contributors were nicknamed as the 'Irish Fireside Club'. Griffith first met William Rooney during 1889 in the *Irish Fireside* editorial room. Arthur Griffith, Patrick Bradley (eds) *Poems and ballads of William Rooney* (Dublin, 1902), introduction.

23. *Nation*, 28 June 1884, 7 and 14 Feb. 1885.

24. Jacqueline Hill, 'The intelligentsia and Irish nationalism in the 1840s', *Studia Hibernica*, vol. 20 (1980), 73–109.

25. 'Concerning a Convert', *United Irishman*, 26 May 1900.

26. 'Advice to Young Irishmen', *United Irishman*, 16 June 1900.

27. 'Advice to Young Irishmen', *United Irishman*, 16 June 1900.

28. NLI, Sweetman papers, Ms 47,585/3, Arthur Griffith to John Sweetman, 18 Sep. 1905.

29. Oliver St. John Gogarty, *It isn't this time of year at all!* (London, 1954), 53; NLI, Sweetman papers, Ms 47,582/7, Maud Gonne to John Sweetman, 7 May [1903].

30. NLI, Eblana Journal of the Leinster Debating Society, Ms 3943.

31. NLI, Minute Book of the Leinster Debating Society, Ms 19935, minute for 7 November 1890. NLI, Eblana Journal of the Leinster Debating Society, Ms 3943, pp 17–18. Michael Seery and James Boland (father of Harry and Gerry Boland), two IRB leaders of the time, managed both this Marlborough Street venue and the Jones Road sports ground, which was later renamed as Croke Park.

32. NLI, Minute Book of the Leinster Debating Society, Ms 19935, minute for 8 Feb. 1889; Eblana Journal of the Leinster Debating Society, Ms 3943, issue for 8 Mar. and 5 May 1889.

33. NLI, Minute Book of the Leinster Debating Society, Ms 19935, minute for 21 Nov. 1890. This led J.E. Masterston, a moderate Dublin socialist and former Land League activist, to join the society. Fintan Lane, *The origins of modern Irish socialism* (Cork, 1997), 181 fn., 151.

34. Brendan McDonnell, 'Tradesmen, labourers and depression 1886-9', *Dublin History Workshop*, 1 (1988), 26–31. The first leader of the Dublin Trades Council, John O'Clohissey, was also mixed up in disputes between rival IRB factions.

35. R.J. Allen (ed.), *Addison and Steele: selections from The Tatler and The Spectator* (New York, 1957), xv. NLI, 'Eblana', Ms 3943, issue for 22 March 1889.

36. NLI, Minute Book of the Leinster Debating Society, Ms 19935, minutes for 12 Apr. 1889, 4 Mar. 1892; Eblana Journal of the Leinster Debating Society, Ms 3943, pp. 213-215. Griffith's interest in the classics was reflected by a lecture he gave (lasting eighty minutes) on the theme 'that ancient civilisation is superior to modern civilisation' and by a brief piece he wrote on the Gracchi brothers in second-century Rome who (reflecting a viewpoint first popularised by Francois-Noel Babeuf) he described as republican martyrs for the idea of liberty. He also gave a talk on the American poet Henry Wadsworth Longfellow.

37. NLI, Eblana Journal of the Leinster Debating Society, Ms 3943, issue for 22 Feb. 1889. He also sometimes demonstrated an unhealthy fascination with morbid subjects, contrasting, for instance, poets like James Clarence Mangan, Thomas Chatterton and Percy Bysshe Shelley not on their literary merits but rather upon their capacity to deal with suicidal tendencies. NLI, Eblana Journal of the Leinster Debating Society, Ms 3943, issue for 5 May 1889.

38. NLI, Eblana Journal of the Leinster Debating Society, Ms 3943, issue for 22 Feb. 1889.

39. *United Irishman*, 6 Oct. 1900, p. 1. This was why many working-class figures of the day admired the legacy of Napoleon. It would also become a demand of the first Dáil Eireann.

40. Seamus O'Sullivan, *Essays and recollections* (Dublin, 1944), 104–111.

41. The Boer War era verse was later collected and published posthumously by Piaras Beaslai as a pamphlet: *Songs, ballads and recitations by famous Irishmen: Arthur Griffith* (Dublin, 1926). The bawdy doggerel was composed by Griffith, with encouragement from Sean McEntee, and recited theatrically by Griffith and George 'Henry' Nichols, an evangelical Protestant friend who fought in the 1916 rising. *Connacht Tribune*, 6 Mar. 1965 (reprinted extracts from diary of Peadar Sweeney); NLI, Griffith papers, acc. 4476, box a, undated press cutting providing an obituary for George Nichols.

42. NLI, Minute Book of the Leinster Debating Society, Ms 19935, minute for 7 November 1890.

43. W.P. Ryan, *The Irish literary revival* (London, 1894), 39–49. NLI, Henry Dixon papers, Ms 35262 (27), programmes of Rathmines National League Literary Society (1887–91).

44. Mary Kettle, wife of the financial spokesman of the Irish Party, recalled that 'in Ireland the ordinary middle class people were unaware of what happened in what were then called the slums. They did not know anything about the people who lived there.' Although a native of Dublin, she only became conscious that slum districts existed near her favourite social haunt (the Gresham Hotel) when informed about this by a New York tourist, who protested that it was disgraceful that anywhere in the civilised world there was such indifference to the plight of the poor as existed in Dublin city. UCD, Tom Kettle papers, LA 32/11, p. 7.

397

45. Fionnuala Waldron, 'Statesmen on the street corners: labour and the Parnell split in Dublin 1890–1892', *Studia Hibernica*, no.34 (2006–07), 151–172.

46. Griffith was reacting to the establishment of the Parnell monument as a means of celebrating John Redmond's achievement of the balance of power in the House of Commons. *Sinn Féin*, 18 June 1910.

47. A particularly noticeable example is Brian Maye, *Arthur Griffith* (Dublin, 1997), 64–68.

48. NLI, Minute book of the Leinster Debating Society, MS 19935, minute for 28 Nov. 1890.

49. This was 41 Rutland (later Parnell) Square. Owen McGee, 'John Clancy (1841–1915)', *Dictionary of Irish Biography*, 2 (Cambridge, 2009).

50. Barry O'Brien judged that without the IRB's support Parnell's candidate (who won only one-third of the vote) could not have run at all. NLI, John O'Leary papers, Ms 5927, R.B. O'Brien to O'Leary, 15 Mar. 1891.

51. NLI, Minute book of the Leinster Debating Society, MS 19935, minutes for 15–19 Dec. 1890.

52. NAI, DMP files, carton 8, Report 1997, Chief Supt. John Mallon, 27 Jan. 1891.

53. NLI, Minute book of the Leinster Debating Society, MS 19935, minute for 6 Feb. 1891. In March 1890, Griffith introduced and defended a polemical motion of debate at the Leinster Literary Society 'that the Catholic Church is opposed to civilisation'. NLI, Minute book of the Leinster Debating Society, MS 19935, minute for 28 Mar. 1890. He lost the debate by one vote.

54. NLI, Minute book of the Leinster Debating Society, MS 19935, minutes for 20 Feb., 27 Feb., 6 Mar., 3 Apr. 1891.

55. NLI, Minute book of the Leinster Debating Society, MS 19935, minute for 6 Feb. 1891. Griffith's maternal cousin Edward Whelan, also a printer, claimed that the French Revolution was inspired by the philosophies of Voltaire and Rousseau. Another speaker saw it as an inevitable result of the role of monarchies in oppressing the poor.

56. Piaras Beaslai (ed.) *Songs, ballads and recitations by famous Irishmen: Arthur Griffith* (Dublin, 1926), 24.

57. *Freeman's Journal*, 14 May 1891 (report of forthcoming convention). This convention was planned a month earlier. *Freeman's Journal*, 14 April 1891. This convention was attended by representatives of IRB-led debating societies in Omagh, Cavan town, Limerick, Kilkenny, Cork, Fermoy, Midleton and Kanturk.

58. *United Ireland*, 6 June 1891; *Evening Telegraph*, 19 June 1891. NAI, DMP files, carton 11, report 3180, Chief Supt. John Mallon, 11 June 1891.

59. This was claimed by an anonymous letter writer to the *Limerick Leader* (18 March 1950); later cited in Sean O'Luing, *Art O Griofa* (Baile Atha Cliath, 1954), 25–26.

60. *Freeman's Journal*, 25 Jul. 1891. As the *Freeman* was allied to Catholic business interests, it would abandon Parnell that September.

61. This event took place on 2 August 1891 as Parnell was on his way to Thurles, Co. Tipperary. Griffith later claimed to have met Parnell briefly at Kingsbridge Station while he was on his way to what would prove to be his last-ever political meeting. Maye, *Griffith*, 65. Parnell's last public meeting was at Creggs, Co. Galway, on 27 September 1891.

62. *Freeman's Journal*, 3 Aug. 1891. NAI, DMP files, carton 8, report 2147, Chief Supt. John Mallon, 3 Aug. 1891.

63. NLI, Minute book of the Leinster Debating Society, MS 19935, minute for 13 Nov. 1891.

64. *United Ireland*, 5 Sept. 1891.

65. *Freeman's Journal*, 18 Sept. 1891.

66. NLI, Minute book of the National Literary Society, Ms 645 (rules of the society).

67. Owen McGee, 'Fred Allan: republican, Methodist and Dubliner', *Dublin Historical Record* (vol.56, 2003). Allan's father, who died in 1881, had worked in Dublin Castle.
68. NLI, Minute book of the Leinster Debating Society, MS 19935, minutes for 15 Jan., 4 Mar. and 11 Mar. 1892.
69. NLI, Minute book of the Leinster Debating Society, MS 19935, minute for 27 Oct. 1892. Rooney, the son of a coachbuilder who had been active in nationalist movements, attended the same Christian Brothers' school as Griffith but they did not meet until several years later. Like Griffith, he had left school at thirteen (to work as a junior clerk in a solicitor's office), was given permission to use various private libraries and became a voracious reader of books by Irish authors over the past century. Arthur Griffith, Patrick Bradley (eds) *Poems and ballads of William Rooney* (Dublin, 1902), introduction.
70. NLI, Minute book of the Leinster Debating Society, Ms 19935, minutes for 11 Nov. to 9 Dec. 1892.
71. Griffith was elected to its Executive Council on 23 May 1892 and Whelan was made its secretary that October. NLI, Griffith papers, acc. 4476, box b, Young Ireland League minute book (1891–93).
72. NLI, Griffith papers, acc.4476, box b, Young Ireland League minute books (1891–96). The MPs in question were William Field, Patrick O'Brien (who had once been in the IRB) and William Redmond (who soon resigned, as did J.P. Quinn of the National League). Many leading journalists joined, including *United Ireland* editor Joseph McGrath (who soon resigned), founding editor of the *Evening Herald* John Wyse Power, John F. Taylor of the Manchester *Guardian*, and J.W. O'Beirne and E.H. Burke of the *Independent*, alongside technical school officials such as L.E. O'Carroll and William O'Leary Curtis and legal officials Henry Dixon and Patrick Lavelle. Writers who joined included W.B. Yeats, George Coffey BL, John Todhunter, Katherine Tynan, T.W. Rolleston, C.H. Oldham, P.J. McCall (an old poet and friend of Griffith), Dublin historian R.J. O'Duffy, Thomas Sherlock, Robert Lynd, and E. Fottrell (sister of Sir George, who soon resigned). The IRB contingent consisted of Fred Allan, John O'Leary and P.J. White of Offaly (Leinster IRB leaders) and its Munster leadership P.N. Fitzgerald, J.K. Bracken and W.M. Stack. Of the dozens of prominent people who attended its initial meeting and enrolled, only three (Patrick O'Brien MP, P.N. Fitzgerald and John O'Leary) thereafter paid the subscription necessary to be admitted to its executive.
73. NLI, Minute book of the Leinster Debating Society, Ms 19935, minutes for 25 Sept. 1891, 5 Feb. 1892.
74. While the Christian Brothers did not support the act in public, the YIL received a letter from the secretary of the Superior General of the order which stated that 'the Christian Brothers are not opposed to the principle of the Compulsory Education Act nor to its getting a fair trial', which indicated that Catholic opposition to the act was indeed more a matter of political tactics than of principle. NLI, Griffith papers, acc. 4476, box b, Young Ireland League minute book (1891–93), minute for 7 Nov. 1893.
75. NLI, Griffith papers, acc.4476, box b, Young Ireland League minute book (1891–93), minute for 10 Jan. 1893 (quote); Young Ireland League minute book (1894–96), minutes for 20 Mar., 17 Apr., 19 June 1894.
76. NLI, Griffith papers, acc.4476, box b, Young Ireland League minute book (1891–93), minute for 5 Dec. 1893.
77. NLI, Griffith papers, acc.4476, box b, Young Ireland League minute book (1894–96), minute for 11 Jan 1894. On this theme, see also *Evening Herald*, 23 July 1892. Alex Blane, a former Irish Party MP for Armagh whose vote dropped from 8,000 to just 50 for supporting Parnell in defiance of the Archbishop of Armagh, became bitterly anticlerical

during the mid-1890s and used both the YIL and the Parnellite press as his vehicle. The church's formation of the *Irish News* in 1891 played a large part in Blane's electoral humiliation during 1892.

78. On this theme, see P.A. Townend, 'Academies of nationality: the reading room and Irish national movements 1838–1905', in L.W. McBride ed., *Reading Irish histories* (Dublin, 2003), 19–39.

79. C.C. O'Brien, *Parnell and his party* (Oxford, 1957), 266; NLI, George Fottrell papers, Ms33670, diary entry for 3 Jan. 1887.

80. NLI, Griffith papers, acc.4476, box b, Young Ireland League minute book (1894–96), minute for 11 Oct. 1894.

81. Patrick Maume, 'William Field (1843–1935)', *Dictionary of Irish Biography*, 3 (Cambridge, 2009), 774–775. Field, who provided (as did Patrick O'Brien) for the family of James Boland when he died, was also a student of ancient Brehon law. William Field, *Governments in Ireland* (Dublin, n.d.). Owen McGee, 'James Boland (1856–95)', *Dictionary of Irish Biography*, 1 (Cambridge, 2009), 638. Owen McGee, 'Patrick O'Brien (1853–1917)', *Dictionary of Irish Biography*, 7 (Cambridge, 2009), 71.

82. This initiative was intended to capitalise upon the British government's intended introduction of the Public Libraries (Ireland) Act (1894). Griffith had acted on a YIL sub-committee to find out what was the general practice in Dublin public libraries regarding their financial management. NLI, Griffith papers, acc.4476, box b, Young Ireland League minute book (1891–93), minute for 11 July 1893.

83. NLI, Griffith papers, acc.4476, box b, Young Ireland League minute book (1894–96), minutes for 20 Feb., 4 Mar., 1 May, 21 May 1894.

84. L.M. Cullen, *Princes and pirates: the Dublin Chamber of Commerce 1783–1983* (Dublin, 1983). T.A. Boylan, T.P. Foley, *Political economy and colonial Ireland* (London, 1992).

85. Martin Maguire, 'The organisation and activism of Dublin's Protestant working class, 1883–1935', *Irish Historical Studies*, (vol. 29,1994), 76–77.

86. NLI, Minute books of the Young Ireland Society, Mss16095 and 19158; minute book of the Leinster Debating Society, Ms 19935 (introductory rules).

87. Royal Economic Society (ed.) *The fiscal relations of Great Britain and Ireland* (Suffolk, 1912). Padraig McGowan, *Money and banking in Ireland* (Dublin, 1990). The Royal Economic Society was originally known as the 'Economics School Society of the University of London'. The price for allowing Irish Catholics political representation in the very self-consciously Protestant British political nation of 1829 had essentially been their total acceptance of this new imperial economy. Indeed, the only new Irish bank that was termed as 'national', founded by Daniel O'Connell for Catholics, was also the only one that established its headquarters in London.

88. Bernard Porter, *Empire and Super Empire* (Yale, 2006), 41. Raymond Dumett, 'Joseph Chamberlain, imperial finance and railway policy', *English Historical Review*, vol. 90 (1975), 292 (quote).

89. A.W. Samuels, 'Some features in recent Irish finance', *Journal of the Statistical and Social Inquiry Society of Ireland* (1907), 1–40.

90. This was the Crime Special Branch (renamed in 1887 as the Crime Branch Special). Some historians, in keeping with the contemporary propaganda of Richard Pigott, have attributed its existence purely to the alleged existence of dangerous secret societies in Ireland (Richard Hawkins, 'Government versus secret societies in the Parnell era', T.D. Williams (ed.) *Secret societies in Ireland* (Dublin, 1973), 113–125), but the purpose of this body was far greater than that as it was integrated with the entire civil administration, in particular the new Resident Magistrate system (Margaret O'Callaghan, *British high*

politics and a nationalist Ireland (Cork, 1994)). The best source on the provenance of its activities is the correspondence of E.G. Jenkinson in British Library, Althorp Papers, Add. 77033–37, including a history of the department written on 26 July 1886 (Add.77036). All its personnel, including five Divisional Magistrates, three Resident Magistrates and two RIC officers, came from an army background.

91. Supported by Sir Robert Giffen of the Imperial Board of Trade, one of Gladstone's ideas was to complement legislation providing for an Irish parliament with no fiscal autonomies by legislating that the financing of the Land Law Act was to become the prerogative of the Irish parliament alone, thereby practically ensuring that its implementation could never be extensive. NLI, Gladstone papers, P3261, 'Secret Memorandum to the Cabinet' (pp 74–75) and 'Secret Memorandum to the Crown' (pp 201–204). His fixed principle regarding the bill was that total control of all finances and security forces in Ireland (including the power to grant the right to raise militias) was to remain with the Imperial Cabinet. He estimated that Ireland's current contribution to the Imperial Treasury in taxes was about £7,500,000 per year, with approximately half of this being spent annually on the civil administration of Ireland and the other half going directly into the Empire's general defence budget, but he believed that his legislation could simultaneously lessen the cost of the Dublin Castle administration and boost Ireland's contribution to Imperial Defence by approximately £1,000,000 per year. Gladstone Papers, P3261, pp 1–4, 22–27. His papers indicate that he spent more time on his proposed parliamentary speech in selling a government of Ireland bill than on the measure itself. He was still nonchalantly toying with various ideas, such as allowing for hereditary British peers to nominate themselves members of an elective Irish House of Commons, after the bill was introduced in Westminster in early April 1886. NLI, Gladstone Papers, P3261, memo for 7 April 1886, page 192; NLI Gladstone papers, P2 875, pp 17–107.

92. NLI, Sir George Fottrell papers, Ms 33670, memos for 25 Apr. 1886 (quote), 27 Apr. 1886, 3 May 1886, 19 Oct. 1886. On this theme, see also Stephen Ball (ed.) *Dublin Castle and the First Home Rule Crisis* (Cambridge, 2008), introduction, and NLI, Gladstone papers, P2875, 'memorandum of W.E. Gladstone to the Liberal party leadership, 27 Jul. 1886', pp 182–183.

93. NLI, Gladstone papers, P2875, p. 149.

94. P.T. Marsh, *Bargaining on Europe: Britain and the First Common Market 1860–92* (Yale, 1999).

95. L.W. MacBride, *The greening of Dublin Castle* (Washington D.C, 1991).

96. L.W. MacBride, *The greening of Dublin Castle* (Washington D.C, 1991).

97. NLI, Henry Dixon papers, Ms 35262 (27), article by 'W.R.' (Rooney) in the programme for the YIL commemoration of the 80th anniversary of Thomas Davis' birth, held on 4 Nov. 1895.

98. The 'Parnellites' of the 1890s, led by John Redmond, were not a party per se but essentially a conglomerate of independent politicians that espoused the old Tory principle of freedom of individual conscience in politics in defiance of the growth of the party whip system. Replies to YIL letters were often received from diverse quarters, including church leaders, 'unionists', Dublin city councillors, the National Education Board and even the Chief Secretary. NLI, Griffith papers, acc. 4476, box b, Young Ireland League minute books (1891–93, 1894–96). Although it ignored Redmond's request to engage in electioneering, the YIL did desire to attend a convention that John Redmond called on the 1893 home rule bill. NAI, DMP files, carton 12, report 2408, Chief Supt. John Mallon, 8 Dec. 1892, attached report of 1 June 1892; NLI, Griffith papers, acc. 4476, box b, Young Ireland League minute book (1891–93), minute for 14 Feb. 1893.

99. NLI, Henry Dixon papers, Ms 35262 (27), programme of the Rathmines National League Literary Society (1890–1); programme of the National Club Literary Society, 1891. NLI, Griffith papers, acc. 4476, box b, Young Ireland League minute book (1894–96).

100. NLI, Henry Dixon papers, Ms 35262 (1)-(2). Dixon became a Sinn Féin activist upon its inception in 1905 and was returned as a Sinn Féin TD in 1918. He opposed the Anglo-Irish Treaty of 1921 and remained a senior clerk in the Dublin Four Courts up until his death in 1926.

101. Dixon proposed, with Griffith's support, that Cole be admitted to the YIL on 31 July 1894. Devereux was proposed as a possible publisher of a YIL magazine on 16 October 1894. NLI, Griffith papers, acc. 4476, box b, Young Ireland League minute book (1894–96).

102. Sean O'Tuama, *The Gaelic League idea* (Dublin, 1973), 17–18.

103. NLI, Griffith papers, acc. 4476, box b, Young Ireland League minute books (1891–93), minute for 23 May 1893.

104. NLI, Griffith papers, acc. 4476, box b, Young Ireland League minute books (1891–93), minute for 15 Aug., 21 Nov. 1893; minute book (1894–96), minute for 10 Apr. 1894. *Irish Weekly Independent*, 14 Apr. 1894. Under the new legislation all Welsh primary schools, as well as all government publications issued in that country, had to be bilingual.

105. NLI, Henry Dixon Papers, Ms 32562 (27), Flyer of Young Ireland League, Jan. 1894. Around the same time, Griffith drew the attention of the YIL Council to the positive work that the Gaelic League was doing in Galway. NLI, Griffith papers, acc. 4476, box b, Young Ireland League minute book (1894–96), minute for 30 Jan. 1894.

106. The replies to this correspondence can be found in NLI, Henry Dixon Papers, Ms 32562 (3)-(20).

107. NLI, Henry Dixon Papers, Ms 32562 (6).

108. NLI, Henry Dixon papers, Ms 32562 (19), (26). Of these fourty-five schools, there were fourteen in Kerry, nine in Galway, eight in Mayo, seven in Cork, three in Waterford and just one in four other counties.

109. NLI, Griffith papers, acc. 4476, box b, Young Ireland League minute books, minutes for 21 Nov., 5 Dec. 1893, 18 Jan. 1894 (Walsh's letter); NLI, Henry Dixon Papers, Ms 32562 (27), Flyer of Young Ireland League, c. Jan. 1894.

110. NLI, Henry Dixon Papers, Ms 32562 (26), copy of resolutions made at the Irish Language Congress.

111. Its Irish Language Congress, which took place during Easter Week of 1894, was attended by representatives from the Society for the Preservation of the Irish Language and Gaelic Union (Sigerson and Wyse Power), the Royal Irish Academy (George Coffey), the Gaelic League (Eoin MacNeill), the National Literary Society, Rooney's Celtic Literary Society and two fairly notable Catholic priests, Fr. Patrick O'Leary (who later became the author 'An t-Athair Peadar O'Laoghaire') and the historian Fr. Denis Murphy S.J., whose death a couple of years later would be lamented by the YIL.

112. *Programme of Oireachtas of the Gaelic League, held at the Rotunda 17 May 1897* (NLI pamphlet collections); Kevin Collins, *Catholic churchmen and the Celtic revival 1848–1916* (Dublin, 2003). By the time of the Gaelic League's 1897 Oireachtas, fifteen of the thirty-three members of its council were senior Catholic churchmen, including the presidents of Blackrock College and Rockwell College, the Dean of St. Patrick's College, Maynooth, and the Superior General of the Christian Brothers. Other members included four Irish Party MPs and five newspaper editors. Fr. Eugene O'Growney was its vice-president, alongside Hyde as its president.

113. William Walsh, *The Irish university question: addresses delivered by the Most Rev. Dr. Walsh* (Dublin, 1890). While the archbishop was correct that the independent Catholic

University, founded by Cardinal Newman in 1854, faced a comparatively difficult financial situation, the British government not only facilitated church management of national schools in Ireland and loans for secondary schools but it had also provided ever since 1795 a very large annual subsidy to Maynooth College to enable the church educate and train its own priests. The chief issue relating to the Catholic University, therefore, was essentially whether or not a large professional class of university graduates could be produced in Ireland who would feel a sense of loyalty to the institutions of the church. The Queen's Colleges, established in Cork, Galway and Belfast in 1845, were not producing such graduates, nor was the Anglican-owned Trinity College.

114. NLI, Griffith papers, acc.4476, box b, YIL minute book, minutes for Oct. 1895 to Mar. 1896; Henry Dixon papers, Ms 35262 (27), article by Rooney in the programme for a Thomas Davis and Young Ireland commemoration, 4 November 1895. Griffith joined Rooney and a few socialists in expressing support for the same policy at Celtic Literary Society meetings towards the close of the decade. NLI, Celtic Literary Society minute book, Ms19934, minute for 14 & 21 Apr. 1899; *United Irishman*, 29 Apr. 1899 (report on Fred Ryan's lecture before the Celtic Literary Society).

115. NLI, Griffith papers, acc.4476, box b, Young Ireland League minute book (1894–96), minute for 18 Feb. 1896 (Walsh's letter). One of Archbishop Walsh's informants within the IRB, James Collins (a public health official with Dublin Corporation), began attending YIL meetings around this time to see if it was being manipulated by anticlerical elements. Later, Sean T. O'Kelly worked to the same end.

116. F.S.L. Lyons, *Culture and anarchy in Ireland 1890–1939* (Oxford, 1979); R.F. Foster, 'Anglo-Irish literature, Gaelic nationalism and Irish politics in the 1890s', British Academy (ed.) *Ireland after the Union* (Oxford, 1989), 61–82.

117. Emmet Larkin, *The Roman Catholic Church and the making of the Irish state 1878–1886* (Dublin, 1975); Stephen Ball (ed.) *Dublin Castle and the first home rule crisis* (Cambridge, 2008).

118. T.W. Rolleston, 'The archbishop in politics: a protest', *Dublin University Review*, vol.2, no.2 (Feb.1886), 98–103; T.W. Rolleston (ed.) *Thomas Davis prose writings* (London, 1889). Rolleston's February 1886 article was timed to coincide with Michael Davitt's negotiation of an independent diplomatic relationship between the papacy and the Irish Catholic hierarchy via the Irish College in Rome.

119. This series was printed in the weekend edition of J.W. Power's *Evening Herald* (13 Feb. 16 July 1892) under a by-line listing Griffith and Rooney as co-authors. As Griffith was more of an enthusiast for the eighteenth century than Rooney, it is likely that this *Evening Herald* series was based mostly upon Griffith's research and writings but was redrafted for publication by Rooney, who had already published one or two pieces. Notwithstanding their slightly macabre title ('Notable Graves: where gifted Irishmen were laid in and around Dublin'), this series consisted of conventional historical biographies rather than an itinerary of graveyards. The chosen subjects were Charles Lucas (13 Feb. 1892), Jonathan Swift (5 Mar. 1892), Patrick Delaney (19 Mar. 1892), Lord Edward Fitzgerald (2 Apr. 1892), The Sheares Brothers (23 Apr. 1892), John Fitzgibbon (14 May 1892), John Philip Curran (4 June 1892) and Charles Kendal Bushe (16 July 1892).

120. *Evening Herald*, 13 Feb. 1892.

121. *Evening Herald*, 4 June 1892.

122. NLI, Minute book of the Leinster Debating Society, Ms 19935, minute for 30 Jan. 1891.

123. *Evening Herald*, 16 July 1892.

124. Michael Keyes, *Funding the nation: money and nationalist politics in nineteenth-century Ireland* (Maynooth, 2011).

125. In addition to promoting Rossa's brief lecture tour in Ireland (Griffith stood alongside Rossa on a platform in Birr, Co. Offaly), Griffith denounced the flunkeyism of (the predominantly Parnellite) Dublin city council for 'unanimously passing a resolution congratulating the Queen of England upon the birth of her great grandson' while failing to confer upon Rossa the position of city marshal. NLI, Griffith papers, acc.4476, box b, Young Ireland League minute book (1894–96), minute for 5 Jun., 11 and 14 July 1894. *Irish Daily Independent*, 3 Mar., 18 July 1894.

126. NLI, Griffith papers, acc.4476, box b, Young Ireland League minute book (1894–96), minutes for 6 Feb., 6 Mar., 3 Apr., 10 Apr., 17 Apr., 24 Apr. 1894. *United Ireland*, 4 Jan. 1894 and *Irish Daily Independent*, 14 April 1894 (reports on YIL meetings). Under YIL auspices, Griffith delivered three public lectures during this period; co-wrote a piece on Joseph Sheridan Le Fanu (*Irish Weekly Independent*, 3 Feb. 1894); made efforts to republish works by Thomas Davis and John Mitchel; and helped to organise republican commemorative demonstrations in Co. Wexford. His YIL lectures were on 'Irish literature of the Jacobin era' (21 Mar. 1893), 'The English Invasion of the 12th century' (14 Nov. 1893) and 'Robert Emmet' (4 Mar. 1894, chaired by O'Leary). *United Ireland*, 10 Mar. 1894. Griffith also chaired one W.B. Yeats lecture to the YIL on 'Irish Fairy Tales', which took place on 31 October 1893. NLI, Griffith papers, acc. 4476, box b, YIL minute books. Yeats claimed (falsely) during 1894 that O'Farrell was in favour of executing Catholic bishops. See John Kelly (ed.), *The collected letters of W.B. Yeats* (Oxford, 1989).

127. NLI, M.J. Lennon papers, Ms 22,293 (9) - Tom Synott and Larry de Lacy's recollections of O'Farrell (who was generally known as 'Charley Farrell'). See also, *The Echo and South Leinster Advertiser* (Enniscorthy), 24 Jan. 1914 (obituary of O'Farrell). He had been an arms agent during the late 1860s around the same time as fellow Wexford IRB man Alfred Aylward began working with Dublin Castle. More recently, after being ambivalent regarding the Land League, he had been of note for founding the GAA in the county.

128. The priest in question was Canon Doyle P.P. and the press cuttings appear in the YIL minute book with the minutes for 4 & 24 Apr. 1894.

129. *Evening Herald*, 28 May 1894 (cutting in YIL minute book).

130. *New Ross Standard*, 21 Apr. 1894. *Enniscorthy Guardian*, 14 Apr. 1894. *Free Press* (Wexford), 2 June 1894 (cuttings in YIL minute book).

131. *Enniscorthy Guardian*, 18 May 1895. *The People* (Wexford), 22 May 1895, *Free Press* (Wexford), 25 May 1895. *The Reporter* (Wexford), 25 May 1895 (cuttings in YIL minute book). Rooney argued that 'there were men in Ireland who regarded the French Revolution as a thing to be abhorred, but there were also men who saw the truth of the principle that underlay the Revolution—the right of man to think and act for himself'. Rooney also claimed that Fr. John Murphy had 'preached loyalty from the altars' up until his own house was burnt down and was never sympathetic to the Irish nationalist ideals of the United Irishmen.

132. NLI, Griffith papers, acc.4476, box b, Young Ireland League minute book (1894–96), minutes for 12 Feb., 28 May 1895. *Irish Weekly Independent*, 30 Jun. 1895 (Bodenstown).

133. *Irish Daily Independent*, 15 March 1895.

134. Griffith took part in Manchester martyr demonstrations in Dublin from 1893–95 (*Irish Daily Independent*, 27 Nov. 1893, 26 Nov. 1894, 25 Nov. 1895) and a 1798 commemoration in County Wicklow during May 1896 (YIL minute book, press cutting attached to minute of 19 May 1896).

135. This annotation is written in pencil in a childish hand beside the YIL minute for 29 Oct. 1895. It was not unusual for those associated with the IRB to be requested to do secret

work, however. Although not a member of the IRB (although his brother and future father-in-law were), Seamus MacManus recalled being sent on a secret service mission relating to the French government during the late 1890s. NAI, Bureau of Military History papers, WS283 (Seamus MacManus), pp3–5.

136. NLI, M.J. Lennon papers, Ms 22, 293 (9) - report of interview with Maud Griffith.

137. Ads for this establishment appeared frequently in the *Evening Herald* during 1892.

138. NLI, Henry Dixon papers, Ms 35,262 (27), advertisement in the programme for the YIL Thomas Davis celebration.

139. NLI, M.J. Lennon papers, Ms 22,293 (1) and (3).

140. The Griffith family lived since 1886 on North Richmond Street (near Mountjoy Square) but by the late 1890s were crowded instead into Frank Griffith's tenement room off Capel Street at 4 Little Britain Street. Sean O'Luing provides the date 1884 for the family's relocation here (O'Luing, *Art Ó'Griofa*, 20), but this seems very unlikely. Soon afterwards Griffith's elder sister, Marcella (who worked as a machinist), contracted tuberculosis; a disease which Griffith may have contracted as well and which would claim his sister's life within a few years. NLI, M.J. Lennon papers, Ms 22,293 (1) and (3). Marcella Griffith died in 1900, aged thirty-three.

141. NLI, George A. Lyons papers, Ms 33675 (L) - draft of article by Lyons, 1933. Lyons later joined Sinn Féin and the IRB (he was arrested during 1909 for 'accidentally' shooting his flatmate) and took part in the 1916 rising.

142. Some of his photographs exist in an album in the NLI, Griffith papers, acc.4476, box a.

143. NLI, Minute book of the Leinster Debating Society, MS 19935, minute for 14 Oct. 1892.

144. Undated press cutting in NLI, Griffith papers, acc.4476, box a.

145. NLI, M.J. Lennon papers, Ms 22,293 (9) - recollections of Maud Griffith. During the early 1890s, Griffith was assigned to night duty at the *Independent* offices. He used to call on Maud only in the morning time (after work), taking her for a brief walk before dropping her home in time for attending an eight-o-clock mass in Gardiner Street church. Brian Maye, *Arthur Griffith* (Dublin, 1997), 29.

146. Seamus O'Sullivan, *Essays and recollections* (Dublin, 1944), 105.

147. NLI, George A. Lyons papers, Ms 33675 (L) - draft of article by Lyons, 1933.

148. NLI, M.J. Lennon papers, Ms 22,293 (9) - recollections of Maud Griffith. For the history of these conspiracies, see Owen McGee, *The IRB* (Dublin, 2005), 212–245.

149. Robert Johnston of Belfast, Ryan's co-leader of the secret IRB breakaway body 'the Irish National Brotherhood', helped sustain these contacts. NAI, Bureau of Military History papers, WS283 (Seamus MacManus), pp1–3. Somewhat inexplicably, the former Dublin IRB leader James Boland, a native of Manchester, had coded messages from General Gordon of Khartoum in his private papers. James Boland papers (private property of Annraoi O'Beolain). This may have related to the activities of James J. O'Kelly as a war correspondent in north Africa c.1884 and O'Kelly and Boland's mutual acquaintance with James O'Connor of Dublin.

150. Hugh Childers, *Financial Relations Report* (London, 1896), 191.

151. NLI, Henry Dixon papers, Ms 35,262 (1), A.J. Kettle to Dixon, 11 Feb. 1911.

152. After a lengthy avoidance of his friends, in November 1896 Griffith attended a Celtic Literary Society lecture on James Clarence Mangan, his favourite Irish poet, and contributed a one-off semi-philosophical essay to 'The Seanachie', the society's handwritten journal, written under his 'J.P. Ruhart' pseudonym. NLI, Minute book of the Celtic Literary Society (1896–1902), Ms 19934, minutes for 25 Nov., 26 Dec. 1896, 7 Jan. 1897.

153. *Irish Daily Independent*, 31 Dec. 1896.

154. It is probable that he hoped to make enough money to help not only himself but also his family. Arthur Griffith (ed.) *Poems and ballads of William Rooney* (Dublin, 1902), 32–33.

155. *Irish Daily Independent*, 31 Dec. 1896.

156. NLI, M.J. Lennon papers, Ms 22,293 (9) - recollections of Maud Griffith.

157. One expression of politicians' appreciation of this ability of Griffith was the willingness of William O'Brien MP, perhaps the most prolific Irish contemporary historian of the day, to commission Griffith to write a political history of post-famine Ireland that appeared in serial form in the Cork *Free Press*.

CHAPTER TWO

1. Erskine Childers, *The framework of home rule* (London, 1911), 120.

2. NLI, Gladstone papers, P2875, memoranda to the cabinet, 8 June, 27 July 1886 (p140, pp182–183). On this theme, see also the relevant correspondence of Earl Spencer, Lord Lieutenant of Ireland, in British Library, Althorp Papers (Add Mss.77033–37, Add Mss44493). Richard Shannon, *Gladstone* (London, 2000), 394–395.

3. A.B. Cooke, J.R. Vincent, *The governing passion: cabinet government and party politics in Britain 1885–86* (London, 1974), 17.

4. Allen Warren, 'Dublin Castle, Whitehall and the formation of Irish policy 1879–92', *Irish Historical Studies*, xxxiv, no.136 (November 2005), 426.

5. British Library, Althorp Papers (Add Mss.77033–37, Add Mss44493). Gladstone also deemed security as the first priority: NLI, Gladstone papers, P3261, memo of Gladstone to cabinet, 4 Feb. 1886; NLI, Gladstone papers P3261, memorandum to cabinet, 2 Mar. 1886 (p155); British Library, Althorp Papers Add.77033, letter of Earl Spencer, 18 Sep. 1884 (quote).

6. Patrick Maume, 'William Martin Murphy (1845–1919)', *Dictionary of Irish Biography*, 6 (Cambridge, 2009), 825–827; 'William Field (1843–1935)', *Dictionary of Irish Biography*, 3 (Cambridge, 2009), 774–775. Murphy and Field were rivals for the St. Patrick's Division parliamentary seat in Dublin. Patrick O'Hea, a very popular Donegal Irish Party MP of the day and close associate of Irish Party treasurer Bishop O'Donnell of Raphoe, resigned from parliament in 1896 to take up gold prospecting in South Africa, as did P.A. Chance, a Kilkenny Irish Party MP best known for being one of its best legal minds.

7. Michael Brown, P.M. Geoghegan, James Kelly (ed.), *The Irish Act of Union* (Dublin, 2001), 57.

8. C.P. Curran, 'Griffith, MacNeill and Pearse', *Studies* (spring 1966), 21–28.

9. 'Zanzibar', *United Irishman*, 23 Sept. 1899.

10. 'Beira', *United Irishman*, 28 April 1900.

11. 'Those English', *United Irishman*, 12 May 1900.

12. 'Delagoa Bay', *United Irishman*, 9 Sept. 1899.

13. 'Zanzibar', *United Irishman*, 23 Sept. 1899.

14. 'Middelburg', *United Irishman*, 4 Aug. 1900.

15. 'Delagoa Bay', *United Irishman*, 9 Sept. 1899.

16. 'Chinese nationalism', *United Irishman*, 23 Sept. 1899.

17. 'The Benevolent Englishman', *United Irishman*, 15 Sept. 1900; 'Barberton', *United Irishman*, 25 Aug. 1900. 'Lydenburg', *United Irishman*, 16 June 1900. On this theme, see also Angus Mitchell, *Roger Casement* (London, 2003).

18. *United Irishman*, 6 July 1901, p.4. The Castlebar IRB leader Anthony McBride, brother of John, wrote to the *United Irishman* to the same effect. *United Irishman*, 16 June 1900.

19. 'Middelburg', *United Irishman*, 4 Aug. 1900.
20. P.A. McCracken, 'Arthur Griffith's South-African sabbatical', *Ireland and South Africa in modern times* (vol. 3, 1996), 230–240.
21. 'Middelburg', *United Irishman*, 4 Aug. 1900. Griffith later told this story of the alleged death threat made against him to Piaras Beaslai and claimed that an Orangeman came to his defence against the Englishman. Piaras Beaslai, 'Arthur Griffith', *The Leader*, 16 Dec. 1944.
22. P.A. McCracken, 'Arthur Griffith's South-African sabbatical', 236–40. In this, Gonne was following up the work of General James MacAdaras and Eugene Davis for the English language Parisian press during the Boulanger controversy of the late 1880s.
23. 'Middelburg', *United Irishman*, 4 Aug. 1900.
24. P.A. McCracken, 'Arthur Griffith's South-African sabbatical', 241.
25. 'Olive Schreiner and the English', *United Irishman*, 9 Feb. 1901.
26. The memoirs of Wilfrid S. Blunt, which were edited and reproduced by Lady Gregory in 1920, are illustrative of this trend in an Anglo-Irish context. There was nothing unusual in this sense about Roger Casement's response to African colonialism in the years to come. Many British contemporaries felt the same.
27. P.A. McCracken, 'Arthur Griffith's South-African sabbatical', 242–249.
28. 'Middelburg', *United Irishman*, 4 Aug. 1900.
29. P.A. McCracken, 'Arthur Griffith's South-African sabbatical', 249–250. On Gillingham's Irish connections, see the references to him in Mark Ryan, *Fenian memories* (Dublin, 1945) and Maud Gonne MacBride, *A servant of the Queen* (London, 1938).
30. *Daily Nation* (Dublin), 13 July 1897. Possibly due to African considerations, Murphy's newspaper actually supported the IRB against the Irish Party in the management of the 1798 centenary movement although it is most likely that this was done to facilitate T.M. Healy's plans to alter the management of Irish Party support bodies. For the history of the 1798 centenary movement, see McGee, *IRB*, 246–265.
31. *United Ireland*, 4 Jan. 1894 (report on a meeting of the Young Ireland League). For the history of the *Irish Republic*, see McGee, *IRB*.
32. D.P. McCracken, 'Ireland's desperadoes of the veld', *Irish Times*, 21 Aug. 2010. This is a review of C. van Onselen, *Masked raiders: Irish banditry in Southern Africa 1880–1899*. (Johannesburg, 2010).
33. K.W. Smith, *Alfred Aylward: the tireless agitator* (Johannesburg, 1983). Aylward, a founder of the IRB in Co. Wexford, was an 'informer' as early as 1866. He operated a Boer commando unit during the war of 1877–1881. Irish-born British citizens in the United States operated the 'fenian' organisations that facilitated the relevant communications networks. Aylward died in Philadelphia in 1889, aged forty-six. Griffith wrote an article on Aylward's career for the *United Irishman* during 1899. Arthur Griffith, 'Alfred Aylward', *United Irishman*, 2 Sep.1899; *Pitt's policy* (Dublin, 1911).
34. James Stephens, *Arthur Griffith* (Dublin, 1922), 8 (quote). *United Irishman*, 27 May 1899 (article on Johannesburg). NLI, Lennon papers, Ms 22,293 (9) - recollections of Maud Griffith.
35. McCracken, 'Arthur Griffith's South-African sabbatical', 251.
36. Sean O'Luing, *Art O Griofa* (Baile Atha Cliath, 1954), 47.
37. McGee, *IRB*, 246–265.
38. Circular of the 1798 Centenary Committee, 22 Feb. 1897. This and most documents of the 1798 Centenary Committee can be found in NLI, Henry Dixon papers, Ms 35262 (26)-(27).

39. Arthur Griffith, *Pitt's policy* (Dublin, 1911).

40. Arthur Griffith, *Pitt's policy* (Dublin, 1911).

41. This was J.K. Ingram, co-founder of the Dublin Statistical Society at Trinity College Dublin. His son Thomas was the author of the chief defence of the Union between Britain and Ireland that was written during the 1880s. Michael Brown, P.M. Geoghegan, James Kelly (ed.), *The Irish Act of Union* (Dublin, 2001), 23–26.

42. *Freeman's Journal*, 13 Sept., 9 Nov. 1897. NLI, Henry Dixon papers, Ms 35262 (1), Rooney to Dixon, 3 Nov. 1897. During 1896 Rooney gave free Irish history classes to the general public in Dublin every week. *Evening Herald*, 25 Sept. 1896.

43. NLI, Minute book of the Celtic Literary Society (1896–1902), Ms 19934, minutes from Oct. 1896-Jan. 1897. In these efforts, Rooney was assisting a notable musician Dr. Annie Patterson, who had joined the Gaelic League. *United Irishman*, 20 May 1899 (editorial).

44. NLI, Henry Dixon papers, Ms 35262 (26), flyer of the 1798 Centenary Committee, reporting resolutions made at a meeting of 12 Mar. 1898.

45. D.P. McCracken, *The Irish Pro-Boers* (Johannesburg, 1989), 134–135.

46. NLI, Henry Dixon papers, Ms 35262 (1), J.W. O'Beirne to Dixon, 6 Jan. '1897' (1898). G.A. Lyons, *Some recollections of Griffith and his times* (Dublin, 1923), 6–7.

47. NLI, Minute book of the Celtic Literary Society (1896–1902), Ms 19934, minutes from Jan. 1899. O'Luing, *Art O'Griofa*, 53.

48. O'Luing, *Art O'Griofa*, 54.

49. *United Irishman*, 13 Apr. 1901 (quote). Allen Library, Alice Milligan papers, IE3180 AM, Milligan to P.J. McCall, 25 Mar. 1896. McCall was a poet, friend and reputed 'kindred spirit' to Griffith, with whom he remained associated up until his death in March 1919.

50. *United Irishman*, 26 Mar. 1899 (editorial).

51. W.L. Féingold, *The revolt of the tenantry* (Dublin, 1984), epilogue; C.B. Shannon, *Arthur Balfour and Ireland* (Washington D.C., 1988), 309. For Dublin Castle's interpretation of this reality, see NAI, CBS files, Home Office précis, carton 3, 25191/s (Aug 1901) and 26398/s (Feb. 1902). Its statisticians estimated 114 county councillors and 486 district councillors elected to local government office immediately after the democratisation of local government in 1898 either were or had been IRB men. Another statistical estimate indicated that such men won 10 per cent of all county council seats, 5 per cent of all district council seats and twenty-three positions as chairmen of either district or county councils in the 1899 local government elections.N.A.I., Crime Special Branch précis reports to the Home Office, carton 2 (1897–1900), files 18240/s, 18257/s, 18259/s, 18263/s, 18272/s, 18287/s, 18340/s, 18345/s, 18488/s, 18586/s, 18696/s, 18595/s, 18711/s, 18733/s, 18846/s, 18851/s, 19071/s, 19074/s, 19100/s, 19257/s (all dating from the spring of 1899). In Cork City, some republicans appear to have occasionally been elected to high municipal office during the mid-1880s, but this seems to have been exceptionable rather than a pattern (W.F. Mandle, *The GAA and Irish nationalist politics* (Dublin, 1987), 20, 67–68). Officially, members of the IRB were allowed to enter municipal office, just as they were allowed to vote in parliamentary elections, if they desired to use that particular outlet to 'exert their proper influence in public affairs', but it does not appear that the IRB, as an organisation, ever had faith in the policy it had first experimented with in 1870, of encouraging its followers to run for local office 'as a means of strengthening the power and influence of the Irish Republic'.

52. Gary Owens, 'Nationalist monuments in Ireland 1870–1914: symbolism and ritual' in Gillespie, Kennedy (eds), *Ireland: Art into History* (Dublin, 1994), 103–117; Nancy Murray, 'Joseph K. Bracken: GAA founder, Fenian and politician', *Tipperary: history and society* (Dublin, 1985), 379–393; Brendan Bracken, 'An Irishman's Diary: J.K. Bracken',

Irish Times, 28 Aug. 2004; NAI, CBS précis reports to the Home Office, carton 2, 18696/s, 19203/s, 19208/s; NAI, CBS files, Home Office précis, carton 3, 25191/s (Aug 1901), 26398/s (Feb. 1902).

53. National Archives (Kew), Gerald Balfour Papers, 30/60/28, Inspector General of RIC to Under Secretary, 6 Jan. 1900.
54. NLI, Gladstone papers P2875, pp182–183; Campbell-Bannermann papers, P1282, memo of 30 Apr.1885; British Library, Gladstone papers, Add. Mss44493; Althorp papers (Add. Mss77033–37); Richard Shannon, *Gladstone* (London, 2000), 394–395.
55. D.P. McCracken, *The Irish Pro Boers* (Johannesburg, 1989).
56. G.A. Lyons to *United Irishman*, 23 Sept. 1899. On the efforts to keep the clubs alive, see *United Irishman*, 4 Mar., 11 Mar., 29 April, 6 May 1899. P.T. Daly (Dublin), Sean O'Keefe (Cork), Robert Johnston (Belfast), Maurice Moynihan (Kerry) and T.B. Kelly (Mayo) were the chief IRB figures involved.
57. *United Irishman*, 1 July 1899.
58. John Devoy, 'The story of Clan na Gael', *Gaelic American*, 8 Sept. 1924.
59. This was replaced around August 1900 by a much briefer and less contentious 'foreign notes' column that was soon phased out.
60. Alan O'Day, 'Frank Hugh O'Donnell (1846–1916)', *Dictionary of Irish Biography*, 7 (Cambridge, 2009), 375–377; Owen McGee, 'John O'Connor Power (1846–1919)', *Dictionary of Irish Biography*, 8 (Cambridge, 2009). Power was the finest orator in the Irish Party. O'Donnell was its authority on foreign affairs; a job later taken over by James J. O'Kelly. All three men had been in the IRB during the 1870s.
61. John O'Leary to *United Irishman*, 28 Mar. 1899.
62. Griffith published sympathetic articles on 'the Jewish enlightenment' and the contribution of Jews to European civilisation ('The Irish school of medicine', *Sinn Féin*, 16 Oct. 1909) and vehemently attacked the Irish Party on the grounds of its call that all Jews be barred from employment in government service ('Irishmen, Jews and "Imperial" Patriots', *Nationality*, 25 Dec. 1915). Griffith's youthful belief that Jews tended to be involved inordinately in usury, founded partly upon the Shakespearian cultural stereotype, was probably influenced by a mentality that was particularly prevalent in Dublin whereby 'the hawkers of goods, [are] called, not by way of reflection on religious connection, but as a reflection on illegitimate trading, the "Jewman"'(Henry Dixon to *United Irishman*, 11 Aug.1900). For instance, Griffith once published a satirical cartoon about bogus sellers of Irish goods in which the bogus trader was referred to as 'Moses O'Toole' (*Sinn Féin*, 11 Dec. 1909). The principle example of anti-Semitism from Griffith occurred during 1904. While in the pay of Catholic fundamentalist John Sweetman, Griffith supported a controversial boycott of Jews in Limerick that was led by a Catholic priest. Griffith justified this action not on religious grounds (the grounds chosen by the priest) or on the grounds of racism, but purely on the basis of alleged usury (*United Irishman*, 23 January, 23 Apr. 1904), but he would seem to have failed to understand the situation in Limerick. Griffith had five close Jewish friends in Dublin, including two doctors and a solicitor. In general, Griffith's mentality regarding the Jews was an extension of his anti-sectarian attitudes. He professed to be against any negative or positive discrimination regarding Jews as much in the case of the member of any religious congregation or race. He also maintained that while the racial nationalism of Zionism was justifiable (a fact that would lead some, rightly or wrongly, to suggest 'Israel represents the triumph of Sinn Féin' ('Jewish nationalism—a comparison', *Sinn Féin*, 16 Mar. 1912, by Aodh de Blacam), any reneging of individual responsibilities by Jews, such as in case of criminal activity (Dreyfus was an alleged traitor), was obviously not.

63. Jerome Ann de Wiel, *The Irish factor 1899-1919* (Dublin, 2008), 127–128. John Devoy, 'The story of Clan na Gael', *Gaelic American*, 8 Sep. 1924, 6 June, 13 June 1925.
64. An attempt was made to blow up Welland Canal Dock in Ontario by two Dubliners and one Irish-American (the leader of the group) who were caught and sentenced to life imprisonment. This was attempted supposedly to prevent Canadian ships bringing supplies to the British troops in southern Africa but it was really intended to gauge reaction in the USA to the British war effort. The British secret service was involved in the plot, which was supposed to have originated with Maud Gonne. National Archives (Kew), Gerald Balfour Papers, 30/60/28, report of Commissioner JJ Jones to Under Secretary, 9 Jan. 1900; NAI, DMP files, carton 7 (packet for 1900), report 5527, JJ Jones, 28 March 1900; NAI, CBS files, Home Office précis, carton 3, 25520/s. C.J. Brannigan, 'The Luke Dillon case and the Welland Canal explosion of 1900', *Niagara Frontier* (vol.24, 1977), 36–44; Maud Gonne MacBride, *A servant of the Queen* (London, 1938). The pro-Boer movement itself, encompassing New York, Chicago, London, Paris, Rotterdam, Johannesburg and Dublin, had far more of an imperial than an Irish context.
65. Both this photograph and the annotated novel can be found in NLI, Griffith papers, acc.4476 (box of printed books).
66. Michael Davitt identified her as a British agent in Dublin as early as 1885 and John Devoy always refused requests of John O'Leary (who was completely won over by Gonne during 1885 upon being introduced to her at C.H. Oldham's Contemporary Club) that he cooperate with her ('Jack Daly', *Gaelic American*, 15 Mar.1924). Devoy called her 'a sinister figure in Irish history' that continued Patrick Casey and Eugene Davis' work for the British consulate in Paris during the 1880s in following the activities of 'the dregs of the Boulangist movement' in Paris City Council. He also noted that 'I cannot believe that Griffith was ever in love with this queer woman.' *Gaelic American*, 8 Sep.1924.
67. *United Irishman*, 12 July 1900. G.A. Lyons, *Some recollections of Griffith and his times* (Dublin, 1923), 10–11.
68. *United Irishman*, 6 Oct. 1900, p.1.
69. NLI, Celtic Literary Society minute book, Ms19934, minute for 14 & 21 Apr. 1899. *United Irishman*, 29 Apr. 1899 (report on Fred Ryan's lecture before the Celtic Literary Society).
70. *United Irishman*, 18 Mar., 25 Mar., 22 Apr. 1899.
71. Although thirty years younger than their author, Griffith was able to highlight inaccuracies in James J. O'Kelly's recollections of the IRB (published in William O'Brien's *Irish People*, Sep.1899-Dec.1900) and to write detailed obituaries for Fenian activists in a manner that almost no contemporary journalist, excepting John Devoy, could match. This may indicate that Griffith was more senior in the movement than was generally known, although it is also likely that this was a reflection of Griffith's photographic (and therefore almost encyclopaedic) memory and his familiarity with various published histories of the Fenians.
72. *United Irishman*, 6 July, 13 July 1901.
73. NAI, CBS files, Home Office précis, carton 2, 22189/s (report of Cork City IRB meeting in June 1900 precis).
74. Fr. Kavanagh to *United Irishman*, 2 June, 9 June 1900. Fr. Kavanagh first wrote against secret societies in the *United Irishman* on 1 Apr 1899 and against anticlericalism on 12 May 1900.
75. 'Some opinions of Fr. Kavanagh I do not believe in', *United Irishman*, 19 May 1900 (quote) and *United Irishman*, 16 June 1900, both written under Griffith's pseudonym of 'Cuguan'. Such arguments had been fairly common in IRB circles. See, for instance, James J. O'Kelly, 'Dawn of Fenianism', *Irish People*, 30 Sep., 7 Oct. 1899 (accounts of his debates with

Jesuits); J.J. O'Kelly, *The Mambi Land* (Philadelphia, 1874), 165. Like O'Kelly, some IRB contributors to the *United Irishman* who criticised Fr. Kavanagh emphasised the church's alleged longstanding hostility to nationalists and republicans in Italy and France, which was deemed morally unjustifiable. The existence of commentaries like these explains why some members of the Catholic religious orders were convinced that the IRB, in common with many nominally revolutionary secret societies on the continent, was a creation of the freemason movement as an adjutant to the British secret service rather than the British government per se. This may perhaps reflect the legacy of the freemason movement having been established with an intentionally international (and financial) focus to compensate for the fact that the Church of England, as a state church, could no longer have an international dimension in the same way as the religious orders provided such a dimension to the national diocesan churches within the Roman Catholic Church. This trend of opinion later shaped the evolution of a British imperial historiography as well as a Protestant interpretation of the Roman Empire in the age of Constantine as a basis of a critique of the Catholic Church and its alleged corruption rooted in an intentionally repressive dogmatism. On this theme, see David Barrett, *A brief history of secret societies* (London, 1997) and Patrick Maume, 'Fenianism as a global phenomenon', in L. Litvack, C. Graham (eds) *Ireland and Europe in the nineteenth century* (Dublin, 2006). Eugene Davis, a Catholic, reputedly did separate intelligence gathering for both Catholic and British agencies in Paris during the mid-1880s. Owen McGee (ed.) *Eugene Davis' Souvenirs of Irish footprints over Europe* (1889, 2nd ed., Dublin, 2006); Christy Campbell, *Fenian fire* (London, 2002).

76. The death of Joseph Poole, witnessed by Griffith as a twelve-year old boy, was one such event. Robert Brennan, *Allegiance* (Dublin, 1950), 211; McGee, *IRB*, 115–116. Griffith's nationalist sympathies made him inclined to be highly defensive about the historical record of any Irish rebel figure. For instance, he turned against F.H. O'Donnell in late June–July 1900 when O'Donnell wrote a pamphlet claiming to have proof that the few United Irish leaders who supported a French invasion after 1794 (nominally to enable an Irish rebellion) had been turned into British *agents provocateurs* to assist Britain's war against revolutionary France purely to delay as long as possible their own convictions following the permanent suppression of the United Irishmen in 1794, hence Tone's secret visits to New York and Paris and his ultimate suicide, once imprisoned. At the same time, however, Griffith once suggested that any Irishman who was foolhardy enough to ever be tempted into joining a secret underground movement pledged to support armed rebellion should first read Henri Le Caron's memoir *Twenty-Five Years in the Secret Service* (London, 1893). A letter of Griffith's to this effect is kept in the NLI manuscript department's 'ALS Signature Collection'. Le Caron was an Englishman named Thomas Beach who posed as a Frenchman in the United States to manipulate US–Canadian relations via the Fenian Brotherhood alongside some ex-French soldiers who did similar work for the British government.

77. Alvin Jackson, 'The failure of unionism in Dublin, 1900', *Irish Historical Studies*, 26 (1989), 377–395.

78. Griffith's speech to the National Council on 22 Oct. 1906, reprinted as Sinn Féin pamphlet no.3 (Dublin, 1907), pp. 3–4; *Sinn Féin*, 25 Oct., 8 Nov. 1913, *Nationality*, 18 Dec. 1915, p. 2.

79. Mary Daly, *Dublin: deposed capital* (Cork, 1984), 266–268; Tom Kennedy (ed.) *Victorian Dublin* (Dublin, 1989), 72–73, 79, 88; Louis Cullen, *Princes and pirates: the history of Dublin Chamber of Commerce* (Dublin, 1983).

80. C.H. Rolleston, *Portrait of an Irishman* (Dublin, 1939), quote from a letter of T.W. Rolleston, pp117–120.

81. Fionnuala Waldron, 'Statesmen on the street corners: labour and the Parnell split in Dublin 1890–92', *Studia Hibernica*, no.34 (2006–07), 151–172.

82. National Archives (Kew), Gerald Balfour Papers, 30/60/28, report of Sir David Harrel to Lord Lieutenant, 11 Jan. 1900; NAI, CBS files, Home Office précis, carton 2, 20989/s, 21270/s, 21614/s, carton 3, 23860/s, 24032/s.

83. Eunan O'Halpin, 'The secret service vote and Ireland', *Irish Historical Studies* (vol.23, 1983); NLI, Campbell-Bannermann papers, P1282, Arnold Morley, secretary to the imperial treasury, to Chief Secretary of Ireland, 12 Mar. 1886; BL Althorp Papers, Add.77035, memorandum on special branch funding, 9 Jan. and 25 June 1885; BL, Althorp Papers, Add.77036, Memorandum of E.G. Jenkinson to cabinet on the history of the Crimes Special Branch Department (Ireland), 26 July 1886. 'Fenian' conspiracies within the Irish diaspora involving the contacting of Britain's perceived international enemies had often been used either as covers for British intelligence gathering or, in the event of actual political disturbances taking place, a means of persuading different countries' intelligence departments (such as the Americans) to cooperate more in Britain's interests on matters that were totally unrelated to Ireland. (BL, Althorp Papers, Add 77033, Jenkinson to Spencer, 3 April 1884; BL, Althorp Papers, Add.77034, Jenkinson to Spencer, 23 January, 14 February and 16 March 1885; O.D. Edwards, 'American diplomats and Irish coercion 1880–83', *Journal of American Studies* (vol.2, 1967), pp213–232). The IRB's traditional decision to maintain close social interactions with members of the Irish militias was not impeded by the anti-enlistment strategy.

84. *United Irishman*, 17 and 24 Feb., 3 Mar. 1900; Mark Ryan to *United Irishman*, 5 May 1900.

85. O'Leary to *United Irishman*, 17 Mar. 1900; *United Irishman*, 14 Apr. 1900. To embarrass Allan, Griffith persuaded James Egan, who had been a political prisoner with John Daly and Tom Clarke and now worked as a corporation official, to issue a public statement against the Queen's visit that Griffith actually wrote for him. G.A. Lyons, *Some recollections of Griffith and his times* (Dublin, 1923), 16–30. Being funded by Maud Gonne, James Connolly had also declared his wish to banish Allan from public life. *Workers Republic*, 13 Aug. 1898, 6 June 1899. Allan to *Workers Republic*, 1 July 1899, and Connolly's reply to Allan's letter, *Workers Republic*, 1 July 1899.

86. NAI, DMP Crime Dept, Précis of Information, carton 6, report 23203/s, John Mallon, 7 Nov. 1900 (summary for Aug-Oct).

87. Piaras Beaslai, 'Arthur Griffith', *The Leader*, 16 Dec. 1944. He trained in Jack Sullivan's well-known gym.

88. NAI, DMP files, carton 7 (packet for 1900), reports 5535–6 and 5548–9, 1–3 and 12 Apr. 1900; *United Irishman*, 7, 14 and 21 Apr. 1900.

89. NAI, DMP files, carton 14, report 5391, JJ Jones, 15 Nov. 1899; NLI, M.J. Lennon papers, MS22293 (1).

90. 'Occasional notes' by T.D. Sullivan MP (undated press cutting, probably *The Irish Catholic and Nation*, 10 Apr. 1900), in NLI, Sean O'Luing papers, Ms 23,516.

91. Initially a Sligo-born customs official and *Irish Times* journalist, then a Dublin publican, together with John 'Jack' Sullivan (an Irish-American boxer who ran a well-known gym at 15 D'Olier Street up until his death in 1916), Clancy had operated a 'republican' network since 1883 that, aside from its connections with the remnants of the original Fenian Brotherhood in the United States (and, indeed, the police), was most noticeable for instigating highly publicised street protest demonstrations and resulting trials that, more often than not, were counterproductive to everything except Clancy's own career. One practical achievement of Clancy's career was to found the Tara Street Baths (now Tara

Street Station) as an alternative to nude swimming in the Liffey, which was popular with poor inner-city youths who could not afford expensive Victorian swimming costumes and thus were not allowed to be present at established bathing places such as Sandymount strand and Kingstown (Dun Laoghaire). Owen McGee, 'John Clancy (1841–1915)', *Dictionary of Irish Biography*, 2 (Cambridge, 2009), 520–521. For Sullivan's career, see the references to the 'Stephenite faction' of the IRB in McGee, *IRB*; *Nationality*, 25 Mar. 1916 (obituary for J.W. Sullivan) and Piaras Beaslai, 'Arthur Griffith', *The Leader*, 16 Dec. 1944.

92. NAI, DMP files, carton 7, Report 5686, Chief Commissioner Jones, 2 Oct. 1900; NAI, DMP précis of information, carton 6, Chief Commissioner Jones, 5 Dec. 1900. NAI, CBS files, Home Office précis, carton 3, 23504/s, Chief Commissioner Jones, 5 Dec. 1900.

93. *United Irishman*, 4 and 21 Aug. 1900.

94. L.W. MacBride, *The greening of Dublin Castle* (Washington D.C., 1991), 92.

95. This aroused intense unionist criticisms. For a contemporary critique of the AOH, see Lord Ashtown (ed.) *The unknown power behind the Irish nationalist party* (London, 1907).

96. *United Irishman*, 6 Oct. 1900.

97. *United Irishman*, 1 Dec. 1900.

98. *United Irishman*, 23 Feb. 1901.

99. McGee, *IRB*, 266–300.

100. *United Irishman*, 21 July 1900.

101. NLI, Douglas Hyde papers, Ms17292, Griffith to 'Mac[Bride]', 3 Aug. 1901.

102. William O'Brien, Desmond Ryan (eds), *Devoy's post bag*, 2 (Dublin, 1953), 347–350; McBride to *United Irishman*, 18 Jan. 1902, 20 May 1903.

103. G.A. Lyons, 'Arthur Griffith and the IRB', *Forum* (Jan. 1950), 6–7; NAI, CBS files, Home Office précis, carton 2, 19172/s, 19425/s, 19650/s (reports Major Gosselin); carton 3, 24896/s, 24928/s (June 1901).

104. *United Irishman*, 24 Oct. 1902.

105. William O'Brien, Desmond Ryan (eds), *Devoy's post bag*, 2 (Dublin, 1953), 347–350.

106. NLI, Sweetman papers, Ms47582 (7), Gonne to Sweetman, 7 May [1903].

107. NLI, Sweetman papers, Ms47582 (7), Sweetman to Gonne (copy), 9 May 1903; Gonne to Sweetman, 10 May [1903].

108. NLI, Sweetman papers, Ms47582 (7), Gonne to Sweetman (no date).

109. UCD, Alderman Cole papers P134, Henry Egan Kenny to Cole, 14 Feb. 1928.

110. Griffith's father was living there when he died in December 1904, aged sixty-six. *Freeman's Journal*, 19 Dec 1904. Upon the death of Griffith's mother in 1919, it appears that the eldest son Bill Griffith returned to Ireland. He was reported to be living in the Summerhill home and working as a registrar in a workhouse when he died, aged fifty-eight, in 1924. *Irish Independent*, 7 Jan. 1924.

CHAPTER THREE

1. NLI, Eblana Journal of the Leinster Debating Society, Ms 3943, issue for 8 Mar. 1889.

2. Hamilton Ffye, *T.P. O'Connor* (London, 1934); Owen McGee, 'Thomas Power O'Connor (1848–1929)', *Dictionary of Irish Biography*, 7 (Cambridge, 2009), 282–283. Griffith was inclined to associate George Bernard Shaw with George Moore's literary example. *United Irishman*, 27 Apr. 1901.

3. 'Journalism and the happy despatch', *Nationality*, 8 Apr. 1916.

4. Arthur Griffith (ed.) *John Mitchel's Jail Journal* (Dublin, 1913), introduction.

5. Kevin Rafter (ed.), *Irish journalism before independence* (Manchester, 2011), introduction.

6. *United Irishman*, 11 May 1901 (obituary for Rooney); Commemorative booklet on Mary Butler O'Nolan (Dublin, 1920).
7. Obituary for 'Sean Ghall', *Irish Press*, 23 Oct. 1936. On being recalled from London by Griffith in 1922, Kenny worked until his retirement as the Dáil librarian. Cuffe wrote anniversary articles about Griffith for the *Sunday Independent* c.1923-c.1940.
8. 'Hurling as a fine art', *Sinn Féin*, 26 Aug. 1913. Griffith credited Cusack, a man with a long journalistic career dating back to the mid century, as being the guiding spirit in founding the GAA.
9. Arthur Griffith, Patrick Bradley (eds) *Poems and ballads by William Rooney* (Dublin, 1902); Seamus MacManus (ed.) *Ethna Carbery: the four winds of Eirinn* (Dublin, 1902); Seamus MacManus (ed.) *William Rooney prose writings* (Dublin, 1909).
10. Griffith, Bradley (eds), *Poems and ballads*, introduction.
11. NLI, Bureau of Military History papers, WS384 (J.J. O'Kelly/Sceilg), p.5.
12. Mary Daly, *Dublin: deposed capital*, 46.
13. Tom Clyde, *Irish literary magazines* (Dublin, 2002), 27.
14. Owen McGee, 'Eugene Davis (1857–1897): a forgotten Clonakilty poet and writer', *Journal of the Cork Historical and Archaeological Society*, vol.109 (2004), 125–136. See also the editorial of *Shamrock*, 1 Sept. 1877.
15. The republican–Catholic debate on Canon Sheehan centred particularly on his novel 'My New Curate' and was partly an extension of the republican–Catholic quarrel surrounding Fr. Kavanagh the previous summer. They can be seen in *United Irishman*, 23 Sept-24 Nov. 1900 (quote 17 Nov.). The anti-republican tenor of Sheehan's writings was seen to stem from their themes of needing to protect Ireland from 'continental poisons'; a hero's declaration 'that the Fenian leaders are all scoundrels receiving secret service money'; and an episode in which 'this "highly-moral" author makes his parish priest forgive the informer and cloak his crime on condition of his cutting his (*the priest's*) garments in the future'. While there were still some republican–Catholic political quarrels at this time (the election of John Daly as mayor of Limerick being one—see Frank O'Connor, *Leinster, Munster and Connacht* (London, 1950), 215), it is likely that a literary anticlericalism influenced some IRB circles due to familiarities with French literary traditions, made evident in Stendhal's *Scarlet and Black*, Victor Hugo's novels, Maupassant's *Bouel de Seuf*, Zola's *Savage Paris* and even in Flaubert's 1848 and 1871 correspondences (although the latter did believe that all French republican secret societies *were* controlled by the police). Meanwhile, a French parallel to Canon Sheehan's sensibilities may be seen in the novels of Francois Mauriac, which were particularly popular with Edwardian UCD students such as Francis Cruise O'Brien and Thomas Kettle.
16. W.B. Yeats, *Collected poems* (London, 1989). Terence Brown and Roy Foster have typified this pantheism as a preoccupation with 'magic'. The role of theosophy in shaping contemporary writers' sensibilities—a trend launched in the 1880s by Juliette Adam's Parisian *Nouvelle Revue* (which was also an alleged home of freemasonry)—evidently shaped Yeats' inspired deviation from the cerebral brand of neo-romanticism championed by Robert Browning and equally distanced him from the self-consciously 'decadent' literature (a deliberate exploration of the extremes of depravity) championed by Catulle Mendes and J.K. Husymans, tormented converts from Judaism and French writers of the 1880s whose example inspired English-language writers during the 1890s via Oscar Wilde's London circle.
17. Rooney felt that only Yeats' earliest verse was 'understandable'. *United Irishman*, 6 May 1899.

18. Cuguan (Griffith's) review of Yeats' collected poems, *United Irishman*, 27 Apr. 1901. The suggestion of stealing a copy of the book was no doubt inspired by the fact that the publisher (Fisher Unwin) had set the very high price of 7s.6d. Hitherto, Griffith considered Mangan the greatest Irish poet. In this review, Griffith credited Yeats with succeeding where Mangan and Ferguson failed in interpreting and giving voice to the Celtic temperament; a fact that Yeats would later cite to his own credit in one of his own verses.

19. NLI, Griffith papers, acc.4476, copies of letters of James Starkey and Griffith to Russell, 16 Dec.1905.

20. *United Irishman*, 2 June 1900 (Cuguan's response to Fr. Kavanagh's opinions, p. 3).

21. *United Irishman*, 29 Apr. 1899.

22. *United Irishman*, 11 Mar. 1899.

23. 'Irish Novelists', *United Irishman*, 22 Apr. 1899. Evidence of an Irish trend against romanticism during the 1880s may perhaps be seen in Eugene Davis' ridiculing of Goethe's sensibilities ('the sorrows of young Werther' etc.) in 1889 despite having translated his verse into English a decade earlier.

24. *United Irishman*, 7 Jan. 1905. Griffith and Yeats debated this issue further in the issues of 28 Jan. and 4 Feb. 1905. Yeats also defended the play in *Samhain*.

25. Piaras Beaslai (ed.) *Songs, ballads and recitations by famous Irishmen: Arthur Griffith* (Dublin, 1926), 3–5, 18–21.

26. *Irish Daily Independent*, 10 June 1892 (speech of Sigerson at launch of National Literary Society). This was despite Sigerson's friendship with IRB leaders, stemming partly from his relationship by marriage to T.N. Underwood and his pioneering study *Modern Ireland* (1868). McGee, *IRB*, 123, 191, 309.

27. W.P. Ryan, *The Irish literary revival* (London, 1894), preface, 130–131.

28. Strangely, Griffith's ineffective satire 'the spooks of the 13th lock' actually proved quite popular (Beaslai (ed.) *Songs, ballads and recitations*). However Griffith was not entirely free from an interest in 'spooks' himself, having once written a short fictional tale, 'The legend of the pale young man', about a youth who meets the ghost of Clarence Mangan in one the latter's favoured Dublin drinking haunts. *United Irishman*, 5 Aug. 1899.

29. Two notable early examples were John Sweetman to the *United Irishman*, 1 Jul. 1899 and Edward Dalton to the *United Irishman*, 16 Sept. 1899.

30. *Irish Weekly Independent*, 17 Aug 1946 (extract from unpublished memoirs of Mary Butler, quoting an English journalist).

31. Michael MacDonagh to *United Irishman*, 15 Apr. 1899. A friend of John O'Connor Power, MacDonagh later used his private papers for a history of the home rule movement.

32. The judgement of academics such as Alice Stopford Green (a professor of medieval history) and John Marcus O'Sullivan (a professor of European history and minister for education) of Griffith's life and times, published in *Studies* (Sep. 1922–Nov. 1923), are instructive in this sense. Although they took the form of a review, the very fact that Griffith's publications were weeklies would have led many contemporaries to associate them with the weekly-only, essentially party-political, newspapers that were launched during the 1880s to target the new skilled working-class vote. Unlike the daily newspapers, these did not usually contain market news or reports on international affairs.

33. 'The place hunter in Irish politics', *Sinn Féin*, 29 Nov. 1913: 'of all hallucinations that is the most insane which inveigles a people to believe that by seeking and accepting the price of corruption it can purchase its liberty'.

34. Griffith's favourite tactic in this regard was to take some episode of contemporary debate and to exaggerate it out of all proportion in an attempt to make it seem

completely absurd. This was usually done in the context of a localised or personalised Irish dispute. Sometimes it was attempted (not necessarily with success) in the context of international relations, an example being an imaginary critique of the idea of 'home rule for England' by an 'Otto Von Balfour, ex-premier of the United Empire of Germany and Great Britain, Berlin, 9 Dec. 1963', written in an attempt to ridicule Arthur Balfour's contemporary stance on home rule for Ireland (*Sinn Féin*, 13 Dec. 1913).

35. Prof. R.M. Henry of Queen's University Belfast on Arthur Griffith, *Studies* (Sept. 1922), 351–352. Henry, an associate of Griffith through the Gaelic League from 1906 onwards, wrote the first history of Sinn Féin in 1920.

36. Quoted in an extract from an unpublished memoir of Máire Butler in *Irish Weekly Independent*, 17 Aug. 1946.

37. NAI, Bureau of Military History papers, WS384 (statement of J.J. O'Kelly), pp 5–6.

38. NLI, Celtic Literary Society minute book, Ms19934, minute for 27 Nov. 1896. W.P. Ryan and Fred Ryan, the most notable Irish socialist thinkers of the day, as well as the still unknown figure of James Connolly, were members of the Celtic at this time.

39. This occurred during July 1902. According to Sceilg, it was the Catholic patrons of the Celtic, T.P. Fox and James Golden, who introduced Griffith to several books on economics. NAI, Bureau of Military History papers, WS384 (statement of J.J. O'Kelly), p. 6.

40. Advertisements for the fifth Oireachtas of the Gaelic League in *An Claidheamh Solus* (May 1901); *Programme of Oireachtas of the Gaelic League* (NLI pamphlet collections).

41. *United Irishman*, 16 Sep., 23 Sep. 1899.

42. Tim G. McMahon, *The Gaelic revival and Irish society 1893–1910* (Syracuse, 2008); Kevin Collins, *Catholic churchmen and the Celtic revival 1848–1916* (Dublin, 2003).

43. To this day, historians have found it difficult to square this circle of debate. Michael Broers has credited Napoleon, far more so than the seventeenth-century English constitutional tradition or the French revolution, with being the inventor of the modern nation state, while Pamela Pilbeam has identified this Napoleonic legacy, as well as the intellectual influence of freemasons, as the root of the ideological debates on modernity that gave birth to the notions of liberalism and republicanism being necessary handmaidens to the nation state. By contrast, Tim Blanning and Adam Zamoyski have associated this glorification of the nation with romanticism in the arts; a mentality that is representative of traditional schools of historical thought in Britain and Ireland. Catholic academics in the United States have reinforced the latter trend.

44. *United Irishman*, 13 Apr. 1901 (editorial).

45. *United Irishman*, 13 Apr. 1901 (editorial).

46. *An Claidheamh Solus*, 18 Mar. 1899 (editorial).

47. *An Claidheamh Solus*, 2 Mar. 1901.

48. 'The New Patriotism', *United Irishman*, 11 Mar.1899.

49. John Mitchel, *Jail journal* (Glasgow, 1870), 25.

50. Griffith's enthusiasm for both music and nationalism led him to judge that contemporary music critics were a little too harsh on the efforts of Sir Arthur Sullivan (also a co-composer of popular operettas) and Augusta Holmes (an Irish-born student of Saint Saens and Faure in Paris) to compose music on Irish themes. *United Irishman*, 6 May 1899.

51. Derek Sayer, *The coasts of Bohemia* (Princeton, 1998), 24–27, 82, 170–180; A.H. Hermann, *A history of the Czechs* (London, 1975). In recent times, this historic legacy has been criticised by Milan Kundera as a negative influence on Czech society.

52. Liam P. O'Riain (W.P. Ryan), *Lessons from modern language movements* (London, 1902).

53. Although Griffith tried to learn Irish, he 'had a constitutional incapacity for learning languages'. It was not until 1918 that Griffith could announce 'with great satisfaction' that he had finally succeeded in reading a relatively simple book in Irish without the aid of a dictionary. NLI, George A. Lyons papers, Ms33,675(L). During the 1890s, the YIL claimed to have succeeded in getting a professor of Irish appointed to a Dublin technical school, while Griffith was delegated to examine how the Royal Irish Academy was looking after its Irish language manuscripts. NLI, Griffith papers, acc. 4476, box b, Young Ireland League minute book (1894–96), minutes for 31 Jul., 11 Sept. 1894. Although he had received schooling from the Christian Brothers, it is far from clear whether or not Griffith knew anything of the Irish language at this time.

54. *United Irishman*, 19 Jan. 1901.

55. 'Irish Nationalism and the Irish Language', *United Irishman*, 19 Jan. 1901.

56. Thomas J. Morrissey S.J., *Towards a national university: William Delany S.J.* (Dublin, 1983); *Thomas A Finlay S.J.* (Dublin, 2004).

57. O.P. Rafferty S.J., *The Catholic Church and the Protestant state: nineteenth-century Irish realities* (Dublin, 2008). On this theme, see also Dermot Keogh, Andrew McCarthy, *The making of the Irish constitution 1937* (Cork, 2007).

58. Patrick Maume (ed.), *D.P. Moran's The Philosophy of Irish Ireland* (Dublin, 2006). George Russell (AE) made a particular issue of this trend. *Controversy in Ireland: an appeal to Irish journalists* (Dublin, 1904).

59. The *Irish Catholic* continued to maintain, for example, that Catholicism was incompatible with both individualism and liberalism. On this theme, see Patrick Maume, *The long gestation* (Dublin, 1999). Some Irish historians have referred to politicians such as Daniel O'Connell as advocates of a 'Catholic liberalism' (Thomas Duddy, *A history of Irish thought* (London, 2002)) but this may be said to be a mistaken idea. O'Connell engaged in debates on 'liberalism' (often associated by contemporaries with a legacy of the French Revolution) but as a Catholic, he had a distinct concept of 'liberty' and, like many educated Catholics who engaged with such debates, frequently distinguished between 'liberty' as a definable and humanist idea that must be promoted and 'liberalism' as a mere political buzzword, without any real humanist connotations or definable meaning. On this theme, see Owen McGee (ed.) *Eugene Davis' Souvenirs of Irish footprints over Europe* (1889, 2nd ed., Dublin, 2006).

60. Patrick Maume, 'William Martin Murphy (1845–1919)', *Dictionary of Irish Biography*, 6 (Cambridge, 2009), 825–827.

61. T.G. McMahon, *The Gaelic revival and Irish society 1893–1910* (Syracuse, 2008). The counter reaction within the Gaelic League was perhaps best demonstrated by the decision of W.P. Ryan, its great champion during 1902, to later write the rather damning critique *The Pope's Green Island* (London, 1912).

62. The programmes for O'Donnell's history lectures to the Gaelic League of London can be found in NLI, Art O'Brien papers.

63. F.H. O'Donnell, *The ruin of education in Ireland* (London, 1903), 26–27, 39–41, 47–50, 57–58, 62–63, 74–75, 77, 81.

64. Many Irish contemporaries equated any suggestion that the Catholic ideal of education was insufficient to accommodate the challenges facing modern political societies solely with a handful of outspoken rationalists in Trinity College, who were popular with neither Protestants nor Catholics but appealed to some intellectuals. Griffith satirised these TCD academics on a frequent basis between 1899 and 1902 by typifying them as egocentric fools. Regarding O'Donnell, a son of Irish parents in England, see Alan O'Day,

'Frank Hugh O'Donnell (1846–1916)', *Dictionary of Irish Biography*, 7 (Cambridge, 2009), 375–377.

65. Tom Kettle, *The day's burden* (1910, reprinted Dublin, 1968). On this theme, see also Cardinal Newman's seminal work *The idea of a university* (Dublin and London, 1854), the founding text of the Catholic University (later renamed by the Jesuits as UCD).

66. G.K. Chesterton, *Heretics* (London, 1905), 174.

67. Tom Kettle, 'Mr. Yeats and the Freedom of the Theatre', *United Irishman*, 14 Jan. 1902. To Kettle's mind, the one essential quality for an Irish writer was 'he must not be a pagan' (*The day's burden*, 55–56). As a barrister, he could not walk into a court assize without wondering whether or not the existence of political systems of any kind was an imposition upon God's law (*The day's burden*, 75–78).

68. Tom Kettle, *The Day's Burden* (Dublin, 1968), 84–85.

69. UCD Archives, Tom Kettle papers, LA134/139. Terence DeVere White, *Kevin O'Higgins* (London, 1948), 179.

70. *United Irishman*, 11 Feb. 1905 (Griffith's critique of Kettle's writings in the *New Ireland Review*).

71. UCD Archives, Tom Kettle papers, LA32/11, p. 3 (recollections of his wife Mary Kettle).

72. Harold Perkin, *The rise of professional society: England since 1880* (London, 1989). This formed the backdrop to the creation during 1880 of the Royal University of Ireland, which amalgamated with the National University of Ireland in 1908.

73. UCD Archives, DeValera papers, P150/49, speech of DeValera on the university question, 19 Feb. 1903.

74. UCD Archives, DeValera papers, P150/49, speech of DeValera on the university question, 19 Feb.1903, and a letter of DeValera to St. Wilfred's Catholic College in England, 13 June 1903 ('my ultimate object is the priesthood').

75. *United Irishman*, 23 and 30 May 1903. When the mayor refused to answer to Griffith, Griffith led a mob armed with sticks that attacked several men present, in the process putting John O'Donnell (the MP for south Mayo, who had defeated John McBride for the seat in 1900) in hospital. NAI, DMP précis, carton 6, 28498/s (May 1903). Reputedly, Griffith had previously been responsible for putting a policeman in hospital (courtesy of a head butt) during the April 1900 Dublin riots.

76. *United Irishman*, 23 May, 30 May, 6 June, 13 June, 4 July 1903. NAI, CBS files, Home Office précis, carton 3, 26763/s, 27019/s, 27804/s, 29702/s. Keating spoke at Bodenstown and outside Dublin City Hall and claimed that the United Irish League, although it had some wealthy supporters, was not popular in Irish-America. Curiously, Keating spoke alongside Patrick Hoctor, a discredited republican within Ireland since 1887, who was then working for a St. Louis business exhibition that was promoted in Ireland by T.W. Rolleston of Horace Plunkett's department at Dublin Castle. Owen McGee, 'Patrick Hoctor (1861–1933)', *Dictionary of Irish Biography*, 4 (Cambridge, 2009). For the history of the United Irish League of America, see Michael Funchion, *Irish American voluntary organisations* (Connecticut, 1983).

77. *United Irishman*, 27 June 1903, 18 July 1903; NAI, CBS précis reports to Home Office, carton 3, 28765/s (July 1903).

78. Both Bodenstown and the IRB's 'Robert Emmet Centenary Demonstration' in September 1903 attracted about 6,000 people who were mostly young Irish–Irelander activists. *United Irishman*, 12 Sept. 1903.

79. *United Irishman*, 20 May, 6 June, 20 June, 18 July, 25 July and 12 Sept. 1903.

80. *United Irishman*, 27 June 1903.

81. For Griffith's defence of O'Brien, see his editorials of October 1903.

82. NLI, MS5943, Griffith to Florence Williams, 4 Nov. 1916.
83. Seamus O'Sullivan, *Essays and recollections* (Dublin, 1944), 104–111.
84. Padraic Colum, *Arthur Griffith* (Dublin, 1959); C.P. Curran, 'Griffith, MacNeill and Pearse', *Studies* (spring 1966), 21–28; Patrick Maume, 'Seamus O'Kelly (1875–1918)', *Dictionary of Irish Biography*, 7 (Cambridge, 2009); William Murphy, 'Darrel Figgis (1882–1925)', *Dictionary of Irish Biography*, 3 (Cambridge, 2009), 775–777; Marie Coleman, 'James Montgomery (1870–1943)', *Dictionary of Irish Biography*, 6 (Cambridge, 2009), 598–599; Patrick Maume, 'Oliver St. John Gogarty (1878–1957)', *Dictionary of Irish Biography*, 4 (Cambridge, 2009), 127–137.
85. NLI, Griffith papers, acc.4476, box a, Griffith to Russell 16 Dec. 1905 (turning down his offer to be an art critic) and undated letters of Griffith to Starkey. NLI, Ms5943, Griffith to Williams, 25 July 1907.
86. R.J. Finneran (ed.) *Letters of James Stephens* (London, 1974), 79 (quote); Sean Ghall, 'Arthur Griffith as I knew him' (undated press cutting, NLI, Sean O'Luing papers, Ms 23,516). Griffith would occasionally attempt to complement his own political articles on various small European nations with an appreciation of some of their finest writers or musicians, a good example being his treatment of Norwegian artists such as Grieg and Ibsen during 1909 (*Sinn Féin*, 6 Nov., 4 Dec. 1909).
87. NLI, Griffith papers, acc.4476, box a, undated letter of Griffith to Starkey (original and photocopy) kept within a photograph book.
88. Kevin Barry (ed.) *James Joyce: occasional, critical and political writing* (London, 2000).
89. James Joyce, *Ulysses* (London, 1968), 704. Joyce's use in his storytelling of real-life figures in the world of Dublin journalism (most notably John Wyse Power renamed as John Wyse Nolan) and his own status as an emigrant in Paris (where he settled with the help of IRB figures) reflected his disinclination to share in the celebrations of Kettle's UCD circle regarding the alleged ascendancy of a 'nationalist [Catholic] Ireland' ever since the mid-1880s, although, generations later, Joyce's novel (after it attained acclaim elsewhere) would often be interpreted as a celebration of UCD and its environs.
90. James Stephens, *Insurrections* (Dublin, 1909), 40 (from 'A Street').
91. Patrick Maume, 'James Stephens (1880–1952)', *Dictionary of Irish Biography*, 9 (Cambridge, 2009). Alongside Colum and Thomas MacDonagh, Stephens also formed the *Irish Review* (1911–1913), to which Griffith contributed. Dermot Bolger's fiction, beginning with *The woman's daughter*, arguably betrayed a debt to Stephens' pioneering example.
92. 'Reparation', *Sinn Féin*, 9 Apr. 1910. Gifford's series of cartoons, published under the title 'Institutions', were published in *Sinn Féin* between January and March 1910.
93. NLI, Ms 3493, 'Eblana' issue for 20 April 1889: 'the maid without a name', by Shanaghagh.
94. 'Those English', *United Irishman*, 12 May 1900.
95. NLI, Sean O'Luing papers, Ms 23,516, 'Arthur Griffith as I knew him' by Sean Ghall (undated press cutting, probably taken from *Young Ireland*, c.Aug-Sep.1922).

CHAPTER FOUR

1. T.M. Kettle, 'Would the Hungarian Policy work?', *New Ireland Review*, vol.22, no. 6 (Feb. 1905), 322–328.
2. Carl Wittke, *The Irish in America* (New York, 1956), 274–276.
3. Patrick Murray (ed.) *Arthur Griffith's The Resurrection of Hungary* (1904, reprinted Dublin, 2003), viii-ix.

4. Dermot Meleady, *John Redmond: the national leader* (Dublin, 2013), 72.
5. John McBride to *United Irishman*, 18 Jan. 1902; *United Irishman*, 8 & 29 Apr. 1899; 'Political ignorance', *United Irishman*, 3 Feb. 1900; 'What is constitutional agitation?' *United Irishman*, 30 May 1903.
6. *United Irishman*, 4 Mar., 11 Mar., 22 Apr., 29 April, 6 May 1899.
7. NLI, Tim Harrington papers, Ms8581 (1) and (3).
8. British Library, Althorp Papers, Add 77032–77037; Owen McGee, *The IRB* (Dublin, 2005), chapter 4.
9. Fr. W.M. Brady [chaplain to Pope Leo XIII], 'A plea for an Anglo-Roman Alliance', *Fortnightly Review* (vol.35, Apr. 1884), 453–462; British Library, Althorp Papers, Add 77032–77037; Stephen Ball (ed.) *Dublin Castle and the First Home Rule Crisis* (Cambridge, 2009); C.C. O'Brien, *Parnell and his party* (Oxford, 1957), 89–90, 128–130; Emmet Larkin, *The Roman Catholic Church and the making of the modern Irish state* (Dublin, 1975).
10. NLI, Sir George Fottrell papers, Ms33670, memos for 31 May, 17 June, 23 June, 5 Aug., 18 Sep., 28 Sep. 1885, 27 Jan.1886.
11. Owen McGee, *The IRB* (Dublin, 2005), 48, 61, 74, 88, 127, 142; British Library, Gladstone papers, Add. Mss4493, letters of Gladstone and E.G. Jenkinson (11–12 Dec. 1885); Richard Shannon, *Gladstone* (London, 2000), 394–395.
12. L.P. Curtis, 'Landlord responses to the Irish land war 1879–1887', *Eire-Ireland*, 38 (fall/winter 2003).
13. D.R.C. Hudson, *The Ireland that we made* (Arkon, 2003), preface. The Catholic hierarchy in both Britain and Ireland were known to be against the severing of the Union. British Library, Althorp Papers, Add.77036–37, letters of 6 Aug., 23 Sep., 20 Dec. 1885, 17 Jan., 24 Jan. 1886.
14. Emmet Larkin, *The Roman Catholic Church and the making of the modern Irish state* (Dublin, 1975); Dermot Keogh, *The Vatican, the bishops and Irish politics* (Cambridge, 1986).
15. Alec Sullivan, 'The American Republic and the Irish National League of America', *American Catholic Quarterly Review* (vol.9, 1884), 35–44; J.P. Rodechko, *Patrick Ford and his search for America* (New York, 1976); F.G. McManamin, *The American years of John Boyle O'Reilly* (New York, 1976).
16. NLI, James Bryce papers, Ms9210, cuttings from *Irish World*, 30 Jan.-13 Mar. 1886. See also James Bryce Killeen (ed.) *The Irish question as viewed by one hundred eminent statesmen of England, Ireland and America* (New York, 1886). Although Irish-Americans expressed deep reservations regarding the terms of Gladstone's bill after its contents were made known, their acceptance of this Anglo-American political consensus nevertheless remained. Michael Funchion, *Irish American voluntary organisations* (Connecticut, 1983).
17. *United Irishman*, 14 Jan. 1905. Griffith was able to use a private letter of Davitt's, dating from August 1902 and expressed anti-British sympathies, in an anti-enlistment pamphlet that was written in defence of the Hungarian Policy. National Council, *Ireland and the British Army* (Dublin, 1906), 18.
18. *United Irishman*, 12 Sept 1903.
19. NLI, Sean O'Luing papers, Ms 23,516, 'Arthur Griffith as I Knew Him' (undated press cutting by Sean Ghall). NAI, DMP reports, précis of information, carton 6, 28965/s, report of 5 Oct. 1903 (summary of events during September).
20. NLI, Sweetman papers, Ms47585/1, Griffith to Sweetman (undated [1904]).
21. Arthur Griffith, *The resurrection of Hungary* (Dublin, 1904), preface.

22. C.C. O'Brien, *Parnell and his party* (Oxford, 1957), 1–2 (quote); R.V. Comerford, *The Fenians in context* (Dublin, 1985), passim.
23. William O'Brien, Desmond Ryan (eds), *Devoy's Post Bag*, 1 (Dublin, 1947), 538.
24. 'Robbery Under Arms', by Nationalist, *United Irishman*, 8 Apr. 1899.
25. Dorothy Thompson, *The Chartists* (Aldershot, 1984), 77.
26. Tim G. McMahon, *Grand opportunity: the Gaelic revival and Irish society 1893–1910* (Syracuse, 2008), 107, 115; Sean O'Tuama (ed.), *The Gaelic League idea* (Dublin, 1972), 34 (recollections of Ernest Blythe, IRB).
27. *United Irishman*, 8 Apr. 1905.
28. NLI, Sweetman papers, Ms47577/7–11; Ms47578/3.
29. NLI, Sweetman papers, Ms47579/1–2, 8; Ms47581/1.
30. NLI, Sweetman papers, Ms47585/1, Griffith to Sweetman (undated [1904]).
31. NLI, Thomas Martin papers, Ms15790; NLI, Sweetman papers, Ms47583/7 (letters of Sweetman and Martin, 1904–1905). Mention of the papal blessing (granted during 1902) was placed on the society's headed notepaper.
32. NLI, James O'Mara papers, Ms 21544 (6), pamphlet of the UILGB Irish Parliament Branch (1906).
33. *United Irishman*, 4 Apr. 1905.
34. NLI, Thomas Martin papers, Ms15790, Healy to Martin, 14 Jul., 27 Jul. 1904.
35. NLI, Sweetman papers, Ms47583/3, Ms47583/6.
36. NLI, Thomas Martin papers, Ms15790, Griffith to Martin, 22 Jul., 29 Jul. 1904 (these communications were sent from Art O'Brien's London Gaelic League headquarters).
37. NLI, Thomas Martin papers, Ms15790 (undated Irish National Society notes).
38. NLI, Sweetman papers, Ms47585/1; Ms47585/3. Sweetman bought £300 of *United Irishman* shares in November 1904 alone, thereby making him practically its owner.
39. It was Mannix who suggested to Sweetman that Griffith's Sinn Féin lecture of 28 Nov. 1905 should be republished as a pamphlet. NLI, Sweetman papers, Ms47584/4, Mannix to Sweetman, 10 Dec. 1905.
40. *United Irishman*, 6 and 13 June, 4 July 1903.
41. *United Irishman*, 18 Feb. 1905.
42. NLI, Sweetman papers, Ms47585/1, Griffith to Sweetman (Dec. 1904).
43. A brilliantly researched survey of Ireland's strategic, or 'diplomatic', importance for foreign powers from 1899–1919 has recently been completed, but its interpretations are weakened by its author's unfamiliarity with the history, or dynamics, of 'fenian' espionage. Jerome Ann de Wiel, *The Irish factor 1899–1919* (Dublin, 2008).
44. Griffith, *The Resurrection of Hungary*, 90–91.
45. Griffith, *The Resurrection of Hungary*, 88–90.
46. [Arthur Griffith], *England's colossal robbery of Ireland: the fiscal relations of the two countries under the Union* (Dublin, 1906), 3–4. It was common knowledge that the Imperial Parliament was overtaxing Ireland by two to three million pounds every year, but it was not as widely known that Gladstone had seen his home rule bills as a means of increasing this level of over-taxation by at least another million. NLI, Gladstone papers, P3261, pp1–4, 22–27, 74–75, 201, 204.
47. Arthur Griffith, *The resurrection of Hungary*, 91–92.
48. Arthur Griffith, *The resurrection of Hungary*, 83–85.
49. Arthur Griffith, *The resurrection of Hungary*, 90.
50. NLI, Sweetman papers, Ms47582/9.
51. NLI, Sweetman papers, Ms47583/5.
52. McMahon, *Grand opportunity*, 144–145.

53. McMahon, *Grand opportunity*, 110–112, 116, 125, 127, 130. McMahon judged that the sum of Gaelic League's educational achievement was to increase the percentage of the urban population with a basic knowledge of Irish, while its status as a spoken language continued to decline.

54. Thomas Morrissey S.J., *Thomas A. Finlay S.J.* (Dublin, 2004), 13. McMahon, *Grand opportunity,* 117–118, 151–152.

55. Carla King, 'Our destitute countrymen on the western coast: relief and development strategies in the congested districts', in Carla King, Conor McNamara (eds) *The west of Ireland* (Dublin, 2011), 161–183.

56. Stephen Gwynn, G.M. Tuckwell, *The Life of the Rt. Hon. Sir Charles Dilke*, 2 (London, 1917), 140; Stephen Ball (ed.) *Dublin Castle and the First Home Rule Crisis* (Cambridge, 2009); British Library, Althorp Papers, Add.77033–37. Fottrell and Jenkinson, the leader of the Crime Special Branch, worked together on occasion, such as in attempting to convict P.N. Fitzgerald, which was Fottrell's first task upon being appointed as the clerk of the Crown in Dublin during October 1884. NAI, CSORP 1885/1410.

57. Patrick Maume, *D.P. Moran* (Dublin, 1996); *The long gestation* (Dublin, 1999).

58. NLI, Sweetman papers, Ms47585/10.

59. This would necessitate that Ginnell form an Independent United Irish League in opposition to the Irish Party's support body. Carla King 'Our destitute countrymen on the western coast: relief and development strategies in the congested districts', in Carla King, Conor McNamara (eds) *The west of Ireland* (Dublin, 2011), 178–180.

60. The papers of the Mansion House Relief Committee that was formed during 1880 with the support of the Catholic hierarchy essentially reflect how great was the divide between the attitudes of Land League radicals and the moderate realism of the Irish Party leadership that was rooted more in financial realities. These papers are held in Dublin City Library and Archives.

61. Thomas Morrissey S.J., *Thomas A. Finlay S.J.* (Dublin, 2004), introduction, 46–47.

62. T.A. Finlay, 'Ethics and economics of poor relief', *Journal of the Statistical and Social Inquiry Society of Ireland* (1907), 43–51; T.A. Finlay, 'The significance of some recent Irish statistics', *Journal of the Statistical and Social Inquiry Society of Ireland* (1912–13), 17–25.

63. Roy Douglas, *Land, people and politics: a history of the land question in the United Kingdom 1878–1952* (London, 1976); J.P.D. Dunbabin, *Rural discontent in nineteenth-century Britain* (London, 1974).

64. The key figure in the rural organisation was Matthew Harris. Owen McGee, Adam Pole, 'Matthew Harris (1825–1890)', *Dictionary of Irish Biography*, 4 (Cambridge, 2009), 480–481. The key figure in the urban organisation was Thomas Brennan. Owen McGee, Des McCabe, 'Thomas Brennan (1853–1912)', *Dictionary of Irish Biography*, 1 (Cambridge, 2009), 816–817. Owen McGee, *The IRB* (Dublin, 2005), 71–78, 293.

65. Arthur Griffith, *How Ireland is taxed* (Dublin, 1907), 5.

66. Thomas Morrissey S.J., *Thomas A. Finlay S.J.* (Dublin, 2004), 97.

67. P. Dempsey, S. Boylan, '(Robert) Lindsay Crawford (1868–1945)', *Dictionary of Irish Biography*, 2 (Cambridge, 2009), 971–973; Patrick Maume, 'Thomas Henry Sloan (1870–1941)', *Dictionary of Irish Biography*, 8 (Cambridge, 2009), 999–1002.

68. Crawford's June 1905 pamphlet *Irish grievances and their remedy* reflected indebtedness to Dublin economic nationalists such as William Field and James McCann and would, in turn, influence Griffith's November 1905 pamphlet *The Sinn Féin policy*.

69. NLI, Sir George Fottrell papers, Ms33670, memo for 5 Dec.1886. This strategy had been first spelt out to Earl Spencer during the late summer of 1884. British Library, Althorp Papers, Add.77033, letters of 25 Aug., 24 Sep.1884.

70. Bernard Porter, *Empire and Super Empire: Britain, America and the world* (Yale, 2006), 59.
71. James McConnel, 'Jobbing with Tory and Liberal: Irish nationalists and the politics of patronage 1880–1914', *Past and Present*, no. 188 (Aug. 2005), 105–131. M.E. Daly, 'The formation of an Irish nationalist elite? Recruiting to the civil service in the decades prior to independence 1870–1920', *Paedogogica Historica*, vol.30, no.1 (1994), 281–301; Martin Maguire, *The civil service and the revolution in Ireland 1912–1938* (Manchester, 2008); Michael Gallagher and Lee Komito, 'Dáil deputies and their constituency work', in Coakley, Gallagher eds *Politics in the republic of Ireland* (2ⁿᵈ ed. Dublin, 1993), 150– 166; Erskine Childers, *The framework of home rule* (London, 1911), chapter 10, pt.3; Royal Economic Society, *The fiscal relations of Great Britain and Ireland* (Suffolk, 1912), 62–63, 67–68.
72. NLI, Sweetman papers, Ms47579/1–2, 8; Ms47581/1; William Field, *Irish railways compared with state owned and managed lines* (Dublin, 1899). William Field, *High rates and railway monopoly in Ireland* (Dublin, 1899); James McCann, *Irish taxation and Irish transit* (Dublin, 1901); 'Thirty years after', *Nationality*, 15 Apr. 1916 (article on Edward Carson).
73. Fr. J.A. Gaughan, *A political odyssey: Thomas O'Donnell, MP for west Kerry* (Dublin, 1983), 22–23.
74. McMahon, *Grand opportunity*, 117–118, 145–147.
75. NLI, Sir George Fottrell papers, Ms33670, memo for 18 Sept 1885.
76. *United Irishman*, 18 Feb. 1905.
77. *United Irishman*, 21 Jan. 1905 (editorial).
78. See his article on the newspaper's 150ᵗʰ anniversary in *Sinn Féin*, 4 Oct. 1913.
79. Kevin Rafter (ed.) *Irish journalism before independence* (Manchester, 2011), 180–183; Ball (ed.) *Dublin Castle and the First Home Rule Crisis*.
80. NLI, Sweetman papers, Ms47576/8 (list of *Freeman* directors in 1893).
81. Virginia Glandon, *Arthur Griffith and the advanced nationalist press* (New York, 1985), 49; NAI, Bureau of Military History papers, WS283 (Seamus MacManus), p10. Prior to 1908 Griffith was also offered jobs as a political journalist for various English newspapers because of 'his flair for pin pointing the economic aspects of a situation' but he likewise turned down these offers. NAI, Bureau of Military History papers, WS848 (Harry Phibbs, ex-CLS), p11. Reputedly, he also turned down an offer to work for Devoy's *Gaelic American*.
82. *United Irishman*, 7 Jan. 1905.
83. *United Irishman*, 14 Jan. 1905 (editorial).
84. T.M. Kettle, 'Would the Hungarian policy work?', *New Ireland Review*, 22 (no.6, Feb. 1905), 325.
85. *United Irishman*, 11 Feb. 1905.
86. *United Irishman*, 14 Jan. 1905 (editorial).
87. Kettle would soon launch a short-lived UCD journal called *The Nationist* to champion this perspective.
88. Kettle, 'Would the Hungarian policy work?', 322, 325, 328.
89. Kettle, 'Would the Hungarian Policy work?' 324–325. This same argument was put forward in *United Ireland*, 26 Dec. 1891.
90. *United Irishman*, 11 Feb. 1905.
91. Arthur Griffith, *The Sinn Féin Policy* (Dublin, 1906), introduction, 2–4. Griffith attributed the birth of the home rule propaganda in 1870 to John Martin, an old republican who was interested in the Hungarian example, rather than to the Tories' anxious reaction to the disestablishment of the Church of Ireland.

92. National Council, *Ireland and the British Army* (Dublin, 1907), 6–7, 26–28. This pamphlet estimated that 75,000 men in Ireland had joined the British army between 1885–1905 and a further 50,000 men enrolled among Irish immigrants in Britain.

93. McGee, *IRB*, chapter 3. The only military dilemma ever faced by Britain in Ireland was how to counterbalance the greater funding requirements of the army and navy elsewhere with the government's budgets for Ireland. E.A. Muenger, *The British military dilemma in Ireland* (Dublin, 1991).

94. NLI, Sir George Fottrell, Ms33670, memos for 28 Jul. 1885, 1 Aug. 1885, 28 Oct. 1885, 24 Sep. 1885 and 12 Mar. 1886. Only the retired figure of Sir Charles Gavan Duffy seemed to think that an immediate establishment of an Irish parliament could make any political sense or was even a possibility. Duffy actually played a significant role in drawing up the home rule bill, but its introduction was essentially a publicity stunt. As Cooke and Vincent have noted, in British political history, writing on the proverbial 'first home rule episode' has always fallen into two categories, with popular journalistic treatments of the subject invariably emphasising its importance and works of serious historical scholarship dismissing it as essentially 'a storm in a teacup'. With regards to party politics, no real 'anti-Gladstone lobby' emerged while the Tories' alleged opposition to Parnell and Gladstone for supposedly threatening the Union was purely for show. A.B. Cooke, J.R. Vincent, *The governing passion: cabinet government and party politics in Britain 1885–86* (London, 1974), 19, 135, 458.

95. NLI, Sweetman papers, Ms47584/1 (Sweetman–Hyde correspondence, Dec. 1905). The arrival of a Liberal government during 1906 would cement this trend.

96. 'The Sinn Féin policy', in Murray (ed.) *The Resurrection of Hungary*, 139–141.

97. *United Irishman*, 7 Jan. 1905.

98. George Moore, *Hail and Farewell! Vale* (London, 1947), 169.

99. Historians have often typified the modernisation of agricultural business practices at this time as evidence of the modernisation of Irish society. Joseph Lee, *The modernisation of Irish society 1848–1918* (Dublin, 1973). This perspective is inclined to overlook the reality that control of this agricultural business market was maintained in Britain and thus the wealth generated was both kept and invested primarily in Britain.

100. P.T. Marsh, *Bargaining on Europe: Britain and the First Common Market 1860–1892* (Yale, 1999), conclusion.

101. 'The Sinn Féin policy', in Murray (ed.) *The Resurrection of Hungary*, 144–145.

102. 'The Sinn Féin policy', in Murray (ed.) *The Resurrection of Hungary*, 144–145.

103. 'The Sinn Féin policy', in Murray (ed.) *The Resurrection of Hungary*, 144–145.

104. Patrick Buckland, *James Craig* (Dublin, 1980), 3–21.

105. *United Irishman*, 29 Apr. 1905.

106. Riobard Ua Fhloinn (Robert Lynd) *The Orangeman and the Nation* (Dublin, 1906), 1–6.

107. *United Irishman*, 28 Jan. 1905.

108. 'The Sinn Féin policy', in Murray (ed.) *The Resurrection of Hungary*, 146–148.

109. 'The Sinn Féin policy', in Murray (ed.) *The Resurrection of Hungary*, 153–160.

110. Arthur Griffith, *How Ireland is taxed* (Dublin, 1907), 3–4.

111. A.W. Samuels, 'Some features in recent Irish finance', *Journal of the Statistical and Social Inquiry Society of Ireland* (1907), 1.

112. A.W. Samuels, 'Some features in recent Irish finance', *Journal of the Statistical and Social Inquiry Society of Ireland* (1907), 2–6, 38–39.

113. 'The Sinn Féin policy', in Murray (ed.) *The Resurrection of Hungary*, 148–152.

114. A.W. Samuels, 'The external commerce of Ireland', *Journal of the Statistical and Social Inquiry Society of Ireland* (1909), 194–197, 217.

115. March, *Bargaining on Europe*, 1–7, 207–211.

116. *United Irishman*, 7 Jan. 1905 (editorial); *The Sinn Féin . Policy* (Dublin, 1906), introduction, p. 2.

117. NLI, Sweetman papers, Ms47585/3, Griffith to Sweetman, 18 Sep. 1905.

118. T.A. Boylan, T.P. Foley, *Political economy and colonial Ireland: the propagation and ideological function of economic discourse in the nineteenth century* (London, 1992).

119. NLI, Sweetman papers, Ms47585/3, Griffith to Sweetman, 18 Sep. 1905.

CHAPTER FIVE

1. C.H. Rolleston, *Portrait of an Irishman: a biographical sketch of T.W. Rolleston* (Dublin, 1939), quoted 121.

2. NLI, Sinn Féin pamphlet collection, pamphlet no.105.

3. With Griffith's support, Martyn took legal action to prevent him from being expelled from the Kildare Street Club after he spoke in defence of the anti-enlistment cause. Philip Rooney, 'Mr. Martyn goes to Court' (undated press cutting in NLI Griffith papers, acc. 4476).

4. J.E. Dunleavy, G.W. Dunleavy, *Douglas Hyde: a maker of modern Ireland* (Oxford, 1991), 314, 322–323.

5. *United Irishman*, 4 March 1905.

6. Boland was also responsible for achieving the YIL goal of encouraging the development of public libraries through the medium of local government. This resulted in the passage of the Public Libraries (Ireland) Act of 1902. Norma McDermott (ed.) *The universities of the people: celebrating Ireland's public libraries* (Dublin, 2003), 19.

7. T.G. McMahon, *Grand opportunity* (Syracuse, 2008), 148–149.

8. Mary Daly, *Industrial development and Irish national identity* (Syracuse, 1992), 4–8; McMahon, *Grand opportunity*, 141, 150.

9. Dunleavy, *Douglas Hyde*, 314; George Russell, *Cooperation and nationality* (Dublin, 1912); Patrick Bolger, *The Irish cooperative movement: its history and development* (Dublin, 1977), 94–95; Mary Daly, 'The economic ideals of Irish nationalism', *Éire-Ireland*, vol.29 (winter 1994), 84–85.

10. Patrick Pearse, *The complete works of P.H. Pearse: political writings and speeches* (Phoenix Press, n.d.), 43.

11. Mary Daly, 'The formation of an Irish nationalist elite? Recruiting to the civil service in the decades prior to independence 1870–1920', *Paedogogica Historica*, vol.30, no.1 (1994), 281–301.

12. Erskine Childers, *The framework of home rule* (London, 1911), chapter 10, pt.3.

13. Gwynn was a prominent and wealthy Dublin unionist who joined the Irish Party during 1906 and was described by Griffith as a man who was employed by the Irish Party 'to look after Mr. Redmond's reputation' by defending it among traditionally critical circles (*Sinn Féin*, 12 July 1913). Gwynn, a senior British army officer in the First World War, later became a director of military intelligence and a posthumous biographer of Redmond. Dermot Meleady, *Redmond: the national leader* (Dublin, 2013), 466–467. During his 1907 public lectures Gwynn once compared Griffith to John Mitchel.

14. 'Details of the procession', *Irish Independent*, 12 Mar. 1906.

15. NAI, DMP files, carton 12, report 2404, Chief Superintendent John Mallon, 25 Nov. 1892.

16. *United Irishman*, 4 March 1905.

17. *Irish Independent*, 7 May 1907.

18. T.M. Kettle, *Home Rule finance* (Dublin, 1911), 2, 22–24.

19. See chapters 1 and 4.

20. NLI, Sweetman papers, Ms47585/3, Griffith to Sweetman, 5 Aug. 1905.

21. Griffith confessed this to his literary friend James Starkey. Carlton Younger, *Arthur Griffith* (Dublin, 1981), 36. Later, Griffith sometimes received information regarding what was happening in high British political circles from Ulster Tories. NLI, Sweetman papers, Ms47587/7, Griffith to Sweetman, 18 May 1912.

22. National Council [John Sweetman] *The purchase of the railways (by the nation)* (Dublin, 1906).

23. William Field, *Irish railways compared with state owned and managed lines* (Dublin, 1899). William Field, *High rates and railway monopoly in Ireland* (Dublin, 1899). At the time, in addition to being President of the Irish Cattle Trades and Stockowners' Association and President of the National Federation of Meat Traders of Great Britain, Ireland and the Isle of Man, Field was a member of a select committee of the House of Commons on railway and canal rates and charges, as well as the MP for St. Patrick's Division, Dublin (1891–1918).

24. L. Paul-Dubois to *Gaelic American*, 22 June, 24 Aug. 1912. Dubois also wrote a book entitled *Contemporary Ireland*, which was translated by Tom Kettle and published in Dublin in 1911.

25. D. Dickson, C. O'Grada (ed.) *Refiguring Ireland* (Dublin, 2003), 280; Mary Daly, *A social and economic history of Ireland since 1800* (Dublin, 1981), 70.

26. Patricia Lavelle, *James O'Mara: a staunch Sinn Féiner* (Dublin, 1961). The attack upon Galway's commercial life during the 1860s (represented partly by the collapse of the *Galway American* newspaper) motivated the Irish nationalism of John Finerty, a future president of the United Irish League of America. Owen McGee, 'John Finerty (1846–1908)', *Dictionary of Irish Biography*, 3 (Cambridge, 2009), 786–787.

27. James McCann, *Irish taxation and Irish transit* (Dublin, 1901). The total value of the agricultural produce of Ireland each year, before the payment of taxes and not counting any farmers' expenses, was roughly £35 million, while the capital of Irish railways raised in a single year was £50 million. *Statist*, 10–17 Feb. 1906 (article by F.W. Crossley); McCann, *Irish taxation and Irish transit*, 4–5.

28. G. Clinton, S. Sturgeon, 'James McCann (1840–1904)', *Dictionary of Irish Biography*, 5 (Cambridge, 2009), 766–767. A self-made Catholic businessman, McCann was originally a Hibernian Bank clerk before succeeding on the Dublin Stock Exchange.

29. National Council [John Sweetman] *The purchase of the railways (by the nation)* (Dublin, 1906).

30. F.W. Crossley, *State purchase of the Irish railways* (Dublin, 1906). Crossley was a railway director and his pamphlet was published by Tourist Development (Ireland) Ltd., 30 Molesworth St., Dublin.

31. J.T. Pim, *The condition of our railways considered with reference to their purchase by the state* (Dublin, 1867); *Purchase of Irish railways, heads of legislation proposed by Rt. Hon. Chicester Fortescue MP, Chief Secretary for Ireland* (Dublin, 1869); 'J.B.', *The Irish church property devoted to the purchase of Irish railways: a letter to the Right Hon. W.E. Gladstone* (London, 1869); Robert Benson, *The amalgamation of railway companies or the alternative to their purchase by the state* (London, 1872). Pim's pamphlet was a reprint of a lecture to the Statistical and Social Inquiry Society of Ireland in December 1866. Benson's pamphlet was focused upon Britain, not Ireland. At that time, the nationalisation proposal failed due to preoccupation with the financial implications of state compensation to the

32. [John Sweetman] *The purchase of the railways (by the nation)* (Dublin, 1906), 3–4.
33. Sweetman argued that Plunkett's department had merely created another army of highly over-paid English officials at Dublin Castle who cared not for Ireland's economic welfare. John Sweetman, *Nationality* (Dublin, 1908), 13–14. Griffith was also frequently critical of Plunkett's Department of Agriculture and Technical Instruction, but he was also capable of acknowledging its work had not entirely negative consequences. 'The Department and Depopulation', *Sinn Féin*, 28 May 1910.
34. [John Sweetman], *The purchase of the railways (by the nation)* (Dublin, 1906), 6–8.
35. Mary Daly, *A social and economic history of Ireland since 1800* (Dublin, 1981), 70.
36. L.M. Cullen, *Princes and pirates: the Dublin Chamber of Commerce 1783–1983* (Dublin, 1983), 63, 66–67, 70–75. On this theme, see also Diarmaid Ferriter, 'Edward Cecil Guinness (1847–1927)', *Dictionary of Irish Biography*, 4 (Cambridge, 2009), 319–320.
37. Pauric Dempsey, 'Andrew Jameson (1855–1941)', *Dictionary of Irish Biography*, 6 (Cambridge, 2009), 951–952.
38. As part of this campaign, Kettle's supporters also produced posthumous biographies of Michael Davitt (1846–1906) in an attempt to deny Sinn Féin the claim to be heirs of the political traditions that Davitt represented. Patrick Maume, *The long gestation* (Dublin, 1999).
39. C.H. Rolleston, *Portrait of an Irishman: a biographical sketch of T.W. Rolleston* (Dublin, 1939), 117–120 (letter of Rolleston to Lady Aberdeen, 5 Sept.1906).
40. Fergus Mulligan, 'William Dargan (1799–1867)', *Dictionary of Irish Biography*, 3 (Cambridge, 2009), 54–57.
41. Timothy R. Harrington, the editor of W.M. Murphy's *Irish Independent*, as well as his relative Timothy C. Harrington, until recently the Lord Mayor of Dublin, suffered a great loss of popularity in Dublin society as a result of this trend. See the entries for both men in *Dictionary of Irish Biography*, 4 (Cambridge, 2009), 474–478.
42. Ken Finlay, *The biggest show in town: record of the international exhibition, Dublin 1907* (Dublin, 2007).
43. A letter of Webb quoted in John Sweetman, *Nationality* (Dublin, 1908), 21. Webb, a treasurer of the United Irish League, wrote to Redmond in June 1906 stating that he was more impressed with the type of people Sinn Féin was winning as supporters than the followers of the United Irish League. In May 1907 he wrote that he was growing more sympathetic to Sinn Féin himself. NLI, Redmond papers, Ms15231/5, Webb to Redmond, 26 June 1906, 29 May 1907.
44. L.M. Cullen, *Princes and pirates: the Dublin Chamber of Commerce 1783–1983* (Dublin, 1983), 63, 66–67, 70–75.
45. 'The "State" and the butter', *Sinn Féin*, 18 June 1910; 'State ownership', *Sinn Féin*, 26 June 1913.
46. A very good example of this was his extrapolation of his initial 1905 programme at a Sinn Féin convention held during the fiscal crisis of 1909 and subsequent economic debates of 1910. *Sinn Féin*, 18 Sep. 1909, 'Sinn Féin and national unity', *Sinn Féin*, 12 Mar. 1910.
47. These Christmas exhibitions of Irish-made goods, known as 'Aonach na Nollaig', were launched in 1908 and held annually up until the First World War.
48. *Sinn Féin*, 7 Jan. 1911, p.1.
49. NLI, Ms47585/3, Sweetman papers, Griffith to Sweetman, 5 Aug.1905.
50. Around the time of the Gaelic League's 1905 St. Patrick's Day collection, the *United Irishman* praised priests for promoting temperance; equated publicans with British

loyalism and the singing of the British national anthem; blacklisted all public houses that failed to close for religious holidays; equated Irish nationalism with the degree to which the rosary was said and hymns were sung in Irish; and Archbishop Walsh was deemed a patriot for having high masses celebrated in the Irish language, using his diocesan influence over City Hall to have liquor licenses withdrawn from the city's workingmen's clubs, and for presiding over Gaelic League St. Patrick's Day processions in which the Christian Brothers marched thousands of school children to St. Patrick's Catholic teacher training college in Drumcondra (*United Irishman*, 18 March-8 April 1905). While Griffith published such religiously-focused writings (written by Máire Butler and supported by Sweetman, president of the Catholic Truth Society), he personally appealed to Catholics not to make fund-raising for church interests their most central concern (the Edwardian era was the great period of cathedral building in the modern history of Catholic Ireland) and to Protestant journalists not to write politically motivated anti-Jesuit tracts. *United Irishman*, 13 Jan. 1906.

51. *United Irishman*, 18 Feb., 29 Apr., 6 May, 13 May, 20 May 1905.

52. Dunleavy, *Douglas Hyde*, 255, 263, 273, 287. President Roosevelt expressed appreciation for the Gaelic League and promised that he would persuade American universities to promote the Irish language. Hyde, judged by the *Irish Independent* to be probably the most popular man in Ireland after the Catholic Primate of Ireland, Archbishop Walsh and John Redmond, was invited to America by John Quinn, a wealthy Irish-American patron of the arts and confrere of W.B. Yeats, who was now suggesting that Ireland's sole destiny was to enhance appreciation of spirituality and the arts in the world.

53. National Council, *Ireland and the British Army* (Dublin, 1906), 6–7, 26–28, 30. The continued influence of the Fenian tradition on Griffith's propaganda was reflected by his reference to a claim made by 'a French diplomat … four years ago' regarding Anglo-Irish relations, that as soon as Irishmen 'ceased to fight her battles she will be forced to give in' to Irish demands for independence because her 'army was composed, by more than half, of Irishmen'.

54. National Council, *The Police and the Nation* (Dublin, 1906).

55. Dublin Students Dungannon Club, *A manifesto to the whole students of Ireland* (Dublin, 1906), pp5–8. The history of the society is provided on pp1–4 of the same leaflet. It argued rather irrationally that, 'following the example of China and India', promoting anti-enlistment and a boycott of British trade would be an effective means of passive resistance to the military strength of imperial powers worldwide. Trinity College students had also played a part in developing the IRB during the 1860s through the Edmund O'Donovan–O'Donovan Rossa connection. O'Donovan was later a leading British war correspondent in Asia and Africa.

56. Christy Campbell, *The Maharajah's Box* (London, 1999). British intelligence supervised developments among potentially troublesome Indian princes who had left for Paris seeking allies with the aid of 'fenian' conspirators who acted as supposedly sympathetic intermediaries.

57. NLI, James O'Mara papers, Ms 21544 (1), Griffith to O'Mara (n.d. [1906–7]). This was a 'Mr. Poysa' from Ceylon (Sri Lanka).

58. NAI, Bureau of Military History papers, WS1 (Thomas Barry); WS26 (P.S. O'Hegarty), pp1–4; Bulmer Hobson, *Ireland: yesterday and tomorrow* (Tralee, 1968), 21.

59. Marnie Hay, *Bulmer Hobson and the nationalist movement in twentieth-century Ireland* (Manchester, 2009), 44, 50–51, 55–58; McMahon, *Grand opportunity*, 106. Reflecting the league's support of denominational education, the Belfast Gaelic League was supported by prominent Church of Ireland and Presbyterian clerics but not by the general Protestant

community or its unionist political representatives. Since the mid-1890s Alice Milligan, John Clarke (the curator of the Linen Hall Library in Belfast), the poet Joseph Campbell and the antiquarian Francis Bigger had been involved in promoting an Irish cultural nationalism among Belfast Protestants, with the financial support of Robert Johnston (IRB treasurer since Oct.1902) and the appreciation of the conservative unionist J.W. Good. This was Hobson's social background.

60. Hay, *Bulmer Hobson*, 67.

61. Judge Daniel Coholan, an American patron of the *Gaelic American*, partly acted in this capacity (he visited Dublin to encourage all IRB leaders to concentrate wholly on the Gaelic League; NAI, British in Ireland microfilm, DMP and RIC monthly précis, 2 July 1906), but Irish figures were also needed. This need arose from the retirement of figures like Patrick Hoctor who, along with F.B. Dineen, was a controversial figure.

62. NAI, British in Ireland microfilm, DMP and RIC monthly précis, 7 May 1906. In the past, John MacBride had maintained that even if Griffith's abstentionist policy worked an Irish provisional government would still need to be backed up by force. McBride to *United Irishman*, 9 Oct. 1904.

63. Bulmer Hobson, *The creed of the Republic* (Belfast, 1907), reprint of article in *The Republic*, entitled 'The mind of the nation'. Hobson, *Ireland yesterday and tomorrow*, 20.

64. The chief dynamic of this situation in terms of its impact on Irish political organisations was essentially the relationship between P.N. Fitzgerald and Michael Davitt and William O'Brien respectively. McGee, *IRB*; John Devoy, *Recollections of an Irish rebel* (New York, 1929), 392.

65. UCD Archives, Denis McCullough papers, P120/29 (1), statement to Bureau of Military History 14 Oct. 1957; NAI, Home Office précis, carton 3, 23860/s, 25049/s, 28150/s, 28377/s; 28429/s, 28634/s; NAI, British in Ireland microfilm, DMP and RIC précis, 7 May 1906; 8 Sep.1908; 1 April 1909; NAI, Bureau of Military History papers, WS26 (P.S. O'Hegarty). Robert Johnston won Devoy's support for the idea of rallying the AOH behind Sinn Féin rather than the Irish Party. McGee, *IRB*.

66. Along with Patrick Hoctor, who worked for a time for Dublin Castle, Dineen was the author of both the clerical–republican controversy of 1887 and the GAA's various bans. Both men were close associates of P.N. Fitzgerald, the Munster IRB leader of the day, who disagreed with their handling of the situation and so denied them promotion within the IRB.

67. NLI, John Redmond papers, Ms15247/7–8 (letters of F.B. Dineen). Regarding P.T. Daly, see NLI, Redmond papers, Ms15243/1 (letter of John Ryan), 15216/3 (letter of John O'Callaghan). Dineen, who took over the management of Jones Road from James Boland and later renamed it Croke Park, actually began his career with the strictly upper-class Irish Amateur Athletics Association. Paul Rouse, 'Frank Brazil Dineen (1863–1916)', *Dictionary of Irish Biography*, 3 (Cambridge, 2009), 327–328.

68. NLI, Redmond papers, Ms15198/1, Denis Johnston to Redmond, 27 June 1907. An example of the internal conflicts within the Irish Party may be found in the suggestion of John Muldoon, the chief legal expert of the Edwardian Irish Party, that the past willingness of Tom O'Donnell and D.D. Sheehan (almost the only pro-labour MP in the party) to write letters to the press criticising the party should be investigated. NLI, Redmond papers, Ms15208 (Muldoon's correspondence, esp. 19 Feb. 1907).

69. Patrick Maume, *The long gestation* (Dublin, 1999), 89.

70. Patricia Lavelle, *James O'Mara* (Dublin, 1961).

71. NLI, Redmond papers, Ms15181/2 (letters of Joseph Devlin to Redmond, June 1907). John Dillon felt that some response should have been made the previous year. NLI,

Redmond papers, Ms15182/12, Dillon to Redmond, 22 Aug., 29 Sep. 1906. According to Richard Hazleton TC, during January 1906 Redmond 'laughed at the suggestion' that Sinn Féin could pose any opposition. NLI, Redmond papers, Ms15193/3, Hazleton to William Field, 17 Dec. 1906.

72. NLI, Redmond papers, Ms15182/15, Dillon to Redmond, 31 June (quote), 1 Oct. 1907.
73. NLI, Redmond papers, Ms15186/1, Redmond to Joseph Dolan, 21 Aug. 1907.
74. When Holmes died in 1910 Griffith published an editorial critiquing his career, beginning with the lines: 'Sir Robert Holmes died on Monday. The public was not impressed by the news. It did not know who Sir Robert Holmes was. Sir Robert Holmes was for many years the real Governor of Ireland'. See 'The Uncrowned King', *Sinn Féin*, 26 Feb. 1910.
75. Arthur Griffith, *How Ireland is taxed* (Dublin, 1907), 5, 8–9.
76. Ronan Fanning, *The Irish Department of Finance 1922-1958* (Dublin, 1978), 1–5.
77. Arthur Griffith, *How Ireland is taxed* (Dublin, 1907), 3, 7–8. This was a republication of a Griffith lecture to the National Council on 16 Sep. 1907. Always keen to draw an eighteenth-century parallel, Griffith also claimed that taxation per head was currently five times higher in Ireland than it had been a century earlier, though, partly as a result, it was actually less in contemporary England than it had been in England a century before.
78. Griffith, *How Ireland is taxed*, 7.
79. *The flowing tide of Sinn Féin* (Dublin, 1907), speech of Griffith at Enniscorthy, Co. Wexford. Gladstone's papers regarding the Government of Ireland Bills (NLI, Gladstone papers, P3261) prove that most of the money that was not reinvested in Ireland went directly into the imperial defence fund to sustain the navy and army in the British colonies.
80. *The flowing tide of Sinn Féin* (Dublin, 1907), letters of Esmonde and James Donohoe J.P., read aloud by John Murphy and Patrick Kehoe at the Enniscorthy demonstration.
81. *The flowing tide of Sinn Féin* (Dublin, 1907), speech of Dolan at Enniscorthy.
82. *The flowing tide of Sinn Féin* (Dublin, 1907), speech of Griffith at Enniscorthy.
83. *The flowing tide of Sinn Féin* (Dublin, 1907), speech of Griffith at Enniscorthy.
84. NLI, James O'Mara papers, Ms 21544 (1), letters from J.P. Farrell MP and E.T. Keane, manager of the *Kilkenny People*, Jun. 1907. Patricia Lavelle, *James O'Mara* (Dublin, 1961), chapter 4. Lavelle was O'Mara's daughter.
85. NLI, Sweetman papers, Ms47585/9, Griffith to Sweetman, 9 May 1907.
86. S.W. Haller, *William O'Brien and the Irish land war* (Dublin, 1990). His wife was Sophie Raffalovich O'Brien.
87. Regarding Esmonde's actions, Redmond wrote that 'no one wants to put any indignity on Sir Thomas Esmonde at all' but it was impossible for him to accept 'a "conditional" member of the party'. NLI, Redmond papers, Ms15247/7, Redmond to Bolger, 15 Aug. 1907.
88. Maume, *Long gestation*, 90.
89. NLI, Sean T. O'Kelly papers, Ms21750. Its total income was £1,123 and total expenses were £1,251.
90. NLI, James O'Mara papers, Ms 21544 (1), C.J. Dolan to O'Mara, 29 May 1907.
91. While there were some sympathisers with Sinn Féin in the provinces, Redmond's supporters knew they were generally isolated individuals confined to a few towns. NLI, Redmond papers, Ms15173/1, letters of J.M.C. Briscoe to Redmond, 7 Aug., 13 Aug. 1907.
92. NLI, James O'Mara papers, Ms 21544 (1), Griffith to O'Mara, 25 Nov. 1907; C.J. Dolan to O'Mara, 26 Nov. 1907.
93. NLI, Sweetman papers, Ms47585/9, Griffith to Sweetman (undated [1907] cover letter for a letter from Fr. Corkley of Dungarvan). The four men who voted for abstention were O'Donnell, Charles J. Dolan, 'Mr. Ganly' (a UIL representative from Longford) and

'someone whose name I did not hear'. Fr. Corkley was a supporter of T.M. Healy who suggested that Sinn Féin should target Sweetman's former constituency of Wicklow East, although Griffith did not believe so, even if 'the UIL, I think, is done for'.

94. NLI, James O'Mara papers, Ms 21544 (1), P.A. McHugh to John Redmond, 1 Jul. 1907. The continued strength of the Irish Party in north Connacht was partly illustrated by the recent return of John O'Dowd in Sligo, an old Land Leaguer and former confrere of P.N. Fitzgerald.

95. NLI, Sweetman papers, Ms47585/9, Griffith to Sweetman, 9 June 1907.

96. Terence McSwiney's Celtic Literary Society in Cork affiliated itself with the National Council and also championed William O'Brien's ideas on the land question. *Sinn Féin*, 5 Oct. 1907. Ex-IRB men of the Parnell era who were now aldermen in Cork City Hall, as well as Sean O'Keeffe, Sean O'Hegarty and their younger Cork IRB following, also sided with 'Sinn Féin'. Seventeen Dublin city councillors now supported the National Council, but only a few other small branches existed in Waterford, Kilkenny, Cavan and Belfast and these generally involved literary rather than political people. This is hardly surprising, considering that the president of the National Council was still Edward Martyn, the director of the Abbey Theatre and a member of the executive of the Gaelic League. The first branch of the National Council in Cork was established in September 1906, and its president was the seventy-year-old republican C.G. Doran (*Sinn Féin*, 3 Nov. 1906) by now a leader of the Cork Historical and Archaeological Society, although he retired shortly thereafter and ultimately died in 1909.

97. NLI, Sweetman papers, Ms47585/9, Griffith to Sweetman, 27 Aug. 1907.

98. NLI, Sweetman papers, Ms47585/9, Griffith to Sweetman, 9 June 1907.

99. NLI, Sinn Féin pamphlet collection, National Council circular, 1 Nov. 1907. The principal 'resident members' were Alderman Thomas Kelly, P.T. Daly T.C., Jennie Wyse Power PLG, T.S. Cuffe, William O'Leary Curtis, Patrick Hughes (also of Dundalk) and Seamus Deakin. The 'non resident members', were Seamus MacManus (USA), Thomas Martin (London), Fr. O'Connolly (a Maynooth professor), Fr. W. Harper C.C., Fr. L. O'Kieran P.P., Bulmer Hobson, Robert Brennan and James Reidy (acting editor of the New York *Gaelic American*). In Kerry, Maurice Moynihan, who became the electoral registrar of Tralee in 1908, formed the first branches of Sinn Féin and promoted both it *and* William O'Brien's All-for-Ireland League until he was struck down by tuberculosis in 1912. J.A. Gaughan, *Tom O'Donnell* (Dublin, 1983), 22–23 (biographical note on Moynihan); NAI, British in Ireland microfilm, DMP and Home Office précis, summary for July 1910.

100. P.T. Daly was later accused of having worked for Dublin Castle at this time. Like James Larkin, he was also accused of misappropriating funds of trade union organisations. P.S. O'Hegarty's understanding of this situation was interesting: NAI, Bureau of Military History papers, WS26 (P.S. O'Hegarty).

101. NLI, Sinn Féin pamphlet collection, National Council circular, 1 Nov. 1907.

102. *Sinn Féin*, 18 Feb. 1911.

103. NLI, Redmond papers, MS15194, Harrington to Redmond, 20 Aug. 1907. Alexander ('Alec') Sullivan, the former president of the Irish National League of America, would also write to Redmond referring to 'the Devoy Sinn Féin element'. NLI, Redmond papers, Ms15236/25, Sullivan to Redmond, 8 Feb. 1910.

104. *United Irishman*, 4 Mar. 1905.

105. The managing director of the Irish Press Agency was J.J. Clancy (MP for North Dublin since 1885), a former member of John O'Leary's Young Ireland Society (1883–1885) but its books and pamphlets were not for sale in Ireland. During 1908 it published a Griffithite flyer *The money argument for home rule* (London, 1908) that was actually written by Tom Kettle.

106. See chapters 1 & 4.

107. [Arthur Griffith], *England's colossal robbery of Ireland: the financial relations of the two countries since the union* (Dublin, 1907), 3–4. Going back no further than 1853, and taking into consideration the British legal rate of interest, Griffith suggested that the amount of money owing to Ireland—by the lowest estimate of the Financial Relations Commission of 1896, is £392,412,000: 'in other words, Ireland has been robbed since 1853—according to the lowest estimate of the British Commission—of double the amount of money which Germany exacted from France in 1871 as a war indemnity—the largest war indemnity known'. Griffith was also fond of pointing out that Gladstone's introduction of an income tax into Ireland in the wake of the great famine encouraged both absentee landlordism and the abandonment of Ireland (especially Dublin) by various businessmen.

108. Arthur Griffith, *How Ireland is taxed* (Dublin, 1907), 9–10.

109. Royal Economic Society (ed.) *The fiscal relations of Great Britain and Ireland* (Suffolk, 1912), 23.

110. Griffith, *How Ireland is taxed*, 9–10.

111. L. Paul-Dubois to *Gaelic American*, 22 June, 24 Aug. 1912. Dubois also wrote a book entitled *Contemporary Ireland*, which was translated by Tom Kettle and published in Dublin in 1911.

112. Padraig McGowan, *Money and banking in Ireland: origins, development and future* (Dublin, 1990), 85.

113. Patrick Buckland, *James Craig* (Dublin, 1980), 3–13.

114. Louis Cullen, *Princes and pirates* (Dublin, 1983).

115. Patricia Lavelle, *James O'Mara* (Dublin, 1961).

116. Jennie Wyse Power gave her own history and critique of the Land League before the Central Branch of Sinn Féin in October 1909 at a meeting chaired by Henry Dixon. *Sinn Féin*, 16 Oct. 1909.

117. Marie O'Neill, *From Parnell to De Valera: a biography of Jennie Wyse Power* (Dublin, 1991); Sheila Carden, *The Alderman: Alderman Tom Kelly and Dublin Corporation* (Dublin, 2007).

118. Charles Dawson, 'Suggested substitutes for the present poor law system', *Social for the Statistical and Social Inquiry of Ireland*, 46 (1906), 428–438; William Lawson, 'Remedies for overcrowding in the city of Dublin', *Social for the Statistical and Social Inquiry of Ireland*, 62 (1908–1909), 230–248; Charles Dawson, 'The Dublin housing question: sanitary and unsanitary', *Social for the Statistical and Social Inquiry of Ireland*, 66 (1912–1913), 91–95.

119. This led to an acceptance by Dublin City Council of the necessity of forming a Housing Committee, although it took four year (1909–1913) before this was eventually established. Carden, *The Alderman*, 113–114.

120. An additional factor, ignored by Griffith, was that private ownership of Irish railways had encouraged the city's businessmen to concentrate upon the development of the south Dublin coastline at the expense of the city itself (hence the creation of the new suburbs).

121. Letter of Griffith, dated 23 Jan. 1919, reproduced in an article by Máire Comerford in *Irish Times*, 26 Jan. 1969. Griffith had made this same argument before in his speech to the National Council on 22 Oct. 1906, reprinted as Sinn Féin pamphlet no.3, Dublin, 1907, pp3–4; and *Sinn Féin*, 25 Oct., 8 Nov. 1913, *Nationality*, 18 Dec. 1915, p2.

122. Arthur Griffith, *The home rule examined* (Dublin, 1912), 13.

123. Maud did come from a political family but she recalled that she never talked about politics with Griffith or anyone else because 'I did not want to, having been brought up in a family in which my father was an ardent Parnellite and my mother a follower of William O'Brien, with consequent frequent disputes on political matters.' NAI, Bureau of Military

History papers, WS205 (Maud Griffith). Harry Phibbs, a former member of the Celtic Literary Society, believed that Maud was related to a McLean family who were involved in the Orange Order. NAI, Bureau of Military History papers, WS848 (Harry Phibbs), p11.

124. Anne Dolan, *Commemorating the Irish civil war* (Cambridge, 2003), 179.

125. R.M. Henry on Arthur Griffith, *Studies*, Sept 1922, 351–352. Professor Henry broke from Sinn Féin (in common with some other long-term readers of Griffith) for being too dogmatic on the compulsory Irish question during 1908 (NLI, Sweetman papers, Ms47586/4, Griffith to Sweetman, 1 Sep. 1908). Griffith had silenced his opposition to the 'no language, no nation' idea as early as 1905, when he annoyed some former *United Irishman* contributors by suggesting that a prosperous and independent Ireland 'is not the complete national ideal … we know no real Irish nationalist whose ideal independent Ireland is not an Irish-speaking independent state.' *United Irishman*, 28 Jan. 1905. Later, in 1920, Henry wrote the first popular history of the Sinn Féin movement.

126. Jerome ann de Wiel, *The Irish factor* (Dublin, 2003), 7, 48–50, 92–94, 127–128.

127. Bulmer Hobson, *Defensive Warfare: a handbook for Irish nationalists* (Belfast, 1907), introduction, 21, 26. The greatest novelty in Hobson's arguments was his call for the nationalisation of Irish trade unions. Less significant was his argument that the 'wholesale massacre of non-combatant people is obsolete' and therefore Irish nationalists could engage in practices such as 'the destruction of means of communication and transit'; actions which he typified as sufficiently 'defensive' in nature that the government would lack the moral authority to act decisively as a coercive aggressor. This was an irrational argument. Hobson, *Defensive Warfare*, 35–43.

128. L.W. White, 'Sean MacDiarmada (1883–1916)', *Dictionary of Irish Biography*, 5 (Cambridge, 2009), 911–914. The 'Aonach na Nollaig' was the annual Christmas exhibition of Irish-made goods.

129. NLI, Sweetman papers, Ms47586/4, Griffith to Sweetman, undated [Apr.1908] and 1 Sep. 1908.

130. NLI, Sweetman papers, Ms47586/4, Sweetman to Griffith (copy), 3 Apr. 1908.

131. NLI, Sweetman papers, Ms47586/4, Griffith to Sweetman (undated [Apr.1908]). To appeal to Sweetman, in criticism of the bill Griffith suggested that it did not bring about 'equality for Catholics in higher education' on the grounds that respective funding for UCD and TCD (with the latter receiving one third extra each year) did not correlate to the sizes of the Catholic and Protestant populations in the country, prompting Griffith to suggest that UCD's annual endowment should be at least four times greater.

132. There are ample illustrations of this in all his private correspondence in NLI, Sweetman papers. In public too, Sweetman was prone to making arguments such as 'if there be any Irish writers who are endeavouring to induce us to give up our faith for the sake of becoming better nationalists' he had a moral obligation, as a lay Catholic, to attempt to locate them and to use his wealth and influence to run them out of public life and, potentially, even deny them their livelihoods: 'I cannot see how being good Catholics prevents our being good Irish nationalists, but, if it does, so much the worse for nationality, as, if we believe in a Creator, we cannot give up our duty to Him for love of country.' (Sweetman to *United Irishman*, 1 Jul. 1899).

133. NLI, Sweetman papers, Ms47587/1, Sweetman to Griffith, 17 Aug. 1909. This was something of an obsession with Sweetman. Ever since his youth in a private Benedictine school in England, Sweetman believed that anticlerical attitudes of any kind could only exist 'amongst the very ignorant' and he sincerely held that 'any anti-clericalism amongst Irish-Irelanders…is the work of Satan who hates to see Ireland rising from slavery.' (Ms47587/1, Sweetman to Fr. Stuart, 17 Aug. 1909). Although he defined himself as an

individualist, Sweetman associated the liberal individualism hinted at by J.S. Mill with the Benedictine philosophy of education of the innately individual nature of every person's intelligence. His pamphlet *Liberty* (Dublin, 1909) partly reflected this outlook, but it is also evident in Sweetman's correspondence throughout his life.

134. Griffith's literary editor Máire Butler (who later died on a pilgrimage to Rome) certainly appreciated Pearse's religiously inspired preoccupation with the notion of martyrdom. She once celebrated the Gaelic League's inspiration by stating 'as Padraic MacPiaras expresses it, many a delegate had been summoned to "the Ard Fhéis of God"'. In turn, 'like Cardinal Newman', all who joined the league inherently had 'a preference for being on the side of the angels. Anyone who throws in his lot with Ireland a Nation might say the same. He joins a godly company … with the blood of martyrs in our veins.' Sursum Corda, *Nationality*, 9 Oct. 1915.

135. NLI, Sweetman papers, Ms47584/4. Sweetman expressed dissatisfaction with the writings of Patrick Pearse on a few occasions (Mss47583/9, 47584/1, 47584/3).

136. NLI, Sweetman papers, Ms47586/4, Sweetman to Griffith (copy), 3 Apr. 1908. W.P. Ryan was the editor of *The Peasant*. James McCann was its owner and founder, although he was dead by the time of the controversy surrounding Ryan.

137. NLI, Sweetman papers, Ms47586/4, Griffith to Sweetman, 1 Sep.1908: 'for months past I have been receiving day-by-day letters from readers urging me to make the appeal'.

138. NLI, Sweetman papers, Ms47586/4, Griffith to Sweetman, 1 Sep.1908. In private, John Dillon was prepared to express sympathy with the compulsory Irish demand but he could not do so publicly without the party's approval. NLI, Douglas Hyde papers, Ms17292, Dillon to Hyde, 15 Apr. 1909.

139. NLI, Sweetman papers, Ms47586/4, Griffith to Sweetman, (undated [Apr.1908]), 1 Sep.1908.

140. NLI, Redmond papers, Ms15197/6, Hyde to Redmond, 5 Oct. 1909.

141. NAI, British in Ireland microfilm, DMP and RIC précis, 1 April 1909, 3 May 1909, 4 May, 2 June, 4 June, 6 July, 2 Sept. 1909. The president of the American AOH Matthew Cummings was also a member of Clan na Gael and therefore unpopular with John O'Callaghan, the leader of the United Irish League of America and a regular correspondent of John Redmond.

142. NLI, Sweetman papers, Ms47586/4, Griffith to Sweetman, 1 Sep.1908.

143. Sweetman wrote letters to the daily press on a regular basis for almost fifty years and kept cuttings of many of them. Several volumes of these can be found in NLI, Sweetman papers (see NLI, Sweetman Family Papers Index, pp143–144).

144. NLI, Sweetman papers, Ms47586/4, Sweetman to Griffith, 28 June 1908.

145. *Sinn Féin* (weekly edition), 18 Sep. 1909 (report on National Council finances).

146. Lacking capital and significant sales, the daily paper was printed on a fourth-hand and antiquated rotary machine and sometimes Griffith could not afford to buy even the reels of newsprint necessary to produce the paper, let alone to hire a staff; a problem that was partly solved when Sean T. O'Kelly managed to persuade the manager of the unionist *Irish Times* to loan them some reels that it took the paper almost a year to repay. 'Irishman's Diary', *Irish Times*, 10 May 1947; Sean T. O'Kelly, 'Arthur Griffith', *Capuchin Annual* (1966), 132–144.

147. Virginia Glandon, *Arthur Griffith and the advanced nationalist press* (New York, 1985), 44–45. Glandon has suggested (pp40–41) that Griffith was earning as large a salary as £200 a year after the formation of *Sinn Féin* in April 1906, although this seems unlikely.

148. On receiving this proposal, Griffith anxiously requested Sweetman's advice but it seems he got no reply. NLI, Sweetman papers, Ms47587/1, Griffith to Sweetman, no date [1909].

149. 'The bursting of the bubble', *Sinn Féin* (weekly edition), 9 Oct. 1909.
150. NLI, Sinn Féin pamphlet collection, pamphlet no.105 (an advertisement of Aug. 1909 for the forthcoming daily edition of *Sinn Féin*): 'Party organs we have in plenty: the time has come to give the nation an organ. The nation is the exclusive property of no party, no sect, no class. The Irish nationalist and Irish unionist, the Irish Catholic and the Irish Protestant, the Irish rich and the Irish poor, are all constituent parts of the nation ... This is not a policy but a fact ... [and] is what a normal press would have taught in Ireland for a 100 years had a normal press existed.' Noting 'that a cargo of turf should be imported into Ireland is ... a fact of more importance to us than that an earthquake should have occurred in Central Asia', Griffith's stated editorial policy reflected his almost narcissistic belief in his capacity to conceive of the nation's best interests.
151. NLI, Sweetman papers, Ms47586/4, Griffith to Sweetman, 1 Sep.1908.
152. Alongside Seamus MacManus, *Gaelic American* figures such as John Devoy, Tom Clarke and Patrick McCartan supported the strategy of getting the AOH in Ireland to support Griffith and Sinn Féin. MacManus' candidate to replace Devlin, John D. Nugent, the national secretary of the AOH (Board of Erin), argued in May 1910 that the AOH (which had 70,000 members) was prepared to support the Irish Party at present, but if it 'did not seem to be winning', the AOH would be willing to support different parties instead. Although Nugent would befriend Dillon, remarks like these help to explain the confidence of men like Patrick Hughes, a leader of Sinn Féin, the AOH and Gaelic League in Dundalk, who proclaimed that the Irish Party would receive 'a rude awakening' in near future regarding the *actual* level of popular support it had in the country. NAI, British in Ireland microfilm, DMP and RIC précis, report for April 1910 (speech of Hughes at Dundalk); report for May 1910 (speech of Nugent at Roscommon). A key factor in preventing the AOH from switching its allegiance to Sinn Féin was that the Irish Party convinced John O'Callaghan, the treasurer of the American AOH who was also a treasurer of the United Irish League of America, to remain loyal to Devlin and Redmond.
153. Patrick Maume, *The long gestation* (Dublin, 1999), 101–103.
154. L.W. White, 'Sean MacDiarmada (1883–1916)', *Dictionary of Irish Biography*, 5 (Cambridge, 2009), 911–914.
155. A copy of the testimonial can be found in NLI, Sweetman papers, Ms47587/1.
156. UCD, Tom Kettle papers, LA32/11, recollections of Mary Kettle, p.10. Mary Kettle's sister, Hanna Sheehy Skeffington, equally hated Griffith and once wrote to the press that the absence of his wife at public meetings indicated his declared support for full women's suffrage (which neither Sweetman nor the Irish Party supported) was insincere and that he was mistreating his wife at home. This attack on Griffith was the one time in Maud (Sheehan) Griffith's life when she wanted to write a letter of protest to the press but she decided against it on Griffith's own advice, as 'he said it was better not, as that would only give her statement more publicity, which was probably what she wanted'. NAI, Bureau of Military History papers, WS205 (Maud Griffith).
157. Sean Ghall [Henry Egan Kenny], 'Arthur Griffith as I knew Him', undated press cuttings in NLI, Sean O'Luing papers, Ms 23,516 (*Young Ireland*, 19 Aug-Sep. 1922).
158. Anne Dolan, *Commemorating the Irish civil war* (Cambridge, 2003) reproduces several of her letters to indicate this, especially in chapter 3.
159. Griffith's surviving letters to Lily Williams (NLI, Ms5943), including a very enthusiastic response to receiving a present of a chess-set, reflected this to some degree. Shortly after Griffith married, he arranged a floral exhibition at the Botanic Gardens. Griffith to Williams, 30 Oct. 1911.

CHAPTER SIX

1. Erskine Childers, *The framework of home rule* (London, 1911), chapter 10.
2. 'Ulster and Home Rule', *Sinn Féin*, 2 Dec. 1910.
3. 'Ireland and the English Protectionists', *Sinn Féin*, 18 Dec. 1909. 'Ireland and Protection', *Sinn Féin*, 2 Oct. 1909.
4. T.M. Kettle, *Home Rule finance: an experiment in justice* (Dublin, 1911), 2, 22–24.
5. *Sinn Féin*, 26 Feb., 16 Apr., 7 May 1910. In order to defend the Irish Party from criticism, the Liberal government later published revised figures, claiming that taxation was being increased by only £535,000, but nobody believed these figures.
6. Ulster Protestant, 'Light on Ulsteria', *The Irish Review: a monthly magazine of Irish literature, art and science*, 1 (May 1912), 122–123. The writer credited William O'Brien with having an intellectually sound conception of nationalism.
7. *Sinn Féin*, 26 Mar. 1910, p.1.
8. Kettle, *Home Rule finance*, 2–3, 7, 27, 77, 81.
9. Griffith offered a critique of this trend in his editorial of *Sinn Féin*, 15 Oct. 1910.
10. Childers, *The framework of home rule*, 185–186. Childers also judged that the 'intensely religious' public attitudes that had developed in Ireland since 1886 had done 'visible good' for the cause of the Empire and therefore must be encouraged even further.
11. Erskine Childers, 'Irish fiscal autonomy', in Royal Economic Society (ed.), *The fiscal relations of Great Britain and Ireland* (Suffolk, 1912), 62–63, 67–68.
12. Ronan Fanning, *The Irish Department of Finance 1922–1958* (Dublin, 1978), 1–5.
13. Childers, *The framework of home rule*, 188, conclusion.
14. Childers, 'Irish fiscal autonomy', 62–63, 67–68; Childers, *The framework of home rule*, chapter 10.
15. Richard Cantillon (1682–1734), an Irish-born French author, considered by many as a founder of modern political economy.
16. 'Our trade and teachers', *Sinn Féin*, 20 Sep. 1913 (quote); 'The case for the unionists [Irish Tories]', *Sinn Féin*, 16 Oct. 1909.
17. As an example of this trend, Griffith noted that young Irish Tories who debated the Sinn Féin Policy with much interest at Church of Ireland Y.M.C.A. meetings no longer considered the Union from this perspective. 'Irish Unionism', *Sinn Féin*, 18 Dec. 1909.
18. Griffith wrote about the origins of the First World War in his editorial 'England, Ireland and America', *Nationality*, 16 Aug. 1919. He also touched upon this theme during his late 1915 *Nationality* editorials on the activities of Jan Smuts and Herbert Kitchener.
19. 'Sinn Féin and the Election, manifesto from the National Council, advice to voters', *Sinn Féin*, 29 Jan. 1910; 'From Ireland's standpoint', *Sinn Féin*, 12 Mar. 1910; 'The balance of power, Redmond's surrender', *Sinn Féin*, 23 Apr 1910; 'Last words on parliamentarianism', *Sinn Féin*, 7 May 1910; 'A council of finance', *Sinn Féin*, 4 June 1910; 'Mr. Redmond's position', *Sinn Féin*, 19 Nov. 1910. James Stephens, the writer, spoke on behalf of Sinn Féin's stance on the budget of April 1910 before Griffith's central branch (*Sinn Féin*, 30 Apr. 1910). Griffith liked to claim that the percentage of people who did not vote in these elections (for example, the 25 per cent of the electorate who did not vote in the second general election) represented Sinn Féin. 'Unionism and the situation', *Sinn Féin*, 24 Dec. 1910.
20. This had led a British government subcommittee, headed by a Scottish civil servant, to recommend financial compensation to Ireland for past over-taxation. Alan O'Day (ed.) *Reactions to Irish nationalism* (London, 1987), chapter 14; H.C.G. Matthew, 'Sir Henry Primrose', *Oxford Dictionary of National Biography* (2004).

21. 'Ostrich policy', *Sinn Féin*, 7 Jan. 1911, 'Ireland pays her way', *Sinn Féin*, 21 Jan. 1911, 'Home Rule will cost you more', *Sinn Féin*, 28 Jan. 1911, 'The Orangeman and Home Rule', *Sinn Féin*, 28 Jan. 1911.

22. Erskine Childers, *The framework of home rule* (London, 1911), chapter 10, pt.3; Erskine Childers, 'Irish fiscal autonomy', 54.

23. Childers, *The framework of home rule*, 144.

24. Childers, *The framework of home rule*, 72–143, 188–229, 339–341 (quote p188); Childers, 'Irish fiscal autonomy'.

25. *Sinn Féin*, 5 Nov. 1910.

26. 'What Home Rule is Not', *Sinn Féin*, 12 Nov. 1910.

27. 'Finance and Home Rule', *Sinn Féin*, 15 Jan 1911. Hitherto, Griffith frequently based his own editorials on articles in the Tory *Irish Times*.

28. NLI, Sweetman papers, Ms47584/6, Sweetman to Griffith, 25 Sep. 1911.

29. Arthur Griffith, 'True and false imperialism', *The Irish Review: a monthly magazine of Irish literature, art and science*, 1 (Aug. 1911), 270–272. Regarding the recent British Imperial Conference, Griffith typified this as a 'fiasco' and argued that it showed that 'the colonies may have a use for imperialism', but 'they have none for English Ascendancy'. In this article, Griffith also noted that 'the title Austrian Empire was a denial of Hungary … There is no longer an Austrian Empire—there is an Austro-Hungarian Empire. There is still a British Empire, not a Brito-Hibernian Empire.'

30. Arthur Griffith, *Pitt's policy* (Dublin, 1911).

31. 'Unionism and Home Rule', *Sinn Féin*, 17 Dec. 1910 (a review by Griffith of a pamphlet by Samuels); Arthur Griffith, 'True and false imperialism', *The Irish Review: a monthly magazine of Irish literature, art and science*, 1 (Aug. 1911).

32. Ironically, this was also a theme of G.A. Birmingham's novel *The Red Hand of Ulster* (London, 1912). Michael Laffan, *The partition of Ireland 1911–1925* (Dundalk, 1983), 22.

33. Arthur Griffith, *Pitt's Policy* (Dublin, 1911).

34. Owen McGee, 'C.H. Oldham (1859–1926)', *Dictionary of Irish Biography*, 7 (Cambridge, 2009), 629–630; C.H. Oldham, 'The economics of industrial revival in Ireland', *Society for the Statistical and Social Inquiry of Ireland*, 61 (1907–08), 175–189. Oldham had originally been a maverick Gladstonian Liberal that led a short-lived Protestant crusade in favour of 'home rule', in which capacity he befriended John O'Leary and founded the journal *North and South*.

35. C.H. Oldham, 'The keystone of Irish finance', in Royal Economic Society (ed.) *The fiscal relations of Great Britain and Ireland* (Suffolk, 1912), 15–33.

36. Arthur Griffith, *Finance of the Home Rule Bill: an examination* (Dublin, 1912), 7–8, 10–12.

37. C.H. Oldham, 'The keystone of Irish finance', in Royal Economic Society (ed.) *The fiscal relations of Great Britain and Ireland* (Suffolk, 1912), 15–33.

38. T.M. Kettle, *Home Rule finance: an experiment in justice* (Dublin, 1911), 28.

39. Kettle, *Home Rule finance*, 14, 21.

40. Kettle, *Home Rule finance*, 74.

41. Kettle, *Home Rule finance*, 79–81; Paul Bew, *Ideology and the Irish question* (Oxford, 1994), 127, 155.

42. 'From Ireland's standpoint', *Sinn Féin*, 12 Mar. 1910. 'A council of finance', *Sinn Féin*, 4 June 1910.

43. NLI, Sinn Féin pamphlet collection, pamphlet no.84.

44. Griffith, 'The Sinn Féin Policy', in Murray (ed.) *The Resurrection of Hungary*, 159–160.

45. *Sinn Féin*, 18 Sep. 1909.

46. *Sinn Féin*, 5 Feb. 1910.

47. This residence, formerly the home of Cardinal Newman and later the headquarters of the Gaelic League, was the Sinn Féin Party headquarters from 1910–1921. In addition to Alderman Kelly, Sheila Carden has identified George Russell and P.T. Daly as early supporters of the Sinn Féin Bank, which possibly helps account for its establishment, while she has also suggested that Griffith's appreciation for the Popular Bank of Milan may have inspired its purpose. Carden, *The Alderman*, 68.

48. NLI, Griffith papers, acc.4476, box b, 'confidential' letter from John Dillon to 'My Dear [George? Sir Charles?] Russell', 26 July 1910: 'please sent me a copy of the paper on the banks alluded to in article in last Saturday's *Statist*. Have you ascertained who is writing these articles in the *Statist*?'.

49. 'The country and the budget', *Sinn Féin*, 26 Feb.1910.

50. L.G. Redmond Howard, *John Redmond* (London, 1910), 330, 339–340.

51. Erskine Childers, *The framework of home rule* (London, 1911), 339, 341.

52. Patrick Bolger, *The Irish cooperative movement: its history and development* (Dublin, 1977), 156–170.

53. Griffith, 'The Sinn Féin Policy', in Murray (ed.) *Resurrection of Hungary*, 141–144.

54. A Cork British army major debated the Sinn Féin policy with Griffith at the Sinn Féin Central Branch in October 1910 ('The policy of withdrawal', *Sinn Féin*, 22 Oct.1910). Griffith was something of a sceptic of the attempts in Cork to revive the city's commercial life: 'if squandering money on deputations to London could have made Cork harbour prosperous, it should now be the most flourishing port in Ireland.' (*Sinn Féin*, 30 Aug. 1913).

55. To this end Sinn Féin had its own 'Industrial Committee', separate from that of the Gaelic League, which claimed to have 'entered into relations with American and continental markets' (*Sinn Féin*, 18 Sep. 1909).

56. For the career of its manager David Kelly, see Sheila Carden, *The Alderman: Alderman Thomas Kelly* (Dublin, 2007).

57. 'Irish money', *Sinn Féin*, 22 Oct. 1910. An imagined positive end result from the formation of a National Land Bank was reflected by one of Griffith's political cartoons at the time. This portrayed agriculture as the root of the Sinn Féin 'tree', but new manufacturing industries were its freshly budding 'branches'. *Sinn Féin*, 4 Mar. 1911, p.1.

58. 'Dublin vindicated', *Sinn Féin*, 4 June 1910, 11 June 1910 (editorial). This anti-royalist initiative was also supported by Henry Dixon, John MacBride, W.T. Cosgrave, Sean Milroy and Francis Sheehy Skeffington.

59. 'Our trade and teachers', *Sinn Féin*, 20 Sep. 1913.

60. *Sinn Féin*, 11 June 1910.

61. *Sinn Féin*, 4 Mar. 1911. A frequent protest of Griffith was that most trained (Catholic) nurses in Ireland were encouraged to emigrate to Britain and were deliberately not being employed by Irish Catholic hospitals, which preferred to hire cheaper staff from abroad, including Britain. Both Catholic schools and hospitals tended to follow this British economic dynamic in terms of labour management almost by necessity owing to the nature of the country's financial institutions.

62. Tom Dunne (ed.), *The National University of Ireland, 1908–2008: centenary essays* (Dublin, 2008), foreword by Garret Fitzgerald.

63. NLI, Sweetman papers, Ms47587/6–7 (letters of Sweetman and Griffith, 1911–1912).

64. NLI, Sweetman papers, Ms47587/6, Griffith to Sweetman, 24 Sep.1911.

65. NLI, Ms18578, letter of Griffith to Patrick MacManus, 13 Sep. 1912. Patrick MacManus was a brother of Seamus MacManus who spent much time in South America. On the security of his promise to sell his family home (which his friends had purchased for £300

but which Griffith felt could fetch £350 due to improvements he had made), he requested a loan of a couple of hundred pounds from Patrick MacManus which, he emphasised, he would not be able to repay for 'at least three years'. Believing that 'Irish politics would enter on a new era and our opportunity would come' following the next home rule episode, Griffith felt that it was necessary to keep his publication alive until such time, as otherwise 'it will be very difficult to resuscitate'.

66. UCD Archives, P163/1, Sinn Féin minute books (Oct.1912-Jan.1913).
67. NLI, Sweetman papers, Ms47587/5.
68. Patrick Maume, 'Sean O'Hegarty (1881–1963)', *Dictionary of Irish Biography*, 7 (Cambridge, 2009), 544–546.
69. Michael Laffan, *The partition of Ireland* (Dundalk, 1983), 22–25, 37, 39.
70. Alvin Jackson, *Sir Edward Carson* (Dublin, 1993).
71. Patrick Buckland, *James Craig* (Dublin, 1980), 3–13.
72. Patrick Buckland, *James Craig* (Dublin, 1980), 11–21, 125.
73. Patrick Bolger, *The Irish cooperative movement* (Dublin, 1977), 166, 366.
74. Patrick Maume, 'Edward James Saunderson (1837–1906)', *Dictionary of Irish Biography*, 8 (Cambridge, 2009), 781–783.
75. Alvin Jackson, 'James Craig (1871–1940)', *Dictionary of Irish Biography*, 2 (Cambridge, 2009), 953–957.
76. Thomas Lough, 'Irish finance', in Royal Economic Society (ed.) *The fiscal relations of Great Britain and Ireland* (Suffolk, 1912), 34–39.
77. *Sinn Féin*, 24 Dec. 1910.
78. Alan Caskey, 'Entrepreneurs and industrial development in Ulster 1850–1914', *Irish Economic and Social History*, vol.12 (1985), 123–124.
79. *Sinn Féin*, 24 Dec. 1910. A more detailed exposition of these arguments can be found in Sean Milroy, *The case of Ulster* (Dublin, 1919), 23–35.
80. 'Ulster humbug', *Sinn Féin*, 19 July 1913.
81. P. Dempsey, S. Boylan, '(Robert) Lindsay Crawford (1868–1945)', *Dictionary of Irish Biography*, 2 (Cambridge, 2009), 971–973.
82. 'Orangemen and the Union', *Sinn Féin*, 2 Aug. 1913 (quote). In 1873, the Grand Orange Lodge voted by 22–18 in favour of the repeal of the Act of Union. However, this vote failed to carry because Lord Enniskillen insisted that a two-thirds majority vote should be required ('Home Rule and the Orangemen', *Sinn Féin*, 4 Oct. 1913). Griffith rarely analysed the financial position of the Church of Ireland, an exception being an analysis published during 1910 in which he credited the church for not giving in entirely to the trend (witnessed in the Catholic Church and elsewhere) of the investment of Irish capital abroad ('Irish money—millions going abroad', *Sinn Féin*, 22 Oct. 1910).
83. *Nationality*, 13 Sep. 1919, p.1.
84. NLI, Sweetman papers, Ms47587/7, Griffith to Sweetman, 18 May 1912.
85. Riobard Ua Fhloinn (Robert Lynd), *The Orangeman and the Nation* (Dublin, 1906), 12–16. In later life, during 1934, Lynd (1879–1949) judged that Griffith was 'the greatest constructive mind—or, at least, the most effective constructive mind—that was ever devoted to Irish politics'. Sean McMahon (ed.) *Robert Lynd's Galway at the Races: selected essays* (Dublin, 1990), 109.
86. Peter Gibbon, *The origins of Ulster unionism: the formation of popular Protestant politics and ideology in 19th century Ireland* (Manchester, 1975) cites the existence of Northern Ireland in 1881. For a treatment of the over-taxation issue, see Paul Bew (later Lord Bew), *Ideology and the Irish question* (Oxford, 1994), 126, 155–159. Elsewhere, Bew has argued that the origins of Ulster unionism 'convey a kind of truth about Gladstone's conversion

to home rule: necessary, just and disastrous—all at the same time'. Myles Dungan (ed.) *Speaking ill of the dead* (Dublin, 2007), 40.

87. Arthur Griffith, 'Home rule and the unionists', *The Irish Review: a monthly magazine of Irish literature, art and science*, 2 (May 1912), 113–118. For a contrary viewpoint, see Andrew Scholes, *The Church of Ireland and the Third Home Rule Bill* (Dublin, 2008). Scholes is a Northern Ireland civil servant with a PhD in history from Queen's University Belfast.

88. Arthur Griffith, 'Home rule and the unionists', *The Irish Review: a monthly magazine of Irish literature, art and science,* 2 (May 1912), 113–118.

89. Arthur Griffith, 'The Sinn Féin Policy', in Murray (ed.) *Resurrection of Hungary*, 139.

90. Arthur Griffith, *When the government publishes sedition* (Dublin, 1915), 6, 9, 10.

91. 'The plunder of Ireland', *Nationality*, 4 Mar. 1916; 'Canto and his Ministers', *Nationality*, 11 Mar. 1916. On this theme, see also 'The protestant church and the Ulster covenant', *Sinn Féin*, 4 Oct. 1913 in which Griffith argued that the Church of Ireland had allowed itself to be abused for political purposes.

92. Tom Feeney, 'Arthur Warren Samuels (1852–1925)', *Dictionary of Irish Biography*, 8 (Cambridge, 2009), 760–761; *Nationality*, 26 Mar. 1918, p.1.

93. J.H. Morgan (ed.), *The new Irish constitution* (London, 1912). The chief contributors to this publication were R.B. O'Brien, Alice Stopford Green, Sir John MacDonnell, Lord Dunraven and Jonathan Pim.

94. NLI, Sweetman papers, Ms47587/7, Sweetman to Griffith 12 Apr. 1912. Griffith replied that the bill was 'very bad'. Griffith to Sweetman, 18 May 1912.

95. Arthur Griffith, *Finance of the Home Rule Bill: an examination* (Dublin, 1912), 9. This was a reprint of articles from *Sinn Féin*, 4 & 11 May 1912.

96. Griffith, *Finance of the Home Rule Bill,* 7–8, 10–12. The Irish parliament was denied the right to pass taxes on any of its exports to Britain, to engage in a direct export trade with other powers and to determine what percentage of revenue raised from whatever taxes it did introduce would be allowed to be used for Irish purposes.

97. Arthur Griffith, *The Home Rule Bill examined* (Dublin, 1912), 14. As an example of this, Griffith cited the granting to non-elective bodies powers of veto over the proposed parliament's bills.

98. Griffith, *Finance of the Home Rule Bill*, 5–7, 22–24.

99. Griffith, *The Home Rule Bill examined*, 5, 16.

100. Griffith, *Finance of the Home Rule Bill*, 10; Griffith, *The Home Rule Bill examined*, 9.

101. Griffith, *The Home Rule Bill examined*, 9.

102. NLI, Sweetman papers, Ms47587/7, Griffith to Sweetman, 18 May 1912.

103. Ronan Fanning, *Fatal path: British government and Irish revolution* (Dublin, 2013), 84.

104. Michael Laffan, *The partition of Ireland* (Dundalk, 1983), 34–37.

105. Ronan Fanning, *Fatal path: British government and Irish revolution* (Dublin, 2013), chapter 3.

106. *Sinn Féin*, 5 July 1913.

107. 'Home rule defined', *Sinn Féin*, 4 Mar. 1911 (quote). On this theme, see also 'The false balance sheet', *Sinn Féin*, 11 Mar. 1911.

108. Arthur Griffith, 'Home rule and the unionists', *The Irish Review: a monthly magazine of Irish literature, art and science*, 2 (May 1912), 118.

109. O'Donnell's two-volume *History of the Irish Parliamentary Party* (London, 1910), drawn partly from his own former experience as a member of that party, is perhaps the most detailed critique of the history of that party in existence. Advertisements for it sometimes appeared in Griffith's publications.

110. This series, entitled 'The place hunter in Irish politics', covering the period 1846–1891, was first published in O'Brien's *Free Press* (Cork) early in 1913 and later reprinted in *Sinn Féin* (13 Sep.-20 Dec. 1913) and again in *Nationality* (Feb.-Apr. 1917).

111. Possibly because the *Evening Telegraph* was the evening edition of the *Freeman's Journal* (a journal Griffith detested), this series ('Irish Revivalists') was published without a by-line (though they sometimes contained initials). John Wyse Power, the husband of Sinn Féiner Jennie Wyse Power, had been the editor of the *Evening Telegraph*, which probably explained why it usually included a report on Sinn Féin meetings. The individuals examined in the series were General Charles Vallancey (15 Mar. 1913), William Halliday (29 Mar. 1913), Edward O'Reilly (12 Apr. 1913), Philip Barron (19 Apr. 1913), George Petrie (3 May 1913), John O'Donovan (10 May 1913), Eugene O'Curry (31 May 1913), William Elliott Hudson (7 Jun. 1913), John Edward Pigot (13 Jun. 1913), Dr. Henthorn Dodd (21 Jun. 1913), Samuel Ferguson (28 Jun. 1913), Archbishop John MacHale (5 Jul. 1913), Bishop William Reeves (19 Jul. 1913), Sir John Gilbert (26 Jul. 1913), Fr. Eugene O'Growney (2 Aug. 1913), Sir William Wilde (9 Aug. 1913) and Rev. Euseby Cleaver (23 Aug. 1913).

112. *Irish Book Lover*, vol.4, Feb 1913, pp119–120.

113. Griffith's *Southern Cross* series was also reprinted in *Sinn Féin*. He suggested that 'if Argentina had passed under British rule in 1807—if her gallant people had not beaten the English back into the sea—she would have to digest a similar bookkeeping' as Ireland did, namely a fraudulent and exploitative form of colonial bookkeeping (reprinted in *Sinn Féin*, 9 Aug. 1913). Bulfin, whose accounts of his cycling tours of Ireland were republished in the *United Irishman* during 1902, died during 1913.

114. Arthur Griffith (ed.) *Mitchel's Jail Journal* (Dublin, 1913); Arthur Griffith (ed.) *Thomas Davis: the thinker and teacher* (Dublin, 1914); Arthur Griffith (ed.) *Meagher of the Sword* (Dublin, 1915); Arthur Griffith (ed.) *James Fintan Lalor* (Dublin, 1918). In *Studies* (June 1915), p299, 'T.C.' (probably Timothy Corcoran S.J., the editor of *Studies*) accused Griffith of making a poor editorial selection of Davis' writings by choosing those that portrayed the old Protestant patriot tradition in too positive a light.

115. Pearse and Griffith's correspondence, suggesting that *Sinn Féin* and *An Claidheamh Solus* work together, was published in *Sinn Féin* on 23 Aug. 1913.

116. UCD Archives, P163/1, Sinn Féin minute books (1912–1913).

117. Hyde to *Sinn Féin*, 26 July 1913.

118. Virginia Glandon, *Arthur Griffith and the advanced nationalist press* (New York, 1985), 98–100.

119. T.G. McMahon, *Grand opportunity*, 150. Aside from Griffith and Larkin, urban labour activists, such as Thomas Johnson and William O'Brien, as well as socialists such as Seamus Hughes (a frequent contributor to Griffith's journal and member of Sinn Féin), joined the Gaelic League because of their belief that initiatives such as the IDA could reverse the trend of urban emigration.

120. Glandon, *Arthur Griffith and the advanced nationalist press*, 100.

121. NLI, Sweetman papers, Ms47587/6, Griffith to Sweetman, 24 Sep. 1911.

122. *Sinn Féin*, 6 Sep. 1913, p.1; 'Troubled Dublin', *Sinn Féin*, 13 Sep. 1913.

123. *Sinn Féin*, 6 Sep. 1913, p.1; 'The economics of the "food-ship"', *Sinn Féin*, 4 Oct. 1913; 'The nation', *Sinn Féin*, 29 Nov. 1913 (quote).

124. 'The cost of living', *Sinn Féin*, 20 Sep. 1913; 'Dublin housing', *Sinn Féin*, 27 Sep. 1913; 'Housing Dublin', *Sinn Féin*, 11 Oct. 1913; 'Three half-pence in the pound', *Sinn Féin*, 1 Nov. 1913 (quote); 'A Sinn Féin housing scheme', *Sinn Féin*, 15 Nov. 1913.

125. 'Strikes and arbitration courts', *Sinn Féin*, 27 Sep. 1913. In this article, Griffith cited France as a positive example of a country that used labour arbitration courts. Elsewhere, he cited New Zealand as another positive example of the same. 'Sinn Féin and the labour question', *Sinn Féin*, 25 Oct. 1913. Griffith also cited the Australian method of holding referendums to solve industrial disputes as a positive example. 'Australia and industrial disputes', *Sinn Féin*, 4 Oct. 1913.
126. 'Our trade and teachers', *Sinn Féin*, 20 Sep. 1913.
127. Irish Banks Standing Committee, *The Control of Banking in the Republic of Ireland* (Dublin, 1984), 138. For the composition of the Dublin Chamber of Commerce, see L.M. Cullen, *Princes and pirates* (Dublin, 1983).
128. Irish Transport and General Workers Union, *The attempt to smash the ITGWU* (Dublin, 1924). This publication published documents dating from 1911–1923 to substantiate the claim that Larkin was a destructive opportunist. A short-lived labour journal that supported the Irish Party, *The Toiler*, denounced both Griffith and Larkin. Glandon, *Arthur Griffith*, 111–112.
129. 'Methodists and Home Rule', *Sinn Féin*, 25 Oct. 1913.
130. Michael Laffan, *The partition of Ireland*, 34–37, 39.
131. *Sinn Féin*, 6 Sep. 1913, p.1; 'Troubled Dublin', *Sinn Féin*, 13 Sep. 1913.
132. 'Sinn Féin and the Labour Question', *Sinn Féin*, 25 Oct. 1913.
133. 'Sinn Féin and the Labour Question by Arthur Griffith', *Sinn Féin*, 25 Oct. 1913. This was one of the few times when Griffith deliberately put his name over one of his own articles.
134. 'Our trade and teachers', *Sinn Féin*, 20 Sep. 1913.
135. Michael Laffan, *The partition of Ireland* (Dundalk, 1983), 34–39.
136. NLI, Redmond papers, Ms15175/2, four communications of Casement to Redmond, Jun.1914. Tom Clarke considered Casement to be Redmond's agent. NAI, Bureau of Military History papers, WS27 (P.S. O'Hegarty) and WS766 (Patrick MacCartan).
137. Captain Robert Monteith, *Casement's last adventure* (Chicago, 1932, republished Dublin, 1953), 262–263.
138. NLI, Redmond papers, Ms15236/5, Patrick Egan (of the United Irish League of America) to Redmond, 24 Nov. 1914; *Scissors and Paste*, 19 Feb. 1915 (republished extract from the London *Times*). On this theme, see also Jerome ann de Viel, *The Irish factor* (Dublin, 2008) and the Casement correspondence in UCD Archives, DeValera papers, P150/1190.
139. 'Home Rule and the Orangeman', *Sinn Féin*, 4 Oct. 1913.
140. *Sinn Féin*, 28 Feb., 28 Nov. 1914.
141. *Sinn Féin*, 21 Mar. 1914.
142. The Sinn Féin Party's latest senior recruits, M.J. O'Rahilly (who liked to be known as 'The O'Rahilly') and Eamon Ceannt (treasurer and secretary of the party), were enthusiastic founders and, in turn, leaders of the Irish Volunteers, although Alderman Tom Kelly, like Griffith, would be a relatively reluctant recruit. Kelly, whose chief political inspiration was his belief in a perpetual deterioration of the Irish Party ever since 1886 (*Sinn Féin*, 22 Feb.1913), feared that the formation of the Irish Volunteers would eclipse Sinn Féin or 'mean the end of Sinn Féin, as we knew it'. Carden, *The Alderman*, 89.
143. *Sinn Féin*, 22 Nov. 1913 (quote); 'The Volunteers', *Sinn Féin*, 6 Dec. 1913.
144. 'The Volunteers', *Sinn Féin*, 20 Dec. 1913.
145. 'The Volunteers', *Sinn Féin*, 6 Dec. 1913.
146. Liam de Roiste of Cork, although a long-term pacifist and member of the IDA, was one of the first volunteers to write to *Sinn Féin* protesting strongly against this proclamation. *Sinn Féin*, 13 Dec. 1913.

147. Not surprisingly, party political divisions mattered little in this development due to the question of national defence. Naval officer Conor O'Brien, a Tory grandson of William Smith O'Brien, facilitated the Irish Volunteer gunrunning with the support of Liberal party figures such as Erskine Childers. F.X. Martin (ed.), *The Howth gun running and the Kilcoole gun running* (Dublin, 1964). Captain Wilfrid Spender and Major F.H. Crawford arranged the Ulster Volunteers' gunrunning at Larne. Alvin Jackson, 'The Larne gunrunning', *History Ireland*, 1 (spring 1993).

148. T.W. Moody, F.X. Martin, F.J. Byrne (eds) *A new history of Ireland*, 8 (Oxford, 1989), 388.

149. 'Ireland and the War', *Sinn Féin*, 8 Aug. 1914.

150. 'Ireland and the War', *Sinn Féin*, 8 Aug. 1914.

151. Accounts for the Irish Volunteers, published in *Eire-Ireland*, 7 Nov. 1914.

152. Ronan Fanning, *Fatal path: British government and Irish revolution 1910–1922* (London, 2012), 130 (quote), introduction.

153. Kevin Kenny (ed.) *Ireland and the British Empire* (Oxford, 2004), 143.

154. Erskine Childers, *The framework of home rule* (London, 1911).

155. Keith Jeffrey (ed.) *An Irish Empire? Aspects of Ireland and the British Empire* (Manchester, 1996).

156. Michael Laffan, *The partition of Ireland* (Dublin, 1983), 24–25.

157. Patrick Buckland, *James Craig* (Dublin, 1980), 36.

CHAPTER SEVEN

1. Articles on South Africa appeared occasionally in Griffith's journals long after 1902, including after the constitutional developments of 1906.

2. Alderman Kelly chaired this demonstration while James Connolly, who formed an Irish Neutrality League with Griffith thereafter, coined the slogan. NLI, Michael Noyk papers, Ms18975, p3.

3. This reality, rooted partly in class differences and the longstanding controversy over Gaelic League management, was reflected by MacNeill's unpublished memoirs (UCD Archives, MacNeill papers, LA1/G/371). Despite the common trajectory and close proximities of their careers from 1892–1922 MacNeill made no mention of Griffith's life or his career whatsoever, except to note that he once shared a prison cell with him alongside Paddy Mahon (the printer of most IRB–Sinn Féin literature ever since 1904).

4. While Tom Clarke had utilised Griffith's *Sinn Féin* to publish letters protesting against alleged Dublin police brutality (Clarke *to Sinn Féin*, 20 Sep, 6 Dec. 1913), the key intermediary between Sinn Féin and the IRB was now Eamon Ceannt, a secretary to both organisations specifically in Dublin and a leader of the Dublin poor law boards.

5. Owen McGee, *The IRB* (Dublin, 2005), 327.

6. Conor Cruise O'Brien, *Parnell and his party* (Oxford, 1957), 2.

7. The most notable war correspondents in its ranks, Edmund O'Donovan and J.J. O'Kelly, had both been close political associates of John Devoy, who also wrote on international affairs although by no means exclusively. In common with William Halpin (the author of the Proclamation of the Irish Republic in January 1867), all three men were former soldiers. Prominent IRB organisers since the 1870s (including John Daly, P.N. Fitzgerald, John MacBride and Tom Clarke) all had some social connections in their family backgrounds with British military figures. Roger Casement's initiation of an association with Devoy during 1914 was essentially rooted in this Victorian tradition. Devoy, *Recollections*.

8. Healy made his debut as a defence lawyer for Fred Allan in November 1884 (Owen McGee, 'Fred Allan', *Dublin Historical Record* (autumn 2003)) and, due to his history of defending IRB activists, was later approached by the Frognoch Prisoners Committee to represent them (NLI, Art O'Brien papers, Ms8442/21). A significant context to this development was the history of 'fenian' amnesty agitations ever since 1869. Healy, who had been a member of the IRB in Britain during the late 1870s, was the first and virtually the only lawyer, prior to the arrival of Charles Wyse Power, who was prepared to tolerate the claim that the 'fenians' could possibly claim 'political status'.

9. NAI, Bureau of Military History papers, WS420 (Charles Wyse Power), pp1–2; WS653 (Mrs. T.M. Sullivan, Healy's daughter, citing chapter 12 of her unpublished memoirs).

10. John Devoy, *Recollections of an Irish rebel* (New York), 392. During the mid-1890s, the IRB's own leadership referred publicly to it as 'that movement just now passing away'. McGee, *IRB*, 227–229.

11. Kathleen Clarke, *Revolutionary woman* (Dublin, 1991), 41; John Devoy, 'Jack Daly', *Gaelic American*, 15 Mar. 1924.

12. *Irish Freedom* was initially managed by the IRB's executive, led by Fred Allan, but with financial assistance from Joseph McGarrity of the Philadelphia Clan na Gael, Patrick MacCartan (formerly of the *Gaelic American*) was able to prompt Allan and his followers to resign from the IRB leadership and surrender control of *Irish Freedom* as a protest against Clan na Gael dictation in the expectation that this would prompt the IRB to stand by them in defence of the movement's organisational independence and re-elect them as leaders. This plan did not work, however. This was a significant personal coup for the Clan and MacCartan, but this had no real repercussions other than to allow MacCartan and Hobson assume editorial control over *Irish Freedom* and Hobson to assume the leadership of a moribund Dublin IRB organisation during 1912. G.Doherty, D. Keogh (eds) *1916* (Cork, 2007), 108–109, 422.

13. Sean T. O'Kelly, 'Arthur Griffith', *Capuchin Annual* (1966), 140–141; F.X. Martin (ed.), *Leaders and men of the 1916 rising* (Dublin, 1967), 62–63; NAI, Bureau of Military History papers, WS3 (Liam O'Briain); WS420 (Charles Wyse Power, son of John); NLI, Michael Noyk papers, Ms18975.

14. The Clan na Gael was raising funds and it intended sending them, if possible, to the Irish Volunteers in Ireland via the IRB. The IRB was a numerous organisation up until the Edwardian era and had always jealously guarded its organisational independence (it frequently resisted any dictation by the Clan). A clear trend emerged in the Edwardian era, however, whereby intelligence reports indicated that 'although the I.R.B. as such has ceased to exist, (our) informant states that the (Supreme) Council, at the instance of the Clan na Gael, has been retained' as its front. In other words, the IRB was now too weak an organisation to have any independence from the Clan na Gael. NAI, DMP and RIC précis, report of Chief Commissioner Wilkins of the DMP to the Inspector General of the RIC, 7 Sep.1909.

15. Sean O'Hegarty, Sean McGarry and Alex McCabe were the most enthusiastic activists in the 1914 reorganisation of the IRB but they managed to get themselves arrested in a relatively short space of time. NAI, Bureau of Military History papers, WS420 (Charles Wyse Power, son of John). McCabe, the successor of John and Joseph McBride (harbour master at Castlebar) as the leader of the Connacht IRB, would later write on international affairs for Griffith's journal (e.g. 'Islam in Ferment', *Nationality*, 26 July 1919). This reflected a strange feature of the history of the Connacht IRB. Although best known for having provided activists for the Land League, some of its leaders (such as Thomas McCauley, who was falsely imprisoned for the infamous 'Crossmolina conspiracy' of 1883

and a grandfather to future Irish president Mary Robinson) were actually keen students of international relations, as indeed was Michael Davitt (Louisa Nally, descendant of P.W. Nally, to author).

16. Sean T. O'Kelly, 'Arthur Griffith', *Capuchin Annual* (1966), 140–141; NAI, Bureau of Military History papers, WS3 (Liam O'Briain), WS205 (Maud Griffith); NLI, Michael Noyk papers, Ms18975.

17. *Eire-Ireland* (editorial), 26 Oct. 1914.

18. 'The militia ballot act: cannot be enforced if Irishmen resist it', *Eire-Ireland*, 26 Oct. 1914. Griffith would soon claim, in a typical example of his wartime propaganda, that the English were exploitatively testing the possibilities of introducing conscription in Ireland and Scotland but not in England itself. *Eire-Ireland*, 3 Nov. 1914.

19. *Eire-Ireland*, 2 Nov. 1914 (editorial).

20. *Eire-Ireland*, 5 Nov. 1914 (republishing a letter of MacNeill to the *Irish Independent*). Many volunteer leaders were remarkably blasé about the accusation of being pro-German. For instance, Desmond Fitzgerald, speaking in Kerry, said that 'some of the police had circulated the story that I had got "German gold". Well, as they know that, they should prosecute me for high treason and then the plain peeler would become a sergeant.' *Eire-Ireland*, 11 Nov. 1914.

21. Tom Dunne (ed.) *The National University of Ireland 1908–2008* (Dublin, 2008), 126–133. Prior to 1885, Walsh had been the president of Maynooth College and, therefore, the chief medium for the British government to fund the education of Catholic priests in Ireland.

22. *Eire-Ireland*, 4 Nov. 1914 (editorial quote): 'it is no baser for an Irish citizen to be in receipt of German bribes than it is for an Irish citizen—or an Irish newspaper—to be in receipt of British bribes.' Several times during the First World War, Griffith accused the *Freeman's Journal*, being a semi-governmental organ, of being in receipt of British secret service money (e.g. 'Latest war news', *Nationality*, 11 Feb. 1916).

23. 'Who is the militarist?', *Eire-Ireland*, 6 Nov. 1914.

24. *Sinn Féin*, 22 Aug. 1914 (quote); 'Grand Orient declares for England', *Eire-Ireland*, 24 Nov. 1914.

25. 'To the readers of Eire-Ireland', signed by Griffith and Sean T. O'Kelly, *Eire-Ireland*, 4 Dec. 1914. On the House of Lords' reaction, see *Eire-Ireland*, 25 Nov. 1914.

26. *Eire-Ireland* was published daily from 26 Oct. to 4 Dec. 1914. *Scissors and Paste* was published twice weekly from 12 Dec. 1914 to 27 Feb. 1915.

27. *Scissors and Paste*, 27 Feb. 1915 (advertisement). The lecture was held on the 4 March and the police seized the office on 2 March. *Irish Times*, 3 Mar. 1915.

28. Another short-lived pro-Irish Volunteer journal, *The Spark*, claimed that Griffith was the most popular nationalist in Dublin at this time. Sheila Carden, *The Alderman* (Dublin, 2007), 93.

29. Two volumes of such press cuttings can be found in NLI, Griffith papers, acc.4476, box a. Griffith's understanding of the course of the war may not have been good. He predicted that Britain could win the support of Japan but not America ('America and Japan', *Eire-Ireland*, 9 Nov. 1914). Earlier, in an attempt to echo the preoccupations of Devoy's *Gaelic American* with Anglo-American relations (which also had a south-American context), Griffith wrote an editorial entitled 'Ireland and Mexico'; a peculiar editorial choice to make in the same week as the Irish Volunteers were formed (*Sinn Féin*, 22 Nov. 1913). Indeed, notwithstanding his own critique of 'Pitt's Policy', Griffith sometimes seemed to be inordinately preoccupied with British foreign policy. For instance, while launching the Sinn Féin Bank, Griffith devoted a whole editorial to a critique of the stance of the *Irish Times* on British foreign policy in the Far East ('Sinn Féin—in China', *Sinn Féin*, 9 Oct. 1909).

30. *Eire-Ireland*, 20 Nov. 1914 (reprinting letter of Sweetman to *Meath Chronicle*). Pearse wrote in the first number of *Eire-Ireland* (26 Oct. 1914) that the volunteers' quarrel with John Redmond was not, as the Irish Party leader claimed, a belief that he had made a secret bargain with the British government—Pearse did not believe this could possibly be true—but rather that his call upon the volunteers 'to take their place in the firing line in the war' was contrary to the volunteers' pledge that the movement's only purpose was 'to secure and to guard the rights and liberties of Ireland', which may or may not include a wartime responsibility to 'defend the shores of Ireland' on behalf of the British government.

31. Marie O'Neill, 'Dublin Corporation in the troubled times 1914–1924', *Dublin Historical Record*, 47 (spring 1994), 60. Clancy died six days before he could take office.

32. *Scissors and Paste*, 19 Feb. 1915 (republished extract from the London *Times*).

33. Patrick Maume, 'John Devoy (1842–1928)', *Dictionary of Irish Biography*, 3 (Cambridge, 2009). On this theme, however, see also NAI, Bureau of Military History papers, WS1070 (Thomas O'Connor).

34. Devoy and Redmond became allies after the fall of Parnell (McGee, *IRB*). Casement's well-publicised American adventure was the inspiration for Arthur Conan Doyle's popular Sherlock Holmes story 'His Last Bow', published during 1915, whereby Holmes, disguised as a Fenian, attends a pro-German Clan na Gael convention in America on behalf of the British government.

35. NLI, Redmond papers, Ms15236/5, Patrick Egan (of the United Irish League of America) to Redmond, 24 Nov. 1914 (Egan refers to the fact that he had denounced Casement in the press).

36. *Eire-Ireland*, 26 Oct. 1914 (report on volunteer convention). Fawsitt, a member of the American AOH, had been a correspondent with the Cork IDA and a business figure of much interest to Griffith.

37. To Redmond's supporters in America, the switch in the editorial policy of the New York *Irish World* was considered a major blow. NLI, Redmond papers, Ms15236/5.

38. Reflecting this, the tumultuous fortunes of Belgian Catholic religious orders (several relocated to Ireland) were presented as symbolical of war's repugnant capacity for social disruption. Patrick Maume, *Long gestation* (Dublin, 1999), 148, 165–167.

39. This recruitment poster is reproduced on the back cover of the American journal *Eire-Ireland*, vol.35, nos.3–4 (fall/winter 2000–2001).

40. J.S. Ellis, 'The degenerate and the martyr: nationalist propaganda and the contestation of Irishness, 1914–1918', *Eire-Ireland* (vol.35, nos.3–4, fall/winter 2000–2001), 7–33.

41. Paul Bew, *Ideology and Irish question* (Oxford, 1994), 124–125; Maume, *Long gestation*, 168–171.

42. Erskine Childers, 'Christian democracy in Belgium', *Studies*, 2 (1913); Charles Dawson, 'The industrial progress of Belgium: an object lesson for Ireland', *Journal of the Society for the Statistical and Social Inquiry of Ireland* (1912), 595–608. In common with Childers, at the time of the 1886 home rule debate, John O'Leary judged that the co-existence of Christian and Liberal parties in Belgium was an example of national politics that was likely to mirror future Irish political developments. John O'Leary, 'Some guarantees for the protestant and unionist minority', *Dublin University Review*, vol.2, no.12 (Dec. 1886), 959–965.

43. Thomas Kettle, *The day's burden* (Dublin, 1968), opening dedication.

44. G.Doherty, D. Keogh (eds) *1916* (Cork, 2007), 264–269.

45. Tom Dunne (ed.) *National University of Ireland* (Dublin, 2008), 133.

46. DeValera acquired personal correspondence of Casement and Clan na Gael leaders and kept them among his own papers. For the 1914–1916 period, see NAI, DeValera papers, P150/1190. According to DeValera himself, he took the IRB oath in the winter of 1914 in order to better follow what was going on within the management of the Irish Volunteers, yet he did not want to become involved in the IRB's secret business. NAI, DeValera papers, P150/472 (statement of DeValera, 7 Jul. 1961).

47. Casement's mission was connected more with Joseph McGarrity than John Devoy and funded via John Kenny, formerly a controversial Clan na Gael treasurer during 1883–1884 (the era of the 'dynamite war', when Devoy had no authority over the Clan's executive). *Gaelic American*, 23 Jan. 1925 (obituary for Kenny). Devoy was connected more with Tom Clarke who, like Devoy, was very ambivalent in his attitude to Casement. Doherty, Keogh (eds) *1916* (Cork, 2007), 113–114; NAI, Bureau of Military History papers, WS27 (P.S. O'Hegarty); WS1070 (Thomas O'Connor).

48. NLI, Michael Noyk papers, Ms18975, p.4. Noyk was a Jewish solicitor and close friend of Griffith.

49. 'Stokes Brothers and Pim, chartered accountants', managed the accounts of the Irish Volunteers. See the balance sheets reproduced in *Eire-Ireland*, 7 Nov. 1914.

50. NLI, Ms5943, Griffith to Florence Williams 4 Nov. 1916 (quote); NLI, Sinn Féin pamphlet collection, 'Sinn Féin in tabloid form (n.d. [1915])' by 'A. Newman'. This presented Griffith's economic nationalist programme in a grossly exaggerated form, claiming that Ireland could easily develop 'the greatest mercantile marine in the world'; that the country's natural resources were 'inexhaustible' and that the moment Sinn Féin's policy was adopted 'emigration would automatically cease' and 'Ireland out of her own riches could support 20 million of a population.'

51. NLI Pamphlet Collection, *O'Donovan Rossa: souvenir of the public funeral 1 August 1915* (Dublin, 1915).

52. That Clarke financed *Nationality* (as he had *Eire-Ireland*) is indicated by the often-repeated claim that MacDermott managed *Nationality*, as he had *Irish Freedom*. L.W. White, Sean MacDiarmada (1883–1916), *Dictionary of Irish Biography*, 5 (Cambridge, 2009), 911–914. However, Clarke and MacDermott do not appear to have had an association with Pim. Meanwhile, J.J. Burke, a former contributor to the *Irish Worker* and *Irish Freedom* while a member of the Liverpool IRB, later became acting-editor for a different edition of *Nationality* and he claimed that *Nationality* was always financed by private 'friends' of Griffith rather than the IRB as an organisation. NLI, Griffith papers, acc.4476 (undated press cutting). Burke was an acting-editor of *Nationality* from November 1918 up until its suppression in September 1919 and thereafter acted similarly for *Young Ireland* up until the beginning of 1922. During 1923, he held the rank of a captain in the National Army.

53. 'Carson and Redmond in 1896', *Nationality*, 29 Jan. 1916; 'Thirty years after', *Nationality*, 15 Apr. 1916 (an article on 'Ned Carson', later 'Sir Edward').

54. Pim claimed that Parnell was an opponent of over-taxation. This had no foundation in fact, however, and probably reflected the prejudiced and retrospective idea that was common to Irish Protestant businessmen that Parnell's fall coincided with a loss of business sense in Irish politics because of the influence of the Roman Catholic Church. Aside from being a sectarian attitude, this attitude was based upon a misreading of the economic context of events of the time. *Nationality*, 1 Jan. 1916 (speech of Pim at a volunteer event chaired by Thomas MacDonagh).

55. *Nationality*, 2 Oct. 1915; 'Crushing militarism', *Nationality*, 9 Oct. 1915; 'The English oligarchs', *Nationality*, 15 Jan. 1916.

56. 'Beware of pickpockets', *Nationality*, 8 January 1916; 'How Ireland is bled', *Nationality*, 15 Jan. 1916. Around this time, Griffith also hastily wrote a pamphlet for the women's movement founded in support of MacNeill's volunteers, Cumann na mBan, called 'Why Ireland is poor'. This was published as part of Pim's *Tracts for the Times* series.

57. 'God save Ireland', and 'The Home Rule Sham', *Nationality*, 15 January 1916.

58. 'Irish War Savings Committee', *Nationality*, 13 Nov. 1915; 'Bankers Manifesto', *Nationality*, 1 Jan. 1916; 'War Economy', *Nationality*, 12 Feb. 1916; 'How to get rich quick', *Nationality*, 25 Feb. 1916.

59. 'Sinn Féin is on the rocks', *Nationality*, 30 Oct. 1915 (reprinting an article on the English press).

60. Dublin Castle estimated that *Nationality* reached a circulation of about 8,000 copies at this time, as opposed to the usual circulation of *Sinn Féin* of about half that figure. Michael Laffan, *Resurrection of Ireland* (Cambridge, 1999), 33.

61. 'The Bulgarian atrocity', *Nationality*, 9 Oct. 1915; *Nationality*, 16 Oct. 1915 (editorial); 'St. George and the Dragons', *Nationality*, 22 Jan. 1916.

62. *Nationality*, 18 Dec. 1915, p.1.

63. *Nationality*, 11 Dec. 1915, pp1–2.

64. 'The prophets of English imperialism', *Nationality*, 22 Jan 1916; 'More jobs', *Nationality*, 20 Nov. 1915: 'for every nationalist jailed in Ulster, one Devlinite, at least, receives a Castle job'.

65. *Nationality*, 27 Nov. 1915, 1 Jan. 1916, 1 Apr. 1916.

66. Griffith gave four historical lectures to the Dublin Gaelic League during early 1916 and the previous November was the chief speaker alongside Pearse at an IRB organised centenary of Mitchel's birth. *Nationality*, 13 Nov. 1915, p3 and p7.

67. MacDermott's assertion that it was meant 'to keep Griffith out' of the Irish volunteer movement (NAI, Bureau of Military History papers, WS28 (P.S. O'Hegarty)), like the desire to keep barristers like Charles Wyse Power out of the movement (WS420), was probably rooted in the belief that they could better serve Irish nationalist aims from outside the movement.

68. Bishop O'Dwyer of Limerick led the protests in this regard. *Nationality*, 20 Nov. 1915, p.1; 27 Nov. 1915, 4 Dec. 1915, 15 Jan.1916, p.1, and 'The Pope's appeal for Peace' (reporting on an article by O'Dwyer in the *North American Review*), *Nationality*, 25 Dec. 1915.

69. Redmond was constantly giving interviews to the New York Catholic press at this time. *Nationality*, 30 Oct. 1915, 1 Jan. 1916; NLI, Redmond papers (Ms15236: American correspondence).

70. *Nationality*, 13 Nov. 1915, pp1–2; 'Roman Question' and 'Grand Orient', *Nationality*, 22 Jan. 1916.

71. For Fr. O'Flanagan's support of Ginnell's anti-rancher agitation, see *Nationality*, 23 Oct. 1915, p1–2. Fr. O'Flanagan's series on British foreign policy, 'The War Game', appeared in *Nationality* from 25 March until 22 April 1916.

72. Fr. P. Browne (ed.), *Collected works of P.H. Pearse: plays, stories and poems* (Dublin, 1917); *The collected works of Patrick Pearse: political writings and speeches* (Phoenix Press, n.d [1917]). Fr. Browne was an academic in Maynooth College.

73. Brendan Walsh, *The pedagogy of protest: the educational thought and work of Patrick H. Pearse* (Bern, 2007).

74. Pearse felt keenly that the Irish Party had been betrayed by the British government's postponement of the Government of Ireland Act and also felt that the deteriorating fortunes of his St. Enda's school was the result of the government's increasingly

unsympathetic attitude towards the Gaelic League. First employed by Tom Clarke as an orator in 1910 (NAI, Bureau of Military History papers, WS1 (Tom Barry)), in the wake of the formation of the Irish Volunteers, Pearse's growing friendship with McDermott and Clarke made him willing to join the IRB.

75. 'Peace in Warsaw', *Nationality*, 23 Oct. 1915; 'A mission for Redmond', *Nationality*, 1 Jan 1916.

76. 'Mr Dillon and the Redmondite volunteers', *Nationality*, 19 Feb. 1916. Both Redmond and Dillon could still justify the existence of MacNeill's Irish Volunteers as a cost-saving measure that was contributing indirectly to the British war effort by guarding the Irish coastline.

77. 'Ireland and the Peace Congress', *Nationality*, 4 Mar. 1916. Griffith characteristically responded to this by writing that 'it is up to the *Freeman* now to describe Cardinal O'Connell as a factionist, a crank, a Sinn Féiner, a pro-German and a dishonest politician'. *Nationality*, 15 Apr. 1916, p.1.

78. Griffith had attended Clarke's initial revolutionary convention of Sep. 1914 alongside John MacBride, Sean T. O'Kelly, Patrick Pearse, Thomas MacDonagh, Eamon Ceannt, Joseph Mary Plunkett and James Connolly and was in frequent contact with them all. Some friends, as well as associates of Sean MacDermott (principally P.S. O'Hegarty), maintained that Griffith knew nothing of what was occurring, although others claimed otherwise. On this theme, see NAI, Bureau of Military History papers, WS420 (Charles Wyse Power, son of John); WS3 (Liam O'Briain); NLI, Michael Noyk papers, Ms18975.

79. NAI, Bureau of Military History papers, WS1070 (Thomas O'Connor). O'Connor, Devoy's envoy to Clarke via a New York–Liverpool shipping company, was interrogated by the American secret service as a result of these developments. The circle of John Kenny, the Clan's intermediary with Casement in Germany (and formerly an initiator of the 'dynamite war' controversy of 1883), probably contained the culprit. On Kenny's career, see the obituary by Devoy in *Gaelic American*, 23 Jan. 1925.

80. Remarkably, Count Plunkett's family decided to contact Roger Casement in Germany, John Devoy in New York and even the Vatican seeking practical or moral support for importing arms and staging a rebellion. While the church naturally did not approve of violence or the idea of a rebellion, it has been claimed that Monsignor O'Riordan, the rector of the Irish College in Rome and the Irish hierarchy's intermediary with the Pope, understood and sympathised with Plunkett's stance. Keogh, Doherty (eds), *1916* (Cork, 2007), 264–269. O'Riordan's statement to the Bureau of Military History indicates a different picture, however, noting that Archbishop Walsh and himself were always unenthusiastic about the existence of the Irish Volunteers. They relied on James Collins and subsequently Sean T O'Kelly for updates on what was happening in the IRB. NLI, Ms27728/1 (copy of O'Riordan's statement to the Bureau), pp7–10.

81. *Nationality*, 4 Mar. 1916; 'The khaki press', *Nationality*, 11 Mar. 1916; 'The plunder of Ireland', *Nationality*, 1 Apr. 1916; 'Twenty five millions!', *Nationality*, 15 Apr. 1916.

82. 'The volunteers at College Green', *Nationality*, 25 Mar. 1916; 'Something new!' (an advertisement for Griffith's lecture to the 2nd Dublin Battalion), *Nationality*, 18 Mar. 1916. Somewhat bizarrely, in mid-April 1916, *Nationality* claimed that the Dublin volunteers had gained 1,400 recruits within the past week. *Nationality*, 15 Apr. 1916, p1.

83. Sean T. O'Kelly, 'Arthur Griffith', *Capuchin Annual* (1966), 142. On the same theme, see WS3 (Liam O'Briain).

84. A good illustration of this was Piaras Beaslaí's introduction to the commemorative booklet *The Grand Concert in Antient Concert Rooms on 9 April 1916, addressed by Eoin MacNeill for equipping the 1st battalion of the Dublin Brigade* (Dublin, 1916).

85. Having been assured on Easter Sunday that no rebellion would take place, Griffith let his wife visit her sister in Cork and promised to look after their two children in her absence. When the rebellion broke out the following day, Griffith was taken by surprise and attempted in vain to get his neighbours to look after the children so he could find out what was going on. By Wednesday or Thursday, he was able to visit MacNeill in Rathfarnham, having travelled there from Clontarf by a circular route on his bicycle. He had also received a letter from MacDermott, in response to a letter sent to the GPO protesting for leaving him in the dark, that it was desired that Griffith would not take part so he could live on and be able to promote their ideals in print afterwards. NAI, Bureau of Military History papers, WS3 (Liam O'Briain), WS7 (Liam O'Briain), pp4–5, WS205 (Maud Griffith); NLI, Michael Noyk papers, Ms18975, 9–11.

86. 'The Lord hath delivered them into our hands!' by 'A.N.', *Nationality* (editorial), 29 Apr. 1916. Pim had recently attempted to create a personality cult regarding Pearse ('The apostle of no compromise', by 'A.N.', *Nationality*, 25 March 1916; 'More tracts for the times', *Nationality*, 29 Apr. 1916) and had also invited Pearse to give a Robert Emmet lecture in Belfast to celebrate the publication of *Ghosts* (*Nationality*, 11 Mar. 1916). Griffith had no doubt that Connolly rather than Pearse was the military leader of the rebellion. NAI, Bureau of Military History papers, WS6 (Liam O'Briain), 4–6; G.Doherty, D. Keogh (eds) 1916 (Cork, 2007), 116–117. Although Pearse stayed with Sean T. O'Kelly the night before the rebellion (NLI, O'Kelly papers, Ms8469/1), the last time Griffith appears to have been in contact with Pearse was on receiving a letter from him in early April. NLI, Griffith papers, acc.4476, box b, letter (copy) of Pearse [to Griffith], 3 Apr. 1916.

87. Sheila Carden, *The Alderman: Alderman Tom Kelly and Dublin Corporation* (Dublin, 2007), 97–101. Kelly and P.J. Little wrote articles about this document for the 1942 Capuchin Annual.

88. The memoirs of Desmond Fitzgerald regarding figures such as M.J. O'Rahilly, Patrick Pearse, Thomas MacDonagh and Joseph Mary Plunkett are quite revealing in this regard. Desmond Fitzgerald, *Desmond's rising: memoirs 1913 to Easter 1916* (Dublin, 1968), esp.140–147.

89. This reflected Connolly's ambitions perhaps more than anyone. Clarke, it would seem, had wished for a larger-scale conflict, but was simply glad *some* rebellion had taken place. G.Doherty, D. Keogh (eds) 1916 (Cork, 2007), 116–117; Desmond Fitzgerald, *Desmond's rising: memoirs 1913 to Easter 1916* (Dublin, 1968), esp.140–147.

90. It seems that a teller within the bank facilitated this, with Pearse's connivance. NAI, Bureau of Military History papers, WS420 (Charles Wyse Power), p7. The Hibernian Bank was considered by many contemporaries to be the 'most Irish bank' because although it had a similar clientele to the National Bank its headquarters was in Dublin rather than London.

91. Owen McGee, 'John Wyse Power (1859–1926)', *Dictionary of Irish Biography*, 8 (Cambridge, 2009), 262; W. Murphy, L. Ni Mhungaile, 'Jennie Wyse Power (1858–1941)', *Dictionary of Irish Biography*, 8 (Cambridge, 2009), 256–257.

92. F.X. Martin (ed.) *Leaders and men of the 1916 rising* (Dublin, 1967), 62–63. This would have been in keeping with the IRB tradition, in which its 'military organisation' had absolutely no standing in itself without the authority of a 'civil organisation'. According to this logic, the 1916 rebel force had to be nominally rebelling on behalf of *some* civil authority but constituted absolutely no authority in itself.

93. Patrick Maume, 'Sean Thomas O'Kelly (1882–1966)', *Dictionary of Irish Biography*, 7 (Cambridge, 2009), 615–619. As Griffith and Alderman Kelly were not involved, they may not have known of this intention, if it existed.

94. Sheila Carden, *The Alderman: Alderman Thomas Kelly and Dublin Corporation* (Dublin, 2007), 104–105.

95. James Stephens, *The insurrection in Dublin* (Dublin, 1916). This was the first account of the rebellion to be published.

96. These were Alderman Tom Kelly, Sean T. O'Kelly T.C. and W.T. Cosgrave T.C. NLI, Sean O'Luing papers, Ms23516 (recollections of W.T. Cosgrave). Sinn Féin also had three representatives on the poor law boards of Dublin, namely Eamon Ceannt, Richard O'Carroll and Jennie Wyse Power.

97. Eunan O'Halpin, 'William Thomas Cosgrave (1880–1961)', *Dictionary of Irish Biography*, 2 (Cambridge, 2009), 880–885. Cosgrave was requested to join the IRB several times but refused. Up until the age of twenty, he was a friend of John Nolan, the leader of the controversial Squad of the Dublin IRB (1892–1900), and later attended Nolan's funeral during 1920. For Nolan's career, see McGee, *IRB*.

98. On the theme of the unutilised political talent within the Gaelic League, see Fergus Campbell, *The Irish establishment 1879–1914* (Oxford, 2009). Campbell argued that little had changed in Irish society since 1879 and therefore the anti-aristocrat focus of the original Irish National Land League of 1879–1881 still had the potential to be revived after 1914.

99. Casement confessed to a priest that he desired to be executed for a secret political motive. NLI, Art O'Brien papers, Ms8447/7, Fr. Ryan to George Gavan Duffy, 12 July 1916.

100. Nationwide petitions were collected in Ireland for Casement to be reprieved. Two hundred and seventy four such petitions, each bearing many signatures, can be found in NLI, Art O'Brien papers, Ms8447/3–5. Forty-two petitions, each bearing many signatures of British public figures, for Casement can be found in NLI, Art O'Brien papers, Ms8447/1–2.

101. David Foxton, *Revolutionary lawyers: Sinn Féin and crown courts in Ireland and Britain 1916–1923* (Dublin, 2008).

102. NLI, Michael Noyk papers, Ms18975, p11 (quoting Piaras Beaslai's recollections in *The Leader*, 16 Dec. 1944). In Reading Jail, Griffith also learnt that the man who was censoring all prisoners' reading material and letters (he was also ably translating for the government all those which were written in Irish) was none other than T.W. Rolleston, who also compiled biographical notes for the government on the many Sinn Féiners whom he had known. NLI, MS5943, Cuguan (Griffith) to Lily Williams, 4 Nov. 1916.

103. NAI, Bureau of Military History papers, WS6 (Liam O'Briain), pp11–12.

104. Most nights in prison, Griffith heard loud explosions nearby because of German Zeppelin bombings in the vicinity; something which led the German prisoners of war (one of 'fourteen nationalities represented in this prison') to attempt to assuage the fears of the twenty-seven Irish prisoners present that they too would be bombed. NLI, MS5943, Griffith to Lily Williams, 29 Nov. 1916 and 'Thursday' [post-25 Dec. 1916]. A slight degree of social bonding took place between the German and Irish prisoners in London ('we have learned to whistle the German War March and the Germans have learned to say "Up Ireland"') and the last action Griffith and fellow Irish prisoners took at Reading just prior to the release in December was to decorate a Christmas tree for the German prisoners.

105. Joost Augusteijn, *From public defiance to guerrilla warfare: the experience of ordinary volunteers* (Dublin, 1996).

106. For the political meaning of the IRB's 'virtually established republic', see Owen McGee, *The IRB* (Dublin, 2005), chapter 1.

107. NLI, MS5943, Griffith to 'Miss Williams' [autumn 1916]. At the time of Roger Casement's execution, Terence MacSwiney and Griffith led the other prisoners in Reading in saying a rosary for his soul before, on Griffith's suggestion, they concluded by singing 'God Save Ireland' in his honour.

108. NLI, Art O'Brien papers, Ms8429/18. Lynch reacted to this by stating that 'there was never intended any suggestion that he, or any of them, had shown any weakness' (Lynch to *Irish Independent*, undated press cutting [probably 17–19 Nov. 1916] in NLI, Griffith papers, acc.4476, box a).

109. NLI, Art O'Brien papers, Ms8435/31.

110. NLI, Art O'Brien papers, Ms8434/10, Ms8435/30; Kathleen Clarke, *Revolutionary woman* (Dublin, 1991).

111. NLI, Ms44614: a letter of Dillon regarding the movements of police officers, with Collins' annotations on the envelope.

112. NLI, Ms5943, letters of Griffith to Lily Williams, 5 Aug., 29 Nov. 1916.

113. Owen McGee, 'James Joseph O'Kelly (1842–1916)', *Dictionary of Irish Biography*, 7 (Cambridge, 2009), 601–603.

114. NAI, Bureau of Military History papers, WS1725 (Patrick O'Keeffe); Manifesto of the Irish Nation League, *Nationality*, 24 Feb. 1917. Appeals by Darrel Figgis for the Irish Nation League to join the National Council went unheeded.

115. Anon., *Arthur Griffith: a study of the founder of Sinn Féin* (Dublin, 1917).

116. NLI, MS5943, Griffith to Williams, 29 Nov. 1916.

117. By December 1916, Sinn Féin in Cork was already making international appeals, sending an address both to the President of the United States and to the Pope. *Nationality*, 17 Feb. 1917, p5. As a credible Sinn Féin Party organisation had not yet been established, this was perhaps a premature action.

118. A recent study of Cork has highlighted the extent to which diverse political interest groups, traditionally marginalised by the Irish Party in order to maintain a single political organisation, became active after 1916 and formed a backdrop to the rise of Sinn Féin. John Borgonovo, *The dynamics of war and revolution: Cork City, 1916–1918* (Cork, 2013). Other localised studies of Irish politics during the First World War may produce similar research findings. Previous examinations of Sinn Féin, such as Michael Laffan, *The resurrection of Ireland* (Cambridge, 1999), tended to follow the same model as past studies of the Irish Party, such as C.C. O'Brien, *Parnell and his party* (Oxford, 1957), in focusing exclusively on a central national executive of the party (i.e. the party administration) rather than the party's actual activities at a local level.

119. 'The work before us', *Nationality*, 17 Feb. 1917.

120. The recollections of Kevin O'Shiel, an Irish Nation League activist who was soon won over to Sinn Féin, regarding party politics during 1917–1918 are revealing in this regard. NAI, Bureau of Military History papers, WS1170.

121. The front page of *Nationality* during 1917 highlighted the extent to which the police courts were busy throughout the year.

122. This misleading idea has been championed by historians such as Peter Hart in studies such as *The IRA and its enemies* (Oxford, 1998) and *The IRA at war* (Oxford, 2000), which attempted to present 'the IRA' as engaged perpetually in a self-styled military conflict from 1916 onwards.

123. These trends have been highlighted in the most detailed and sophisticated study of police reports during 1914–1921 yet completed, Benjamin Grob-Fitzgibbon, *Turning points of the Irish revolution* (New York, 2007).

124. On this theme, see Peter Martin, *Irish peers 1909–1924* (MA, UCD, 1998).

125. It has been suggested that militancy arose in Ireland at this time. Conor Kostick, *Revolution in Ireland: popular militancy 1917–1923* (Cork, 2009). However, these arguments have not been based on an understanding of the economy of Ireland up until that time. A useful survey on this theme is Emmet O'Connor, 'Active sabotage in industrial conflict 1917–1923', *Irish Economic and Social History*, 12 (1985), 50–62.

126. C.H. Oldham, 'Changes in Irish exports during twelve years', *Journal of the Statistical and Social Inquiry of Ireland* (1918–19), 548–551.

127. 'The Sinn Féin Policy' in Murray (ed.), *Resurrection of Hungary*, 144 (quote).

128. Manifesto of the Irish Nation League, *Nationality*, 24 Feb. 1917.

129. Michael Laffan, *The resurrection of Ireland* (Cambridge, 1999), 96–97.

130. NLI, Michael Noyk papers, Ms18975, p16. Professor Thomas Dillon of the UCD and later UCG chemistry department, a former militant supporter of Kettle's Young Ireland Branch of the United Irish League, would later (1953) write a very critical, influential and unsympathetic treatment of Griffith's activities at this time that would seem to have coloured unduly by his career-long opposition to him. UCD Archives, DeValera papers, P150/575, 'Arthur Griffith and the reorganisation of Sinn Féin 1917'. Regarding this article, DeValera himself wrote (annotated comment, 21 Mar. 1963) that the attempt to portray Griffith as an anti-republican figure was mistaken, as was the claim of the existence of a mutual hostility between himself and Griffith: 'we were all the time good friends and continued so until the Treaty was signed.'

131. *Nationality*, 26 May 1917.

132. NLI, Henry Dixon papers, Ms35262/1, Lloyd George to Dixon.

133. Archbishop Walsh's letter to the Irish press, 7 May 1917, reprinted in *Nationality*, 2 Feb. 1918, p.1. At the time, the Catholic hierarchy were concentrating their financial resources primarily upon launching a major new Irish missionary campaign to the Far East. A fund-collection for this campaign was advertised in most newspapers, including Griffith's.

134. He suggested that the rise of Sinn Féin meant that 'the sale was averted', *Nationality*, 2 Feb. 1918, p.1.

135. Patrick Maume, 'William Martin Murphy' (1845–1919)', *Dictionary of Irish Biography*, 6 (Cambridge, 2009), 825–827. Griffith considered that Murphy's ideas regarding home rule were, by far, the best that were put forward at the Irish Convention, although he also emphasised the problem that Ireland could be still taxed for an English war under Murphy's scheme. *Irish Independent*, 24 May 1917 (report of Griffith's speech at a Sinn Féin convention). On this occasion, Griffith also claimed to be hopeful that while Lloyd George claimed that the British government would never concede more to Ireland than it had offered to the Irish Party, 'the England of 1917 is not the England of 1913, and the England of 1918 will not be the England of 1917', while 'Sinn Féin will outlive Mr Lloyd George and anything the English Government can do against it.' UCD Archives, DeValera papers, P150/575. Eamon DeValera later requested copies of Murphy's letters regarding Plunkett's convention in order to give him some information he could use for his own lecture tour in the United States. UCD Archives, P150/727, DeValera to Griffith, 13 Aug. 1919.

136. *Nationality*, 22 Sep. 1917, p1.

137. The *Irish Independent*'s 'generalissimo' advertisements appeared in *Nationality* throughout the autumn and winter of 1918. Historians have traditionally underestimated the significance of Murphy and his press at this time (UCD library contains copies of the *Irish Times*, the Tory party journal, and the *Freeman's Journal*, the Irish Party journal, as the chief national newspapers in Ireland at this time. It also includes some small radical newspapers, including James Larkin's. However, it does not include the *Irish Independent*).

138. For a general analysis of the history of the *Irish Independent* at this time, see Mark O'Brien, Kevin Rafter (eds) *Independent Newspapers: a history* (Dublin, 2012).

139. Laffan, *Resurrection of Ireland*, 98–99. The manner of Collins' theatrical entry virtually repeated that adopted by P.N. Fitzgerald on entering the famed Kilkenny by-election of December 1890. R.B. O'Brien, *The life of Parnell* (1898, 2nd ed., London, 1910), 515.

140. Moynihan to *Kerry Sentinel*, 19 May 1917, reproduced in Deirdre McMahon (ed.), *The Moynihan brothers in peace and war 1908–1918* (Dublin, 2004), 155–156.

141. This pamphlet was published anonymously but its author (a former secret service activist among the Irish abroad) was identified in Christy Campbell, *Fenian fire: the British government plot to assassinate Queen Victoria* (London, 2000). See the references to 'the Black Pamphlet' and 'Capt. Stephens' in that book's index.

142. Professor John [Eoin] MacNeill, 'War and reconstruction: Irish settlement', *The English Review* (1917), 253–262 (written in response to Stephens' article in the same). A copy of MacNeill's article can be found in NLI, Art O'Brien papers, Ms8457/8.

143. 'Ireland and England', *Nationality*, 8 Sep. 1917 (editorial).

144. Erskine Childers, *The framework of home rule* (London, 1911), chapter 10, part c (p.195).

145. *Nationality*, 21 July 1917 (editorial).

146. NLI, Redmond papers, Ms15182/24, Dillon to Redmond, 13 Apr. 1917 (written at the time of the McGuinness campaign).

147. T.A. Finlay, 'The significance of some recent Irish statistics', *Journal of the Statistical and Social Inquiry Society of Ireland* (1912–13), 17–25. Fr. Finlay was actually the president of this society for a time, i.e. when W.M. Murphy was chairman of the Dublin Chamber of Commerce (1912–1913).

148. Rt. Hon Thomas Lough MP, 'Irish finance', in Royal Economic Society (ed.) *The fiscal relations of Great Britain and Ireland* (Suffolk, 1912), 38–39.

149. NLI, Sweetman papers, Ms47587/7, Griffith to Sweetman, 18 May 1912. Griffith was fond of typifying Plunkett as a man 'who was wandering around in the faith that he had a mission from heaven—it was really from Mr. Arthur Balfour—to disinfect Irish politics'. 'Neutral [T.P.] Gill', *Nationality*, 20 Nov. 1915 (Gill was secretary to Plunkett's department).

150. P. Dempsey, S. Boylan, '(Robert) Lindsay Crawford (1868–1945)', *Dictionary of Irish Biography*, 2 (Cambridge, 2009), 971–973.

151. Patrick Maume, *The long gestation* (Dublin, 1999), 240.

152. This was a common argument in both *An Claidheamh Solus* as well as Griffith's publications *Sinn Féin* and *Nationality*. Griffith had sided with the argument that the government was deliberately punishing, or provoking, the Gaelic League because of its anti-war stance, not least by withdrawing all funding for Irish language teaching. This would have been the popular Gaelic League view and it surfaced frequently from December 1905 onwards.

153. *Nationality*, 22 Jan. 1916, pp1–2.

154. 'The finance of the charter of liberty', *Nationality*, 24 Feb. 1917. This was a summary of British economy policy between 1816 and 1896, arguing that it had continued unaltered in its treatment of Ireland.

155. *Nationality*, 6 Nov. 1915, p1.

156. 'Customs and Excise', *Nationality*, 27 Apr. 1918 (a reprint from *Sinn Féin* at the time of the Government of Ireland Bill debate in 1913).

157. 'Customs and Excise', *Nationality*, 27 Apr. 1918 (a reprint from *Sinn Féin* at the time of the Government of Ireland Bill debate in 1913).

158. *Nationality*, 11 May 1918.

159. *Nationality*, 2 Feb. 1918, p.1; 'Federalism and fraud', *Nationality*, 6 Apr. 1918; *Nationality*, 13 Apr. 1918, p.1; 'Colonial home rule', *Nationality*, 20 Apr. 1918; 'Masked words', *Nationality*, 11 May 1918.

160. 'Why food and coal are dear', *Nationality*, 17 Feb. 1917.

161. *Nationality*, 27 Oct. 1917, p1.

162. *Nationality*, 8 June 1918, p.1.

163. *Nationality*, 27 Oct. 1917.

164. *Nationality*, 5 Jan. 1918, p.1.

165. C.H. Oldham, 'The incidence of emigration on town and country life in Ireland', *Journal of the Statistical and Social Inquiry Society of Ireland* (1914), 207–218 (quote p.216); 'The economic interests involved in the present war', *Journal of the Statistical and Social Inquiry Society of Ireland* (1914–15), 269–280; 'Industrial Ireland under free trade', *Journal of the Statistical and Social Inquiry Society of Ireland* (1916–17), 383–398; 'Changes in Irish exports during twelve years', *Journal of the Statistical and Social Inquiry Society of Ireland* (1918–19), 541–553; 'Changes in the export industries of Ireland 1904–1916', *Journal of the Statistical and Social Inquiry Society of Ireland* (1918–19), 629–637.

166. *Nationality*, 27 Oct. 1917, p.1.

167. *Nationality*, 27 Oct. 1917, p.1, *Nationality*, 5 Jan. 1918, p.1.

168. *Nationality*, 24 Nov. 1917, p.1.

169. R.J. Kelly K.C., 'The recent British bank amalgamations and Ireland', *Journal of the Statistical and Social Inquiry Society of Ireland* (1918–19), 642–674 (quote p.650).

170. 'Twenty-five millions!', *Nationality*, 15 Apr. 1916; *Nationality*, 4 May 1918, p1. The budget of 1918 involved the withdrawal of £35million in revenue from Ireland with a maximum of £12millon to be returned for expenditure on the Dublin Castle administration.

171. W.E. Vaughan (ed.) *A new history of Ireland*, 6 (Oxford, 1989), 342–350.

172. 'The business basis of unionism', *Nationality*, 26 Mar. 1918.

173. *Nationality*, 12 Jan. 1918.

174. *Nationality*, 26 Jan. 1918; *Nationality*, 24 Nov. 1917, p.1. In the latter article, Griffith candidly admitted his discovery that 'the National Bank has become a London bank, as was shown recently by the *Economist*', although it was common knowledge in the business and financial world that the National Bank had essentially always been a London bank ever since its formation by Daniel O'Connell in the 1830s.

175. 'Munster and Leinster Bank', *Nationality*, 2 Feb. 1918.

176. 'National Bank', *Nationality*, 16 Mar. 1918.

177. 'Hibernian Bank', *Nationality*, 9 Feb. 1918.

178. 'National Bank', *Nationality*, 16 Mar. 1918.

179. 'Hibernian Bank', *Nationality*, 9 Feb. 1918.

180. 'National Bank', *Nationality*, 16 Mar. 1918.

181. Lionel Smith Gordon, *The place of banking in the national programme* (Dublin, 1921).

182. *Nationality* remained in print until September 1919. Thereafter, Griffith operated *Young Ireland*.

183. *Nationality*, 24 Nov. 1917 & 5 Jan. 1918 contain good early expressions of this argument.

184. *Nationality*, 3 Mar. 1917, p1.

185. *Nationality*, 12 Jan. 1918.

186. *Sinn Féin*, 21 Mar. 1914.

187. Very few (including Thomas Martin of London) were actually in favour of Griffith remaining president and the IRB were encouraged to support DeValera's candidacy. NAI, Bureau of Military History, WS767 (Patrick Moylett), p13; WS279 (Seamus Dobbyn), p14.

188. NAI, DeValera papers, P150/575, report of Sinn Féin Ard Fheis, 25 Oct. 1917 and text of DeValera's speech: 'the only banner under which our freedom can be won at the present time is the republican banner. It is an Irish republic that we have a chance of getting international recognition for. Some of us would wish, having got that recognition, to have a republican form of government. Some might have faults to find with that and prefer other forms of government. This is not the time for discussion on the best forms of government. But we are all united on this—that we want complete and absolute independence. Get that, and we will agree to differ afterwards'.

189. T.W. Moody, F.X. Martin, F.J. Byrne (eds) *A new history of Ireland*, 8 (Oxford, 1989), 394.

190. Patricia Lavelle, *James O'Mara* (Dublin, 1961). Fogarty had been a particularly outspoken critic of the British government for imprisoning Irish Volunteers during 1917. NLI, Sinn Féin pamphlet collection, flyer 60.

191. Michael Laffan, *The resurrection of Ireland* (Cambridge, 1999), 177–179.

192. Laffan, *Resurrection of Ireland*, 199.

193. *Nationality*, 9 Mar., 23 Mar., 30 Mar., 6 Apr., 20 Apr. 1918. Addresses of welcome to Griffith issued by Sinn Féin branches in Strabane, Bundoran, Cavan and Waterford can be found in NLI, Griffith papers, acc.4476, box b.

194. *Nationality*, 19 Jan. 1918, p.1.

195. *Nationality*, 19 Jan. 1918, p.1; *Nationality*, 2 Mar. 1918, p.1; *Nationality*, 27 Apr. 1918, p.1.

196. *Nationality*, 2 Feb., 9 Feb., 13 Apr. 1918.

197. William O'Brien, Desmond Ryan (eds) *Devoy's post bag*, 2 (Dublin, 1953), 520–522.

198. The recollections of Kevin O'Shiel regarding the respective roles of the Irish Party and Sinn Féin in organising this development are instructive. NAI, Bureau of Military History papers, WS1170.

199. *Nationality*, 27 Apr. 1918, p.1.

200. *Nationality*, 4 May 1918, p.1.

201. *Young Ireland*, 19 Feb. 1918.

202. *Nationality*, 27 Apr. 1918, p.1; *Nationality*, 18 May 1918, p.1; *Nationality*, 25 May 1918, p.1 (on Carson); *Nationality*, 1 June 1918 (editorial, including comment on Devoy).

203. Sinn Féin leaders such as DeValera, MacNeill, Plunkett, Sean T. O'Kelly, W.T. Cosgrave, Sean Milroy and Joseph McGuinness addressed meetings in Cavan in favour of Griffith (*Nationality*, 4 May, 18 May 1918), while Irish Party leaders such as John Dillon, Stephen Gwynn, John Muldoon, J.P. Boland, David Sheehy, Tom O'Donnell, John O'Connor and William Doris addressed meetings in Cavan in opposition to Griffith (*Nationality*, 11 May, 18 May 1918).

204. This was Joseph Dowling. His arrival in Ireland at this time, with a letter supposedly from the German government apologising to Sinn Féin for failing to provide support for the 1916 rising, was a very strange episode that did Sinn Féin harm. NAI, Bureau of Military History papers, WS1170 (Kevin O'Shiel). Despite its incredibility, Dowling's case would also become a subject for agitations by Irish political prisoner organisations, especially Art O'Brien's new 'Roger Casement Central Branch' of Sinn Féin in London. Regarding Dowling, see the references to him in NLI, Art O'Brien Papers Collection List No.150.

205. *Nationality*, 25 May 1918, p.1.

206. UCD Archives, MacNeill papers, LA1/G/371, p118.

207. *Nationality*, 25 May 1918, p.1, 1 June 1918, p.1.

CHAPTER EIGHT

1. Sinn Féin leaders such as DeValera, MacNeill, Plunkett, Sean T. O'Kelly, W.T. Cosgrave, Sean Milroy and Joseph McGuinness addressed meetings in Cavan in favour of Griffith (*Nationality*, 4 May, 18 May 1918), while Irish Party leaders such as John Dillon, Stephen Gwynn, John Muldoon, J.P. Boland, David Sheehy, Tom O'Donnell, John O'Connor and William Doris addressed meetings in Cavan in opposition to Griffith (*Nationality*, 11 May, 18 May 1918).

2. Griffith had not been sure of victory ('we awaited the result with some anxiety') but he had felt confident that voters would not 'be intimidated or duped' by Lord Londonderry's support of the rival Irish Party candidate whilst claiming that the British government was willing to surrender to the principle of Irish self-government. NLI, Griffith papers, acc.4476, box b, letter to Thomas Martin, 22 Jul. 1918.

3. *Nationality*, 29 June 1918. Michael Laffan, *The resurrection of Ireland* (Cambridge, 1999), 147–148. Dillon absolutely hated Griffith for having 'poured forth a torrent of the most disgusting and infamous abuse and calumny of the Irish Party'. Griffith defeated J.F. O'Hanlon by 3,785 votes to 2,581 in mid-June.

4. NLI, Griffith papers, acc.4476, box b, letters to John Murphy (manager of *Nationality*), 22 and 26 Jun. 1918 (incomplete); letter to Thomas Martin, 22 Jul. 1918; letter dated 23 Aug. 1918 to an unidentified Gaelic Leaguer.

5. R.B. McDowell, *The Irish Convention 1917–1918* (London, 1970), 55.

6. Patrick Maume, 'William St. John Broderick, 1st Earl of Midleton (1856–1942)', *Dictionary of Irish Biography*, 1 (Cambridge, 2009), 860–863.

7. Peter Martin, *Irish peers 1909–1924* (unpublished MA, UCD, 1998), 132–135, 162–170.

8. *Irish Times*, 26 Nov. 1909.

9. Peter Martin, *Irish peers*, 139.

10. Harold Perkin, *The rise of professional society: England since 1880* (London, 1989).

11. Roy Douglas, *Land, people and politics: a history of the land question in the United Kingdom 1878–1952* (London, 1976). On this theme, see also chapter four.

12. Peter Martin, *Irish peers* (unpublished MA, UCD, 1998), 10–12. Lord Killanin of Galway led this protest.

13. Many historians have accepted the historic view in some Irish Party circles of the IRB that it was a manifestation of 'Young England' inspired 'Young Ireland' anti-liberalism. James Quinn, 'John Mitchel and the rejection of the nineteenth century', *Eire Ireland*, 38 (fall/winter 2003), 90–108; Patrick Maume, 'Young Ireland, Arthur Griffith and republican ideology', *Eire Ireland*, 34 (summer 1999), 155–174; Patrick Maume, 'The ancient constitution: Arthur Griffith and his intellectual legacy to Sinn Féin', *Irish Political Studies*, 10 (1995), 123–137; D.G. Boyce, *Nationalism in Ireland* (London, 1982), passim. What this 'liberalism' meant in the context of the time, however, is a highly debatable issue (support for Gladstone was not necessarily a liberal choice).

14. Martin, *Irish peers*, 11 (quoting Lord Killanin).

15. This responsibility was given to Fr. O'Flanagan in June 1918. See the account of the party's progress in *Programme of the Sinn Féin Ard Fheis, 29 Nov. 1918* (Dublin, 1918).

16. *Nationality*, 1 June 1918 (editorial). O'Kelly, a literary man and experienced journalist with very many newspapers (including the *Leinster Leader* and *Freeman's Journal*), once attempted to form a branch of Sinn Féin in Naas. Patrick Maume, 'Seamus O'Kelly (1875–1918)', *Dictionary of Irish Biography*, 7 (Cambridge, 2009).

17. NLI, Sinn Féin pamphlet collection, especially flyers 55–60.
18. Michael Laffan, *The resurrection of Ireland: the Sinn Féin Party 1916–1923* (Cambridge, 1999), chapter 6.
19. Ronan Fanning, *Fatal path* (Dublin, 2013).
20. *Nationality*, 16 Mar. 1918. It was noted, however, that the Attorney General for England and Commander-in-Chief of the British army in Ireland were at Redmond's graveside.
21. Patrick Maume, 'Patrick O'Donnell (1856–1927)', *Dictionary of Irish Biography*, 7 (Cambridge, 2009), 397–399.
22. Peter Martin, *Irish peers* (unpublished MA, UCD, 1998), 163–165.
23. Frank Callanan, 'John Dillon (1851–1927)', *Dictionary of Irish Biography*, 3 (Cambridge, 2009), 296–302.
24. The Earl of Longford and T.P. O'Neill, *Eamon DeValera* (Dublin, 1970), 72–74; NAI, Bureau of Military History papers, WS1170 (Kevin O'Shiel).
25. Dillon viewed this development as something that he and the Catholic hierarchy had arranged between them. Patrick Maume, *The long gestation* (Dublin, 1999), 206.
26. Letters of Fr. O'Flanagan to the *Freeman's Journal* and the *Leader*, quoted in Paul Bew, *Ireland* (Oxford, 2007), 387.
27. *Sinn Féin*, 10 Jan. 1914 (editorial).
28. *Nationality*, 2 Nov. 1918, 9 Nov. 1918 (quote).
29. Aodh de Blacam, *Towards the Republic* (London and Dublin, 1918). Later, de Blacam worked for the *Irish Times*.
30. Michael Doorley, *Irish-American diaspora nationalism: the Friends of Irish Freedom* (Dublin, 2005), 52.
31. David Fitzpatrick, *Harry Boland's Irish revolution* (Cork, 2003), 103–110.
32. *Programme for Sinn Féin Ard Fheis 29 Oct. 1918* (Dublin, 1918), resolutions no. 6b, 22, 47 and 50.
33. Professor John [Eoin] MacNeill, 'War and reconstruction: Irish settlement', *English Review* (Sep. 1917), 252–262.
34. Eoin MacNeill, *Daniel O'Connell and Sinn Féin* (Dublin, n.d.).
35. NAI, Bureau of Military History papers, WS205 (Maud Griffith).
36. *Nationality*, 15 Feb. 1919, p.1. In this literary tradition, see also Michael Collins, *The path to freedom* (Dublin, 1922).
37. *Nationality*, 23 Nov. 1918, p.1.
38. For biographical information on Burke, see his obituary for Pierce McCann in *Nationality*, 15 Mar. 1919 and his autobiographical article 'Suspect' in *Young Ireland*, 24 Dec. 1921.
39. *Nationality*, 13 Dec, 21 Dec (quote), 28 Dec. 1918 .
40. Archbishop Walsh to an unidentified newspaper 4 Dec. 1918, quoted in *Nationality* editorial, 7 Dec. 1918.
41. *Nationality*, 30 Nov. 1918, p1; *Nationality*, 7 Dec. 1918, p.1; *Nationality*, 14 Dec. 1918, p.1.
42. *Nationality*, 23 Nov. 1918, p1 Incidentally, A.W. Samuels retained his seat as representative of the University of Dublin (Trinity College), where no nationalist candidates ran.
43. Field would continue to represent meat traders' concerns on this body up until 1932. Patrick Maume, 'William Field (1843–1935)', *Dictionary of Irish Biography*, 3 (Cambridge, 2009), 774–775.
44. Sean Collins, 'Frank Thornton (1891–1965)', *Dictionary of Irish Biography*, 9 (Cambridge, 2009), 358–359. For Collins' use of Field's name, see his IRB correspondence with Boland in UCD Archives, DeValera papers, P150/1125.
45. This meant that even if they desired to take their parliamentary seats at Westminster they could not.

46. *Nationality*, 4 Jan. 1919, p.1.
47. Westminster Diocesan Archives, BO1/72, Cardinal Logue to James O'Connor (copy), 1 Mar. 1918. O'Connor, an Irish Party supporter, had been prised to become Attorney General for Ireland during 1914 before his candidacy was dismissed by Asquith; a source of grievance to Dillon and Redmond.
48. The degree to which the clergy had sided with Sinn Féin in expressing their attitude towards the question of conscription had led Walter Long, who replaced Lloyd George as head of the cabinet's 'Irish committee', to consider arresting clergymen alongside Sinn Féiners in May 1918. This led the Irish hierarchy to issue a protest to the government via the Catholic Cardinal of Westminster. Westminster Diocesan Archives, BO1/72, Cardinal Bourne to Walter Long, 17 May 1918 (copy).
49. Bertram Windle, the president of University College Cork, felt strongly that the hierarchy (especially a Bishop Kelly) were responsible for splitting and destroying the Irish Party, regarding which he noted bitterly that 'God may forgive him. I never will.' Westminster Diocesan Archives, BO 1/72, Bertram Windle to Cardinal Bourne, 29 Aug. 1918. On the same theme, see Owen McGee, 'David Sheehy (1844–1932)', *Dictionary of Irish Biography*, 8 (Cambridge, 2009), 886–887. As with many party political attitudes, Windle's irrational anger was essentially rooted in questions of patronage: now that the NUI Chancellor Archbishop Walsh had gone pro-Sinn Féin, Windle's days as the president of UCC were numbered. Nevertheless, there was a strong likelihood that many Irish Party supporters who had formerly achieved influence, employment and patronage through its political networks would do all they could to sabotage Sinn Féiners' challenge to their social status, just as many Sinn Féiners would desire to use politics as a means to supplant Irish Party members' social prestige.
50. NLI, Thomas Martin papers, Ms 15790, Cole to Martin, 21 Jan. 1919.
51. Peter Martin, *Irish peers* (unpublished MA, UCD, 1998), 169–170.
52. Bridget Hourican, 'Arthur Kenlis Maxwell (1879–1957)', *Dictionary of Irish Biography*, 6 (Cambridge, 2009), 446.
53. Although largely protected in prison from the deadly influenza epidemic that was affecting many at the time, Griffith noted that his good friend Joseph MacBride (brother of John), 'the oldest of the prisoners here', and Denis McCullough had caught a slight dose, were not well and, on the whole, 'it is a very sick and tired atmosphere'. To keep fit and to relieve boredom, Griffith frequently played handball with Desmond Fitzgerald, wrote sonnets with Sean McEntee, admired the architecture of Gloucester Cathedral from his prison cell window and tried (with some success, for the first time) to learn the Irish language. NLI, Griffith papers, acc.4476, box b, letter from Gloucester Prison to James Starkey, 17 Oct. 1918.
54. NLI, Griffith papers, acc.4476, box b, letter of Edward Duffy, election agent in Cavan, to Griffith, 6 Dec. 1918.
55. NLI, Thomas Martin papers, Ms 15790, Griffith to Martin from Gloucester Prison, 16 Jul. 1918; MS5943, Griffith to Lily Williams, 19 June 1918; NLI, Griffith papers, acc.4476, box b, letter of 2 November 1918 and draft of a letter 'to the editor Gloucester *Diamond*'. He won 10,442 votes in Tyrone, defeating the unionist candidate (who won 7,696 votes).
56. Letter of Griffith, dated 23 Jan. 1919, reproduced in an article by Máire Comerford in *Irish Times*, 26 Jan. 1969.
57. Secret programme of Griffith reproduced in article in *Irish Times*, 26 Jan. 1969.
58. Secret programme of Griffith reproduced in article in *Irish Times*, 26 Jan. 1969.
59. Secret programme of Griffith reproduced in article in *Irish Times*, 26 Jan. 1969.
60. *Nationality*, 11 Jan. 1919, p.1.

61. Secret programme of Griffith reproduced in article in *Irish Times*, 26 Jan. 1969.

62. This was during Egan's tenure as US minister for Chile (1888–1892). Owen McGee, 'Patrick Egan (1841–1919)', *Dictionary of Irish Biography*, 3 (Cambridge, 2009), 592–593.

63. Owen McGee, 'Joseph Patrick MacDonnell (1842–1908)', *Dictionary of Irish Biography*, 5 (Cambridge, 2009).

64. Secret programme of Griffith reproduced in article in *Irish Times*, 26 Jan. 1969.

65. Secret programme of Griffith reproduced in article in *Irish Times*, 26 Jan. 1969.

66. Fitzpatrick, *Harry Boland's Irish revolution*, 114–116.

67. NLI, Art O'Brien papers, Ms8426/41, DeValera to O Briain, 25 Mar. 1919; Westminster Diocesan Archives, Cardinal Bourne papers, BO5/36a (flyer of the Catholic Union of Great Britain); BO5/87(1), untitled press cuttings on the same theme.

68. Emmet Larkin, *The Roman Catholic Church and the making of the Irish state 1878–1886* (Dublin, 1975).

69. NLI, Griffith papers, acc.4476, box b, DeValera to Brugha, 1 March 1919.

70. Patrick Maume, 'Timothy Corcoran (1872–1943)', *Dictionary of Irish Biography*, 2 (Cambridge, 2009), 848–849.

71. Kathleen Clarke, *Revolutionary woman* (Dublin, 1991), 141–142.

72. The fact that DeValera's confidential letter to Brugha ended up in the Griffith family's possession may indicate that Brugha did not agree with DeValera's stance on the IRB. Kathleen Clarke (*Revolutionary woman*, p142) implies that Brugha later realised that it was a mistake to argue after 1916 that 'the IRB must go!' and so abandoned that stance. The posthumous writings on Brugha by Sceilg played a large part in substantiating the idea, however, that the IRB and Brugha were perpetually at loggerheads because the former was a sinister cabal.

73. NLI, Griffith papers, acc.4476, box b, DeValera to Brugha, 1 March 1919.

74. NLI, Sinn Féin pamphlet collection, flyer no.73 (an Irish Party flyer in criticism of Sinn Féin) The Irish Party also produced a pamphlet at this time called *The vagaries of Sinn Féin* (Dublin, 1918) which typified the Sinn Féin Policy as an invention of Maud Gonne twenty years previously that had achieved and could achieve nothing. The Sinn Féin counter argument (NLI, Sinn Féin pamphlet collection, flyer no.86) was that the British cabinet could claim to speak on behalf of the Irish Party so long as it sat in Westminster and this was precisely why it was now necessary to abstain from Westminster if Ireland was to have an independent voice at the Peace Conference.

75. Tom Dunne (ed.) *The National University of Ireland 1908–2008* (Dublin, 2008), 133–136.

76. DeValera's membership of the IRB (who would nickname him 'Dev') c.Nov.1914–Apr.1916 being the chief difference.

77. *Nationality*, 11 Jan. 1919, p.1.

78. NLI, Art O'Brien papers, Ms8426/41, DeValera to O Briain, 25 Mar. 1919 (quote).

79. A useful survey of this trend is Benjamin Grob-Fitzgibbon, *Turning points of the Irish revolution* (New York, 2007). A common, but mistaken, idea is to attribute the beginning of these developments to the activities of Ernest O'Malley's circle (Dan Breen and Sean Treacy) due to their having taken an offensive on the same day as the Dáil first met.

80. The degree to which this was common is evident from many of the recollections of junior volunteers in the Bureau of Military History witness statements. Their local commanders evidently made these decisions based purely upon an assessment of their own situation or locality (surrounding towns and villages) rather than nationwide considerations or from following orders of a disciplined national command.

81. A good source for Clarke's personality in this regard is his correspondence in the John Daly papers at the University of Limerick, as well as his reflections in his prison memoirs

on Orangemen whom he knew in prison. These prison memoirs were first published in *Irish Freedom* and were later republished by P.S. O'Hegarty in book format as *Glimpses of an Irish felon's prison life* (Dublin, 1922).

82. Marie Coleman, William Murphy, 'Diarmuid O'Hegarty (1892–1958)', *Dictionary of Irish Biography*, 7 (Cambridge, 2009), 541–542.
83. *Nationality*, 4 May 1918.
84. This was the London office of the Guaranty Trust Company of New York, where Collins worked from July 1914-December 1915 before he moved to Dublin. W.T. Cosgrave, 'Michael Collins (1890–1922)', *Dictionary of National Biography 1922–1930* (Oxford, 1937), 199–200. Collins worked as a clerk in the West Kensington Post Office Savings Bank from 1906–1910 before working for a London stockbroker (1910–14). He had joined the IRB in 1909 via the London GAA.
85. M.A. Hopkinson, 'Michael Collins (1890–1922)', *Dictionary of Irish Biography*, 2 (Cambridge, 2009).
86. Earl of Longford, T.P. O'Neill, *Eamon DeValera* (Dublin, 1970), 96.
87. NLI, Art O'Brien Papers Collection List No.150, section IV.ii.5–7.
88. NLI, Art O'Brien Papers Collection List No.150, section IV.ii.5.
89. During the mid-1880s, amongst laymen, Michael Davitt, Eugene Davis, Alec Sullivan, John Sweetman and John Boyle O'Reilly were among the most notable individuals responsible for forming these links. The *Times* propaganda campaign launched against Sullivan for being an alleged terrorist ally of Parnell ('the dynamite war') was a cover for the British consulate's distaste for the American Catholic Church and its desire to discredit it and negate its political influence in America (reputedly, this factor had previously played a part in the demise of Thomas D'Arcy McGee). Nevertheless, Irish historians to this day have uncritically accepted the *Times* judgement and understanding of everything from the 'dynamite war' to the *Times* Commission and the murder of Dr. Cronin due to the extent of British academic writings on the subject and Irish historians' lack of research upon American Catholic history.
90. *Nationality*, 15 Mar. 1919, p.1; 29 Mar. 1919 (editorial), 24 May 1919, p.1 (quote from Ian MacPherson, Chief Secretary); 7 June 1919 (quoting the *Freeman's Journal* and *Irish Times*).
91. Brugha was appointed as the Dáil's nominal 'minister of defence'. Having been wounded in 1916 and an IRB organiser prior to that, Brugha had the reputation of being a military man but he was far more of a no-nonsense businessman (his Lalor candle factory had a complete monopoly over all Catholic Church candle usage in Ireland) who was well suited temperamentally to acting like a party whip. His mission, shared by his associate in Dublin Catholic confraternities 'Sceilg' (J.J. O'Kelly, who was appointed chairman for most Dáil sessions), was less to defend the Dáil militarily (there was no such established, or sitting, body to defend) than to defend it administratively, issuing orders to all Irish Volunteer and Sinn Féin circles to begin transacting their business more through the Dáil's channels (meaning communicating with either Diarmuid O'Hegarty or a few departmental secretaries) rather than through their own organisations. Griffith particularly admired Brugha, an old friend who maintained a personal yet good-natured rivalry with Griffith ever since their days as mutual sparring partners in amateur Dublin boxing tournaments twenty years previously (NLI, Griffith papers, acc.4476, box b, letter of Senator Michael Hayes to Nevin Griffith B.L. (Griffith's son), 29 Sep. 1950), for his enabling work in this regard.
92. *Nationality*, 30 Aug. 1919 (report of Sinn Féin Party secretaries and treasurers at the party's national convention).

93. *Nationality*, 25 Jan. 1919 (article entitled 'Ireland and President Wilson').

94. *Nationality*, 22 Feb. 1919.

95. See, for instance, the manner in which the minutes of the Sinn Féin central branch were kept during 1912–1913. UCD Archives, P163/1, Sinn Féin minute books (1912–1913).

96. The Government Stationary Office, *Dáil Eireann, miontuaric an chead Dala 1919–1921* (Dublin, 1994).

97. The paper announced in both April and June 1919 that Griffith would soon resume his editorship. It appears that he certainly resumed this responsibility by August, when the paper doubled in size, although this may well have been done in only a part-time fashion with its hitherto acting editor (J.J. Burke) and sub-editor (Sean Milroy) continuing to do much of the work.

98. 'Export of Irish money', *Nationality*, 25 Jan. 1919.

99. Patrick Maume, *The long gestation*; Laffan, *Resurrection of Ireland*, 16–17, 214, 223 (quote)-224.

100. 'Ireland and Sweden', *Nationality*, 9 Aug. 1919.

101. *Nationality*, 23 Aug. 1919.

102. Griffith's figures here were slightly out of date, as they dated from 1914. He cited the value of Britain's trade with various countries as follows: USA (£173 million), Ireland (£135 million), Germany (£70 million), France (£63 million), Holland (£38 million), Russia (£32 million), Belgium (£24 million), Spain (£21 million), Italy (£21 million), Japan (£12.5 million), Austria-Hungary (£7 million) and Portugal (£6 million). *Nationality*, 12 Jul. 1919 (these figures were first reproduced in an article entitled 'Irish trade' in *Nationality*, 22 Apr. 1916).

103. 'Sinn Féin', *Nationality*, 12 July 1919.

104. 'Free trade', *Nationality*, 16 Aug. 1919. The deliberate shut down of Cork–USA shipping routes by Britain prior to the First World War in favour of Southampton was continued and was seen by Griffith as deliberate effort to prevent the opening of Irish trading routes. Cork was one area that certainly did not do well financially out of the First World War. John Borgonovo, *The dynamics of war and revolution* (Cork, 2013), 156–160.

105. Speeches of Griffith made at monster rallies held in Cootehill and Ballyjamesduff, Co. Cavan, *Nationality*, 5 Apr. 1919, 16 Aug. 1919 (quote).

106. *Nationality*, 19 Jan. 1918, p.1.

107. *Nationality*, 6 Sep. 1919, p.6.

108. 'Sinn Féin!', *Nationality*, 12 Jul. 1919.

109. Sylvester Ó Muirí, *The state and the sea fisheries of the south and west coasts of Ireland 1922–1972* (Dublin, 2013), introduction.

110. *Nationality*, 19 July 1919; *Nationality*, 2 Aug. 1919, p.1. 'The Reconstruction and Federation of Irish Industries Ltd' was one such firm. This was quite possibly an indication that Ireland was perceived by the general business community across the United Kingdom to be in a state of instability.

111. Ads for Duggan's company began to appear in *Nationality* in early March 1919. Thereafter, dubious sounding firms such as 'Taxes Recovery Ltd' were established, which advised people to send all their bank account details in the post in advance of a consultation.

112. *Nationality*, 22 Feb. 1919.

113. *Nationality*, 9 Aug. 1919.

114. *Nationality*, 9 Aug. 1919.

115. *Nationality*, 23 Aug. 1919.

116. The Government Stationary Office, *Dáil Eireann, miontuaric an chead Dala 1919–1921* (Dublin, 1994), 120–123. Sean Etchingham, Alderman Thomas Kelly, Alderman Walter

Cole and Darrel Figgis led these departments, although the latter was essentially a literary man only. All had been associated with Sinn Féin since 1906. This was also true of the principal European counsels Sean T. O'Kelly and Gavan Duffy. Nominally in support of the commission on resources, P.S. O'Hegarty's new 'Irish Book Shop' on Dawson Street was involved in drawing up proposed reading material for members of all Sinn Féin branches, which included studies on proportional representation and how to analyse the performance of local industries. NLI, Sinn Féin pamphlet collection, flyers 91, 97 and 100.

117. *Nationality*, 30 Aug. 1919.
118. L.W. White, 'Joseph MacDonagh (1883–1922)', *Dictionary of Irish Biography*, 5 (Cambridge, 2009), 917–919.
119. The Government Stationary Office, *Dáil Eireann, miontuaric an chead Dala 1919–1921* (Dublin, 1994), 127–131.
120. UCD Archives, DeValera papers, P150/727, Griffith to DeValera, 29 Aug. 1919.
121. *Nationality*, 30 Aug. 1919; Government Stationary Office, *Dáil Eireann*, 132–150. Collins also wrote to DeValera regarding the Fenian bonds. UCD Archives, DeValera papers, P150/726, letter 6 Oct.1919.
122. UCD Archives, DeValera papers, P150/726, Griffith to DeValera, 8 Dec. 1919.
123. UCD Archives, DeValera papers, P150/727, DeValera to Griffith, 9 Aug. 1919. This reflected the fact that President Wilson had responded to a US senate declaration that Versailles should be willing to hear DeValera, Griffith and Plunkett by stating to an Irish-American delegation that the American government 'could not take up the case of Ireland officially'. *Nationality*, 21 June 1919, p.1.
124. Plunkett's initiative had led to the formation of the Irish Dominion League, although this was almost universally considered a mere propagandistic exercise that meant nothing in practice.
125. UCD Archives, DeValera papers, P150/727, DeValera to Griffith, 28 June, 9 Aug. 1919 (quote), 13 Aug., 19 Aug. 1919. Griffith sent him such material on 29 July, 8 August and 18 August with cover letters.
126. UCD Archives, DeValera papers, P150/727, DeValera to Griffith, 13 Aug., 21 Aug. 1919.
127. *Nationality*, 9 Aug., 30 Aug. 1919, p.1 (quote).
128. Griffith's speech at a monster rally in Ballyjamesduff, Co. Cavan, *Nationality*, 16 Aug. 1919. *Nationality* had adopted this tone since January 1919 under J.J. Burke's acting editorship.
129. 'The coming of America', *Nationality*, 2 Aug. 1919.
130. 'England, Ireland and America', *Nationality*, 16 Aug. 1919.
131. 'The Paris conference', *Nationality*, 21 June 1919. This was essentially the first article in *Nationality* to admit that President Wilson was not going to champion Ireland's cause.
132. 'The American delegation', *Nationality*, 10 May 1919.
133. Michael Laffan, *The resurrection of Ireland*, 223.
134. Michael Laffan, *The resurrection of Ireland*, 214.
135. 'The perils of Europe', *Nationality*, 16 Aug. 1919.
136. *Nationality*, 23 Aug. 1919, p.2.
137. *Nationality*, 23 Aug. 1919, p.2.
138. *Nationality*, 30 Aug. 1919 (report on meeting of Dáil Eireann).
139. NLI, McKenna Napoli papers, Ms22738, statement of Griffith on the suppression of the Dáil, Sept 1919; Ms22739, 'presidential statement' of Griffith at Sinn Féin Ard Fheis, 25 Nov. 1919.
140. In this he was quoting a French economist, Leon Polier. *Nationality*, 16 Aug. 1919.

141. 'The financial boycott of Ireland', *Nationality*, 9 Aug.1919.
142. UCD Archives, DeValera papers, P150/726, Collins to DeValera, letters Dec.1919–Feb.1920.
143. *Nationality*, 5 July 1919, p.3.

CHAPTER NINE

1. Arthur Mitchell, *Revolutionary government in Ireland: Dáil Eireann 1919–1922* (Dublin, 1995), 347.
2. Ronan Fanning, *Fatal path* (Dublin, 2013), 274–275.
3. Griffith made the 'presidential statement' at the Sinn Féin Ard Fheis on 25 November 1919. NLI, Kathleen McKenna Napoli papers, Ms22739.
4. *Nationality*, 30 Aug. 1919; The Government Stationary Office, *Dáil Eireann, miontuaric an chead Dala 1919–1921* (Dublin, 1994), 149, 154–155.
5. T. Duff, J. Hegarty, M. Hussey, *The story of the Dublin Institute of Technology* (Dublin, 2000), 1–13; James Cooke, 'Louis Ely O'Carroll 1863–1943' (unpublished article, courtesy of author).
6. NLI, Sinn Féin pamphlet collection, flyers 61 and 88.
7. A Catholic secret society known as the 'Irish Vigilance Club' was established after the formation of Dáil Eireann to mobilise Catholics against a 'subtle plot' of 'the ultra nationalists' to undermine 'faith and fatherland' in Ireland by overlooking the need to rely on exclusively Catholic channels (NLI, Sweetman papers, Ms47592/1). It is likely that many Catholic fraternities felt similarly, to a greater or lesser extent.
8. Owen McGee, 'Fred Allan (1861–1937)', *Dublin Historical Record*, 56, no.2 (autumn 2003), 211–213; Patrick Maume, 'William Field (1843–1935)', *Dictionary of Irish Biography*, 3 (Cambridge, 2009), 774–775.
9. Sheila Carden, *The Alderman: Alderman Thomas Kelly and Dublin Corporation* (Dublin, 2007), 163, 187–188. Kelly was the brother of Alderman Kelly. The offices of Michael Staines' Irish National Assurance Company were likewise sacked.
10. As Cosgrave noted, the Irish Volunteers were 'later known popularly, though erroneously, as the "Irish republican army"'. W.T. Cosgrave, 'Michael Collins (1890–1922)', *Dictionary of National Biography 1922–1930* (Oxford, 1937), 200.
11. 'Fenians' became a nickname in the British press for nationalists in Ireland after 1865, although the only 'Fenians' of the time were a public and entirely legal freemason style movement in the United States, the Fenian Brotherhood. This was a separate organisation to all nationalist movement within Ireland, including the secret Irish revolutionary brotherhood. On this theme, see Owen McGee, 'Soldiers and propagandists: the impact of the American Fenian Brotherhood on Irish politics', *History Studies*, 8 (2007), 1–16.
12. This decision was taken on 19 August 1919 and the debate on the decision was illustrative of its meaning. The Government Stationary Office, *Dáil Eireann, miontuaric an chead Dala 1919–1921* (Dublin, 1994), 151–153.
13. W.T. Cosgrave, 'Michael Collins (1890–1922)', *Dictionary of National Biography 1922–1930* (Oxford, 1937), 200.
14. NLI, Sinn Féin pamphlet collection, flyers nos.106 (mentioning Dáil decrees of 10 Apr. 1919), 108 and 111. As the volunteers were very poorly equipped, Brugha also worked to import arms. This was a task for which Collins offered him some purely logistical

assistance in his capacity as the volunteers' intelligence officer. NAI, Bureau of Military History papers, WS767 (Patrick Moylett).

15. Richard Sinnott, *Irish voters decide* (Manchester, 1995), 27–28.

16. *Sinn Féin*, 9 Nov. 1912 (editorial).

17. UCD Archives, DeValera papers, P150/727, DeValera to Griffith, cablegram Jan. 1920.

18. NLI, Kathleen McKenna Napoli papers, Ms22736-7.

19. NLI, Kathleen McKenna Napoli papers, Ms22739 (statement of Griffith at the November 1919 Ard Fheis).

20. NLI, Art O'Brien papers, Ms8427/45 (Collins correspondence for Nov.-Dec.1919). The sister in question was a Mrs. Newman who lived in South Kensington. Later, the London Office met in the private home of J.P. McDonnell, the solicitor of the Irish Self-Determination League. NAI, Bureau of Military History papers, WS860 (Elizabeth McGinley, formerly Lily Brennan, secretary to the London Office).

21. Patrick Maume, 'A nursery of editors: the Cork Free Press 1910–1916', *History Ireland*, 15, no.2 (Mar/Apr.2007), 42–46. The *Cork Free Press* was the successor of the *Cork Accent* as the organ of William O'Brien MP in support of the All-for-Ireland League.

22. That this was the principal business of the London Office, alongside working for Irish political prisoners in Britain via solicitor J.P. McDonnell, is shown by the contents of the Art O'Brien Papers in the National Library of Ireland.

23. Ronan Fanning, *The Irish Department of Finance 1922-1958* (Dublin, 1978), 7–13; John McColgan, *British policy and the Irish administration 1920-1922* (Dublin, 1983).

24. William Sheehan, *Fighting for Dublin: the British battle for Dublin 1919-1921* (Cork, 2007), 10–11. O'Malley directed Dan Breen and Sean Treacy who, also without authority from the Irish Volunteer executive, committed outrages at Soloheadbeg, Co. Tipperary on 21 January 1919 (the same day as the Dáil first met); an event which O'Malley later cited as marking the beginning of 'the IRA war' for Irish independence; an attitude that would ultimately shape a lot of people's sense of the history of the time.

25. Collins was correct about what Bell was doing. John McColgan, *British policy and the Irish administration 1920-1922* (Dublin, 1983), 10. For a description of Collins' work in this regard, see Ronan Fanning, *The Irish Department of Finance 1922-1958* (Dublin, 1978), chapter one.

26. NLI, Art O'Brien Papers Collection List No.150, IV.ii.1, VI.i, introduction.

27. NLI, Art O'Brien papers, Ms8432/8 (souvenir booklet for this event). See also Ms8421/10–11, Ms8425/28 and Ms8433/51.

28. Elizabeth McGinley, who worked as secretary of the Dáil's London Office, recalled that McGrath was an occasional caller there, whereas Sam Maguire was a daily caller on the office and the regulator of all courier work between Dublin and the London Office and was also in charge of the local Irish Volunteers/IRA (NAI, Bureau of Military History papers, WS860). However, the actual surviving papers of the London Office (NLI, Art O'Brien papers) indicate that Sean McGrath, who went under various aliases, performed all the work she ascribed to Maguire, who does not feature in the O'Brien papers at all. They were evidently two different men, however. Maguire died in Cork in 1927 whereas McGrath was still alive to make a statement to the Military Service Pensions scheme during the mid-1930s. Maguire was evidently an assistant of McGrath, as was William (Liam) McCarthy (his letters survive in the O'Brien papers). Later, Maguire and McCarthy would have GAA trophies named after them.

29. The papers of the Irish Self-Determination League of Great Britain and the British wing of Sinn Féin can be found in NLI, Art O'Brien papers. In founding a Sinn Féin Party

organisation in Britain during 1918, the work of Sean Milroy (also chief Sinn Féin's spokesman on the Ulster question) seems to have differed from past work by the likes of P.S. O'Hegarty in founding Sinn Féin clubs in Britain in that the latter were not a part, or an extension, of an Irish party organisation.

30. These included Arthur Lynch's English Republican League of 1917 and the English Republican Brotherhood (ERB) of the early 1870s (republicanism, generally associated with the still revolutionary notion of democracy, was popular with liberal-minded English university students, including a young John Morley, at that time owing to a sense of excitement at events in France). The most notable example of Irish radicalisms within English political organisations was the Home Rule Confederation of Great Britain (1873–1882), which not only launched the careers of T.P. O'Connor, T.M. Healy and C.S. Parnell but also had a republican press during the early-to-mid 1870s. Alan O'Day, 'The political organisation of the Irish in Britain 1867–90', Swift, Gilley (eds) *The Irish in Britain 1815–1939* (London, 1989), 193–198. On a similar theme, see Alan O'Day, *The English face of Irish nationalism* (London, 1977).

31. Sam Davies, 'A stormy political career: P.J. Kelly and Irish nationalism and labour politics in Liverpool, 1891–1936', *Transactions of the Historic Society of Lancashire & Cheshire*, vol.148 (1999), 147–189. *Irish Times*, 2 Dec. 1936 (obituary for P.J. Kelly). Kelly was a native of Tyrone who had first entered politics during 1891 as a member of Mark Ryan's (Parnellite) Irish National League of Great Britain. In this capacity, he came to know Griffith slightly during the 1890s.

32. Patrick Maume, 'Charles Diamond (1858–1934)', *Dictionary of Irish Biography*, 3 (Cambridge, 2009), 250–252.

33. The republican-style political rebellion against the organisation of the UIL in both Ireland and Britain during the First World War—represented by the actions of the likes of Tom Clarke and Arthur Griffith in Dublin, and Art O'Brien and Michael Collins in London— seems to have been the essential basis, or impetus, of the IRB's political reorganisation after 1916.

34. Westminster Diocesan Archives, Cardinal Bourne papers, BO5/87 (2).

35. The fact that Sean MacGrath, its very active national organiser, was a railway station foreman by day and a member of the IRB did not do much to establish a political profile for the organisation.

36. NLI, Art O'Brien papers, Ms8427/18 (quote). Other of O'Brien's communications with the Scottish nationalists can be found in Ms8426/17, Ms8433/28, Ms8448/7, Ms8426/19, Ms8418/7, Ms8435/27, Ms8421/21, Ms8460/49, Ms8428/21, Ms8429/16, Ms8436/19, Ms8432/30 and Ms8426/36.

37. Elaine McFarland, *John Ferguson* (East Lothian, 2003).

38. Cameron and Ferguson (Glasgow) printed virtually all the 'Young Ireland' books, as well as some IRB prison memoirs, that were available in Ireland during the period 1860–1900 after the collapse of James Duffy and Co. (Dublin). Ferguson was a Belfast Presbyterian by birth.

39. B.P. Murphy, *John Chartres: mystery man of the treaty* (Dublin, 1995), 18–22.

40. Bernard Porter, *Empire and Super Empire: Britain, America and the world* (Yale, 2006), 42.

41. Erskine Childers, *A strikebreaking army at work* (London, 1919). The *Daily Herald* attempted to interview Griffith after it published its own manifesto, 'a policy for Ireland', on 23 July 1920. NLI, Griffith papers, acc.4476, box b (draft of a handwritten list of points by Griffith in response to the *Daily Herald*).

42. On the *Daily News* during the 1880s, see Christy Campbell, *Fenian fire: the British government's plot to assassinate Queen Victoria* (London, 2000). Curiously, at the time of

his most militant editorials during January-March 1919, J.J. Burke frequently championed the *Daily News* in the pages of *Nationality*.

43. Erskine Childers, *Military rule in Ireland* (Dublin, 1920), 49 (quote).

44. NLI, Art O'Brien papers, Ms8429/11.

45. Erskine Childers, *Military rule in Ireland* (Talbot Press, Dublin, 1920). The French translation was published as *La terreur militaire en Irelande* (Paris, 1920) and the Spanish translation, which included a couple of additional articles, was published as *La tragedia de Irlanda* (Barcelona, 1920).

46. The Government Stationary Office, *Dáil Eireann, miontuaric an chead Dala 1919-1921* (Dublin, 1994), 78. On this occasion, in response to a query from Alderman Kelly, DeValera also argued that 'they had not yet an education or public health [ministry], but they should add them if they found it necessary'.

47. Bank of Ireland Archives, 'Synopsis of the decisions of the committee' (Irish Banks Standing Committee, 1925), 1–4.

48. Bank of Ireland Archives, 'Synopsis of the decisions of the committee' (Irish Banks Standing Committee, 1925), 1–4.

49. F.S.L. Lyons (ed.) *Bank of Ireland 1783-1983* (Dublin, 1983), 55–56.

50. Paul Rouse, Marc Duncan, *Handling change: a history of the Irish Bank Officials' Association* (Cork, 2012), 20–30; Irish Banks Standing Committee, *The control of banking in the Republic of Ireland* (Dublin, 1984), 139.

51. Irish Banks Standing Committee, *The control of banking in the Republic of Ireland* (Dublin, 1984), 140; Bank of Ireland Archives, 'Synopsis of the decisions of the committee' (Irish Banks Standing Committee, 1925), 4.

52. The Government Stationary Office, *Dáil Eireann, miontuaric an chead Dala 1919-1921* (Dublin, 1994), 157–166 (quote 158).

53. The Government Stationary Office, *Dáil Eireann, miontuaric an chead Dala 1919-1921* (Dublin, 1994), 167–186 (quote 179).

54. Marie Coleman, 'Kevin Roantree O'Sheil (1891–1970)', *Dictionary of Irish Biography*, 7 (Cambridge, 2009), 947–948. O'Shiel also authored *The Making of a Republic* (Dublin, 1920), a study of the foundation of the United States (with a final chapter on Ireland), a signed copy of which, dedicated to Griffith, can be found in NLI, Griffith papers, acc. 4476.

55. Daire Hogan, *The legal profession in Ireland 1789-1922* (Naas, 1986), 145.

56. Daire Hogan, *The legal profession in Ireland 1789-1922* (Naas, 1986), 144–150.

57. The Government Stationary Office, *Dáil Eireann, miontuaric an chead Dala 1919-1921* (Dublin, 1994), 180–183, 186.

58. Government Stationary Office, *Dáil Eireann*, 185.

59. Government Stationary Office, *Dáil Eireann*, 185.

60. NAI, Bureau of Military History papers, WS1170 (Kevin O'Sheil).

61. *Dáil Eireann, Debate on the Treaty between Great Britain and Ireland, signed in London on the 6th December 1921: Sessions 14 December 1921 to 10 January 1922* (Dublin, 1922), 151.

62. An undated press cutting (probably from the *Times* during the summer of 1920) regarding this Westminster debate can be found in NLI, Art O'Brien papers, Ms8432/10.

63. The recollections of Seamus Dobbyn, an Ulster IRB leader, are particularly instructive here. NAI, Bureau of Military History papers, WS279 (Seamus Dobbyn), pp12–18.

64. A good example of such activities can be found in the recollections of Frank Donnelly of Armagh City. NAI, Bureau of Military History papers, WS941 (Frank Donnelly).

65. NLI, Kathleen McKenna Napoli papers, Ms22743 (Griffith's statement on the Derry riots intended for publication, June 1920). In the light of this stance by the Dáil, Collins did not

appreciate the fact that the Catholic bishop of Cork, Daniel Cohalan, directly challenged the British government to set up an independent commission on the murder of Lord Mayor MacCurtain of Cork, which he believed would prove that Inspector Swanzy of the Special Branch, who was shot dead in Lisburn five months later, was behind the murder.

66. Churchill Archives, Lord Hankey papers, HNKY1/5, diary entry for 5 Oct. 1920 (pp155–156). Hankey also noted in his diary that Lloyd George had said that a couple of 'eminent Irish nationalists' in Westminster (i.e. Irish Party MPs) had told him in confidence regarding the reprisals that 'they ought not to be stopped' because they had a positive effect in manipulating public opinion to the British government's advantage.

67. The principal peers in question were Baron Anthony MacDonnell, a former leader of the Indian and Irish administrations, and Sir John R. O'Connell (PhD, NUI) who had recently written an extensive panegyric on behalf of British imperial administrations worldwide in his study 'The foundations of colonial self-government', *Society for the Statistical and Social Inquiry of Ireland* (1916–1917), 419–459. Among the NUI academics that now supported Plunkett were Professor Mary Hayden of the UCD History department. All these figures began attended meetings of Plunkett's association during the summer or autumn of 1920.

68. On this theme, see Hamilton Ffye, *T.P. O'Connor* (London, 1934), still the best biography of T.P. written to date.

69. NLI, Kathleen MacKenna Napoli Papers, Ms22739 and Ms22742 (quotes); Government Stationary Office, *Dáil Eireann*, statements of the acting president (Griffith) at each meeting from 1919–1920.

70. Griffith was inclined to make similar grandiose claims in private messages sent to DeValera. UCD, DeValera papers, P150/727, address of 17 Mar. 1920; NLI, Kathleen MacKenna Napoli papers, Ms22736.

71. Michael Doorley, *Irish-American diaspora nationalism: the Friends of Irish Freedom 1916–1935* (Dublin, 2005), 105–121.

72. Michael Funchion (ed.) *Irish-American voluntary organisations* (Greenport, 1983),185, 205. This trend began after 1886. It did not exist prior to 1884.

73. DeValera was sensitive regarding how Devoy's criticisms might be read in Dublin (UCD Archives, DeValera papers, P150/727, DeValera to Griffith, 17 Feb.1920) but Griffith would soon write a strong criticism to Devoy, arguing that he must stand by DeValera (UCD Archives, DeValera papers, P150/727, address of Griffith, 23 June 1920). This may have played a part in convincing Devoy thereafter that he had grown out of touch with Irish realities and thus should consider retiring. On behalf of the IRB Supreme Council, Collins also wrote to Devoy criticising him for denouncing DeValera for making his Cuban proposal (UCD Archives, DeValera papers, P150/1125, Collins to Boland, 26 Apr. 1920).

74. Owen McGee, 'John Finerty (1846–1908)', *Dictionary of Irish Biography*, 3 (Cambridge, 2009), 786–787.

75. F.M.Carroll, 'Joseph McGarrity (1874–1940)', *Dictionary of Irish Biography*, 5 (Cambridge, 2009), 1011–1013.

76. F.M. Carroll, *Money for Ireland: finance, diplomacy, politics and the first Dáil Eireann loans, 1919–1936* (London, 2002).

77. UCD, DeValera papers, P150/727, Griffith–DeValera correspondence (1919–1920).

78. UCD, DeValera papers, P150/727, DeValera to Griffith, 13 Aug. 1919.

79. UCD, DeValera papers, P150/1132, confidential memorandum of DeValera for forwarding to the Dáil cabinet, 15 Apr. 1920.

80. O'Kelly succeeded in making an address to the Pope in May 1920. A copy of his address and his correspondence with DeValera on the matter can be found in UCD, DeValera papers, P150/731. O'Kelly's success in acquiring an audience with the Pope was enabled by Monsignor John Hagan of the Irish College at Rome who was more willing to correspond with members of the Dáil ministry than his predecessor Monsignor O'Riordan. Patrick Long, 'John Hagan (1873–1930)', *Dictionary of Irish Biography*, 4 (Cambridge, 2009), 353–354.

81. NLI, Griffith papers, acc.4476, box b, copy of DeValera memorandum to Griffith, 27 Aug. 1920. Griffith had received a memorandum a fortnight earlier emphasising that DeValera 'has definitely decided to retire from public speaking here'. UCD, DeValera papers, P150/727, memo 11 Aug. 1920.

82. A Clan na Gael address to the IRB Supreme Council (attached to Devoy's letter of 17 Aug. 1920 in DeValera Papers, P150/1154), emphasised that 'the defeat of English intrigues in America is essential to success; that this can only be achieved by Irishmen here working as citizens of the US, guided by men who have intimate knowledge of American affairs, and that therefore there should be constant consultation between you and us as to the measures that concern purely American affairs. So that your hopes may not be raised too high as to possibilities, we would remind you that our people here are less than a fifth of the total population, that scarcely more than a tenth of that fifth are directly interested in the Irish cause and that our power to influence public measures that concern Ireland depends largely on our supposed, rather than our actual strength, and on our ability to make combinations with other and friendly sections of the American people, who still require enlightenment on the Irish question.'

83. Doorley, *Irish-American diaspora nationalism*, 133.

84. NLI, Griffith papers, acc.4476, box b, copy of DeValera memorandum to Griffith, 27 Aug. 1920. Griffith had received a memorandum a fortnight earlier emphasising that DeValera 'has definitely decided to retire from public speaking here'. UCD, DeValera papers, P150/727, memo 11 Aug. 1920.

85. Owen McGee, 'John Savage (1828–1888)', *Dictionary of Irish Biography*, 8 (Cambridge, 2009).

86. Kevin O'Shiel, *The making of a republic* (Dublin, 1920), foreword (quotes), 139. A signed copy of O'Shiel's book, dedicated to Griffith, can be found in NLI, Griffith papers, acc. 4476.

87. Churchill Archives, Lord Hankey Papers, HNKY1/5, diary entry for 1 Jan. 1921 (p.185).

88. DeValera's idea was published in an interview in the Westminster *Gazette* on 7 Feb. 1920. It generated controversy because of Devoy's understanding that Cuba was inherently a despised satellite state of the United States and not truly independent. On this theme, see Doorley, *Irish-American diaspora nationalism*, 110–121.

89. NLI, Griffith papers, acc.4476, boxes a and b. Griffith wrote regularly to DeValera regarding the activities of such journalists. UCD Archives, DeValera papers, P150/727.

90. NLI, Griffith papers, acc.4476, box a, letter from Alfred T. Davies, 28 July 1920. Davies wrote to Art O'Brien fairly regularly and also appealed to him to persuade Griffith to open negotiations. NLI, Art O'Brien papers, Ms8427/25.

91. The best study of this work to date is probably still John McColgan, *British policy and the Irish administration 1920–1922* (Dublin, 1983).

92. NAI, Bureau of Military History papers, WS216 (W.T. Cosgrave).

93. This is the perspective that he voiced in W.T. Cosgrave, 'Michael Collins (1890–1922)', *Dictionary of National Biography 1922–1930* (Oxford, 1937), 199–201.

94. NLI, Kathleen MacKenna Napoli papers, Ms22740 (incomplete draft of Griffith's intended reply).
95. Government Stationary Office, *Dáil Eireann*, 191 (minutes for 6 Aug. 1920 session).
96. Government Stationary Office, *Dáil Eireann*, 192–194 (minutes for 6 Aug. 1920 session). Collins also opposed the boycott but was preoccupied with the question of the Belfast banks. He wrote to Boland at the time (UCD Archives, DeValera papers, P150/1125, letter of 14 Aug. 1920) that when forwarding American funds, 'please see that a draft is not drawn on one of the Belfast Banks, or any Bank having its head office in that city, or elsewhere than in Dublin or Cork'.
97. NLI, Sinn Féin pamphlet collection, flyers 62, 64–66 (listing Dáil decrees).
98. Government Stationary Office, *Dáil Eireann*, 233, 212 (minutes for 17 Sep. 1920).
99. For instance, P.S. O'Hegarty, a fellow traveller if never quite an ally of Griffith in Sinn Féin debates since 1907, would later place much emphasis on the claim that Griffith supported the boycott in his influential publication *The Victory of Sinn Féin* (Dublin, 1924) and criticised him on this basis. It might be noted that, at the actual time of the boycott, O'Hegarty was an associate of Denis McCullough, a fellow former IRB leader who, as a Belfast city councillor, was actually one of the authors of the boycott.
100. To date, no histories of the Sinn Féin Party in Ulster have been written. There have been, however, histories of 'the northern IRA' by authors such as Tim Pat Coogan, John Regan and Robert Lynch.
101. The Presbyterian Griffiths of Cavan would write to Griffith in January 1922, offering him congratulations for being elected president of the Dáil while stating that they still remained opposed to his Irish nationalist politics. In the wake of Griffith's death, they offered to help Maud look after her two children. NLI, M.J. Lennon papers, Ms 22,293 (9)—recollections of Maud Griffith.
102. This was Bernard O'Rourke, a former Irish Party supporter. Terence Dooley, *Inniskeen, 1912–1918: the political conversion of Bernard O'Rourke* (Maynooth, 2004). Eamon Donnelly acted as a manager of the National Loan scheme in Ulster.
103. Eamon Donnelly's papers have recently been donated to the Newry and Mourne museum.
104. Government Stationary Office, *Dáil Eireann*, 231–232 (minutes for 17 Sep. 1920).
105. Owen McGee, 'Henry Harrison (1867–1954)', *Dictionary of Irish Biography*, 4 (Cambridge, 2009). Harrison's foremost publication of the theme of partition was *Ulster and the British Empire* (Dublin and London, 1939).
106. Captain Henry Harrison M.C. [later O.B.E.], *The peace conference 1920 and its betrayal* (Dublin, 1920), 9. This was a publication of Plunkett's Irish Dominion League.
107. Arthur Mitchell, *Revolutionary government in Ireland: Dáil Eireann 1919–1922* (Dublin, 1995), 204. The degree to which the Dáil courts were ever a valid enterprise has sometimes been a subject of debate among historians. On this theme, see Mary Kotsonouris, *Retreat from revolution: the Dáil courts 1920–1924* (Dublin, 1994). It might be suggested that the Dáil's prior resolution (19 August 1919) 'that clergymen be *ex-officio* justices' in its arbitration courts, just as they had formerly been given the right to be *ex-officio* officers in all party branches of Redmond's United Irish League, served to convince many contemporaries that were merely a party-political manifestation of Sinn Féin that would simply co-exist with the institutions of the British state until such time as an Anglo-Irish political settlement for Southern Ireland was formally settled or even imposed.
108. Churchill Archives, Lord Hankey Papers, HNKY1/5, diary entry for 5 Oct. 1920 (pp155–156).
109. Churchill Archives, Lord Hankey Papers, HNKY1/5, diary entry for 7 Sep. 1920 (p.154).
110. Arthur Mitchell, *Revolutionary government in Ireland*, 164–165, 204.

111. Ronan Fanning, *The Department of Finance 1922–1958* (Dublin, 1978), 24.
112. Surviving correspondence of Parry relating to the Dáil bank scheme and many other matters can be found in NLI, Art O'Brien papers (see the references to him in NLI, Collection List No.150).
113. This biographical information on Lionel Smith Gordon is based upon a newspaper article published about him while in the United States as a Dáil envoy during 1924. *Evening Independent* (St. Petersburg, Florida), 14 Jan. 1924. This article can easily be found online. See also Patrick Bolger, *The Irish cooperative movement* (Dublin, 1977).
114. On this theme, see the references to Briscoe in B.P. Murphy, *John Chartres: mystery man of the treaty* (Dublin, 1995). Chartres became a Dáil envoy in Germany during 1921.
115. Art O'Brien later explained to Henry Dixon (NLI, Art O'Brien papers, Ms8461/17, letter of 22 July 1926) that Briscoe was Collins' intermediary with German bankers. Collins wrote to Boland in May 1920 requesting that American funds be transferred for the sake of the Land Bank. Funds arrived in August and more were prepared in September. UCD Archives, DeValera papers, P150/1125, letters of 12 May, 14 Aug., 22 Sep. 1920.
116. David Fitzpatrick, *Harry Boland's Irish revolution* (Cork, 2003), quoted p.10.
117. On the debate regarding the League of Nations, see Doorley, *Irish-American diaspora nationalism*.
118. John Devoy, 'The story of Clan na Gael', *Gaelic American*, 13 June 1925.
119. Boland corresponded with Collins, the IRB treasurer, regarding this. Their correspondence was later acquired by DeValera and can be found in UCD Archives, DeValera papers, P150/1125. DeValera also acquired Devoy's correspondence with Boland (P150/1154).
120. On this theme, see Sister Mary Veronica Tarpey [of Villanova], *Joseph McGarrity and his role in the struggle for Irish independence* (New York, 1976) and F.M. Carroll, 'Joseph McGarrity (1874–1940)', *Dictionary of Irish Biography*, 5 (Cambridge, 2009).
121. Gabriel Doherty, Dermot Keogh (eds) *1916* (Cork, 2007), 422; Owen McGee, *The IRB* (Dublin, 2005), 179–183, 281, 307, 352.
122. UCD Archives, DeValera Papers, P150/1125, Boland to Collins, 22 Sep. 1920.
123. The IRB Supreme Council wrote to Boland emphasising these matters both before and after Boland initiated the break with the Clan na Gael. UCD Archives, DeValera papers, P150/1125, Supreme Council communications to Boland, 26 Apr. 1920, Collins letters to Boland, 19 Nov. 1920, 7 Feb., 7 Mar. 1921. This formed the tone of the subsequent correspondence of Collins and Boland, who first wrote to Collins regarding his unilateral decision to sever the link between the two organisations on 4 Nov. 1920 and wrote on 30 Mar. 1921 requesting that the IRB recognise McGarrity's new organisation as its official partner; a question regarding which no action whatsoever would be taken until a hesitant and inconclusive response to McGarrity's visiting Dublin was made in Feb. 1922. Although the Supreme Council wrote to the Clan executive regarding the 'generally entirely satisfactory' relationship between the two bodies as late as 1 Oct. 1920, two reasons for Collins to accept Boland's judgement were that Boland generally equated the issue of supporting DeValera's demands in America as a question of defending the IRB's autonomy from the Clan (Boland to Collins, 27 Aug.1920) and the fact that Collins himself did not appreciate that he was mentioned by name in a *Gaelic American* article of 11 Sep. in a manner that he deemed 'a breach of faith' (Collins to Boland, 27 Sep., 15 Oct. 1920). Collins also noted to Boland (3 July 1920) that 'you know there is no feeling at home now of looking to America in the way former generations look to Westminster'.
124. UCD Archives, DeValera papers, P150/1125, Collins to Boland, 17 Nov. 1920: 'Their negotiations with Egypt have broken down; all their dreams in Greece have been shattered and they must look forward to another army of occupation there; the Turks are joining the

Bolsheviks and will menace the British position in the near East; the Arabs are fighting it and menacing it in the middle East; the Indians are doing a little, and the Burmese Mission to London, to state their claims for better government, has been sadly disillusioned in its expectations from the promises of British Ministers. We can look forward with hope.'

125. Griffith's action in this regard is referred to in UCD Archives, DeValera papers, P150/1125, Collins to Boland, 14 Aug. 1920.

126. For a large selection of material relating to the MacSwiney episode, see NLI, Art O'Brien papers Collection List no.150, section III.iii. Copies of Griffith's statement, alongside those of many other figures, can be found in the publicity material in Ms8446/16–19.

127. NLI, Griffith papers, acc.4476, box b, letter of Senator Michael Hayes to Nevin Griffith B.L. (Griffith's son), 29 Sep. 1950.

128. Hankey's response was to go to Dublin himself to secretly attend the funerals of the plain-clothes British officers. In his diary, Hankey also noted that the killings had the affect of causing the British cabinet's attitude towards Ireland to swing from 'extreme apathy to almost panicky activity'. Churchill Archives, Lord Hankey Papers, HNKY1/5, diary entry for 25 Nov. 1920 (pp 169–170).

129. Churchill Archives, Lord Hankey Papers, HNKY1/5, diary entry for 1 Jan. 1921 (p.188). Although Ireland was still not a priority, Lloyd George would now keep the whole cabinet standing in waiting for a day 'on the chance of meeting in consequence of some message from the Sinn Féiners brought over by [?] Lynch'.

130. Patrick Moylett, 'The secret peace talks 1920–1921', *Irish Times*, 15–17 Nov. 1965. This series of newspaper articles was drawn from a hundred-page long statement made in 1952: NAI, Bureau of Military History papers, WS767 (Moylett).

131. NAI, Bureau of Military History papers, WS979 (Robert Barton), pp18–19; WS767 (Patrick Moylett), pp18–19. Moylett did not like the choice of bank directors, who initially included Dáil figures such as Barton and Blythe but was extended to include figures like Lionel Smith Gordon, James MacNeill, Conor Maguire, Erskine Childers and some men who were deemed to be ex-Irish Party supporters.

132. Letter of Griffith to Moylett, 16 Nov. 1920, reproduced in *Irish Times*, 16 Nov. 1965.

133. NLI, Art O'Brien papers, Ms8426/7, Collins to O'Brien, 14, 15 and 17 Dec. 1920. Collins suspected that Moylett was actually working on behalf of Captain Stephen Gwynn, formerly of the Irish Party and an intermediary between the Irish Dominion League and Alfred Cope at Dublin Castle.

134. NAI, Bureau of Military History papers, WS767 (Patrick Moylett), pp75–76. For the Earl of Denbigh's prior work with the Catholic Union of Great Britain regarding Ireland, see Youssef Taouk, 'We are alienating the splendid Irish race: British Catholic response to the Irish conscription controversy of 1918', *Journal of Church and State*, 48 (2006), 601–622.

135. NLI, Art O'Brien papers, Ms8430/10–12, Ms8426/7 (correspondence of Collins and O'Brien, Jan. 1921).

136. NLI, Art O'Brien papers, Ms8426/7, Collins to O'Brien, 15 Dec., 21 Dec. 1920, 5 Jan. 1921.

137. A notebook containing Griffith's account of the progress of his hunger strike (testing how he felt when he did not eat or drink but kept smoking heavily as usual) can be found in NLI, Griffith papers, acc.4476, box b.

138. NLI, Kathleen MacKenna Napoli papers, MS 22744 (notes of Griffith in jail, [11] Dec 1920).

139. Sam Davies, 'A stormy political career: P.J. Kelly and Irish nationalism and labour politics in Liverpool, 1891–1936', *Transactions of the Historic Society of Lancashire & Cheshire*, vol.148 (1999), 147–189.

140. Peter Hart, 'The IRA in Britain 1919–1923', *English Historical Review*, 115, no.460 (Feb.2000), 98–99. For the resulting political prisoners issues, see NAI, Art O'Brien Papers Collection List No.150, sections 3 and 8.

141. NLI, Art O'Brien papers, Ms8429/11, Collins to MacGrath, 9 Oct. 1919.

142. NLI, Art O'Brien papers, Ms8426/38, Collins to O'Brien, 18 Feb. 1921.

143. This is indicated by some material held in the Art O'Brien papers, such as NLI, Ms8419/2, Ms8424/13, Ms8432/9.

144. Churchill Archives, Lord Hankey Papers, HNKY1/5, diary entry for 25 Nov. 1920 (pp169–170). The attack occurred on 27 November 1920. See also the reports of the London *Times* on the question of 'the IRA' for 24–28 Nov. 1920.

145. 'The secret peace talks', *Irish Times*, 16 Nov. 1965; NAI, Bureau of Military History papers, WS767 (Moylett), pp61–62.

146. This was indicated by a memoir of a London Irish Volunteer—Joe Good, *Enchanted by dreams* (Dublin, 1996), 130–144—while Garret Fitzgerald, son of Desmond Fitzgerald, once referred to this idea regarding Brugha while talking about Griffith's legacy. *Irish Times*, 17 June 1970. As Brugha was relatively close to the church and also issued orders to volunteers to prevent disturbances, it is doubtful that he really was in favour of outrages, notwithstanding his 'hardline temperament' (an impression made upon many contemporaries simply due to his cold manner).

147. Westminster Diocesan Archives, Cardinal Bourne papers, BO5/36a.

148. There was some justification for this belief. The London *Times* had desired that Mannix would persuade the Irish bishops to sue for peace on behalf of the British government but upon meeting him, the editor of the *Times* judged that Mannix was unlikely to comply. Westminster Diocesan Archives, Cardinal Bourne papers, BO5/36a, Wickham Stead to Cardinal Bourne, 9 Aug. and 12 Aug. 1920.

149. NLI, Art O'Brien papers, Ms8426/7, Collins to O'Brien, 12 and 28 Jan. 1921 (with attached communication from DeValera to Collins).

150. The Government Stationary Office, *Dáil Eireann minutes 1919–1921* (Dublin, 1994), 140–150.

CHAPTER TEN

1. For a list of the names of the executed volunteers, see NLI, Art O'Brien papers, Ms8442/14. Fourteen were executed in Cork prisons and nine were executed in Mountjoy prison in Dublin. How long Griffith continued his hunger strike in Mountjoy, sustained by his heavy smoking habit, is unknown. Like most people, it is doubtful that he could do so for more than a week or two.

2. The chapter on Ireland in John Turner, *Lloyd George's secretariat* (Cambridge, 1980) is a particularly good source on how the Irish Party worked for the British government behind the scenes in attempting to bring Sinn Féin into line with existing consensuses regarding Anglo-Irish relations and the role of the Catholic Church therein, established during 1884–1886. Hankey also noted in his diary that Lloyd George had said that a couple of 'eminent Irish nationalists' in Westminster (i.e. Irish Party MPs) had told him in confidence that the policy of reprisals 'ought not to be stopped' because they had a positive effect in manipulating public opinion to the British government's advantage. Churchill Archives, Lord Hankey papers, HNKY1/5, diary entry for 5 Oct. 1920 (pp 155–156).

3. Chesterton's pamphlet *How to solve the Irish question* (Montreal, 1921) and his associated flyers 'the delusion of the double policy' and 'what are reprisals?' can be found in

Westminster Diocesan Archives, Cardinal Bourne papers, BO5/87 (2). Robert Lindsay Crawford of the Irish Self-Determination League in Canada published Chesterton's pamphlet.

4. The impact of this arson campaign on English public opinion was reflected by Chesterton's lament that a campaign of 'indiscriminate destruction … will be what is remembered', not the existence of a democratic movement in favour of political self-determination within Ireland.

5. Westminster Diocesan Archives, Cardinal Bourne papers, BO5/87 (2), BO5/36a (press cutting regarding Dillon, 27 Jan. 1921). Both the High Sheriff of Dublin and an official representing the Catholic members of the RIC wrote to Cardinal Bourne, thanking him for his stance against Sinn Féin.

6. Westminster Diocesan Archives, Cardinal Bourne papers, BO5/87 (2), W.T. Kerr (leader of the Catholic Union of Great Britain) to Cardinal Bourne, 10 Dec. 1920. Kerr was also a decorated royal navy officer.

7. Westminster Diocesan Archives, Cardinal Bourne papers, BO5/87 (2), Count Plunkett to Cardinal Bourne, 23 Feb. 1921.

8. For the Vatican's response to the appointment, see Westminster Diocesan Archives, Cardinal Bourne papers, BO 1/72, Lord Fitzalan to Cardinal Bourne, 9 Apr. 1921. The Irish hierarchy were also pleased. Whitehall still considered them to be relatively uncooperative, however. For instance, when the Archbishop of Tuam met Chief Secretary Hamar Greenwood at Lloyd George's request, to the Prime Minister's irritation, the archbishop went directly from the interview to inform DeValera what had transpired. Cardinal Bourne papers, BO1/72 (copy of a letter from the Archbishop's House to Lloyd George, 25 Apr. 1921). The British Foreign Office desired to keep its dealings with the Vatican completely out of the press, fearing Protestant criticisms (Lord Fitzalan to Cardinal Bourne, BO 1/72, 31 Mar. 1921). Reflecting this trend, the appointment of a Catholic Viceroy motivated Edward Carson to formally announce his political retirement (this being the moment when James Craig officially assumed leadership of the Ulster Unionist Party for the first time). Collins' last intelligence insights before the IRB fell apart in February 1921 included an awareness that British military figures were suggesting to Whitehall that a perceived South Africa–Ireland political parallel should be explored (NLI, Art O'Brien papers, Collins to O'Brien, 30 Dec.1920, 5 Jan., 12 Jan.1921); a practically useless piece of intelligence because an Irish association in South Africa, led by P.J. Little, already knew that Jan Smuts, a politically astute former military officer turned governor in South Africa, was planning to confer both with DeValera and the British government in precisely this matter with the support of Tom Casement (brother of Roger). Reflecting this, many figures, including several Irish Party leaders, believed that the nature of Smuts' British colony in South Africa was a very suitable model for settling the Anglo-Irish security relationship. A joint preoccupation with matters in Rome and the likelihood of an Irish settlement along South African lines can be seen in letters sent to O'Brien by Maurice Moore in South Africa (Ms8429/1) and Sydney Parry in Rome (Ms8429/41). Moore entered into communications with Fr. O'Flanagan and the Sinn Féin executive in the winter of 1920 as part of the Irish Party's effort to negotiate a political surrender (NAI, Bureau of Military History papers, WS767, Patrick Moylett, p79). He had effectively been the leader of the National Volunteers (see NLI, Redmond papers), in which capacity he had employed Childers and Barton as his secretaries (NAI, Bureau of Military History papers, WS979, Robert Barton, pp8–9) and knew Roger Casement well. An admirer of DeValera from 1921 onwards, later he would become a founder of Fianna Fáil.

9. NLI, Art O'Brien papers, Ms8429/1, DeValera to O'Brien, 24 Apr. 1921.

10. This was the Earl of Longford, Frank Pakenham, who, although a man contemptuously ignored by Griffith, was a friend to both Griffith's predecessor and successor as the president of Sinn Féin, John Sweetman and Eamon DeValera.

11. Lord Longford, *Peace by ordeal* (London, 1935).

12. NLI, Art O'Brien papers, Ms8430/12, Collins to O'Brien, 17 Jan. 1921, forwarding a communication from DeValera. Griffith's ministry hitherto, 'home affairs', was now granted to Austin Stack.

13. NLI, Art O'Brien papers, Ms8429/1. While fluent in Spanish and appreciative of the offer, O'Brien declined. The job went instead to a relative Marie O'Brien, who worked with the Irish College in Salamanca in attempting to influence Spanish journalists up until the Dáil's Spanish publicity office was closed down a year later. NLI, Art O'Brien papers, Ms8421/27, Ms8426/30.

14. NLI, Art O'Brien Papers, Collection List No.150, section VI.i. As the conference approached, Elizabeth McGinley, formerly of the London Office, effectively took on the responsibilities initially given to Ms. Hughes and was sent to Paris (NAI, Bureau of Military History papers WS860). This was partly why Paris, not Montreal, ultimately became the host city of the event, held in January 1922.

15. For the history of this newspaper, which would become the most significant base of DeValera's American political support in the years ahead, see J.P. Rodechko, *Patrick Ford and his search for America* (New York, 1976). Robert was the son of Patrick. For the history of the Finerty family, see Owen McGee, 'John Finerty (1846–1908)', *Dictionary of Irish Biography*, 3, pp786–787, and the section for UILA correspondence in NLI, John Redmond Papers Collection List No.118.

16. Although the Clan na Gael–IRB link was not re-established, Boland would attempt to persuade the IRB to ally itself with the new breakaway organisation formed by Joe McGarrity. UCD Archives, DeValera Papers, P150/1125 (IRB Supreme Council correspondence of Collins and Boland).

17. NLI, Art O'Brien papers, Ms8421/1, Ms8426/32. For Collins and Boland's prior work in setting up this system, see UCD Archives, DeValera Papers, P150/1125 (IRB Supreme Council correspondence of Collins and Boland) and P150/1154 (Clan na Gael correspondence of Boland and Devoy).

18. This was an extension of the fact that hitherto Collins had managed the Dail's accounts through Art O'Brien's London Office, which had now diminished in importance. Collins continued to correspond primarily with O'Brien, however, up until 1922 (NLI, Art O'Brien Papers).

19. NAI, Bureau of Military History papers, WS767 (Patrick Moylett), pp82–83 (quoting Fahy). The memory of this perspective in Irish political folklore might have influenced unduly some recent historical studies such as B.P. Murphy, *John Chartres: mystery man of the treaty* (Dublin, 1995).

20. NLI, Art O'Brien papers, Ms8430/11, Collins to O'Brien, 31 Dec.1920; Ms8430/12, Collins to O'Brien, 3 Jan. 1921.

21. DeValera's understanding of the situation Griffith's cabinet faced during 1920 may be seen in his comment to Art O'Brien (NLI, Art O'Brien papers, Ms8429/1, DeValera to O'Brien, 19 Mar. 1921) that 'how you managed to keep all the irons hot which you were expected to in the past is more than I know. M.C. [Collins] was in the same boat. You are paying the penalty now with your health and M.C. ran it very close more than once too. This fight isn't a question of mere "spurt", so we must not run ourselves out in the early part of the race.'

22. This was a Major Robinson. NAI, Bureau of Military History papers, WS767 (Patrick Moylett), p82.

23. Sheila Carden, *The Alderman: Alderman Tom Kelly and Dublin Corporation* (Dublin, 2007), 185. An 'American Committee for Relief in Ireland' led by Cardinal Gibbons of Baltimore was also established at this time.

24. For sources on the activities and personnel of these political prisoners' bodies, see NLI, Art O'Brien Papers Collection List No.150, sections III, V and VIII. Many members of the Catholic religious orders, such as the Augustinians, Dominicans and especially the Capuchins, had already attained great popularity within Sinn Féin's ranks due to their acceptance of the responsibility ever since 1916 to act as neutral intermediaries with the political prisoners. Dr. Brian Kirby of the Capuchin Archives, Dublin, can point interested scholars in the direction of valuable sources on this theme. See also the papers relating to Terence MacSwiney's hunger strike in NLI, Art O'Brien papers.

25. The papers of the Mansion House Relief Committee of 1880–1882 are held in the Dublin City Library and Archives, Pearse Street, Dublin 2. On the degree to which this body superseded the significance of the Land League organisation, see R.V. Comerford, *The Fenians in context* (Dublin, 1985), chapter 8 ('a different revolution, 1878–1882'), Dana Hearne (ed.) *The tale of a great sham, by Anna Parnell* (Dublin, 1986) and C.C. O'Brien, *Parnell and his party* (Oxford, 1957), chapters 1–4.

26. On this theme, see Fergus Campbell, *The Irish establishment 1879–1914* (Oxford, 2009).

27. The *Cumann* would also treat the cultural subject of Irish history.

28. See the Liberal Party publication, J.H. Morgan (ed.) *The new Irish constitution* (London, 1912).

29. On the Stopford family, see Leon O'Broin, *Protestant nationalists in revolutionary Ireland: the Stopford connection* (Dublin, 1985), Angus Mitchell, *Roger Casement* (London, 2003) and a book with a bizarrely personality-centred title: Royal Irish Academy (ed.) *Roger Casement in Irish and World History* (Dublin, 2006).

30. Obituary of Griffith by Green in *Studies*, Sep. 1922, p344. Due to her great wealth and family political connections (not her academic skills), Alice Stopford Green had been a party to many high-political debates on Ireland between 1911 and 1921, usually in total opposition to Griffith's contemporaneous stances in the press. Regarding Griffith, she judged that 'his poverty was his great disaster' and that 'the shining of the new light, flashed out by Griffith from dark places' could ultimately only appeal to his fellow poor men.

31. DeValera was a student of MacNeill's work in India. See Eamon DeValera, *Ireland and India* (New York, 1920), cited in Doorley. Sir John O'Donnell had previously made notable contributions to Liberal Party publications (his views on single or double chambered parliaments had been a subject of analysis in *Sinn Féin* during 1912) but the best illustration of his understanding of Ireland was his complex analysis of imperial administrations, 'the foundations of colonial self-government', in *Journal of the Society for the Statistical and Social Inquiry of Ireland* (1916–1917), 419–459.

32. The *Cumann's* personnel and its lecture programmes were advertised in all its publications, the most interesting of which was Lionel Smith Gordon, *The place of banking in the national programme* (Dublin, 1921).

33. Pauric Dempsey, 'Andrew Jameson (1855–1941)', *Dictionary of Irish Biography*, 6 (Cambridge, 2009), 951–952; Patrick Maume, 'William St. John Broderick, Earl of Midleton (1856–1942)', *Dictionary of Irish Biography*, 1 (Cambridge, 2009), 860–863. Barry Egan, the deputy mayor of Cork, would handle the challenge of attempting to promote the idea of a truce in Cork.

34. Patrick Maume, 'Timothy Corcoran (1872–1943)', *Dictionary of Irish Biography*, 2 (Cambridge, 2009), 848–849.

35. NAI, Bureau of Military History papers, WS979 (Robert Barton), pp17–19. Patrick Moylett was not impressed by the fact that James MacNeill was the only Catholic director of the company; a significant illustration, in the light of Moylett's standing as a leading businessman of Galway and Ballina, of the degree to which sectarian attitudes governed contemporary Irish businessmen's attitudes (WS767, pp18–19).

36. Lionel Smith Gordon, *The place of banking in the national programme* (Dublin, 1921), 11–12. Smith Gordon cited publicly the Irish Banks Standing Committee's secret standard ratio of interest rates for investments against those on offer by banks in Britain. These were so designed to make it inherently more profitable (by at least a 1½ per cent margin) for all major Irish investors, including the banks themselves, to invest their funds in Britain rather than in Ireland. Gordon claimed falsely, however, that this was a matter that had been determined exclusively by the Irish bank's shareholders (Lionel Smith Gordon, *The place of banking in the national programme* (Dublin, 1921), 5–6, 11–12). In reality, these interest rates had been determined the previous May exclusively by the directors of each affiliated bank on the Irish Banks Standing Committee without consultation with any party but themselves and the Bank of England. This may be explained partly by Smith Gordon's admission that 'English and Irish banks find it profitable to join forces with one another, either by a joint working arrangement or a formal amalgamation.'

37. Michael Collins, *The path to freedom* (Dublin, 1922), 116–117.

38. Lionel Smith Gordon, *The place of banking in the national programme* (Dublin, 1921), 6–7.

39. Lionel Smith Gordon, *The place of banking in the national programme* (Dublin, 1921), 6–7.

40. Lionel Smith Gordon, *The place of banking in the national programme* (Dublin, 1921), 8.

41. Lionel Smith Gordon, *The place of banking in the national programme* (Dublin, 1921), 8, 11–14.

42. This was the model employed by the National Land Bank.

43. Lionel Smith Gordon, *The place of banking in the national programme* (Dublin, 1921), 8, 11–14.

44. Brendan Lynn, 'Joseph MacRory (1861–1945)', *Dictionary of Irish Biography*, 6 (Cambridge, 2009), 182–183.

45. Tom Dunne (ed.) *The National University of Ireland 1908–2008* (Dublin, 2008), 135–136. DeValera received formal notification of his appointment by telegram upon his arrival in London in July 1921 to negotiate with Lloyd George (NLI, Art O'Brien papers, Ms8429/2) but he did not officially take up the responsibility until 19 December 1921 in the midst of a Dáil debate on an Anglo-Irish agreement. DeValera would remain NUI Chancellor until his death in 1975.

46. Anne Dolan, *Commemorating the Irish civil war: history and memory* (Cambridge, 2009), quoting the Cork IRB leader Florence O'Donoghue, p.150.

47. Letter of Smuts to DeValera, reproduced in St. John Ervine, *Craigavon* (London, 1949), 650–651.

48. NLI, Art O'Brien papers, Ms8429/1, DeValera to O'Brien, 24 Apr., 4 May 1921 regarding the progress of his meetings with Lord Derby.

49. NLI, Art O'Brien papers, Ms8429/1, DeValera to O'Brien, 24 Apr., 4 May 1921.

50. For a recent, more positive, appraisal of the Napoleonic legacy, see the writings of Michael Broers.

51. Gerard Hogan, 'George Gavan Duffy (1882–1951)', *Dictionary of Irish Biography*, 3 (Cambridge, 2009), 510–512. A good examination of the evolution of a school of

Irish constitutional thought from this Catholic basis can be found in an article by Joseph Crehan S.J. in *Studies*, 40 (1951), 158–166.

52. W.H. Krautt, *Ground truths* (Dublin, 2014), 155–156.

53. W.T. Cosgrave, 'Michael Collins (1890–1922)', *Dictionary of National Biography 1922–1930* (Oxford, 1937), 199–201.

54. Churchill Archives, CHAR22/11/36, report of 'H' to Secretary of State, 27 Jan. 1922, regarding the still extant liaison arrangements of June 1921.

55. Churchill Archives, CHAR22/8, report of Sir John Anderson to Churchill, 30 Dec. 1921.

56. Dáil Eireann, *Debate on the treaty between Great Britain and Ireland* (Dublin, 1922), 30–32.

57. Prior to his appointment at Dublin Castle, Cope was head of the detective department in the imperial department of customs and excise and, alongside James Craig, a secretary to a newly created ministry of pensions. Richard Hawkins, P.J. Dempsey, 'Sir Alfred William ('Andy') Cope (1877–1954)', *Dictionary of Irish Biography*, 2 (Cambridge, 2009), 836–838.

58. NLI, Kathleen MacKenna Napoli Papers, Ms22745, Griffith's statement to press representatives in London, July 1921.

59. [Erskine Childers (ed.)] *The constructive work of Dáil Eireann* (Dublin, 1921); [Erskine Childers (ed.)] *Dáil Eireann, miontuaric an Chead Dala 1919–1921* (1st ed., Dublin, 1921). 'The work of the republic' series began in *Young Ireland* on 16 August 1921.

60. A truly remarkable photograph can be seen in Jim Ring, *Erskine Childers* (London, 1996) of DeValera and Childers in a private discussion on board a steamship between Dun Laoghaire and Holyhead in July 1921 with Griffith visible in the distance looking on with a look of contempt on his face.

61. NAI, Bureau of Military History papers, WS767 (Patrick Moylett), p87.

62. Westminster Parliamentary Archives, Lloyd George Papers, F25/1/42, Tom Jones to Lloyd George, 15 Jun 1921 (report on Irish Situation Committee meeting).

63. The RIC were armed but generally kept their arms in barracks.

64. This was the Bureau of Military History, which was established in 1942 and continued to operate up until 1953.

65. T.M. Healy, as chief defence lawyer for the Irish Volunteers, knew Lynch in his capacity as a thrice-paroled private in the British army. Frank Callanan, *T.M. Healy* (Cork, 1996), 607. It was not uncommon for the most militant of volunteer leaders to have been men who had a prior interest in an army career. For instance, Ernie O'Malley's original great ambition was to serve in the British army. Richard English, 'Ernest Bernard O'Malley (1897–1957)', *Dictionary of Irish Biography*, 7 (Cambridge, 2009), 677–678.

66. Photographs of MacSwiney's funeral procession can be see in NLI, Art O'Brien papers, Ms8446/3, Ms8450/5, Ms8440/22.

67. Westminster Parliamentary Archives, Lloyd George Papers, F/25/2/13, H.A.L. Fisher to the Prime Minister, 4 Sep.1921.

68. Westminster Diocesan Archives, Cardinal Bourne Papers, BO 1/72, Lord Fitzalan to Cardinal Bourne, 22 Aug., 3 Sep. 1921. Westminster Parliamentary Archives, Lloyd George Papers, F/25/2/13, H.A.L. Fisher to the Prime Minister, 4 Sep.1921. The Viceroy also suggested that the many public drills by the IRA and its drive for fresh recruits was actually a good thing, as 'it keeps their young men under discipline and control' and made them 'a better [or easier] target if hostilities should recommence'.

69. Westminster Parliamentary Archives, Lloyd George Papers, F25/2/2 and F25/2/7 (reports to the Prime Minister of meetings of Tom Jones, assistant cabinet secretary, with O'Brien, Aug.1921).

70. Westminster Parliamentary Archives, Lloyd George Papers, F/25/2/15, 'George M.' to Tom Jones [Sep. 1921]; F/25/2/13, Fisher to Prime Minister 4 Sep. 1921 (forwarding communication from Cope).

71. Westminster Parliamentary Archives, Lloyd George Papers, Lloyd George Papers, F/25/2/18, DeValera to Lloyd George (signed telegram forwarded by Cope), 19 Sep. 1921.

72. Westminster Parliamentary Archives, Lloyd George Papers, F25/1/19, Maurice Hankey to Prime Minister (in Gairloch, Scotland), 27 Sep. 1921 (with attached intelligence communication). This item is numbered F25/1/19, but filed at F/25/2/19.

73. Westminster Parliamentary Archives, Lloyd George Papers, F25/1/19, Maurice Hankey to Prime Minister (in Gairloch, Scotland), 27 Sep. 1921 (with attached intelligence communication). This item is numbered F25/1/19, but filed at F/25/2/19.

74. With regards to the significance or value of Hankey's communication, it should be noted that he was the director of British intelligence worldwide and, therefore, did not report on Irish affairs on a general rule, this being a matter only for those junior military officers who worked with the Irish police services, under the Home Office. On Hankey's career generally, see John Turner, *Lloyd George's secretariat* (Cambridge, 1980) and Stephen Roskill, *Hankey: man of secrets* (2 volumes, London, 1972). The chapter on Ireland in the former publication is a particularly good source on how the Irish Party worked for the British government behind the scenes in attempting to bring Sinn Féin into line with existing consensuses regarding Anglo-Irish relations and the role of the Catholic Church therein, established during 1884–1886.

75. Dáil Eireann, *Debate on the treaty between Great Britain and Ireland, signed in London on 6 December 1921: sessions 14 Dec.1921 to 10 January 1922* (Dublin, 1922), speeches of David Kent, Sean McEntee and Mary MacSwiney on 10 December.

76. In the Churchill Archives in Cambridge, there is an extensive correspondence of Churchill relating to Irish matters dating from 1921–1922 but of the relevant material (CHAR 22/8 - CHAR 22/14) all correspondence dating from mid-September until late December 1921 is withdrawn on orders of the British government due to its sensitivity.

77. Arthur Mitchell, *Revolutionary government: Dáil Eireann 1919-1922* (Dublin, 1995), 348–349.

78. For Duffy's work in this regard, see the papers relating to J.P. MacDonnell in NLI, Art O'Brien papers, as well as David Foxton, *Revolutionary lawyers: Sinn Féin and crown courts in Ireland and Britain 1916-1923* (Dublin, 2008).

79. NLI, Art O'Brien papers, Ms8428/5, DeValera to O'Brien (forwarding a request of the British department of defence), 26 Oct. 1921, and O'Brien's reply.

80. On this clerical level, the British side during the subsequent negotiations benefited from the fact that highly professional civil servants produced detailed reports on the negotiations almost instantaneously for the whole cabinet's information. As the Dáil lacked its own civil service, these British cabinet reports were also given to the Irish side for their own information.

81. When Churchill demanded that Britain must retain control of all naval bases on the Irish coastline owing to their importance to submarine warfare, Collins replied that 'people in Ireland have no desire to build submarines; it would be a mad cap thing!' Even though he noted that the Dáil might want a small navy, Collins suggested that Britain might be granted a right to inspect Irish coast stations without actually governing them. This was because the Irish could appreciate that if 'the British navy is beaten the neutrality of Ireland does not matter a damn'. Collins' effort to raise the question of neutrality in this manner was effectively silenced thereafter, however, when Childers made the basis of the defence negotiations a four-way theoretical debate between himself, Churchill,

Birkenhead and Lord Beatty (leader of the Royal Navy), about the degree to which the renaming of the Empire as a Commonwealth over the past couple of years had or had not affected each of the British dominions' need to surrender control of their ports to the imperial navy in the event of war. Westminster Parliamentary Archives, Lloyd George Papers, F25/2/32, Tom Jones to Prime Minister, 14 Oct. 1921; NLI, Art O'Brien papers, Ms8425/8 (copies of government reports on defence meetings).

82. W.T. Cosgrave, 'Arthur Griffith (1872–1922)', *Dictionary of National Biography 1922–1930* (Oxford, 1937), 368; Kathleen Clarke, *Revolutionary woman* (Dublin, 1991), 189.

83. Arthur Mitchell, *Revolutionary government*, 76, 325. Mitchell is here drawing on Duffy's later statement to the Bureau of Military History (1942–1953).

84. Westminster Diocesan Archives, Cardinal Bourne papers, BO5/87 (2), undated letter of the members of the St. George's Cathedral Congregation together with contemporary letters and news-cuttings.

85. *Daily Express*, 17 Oct. 1921. This nervousness was seen to stem from a visible physical reaction: they 'quailed before an ordeal of handshaking' with members of the English public. MacRory said a regular mass for the delegation in a small north London chapel with Mark Ryan also in attendance.

86. NLI, Art O'Brien papers, Ms8428/15.

87. NLI, Griffith papers, acc.4476, box b, telegram.

88. Her letters from 1916 and 1918–1919 can be found in prison records in National Archives (Kew), HO144/1458/316093.

89. David Lloyd George, *Is it peace?* (London, 1924), 271–272; NLI, Griffith papers, acc.4476, box b, Michael Hayes to Nevin Griffith, 29 Sep.1950, based on an interview with the latter's mother (quote).

90. NAI, Bureau of Military History papers, WS205 (Maud Griffith).

91. Keith Middlemas (ed.) *Thomas Jones, Whitehall diary, vol.3* (London, 1971), 116 (quote, letter of Lloyd George to DeValera), 119–120. This text of the proposal of 20 July can be seen in Fanning, Kennedy, Keogh, O'Halpin (eds) *Documents on Irish foreign policy vol.1, 1919–1922* (Dublin, 1998), 236–238.

92. NLI, Griffith papers, acc.4476, box b, page of manuscript notes, marked 'p.81'. Pages numbered prior to page eighty-one do not appear to have survived.

93. The Catholic Viceroy of Ireland had maintained that undoing the partition of Ireland was impossible. He did consider, however, that an Anglo-Irish agreement between Dublin and London would be likely to alter the impact that partition might have on the country's political evolution. Westminster Diocesan Archives, Cardinal Bourne Papers, BO 1/72, Lord Fitzalan to Cardinal Bourne, 22 Aug., 3 Sep. 1921.

94. NLI, Griffith papers, acc.4476, box b, manuscript note marked 'p.81'. These notes, like most of Griffith's letters, are written in pencil (reputedly, or at least according to an obituary in the *Review of Reviews*, he always carried dozens of blunt pencils in his pockets, along with spare shoelaces for his orthopaedic boots and some rosary beads).

95. Westminster Parliamentary Archives, Lloyd George Papers, F21/1/2- 3. For southern unionists efforts in this regard, see Peter Martin, 'Irish peers 1909–1924' (unpublished MA, UCD, 1998).

96. NLI, Griffith papers, acc.4476, box b, manuscript notes 'p.82', 'p.84'. Pages numbered prior to page eighty-one do not appear to have survived.

97. NLI, Griffith papers, acc.4476, box b, manuscript notes 'p.82', 'p.83', 'p.84'.

98. Owen McGee, 'Thomas Power O'Connor (1848–1929)', *Dictionary of Irish Biography*, 7 (Cambridge, 2009), 283.

99. NLI, Griffith papers, acc.4476, box b, manuscript notes p.84: 'debt—establish'.
100. NLI, Griffith papers, acc.4476, box b, manuscript notes 'p.83'.
101. Richard Lloyd George, *Lloyd George* (London, 1960), 26; David Lloyd George, *Is it peace?* (London, 1924), 267–270.
102. Westminster Parliamentary Archives, Lloyd George Papers, F/21/1/1, Griffith to Lloyd George, 2 Nov. 1921.
103. Ronan Fanning, *Fatal path* (Dublin, 2013), 282, 290.
104. Ronan Fanning, *Fatal path* (Dublin, 2013), 293–294.
105. Lloyd George Papers, F/10/3/3, Lloyd George to Churchill, 8 Jun. 1922.
106. Fanning, Kennedy, Keogh, O'Halpin (eds) *Documents on Irish foreign policy vol.1, 1919–1922* (Dublin, 1998), 292.
107. Fanning, Kennedy, Keogh, O'Halpin (eds) *Documents on Irish foreign policy vol.1, 1919–1922* (Dublin, 1998), 276 (letter of Griffith to DeValera, 14 Oct. 1921).
108. Fanning, Kennedy, Keogh, O'Halpin (eds) *Documents on Irish foreign policy vol.1, 1919–1922* (Dublin, 1998), 275, 282, 292.
109. Keith Middlemas (ed.) *Thomas Jones, Whitehall diary, vol.3* (London, 1971), 160.
110. Westminster Parliamentary Archives, Lloyd George papers, F/25/2/54, Craig to Lloyd George. The fact of Craig's dealings with the Prime Minister regarding Griffith's actions were not made known to the public until 13 December 1921.
111. Fanning, Kennedy, Keogh, O'Halpin (eds) *Documents on Irish foreign policy vol.1, 1919–1922* (Dublin, 1998), 305–309 (letters of Griffith to DeValera, 9–15 Nov. 1921).
112. Printed copies of the altered statement are also held in Westminster Parliamentary Archives, Lloyd George Papers, F/21/1/1.
113. A copy of Griffith's original letter, including the statement that he could not accept the Crown without Irish unity, was distributed to and held by the Dáil's London Office (NLI, Art O'Brien papers, Ms8430/28) but among Lloyd George's altered copies of the statement (Westminster Parliamentary Archives, Lloyd George Papers, F/21/1/1) is actually a copy of the statement *on Dáil Eireann headed notepaper* that omits this final section. The source of this particular copy remains unknown.
114. Tom Jones, the assistant cabinet secretary, had to face stern criticisms from the Irish delegation for this. Westminster Parliamentary Archives, Lloyd George Papers, F/25/2/38, telegram of Jones to Prime Minister, 29 Oct. 1921; F/25/2/43, Jones to Prime Minister, 19 Nov. 1921.
115. Keith Middlemas (ed.) *Thomas Jones, Whitehall diary, vol.3* (London, 1971), 161.
116. Westminster Parliamentary Archives, Lloyd George Papers, F/25/2/48, Tom Jones to John Chartres (marked 'secret and urgent'), 25 Nov. 1921.
117. Dáil Eireann, *Debate on the treaty between Great Britain and Ireland, signed in London on 6 December 1921: sessions 14 Dec.1921 to 10 January 1922* (Dublin, 1922), 98 (speech of Eamon Duggan).
118. Fanning, Kennedy, Keogh, O'Halpin (eds) *Documents on Irish foreign policy vol.1, 1919–1922* (Dublin, 1998), 293.
119. Fanning, Kennedy, Keogh, O'Halpin (eds) *Documents on Irish foreign policy vol.1, 1919–1922* (Dublin, 1998), 318–319; Maryann Gialanella Valiulis, *Portrait of a revolutionary: General Richard Mulcahy and the founding of the Irish Free State* (Dublin, 1992), 105–109; Westminster Parliamentary Archives, Lloyd George Papers, F/25/2/48, Tom Jones to John Chartres (marked 'secret and urgent'), 25 Nov. 1921.
120. Westminster Parliamentary Archives, Lloyd George Papers, F/25/2/51, Tom Jones to Prime Minister, 4 Dec. 1921.

121. Collins would place particular emphasis on this point in the near future. Dáil Eireann, *Debate on the treaty between Great Britain and Ireland, signed in London on 6 December 1921: sessions 14 Dec.1921 to 10 January 1922* (Dublin, 1922), 30–32.

122. Fanning, Kennedy, Keogh, O'Halpin (eds) *Documents on Irish foreign policy vol.1, 1919–1922* (Dublin, 1998), 239–246 (quote p. 241).

123. DeValera would state that, as a Catholic, he was actually morally opposed to oath taking of any kind, viewing it as a denial of human free will. Dáil Eireann, *Debate on the treaty between Great Britain and Ireland, signed in London on 6 December 1921: sessions 14 Dec.1921 to 10 January 1922* (Dublin, 1922), 24–27.

124. Fanning, Kennedy, Keogh, O'Halpin (eds) *Documents on Irish foreign policy vol.1, 1919–1922* (Dublin, 1998), 318–319 (quoting DeValera to Boland, 29 Nov.1921): 'I appreciate all that WAR means to our people and what my misgivings are as to the outcome of war … If I appear with those who choose war it is only because the alternative is impossible without dishonour. For us to recommend that our people should subscribe with their lips to an allegiance which they could not render in their hearts would be to recommend to them subscription to a living lie and the abandonment of the supreme issue in the struggle through centuries.'

125. Brendan Lynn, 'Joseph MacRory (1861–1945)', *Dictionary of Irish Biography*, 6 (Cambridge, 2009), 182–183.

126. Collins' perpetual preoccupation with and deep involvement in the question of the fate of Irish political prisoners in Britain throughout 1921 and well into 1922 is evidenced by his correspondence in NLI, Art O'Brien papers.

127. Lloyd George wrote to Griffith on this matter in early December. Westminster Parliamentary Archives, Lloyd George Papers, F21/1/2- 3.

128. This would be reflected by Lord Iveagh, the owner of Guinness Breweries, and Andrew Jameson, the Director of Bank of Ireland, writing to Midleton that if they demanded too much they might be considered responsible for 'breaking the treaty'. Peter Martin, 'Irish peers', quoted p198.

129. Westminster Parliamentary Archives, Lloyd George Papers, F/25/2/51, Tom Jones to Prime Minister, 4 Dec. 1921.

130. According to Jones, Griffith even suggested that if Craig was willing to make such a public gesture, 'then the South will give all the safeguards you want to the North and will not ask for a Boundary Commission'. This may well, however, have been a simple admission by Griffith that the Boundary Commission idea was useless, although Bishop MacRory considered otherwise (NLI, Griffith papers, acc. 4476, box b, memo sent to Griffith).

131. Westminster Parliamentary Archives, Lloyd George Papers, F/25/2/51, Tom Jones to Prime Minister, 4 Dec. 1921.

132. Westminster Parliamentary Archives, Lloyd George Papers, F/25/2/51, Tom Jones to Prime Minister, 4 Dec. 1921.

133. Fanning, Kennedy, Keogh, O'Halpin (eds) *Documents on Irish foreign policy vol.1, 1919–1922* (Dublin, 1998), 354 (report by Barton on meeting of 5 Dec.1921).

134. Westminster Parliamentary Archives, Lloyd George Papers, F/25/2/51, Tom Jones to Prime Minister, 4 Dec. 1921.

135. Westminster Parliamentary Archives, Lloyd George Papers, F/26/1/17, Tom Jones to Prime Minister, 17 Mar. 1922.

136. Fanning, Kennedy, Keogh, O'Halpin (eds) *Documents on Irish foreign policy vol.1, 1919–1922* (Dublin, 1998), 359 (clause 15 of the 'articles of agreement for a treaty between Great Britain and Ireland').

CHAPTER ELEVEN

1. Keith Middlemas (ed.) *Thomas Jones, Whitehall diary, vol.3* (London, 1971), 161.
2. Churchill Archives, CHAR22/13/40–41, letter [of Lord Londonderry?] to Churchill, 22 May 1922; CHAR22/13/58–60, 'Charley' [Lord Londonderry?] to 'WSC' [Churchill], 25 May 1922 (quote).
3. Kathleen Clarke, *Revolutionary woman* (Dublin, 1991), 192; John Borgonovo (ed.) *Florence and Josephine O'Donoghue's War of Independence* (Dublin, 2006). This resolve formally manifested itself in an IRB Supreme Council circular letter of 12 December 1921, the last circular to be issued in the sixty-four year history of that historic organisation. Florence O'Donoghue, *No other law* (Dublin, 1954), 193.
4. Michael Collins, *The path to freedom* (Dublin, 1922), 116–117.
5. Churchill Archives, CHAR22/11/38, Fitzalan to Churchill, 27 Jan. 1922 (citing Bishop Fogarty, the Sinn Féin Party treasurer).
6. NAI, Dáil Eireann papers, DE1/4, cabinet minute 12 Jan. 1922.
7. F.M. Carroll, 'Thomas D'Arcy McGee (1825–68)', *Dictionary of Irish Biography*, 5 (Cambridge, 2009), 1017–1019; Patrick Maume, 'Charles Gavan Duffy (1816– 1903)', *Dictionary of Irish Biography*, 3 (Cambridge, 2009), 505–509. With some advice from James Bryce and John O'Leary, Duffy alone actually attempted to draft a *written* Irish constitution in 1886 (something that Gladstone, obviously, would not attempt to do), although his ideas (partly reflecting his age) were about as conservative as Midleton's ideas in 1918! His son did play a part in drafting the Irish constitutions of 1922 and 1937.
8. For the role of the Irish Party in attempting to sabotage the Dáil, see the chapter on Ireland in John Turner, *Lloyd George's secretariat* (Cambridge, 1980). The British Catholic anti-Dáil agitation meant principally the activities of the Catholic Union of Great Britain, established to protect the papacy's temporal power during 1871 and which had worked with the Irish Party to secure a truce from December 1920 onwards. For the history of this body, see Youssef Taouk, 'We are alienating the splendid Irish race: British Catholic response to the Irish conscription controversy of 1918', *Journal of Church and State*, 48 (2006), pp. 601–622, esp. p. 610.
9. Westminster Parliamentary Archives, Lloyd George Papers, Maurice Hankey to Prime Minister, 27 Sep. 1921, with attached intelligence communication (this item is numbered F25/1/19, but filed at F/25/2/19).
10. DeValera had worked with Leslie in the summer of 1919 (UCD Archives, DeValera papers, P150/727, DeValera to Griffith Aug.1919) and, reflecting the continuity of the post-1884 American political situation, British figures like Leslie (a cousin of Churchill) were essentially the chief political figures in the New York Irish social world even if the public, or popular, face of New York Irish Catholic opinion was represented by the Ford family's *Irish World*, which now became DeValera's greatest supporter, and to a lesser extent Devoy's *Gaelic American* (established in 1903 as a fenian rival to the *Irish World*).
11. Churchill Archives, CHAR22/11/1, Sir Shane Leslie to Churchill, 2 January 1922: 'the bishops seem to think it really can be settled. Many congratulations.'
12. NLI, Art O'Brien papers, Ms8428/4. See also the explanatory note for this reference in NLI, Art O'Brien Collection List No.150. It might also be noted that Markievicz, like all Irish political activists since 1917 who did not risk arrest by availing of the IRB's secret courier system, was necessarily applying for a British passport at this time so she could travel abroad (Ms8424/1, Ms8428/19).

13. Gerard Keown, 'The Irish race conference 1922 reconsidered', *Irish Historical Studies,* xxxiii, no.127 (May 2001), 365–376 (quote p376).

14. Dáil Eireann had a constitution for its own assembly but it did not produce a proposed constitution for an Irish state. Draft constitutions discussed during the Anglo-Irish negotiations of October 1921–December 1921 were based on British proposals (usually revised by Childers), not a constitution drawn up by members of Dáil Eireann.

15. Churchill Archives, CHAR22/11/57, Churchill to Sir John Anderson, 31 Jan. 1922.

16. Ronan Keane, 'Hugh Kennedy (1879–1936)', *Dictionary of Irish Biography,* 5 (Cambridge, 2009), 111–113; Gerard Hogan, 'George Gavan Duffy (1882–1951)', *Dictionary of Irish Biography,* 3 (Cambridge, 2009), 510–521; R.D. Marshall, 'William Evelyn Wylie (1881–1964)', *Dictionary of Irish Biography,* 9 (Cambridge, 2009), 1059–1061; Patrick Maume, 'James Henry Mussen Campbell (1851–1931)', *Dictionary of Irish Biography,* 2 (Cambridge, 2009), 289–292; Daire Hogan, *The legal profession in Ireland 1789–1922* (Naas, 1986); David Foxton, *Revolutionary lawyers: Sinn Féin and crown courts in Ireland and Britain 1916–1923* (Dublin, 2008).

17. Churchill Archives, CHAR22/8/14–20, Cope to Churchill, 23 Dec. 1921; CHAR22/8, 'J.M.S.' (James Masterston Smith) to Churchill, 29 Dec. 1921 (report of the Irish Situation Committee, 'containing matter unsuitable for presentation to the Irish leaders'); CHAR22/8, Sir John Anderson to Churchill, 30 Dec. 1921. Although he acted as a defence lawyer for republicans since 1884, Healy, by virtue of his very status as a defence lawyer, also had 'a great relationship with the DMP for nearly forty years': CHAR22/11/48, Healy to Churchill, 30 Jan. 1922.

18. Arthur Mitchell, *Revolutionary government,* 76, 325.

19. Churchill Archives, CHAR22/11/2, Craig to Churchill, 11 Jan. 1922.

20. *Sinn Féin,* 28 Jan. 1911, p.1.

21. A good source on the role of Birkenhead (F.E. Smith) in the negotiations is Keith Middlemas (ed.) *Thomas Jones, Whitehall diary, vol.3* (London, 1971).

22. Churchill Archives, CHAR22/8/31, Fisher to Churchill, 23 Jan. 1922.

23. Keith Middlemas (ed.) *Thomas Jones, Whitehall diary, vol.3* (London, 1971), 160.

24. Fanning, Kennedy, Keogh, O'Halpin (eds) *Documents on Irish foreign policy vol.1, 1919–1922* (Dublin, 1998), 354.

25. Regarding the latter, Hankey was advising Churchill that 'it becomes very important to know what the other fellow is doing before he does it. People are sent to find out on both sides. Sometimes they get caught and punished … we went through all this with Germany in the years before the war, as I can testify. What a ghastly disaster it would be if such a process began between Great Britain and the United States'. Churchill Archives, CHAR25/2, Hankey to Churchill, 4 July 1921. By contrast, Lloyd George was generally sympathetic to the idea of encouraging American financial investment in Britain and sidelining concerns regarding international espionage and naval races.

26. Churchill Archives, CHAR22/8/8, Churchill to 'W.S.B.' [W.B. Spender?], 15 Sep. 1921.

27. Churchill Archives, CHAR22/8/20–22, report of the Irish Situation Sub-Committee to the Secretary of State, 29 Dec.1921. This new subcommittee, whose concerns 'contains matter unsuitable for presentation to the Irish leaders', consisted of Sir John Anderson (Dublin Castle), Sir Otto Niemeyer (financial controller of the treasury and director of Bank of England), Sir Herbert Creedy (War Office), C.T. Davis (Colonial Office), S.G. Tallents (secretary to the Lord Lieutenant) and Lionel Curtis (advisor to PM).

28. Churchill Archives, CHAR22/8, Sir John Anderson to Churchill, 30 Dec. 1921.

29. Richard Lloyd George, *Lloyd George* (London, 1960), 201–203.

30. Churchill Archives, CHAR22/11/2, Craig to Churchill, 11 Jan. 1922.

31. NLI, Kathleen Napoli MacKenna papers, Ms22749, Ms22753.

32. A side-product of the defence or security arrangements launched in June 1921 was the question of upon what basis Irish defence forces were to be organised; a fact that had led many government officials (from December 1920 onwards) to look to examples in British colonies. Although Jan Smuts' South African colony was the principal example considered, the very fact of the persistence of conflict in Egypt (which was sending delegations to London at the same time as Ireland, requesting similar treatment to the Dáil) led to the request made to Emmet Dalton (who had been a senior British army officer who became involved in the IRA) to deal directly with the Egyptian delegation. This was done notwithstanding Griffith's opposition to the idea of the Dáil dealing with any Egyptian delegation. Dalton later became a National Army officer and, after retiring in 1923, ultimately launched Ardmore film studios. For his liaisons with the Egyptians, see the references to Egypt in NLI, Art O'Brien papers, Collection List No.150.

33. Fanning, Kennedy, Keogh, O'Halpin (eds) *Documents on Irish foreign policy vol.1, 1919–1922* (Dublin, 1998), pp. 239–246 (quote p. 241). It was Childers, in conjunction with Royal Navy personnel, who arranged the Howth and Kilcoole gunrunning of 1914, not the IRB (it had no such facilities to enable it to perform such work). This reflected Childers' motive in calling upon the British government during 1911 to create volunteer forces, for local Irish defence, as a cost-saving measure for imperial defence generally in the forthcoming European war.

34. Frank Callanan, *T.M. Healy* (Cork, 1996), 603.

35. Arthur Griffith, *Arguments for the treaty* (Dublin, 1922), 9.

36. NLI, Kathleen MacKenna Napoli papers, MS22751.

37. Dáil Eireann, *Debate on the treaty between Great Britain and Ireland, signed in London on 6 December 1921: sessions 14 Dec.1921 to 10 January 1922* (Dublin, 1922), 7–8.

38. Dáil Eireann, *Debate on the treaty between Great Britain and Ireland, signed in London on 6 December 1921: sessions 14 Dec.1921 to 10 January 1922* (Dublin, 1922), 7–8.

39. Dáil Eireann, *Debate on the treaty between Great Britain and Ireland, signed in London on 6 December 1921: sessions 14 Dec.1921 to 10 January 1922* (Dublin, 1922), 10–15.

40. Arthur Griffith, *Arguments for the treaty* (Dublin, 1922), 6, 8–9, 19.

41. Dáil Eireann, *Debate on the treaty between Great Britain and Ireland, signed in London on 6 December 1921: sessions 14 Dec.1921 to 10 January 1922* (Dublin, 1922), 19–21.

42. Dáil Eireann, *Debate on the treaty between Great Britain and Ireland*, 96–98.

43. UCD, DeValera papers, P150/575 (report on Sinn Féin Ard Fheis, 25 Oct. 1917).

44. Dáil Eireann, *Debate on the treaty between Great Britain and Ireland*, 24–27.

45. Dáil Eireann, *Debate on the treaty between Great Britain and Ireland*, 130.

46. Dáil Eireann, *Debate on the treaty between Great Britain and Ireland*, 24–27.

47. NLI, Art O'Brien papers, Ms8425/17 (publicity material relating to an anti-treaty fund-raising tour in America, quote from speech of Muriel MacSwiney). On this theme, see also Countess Markievicz's press articles during the summer of 1922.

48. Dáil Eireann, *Debate on the treaty between Great Britain and Ireland*, 24–27.

49. Dáil Eireann, *Debate on the treaty between Great Britain and Ireland*, 28–29. Plunkett justified this latter point by arguing that 'I will never sacrifice the independence of Ireland simply for the purpose of securing a cessation of warfare', to which one might have reasonably retorted what 'warfare' was he referring to? Sean T. O'Kelly referred disparagingly to the peace agreement as 'a dictated peace' (p65). In a similar vein, Austin Stack claimed that he personally recognised, even if nobody else in the world did, that at no stage in history did the British government ever exercise the slightest political authority over the island of Ireland (pp. 27–28).

50. Arthur Griffith, *Arguments for the treaty* (Dublin, 1922), 8–9, 12.
51. Westminster Diocesan Archives, Cardinal Bourne papers, BO 1/72, a copy of a letter Archbishop Byrne of Dublin to (ex-Under Secretary) James MacMahon, 29 Jan. 1922; a copy of Lord Fitzalan's reply, 29 Jan. 1922, and Lord Fitzalan to Cardinal Bourne, 1 Feb. 1922. Churchill Archives, CHAR22/11/43.
52. Regarding the Church's support for DeValera's stance, Bishop Fogarty, the Sinn Féin Party treasurer, told Lord Fitzalan that this would be done 'not so much on political grounds as with sympathy for him in his misfortunes' (Churchill Archives, CHAR22/11/38, Fitzalan to Churchill, 27 Jan. 1922). This essentially reflected a willingness to portray DeValera as an iconic and victimised, or 'misfortunate', figure, partly in order to give symbolical representation to the church's grievances.
53. Dáil Eireann, *Debate on the treaty between Great Britain and Ireland*, 34–36.
54. Dáil Eireann, *Debate on the treaty between Great Britain and Ireland*, 30–32.
55. Dáil Eireann, *Debate on the treaty between Great Britain and Ireland*, 9.
56. Arthur Griffith, *Arguments for the treaty* (Dublin, 1922), 13–14.
57. Dáil Eireann, *Debate on the treaty between Great Britain and Ireland*, 26–27.
58. Arthur Griffith, *Arguments for the treaty* (Dublin, 1922), 18–19.
59. Dáil Eireann, *Debate on the treaty between Great Britain and Ireland*, 38–41.
60. Dáil Eireann, *Debate on the treaty between Great Britain and Ireland*, 48–49, 86–88.
61. Churchill Archives, CHAR22/8/14–20, Cope to Churchill, 23 Dec. 1921 (quote); CHAR22/11/1, Leslie to Churchill, 2 Jan.1922.
62. P.J. Dempsey, Shaun Boylan, 'Robert Childers Barton (1881–1975)', *Dictionary of Irish Biography*, 1 (Cambridge, 2009), 361–363.
63. The very popular satirical magazine, *Dublin Opinion*, was founded as a direct result of the farcical and pitiable character of most TDs' behaviour in the so-called 'treaty debates'. *Thirty years of Dublin Opinion* (Dublin, 1952).
64. Dáil Eireann, *Debate on the treaty between Great Britain and Ireland*, 96.
65. Dáil Eireann, *Debate on the treaty between Great Britain and Ireland*, 75. Sean Etchingham, followed by Máire O'Callaghan (wife of the murdered mayor of Limerick, an old friend of Griffith) and Sean T. O'Kelly, all used Barton's admission as a basis for a direct attack on Griffith, accusing him of being a renegade to his old beliefs. The term 'treaty of terror' was coined by Etchingham (Dáil Eireann, *Debate on the treaty between Great Britain and Ireland*, 53–65).
66. Dáil Eireann, *Debate on the treaty between Great Britain and Ireland*, 46–47. Griffith would defend this stance by citing Abraham Lincoln.
67. Arthur Griffith, *Arguments for the treaty* (Dublin, 1922), 5, 16–18.
68. NLI, Griffith papers, acc.4476, box a and box b (copy).
69. Dáil Eireann, *Debate on the treaty between Great Britain and Ireland*, 30 (speech of Collins).
70. Dáil Eireann, *Debate on the treaty between Great Britain and Ireland*, 20–21.
71. Dáil Eireann, *Debate on the treaty between Great Britain and Ireland*, 74–75.
72. Dáil Eireann, *Debate on the treaty between Great Britain and Ireland*, 150.
73. *Nationality*, 4 May 1918, p.1.
74. Arthur Griffith, *Arguments for the treaty* (Dublin, 1922), 12–14.
75. Dáil Eireann, *Debate on the treaty between Great Britain and Ireland*, 111–113.
76. Dáil Eireann, *Debate on the treaty between Great Britain and Ireland*, 88–90.
77. Michael Laffan, *The resurrection of Ireland* (Cambridge, 1999), 370–372.
78. NAI, Dáil Eireann papers, DE1/4, cabinet minutes for 11 and 13 Jan. 1922.
79. NAI, Dáil Eireann papers, DE1/4, cabinet minute 3 Feb. 1922.

80. NAI, Dáil Eireann papers, DE1/4, cabinet minute 3 Feb. 1922. Gavan Duffy and Griffith were ready to appoint Thomas Hughes Kelly in place of Sean T. O'Kelly at Paris. Griffith received communications from the French and Canadian governments during 1922, possibly partly due to the past efforts (during 1911) of Lord Killanin, supported by the Dublin Corporation, to promote Irish business links in such countries before the British government vetoed these efforts, as well as the more recent efforts of Michael MacWhite.

81. NAI, Dáil Eireann papers, DE1/4, cabinet minute for 24 Jan. 1922. To facilitate this, Griffith acquired the services of Gearoid O'Lochlain as his personal secretary and Lily O'Brennan as his personal typist.

82. NAI, Dáil Eireann papers, DE1/4, cabinet minute 27 Jan 1922.

83. NAI, Dáil Eireann papers, DE1/4, cabinet minute for 23 Feb. 1922.

84. Arthur Griffith, *Arguments for the treaty* (Dublin, 1922), 6–9.

85. Arthur Griffith, *The Home Rule Bill examined* (Dublin, 1912), 10: 'If England tomorrow eliminated the name of God from the oath she administers to her legislators, as her ally on the continent [the republican French state] has done, Ireland must erase the name of God also. I do not contest the liberty of any Irishman to hold heterodox views on religion but I declare it an insult to the whole Irish people that the English Parliament should claim the right to make them ignore the Almighty. The terms of the oath imposed on Irish legislators must not be subject to the belief or disbelief of a foreign and materialistic people.'

86. Arthur Griffith, *How Ireland is taxed* (Dublin, 1907), 4.

87. Sean T. O'Kelly, 'Arthur Griffith', *Capuchin Annual* (1966).

88. Arthur Griffith, 'True and false imperialism', *The Irish Review: a monthly magazine of Irish literature, art and science*, 1 (Aug. 1911), 270–272.

89. Arthur Griffith, *The Home Rule Bill examined* (Dublin, 1912), 4.

90. Arthur Griffith, *The Home Rule Bill examined* (Dublin, 1912), 4.

91. Arthur Griffith, *Arguments for the treaty* (Dublin, 1922), 6–9.

92. Churchill Archives, 22/8/20–22, report of the Irish Situation Sub-Committee to the Secretary of State, 29 Dec.1921. This new subcommittee consisted of Sir John Anderson (Dublin Castle), Sir Otto Niemeyer (financial controller of the treasury and director of Bank of England), Sir Herbert Creedy (War Office), C.T. Davis (Colonial Office), S.G. Tallents (secretary to the Lord Lieutenant) and Lionel Curtis (advisor to PM).

93. Churchill Archives, CHAR22/11/[72], report of Irish Situation Committee to Secretary of State, 6 Feb. 1922. When Craig was surprised at the extent of Collins' expectations from the Boundary Commission, he told him that this was not what the Prime Minister had said in parliament, to which Collins replied that he did not read the speeches of the Prime Minister in parliament. CHAR22/11/69–70, 'F' to 'Hamar [Greenwood]', 9 Feb. 1922.

94. Griffith, Gavan Duffy and Cosgrave formed a subcommittee to deal with the matter of civil servants, requesting that they swear allegiance to the Dáil. NAI, Dáil Eireann papers, DE1/4, cabinet minute 27 Jan 1922.

95. Churchill Archives, CHAR22/11/[72], report of Irish Situation Committee to Secretary of State, 6 Feb. 1922.

96. NAI, Dáil Eireann papers, DE1/4, cabinet minute for 17 Feb 1922.

97. Churchill Archives, CHAR22/11/71, copy of letter sent to Collins on behalf of Churchill, dated 3 Feb.1922.

98. Dáil Eireann, *Debate on the treaty between Great Britain and Ireland*, 26–27. The nominal convening of a Southern Ireland parliament under the terms of the agreement was a matter that essentially determined the meaning of the 'common citizenship' principle, at least as far as Britain was concerned.

99. *Nationality*, 9 Aug., 30 Aug. 1919, p.1.

100. Tom Dunne (ed.) *The National University of Ireland 1908–2008* (Dublin, 2008), 136.

101. Churchill Archives, CHAR22/11/20, 'Crowe' to Lord Harding (Foreign Office, Paris), 14 January 1922 (a communication that was also forwarded by Churchill for the Prime Minister's attention).

102. Arthur Griffith, *Arguments for the treaty* (Dublin, 1922), 21–24, 6–7, 16–18.

103. Michael Laffan, *The resurrection of Ireland* (Cambridge, 1999), 370–372.

104. Westminster Parliamentary Archives, Lloyd George papers, F/26/1/17, Tom Jones to Prime Minister, 17 Mar. 1922.

105. Westminster Parliamentary Archives, Lloyd George Papers, F/21/1/7, Lloyd George to Griffith, 1 June 1922.

106. Westminster Parliamentary Archives, Lloyd George Papers, F/21/1/8, Griffith to Lloyd George, 2 June 1922 (copy). The original copy of this letter is at F/26/1/39.

107. NAI, Dáil Eireann papers, DE4/6/7, cabinet minutes 2–5 June 1922.

108. Erskine Childers, *Clause by clause: a comparison between the treaty and document no.2* (Manchester, 1922), 2–4.

109. Robert Barton, *The truth about the treaty and document no.2* (Manchester, 1922), 3–4.

110. NAI, Dáil Eireann papers, DE1/4, cabinet minute for 17 Feb. and 27 Feb. 1922.

111. Arthur Griffith, *Arguments for the treaty* (Dublin, 1922), 26–28.

112. Ronan Fanning, *The Irish Department of Finance 1922–1958* (Dublin, 1978), 30–33.

113. Churchill Archives, CHAR22/8/16, Cope to Churchill, 23 Dec. 1921.

114. F.S.L. Lyons (ed.) *Bank of Ireland 1783–1983* (Dublin, 1983), 55–56.

115. Bank of Ireland Archives, 'Synopsis of the decisions of the committee' (Irish Banks Standing Committee, 1925), 5.

116. Ronan Fanning, *The Irish Department of Finance 1922–1958* (Dublin, 1978), chapter two.

117. NAI, Dáil Eireann papers, DE1/4, cabinet minute for 24 Feb. 1922.

118. Westminster Diocesan Archives, Cardinal Bourne Papers, BO1/72, Lord Fitzalan to Cardinal Bourne, 1 Feb. 1922.

119. Mark O'Brien, Kevin Rafter (eds) *Independent Newspapers: a history* (Dublin, 2012), 47–48, 61–62.

120. NLI, Griffith papers, acc.4476, box a, DeValera to 'Art O'Griobhta, President of the Republic', 10 Mar. 1922. Griffith's reply to DeValera on this matter of election registers was submitted to cabinet and approved on 24 March 1922 (NAI, Dáil Eireann papers, DE1/4, cabinet minute for 24 Mar. 1922). A draft of the same can also be seen in NLI, Griffith papers, acc.4476, box a.

121. Churchill Archives, CHAR22/8, Sir John Anderson to Churchill, 30 Dec. 1921.

122. Westminster Parliamentary Archives, Lloyd George papers, F/10/6/3, Collins to Lloyd George, 9 Feb. 1922.

123. Westminster Parliamentary Archives, Lloyd George papers, F/26/1/17 and F26/1/24, Tom Jones to Prime Minister, 17 and 24 Mar. 1922.

124. Churchill Archives, Lord Hankey papers, HNKY1/5, diary entry for 7 Sep. 1920 (p.154); Westminster Parliamentary Archives, Lloyd George Papers, F25/1/42, Tom Jones to Lloyd George, 15 Jun. 1921 (report on Irish Situation Committee meeting).

125. Westminster Parliamentary Archives, Lloyd George Papers, F/25/2/24, Arthur Balfour to Sir Maurice Hankey, 30 Sep. 1921.

126. This was reflected by Lord Iveagh, the owner of Guinness Breweries, and Andrew Jameson, the Director of Bank of Ireland, writing to Midleton that if they demanded too much they might be considered responsible for 'breaking the treaty'. Peter Martin, 'Irish peers' (MA, UCD, 1998), quoted p.198.

127. Peter Martin, 'Irish peers' (MA, UCD, 1998), 193–198.

128. Ian Kenneally, *The Paper Wall* (Cork, 2008), 78, 98–99.

129. Interview with Lionel Smith Gordon published in the *Evening Independent* (St. Petersburg, Florida), 14 Jan. 1924.

130. L.M. Cullen, *Princes and pirates: the Dublin Chamber of Commerce 1783–1983* (Dublin, 1983), 96; Eunan O'Halpin, 'William Thomas Cosgrave (1880–1961)', *Dictionary of Irish Biography*, 2 (Cambridge, 2009), 880–885.

131. Bank of Ireland Archives, 'Synopsis of the decisions of the committee' (Irish Banks Standing Committee, 1925), memo for 14 June 1922.

132. L.M. Cullen, *Princes and pirates*, 85.

133. John Patrick Dunne, 'Poverty problems for a patriot parliament', *Journal of the Society for the Statistical and Social Inquiry of Ireland*, vol.74–76 (1921–1923), 189–198. This was quite possibly the same J.P. Dunne who misappropriated the funds of the Wolfe Tone Clubs in 1899, probably at the request of the Irish Party.

134. 'Hints for historians', *Irish Times*, 23 Mar. 1922. Susan Mitchell, although primarily a literary figure, was the assistant to George Russell in the Irish Agricultural Organisation Society and the author of these comments, which met with Green's approval.

135. Regarding the Church's support for DeValera's stance, Bishop Fogarty, the Sinn Féin Party treasurer, told Lord Fitzalan that this would be done 'not so much on political grounds as with sympathy for him in his misfortunes' (Churchill Archives, CHAR22/11/38, Fitzalan to Churchill, 27 Jan. 1922).

CHAPTER TWELVE

1. W.T. Cosgrave, 'Arthur Griffith (1872–1922)', *Dictionary of National Biography 1922–1930* (Oxford, 1937), 364–368; NLI, Ms22812 (manuscript draft of Kevin O'Higgins' account of the origins of the civil war—quote).

2. The massive collection of British press cuttings from 1922 within the Art O'Brien papers in the National Library of Ireland is an excellent source for this subject. See NLI, Art O'Brien Collection List No.150.

3. Robert Barton, *The truth about the treaty and document no.2* (Manchester, 1922); Erskine Childers, *Clause by clause: a comparison between the treaty and document no.2* (Manchester, 1922).

4. See the provisional constitution of Cumann na Poblachta, reproduced as an appendix in Ann Matthews, *Dissidents* (Cork, 2012).

5. NAI, Dáil Eireann papers, DE2/514, letter of Fr. J O'Sullivan OP (Rome) included within letter of J. Robinson, 25 Apr.1922. This is included in a folder relating to Collins and O'Kelly. Sean T. did have one sympathetic Roman listener in Monsignor Hagan. Patrick Long, 'John Hagan (1873–1930)', *Dictionary of Irish Biography*, 4 (Cambridge, 2009), 353–354.

6. On this theme, see Fearghal McGarry (ed.) *Republicanism in modern Ireland* (Dublin, 2003).

7. UCD Archives, DeValera papers, P150/1171, Joe Begley to Harry Boland, 30 Mar. 1922 (summarising Devoy's arguments in the *Gaelic American*). Devoy's journalism at this time has been examined well by Michael Doorley in the context of American politics at the time. For the history of Devoy's involvement in American politics prior to the first world war, see Owen McGee, 'Soldiers and propagandists: the impact of the American Fenian Brotherhood on Irish politics', *History Studies*, 8 (2007), 1–16.

8. NAI, Dáil Eireann papers, DE1/4, cabinet minutes for 12, 16 and 24 Jan.1922.

9. NAI, Dáil Eireann papers, DE1/4, cabinet minute for 17 Feb. 1922.

10. NAI, Dáil Eireann papers, DE1/4, cabinet minute for 15 Mar. 1922.

11. NAI, Dáil Eireann papers, DE1/4, cabinet minute for 15 Mar. 1922.

12. NAI, Dáil Eireann papers, DE1/4, cabinet minutes for 24 Feb., 27 Feb., 15 Mar., 21 Mar., 4 Apr. 1922.

13. Marie Coleman, 'Oscar Traynor (1886–1963)', *Dictionary of Irish Biography*, 9 (Cambridge, 2009), 456–457.

14. NAI, Dáil Eireann papers, DE1/4, cabinet minutes for 4 Apr. and 10 Apr. 1922.

15. Mark O'Brien, Kevin Rafter (eds) *Independent newspapers*, 48.

16. F.M. Carroll, 'Joseph McGarrity (1874–1940)', *Dictionary of Irish Biography*, 5 (Cambridge, 2009), 1011–1013; UCD Archives, DeValera papers, P150/1125, Boland to Collins, 14 Mar. 1921.

17. UCD Archives, DeValera papers, P150/1125, Collins to Boland, 3 July 1920.

18. NAI, Dáil Eireann papers, DE1/4, cabinet minute for 15 Mar. 1922. Commenting on Devoy's information, 'the Minister of Finance [Collins] was of opinion that this money was withdrawn by DeValera under power of attorney in order to transfer it to other banks'. Appreciation for Devoy's work in attempting to assist the Dáil cabinet in this way evidently motivated Cosgrave and Fitzgerald's later extension of an invitation to him to receive a state reception in 1924.

19. Dáil Eireann, *Debate on the treaty between Great Britain and Ireland, signed in London on 6 December 1921: sessions 14 Dec.1921 to 10 January 1922* (Dublin, 1922), 35.

20. Fanning, Kennedy, Keogh, O'Halpin (eds) *Documents on Irish foreign policy vol.1, 1919– 1922* (Dublin, 1998), 318–319.

21. On this theme, see the IRB Supreme Council circular to the Clan of 26 Apr.1920 in UCD Archives, DeValera papers, P150/1125. Devoy implicitly trusted Clarke's judgment in such matters and did not have an opinion himself whether or not Clarke was correct in calling for a rebellion in Ireland in 1916.

22. UCD Archives, DeValera papers, P150/1171 (Boland correspondence).

23. UCD Archives, DeValera papers, P150/1171, Peter Drury, Merchants Bank, to Boland, 6 Feb.1922; receipt of 28 Feb.1922; letter of McGarrity (in Cork) to Boland, 22 Apr.1922, noting receipt of funds by Traynor, Mellows and O'Connor.

24. UCD Archives, DeValera papers, P150/1171, Boland to McGarrity, 12 Apr.1922.

25. Letter of Liam Mellows, 'secretary to the army council Four Courts', to the cabinet, quoted in NAI, Dáil Eireann papers, DE1/4, cabinet minute for 21 Apr. 1922.

26. UCD Archives, DeValera papers, P150/1171, Lynch to Boland, 24 Apr. 1922.

27. UCD Archives, DeValera papers, P150/1171, Boland to Liam Lynch, 20 Apr.1922. Contrary to the claims of Black and Tans at Templemore, in fact a chief of police appointed by the ministry of home affairs to Templemore (Simon Donnelly) was found by the Dáil cabinet to be working for the IRA. NAI, Dáil Eireann papers, DE1/4, cabinet minute for 4 Apr.1922.

28. UCD Archives, DeValera papers, P150/1171, Boland to Lynch, 30 May 1922.

29. The previous spring and summer, Boland tried to arrange the purchase and transportation to Ireland of many machine guns in America; a foolish scheme that unsurprisingly backfired, and led him to write to Brugha (then minister for defence) that 'I regret very much if my action has caused you any embarrassment, and will be more careful in future in doing unauthorised work.' UCD Archives, DeValera papers, P150/1128, Boland– Brugha correspondence (quote from letter of 21 July 1921).

30. Jennie Wyse Power, a party treasurer and trustee of the defunct Sinn Féin People's Bank Ltd., temporarily froze the accounts of Sinn Féin to prevent them being used against the Dáil, but other party members who had as lengthy party records as Power, such as Sean T.

O'Kelly, Henry Dixon and Margaret Buckley (wife to Griffith and Rooney's one-time aide Patrick Buckley)—all of whom opposed the treaty—opposed this move. Bishop Fogarty, the chief Sinn Féin Party treasurer after 1918, decided not to take sides in this matter. William Murphy, Lesa Ní Mhungaile, 'Jenny Wyse Power (1858–1941)', *Dictionary of Irish Biography*, 8 (Cambridge, 2009), 256–257; Frances Clarke, 'Margaret (Goulding) Buckley', *Dictionary of Irish Biography*, 1 (Cambridge, 2009), 973–974; Sean T. O'Kelly, 'Arthur Griffith', *Capuchin Annual* (1966), 132–150.

31. P.S. O'Hegarty, *The victory of Sinn Féin* (Dublin, 1924), 8.
32. On this theme, see Owen McGee, *The IRB* (Dublin, 2005), chapter 1; Owen McGee, 'Soldiers and propagandists: the impact of the American Fenian Brotherhood on Irish politics', *History Studies*, 8 (2007), 1–16.
33. Sean T. O'Kelly was primarily responsible for propagating these ideas. Later, he professed to have only discovered many years afterwards that Collins had been working to maintain a peaceable republican unity rather than doing anything to split the Dáil or volunteers' ranks from December 1921 onwards. Sean T. O'Kelly, 'Arthur Griffith', *Capuchin Annual* (1966). Like Brugha, O'Kelly himself had left the IRB after 1916 at the church's request. His political confusion during 1922 may be said to have partly been because he had formerly been the Dáil's chief consul on the European continent and, for this very reason, prior to the treaty debates in December 1921, he had never attended a single Dáil session and so was not particularly well informed of the dynamics of the political situation in Dublin.
34. NLI, Sinn Féin pamphlet collection, ILB300p13 (item 118).
35. NLI, Art O'Brien papers, Ms8430/31.
36. Westminster Diocesan Archives, Cardinal Bourne papers, BO1/72, Lord Fitzalan to Cardinal Bourne, 1 Feb. 1922.
37. NLI, Kathleen MacKenna Napoli papers, Ms22760.
38. Richard English, 'Ernest Bernard O'Malley (1897–1957)', *Dictionary of Irish Biography*, 7 (Cambridge, 2009), 677–678; Pauric Dempsey, 'Thomas Derrig (1897–1956)', *Dictionary of Irish Biography*, 3 (Cambridge, 2009), 185–186. The willingness of Derrig, the headmaster of the Ballina Technical School with a degree in commerce and a supporter of the idea of industrial development, to take up a stance that was so militantly opposed to Griffith was symbolic of the failure of nationalists to develop an economic platform that could unite Sinn Féin. It had recently been brought to the cabinet's attention that P.J. Ruttledge, the anti-treaty chairman of Mayo County Council, was attempting to introduce rates for 'the IRA' without reference to Dáil Eireann. NAI, Dáil Eireann papers, DE1/4, cabinet minute for 31 Mar. 1922.
39. NLI, Kathleen MacKenna Napoli papers, Ms22759.
40. *Freeman's Journal*, 19 Aug. 1922.
41. NAI, Dáil Eireann papers, DE1/4, cabinet minute for 10 Apr. 1922.
42. Westminster Diocesan Archives, Cardinal Bourne papers, BO 1/72, Lord Fitzalan to Cardinal Bourne, 22 Apr. 1922.
43. NAI, Dáil Eireann papers, DE1/4, cabinet minute for 13 Apr. 1922.
44. NAI, Dáil Eireann papers, DE1/4, cabinet minute for 21 Apr. 1922.
45. T.W. Moody, F.X. Martin (eds) *A new history of Ireland*, 8 (Oxford, 1989), 401.
46. Westminster Diocesan Archives, Cardinal Bourne papers, BO 1/72, Lord Fitzalan to Cardinal Bourne, 22 Apr. 1922.
47. UCD Archives, DeValera Papers, P150/1172, P150/1191.
48. Churchill Archives, CHAR22/8, Sir John Anderson to Churchill, 30 Dec. 1921.
49. See his letters to Art O'Brien in NLI, Ms8421/8, Ms8427/30.

50. Frances Clarke, 'Charlotte Despard (1844–1939)', *Dictionary of Irish Biography*, 3 (Cambridge, 2009), 188–189.

51. Ann Matthews, *Dissidents* (Cork, 2012).

52. Although Cumann na mBan had existed since 1914 and Louise Gavan Duffy, as secretary, was also (for a brief time) a secretary of the Irish National Aid and Volunteers Dependents Fund, the organisation did not really come into its own until after taking up the political prisoners issue in 1922. Ann Matthews, *Dissidents* (Cork, 2012).

53. NAI, Dáil Eireann papers, DE1/4, cabinet minute for 15 Mar. 1922.

54. Stephen O'Mara's refusal to cooperate with the Dáil in New York forced the cabinet by April to consider removing him as a trustee (NAI, Dáil Eireann papers, DE1/4, cabinet minute for 4 Apr. 1922). It was soon felt necessary to try and change the trustees, replacing Bishop Fogarty with W.T. Cosgrave and Stephen O'Mara with P.J. Little (cabinet minute for 21 April). This may have prompted Eoin MacNeill to express a desire to resign from the ministry (DE4/6/7, cabinet minute for 2 May 1922).

55. NAI, Dáil Eireann papers, DE4/6/7, cabinet minutes for 2–3 May 1922.

56. UCD Archives, DeValera papers, P150/1132, letter of 'D' to Boland, 1 Jan.1921; DeValera statement on the White Cross from 4 Feb.1921, and DeValera to Dr. Gertrude Kelly (New York), 28 Feb. 1921.

57. NAI, Dáil Eireann papers, DE1/4, cabinet minutes for 15 Mar., 10 Apr. 1922.

58. It was the publicity (and shock in British political circles) surrounding 'Bloody Sunday' alone that gave Collins the reputation in the British and in turn Irish press as 'an IRA' leader six months later. However, not only was there no such organisation as 'the IRA' but the only contribution of Collins, as a leader of the IRB, to the Irish Volunteers had been in his attempt to do intelligence work to aid Mulcahy and Brugha in defending the Dáil. During the treaty negotiations, British leaders spoke to Collins as if he had control of an Irish army. Collins dismissed this idea, noting that he had, perhaps, only a few thousand supporters, whereas the Irish Volunteers had well over ten thousand members. Richard Lloyd George, *Lloyd George* (London, 1960), 200. Neither the British cabinet nor the Irish public evidently understood what he meant in making this distinction. However, Collins was evidently referring to the fact that, aside from his responsibilities as the Dáil's minister for finance, he had no authority, except as a leader of the IRB. Mulcahy had been an ordinary member of that organisation for a time but was never a member of its executive.

59. These were sometimes also referred to as 'mutineers' or 'IRP'; evidently meaning a self-styled police who were not willing to act as the Dáil's police.

60. NAI, Dáil Eireann papers, DE1/4, cabinet minutes for 10 Apr., 13 Apr., 21 Apr. 1922.

61. Government Stationary Office, *Dáil Eireann*, 192–194 (minutes for 6 Aug. 1920 session).

62. L.W. White, 'Joseph MacDonagh (1883–1922)', *Dictionary of Irish Biography*, 5 (Cambridge, 2009), 917–919. MacDonagh, an anti-treatyite, died in prison from illness on Christmas Day 1922.

63. Reflecting Griffith's resolution of August 1920 that the Dáil considered that the imposition of religious or political tests of employment should be illegal, the Dáil cabinet reported in January 1922 (minute for 24 Jan.) that 'these tests are now to be withdrawn', owing to a belief that the situation was being resolved.

64. L.M. Cullen, *Princes and pirates: the Dublin Chamber of Commerce 1783–1983* (Dublin, 1983), 96; Eunan O'Halpin, 'William Thomas Cosgrave (1880–1961)', *Dictionary of Irish Biography*, 2 (Cambridge, 2009), 880–885.

65. NAI, Dáil Eireann papers, DE1/4, cabinet minutes 27 Jan., 24 Feb., 7 Mar. 1922.

66. NAI, Dáil Eireann papers, DE1/4, cabinet minutes 17 Feb., 24 Feb. 1922.

67. NAI, Dáil Eireann papers, DE1/4, cabinet minute for 12 Jan. 1922.
68. NAI, Dáil Eireann papers, DE1/4, cabinet minutes for 15 Mar., 21 Mar. 1922 (see also NLI, Art O'Brien papers). The names of the Belfast committee representatives that met the Dáil cabinet were Dr. McNabb and Fr. Hasson, who opposed the revival of the boycott, and 'F. Crummie' and 'Mr. Chambers', who wanted it revived by means of the Dáil sending men to Belfast to burn properties.
69. NAI, Dáil Eireann papers, DE1/4, cabinet minute for 24 Mar. 1922.
70. NAI, Dáil Eireann papers, DE1/4, cabinet minute for 4 Apr. 1922.
71. Churchill Archives, CHAR22/13/11.
72. W.T. Cosgrave, 'Arthur Griffith 1872–1922', *Dictionary of National Biography 1922–30* (Oxford, 1937).
73. See the correspondence for April 1922 in NLI, Art O'Brien papers. Quiet recently, Art O'Brien's personal solicitor, J.P. MacDonnell, was 'given a commission to visit Irish prisoners in English jails as official solicitor to the Govt.' on the suggestion of Gavan Duffy (NAI, Dáil Eireann papers, DE1/4, cabinet minute 3 Feb. 1922), who knew MacDonnell well due to the fact that they were both long-time members of the legal profession in London.
74. For the Collins–O'Brien controversy, see NLI, Art O'Brien Papers, Collection List No.150, section VI; Fanning, *Irish department of finance*, chapter 2.
75. Richard Lloyd George, *Lloyd George* (London, 1960), 199.
76. NAI, Dáil Eireann papers, DE4/6/7, cabinet minute for 28 April 1922.
77. David Foxton, *Revolutionary lawyers* (Dublin, 2008). Sean Moylan's legal representative was a senior King's Councillor who also acted as a personal intermediary between him and Kevin O'Higgins. NAI, Dáil Eireann papers, DE4/6/7, cabinet minute for 28 April 1922.
78. Since the truce of 10 July 1921, 4,900 rifles had been handed over to the Northern Ireland government from army stocks in Dublin and these were then held at Carrickfergus Castle. There were 4,400 rifles still available in Dublin, 1,887 belonging to the British army and 2,523 belonging to the RIC. Churchill Archives, CHAR22/13/15, H.J. Creedy (War Office) to Masterston Smith.
79. Churchill Archives, CHAR22/13/3, Churchill to Cope, 2 May 1922.
80. Churchill Archives, CHAR22/13/19–20, report of Earl of Cavan to Churchill, 10 May 1922. It was intended relocating British forces in Cork to Ulster.
81. NAI, Dáil Eireann papers, DE1/4, cabinet minute for 25 Apr.1922; DE4/6/7, cabinet minutes for 2–3 May 1922.
82. Churchill Archives, CHAR22/13/8, Cope to Masterston Smith, 6 May 1922.
83. UCD Archives, DeValera papers, P150/1171, Boland to McGarrity, 30 May 1922.
84. Churchill Archives, CHAR22/13/8, Cope to Masterston Smith, 6 May 1922.
85. This perception was shared by non-IRB figures, including W.T. Cosgrave. See his comments regarding the 'Sinn Féin Volunteers', 'the Irish Republican Brotherhood' and the 1916 rising in W.T. Cosgrave, 'Arthur Griffith (1872–1922)', *Dictionary of National Biography 1922–1930* (Oxford, 1937).
86. David Fitzpatrick, *Harry Boland's Irish revolution* (Cork, 2003), 18–30, photo caption 2a (quote).
87. *Acta Sanctae Sedis* (5ᵗʰ ed., Rome, 1872–1911), V (1911), p.389, quoted in translation from Latin by Fr. William D'Arcy in *The Fenian movement in the United States* (Washington D.C., 197), 329.
88. Chrissy Osborne, *Michael Collins himself* (Cork, 2013), 75–80. Moya O'Connor was daughter of James O'Connor (1836–1910) and niece of John O'Connor (1849–1908) from

the Glen of Imaal, Co. Wicklow. For their republican careers, see the entries on them in the *Dictionary of Irish Biography* or Owen McGee, *The IRB* (Dublin, 2005).

89. John Newsinger, *Fenianism in mid-Victorian Britain* (London, 1994), quoted 54–55. William G. Halpin, a Meath-born American soldier, drafted this proclamation in London in January 1867.

90. Owen McGee, 'Thomas Power O'Connor (1848–1929)', *Dictionary of Irish Biography*, 7 (Cambridge, 2009); Owen McGee, *The IRB: the Irish Republican Brotherhood from the Land League to Sinn Féin* (Dublin, 2005).

91. 'Building up Ireland: the resources of Ireland', in Michael Collins, *The path to freedom* (Dublin, 1922), 106–117 (quote 109).

92. Michael Collins, *The path to freedom* (Dublin, 1922), 50, 126.

93. P.S. O'Hegarty, *A history of Ireland under the Union* (London, 1952), 754–787.

94. Brian Maye, *Arthur Griffith* (Dublin, 1997), 1 (quote).

95. UCD Archives, DeValera papers, P150/1171, unsigned letter of Boland (possibly to W.H. O'Brien), 21 June 1922.

96. UCD Archives, DeValera papers, P150/1171, Boland to McGarrity, 22 June 1922.

97. NAI, Dáil Eireann papers, DE1/4, cabinet minutes for 25 Apr., 26 Apr. 1922. Griffith's response was to decide that 'the Dáil reassemble on Wed 3 May and continue in session for 2 days a week until the elections, the hours of session to be 3–7pm' (cabinet minute for 28 Apr.).

98. NAI, Dáil Eireann papers, DE1/4, minute for 28 Apr.1922; DE4/6/7, minute for 2 May 1922.

99. NAI, Dáil Eireann papers, DE4/6/7, cabinet minute for 3 May 1922 (this motion was scribbled out, possibly by Mulcahy, at a later date).

100. NAI, Dáil Eireann papers, DE4/6/7, cabinet minute for 5 May 1922.

101. NLI, Art O'Brien papers, Ms8460/8, DeValera to O'Brien, 4 July 1922.

102. Westminster Parliamentary Archives, Lloyd George Papers, F/26/1/31, Tom Jones to Prime Minister, 17 May 1922.

103. The legacy of DeValera's threats about 'two armies' to Mulcahy in November 1921 may have forced the latter into taking such action. Mulcahy himself would later claim that when Catholic priests arranged for him a secret meeting with DeValera during 1922, separately from Griffith's secret meeting at the Archbishop's Palace on 10 April, he found that DeValera was unwilling to take any responsibility for the course of public events, as if he inherently enjoyed a form of diplomatic immunity, while he simultaneously expressed a strong sense of identification with Rory O'Connor's IRA dissidents who had occupied the Four Courts, claiming that they were his fellow 'men of faith'. M.G. Valiulis, *Portrait of a revolutionary* (Dublin, 1992), 175.

104. NAI, Dáil Eireann papers, DE1/4, cabinet minute for 23 Feb. 1922.

105. Westminster Parliamentary Archives, Lloyd George papers, F/10/3/48, Cope to Curtis, 8 Sep. 1922.

106. NAI, Bureau of Military History papers, WS205 (Maud Griffith).

107. Arthur Griffith, *Arguments for the treaty* (Dublin, 1922), 9.

108. Westminster Parliamentary Archives, Lloyd George Papers, F/26/1/31, Tom Jones to Prime Minister, 17 May 1922; David Foxton, *Revolutionary lawyers*.

109. Arthur Griffith, *Arguments for the treaty* (Dublin, 1922), 24–25.

110. Arthur Griffith, *Simply gamblers* (Dublin, 1922), 2–4.

111. Churchill Archives, CHAR22/13/25, W.S.C. [Churchill] to Austen [Chamberlain], 13 May 1922.

112. NAI, Dáil Eireann papers, DE4/6/7, cabinet minute for 18 May 1922.

113. Churchill Archives, CHAR22/13/40–41, letter [of Lord Londonderry?] to Churchill, 22 May 1922; CHAR22/13/58–60, 'Charley' [Lord Londonderry?] to 'WSC' [Churchill], 25 May 1922 (quote).

114. Churchill Archives, CHAR22/13/55–56, letter of 'Limerick Man' to Lionel Curtis, 25 May 1922. This 'Limerick man', although relatively elderly, felt sure that this was probably the opinion of about 85 per cent of the Irish population.

115. NAI, Dáil Eireann papers, DE4/6/7, cabinet minute for 5 May 1922. If the next election was not to be properly contested, Joseph McGuinness felt a 60 per cent majority of seats for the government party should be provided for and that Griffith alone should determine all ministerial appointments. NAI, Dáil Eireann papers, DE4/6/7, cabinet minute for 15 May 1922.

116. NAI, Dáil Eireann papers, DE4/6/7, cabinet minute for 6 May 1922.

117. NAI, Dáil Eireann papers, DE4/6/7, cabinet minute for 15 May 1922.

118. NAI, Dáil Eireann papers, DE4/6/7, cabinet minute for 18 May 1922.

119. NAI, Dáil Eireann papers, DE4/6/7, cabinet minute for 25 May 1922.

120. NAI, Dáil Eireann papers, DE4/6/7, cabinet minute for 3 June 1922.

121. NAI, Dáil Eireann papers, DE4/6/7, cabinet minutes for 24–25 May 1922. Remarkably, the advice of Patrick MacCartan, an anti-treatyite, was seemingly relied upon in this matter.

122. Westminster Parliamentary Archives, Lloyd George papers, F/26/1/33, Tom Jones to Prime Minister, 29 May 1922.

123. Westminster Parliamentary Archives, Lloyd George papers, F/26/1/31, Tom Jones to Prime Minister, 17 May 1922.

124. Westminster Parliamentary Archives, Lloyd George Papers, F/21/1/7, Lloyd George to Griffith, 1 June 1922.

125. Westminster Parliamentary Archives, Lloyd George Papers, F/21/1/8, Griffith to Lloyd George, 2 June 1922 (copy). The original copy of this letter is at F/26/1/39. Griffith emphasised that the constitution was drafted by men to whom 'the only instructions which the Provisional Government gave…were printed copies of the Treaty' and therefore it 'represents the work of an independent committee acting upon their own independent interpretation of the Treaty, approaching it with minds biased in its favour'. On one point, however, Griffith reassured the British Prime Minister and left absolutely no room for doubt, namely that 'it is intended that the Irish Free State shall be not merely associated with but a member of the Community of Nations known as the British Empire and on the basis of common citizenship as explicitly provided by the Treaty.'

126. Westminster Parliamentary Archives, Lloyd George Papers, F/26/1/33, Tom Jones to Prime Minister, 29 May 1922.

127. Churchill Archives, CHAR22/13/88, Proclamation of Viscount Fitzalan, governor general of Southern Ireland, 27 May 1922.

128. NAI, Dáil Eireann papers, DE4/6/7, cabinet minute for 26 June 1922.

129. Churchill Archives, CHAR22/13/70–72, Bernard to Midleton, 23 May 1922. It was intended relocating British forces in Cork to Ulster. Churchill Archives, CHAR22/13/19–20, report of Earl of Cavan to Churchill, 10 May 1922 ('secret').

130. Churchill Archives, CHAR22/13/74, report of Earl of Cavan's Imperial Defence committee on Ireland, 26 May 1922.

131. Westminster Parliamentary Archives, Lloyd George papers, F/26/1/38, Churchill to Collins, 6 June 1922 (copy). In the past, Churchill's approach to temporarily having to deal with Ireland was characterised not only by impatience but also an awareness that he did not really know anything about the state of public opinion within Ireland, emphasising to Dublin Castle that 'you must let me know if there is anything in particular that they

don't want said'. Churchill Archives, CHAR22/11/57, Churchill to Sir John Anderson, 31 Jan. 1922.

132. Churchill Archives, CHAR22/13/174–176. Major General A.M. Cameron, an Ulster commander, attempted to dispute this.

133. Westminster Parliamentary Archive, Lloyd George Papers, F/10/3/3, Lloyd George to Churchill, 8 June 1922. Craig wrote regularly to Churchill in May–June 1922 emphasising his willingness to accept *any* plan for increasing funding for the British army in Ulster because of Stormont's lack of any substantive revenue scheme of its own for policing and defence.

134. Westminster Parliamentary Archive, Lloyd George Papers, F/26/1/35–38, Cope to Churchill, 5 June 1922.

135. Richard Lloyd George, *Lloyd George* (London, 1960), introduction, 201; Dominic Sandbrook, *David Lloyd George: the great outsider* (London, 2010). The famous label 'the man who won the war' was given to Lloyd George by an appreciative British press, yet somehow it has often been cited as a supposed label Griffith applied to Collins. What Griffith actually said of Collins was as follows: 'He was the man who made this situation: he was the man—and no one knows it better than I do during a year and a half how he worked—whose matchless energy and indomitable will carried Ireland through that terrible crisis; and if I had any ambition about political affairs or history, and if my name is to go down to history, I want it associated with the name of Michael Collins. Michael Collins was the man who fought the Black-and-Tan terror until England was forced to offer terms of peace.' Tomas S. Cuffe, 'Arthur Griffith's tenth anniversary', *Sunday Independent*, 7 Aug. 1932.

136. NAI, Dáil Eireann papers, DE4/6/7, cabinet minutes of 2–3 June 1922.

137. NAI, Dáil Eireann papers, DE4/6/7, cabinet minutes of 5 June 1922.

138. Mulcahy's arrangement for the IRA army council was as follows: Rory O'Connor, Liam Mellows and Sean Moylan (Four Courts), Richard Mulcahy, Eoin O'Duffy, Gearoid O'Sullivan (Dáil), Diarmuid O'Hegarty and Florence O'Donoghue (neutrals). O'Hegarty, the former cabinet secretary, actually resigned from the Dáil cabinet on 24 February 1922.

139. NAI, Dáil Eireann papers, DE4/6/7, cabinet minutes of 5 June 1922.

140. Justice Hugh Kennedy was working with Griffith in this matter, while three Catholic bishops, including Archbishop Byrne of Dublin, were requesting to see the constitution before it was published. NAI, Dáil Eireann papers, DE4/6/7, cabinet minute of 12 June 1922.

141. NAI, Dáil Eireann papers, DE4/6/7, cabinet minutes of 9–12 June 1922.

142. Westminster Parliamentary Archive, Lloyd George Papers, F/10/3/3, Lloyd George to Churchill, 8 June 1922.

143. UCD Archives, DeValera papers, P150/1171, Boland to McGarrity, 22 June 1922. Gavan Duffy met with Hayes, O'Higgins, McGrath and Lynch on 15 June and although McGrath objected to the oath and king terminology in a draft constitution in their hands, O'Higgins favoured publishing it.

144. T.W. Moody, F.X. Martin (eds) *A new history of Ireland*, 8 (Oxford, 1989), 403. The thirty-four non-Sinn Féin representatives have been typified as seventeen labour candidates, ten independents and seven farmer candidates.

145. Churchill Archives, CHAR22/13/202, copy of extract of 'M.C.' to 'H.L.' [Collins to Hazel Lavery], 25 June 1922, sent by Lavery to Churchill.

146. Chrissy Osborne, *Michael Collins himself* (Cork, 2013), 75–85.

147. Westminster Parliamentary Archives, Lloyd George papers, F/26/1/31, Tom Jones to Prime Minister, 17 May 1922.

148. NAI, Dáil Eireann papers, DE4/6/7, cabinet minute for 23 June 1922.
149. Westminster Parliamentary Archives, Lloyd George papers, F/10/6/4, Lloyd George to Collins, 22 Jun 1922. The basis of the claim regarding Reginald Dunne, the ex-British soldier, rested purely on the fact that he was a man who was imprisoned in England before on IRA charges and the supposition that the assassin was probably a sympathiser with the men in the Four Courts. The 'documents' found on him was merely a single letter from June 1921 that had 'no relation to recent events'. Lloyd George papers, F/10/3/14, Lionel Curtis to Lloyd George, 1 Jul. 1922. For Dunne's trial, see the relevant papers in NLI, Art O'Brien papers, Collection List No.150.
150. Westminster Parliamentary Archives, Lloyd George papers, F/10/6/4, Lloyd George to Collins, 22 Jun 1922.
151. NAI, Dáil Eireann papers, DE4/6/7, cabinet minute for 23 June 1922.
152. NAI, Dáil Eireann papers, DE4/6/7, cabinet minute for 23 June 1922.
153. Churchill Archives, CHAR22/13/202, copy of extract of 'M.C.' to 'H.L.' [Collins to Hazel Lavery], 25 June 1922, sent by Lavery to Churchill.
154. NAI, Dáil Eireann papers, DE4/6/7, cabinet minute for 26 June 1922. This is the last surviving minute of Griffith's cabinet.
155. Westminster Parliamentary Archives, Lloyd George Papers, F/10/3/9, Cope to Curtis (copy of telegram), 29 Jun. 1922. Emmet Dalton commanded the troops that fired the artillery.
156. NLI, Kathleen MacKenna Napoli papers, Ms22764. Similar statements, calling for a reunification of the army, and a recruitment drive for the National Army were published in Griffith's *Young Ireland*.
157. NLI, Art O'Brien papers, Ms8460/8, DeValera to O'Brien, 4 July 1922; Ms8425/19, copy of DeValera's address 'to the people of America' (4 Jul.1922).
158. Westminster Parliamentary Archives, Lloyd George Papers, F/10/3/13, Churchill to Cope, 1 Jul. 1922.
159. Robert Brennan, *Allegiance* (Dublin, 1950), 344–348. Brennan, a long-term friend of Griffith, felt grieved to find himself on opposite sides during the treaty disputes.
160. Westminster Parliamentary Archives, Lloyd George papers, F/10/3/48, Cope to Curtis, 8 Sep. 1922.
161. *Poblacht na hEireann War News*, 29–30 June 1922: 'Eamon DeValera is on acting service with the Dublin Brigade [of the IRA] … Black and Tans and British Soldiers are dressed in Free State uniforms.'
162. 'Government by the IRB', *Poblacht na hEireann War News*, 25 July 1922; 'The real test', *Poblacht na hEireann War News*, 7 Aug. 1922; 'Government by Secret Society', *Poblacht na hEireann War News*, 7 Aug. 1922; 'Commandant General Oliver Cromwell' and 'Contemptible Soldiers', *Poblacht na hEireann War News*, 15 Aug. 1922; *Poblacht na hEireann War News*, 22 Aug. 1922, p. 1 and article on George Gavan Duffy's resignation. Similar arguments were championed in Countess Markievicz's *The Republican War Bulletin* (a typescript rather than a professionally printed organ).
163. David Fitzpatrick, *Harry Boland's Irish revolution* (Cork, 2003), 2.
164. The former illustration has recently been reproduced as the front cover of Bill Kissane, *The politics of the Irish civil war* (Oxford, 2007). The latter illustration can be seen in Michael Laffan, *The resurrection of Ireland* (Cambridge, 1999), 435. Perhaps her most poignant cartoon, which was almost worthy of her odd sister, appeared in her *Republican War Bulletin*, featuring a mother and child kissing goodbye to their father with the caption: 'Say goodbye to Daddy. He's going out to fight for the Republic.'
165. NLI, Kathleen MacKenna Napoli papers, Ms22764.

166. NLI, Sean O'Luing papers, Ms23516, undated press cuttings regarding Gogarty's medication examinations of Griffith.
167. NLI, Kathleen MacKenna Napoli papers, Ms22779, report of Collins, dated 19 Aug. 1922.
168. A handwritten copy of terms of a truce agreement can be seen in NLI, Art O'Brien papers, Ms8430/24. This was presented to O'Brien on 23 August and was evidently made possible by the fall of Cork City to the National Army on 11 August.
169. Westminster Parliamentary Archives, Lloyd George papers, F/10/3/48, Cope to Curtis, 8 Sep. 1922. In the wake of Collins' death, some Catholic clergy attempted to step into his shoes of attempting to negotiate a truce; a move that led in October 1922 to a declaration by the diocesan clergy that virtually excommunicated members of the IRA by defending the moral authority of 'national soldiers' (presumably a reference to the National Army). At the level of the monastic or spiritual church, the religious orders (as they had done in the past) would both offer humanitarian assistance to IRA political prisoners and, reflecting their positive relationship with Sean T. O'Kelly, would soon successfully persuade the Vatican to issue a call upon Dublin and London to treat these unfortunate men with respect and not to provoke any more hostilities in the unfortunate country of Ireland. Monastic clergy would also play a leading role in attempting to appease IRA men who were imprisoned during and after 1922 (UCD Archives, Richard Mulcahy papers).
170. On 15 March, Griffith's cabinet 'decided that injunctions restraining proceedings in ex-enemy courts will not, in future, be issued except on the authority of the full Supreme Court of Dáil Eireann'. NAI, Dáil Eireann papers, DE1/4, minute for 15 Mar. 1922.
171. Westminster Parliamentary Archives, Lloyd George papers, F/10/3/49, Cope to Curtis, 9 Sep. 1922; Pauric Dempsey, 'Diarmuid Crowley (1875–1947)', *Dictionary of Irish Biography*, 2 (Cambridge, 2009), 1049–1051. Cope described Duggan as 'the only signatory who has neither died nor ratted'.
172. Westminster Parliamentary Archives, Lloyd George papers, F/10/3/37, Churchill to Cope, 24 Aug. 1922.
173. Reputedly, Griffith had intended Oliver St. John Gogarty for such a role. Patrick Maume, 'Oliver St. John Gogarty (1878–1957)', *Dictionary of Irish Biography*, 4 (Cambridge, 2009), 123–127.
174. Frank Callanan, *T.M. Healy* (Cork, 1996), 596.
175. Westminster Parliamentary Archives, Lloyd George papers, F/10/3/49, Curtis to Churchill, 17 Sep. 1922.
176. Just prior to the signing of the truce between General Macready and Richard Mulcahy, the British cabinet's Irish Situation Committee was fully prepared to consider the execution of every member of the Dáil and the shooting of 100 Sinn Féiners every week. While the opinion of the politicians naturally outweighed those of the soldiers in the Irish Situation Committee, even the political opponents of sending the army into Ireland for the first time had believed that the leaders of the Dáil, including the (then) imprisoned Griffith, must be tried for treason some day, and among these politicians Arthur Balfour alone dissented to suggest 'transportation rather than hanging as a punishment' following their inevitable conviction. At the same time, however, the Irish Situation Committee judged that the true leaders of the Irish nationalist conspiracy—'the *active* members of the Irish Republican Government, together with the I.R. Army and I.R. Brotherhood'—had only ever been a very small and enthusiastic minority within the nominal membership of Dáil Eireann, let alone Irish political society as a whole, this being a reason why it was judged that it might not be necessary to pursue the transportation or hanging solution. Westminster Parliamentary Archives, Lloyd George Papers, F25/1/42, Tom Jones to Lloyd George, 15 Jun 1921 (report on Irish Situation Committee meeting). In this respect, a great irony

regarding the outbreak of hostilities in Ireland after June 1922 was the alleged discovery of an IRA circular of Ernest O'Malley in the possession of Thomas Derrig that called for the execution of every member of Dáil Eireann. Pauric Dempsey, 'Thomas Derrig (1897–1956)', *Dictionary of Irish Biography*, 3 (Cambridge, 2009), 185–186. O'Malley was allowed by Dublin Castle to flee to America not long after ordering the destruction of all infrastructure for Irish businesses, especially the railways. For an appreciative appraisal of O'Malley's career, see Richard English, *Ernest O'Malley: IRA intellectual* (Oxford, 1998).

177. Arthur Griffith, *Arguments for the Treaty* (Dublin, 1922), 15.

178. *Poblacht na hEireann War News*, Oct.-Nov. 1922; Pauric Dempsey, 'Thomas Derrig (1897–1956)', *Dictionary of Irish Biography*, 3 (Cambridge, 2009), 185–186.

179. Peter Martin, 'Irish peers', 197–198.

180. T.W. Moody, F.X. Martin (eds) *A new history of Ireland*, 8 (Oxford, 1989), 404.

181. Patrick Maume, 'William St. John Broderick, 1st Earl of Midleton (1856–1942)', *Dictionary of Irish Biography*, 1 (Cambridge, 2009), 860–863; Peter Martin, *Irish peers 1909–1924* (MA, UCD, 1998), 197–198.

182. Midleton would use an interpretation of modern Irish history to justify his overall interpretation of contemporary Irish politics and, in turn, was considered by many English commentators to be 'the greatest living authority on Ireland'. *London Standard* blurb on the cover of The Earl of Midleton K.P., *Ireland: dupe or heroine* (London, 1932).

183. Diarmuid Crowley, who had been a prominent member of the Dáil courts system, was perhaps the most senior legal figure to attempt to justify this stance. He was an outspoken critic of Mulcahy's disbandment of the Dáil courts but, as in the case of many anti-treaty Irish Volunteers, his personal salary claims were a motivation for the stance that he took. Pauric Dempsey, 'Diarmuid Crowley (1875–1947)', *Dictionary of Irish Biography*, 2 (Cambridge, 2009), 1049–1051.

184. Eunan O'Halpin, 'William Thomas Cosgrave (1880–1961)', *Dictionary of Irish Biography*, 3 (Cambridge, 2009), 883.

185. Eunan O'Halpin, 'William Thomas Cosgrave (1880–1961)', *Dictionary of Irish Biography*, 3 (Cambridge, 2009), 881–885.

186. W.T. Cosgrave, 'Arthur Griffith (1872–1922)', *Dictionary of National Biography 1922–1930* (Oxford, 1937), 364–368.

187. W.T. Cosgrave, 'Arthur Griffith (1872–1922)', *Dictionary of National Biography 1922–1930* (Oxford, 1937), 364–368.

CHAPTER THIRTEEN

1. Cosgrave became a founder of the Fine Gael party in 1934 and six party branches would later be named after Griffith. Over time, Dublin Corporation renamed a bridge, a road and a barracks after Griffith. Anne Dolan, *Commemorating the Irish civil war* (Cambridge, 2003), 101. A historian of Fine Gael has also produced a biographical survey of past literature on Griffith in an attempt to stimulate greater debate upon his career. Brian Maye, *Arthur Griffith* (Dublin, 1997).

2. Griffith's personal assets upon his death were based on his shareholding in *Young Ireland*, as well as this company's debts. A government enquiry found that this would have left him with a total wealth of £289. It was decided that Maud Griffith would be allowed a pension of £1,000 a year to provide for her and her two children. NAI, Dáil Eireann papers, S6187. Griffith's older brother Bill died in 1924 while a workhouse supervisor in Summerhill. While it was considered, there does not appear to have been an allowance made for his younger sister Frances or younger brother Frank, both of whom lived until

1949. Dr. Barry Kennerk has informed the author that Frances ('Fanny') Griffith was practically adopted into his mother's family, the Careys, during the 1940s after she was found living alone and in great poverty on Gardiner Street. Nevertheless, press reports indicate that both Maud Griffith and W.T. Cosgrave attended her funeral a few years later as the chief mourners.

3. 'Financially ruined: Mr. Collins' confession', *Poblacht na hEireann War News*, 17 August 1922.

4. St John Ervine, *Craigavon* (London, 1949), 283.

5. Churchill Archives, CHAR22/14/18–19, report on the Shaw Commission; CHAR22/14/11, Churchill to Curtis, 7 Jul. 1922 (quote); Henry Harrison, *Ulster and the British Empire* (London, 1939), 36–40.

6. Mary Daly, 'Government finance for industry in the Irish Free State: the Trade Loans (Guarantee) Acts', *Irish Economic and Social History*, vol.11 (1984), 73–74.

7. John Busteed, 'Economic barometers', *Journal of the Society for the Statistical and Social Inquiry of Ireland*, 79–80 (1926), 282.

8. C.H. Oldham, 'Reform', *Journal of the Statistical and Social Inquiry Society of Ireland*, 79–80 (1926), 206, 211. In the southern unionist *Irish Times*, C.H. Oldham earned the reputation of being a Griffithite Irish nationalist ideologue shortly before his death in 1926 by arguing that it was necessary for the Irish government to work hand-in-hand with economists in following Griffith's dictum of the necessity of Ireland looking far beyond the United Kingdom to understand its place in the modern world. *Irish Times*, 22 and 24 Feb. 1926 (obituary for Oldham). This reflected the fact that, shortly before he died, Oldham, as president of the Society for the Statistical and Social Inquiry of Ireland, persuaded this traditionally unionist society to become sympathetic towards the Irish Free State's Department of Industry and Commerce.

9. At the close of the disturbances of July 1922–April 1923 and in the wake of deals made by Cosgrave with the banks regarding the retention of the land annuities, some tariffs were nominally introduced by the Irish Free State but these were made meaningless by the government's inability to form a monetary policy and the formal absence of trading rights; the latter being a matter that first began to be dealt with by legislation passed during 1924 prior to the imperial negotiations that led to the Balfour Declaration. Mary Daly, 'Government finance for industry in the Irish Free State: the Trade Loans (Guarantee) Acts', *Irish Economic and Social History*, vol.11 (1984), 73–93. In this sense, it is not really correct to speak of an Irish protectionism as a potentially relevant concept to the history of Irish state after 1927 and prior to the repatriation of the Irish state's exchequer account in 1972.

10. *Poblacht na hEireann War News*, 24 Aug. 1922. This would be a mantra for the remainder of DeValera's career.

11. No history of the bank raids of 1922–1923 has been written, partly due to lack of public access to the relevant sources, although newspapers should be able to provide a good outline history, despite the state-controlled press censorship of the time. An interesting piece of oral history is that the author's late father Donard McGee joined the Hibernian Bank in 1955 and was requested in 1957 to do a tour of branches of the Hibernian Bank with a view to examining their ledgers and ensuring that they were in proper order for a forthcoming merger with the Bank of Ireland (1958). He was surprised to discover and to subsequently have to report that almost every branch suffered robberies during 1922–23 and that this was generally either facilitated or performed by the bank staff themselves, who were frequently replaced and yet their replacements proved no more reliable. This would seem to indicate that the perception was widespread at the time that the country was in a state of total financial collapse.

12. Ernest O'Malley was reputedly responsible for launching this sabotage campaign. His letters have recently been reproduced in an edited volume entitled *No surrender here!* O'Malley is perhaps still best known for his personal recollections from the late 1950s about other men's wounds. Recently, an outline history of the attack on the railways has been produced. Bernard Share, *In time of civil war: the conflict on the Irish railways 1922–1923* (Cork, 2006). For a critical appraisal of O'Malley's career, see Richard English, *Ernie O'Malley: IRA intellectual* (Oxford, 1999).

13. H.C. Casserley, *Outline of Irish railway history* (London, 1974), 147.

14. W.E. Wylie, formerly chief law advisor to Dublin Castle (who irritated Hugh Kennedy, the creator of the Irish Free State's constitution, to no end by continuing to refer to the state on all government correspondence as 'Southern Ireland') later became the director of Córas Iompair Éireann (C.I.E., established 1945) without altering this business arrangement. R.D. Marshall, 'William Evelyn Wylie (1881–1964)', *Dictionary of Irish Biography*, 9 (Cambridge, 2009), 1059–1061. C.I.E. was nationalised in 1950, three years after the formation of British Rail, but the infrastructure of the Irish transport industry was largely determined before then. Reflecting this, many Irish railway lines were simply abandoned while partition broke up those that had now cross-border dimensions.

15. Michael Laffan, *The partition of Ireland 1911–1925* (Dundalk, 1983).

16. At the request of the Bank of Ireland, the legacy of press censorship launched in 1914 continued. Reflecting this, Cosgrave necessarily ordered that Griffith's newspaper *Young Ireland* cease publication in December 1922; a move that annoyed the widowed Maud Griffith. Although concerned primarily with her own private family matters, she used the sale of the *Young Ireland* franchise, combined with some of the Griffiths' own personal savings (arising almost entirely from the sales of *Nationality* and *Young Ireland* since 1917), to create a new organ, the *United Irishman*, in February 1923 under the editorship of Sean Milroy to propagate the views of 'the late president'. This journal lasted until 1924.

17. Sean Milroy, *The Tariff Commission and Saorstat economic policy* (Dublin, 1926).

18. Sean Milroy, *The Tariff Commission and Saorstat economic policy* (Dublin, 1926); *The case of Ulster* (1919, 2nd ed., Dublin, 1922).

19. A committee of inquiry found that an effort was made to revive the IRB after April 1923 in an effort to promote army unity negotiations but doing so merely helped to undermine the same goal by breeding suspicions of the working of secret hands. UCD, Eoin MacNeill papers, LA1/G/258, Army Enquiry Committee Report, 7 June 1924. This had nothing to do with Milroy and Joseph McGrath's national group beyond the fact that some soldiers concerned with their careers had also approached them. Mulcahy, as leader of the defence forces between 1922–1924, relied largely on priests in an effort to restore unity in old volunteer circles by approaching imprisoned men (see UCD Archives, Mulcahy papers). It seems that it was decided in 1924 that funds formerly held by the IRB were supposed to be used to commission a history of that now disbanded organisation. UCD Archives, Martin Conlon papers, P97/3(2). Such a publication never appeared. Liam Tobin and Emmet Dalton, an ally of Robert Barton, were largely responsible for instigating a controversy regarding the army at this time in order to make the institutionalisation of the Defence Forces (est.1924) more difficult. They claimed to be acting in the name of 'the IRA Organisation'. Patrick Long, 'Liam Tobin (1899–1963)', *Dictionary of Irish Biography*, 9 (Cambridge, 2009).

20. Sean Milroy, *The Tariff Commission and Saorstat economic policy* (Dublin, 1926).

21. Joe Lee, *Ireland 1912–1985* (Cambridge, 1989), 118.

22. During 1920 Keynes was still an absolute advocate of the centrality of tariff walls to international relations and commerce (*The Economic Consequences of the Peace* (New

York, 1920)). His success in persuading British governments during the 1930s to consider the formation of an economic policy based on international exchange rates for various currencies and to combine this with a concern with developing welfare programmes led him to be celebrated in Britain as a great thinker but it could well be argued that the essential dynamic to his career was the same practical, non-theoretical, political issue that had divided Churchill from Lloyd George in British politics during the 1920s and early 1930s; namely, a willingness to concede to American financial supremacy.

23. Joseph Lee, *Ireland 1912–1985* (Cambridge, 1989), 109–110.
24. Louis Cullen has suggested that the creation of such imperial war debts played a key role in the development of banking, as represented by the origins of both the Bank of England in the 1690s and the origins of the Bank of Ireland during the 1780s. L.M. Cullen, *Economy, trade and Irish merchants at home and abroad 1600–1988* (Dublin, 2012), 211–212.
25. Brendan Bracken, an Irishman who virtually became Churchill's adopted son, defended Churchill's policy by forming new financial publications in London, while Henry Harrison, as the Irish correspondent of the *Economist*, was not so favourable to it. C.E. Lysaght, 'Brendan Bracken (1901–58)', *Dictionary of Irish Biography*, 1 (Cambridge, 2009), 755–756.
26. Donal P. Corcoran, *Freedom to achieve freedom: the Irish Free State 1922–1932* (Dublin, 2013), 142.
27. Erskine Childers, *The framework of home rule* (London, 1911); L.M. Cullen, *Irish national income in 1911 and its context* (Dublin, 1995).
28. M.E. Daly, 'The economic ideals of Irish nationalism: frugal comfort or lavish austerity?', *Eire-Ireland*, 29 (winter 1994), 77–100.
29. Marie O'Neill, *From Parnell to DeValera: a biography of Jennie Wyse Power 1858–1941* (Dublin, 1991); Sheila Carden, *The Alderman: Alderman Tom Kelly (1868–1942) and Dublin Corporation* (Dublin, 2007).
30. M.E. Daly, 'The economic ideals of Irish nationalism: frugal comfort or lavish austerity?', *Eire-Ireland*, 29 (winter 1994), 77–100. During 1926 the National Land Bank was bought out by the Bank of Ireland and converted into a 'National City Bank', as a Bank of Ireland owned subsidiary, the following year. During 1995, the Bank of Ireland published an outline history of the National City Bank, which used to feature a bust of Collins (later removed to Merrion Square park) in its College Green headquarters and nominally existed until 1968. This pamphlet also features a fine survey of the history of the National Land Bank as its first chapter. It also noted how the churches, unlike TDs, refused to support either it or the National City Bank by opening accounts. Eoin Ryan, *An Irish banking revolution* (Dublin, 1995), 3–33.
31. Bank of Ireland Archives, 'Synopsis of the decisions of the committee' (Irish Banks Standing Committee, 1925), minute for 24 June 1922.
32. John Horgan, *Sean Lemass: the enigmatic patriot* (Dublin, 1997); Bryce Evans, *Sean Lemass: democratic dictator* (Cork, 2011). Horgan's grandfather J.J. Horgan wrote the classic anti-Griffith text *Parnell to Pearse* (Dublin, 1949).
33. Alvin Jackson, 'Ireland, the Union and Empire, 1800–1960', in Kevin Kenny (ed.) *Ireland and the British Empire* (Oxford, 2004), 143.
34. Sean Milroy, *The Tariff Commission and Saorstat economic policy* (Dublin, 1926), 25, 38.
35. During the mid-1920s, just as *An Phoblacht* managed to make ex-Irish Volunteer concerns a live issue in labour politics, Henry Harrison simultaneously championed the exact same labour issue relentlessly on behalf of ex-British soldiers. Brian Hanley, *The IRA 1926–1936* (Dublin, 2002); Owen McGee, 'Henry Harrison (1867–1954)', *Dictionary of Irish Biography*, 4 (Cambridge, 2009).

36. The correspondence of John Sweetman, who supported DeValera from 1928 onwards due to the latter's perceived dependence on papal encyclicals for political inspiration, with various priests regarding tensions in Irish politics between 1928 and 1933 are revealing in this regard. See NLI, Sweetman Papers, Collection List No.156.

37. NLI, Sweetman papers, Ms47,565/4.

38. *Poblacht na hEireann War News*, 24 Aug. 1922. This would be a mantra for the remainder of DeValera's career.

39. It was not until the spring of 1926 that London withdrew the last of its own personnel from the provisional Irish Free State administration at Dublin Castle. Gerard O'Brien, *Irish governments and the guardianship of historical records 1922–72* (Dublin, 2004), 17, 23–31, 36–38, 52–53, ft.10. On this theme, see also D.A. Chart, 'The Public Record Office of Northern Ireland, 1924–36', *Irish Historical Studies*, vol.1, no.1 (Mar. 1938), 42–57; Kenneth Darwin, 'The Irish record situation', *Journal of the Society of Archivists*, vol.2, no.8 (Oct. 1963), 364–365; John McColgan, *British policy and the Irish administration 1920–22* (London, 1983), 27, 32, 41. The fact that the banks refused to offer any financial support to the Dàil until after hostilities broke out in June 1922 was a source of grievance to many contemporaries. On this theme, see the reports on DeValera and the banks in *Irish Times*, 10 May 1923, and *Irish Independent,* 20 July 1923.

40. Ronan Fanning, *Independent Ireland* (Dublin, 1983), 188–204.

41. On this theme, see L.W. McBride (ed.) *Reading Irish histories: texts, contexts and memory in modern Ireland* (Dublin, 2003). For a more popular historical treatment of the same subject, see R.F. Foster, *The Irish story* (London, 2001).

42. The Government Stationary Office, *Dáil Eireann, miontuaric an chead Dala 1919–1921* (Dublin, 1994), 78.

43. Padraig McGowan, *Money and banking in Ireland* (Dublin, 1990), 33.

44. Dermot Meleady, *John Redmond: the national leader* (Dublin, 2013), 466–467. Stephen Gwynn and William Redmond's National League party of the 1920s was initially allied with Fianna Fàil and later amalgamated with Cumann na nGaedhael to form Fine Gael. This was James Dillon's entry point into politics.

45. R.F. Foster, 'Revisiting the Ireland of John Redmond', *Irish Times*, 25 Jan. 2014.

46. UCD Archives, P150/575, a 1953 article of Dr. Thomas Dillon of University College Galway on the reorganisation of Sinn Féin in 1917. DeValera himself wrote a comment on this paper. Regarding the claim that Griffith had a first object of a King, Lords and Commons of Ireland, DeValera wrote that 'this is quite untrue. There is no foundation for it whatever'. DeValera also emphasised that 'we were all the time good friends, and continued so until the Treaty was signed' (annotation made 21 Mar. 1963).

47. T.K. Whitaker, 'Ireland's external assets', *Journal of the Society for the Statistical and Social Inquiry of Ireland*, vol.102 (1948–1949), 192–209.

48. Ben Tonra, Michael Kennedy, John Doyle, Noel Dorr (eds) *Irish Foreign Policy* (Dublin, 2012), 23–25.

49. On this theme, see Dermot Keogh, Gabriel Doherty (eds) *1916* (Cork, 2007), 119.

50. NAI, Bureau of Military History papers, WS384 (Sceilg).

51. B.P. Murphy, 'John Joseph O'Kelly (1872-1957)', *Dictionary of Irish Biography*, 7 (Cambridge, 2009), 603–608; *Patrick Pearse and the lost republican ideal* (Dublin, 1991).

52. Frank Callanan, 'In the name of God and of the dead generations: nationalism and republicanism in Ireland', in Richard English, J.M. Skelly (eds) *Ideas matter: essays in honour of Conor Cruise O'Brien* (Dublin, 1998).

53. It has recently been judged, with approval, that 'the civil war may have ended militarily' but it also marked 'the opening shots of a hard-fought historical war' that shows no sign

of abating. Diarmuid Ferriter, *Judging Dev* (Dublin, 2007), quoted 13. It has also been deemed a 'blasphemy' that a memorial to Griffith can exist within a single Catholic chapel in the country and judged that all within Irish society who 'attest smugly to the end of bitterness' should realise that not only will this not be tolerated but also 'the race is far from run'. Anne Dolan, *Commemorating the Irish civil war: history and memory 1923–2000* (Cambridge, 2003), 105, 202. A recent book has claimed that, during Sceilg's lifetime, the IRA existed within RTE, a state-controlled media service, to serve as a cultural watchdog to protect a sense of Irish national identity from all potential enemies within Irish society. Brian Hanley, Scott Millar, *The lost revolution* (Dublin, 2008).

54. Owen McGee, 'David Sheehy (1844–1932)', *Dictionary of Irish Biography*, 8 (Cambridge, 2009). Francis Cruise O'Brien's son, Conor, was inspired to do a history PhD at Oxford on Parnell's party because in his youth he knew David Sheehy who in turn introduced him to Henry Harrison. This is why the seminal study C.C. O'Brien, *Parnell and his party* (Oxford, 1957) is dedicated to Sheehy and Harrison, who inspired its thesis and creation.
55. Brian Farrell (ed.) *The Irish parliamentary tradition* (Dublin, 1973); Alan Ward, *The Irish constitution tradition: responsible government and modern Ireland 1782–1992* (Washington, 1994).
56. A project of this title is currently underway under Professor Eunan O'Halpin of the 'Bank of Ireland Centre for Contemporary Irish History' in Trinity College Dublin with funding from British and American universities.
57. John Regan, *The Irish counter revolution 1921–1936* (Dublin, 1999).
58. See, for instance, Peter Hart, *The IRA at war 1916–1923* (Oxford, 2000).
59. Brendan O'Cathaoir, 'Playing the Orange Card', *Irish Times*, 3 May 2014; Ronan Fanning, *Fatal path* (Dublin, 2013); Kevin Matthews, *Fatal influence* (Dublin, 2004).
60. Nicholas Mansergh, *The Irish question 1840–1921* (London, 1940, 2nd ed., 1965), 238, 288.
61. Keith Jeffrey, '(Philip) Nicholas Seton Mansergh (1910–1991)', *Dictionary of Irish Biography*, 6 (Cambridge, 2009), 351–352.
62. The Earl of Midleton K.P., *Ireland: dupe or heroine* (London, 1932).
63. The Irish state's reliance during the 1960s upon F.X. Martin, a noteworthy Augustinian monk, social activist and medieval historian, to look after the fiftieth-anniversary of the 1916 rising celebrations, as well as to produce a history of the same, was a noteworthy example of this.
64. Emmet Larkin, *The Roman Catholic Church and the making of the Irish state 1878–1886* (Dublin, 1975), 396.
65. Conor McCabe, *Sins of the father* (Dublin, 2011).
66. Maura Adshead, Peadar Kirby, Michelle Millar (eds) *Contesting the state: lessons from the Irish case* (Manchester, 2008), quote p46 (Joe Lee).
67. M.E. Daly, 'The economic ideals of Irish nationalism: frugal comfort or lavish austerity?', *Eire-Ireland*, 29 (winter 1994), 77–100.
68. M.E. Daly, 'The Irish Free State/Eire/Republic of Ireland/Ireland: a country by any other name?', *Journal of British Studies*, 46 (January 2007), 72–90.
69. During June 1922, three Catholic bishops, including Archbishop Byrne of Dublin, demanded that the Dáil cabinet allow them to see its proposed constitution before it was published. NAI, Dáil Eireann papers, DE4/6/7, cabinet minute of 12 June 1922.
70. Articles on the significance of the treaty agreement that appeared during 1922–1923 in *Studies* and other NUI journals generally focused exclusively on the taking oaths of allegiance as an essentially ethical or theological issue and considered no other question.
71. In both Northern Ireland and the south, Protestants as much as Catholics opposed British support for state-controlled education during 1922. Westminster Diocesan Archives, BO

1/72, Lord Fitzalan to Cardinal Bourne, 1 Feb. 1922; D.H. Akenson, *Education and enmity* (New York, 1973). Along with Eoin MacNeill and Michael Hayes (with whom he formed a virtual NUI triumvirate in the Dáil), DeValera had spent many years involved in the politics of education, from his youthful studies of Catholics' responses to the education programmes of Sir Robert Peel and Lord Palmerston's governments during the early-Victorian period through to his effective replacement during 1915 of Tom Kettle (of Redmond's Irish Party) as Archbishop Walsh's champion in the politics of education at UCD. As such, DeValera was as well equipped to act as an effective minister for education for any prospective Irish parliament as MacNeill and Hayes (two old supporters of Redmond, both of whom would eventually assume such responsibilities). That was his intellectual forte or professional skill; hence his succession of the redoubtable Archbishop Walsh as NUI Chancellor. Were it not that the secularist Liberal government of 1906 withdrew British state funding for the Gaelic League, it is quite possible that Pearse would never have become enamoured with conspiracy theories regarding the existence of a 'murder machine' designed to kill the Gaelic League ideal of education and that the somewhat similar politics of DeValera and many other Gaelic League nationalists, as Catholic educationalists, would not have become so opposed to the British government around the same time Pearse did, particularly after the outbreak of the First World War imposed censorship upon the expression of Irish Catholic opinion.

72. Diarmaid Ferriter, *Judging Dev* (Dublin, 2007), quoted 195.
73. M.E. Daly, K.T. Hoppen (eds), *Gladstone: Ireland and beyond* (Dublin, 2011). This book consists of papers for a historical conference organised by the Department of the Taoiseach to celebrate Gladstone's legacy for Ireland. On this theme, see also the celebratory writings about Gladstone by Martin Mansergh, the official 'historical advisor' to the Irish government, in *The legacy of history* (Cork, 2003).
74. This was both the motive and the theme of Oliver St. John Gogarty's poetic tribute to Griffith in *Free State*, 19 Aug. 1922: 'He fought as many fights as Conn the Fighter [a Fenian]; and all alone he fought, without a friend to make his sword arm lighter, unblindable, unbought. He held his shield until the waves resounded, the men of Ireland woke, He made the loud tyrannical foe dumb-founded and then relax his yoke. Inglorious in the gap: by many a hater, the scoffing word was said. He heard from those who had betrayed him "traitor!": the Cross-gained and Cross-bred [Irish clericalist public figures]. He shook from him off with a grand impatience, the flesh uncomforted, and passed among the captains in whom nations live when these men are dead.'
75. Kevin O'Shiel might be considered as one who refused to accept this consensus. He was shocked (P.S. O'Hegarty considerably less so) by the extent to which the Sinn Féin Party now ridiculed and dismissed Griffith in the exact same manner as the Irish Party did in yesteryear, all under the new umbrella accusation (defined by Childers, no less) of supposedly not being a republican: he was 'a plotter against the Church', 'a nobody', 'an immoral man with an evil record', 'a factionist working in the pay of the unionists to smash home rule' or even an inherently untrustworthy 'Welshman without a drop of Irish blood in his veins' (Kevin O'Shiel, 'The reign of the people', *United Irishman*, 17 Mar. 1923). Although he had been a very senior legal advisor to the Dáil between 1920–1922, O'Shiel was soon retired from Irish public life. Incidentally, Griffith was a Catholic and regular attendant at Mass in adulthood. He admired the Dominican ideal of Catholic education of combining high standards of education with a sworn vow to work among the populace at large. He did not admire the Jesuit ideal of education. John Sweetman supported the Benedictine ideal of education, the most individualistic of Catholic theories of education but one that was almost non-existent in Ireland.

76. During July 1922, *Poblacht na hEireann War News* repeatedly defined the 'military dictatorship' of the IRB as constituting a triumvarite of Michael Collins, Richard Mulcahy and Eoin O'Duffy; a perspective recently championed by historians John Regan and Fearghal McGarry. It seems clear, however, that Collins, Mulcahy and O'Duffy, although each officers of the National Army, constituted no such particular clique, the motivation of Childers' argument evidently being rooted in a desire to affect public perceptions of whatever O'Duffy and his fellow Ulster Irish Volunteers either were or had been doing.

77. R.V. Comerford, *The Fenians in context: Irish politics and society 1848–1882* (2nd ed., Dublin, 1998), 194; R.V. Comerford, 'Republicans and democracy in modern Irish politics', in Fearghal McGarry (ed.) *Republicanism in modern Ireland* (Dublin, 2003), 8, 20.

78. John Regan's review of Brian Maye's 'Arthur Griffith' in *Irish Times*, 4 Nov. 1997.

79. On this theme, see Frank Callanan, *T.M. Healy* (Cork, 1996).

80. *Nation*, 20 Feb. 1886 (editorial). The editorial board of the *Nation* at this time was T.M. Healy MP, T.D. Sullivan MP, J. J. Clancy MP, Dan Crilly MP, Thomas Sexton MP, Donal Sullivan MP, D.B. Sullivan BL (supplement to the *Nation*, 16 Jan. 1886).

81. Ex-plenipotentiary George Gavan Duffy was the principal man involved; a fact that, it has been claimed, was hidden from Fianna Fáil supporters. As DeValera's choice as secretary to the department of the Taoiseach, Maurice Moynihan, who supported Griffith during 1922 and was the son of Griffith's chief supporter in Kerry of the same name, also played a part in this process. Gerard Hogan, 'George Gavan Duffy (1882–1951)', *Dictionary of Irish Biography*, 3 (Cambridge, 2009), 510–512; Deirdre McMahon, 'Maurice Moynihan (1902–99)', *Dictionary of Irish Biography*, 6 (Cambridge, 2009), 731–734.

82. Joseph Crehan S.J., 'Freedom and Catholic power', *Studies*, 40 (1951), 158–166. This is a review of a book by the chief American anti-Vatican polemicist, Paul Blanshard, *The Irish and Catholic Power*, in which the author admitted that he could actually find no flaws whatsoever in the Vatican-inspired, Christian Democratic, ethos of DeValera's constitution, and found that studying it was actually a learning and educational process for himself. For the question of the degree to which the Jesuits were involved in drafting the constitution, see Dermot Keogh, *The making of the Irish constitution 1937* (Cork, 2007) and *The Vatican, the bishops and Irish politics 1919–1939* (Cambridge, 1986).

83. Joe Humphreys, *God's entrepreneurs: how Irish missionaries tried to change the world* (Dublin, 2010). The overt Christian ethos of the Irish state may also be said to have been reflected by the decision to name the planes of the state's airline Aer Lingus after the first Irish Christian missionaries and the fact that, since the 1990s, a significant percentage of the state's annual GDP is given to 'Irish National Aid' (a Christian missionary organisation in Africa), this being a continuation of a policy launched in the 1950s to emphasise the Irish state's definition of its foreign policy (which effectively began in 1949) as a self-consciously Christian one. Ben Tonra, Michael Kennedy, John Doyle, Noel Dorr (eds) *Irish Foreign Policy* (Dublin, 2012), 152–158.

84. *Poblacht na hEireann War News*, 5 July 1922: 'Craig blesses Collins'.

85. *Poblacht na hEireann War News*, 28 Dec. 1922; *Poblacht na hEireann War News*, 26 Oct. 1922.

86. During DeValera's 1928 American tour, which was intended to rival W.T. Cosgrave's simultaneous American tour to promote Irish businesses, he was quoted in the American press as saying that all current leaders of the Irish Defence Forces were traitors that deserved to be executed and, in defence of this idea, noted that he suspected that the IRB still secretly existed in its ranks. One such press cutting can be found within Fr. Martin Mahony's correspondence in NLI, Sweetman papers, Ms47604/12. There is no evidence to substantiate DeValera's suspicions regarding the survival of the IRB within the Defence

Forces. A surviving 1937 letter of 'MacEoin [?]' from the Fine Gael Party headquarters may seem to substantiate the theory that it still existed by making a seeming, albeit very oblique, reference to the IRB in the present tense (NLI, George A Lyons papers, Ms33675/a/2). An IRB account certainly still existed at this time but it had not been in use since 1922 (see UCD Archives, Martin Conlon papers, P97/3).

87. In Defence Forces flag protocol the Irish tricolour is to be used to give a military salute to a Consecrated Host during the Elevation at a Catholic Mass but on no other occasion. Lt. Col. James McGee (1923–1998), an uncle of the author, once explained this to the author's late father. Lt. Colonel McGee was in charge of the Defence Forces' Army School of Music prior to his retirement in 1988 and, to date, is the longest serving member of the Defence Forces in Irish history (1938–88). He joined the army band as a boy and is the author of the current arrangement of *Amhran na bhFiann* for all presidential occasions.

88. P.S. O'Hegarty, *The victory of Sinn Féin* (Dublin, 1924), 86–87. There was a conventional Christian wisdom to this perception. Pilate was a soldier. Christ was not.

89. Robert Brennan, *Allegiance* (Dublin, 1950), 344–348. DeValera looked up to Childers as the 'noblest' man he ever met and judged that he 'died the Prince that he was'. At the same time, however, DeValera valued Childers' assistance in defending his own political stance during 1922 'not so much on account of what he was doing' but simply 'because of what he could [potentially] do under new conditions'. UCD Archives, DeValera papers, P150/1195, DeValera to McGarrity, 28 Nov. 1922.

90. Anne Dolan, *Commemorating the Irish civil war: history and memory 1923-2000* (Cambridge, 2003), 56, 100 (quote).

91. Diarmuid Ferriter, *The transformation of Ireland 1900–2000* (London, 2005), 260.

92. Garret Fitzgerald, *Reflections on the Irish state* (Dublin, 2003), ix.

93. R.F. Foster, *The Irish story: telling stories and making it up in Ireland* (London, 2001); *The luck of the Irish* (London, 2005); Diarmuid Ferriter, *The transformation of Ireland* (London, 2005).

94. Helen O'Connell, *Ireland and the fiction of improvement* (Oxford, 2005).

95. For instance, there have been very many studies that have referred to forces of Catholicism and Protestantism in modern Ireland but very few studies completed (almost none) of the histories of Catholic and Protestant faith congregations and their missionary work despite the fact that this was their primary focus of attention, both personally and financially, aside from schools and hospitals.

96. Patrick Lynch, 'The social revolution that never was', in T.D. Williams (eds), *The Irish struggle 1916–1926* (London, 1966), quote 41.

97. T.D. Sullivan, *A.M. Sullivan* (Dublin, 1885), 7. The writings of A.M. Sullivan are a particularly good source on this theme. Occasional expressions of appreciation for republicanism by (non-fenian) Irish Catholics may be found in the writings of T.D. McGee, Eugene Davis and George Sigerson, although these men, excepting Sigerson (his *Modern Ireland* of 1868 is a significant text), lived most of their adult lives outside Ireland. The expulsion of prominent 1848 Catholic rebels from Ireland such as John Savage and T.F. Meagher may be said to have contributed to this trend.

98. Aidan Clarke, 'Robert (Robin) Walter Dudley Edwards (1909–1988)', *Dictionary of Irish Biography*, 3 (Cambridge, 2009), 583–585 (quote); R.V. Comerford, 'Theodore William Moody (1907–1984)', *Dictionary of Irish Biography*, 6 (Cambridge, 2009), 606–608.

99. O'Brien was originally co-secretary of the Munster IRB organisation alongside P.N. Fitzgerald before his apprenticeship as a journalist with the *Freeman's Journal* prompted him to leave the IRB (1876) and, later, become editor of *United Ireland* (1881–90). His initiatives included launching the Plan of Campaign (1886), United Irish League (1898)

and All-for-Ireland League (1910). In his final years, he sided with Sinn Féin academics against Irish Party figures in the management of University College Cork (he was very disillusioned with the treaty settlement) before welcoming the establishment of Fianna Fáil. The 1928 biography by Michael MacDonagh, an old *Freeman* colleague, is arguably still the best.

100. There are too many titles to be listed here, but the title of a recent study Brian Jenkins, *The fenian problem: insurgency and terrorism in a liberal state 1858–1874* (London, 2008) reflects the persistence of this school of writing. Other contemporary scholars in this field may be said to include Charles Townsend, whose seminal *Political violence in Ireland 1848–1918* (London, 1983) has recently been capped by a study entitled *The Republic* (London, 2013), in which the idea that the IRA Army Council established in November 1922 constituted the government of Ireland and a continuity from the original counter-state programme of the Dáil established in 1919 is given some credence; a perspective that may seem to fit with the common argument in Ireland that the IRA ceasefire in April 1923 constituted the end of 'the Irish revolution'.

101. Padraig Colum, *Arthur Griffith* (Dublin, 1959). The most recent study along these lines has been Anthony J. Jordan, *Arthur Griffith: with James Joyce and W.B. Yeats in liberating Ireland* (Dublin, 2013), which was positively reviewed by Brian Maye, author of *Arthur Griffith* (Dublin, 1997), for 'connecting a trio of titans' in the world of letters (*Irish Times*, 4 Jan. 2014). Since James Dillon (son of John) took over from W.T. Cosgrave as the leader of Fine Gael, Garrett Fitzgerald may be typified as the only Irish political leader to have cited Griffith as a positive inspiration for future political leaders (*Irish Times*, 17 June 1970).

102. George Aston KCB, 'The Irish Free State and British "Empire" Defence', *Fortnightly Review* (Sept. 1922), 411.

103. Recent examples may be said to include Andrew Roberts, *A history of English speaking peoples since 1900* (London, 2005) or even Eric Hobsbawm, *Age of extremes: the short twentieth century 1914–1991* (London, 1994), both of which espouse an Anglocentric worldview; the latter from the point of a native of the final British imperial colony in Egypt, brought to London to champion a Marxist ideology on behalf of the state. For a popular historical treatment of the same, see Niall Ferguson, *Empire: how Britain made the modern world* (London, 2006).

104. John Redmond, *Historical and political addresses 1883–1897* (Dublin, 1898); Michael Davitt, *Leaves from a prison diary* (Dublin, 1885); *The fall of feudalism* (New York, 1904).

105. NAI, DICS files, carton 3 (police biography of T.P. O'Connor).

106. Review of Stuart Laycock, *All the countries we've ever invaded* (London, 2012) in *Daily Telegraph*, 4 Nov 2012.

107. Alvin Jackson, *Ireland 1798–1998: politics and war* (London, 1999); Paul Bew, *Ireland: the politics of enmity 1798–2006* (Oxford, 2007); Henry Patterson, *The persistence of conflict* (London, 1995); Colin Reid (ed.) *From Parnell to Paisley: constitutional and revolutionary politics in modern Ireland* (Dublin, 2010).

108. The traditions born during Bryce's youth of encouraging Protestants within Ireland to subscribe to myths regarding 1641 or 1690 and Catholics within Ireland to subscribe to myths regarding 1649 (as if Cromwell had robbed every 'Irish' family of their land) reflected nothing if not a determination to write histories of Ireland that emphasised communal conflict above all else, as if the story of Ireland was inherently one of centuries of perpetual and unrelenting communal enmity and strife ('war'). It is debatable whether or not this tradition has ever truly ceased, while the employment of national identity debates within Ireland as if this was the sole purpose of historical studies (regarding

which every public figure, journalist and even artist in Ireland is expected to express an opinion, even if they have never studied history, as if this was a matter of current affairs) has certainly done nothing to minimise this trend.

109. The Bureau of Military History and Military Pensions Service Act records of the 1940s have recently been released to the public to coincide with republications of the series of recollections produced by Florence O'Donoghue (and, later, Anvil Press of Tralee) from around the same time period. The title of some of these publications (e.g. 'With the IRA [?] in the fight for freedom: *the red path of glory*' [my italics]) were, and are, misleading, in their tendency to portray the Irish Volunteers as Marxist revolutionaries, however. This was something that neither the contents of these publications nor O'Donoghue's own views would validate, although the adoption of such book titles probably helped to sell a few extra copies in their day.

110. Many close Anglo-Irish parallels naturally exist in modern history and not least of these was the reality that an aristocratic social ideal was essentially a norm of political life in the nineteenth and early-twentieth centuries to a far greater extent than many mid to late twentieth-century historians of 'the course of history' or 'modernisation' (the intellectual legacy of Marxist and modernist ideologies respectively) generally cared to admit. Belfast Presbyterian clergymen were fond of noting in the Land League days that 'you will never find an honest Presbyterian who is not, at heart, a republican', but just as was the case regarding the input of the self-styled 'brothers-in-a-republic' in encouraging political activism elsewhere in Ireland (most of these naturally did not like the social significance of the contemporary rhetoric of 'uncrowned kings') the mere existence of such egalitarian sympathies frequently did not count for a whole lot in terms of altering the internal dynamics of Irish political society, even irrespective of the limitations imposed by the Union (Owen McGee, *The IRB* (Dublin, 2005), chapter 3 and 5). Similarly, when Keir Hardie was elected as the 'first workingman' in the imperial parliament in 1892, he marched on the House of Commons to La Marseillaise (then, still the chief international anthem of democracy or 'republicanism') but, as was the case with the very many nationalist demonstrations in Ireland that had long used the exact same republican symbolism (especially during the Land League days), as soon as his march was over nothing had actually changed. Although many spoke of a republican revolution having taken place in Ireland during the late 1910s, the legacy of pre-1914 politics in shaping Irish political culture remained significant.

111. Peter Hart, *The IRA at war 1916–1923* (Oxford, 2000); Paul McMahon, *British spies and Irish rebels: British intelligence and Ireland 1916–1945* (Suffolk, 2008). The Fianna Fáil journalist historian Tim Pat Coogan may perhaps be said to have helped launch this school of writing.

112. Excepting Richard Hawkins, few historians have analysed this system to date.

113. Elizabeth Muenger, *The British military dilemma in Ireland* (Dublin, 1991).

114. T.K. Daniel, 'Griffith on his noble head', *Irish Economic and Society History*, vol.3 (1976), 55–65.

115. 'Economic nationalism', in R.P. Davis, *Arthur Griffith and non-violent Sinn Féin* (Anvil Press, Tralee, 1974), quote 135.

116. Richard Davis, *Arthur Griffith* (Dundalk, 1976), 36.

117. R.P. Davis, 'Griffith and Gandhi: a study in non-violent resistance', *Threshold*, vol.3, no.2 (summer 1959), 29–44; Sean O'Luing, 'Arthur Griffith: thoughts on a centenary', *Studies* (summer 1971), 127–138; R.P. Davis, *The Young Ireland movement* (Dublin, 1987).

118. Sean O'Luing, 'Arthur Griffith and Sinn Féin', in F.X. Martin (ed.) *Leaders and men of the Easter rising 1916* (London, 1967), 65; Sean O'Luing, *Art O Griofa* (Baile Atha Cliath, 1954).

119. The impact such conflicting ideas have had on Irish historical studies may perhaps be witnessed in the contrast in perspective between Colonel Maurice Walsh's (formerly of the Defence Forces) *G2: in defence of Ireland* (Cork, 2010) and many other historical studies, including Eunan O'Halpin, *Defending Ireland: the Irish state and its enemies since 1922* (Oxford, 1999).

120. Michael Laffan, *The resurrection of Ireland* (Cambridge, 1999), 223. On this theme, see also Garret Fitzgerald, *Ireland in the world: further reflections* (Dublin, 2005), 23–37.

121. Erskine Childers, *The framework of home rule* (London, 1911).

122. T.S.C., 'Cavan's choice', *Nationality*, 8 June 1918 'T.S.C.' was Thomas Shine Cuffe, a working-class historian of Dublin who was reacting to the publication of Anon., *Arthur Griffith: a study of the founder of Sinn Féin* (Dublin, 1917). The author of this pamphlet admitted to knowing nothing whatsoever of Griffith but nevertheless proclaimed him to be 'a genius' (pp. 2–3) owing to his growing political association with Fr. O'Flanagan.

123. W.T. Cosgrave, 'Arthur Griffith (1872–1922)', *Dictionary of National Biography 1922–1930* (Oxford, 1937), 368.

124. D. Dickson, C. O'Grada (ed.) *Refiguring Ireland* (Dublin, 2003), 277, 283.

125. One of Ireland's premier economic historians Louis Cullen, a graduate of the London School of Economics before becoming an Irish civil servant, has focused primarily on the eighteenth century as a basis for interpreting modern Irish economic history. His interpretative framework for understanding the evolution of Ireland ever since the eighteenth century has focused on the idea that this is 'not really an Irish story at all…it is just one regional consequence of the most important event in modern economic history, namely the British Industrial Revolution'. This school of writing has also judged that the failure in Ireland to develop industries was simply the result of poor entrepreneurship by Irish businessmen and good entrepreneurship by English and Scottish businessmen who proved their superiority in business matters by establishing the only successful industrial firms in Dublin or Belfast under the Union. L.M. Cullen (ed.) *The formation of the Irish economy* (Cork, 1968); Cormac O'Grada, *Ireland: a new economic history 1780–1939* (Oxford, 1994), 314, 325, 349–353, 376. The significance of London's control of the Irish state's accounts and, in effect, the Irish banks, is essentially ignored. The tendency of modern-day historians to emphasise the great continuities in the Anglo-Irish economic relationship before and after partition as a supposedly inherently positive factor in Irish life is essentially a fall-out from this perspective. Cormac O'Grada, *Ireland: a new economic history 1780–1939* (Oxford, 1994); C. O'Grada, B.M. Walsh, 'Did (and does) the Irish border matter?', *Working Papers in British-Irish Studies* (no.60, 2006). Similarly, in Louis M. Cullen, *Irish national income in 1911 and its context* (Dublin, 1995), an attempt to contextualise the state of the economy during 1911 was carried out exclusively by comparing the situation during 1911 with that during 1926, but is it correct to speak about an 'Irish national income' in 1911? The amalgamation of the British and Irish exchequers since 1816 surely means that it would be inappropriate to speak of anything other than a British labour market in Ireland from this time onwards.

126. Patrick Buckland, *James Craig* (Dublin, 1980), 94–100, 115–125.

127. Alvin Jackson, *Sir Edward Carson* (Dundalk, 1993); Myles Dungan (ed.), *Speaking ill of the dead* (Dublin, 2007), 40 (quote from Paul Bew). One consequence of these trends in terms of Belfast cultural life may perhaps be seen in the fact that the worlds of James Bryce, Francis Joseph Bigger (perhaps the principal rival to George Sigerson, a fellow Ulsterman, as Ireland's supreme cultural nationalist scholar) and Robert Lynd (a lifelong sympathiser with Griffith's ideals) would soon essentially become written out of history

altogether in the name of a self-consciously Protestant polity that, for one reason or another, was not ashamed to make a martyr out of Robert Harbinson's 'Tattoo Lily'.

128. British and Irish public figures, as well as some scholars, meet annually in Parnell's name for Ireland's top 'historical' summer school as a means of discussing Ireland's contemporary political predicaments. According to this logic, would it not be safely presumed that the best means of the United Kingdom, Germany and the United States to develop a deeper understanding of what political predicaments they may ever face in the current day would be by meeting as a 'historical' summer school in the name of the ideals of Parnell's contemporaries such as Benjamin Disraeli, Otto Von Bismarck and Grover Cleveland and, in the process, abandoning both historical studies and all forms of intelligible thought altogether?

129. Carlton Younger, *A state of disunion* (London, 1972), 199; Buckland, *James Craig*, 57–58.

130. Bernard Porter, *Empire and Super Empire: Britain, America and the world* (Yale, 2006), 59.

131. James McConnel, 'Jobbing with Tory and Liberal: Irish nationalists and the politics of patronage 1880–1914', *Past and Present*, no. 188 (Aug. 2005), 105–131. M.E. Daly, 'The formation of an Irish nationalist elite? Recruiting to the civil service in the decades prior to independence 1870–1920', *Paedogogica Historica*, vol.30, no.1 (1994), 281–301; Martin Maguire, *The civil service and the revolution in Ireland 1912–1938* (Manchester, 2008); Michael Gallagher and Lee Komito, 'Dáil deputies and their constituency work', in Coakley, Gallagher eds *Politics in the republic of Ireland* (2nd ed. Dublin, 1993), 150–166; Erskine Childers, *The framework of home rule* (London, 1911), chapter 10, pt.3; Royal Economic Society (ed.) *The fiscal relations of Great Britain and Ireland* (Suffolk, 1912), 62–63, 67–68.

132. Mary Daly, *Industrial development and Irish national identity 1922–1939* (Syracuse, 1994), 4–8.

133. Padraig McGowan, *Money and banking in Ireland* (Dublin, 1990), 85. This intention led to a conference in TCD during 1968 involving Bank of England representatives and various European banking figures to discuss this issue. The Institute of Bankers in Ireland, *Economic planning and the banking system* (Dublin, 1968). Such developments also led to a renewed interest in Ireland by the 1970s in the pursuit of economic thinking and analyses with a view to formulating an Irish monetary policy. J.W. O'Hagan (ed.) *The economy of Ireland: policy and performance* (Dublin, 1975). Since its eighth edition, this book has been titled *The economy of Ireland: policy and performance of a European region* (Dublin, 2000).

134. Conor McCabe, *Sins of the father: tracing the decision that shaped the Irish economy* (Dublin, 2011), quote 133. See also footnote 39.

135. The Irish Banks Standing Committee, *The control of banking in the Republic of Ireland* (Dublin, 1984), 157, passim.

136. Maura Adshead, Peadar Kirby, Michelle Millar (eds), *Contesting the state: lessons from the Irish case* (Manchester, 2008), 81.

137. This was certainly the case in France. The Institute of Bankers in Ireland, *Economic planning and the banking system* (Dublin, 1968), 107–109.

138. This legacy would be identified as a growing challenge after the establishment of the Irish Financial Services Centre (Philip Bourke, R.P. Kinsella, *The financial services revolution: an Irish perspective* (Dublin, 1988)) as well as the unification of the British and Irish stock exchanges in 1973 as an intentional counter to the fact that the Irish state's exchequer account was, from 1972 onwards, now held in the Bank of Ireland. Price Waterhouse, *International banking—Dublin* (Dublin, 1985), chapter 1.

139. Pauric Dempsey, 'Charles Gordon Campbell, 2nd Baron Glenavy (1885–1961)', *Dictionary of Irish Biography*, 2 (Cambridge, 2009), 281–282.
140. Maurice Moynihan, *Currency and central banking in Ireland 1922–1960* (Dublin, 1975); Padraig McGowan, *Money and banking in Ireland* (Dublin, 1990).
141. Ronan Fanning, 'The resurrection of Michael Collins', *Sunday independent*, 5 Jan.1997.
142. A Fianna Fáil newspaper editor Tim Pat Coogan (who wrote the first IRA history for the London book market during the 1960s) wrote a biography claiming that Collins was in favour of making armed attacks upon Northern Ireland and ordered the assassination of Henry Wilson. Peter Hart's *The Real Mick* also attempted to substantiate such interpretations. This does not fit the historical record, however, and indicates a failure by Coogan (and, in turn, others) to interpret the relevant sources. Coogan's biography of Collins led to Neil Jordan's film *Michael Collins*, after which Ronan Fanning interpreted Collins career as one of 'the successful use of urban guerrilla violence' and deemed this a principle of international significance in modern history and of particular relevance to the Northern Ireland troubles (*Sunday Independent*, 5 Jan.1997). A book resulting from the debate arising from the film, G. Doherty, D. Keogh (eds) *Michael Collins and the making of the Irish state* (Cork, 1998), indicates that academic historians generally accept the perception of Collins' career championed by Coogan. This means that almost all historians ignore the fact that Collins felt that the methods of resistance he had employed, purely to protect a finance ministry from political intrigues, were redundant by February 1921; the same time as the Dail's Land Bank began to be regulated by the British state system and Collins' name first began appearing, much to his chagrin, in the British press as a fictitious urban guerrilla warfare 'IRA' leader with a large bounty on his head. The dynamics and controversies in Collins' career seem to be most explainable according to the history of the IRB, an organisation whose history is very difficult to reconstruct and long predated Collins' arrival in Irish politics.
143. Ronan Fanning's unique study *The Irish Department of Finance 1922–1958* (Dublin, 1978) highlights the fact that Joseph Brennan and other civil servants who arrived from London came to determine the activities of the finance ministry of the Provisional Government more so than Collins himself, although the fact that Collins was waiting for a transfer of powers to the Dáil (for which he was still the finance minister; he did not have this responsibility for the Provisional Government) and continued to espouse the principle of repatriating sterling assets (see *The Path to Freedom*) would seem to indicate that it is mistaken to assume that Collins had committed himself to allowing London and the Government of Ireland Act determine a future Irish governmental policy on finance, although many contemporary *Freeman's Journal* readers, i.e. Irish Party supporters, no doubt hoped that he had.
144. Donal P. Corcoran, *Freedom to achieve freedom: the Irish Free State 1922–1932* (Dublin, 2013), 64.
145. During the 'treaty debates'—the historical significance of which have often been greatly overestimated—Griffith argued that he had 'always' had stern critics who claimed that he gave 'bad advice' to the Irish public, but he believed that he 'had never concealed from the Irish people anything vital to their interests to know' and even if his advice was never followed, he believed that he 'had never deceived them' about where their best material interests and, in turn, their best political interests lay. Arthur Griffith, *Arguments for the Treaty* (Dublin, 1922), 16–18. This was essentially his understanding of what a citizen's responsibility should be. The fact that during 1922 Catholic literary writers like James Joyce celebrated the idea that a good Irish citizen is a contradiction in terms is largely irrelevant here. Recently, UCD library has renamed itself in honour of Joyce.

146. See, for example, 'Historian criticises 1916 generation', *Irish Times*, 15 Mar. 2011.

147. P.S. O'Hegarty, *The victory of Sinn Féin* (Dublin, 1924), 119.

148. Maura Adshead, Peadar Kirby, Michelle Millar (eds), *Contesting the state: lessons from the Irish case* (Manchester, 2008), 126, 170, 176–177; Ben Tonra, Michael Kennedy, John Doyle, Noel Dorr (eds) *Irish Foreign Policy* (Dublin, 2012), 190–199.

149. Maura Adshead, Peadar Kirby, Michelle Millar (eds), *Contesting the state: lessons from the Irish case* (Manchester, 2008), 4.

150. On this theme, see Brendan O'Donoghue, 'John Garvin (1904–86)', *Dictionary of Irish Biography*, 4 (Cambridge, 2009), 35–37; L.W. White, 'Leon O'Broin (1902–90)', *Dictionary of Irish Biography*, 7 (Cambridge, 2009), 100–102; Deirdre McMahon, 'Maurice Moynihan (1902–99)', *Dictionary of Irish Biography*, 6 (Cambridge, 2009), 731–734. Garvin, O'Broin and Moynihan were all supporters of Griffith in 1922.

151. J.J Lee, *Ireland 1912–1985* (Cambridge, 1989), 288.

152. J.F. O'Connor, 'Article 50 of Bunreacht na hEireann and the unwritten English constitution of Ireland', in J.P. O'Carroll, J.A. Murphy (ed.), *De Valera and his times* (Cork, 1983), 173–181. Upon this basis, the British Government's Ireland Act of 1949 recognised that Éire/Republic of Ireland, although no longer a part of the commonwealth, was 'not a foreign country'. This ruling is partly why (irrespective of the question of EU membership) Irish citizens can still seek work in Britain and British citizens can still seek work in Ireland without having to become a naturalised citizen and even acquire voting rights, if they so desire, with the consent of the relevant Attorney Generals.

Bibliography

Newspapers and Journals

United Irishman (1899–1906)

Sinn Féin

Scissors and Paste

Eire-Ireland

Nationality

Young Ireland

Freeman's Journal

Irish Independent

Irish Weekly Independent

Sunday Independent

An Claidheamh Solus

Gaelic American

Irish Times

Citizen and Irish Artisan

Nation

Dublin University Review

New Ireland Review

Journal of the Statistical and Social Inquiry Society of Ireland

The Irish Review

Workers Republic

The Leader

Studies

Poblacht na hEireann War News

Republican War Bulletin

The Separatist

Free State

United Irishman (1923–1924)

Irish Press

Archives and Libraries in Ireland

National Archives
Dáil Eireann papers (especially cabinet minutes, DE1/4, DE4/6/7)
Bureau of Military History papers
DMP files, RIC monthly précis and CBS files

UCD Archives
Eamon DeValera papers (includes Harry Boland's papers)
Eoin MacNeill papers
Thomas Kettle papers
Walter Cole papers
Sinn Féin minute books (1912–1913)
Martin Conlon papers
Richard Mulcahy papers
Denis McCullough papers
Desmond Ryan papers

National Library of Ireland Manuscripts Department
Arthur Griffith papers (acc.4476, acc.4476, box a, acc.4476, box b)
Leinster, Celtic and National Literary Societies minute books (including the 'Eblana Journal')
Sinn Féin Flyer Collection (bound volume, held in Main Reading Room, ILB300p13.)
M.J. Lennon Papers
Sean O'Luing papers
Henry Dixon Papers
John O'Leary Papers
James Bryce papers
John Redmond Papers
Sweetman Papers
Sean T. O'Kelly papers
Florence Williams papers
George A. Lyons papers
Douglas Hyde papers

Thomas Martin papers
James O'Mara papers
Tim Harrington papers
Michael Noyk papers
George Fottrell papers
Art O'Brien Papers
Kathleen McKenna Napoli papers
Kevin O'Higgins papers (Ms22812)

Bank of Ireland Archives
Irish Banks' Standing Committee report (1925)

University of Limerick
John Daly papers

Archives within the United Kingdom

Westminster Parliamentary Archives
David Lloyd George papers (F10/3, F10/6, F21/1, F25/1, F25/2, F26/1)

Westminster Diocesan Archives
Cardinal Bourne papers (BO1/72, BO5/36)
Cardinal Manning papers

Churchill Archives
Winston Churchill papers (CHAR 22/8 - 22/14, CHAR25/2)
Maurice Hankey papers (HNKY 1/5)

National Archives (Kew)
Griffith Prison Records (HO144/1458/316093)
Gerald Balfour Papers (PRO 30/60/28)

British Library
Althorp [Lord Spencer] Papers (Add Mss.77033–37, Add Mss44493)
W.E. Gladstone papers (microfilm copies in NLI, p.2875, p.3261)
Henry Campbell-Bannermann papers (microfilm copies in NLI, p.1282)

Books, Pamphlets and Articles by Arthur Griffith's contemporaries

The Government Stationary Office, *Dáil Eireann, miontuaric an chead Dala 1919–1921* (Dublin, 1994)

[Childers, Erskine (ed.)] *The constructive work of Dáil Eireann* (Dublin, 1921)

Dáil Eireann, *Debate on the treaty between Great Britain and Ireland* (Dublin, 1922)

Fanning R., Kennedy M., Keogh D., O'Halpin E. (eds) *Documents on Irish foreign policy vol.1, 1919–1922* (Dublin, 1998)

Anon., *Arthur Griffith: a study of the founder of Sinn Féin* (Dublin, 1917)

Ashtown, Lord (ed.) *The unknown power behind the Irish nationalist party* (London, 1907)

Barton, Robert, *The truth about the treaty and document no.2* (Manchester, 1922)

Beaslai, Piaras (ed.) *Songs, ballads and recitations by famous Irishmen: Arthur Griffith* (Dublin, 1926)

----------, *The Grand Concert in Antient Concert Rooms on 9 April 1916, addressed by Eoin MacNeill for equipping the 1st battalion of the Dublin Brigade* (Dublin, 1916)

Brennan, Robert, *Allegiance* (Dublin, 1950)

Browne, P. (ed.) *Collected works of P.H. Pearse: plays, stories and poems* (Dublin, 1917)

Busteed, John, 'Economic barometers', *Journal of the Society for the Statistical and Social Inquiry of Ireland*, 79–80 (1926)

Chesterton, G.K., *Heretics* (London, 1905)

----------, *How to solve the Irish question* (Montreal, 1921)

Childers, Erskine, *The framework of home rule* (London, 1911)

----------, 'Christian democracy in Belgium', *Studies*, 2 (1913)

----------, *A strikebreaking army at work* (London, 1919)

----------, *Military rule in Ireland* (Dublin, 1920)

----------, *Clause by clause: a comparison between the treaty and document no. 2* (Manchester, 1922)

Clarke, Kathleen, *Revolutionary woman* (Dublin, 1991)

Clarke, Tom, *Glimpses of an Irish felon's prison life* (Dublin, 1922)

Collins, Michael, *The path to freedom* (Dublin, 1922)

Cosgrave, W.T., 'Arthur Griffith (1872–1922)', *Dictionary of National Biography 1922–1930* (Oxford, 1937), 364–368

----------, 'Michael Collins (1890–1922)', *Dictionary of National Biography 1922–1930* (Oxford, 1937), 199–200

Crossley, F.W., *State purchase of the Irish railways* (Tourist Development (Ireland) Ltd., Dublin, 1906)

Curran, C.P., 'Griffith, MacNeill and Pearse', *Studies* (spring 1966), 21–28

Dawson, Charles, 'Suggested substitutes for the present poor law system', *Social for the Statistical and Social Inquiry of Ireland*, 46 (1906), 428–438

----------, 'The industrial progress of Belgium: an object lesson for Ireland', *Journal of the Society for the Statistical and Social Inquiry of Ireland* (1912), 595–608

----------, 'The Dublin housing question: sanitary and unsanitary', *Social for the Statistical and Social Inquiry of Ireland*, 66 (1912–1913), 91–95

De Blacam, Aodh, *Towards the Republic* (London and Dublin, 1918)

Dublin Students Dungannon Club, *A manifesto to the whole students of Ireland* (Dublin, 1906)

Dunne, John Patrick, 'Poverty problems for a patriot parliament', *Journal of the Society for the Statistical and Social Inquiry of Ireland*, 74–76 (1921–1923), 189–198

Ervine, St. John, *Craigavon* (London, 1949)

Field, William, *Irish railways compared with state owned and managed lines* (Dublin, 1899)

----------, *High rates and railway monopoly in Ireland* (Dublin, 1899)

Finlay, T.A., 'Ethics and economics of poor relief', *Journal of the Statistical and Social Inquiry Society of Ireland* (1907), 43–51

----------, 'The significance of some recent Irish statistics', *Journal of the Statistical and Social Inquiry Society of Ireland* (1912–13), 17–25

Gogarty, Oliver St. John, *Sackville Street: three classic volumes of autobiography* (Suffolk, 1988)

Griffith A., Bradley P. (eds) *Poems and ballads of William Rooney* (Dublin, 1902)

Griffith, Arthur, *The resurrection of Hungary* (Dublin, 1904)

----------, *The Sinn Féin Policy* (Dublin, 1906)

National Council [Griffith, Arthur], *England's colossal robbery of Ireland: the fiscal relations of the two countries under the Union* (Dublin, 1906)

----------, *The Police and the Nation* (Dublin, 1906)

----------, *How Ireland is taxed* (Dublin, 1907)

National Council [Griffith ed.], *The Flowing Tide of Sinn Féin* (Dublin, 1907)

Griffith, Arthur, *Pitt's policy* (Dublin, 1911)

----------, 'True and false imperialism', *The Irish Review: a monthly magazine of Irish literature, art and science*, 1 (Aug. 1911)

----------, 'Home rule and the unionists', *The Irish Review: a monthly magazine of Irish literature, art and science*, 2 (May 1912)

----------, *The home rule bill examined* (Dublin, 1912)

----------, *Finance of the Home Rule Bill: an examination* (Dublin, 1912)

---------- (ed.) *John Mitchel's Jail Journal* (Dublin, 1913)

---------- (ed.) *Thomas Davis: the thinker and teacher* (Dublin, 1914)

---------- (ed.) *Meagher of the Sword* (Dublin, 1915)

----------, *When the government publishes sedition* (Dublin, 1915)

[Arthur Griffith], *Why Ireland is poor* (Dublin, 1915)

Griffith A., Fogarty L. (eds) *James Fintan Lalor* (Dublin, 1918)

Griffith, Arthur, *Arguments for the treaty* (Dublin, 1922)

----------, *Simply gamblers* (Dublin, 1922)

Harrison, Henry, *The peace conference 1920 and its betrayal* (Dublin, 1920)

----------, *Ulster and the British Empire* (Dublin and London, 1939)

Henry, R.M., *The evolution of Sinn Féin* (Dublin, 1920)

Hobson, Bulmer, *The creed of the Republic* (Belfast, 1907)

----------, *Defensive Warfare: a handbook for Irish nationalists* (Belfast, 1907)

----------, *Ireland: yesterday and tomorrow* (Tralee, 1968)

Irish Transport and General Workers Union, *The attempt to smash the ITGWU* (Dublin, 1924)

Joyce, James, *Ulysses* (1922, republished London, 1968)

Kelly, R.J., 'The recent British bank amalgamations and Ireland', *Journal of the Statistical and Social Inquiry Society of Ireland* (1918–19), 642–674

Kettle, T.M., 'Would the Hungarian Policy work?', *New Ireland Review*, vol.22, no.6 (Feb. 1905), 322–328

----------, *The day's burden* (1910, reprinted Dublin, 1968)

----------, *Home Rule finance* (Dublin, 1911)

Lawson, William, 'Remedies for overcrowding in the city of Dublin', *Social for the Statistical and Social Inquiry of Ireland*, 62 (1908–1909), 230–248

Lloyd George, David, *Is it peace?* (London, 1924)

Lynd, Robert (Riobard Ua Fhloinn), *The Orangeman and the Nation* (Dublin, 1906)

Lyons, G.A., *Some recollections of Griffith and his times* (Dublin, 1923)

MacBride, Maud Gonne, *A servant of the Queen* (London, 1938)

McCann, James, *Irish taxation and Irish transit* (Dublin, 1901)

McMahon, Sean (ed.) *Robert Lynd's Galway at the Races: selected essays* (Dublin, 1990)

MacManus, Seamus (ed.) *William Rooney prose writings* (Dublin, 1909)

MacNeill, John [Eoin], 'War and reconstruction: Irish settlement', *The English Review* (1917), 253–262

MacNeill, Eoin, *Daniel O'Connell and Sinn Féin* (Dublin, n.d.)

Maume, Patrick (ed.) *D.P. Moran's The Philosophy of Irish Ireland* (1898, 2nd ed. Dublin, 2006)

Middlemas, Keith (ed.) *Thomas Jones, Whitehall diary,* vol.3 (London, 1971)

Midleton, Lord, *Ireland: dupe or heroine* (London, 1932)

Milroy, Sean, *The case of Ulster* (Dublin, 1919, 2nd ed., Dublin, 1922)

-----------, *The Tariff Commission and Saorstat economic policy* (Dublin, 1926)

Monteith, Robert, *Casement's last adventure* (Chicago, 1932, republished Dublin, 1953)

Moore, George, *Hail and Farewell! Vale* (London, 1947)

Morgan, J.H. (ed.) *The new Irish constitution* (London, 1912)

Murray, Patrick (ed.) *Arthur Griffith's The Resurrection of Hungary* (1904, reprinted Dublin, 2003)

National Council, *Ireland and the British Army* (Dublin, 1907)

National Council [John Sweetman], *The purchase of the railways (by the nation)* (Dublin, 1906)

O'Brien W., Ryan D. (eds) *Devoy's Post Bag*, 2 vols. (Dublin, 1948, 1953)

O'Donnell, F.H., *The ruin of education in Ireland* (London, 1903)

-----------, *History of the Irish Parliamentary Party*, 2 vols. (London, 1910)

O'Hegarty, P.S., *The victory of Sinn Féin* (Dublin, 1924)

-----------, *A history of Ireland under the Union* (London, 1952)

O'Kelly, Sean T., 'Arthur Griffith', *Capuchin Annual* (1966), 132–144

O'Leary, John, 'Some guarantees for the protestant and unionist minority', *Dublin University Review*, vol.2, no.12 (Dec. 1886), 959–965

Oldham, C.H., 'The economics of industrial revival in Ireland', *Society for the Statistical and Social Inquiry of Ireland*, 61 (1907–08), 175–189

-----------, 'The keystone of Irish finance', in Royal Economic Society, *The fiscal relations of Great Britain and Ireland* (Suffolk, 1912), 15–33

-----------, 'The incidence of emigration on town and country life in Ireland', *Journal of the Statistical and Social Inquiry Society of Ireland* (1914), 207–218

-----------, 'The economic interests involved in the present war', *Journal of the Statistical and Social Inquiry Society of Ireland* (1914–15), 269–280

----------, 'Industrial Ireland under free trade', *Journal of the Statistical and Social Inquiry Society of Ireland* (1916–17), 383–398

----------, 'Changes in Irish exports during twelve years', *Journal of the Statistical and Social Inquiry Society of Ireland* (1918–19), 541–553

----------, 'Changes in the export industries of Ireland 1904–1916', *Journal of the Statistical and Social Inquiry Society of Ireland* (1918–19), 629–637

----------, 'Reform', *Journal of the Statistical and Social Inquiry Society of Ireland*, 79–80 (1926)

O'Shiel, Kevin, *The Making of a Republic* (Dublin, 1920)

O'Sullivan, Seamus [James Starkey], *Essays and recollections* (Dublin, 1944)

Pearse, Patrick, *The complete works of P.H. Pearse: political writings and speeches* (Phoenix Press, n.d.)

Pim, J.T., *The condition of our railways considered with reference to their purchase by the state* (Dublin, 1867)

[Pim, Herbert] A. Newman, *Sinn Féin in tabloid form* (n.d. [1915])

Royal Economic Society (ed.) *The fiscal relations of Great Britain and Ireland* (Suffolk, 1912)

Russell, George, *Controversy in Ireland: an appeal to Irish journalists* (Dublin, 1904)

----------, *Cooperation and nationality* (Dublin, 1912)

Ryan, Mark, *Fenian memories* (Dublin, 1945)

Ryan, W.P., *The Irish literary revival* (London, 1894)

----------, *Lessons from modern language movements* (London, 1902)

----------, *The Pope's Green Island* (London, 1912)

Samuels, A.W., 'Some features in recent Irish finance', *Journal of the Statistical and Social Inquiry Society of Ireland* (1907), 1–40

----------, 'The external commerce of Ireland', *Journal of the Statistical and Social Inquiry Society of Ireland* (1909), 194–217

Sinn Féin, *Programme of the Sinn Féin Ard Fheis, 29 Nov. 1918* (Dublin, 1918)

Smith Gordon, Lionel, *The place of banking in the national programme* (Dublin, 1921)

Stephens, James, *Insurrections* (Dublin, 1909)

----------, *The insurrection in Dublin* (Dublin, 1916)

----------, *Arthur Griffith* (Dublin, 1922)

Sweetman, John, *Nationality* (Dublin, 1908)

----------, *Liberty* (Dublin, 1909)

Walsh, William, *The Irish university question: addresses delivered by the Most Rev. Dr. Walsh* (Dublin, 1890)

Secondary sources (recent books, pamphlets and articles)

Adshead M., Kirby P., Millar M. (eds) *Contesting the state, lessons from the Irish case* (Manchester, 2008)

Ball, Stephen (ed.) *Dublin Castle and the First Home Rule Crisis* (Cambridge, 2008)

Barry, Kevin (ed.) *James Joyce: occasional, critical and political writing* (London, 2000)

Bew, Paul, *Ireland* (Oxford, 2007)

Bolger, Patrick, *The Irish cooperative movement: its history and development* (Dublin, 1977)

Borgonovo, John, *The dynamics of war and revolution: Cork City, 1916–1918* (Cork, 2013)

Boylan T., Foley T., *Political economy and colonial Ireland: the propagation and ideological function of economic discourse in the nineteenth century* (London, 1992)

Brown M., Geoghegan P., Kelly J. (eds) *The Irish Act of Union* (Dublin, 2001)

Buckland, Patrick, *James Craig* (Dublin, 1980)

Callanan, Frank, *T.M. Healy* (Cork, 1996)

Carden, Sheila, *The Alderman: Alderman Tom Kelly and Dublin Corporation* (Dublin, 2007)

Carroll, F.M., *Money for Ireland: finance, diplomacy, politics and the first Dáil Eireann loans, 1919–1936* (London, 2002)

Caskey, Alan, 'Entrepreneurs and industrial development in Ulster 1850–1914', *Irish Economic and Social History*, vol.12 (1985), 123–124

Casserley, H.C., *Outline of Irish railway history* (London, 1974)

Clyde, Tom, *Irish literary magazines* (Dublin, 2002)

Collins, Kevin, *Catholic churchmen and the Celtic revival 1848–1916* (Dublin, 2003)

Colum, Padraic, *Arthur Griffith* (Dublin, 1959)

Cooke A., Vincent J., *The governing passion: cabinet government and party politics in Britain 1885–86* (London, 1974)

Corcoran, Donal P., *Freedom to achieve freedom: the Irish Free State 1922–1932* (Dublin, 2013)

Crehan, Joseph S.J., 'Freedom and Catholic power', *Studies*, 40 (1951), 158–166

Cronin, Mary, *Country, class or craft?: the politicisation of the skilled artisan in nineteenth-century Cork* (Cork, 1994)

Cullen, L.M. (ed.) *The formation of the Irish economy* (Cork, 1968)

Cullen, L.M., *Princes and pirates: the Dublin Chamber of Commerce 1783–1983* (Dublin, 1983)

-----------, *Irish national income in 1911 and its context* (Dublin, 1995)

-----------, *Economy, trade and Irish merchants at home and abroad 1600–1988* (Dublin, 2012)

Daly, Mary, *A social and economic history of Ireland since 1800* (Dublin, 1981)

-----------, *Dublin: deposed capital* (Cork, 1984)

-----------, 'Government finance for industry in the Irish Free State: the Trade Loans (Guarantee) Acts', *Irish Economic and Social History*, vol.11 (1984), 73–93

-----------, *Industrial development and Irish national identity 1922–1939* (Syracuse, 1994)

-----------, 'The formation of an Irish nationalist elite? Recruiting to the civil service in the decades prior to independence 1870–1920', *Paedogogica Historica*, vol.30, no.1 (1994), 281–301

-----------, 'The economic ideals of Irish nationalism: frugal comfort or lavish austerity?', *Eire-Ireland*, 29 (winter 1994), 77–100

-----------, 'The Irish Free State/Eire/Republic of Ireland/Ireland: a country by any other name?", *Journal of British Studies*, 46 (January 2007), 72–90

Daniel, T.K., 'Griffith on his noble head', *Irish Economic and Society History*, vol.3 (1976), 55–65

Davis, R.P., 'Griffith and Gandhi: a study in non-violent resistance', *Threshold*, vol.3, no.2 (summer 1959), 29–44

-----------, *Arthur Griffith and non-violent Sinn Féin* (Tralee, 1974)

De Wiel, Jerome Ann, *The Irish factor 1899–1919* (Dublin, 2008)

Dickson D., O'Grada C. (eds) *Refiguring Ireland* (Dublin, 2003)

Doherty G., Keogh D. (eds) *1916* (Cork, 2007)

Dolan, Anne, *Commemorating the Irish civil war* (Cambridge, 2003)

Doorley, Michael, *Irish-American diaspora nationalism: the Friends of Irish Freedom 1916–1935* (Dublin, 2005)

Douglas, Roy, *Land, people and politics: a history of the land question in the United Kingdom 1878–1952* (London, 1976)

Duff T., Hegarty J., Hussey M., *The story of the Dublin Institute of Technology* (Dublin, 2000)

Dungan, Myles (ed.), *Speaking ill of the dead* (Dublin, 2007)

Dunleavy, J.E., Dunleavy G.W., *Douglas Hyde: a maker of modern Ireland* (Oxford, 1991)

Dunne, Tom (ed.), *The National University of Ireland, 1908–2008: centenary essays* (Dublin, 2008)

Fanning, Ronan, *The Irish Department of Finance 1922–1958* (Dublin, 1978)

-----------, *Independent Ireland* (Dublin, 1983)

-----------, *Fatal path: British government and Irish revolution* (Dublin, 2013)

Ferriter, Diarmuid, *Judging Dev* (Dublin, 2007)

-----------, *The transformation of Ireland 1900–2000* (London, 2005)

Finlay, Ken, *The biggest show in town: record of the international exhibition, Dublin 1907* (Dublin, 2007)

Finneran, R.J. (ed.) *Letters of James Stephens* (London, 1974)

Fitzgerald, Garret, *Reflections on the Irish state* (Dublin, 2003)

-----------, *Ireland in the world: further reflections* (Dublin, 2005)

Fitzpatrick, David, *Harry Boland's Irish revolution* (Cork, 2003)

Foxton, David, *Revolutionary lawyers: Sinn Féin and crown courts in Ireland and Britain 1916–1923* (Dublin, 2008)

Glandon, Virginia, *Arthur Griffith and the advanced nationalist press* (New York, 1985)

Grob-Fitzgibbon, Benjamin, *Turning points of the Irish revolution* (New York, 2007)

Hart, Peter, *The IRA at war* (Oxford, 2000)

Hay, Marnie, *Bulmer Hobson and the nationalist movement in twentieth-century Ireland* (Manchester, 2009)

Hogan, Daire, *The legal profession in Ireland 1789–1922* (Naas, 1986)

Institute of Bankers in Ireland, *Economic planning and the banking system* (Dublin, 1968)

Irish Banks Standing Committee, *The control of banking in the Republic of Ireland* (Dublin, 1984)

Jackson, Alvin, *Sir Edward Carson* (Dundalk, 1993)

Jackson, Alvin, 'The failure of unionism in Dublin, 1900', *Irish Historical Studies*, 26 (1989), 377–395

Kenneally, Ian, *The Paper Wall* (Cork, 2008)

Kenny, Kevin (ed.) *Ireland and the British Empire* (Oxford, 2004)

Keogh D., McCarthy A., *The making of the Irish constitution 1937* (Cork, 2007)

Keogh, Dermot, *The Vatican, the bishops and Irish politics* (Cambridge, 1986)

Keyes, Michael, *Funding the nation: money and nationalist politics in nineteenth-century Ireland* (Dublin, 2011)

Krautt, W.H., *Ground truths* (Dublin, 2014)

Laffan, Michael, *The partition of Ireland 1911–1925* (Dundalk, 1983)

----------, *The resurrection of Ireland* (Cambridge, 1999)

Larkin, Emmet, *The Roman Catholic Church and the making of the Irish state 1878–1886* (Dublin, 1975)

Lavelle, Patricia, *James O'Mara: a staunch Sinn Féiner* (Dublin, 1961)

Lee, Joseph, *The modernisation of Irish society 1848–1918* (Dublin, 1973)

----------, *Ireland 1912–1985* (Cambridge, 1989)

Lloyd George, Richard, *Lloyd George* (London, 1960)

Longford, Lord, *Peace by ordeal* (London, 1935)

Longford, Lord, O'Neill, T.P., *Eamon De Valera* (Dublin, 1970)

Lyons, F.S.L. (ed.) *Bank of Ireland 1783–1983* (Dublin, 1983)

Maguire, Martin, *The civil service and the revolution in Ireland 1912–1938* (Manchester, 2008)

Marsh, P.T., *Bargaining on Europe: Britain and the First Common Market 1860–92* (Yale, 1999)

Martin, F.X. (ed.), *Leaders and men of the 1916 rising* (Dublin, 1967)

Martin, Peter, *Irish peers 1909–1924* (unpublished MA, UCD, 1998)

Matthews, Ann, *Dissidents* (Cork, 2012)

Maume, Patrick, *D.P. Moran* (Dublin, 1996)

----------, *The long gestation* (Dublin, 1999)

----------, 'A nursery of editors: the Cork Free Press 1910–1916', *History Ireland*, 15, no.2 (Mar/Apr.2007), 42–46

Maye, Brian, *Arthur Griffith* (Dublin, 1997)

MacBride, L.W., *The greening of Dublin Castle* (Washington D.C, 1991)

---------- (ed.) *Reading Irish histories: texts, contexts and memory in modern Ireland* (Dublin, 2003)

McCabe, Conor, *Sins of the father: tracing the decision that shaped the Irish economy* (Dublin, 2011)

McColgan, John, *British policy and the Irish administration 1920–1922* (Dublin, 1983)

McConnel, James, 'Jobbing with Tory and Liberal: Irish nationalists and the politics of patronage 1880–1914', *Past and Present*, no. 188 (Aug. 2005), 105–131

McCracken, D.P., *The Irish Pro-Boers* (Johannesburg, 1989)

McCracken, P.A., 'Arthur Griffith's South-African sabbatical', *Ireland and South Africa in modern times* (vol. 3, 1996), 230–240

McDermott, Norma (ed.) *The universities of the people: celebrating Ireland's public libraries* (Dublin, 2003)

McGarry, Fearghal (ed.) *Republicanism in modern Ireland* (Dublin, 2003)

McGee, Owen, *The IRB* (Dublin, 2005)

McGowan, Padraig, *Money and banking in Ireland: origins, development and future* (Dublin, 1990)

McGuire J., Quinn J. (eds.) *Dictionary of Irish Biography*, 9 vols. (Cambridge, 2009)

McMahon, T.G., *The Gaelic revival and Irish society 1893–1910* (Syracuse, 2008)

Meleady, Dermot, *John Redmond: the national leader* (Dublin, 2013)

Mitchell, Angus, *Roger Casement* (London, 2003)

Mitchell, Arthur, *Revolutionary government in Ireland: Dáil Eireann 1919–1922* (Dublin, 1995)

Moody T.W., Martin F.X., Byrne F.J. (eds) *A new history of Ireland*, 8 (Oxford, 1989)

Morrissey, Thomas S.J., *Towards a national university: William Delany S.J.* (Dublin, 1983)

----------, *Thomas A Finlay S.J.* (Dublin, 2004)

Moynihan, Maurice, *Currency and central banking in Ireland 1922–1960* (Dublin, 1975)

Murphy, B.P., *John Chartres: mystery man of the treaty* (Dublin, 1995)

O'Brien M., Rafter K. (eds) *Independent Newspapers: a history* (Dublin, 2012)

O'Carroll, J.P., Murphy, J.A. (eds) *DeValera and his times* (Cork, 1983)

O'Grada, Cormac, *Ireland: a new economic history 1780–1939* (Oxford, 1994)

O'Grada C., Walsh B., 'Did (and does) the Irish border matter?', *Working Papers in British–Irish Studies*, no.60 (2006)

O'Luing, Sean, *Art O Griofa* (Baile Atha Cliath, 1954)

----------, 'Arthur Griffith: thoughts on a centenary', *Studies* (summer 1971), 127–138

O'Neill, Marie, *From Parnell to DeValera: a biography of Jennie Wyse Power* (Dublin, 1991)

----------, 'Dublin Corporation in the troubled times 1914–1924', *Dublin Historical Record*, 47 (spring 1994)

Osborne, Chrissy, *Michael Collins himself* (Cork, 2013)

Perkin, Harold, *The rise of professional society: England since 1880* (London, 1989)

Porter, Bernard, *Empire and Super Empire: Britain, America and the world* (Yale, 2006)

Prunty, Jacinta, *Dublin slums 1800–1925* (Dublin, 1999)

Rafferty, Oliver S.J., *The Catholic Church and the Protestant state: nineteenth-century Irish realities* (Dublin, 2008)

Rafter, Kevin (ed.), *Irish journalism before independence* (Manchester, 2011)

Rolleston, C.H., *Portrait of an Irishman: a biographical sketch of T.W. Rolleston* (Dublin, 1939)

Rouse P., Duncan M., *Handling change: a history of the Irish Bank Officials' Association* (Cork, 2012)

Sheehan, William, *Fighting for Dublin: the British battle for Dublin 1919–1921* (Cork, 2007)

Swift R., Gilley T. (eds) *The Irish in Britain 1815–1939* (London, 1989)

Taouk, Youssef, 'We are alienating the splendid Irish race: British Catholic response to the Irish conscription controversy of 1918', *Journal of Church and State*, 48 (2006), 601–622

Tonra B., Kennedy M., Doyle J., Dorr N. (eds) *Irish Foreign Policy* (Dublin, 2012)

Turner, John, *Lloyd George's secretariat* (Cambridge, 1980)

Valiulis, Maryann Gialanella, *Portrait of a revolutionary: General Richard Mulcahy and the founding of the Irish Free State* (Dublin, 1992)

Vaughan, W.E. (ed.) *A new history of Ireland*, 6 (Oxford, 1989)

Waldron, Fionnuala, 'Statesmen on the street corners: labour and the Parnell split in Dublin 1890–1892', *Studia Hibernica*, no.34 (2006–07), 151–172

Warren, Allen, 'Dublin Castle, Whitehall and the formation of Irish policy 1879–92', *Irish Historical Studies*, xxxiv, no.136 (November 2005)

Whitaker, T.K., 'Ireland's external assets', *Journal of the Society for the Statistical and Social Inquiry of Ireland*, vol.102 (1948–1949), 192–209

White, Terence DeVere, *Kevin O'Higgins* (London, 1948)

Younger, Carlton, *A state of disunion* (London, 1972)

----------, *Arthur Griffith* (Dublin, 1981)

Index